Cornered!

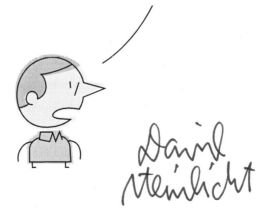

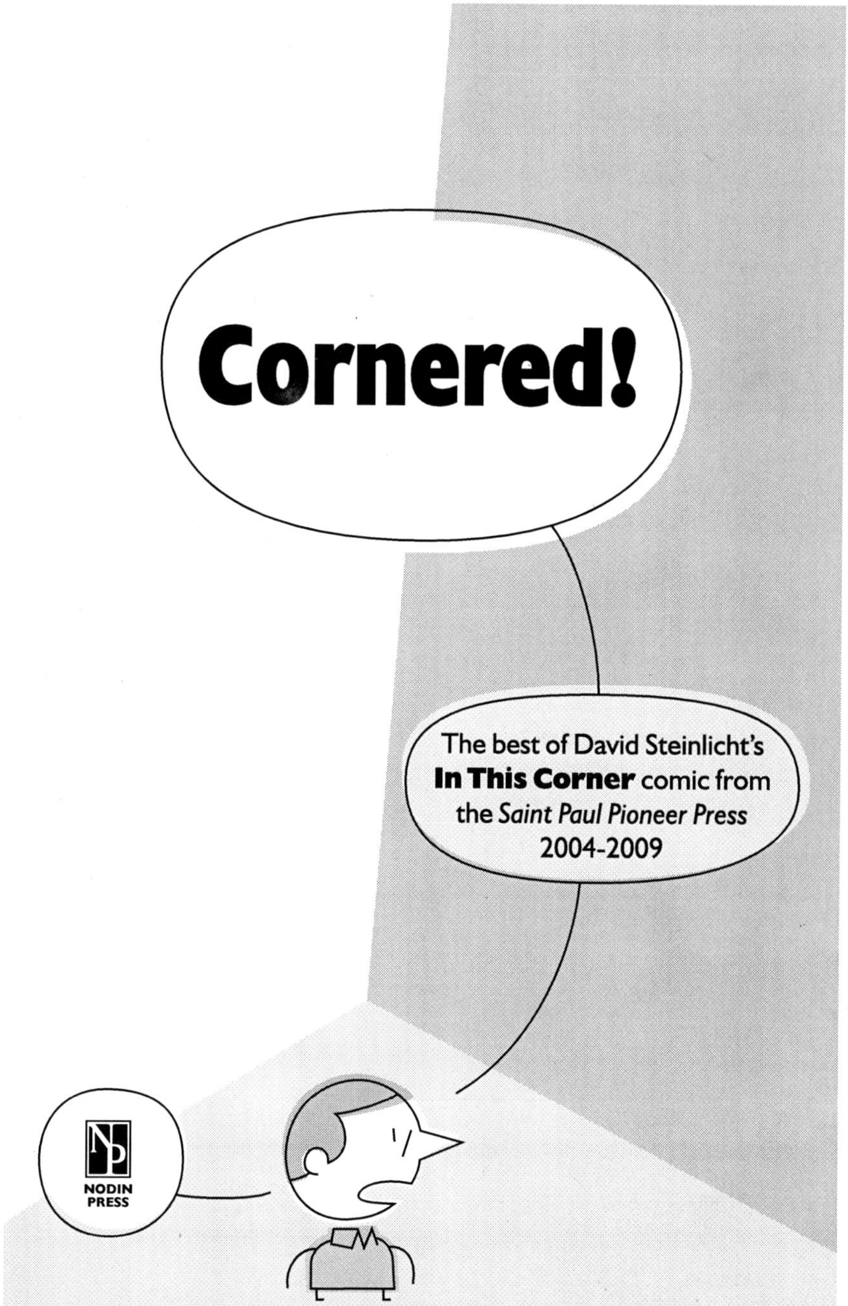
Cornered!
The best of David Steinlicht's **In This Corner** comic from the *Saint Paul Pioneer Press* 2004-2009
NODIN PRESS

These comics were first published in the St. Paul Pioneer Press
and on the Web sites twincities.com and cornercomic.com

You could write the author at davidsteinlicht@yahoo.com

ISBN: 978-1-932472-95-0
Library of Congress Control Number: 2009940888

Any resemblance to actual persons, living or dead, without
satirical or humorous intent, is coincidental.

Author photo by Ben Garvin, bengarvin.com

Cover and book design by David Steinlicht.
Who wants to know the fonts used in this book?
Only me? Well, okay…. But here they are anyway:
Frutiger, Stainless, Gill Sans, Bell Centennial and Aurora.

Printed on recycled paper by BookMobile in
Minneapolis, Minnesota, USA.

Nodin Press, LLC
530 N. 3rd Street
Suite 120
Minneapolis, MN 55401

Introduction and so forth

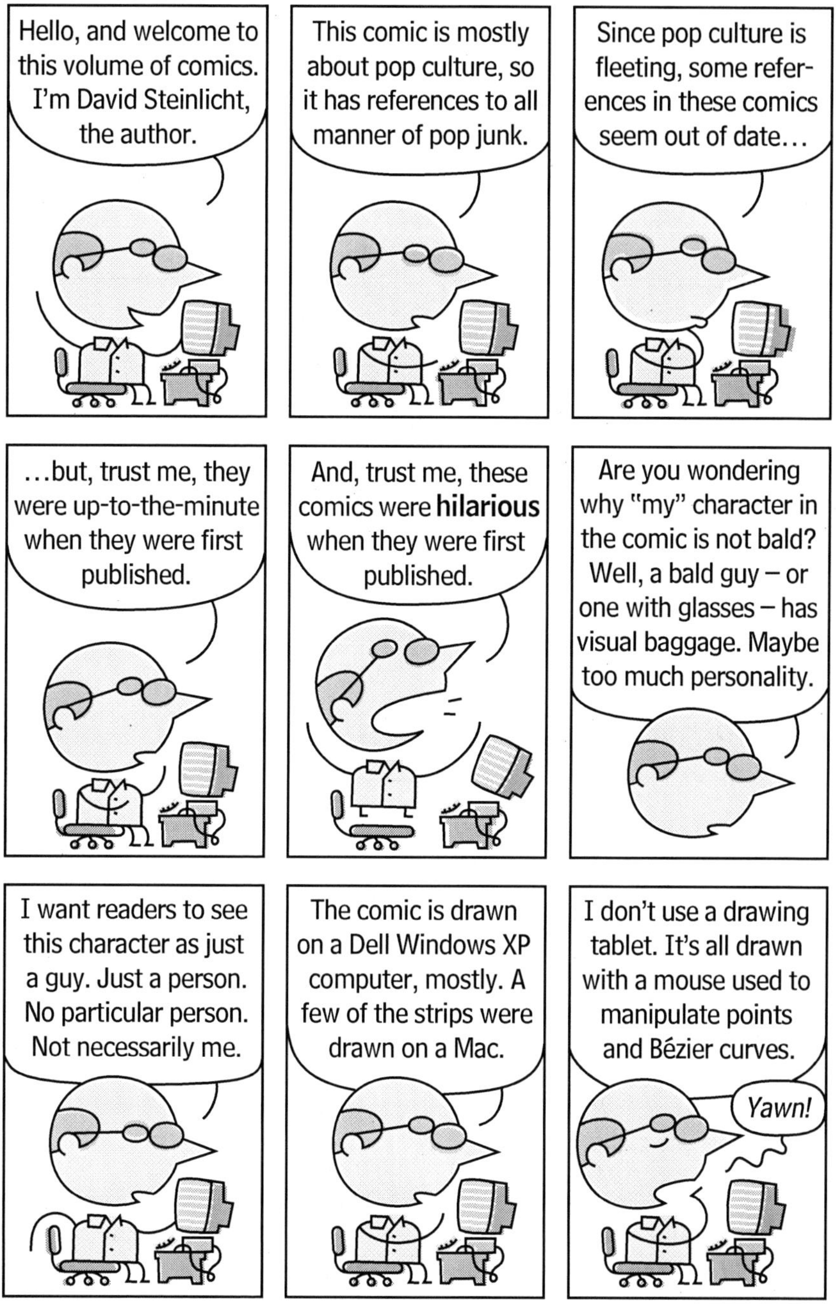

Hello, and welcome to this volume of comics. I'm David Steinlicht, the author.
This comic is mostly about pop culture, so it has references to all manner of pop junk.
Since pop culture is fleeting, some references in these comics seem out of date...
...but, trust me, they were up-to-the-minute when they were first published.
And, trust me, these comics were **hilarious** when they were first published.
Are you wondering why "my" character in the comic is not bald? Well, a bald guy – or one with glasses – has visual baggage. Maybe too much personality.
I want readers to see this character as just a guy. Just a person. No particular person. Not necessarily me.
The comic is drawn on a Dell Windows XP computer, mostly. A few of the strips were drawn on a Mac.
I don't use a drawing tablet. It's all drawn with a mouse used to manipulate points and Bézier curves.
Yawn!

Continued...

For five years, "In This Corner" has appeared weekly in the St. Paul Pioneer Press newspaper...

...that's a daily paper. Published every day. Full of news. Delivered right to your door. It's kind of a cool idea.

First, many thanks to Heidi Raschke, the features editor, for suggesting I do a comic.

Thank you, too, to Thom Fladung, the editor of the paper, and Lauri Hopple, my boss at the paper, for letting me take the time to do the comic.

Special thanks to Dan Kelly, my first reader, idea guy and fix-it specialist.

Might I mention the contributions of copy editors Dana Davis and Kathy Derong? Thanks for catching numerous mistakes.*

For ideas and help, thanks to Kraig Odden, Kathy Berdan, Susan Guernsey, Amy Nelson, Mary Divine, Ben Garvin (photo on p. 25), Kevin Cusick, Dennis Lien, Julio Ojeda-Zapata, Lisa Legge and Ruth Weleczki.

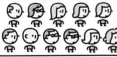

And thank you to Karl Raschke, John Vincent and Brian Henderson for posting the comics on twincities.com.

(Read my comics on cornercomic.com and allsmall.net)

Finally and always, thank you, Delores.

dst

*Any mistakes that remain are all mine.

July 2009

Four months later...

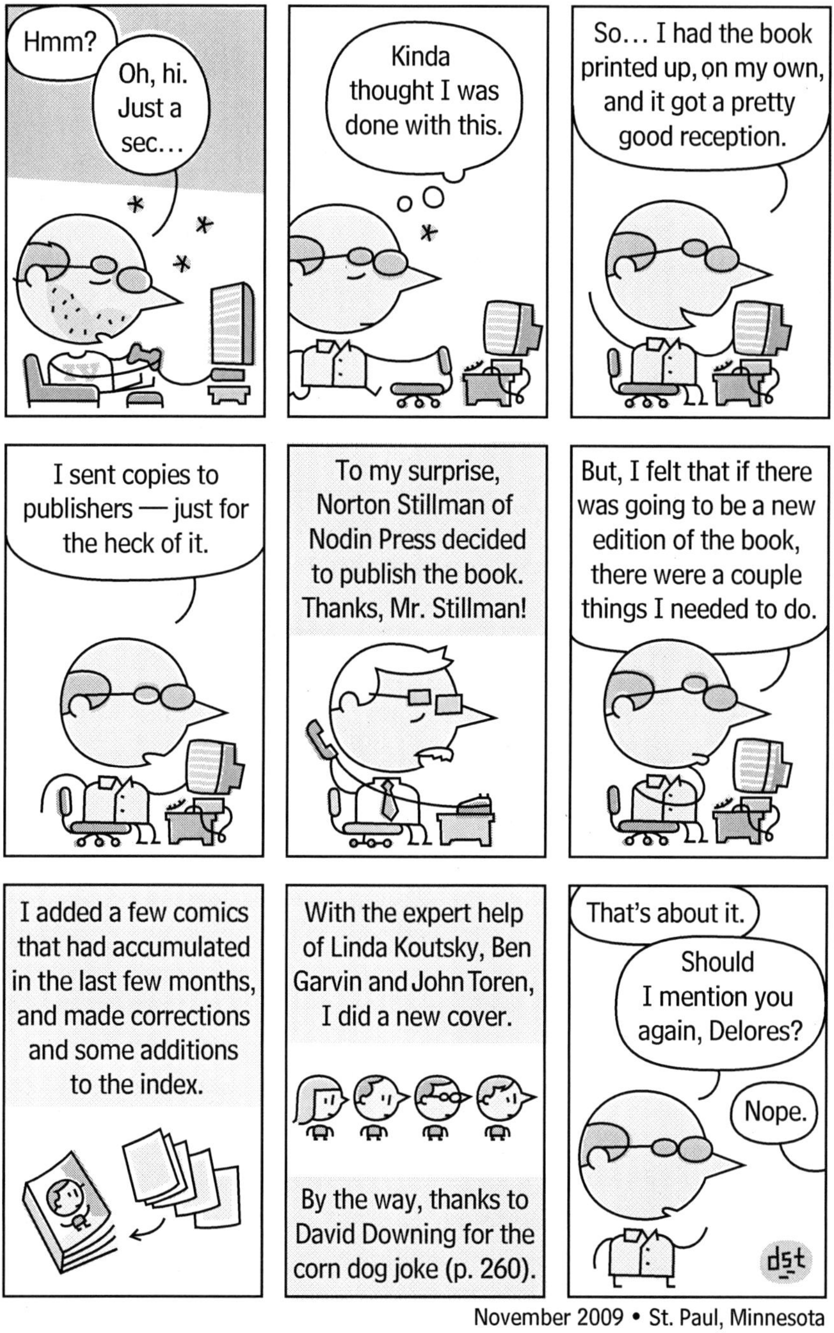

Hmm?
Oh, hi. Just a sec…
Kinda thought I was done with this.
So… I had the book printed up, on my own, and it got a pretty good reception.
I sent copies to publishers — just for the heck of it.
To my surprise, Norton Stillman of Nodin Press decided to publish the book. Thanks, Mr. Stillman!
But, I felt that if there was going to be a new edition of the book, there were a couple things I needed to do.
I added a few comics that had accumulated in the last few months, and made corrections and some additions to the index.
With the expert help of Linda Koutsky, Ben Garvin and John Toren, I did a new cover.
By the way, thanks to David Downing for the corn dog joke (p. 260).
That's about it.
Should I mention you again, Delores?
Nope.
dst

November 2009 • St. Paul, Minnesota

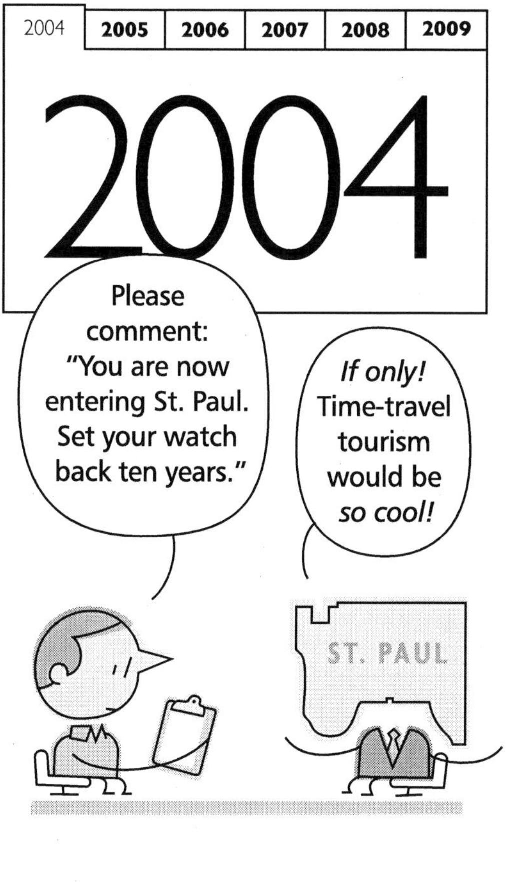
2004
2005
2006
2007
2008
2009
2004
Please comment: "You are now entering St. Paul. Set your watch back ten years."
If only! Time-travel tourism would be *so cool!*
ST. PAUL

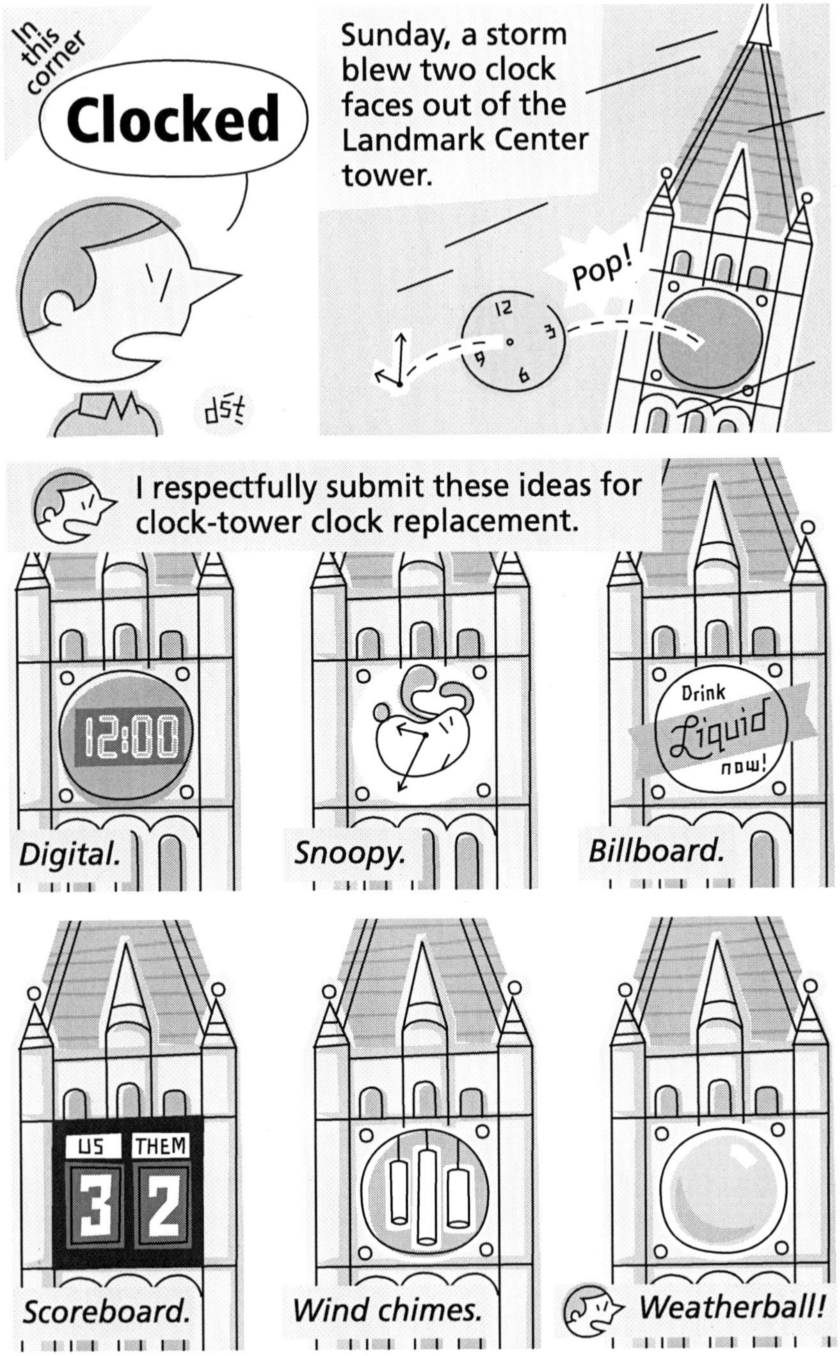
In this corner
Clocked
dst
Sunday, a storm blew two clock faces out of the Landmark Center tower.
Pop!
I respectfully submit these ideas for clock-tower clock replacement.
12:00
Digital.
Snoopy.
Drink Liquid now!
Billboard.
US
THEM
3
2
Scoreboard.
Wind chimes.
Weatherball!

April 15, 2004

DAVID STEINLICHT, PIONEER PRESS

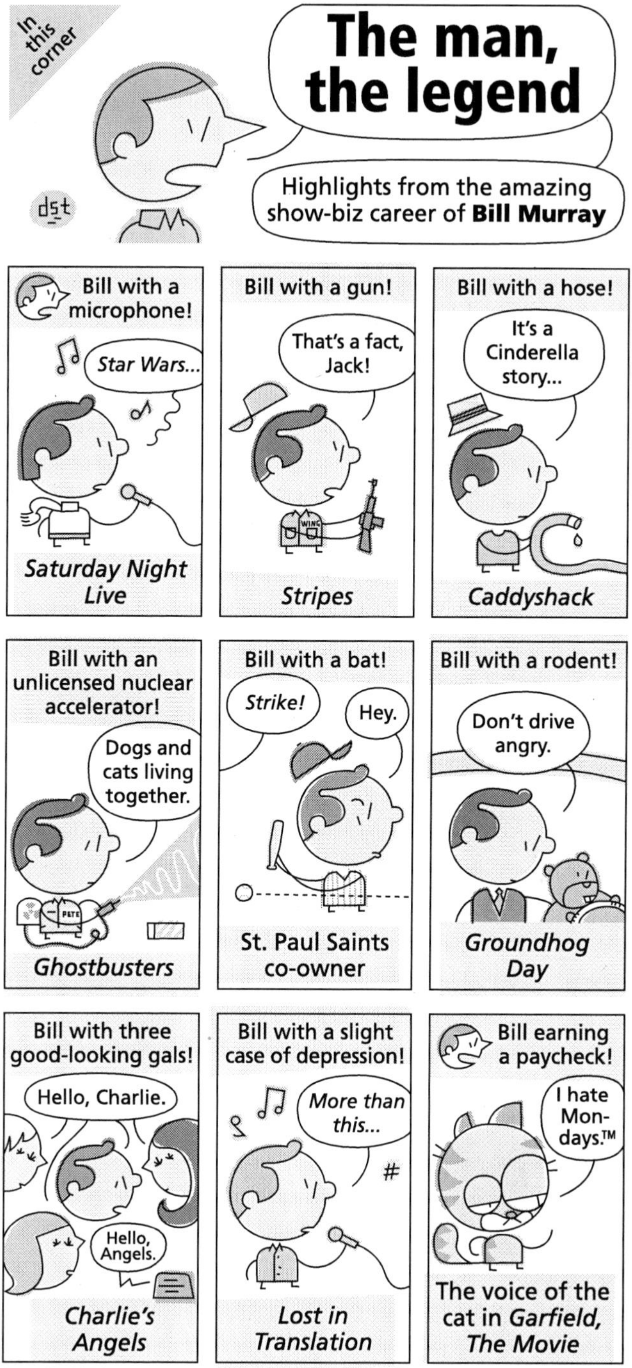
In this corner
dst
The man, the legend
Highlights from the amazing show-biz career of Bill Murray
Bill with a microphone!
Star Wars...
Saturday Night Live
Bill with a gun!
That's a fact, Jack!
WING
Stripes
Bill with a hose!
It's a Cinderella story...
Caddyshack
Bill with an unlicensed nuclear accelerator!
Dogs and cats living together.
PETE
Ghostbusters
Bill with a bat!
Strike!
Hey.
St. Paul Saints co-owner
Bill with a rodent!
Don't drive angry.
Groundhog Day
Bill with three good-looking gals!
Hello, Charlie.
Hello, Angels.
Charlie's Angels
Bill with a slight case of depression!
More than this...
#
Lost in Translation
Bill earning a paycheck!
I hate Mon-days.™
The voice of the cat in Garfield, The Movie

June 13, 2004 DAVID STEINLICHT, PIONEER PRESS

In this corner

Make your next movie here, **Jackie Chan!**

Around Minnesota In 8 Days!

dst

Day 1 Boundary Waters canoe chase

Day 2 Battle with Leech Lake walleye

Day 3 Sword fight on the Spoonbridge

Day 4 Verbal joust with Garrison Keillor

...Pastor Torvaldson says to Lena...

?

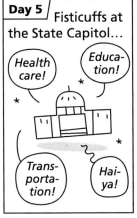

Day 5 Fisticuffs at the State Capitol...

Health care!

Educa-tion!

Trans-porta-tion!

Hai-ya!

Day 6 ... spins off into Jackie vs. Jesse!

Put out that cigar, please!

Make me!

Day 7 A day of recuperation at the Mayo Clinic.

Wheelchair fight!

Day 8 Finale fight destroys the Mall of America (computer-generated special effects, of course).

June 24, 2004

DAVID STEINLICHT, PIONEER PRESS

Note: Jackie Chan's then-current movie was *Around the World in 80 Days*.
Also, Jesse Ventura was not in office at that time, but match-up that would be.

4

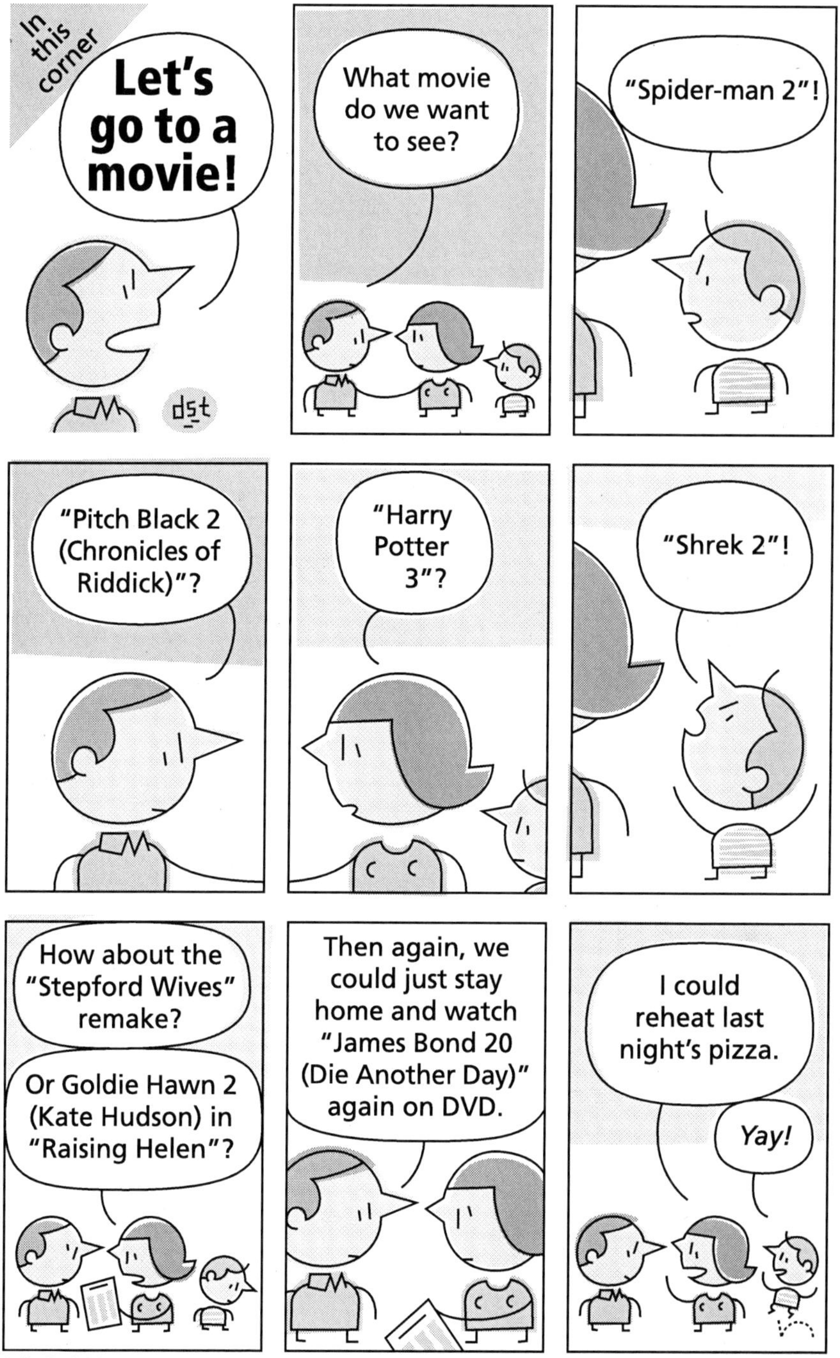
In this corner
Let's go to a movie!
dst
What movie do we want to see?
"Spider-man 2"!
"Pitch Black 2 (Chronicles of Riddick)"?
"Harry Potter 3"?
"Shrek 2"!
How about the "Stepford Wives" remake?
Or Goldie Hawn 2 (Kate Hudson) in "Raising Helen"?
Then again, we could just stay home and watch "James Bond 20 (Die Another Day)" again on DVD.
I could reheat last night's pizza.
Yay!

July 2, 2004

DAVID STEINLICHT, PIONEER PRESS

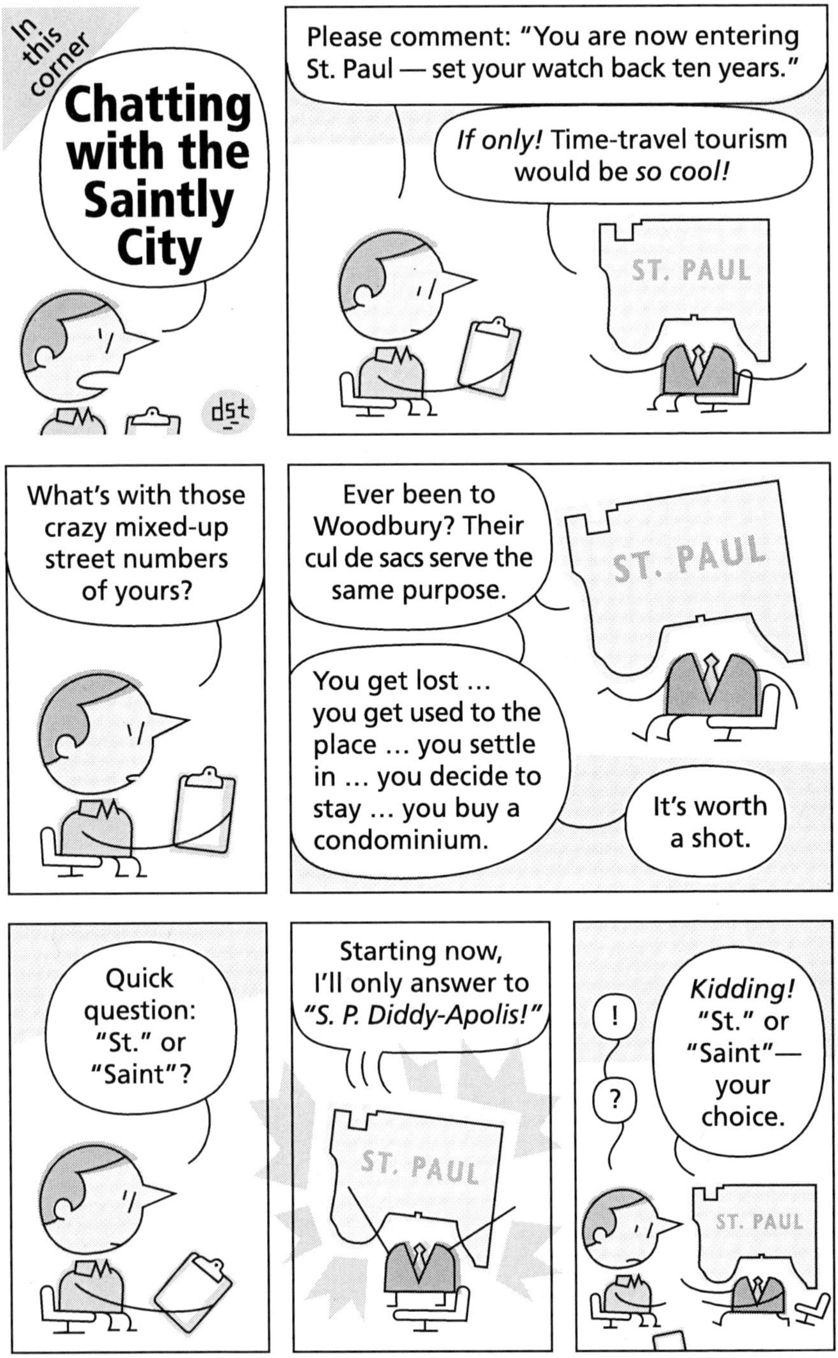
In this corner
Chatting with the Saintly City
dst
Please comment: "You are now entering St. Paul — set your watch back ten years."
If only! Time-travel tourism would be *so cool!*
ST. PAUL
What's with those crazy mixed-up street numbers of yours?
Ever been to Woodbury? Their cul de sacs serve the same purpose.
You get lost ... you get used to the place ... you settle in ... you decide to stay ... you buy a condominium.
It's worth a shot.
Quick question: "St." or "Saint"?
Starting now, I'll only answer to *"S. P. Diddy-Apolis!"*
!
?
Kidding! "St." or "Saint"— your choice.

July 9, 2004 DAVID STEINLICHT, PIONEER PRESS

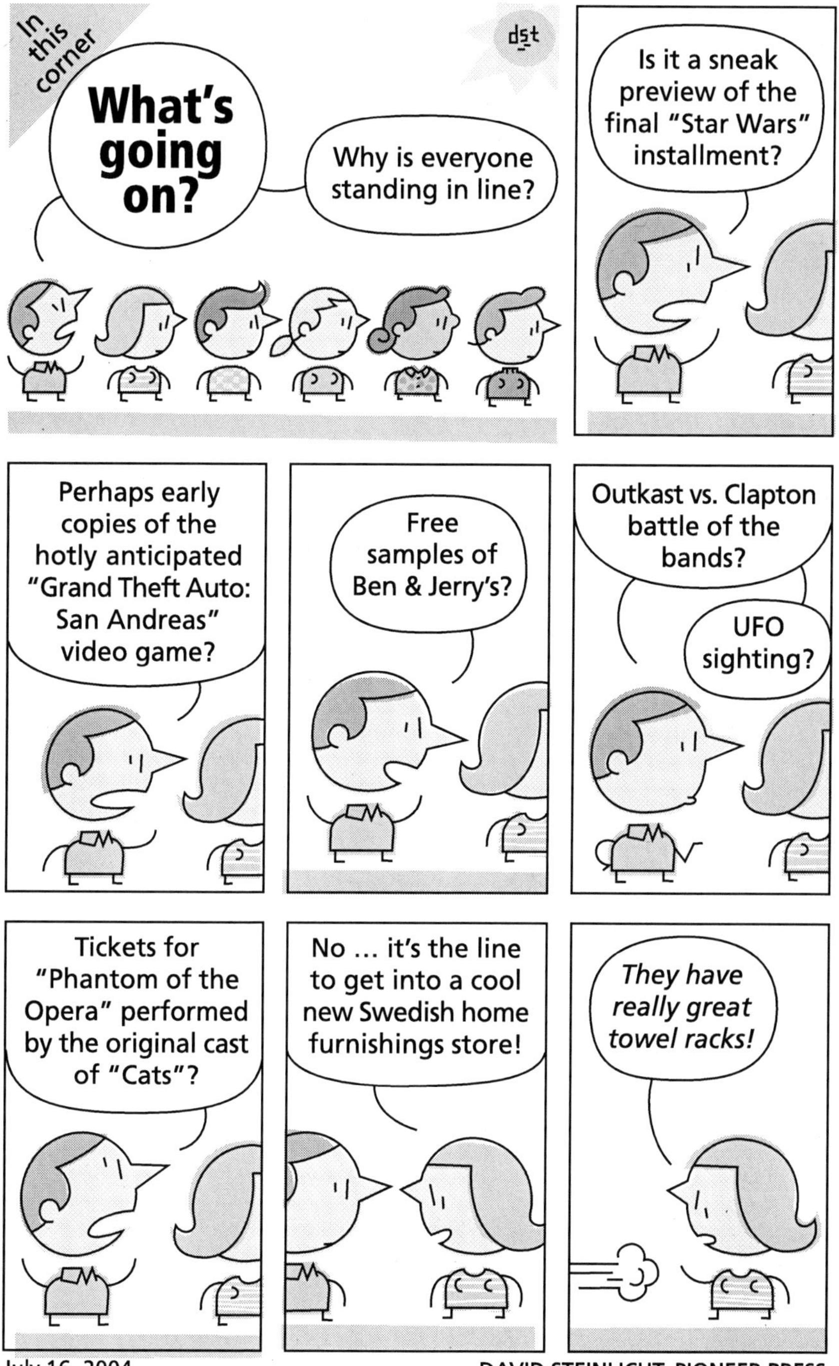
In this corner
dst
What's going on?
Why is everyone standing in line?
Is it a sneak preview of the final "Star Wars" installment?
Perhaps early copies of the hotly anticipated "Grand Theft Auto: San Andreas" video game?
Free samples of Ben & Jerry's?
Outkast vs. Clapton battle of the bands?
UFO sighting?
Tickets for "Phantom of the Opera" performed by the original cast of "Cats"?
No ... it's the line to get into a cool new Swedish home furnishings store!
They have really great towel racks!

July 16, 2004

DAVID STEINLICHT, PIONEER PRESS

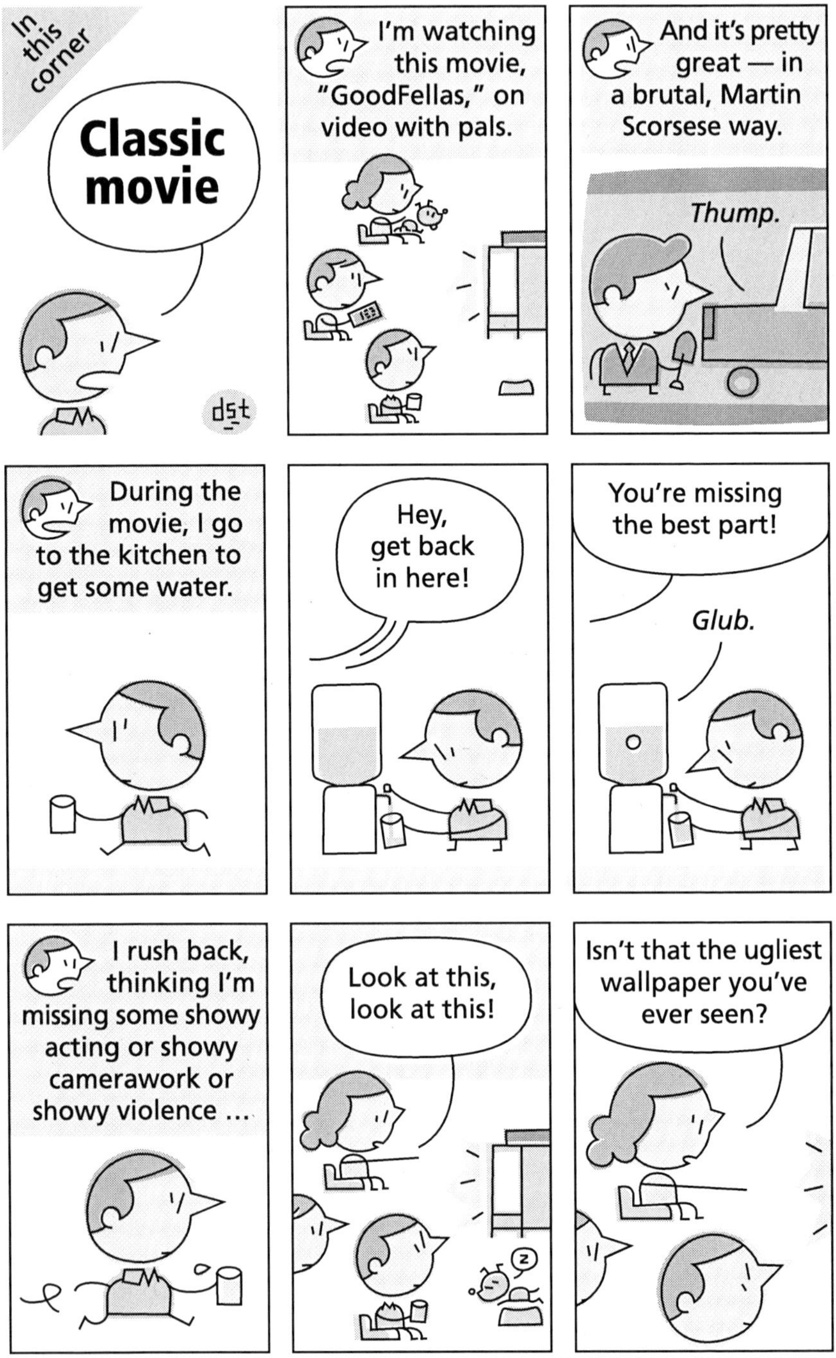
In this corner
Classic movie
dst
I'm watching this movie, "GoodFellas," on video with pals.
And it's pretty great — in a brutal, Martin Scorsese way.
Thump.
During the movie, I go to the kitchen to get some water.
Hey, get back in here!
You're missing the best part!
Glub.
I rush back, thinking I'm missing some showy acting or showy camerawork or showy violence ...
Look at this, look at this!
Isn't that the ugliest wallpaper you've ever seen?

July 23, 2004

DAVID STEINLICHT, PIONEER PRESS

In this corner

New diet fad

dst

How've you been? You look great! Relaxed and happy.

I'm on a new diet.

Really?

Yeah. It's not for everyone. It's kinda strict.

Tell me about it.

It's an information diet. I try to indulge in less information overall and then only in high-quality information.

I've cut back on my network and cable news viewing almost entirely. Restricted my consumption of infomercials.

Lowered my intake of docudramas, while bulking up on library books — hard cover *and* paperback.

Reality television is out altogether. I still visit a few Internet news sites.

And I've eliminated watching any and all yelling heads programs. They're just bad for my blood pressure.

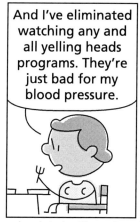

Newspapers? Magazines?

Only if printed with soy-based ink.

Sounds healthly.

Please note: The Pioneer Press is printed with soy-based ink.
July 30, 2004   DAVID STEINLICHT, PIONEER PRESS

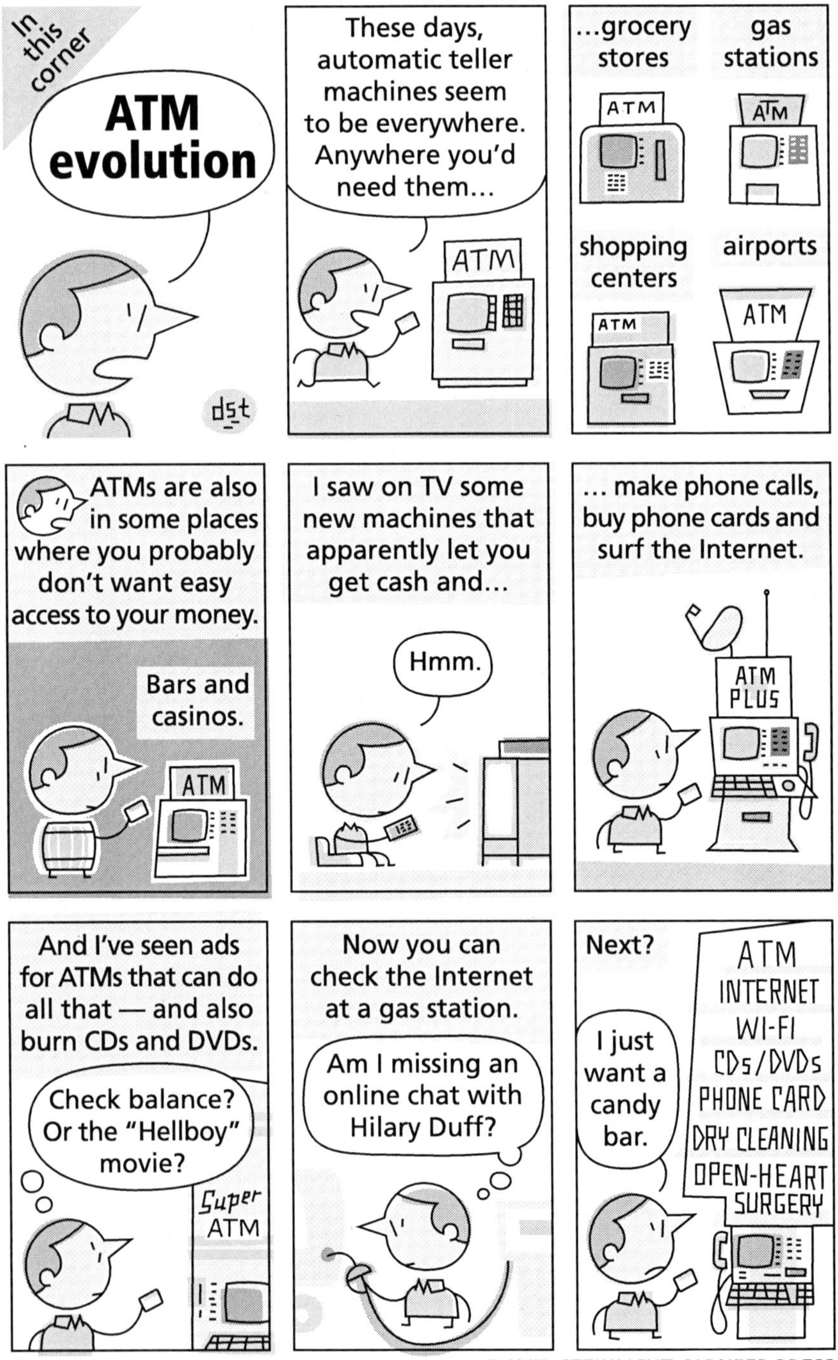
In this corner
ATM evolution
dst
These days, automatic teller machines seem to be everywhere. Anywhere you'd need them...
ATM
...grocery stores
gas stations
shopping centers
airports
ATM
ATM
ATM
ATM
ATMs are also in some places where you probably don't want easy access to your money.
Bars and casinos.
ATM
I saw on TV some new machines that apparently let you get cash and...
Hmm.
... make phone calls, buy phone cards and surf the Internet.
ATM PLUS
And I've seen ads for ATMs that can do all that — and also burn CDs and DVDs.
Check balance? Or the "Hellboy" movie?
Super ATM
Now you can check the Internet at a gas station.
Am I missing an online chat with Hilary Duff?
Next?
I just want a candy bar.
ATM
INTERNET
WI-FI
CDs/DVDs
PHONE CARD
DRY CLEANING
OPEN-HEART SURGERY

Aug. 6, 2004

DAVID STEINLICHT, PIONEER PRESS

Prepare for the Fair

In this corner

dst

Minnesota's State Fair is fast approaching. Participants hope for the best.

Blue ribbon
or
red ribbon
or
chicken taco.

Pork chop on a stick
or
sausage on a stick
or
about-a-foot-long hot dog.

Milking demo
or
vanilla milkshake
or
all-you-can-drink-for-$1 milk.

Corn roast
or
kettle corn
or
cow feed.

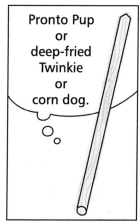

Pronto Pup
or
deep-fried Twinkie
or
corn dog.

Cheese sandwich
or
cheeseburger
or
deep-fried cheese curds.

Grandstand:
Clay Aiken
or
bandshell:
Shawn Colvin
or
under the Grandstand:
Miracle Knife guy.

Fries
or
fries
or
uh, fries.

Aug. 13, 2004

DAVID STEINLICHT, PIONEER PRESS

Goodbye, Charlie

dst

St. Paul's fiberglass tribute to Charles Schulz's Peanuts cartoon is currently in its fifth — and most probably final — year.

Slurp.

Memorable past statues:

"I'm feeling a little fragile Snoopy"

"Only $12.95 for 4x9 particle board Peppermint Patty"

"Uma Van Pelt"

"Supersized Linus"

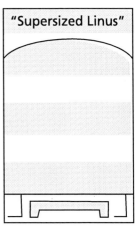

"SnowMN, bobblehead-hockey-player Schroeder"

"Bram Stoker's *Voodstock*"

"Good grief, your job's been offshored, Charlie Brown!"

Aug. 20, 2004

DAVID STEINLICHT, PIONEER PRESS

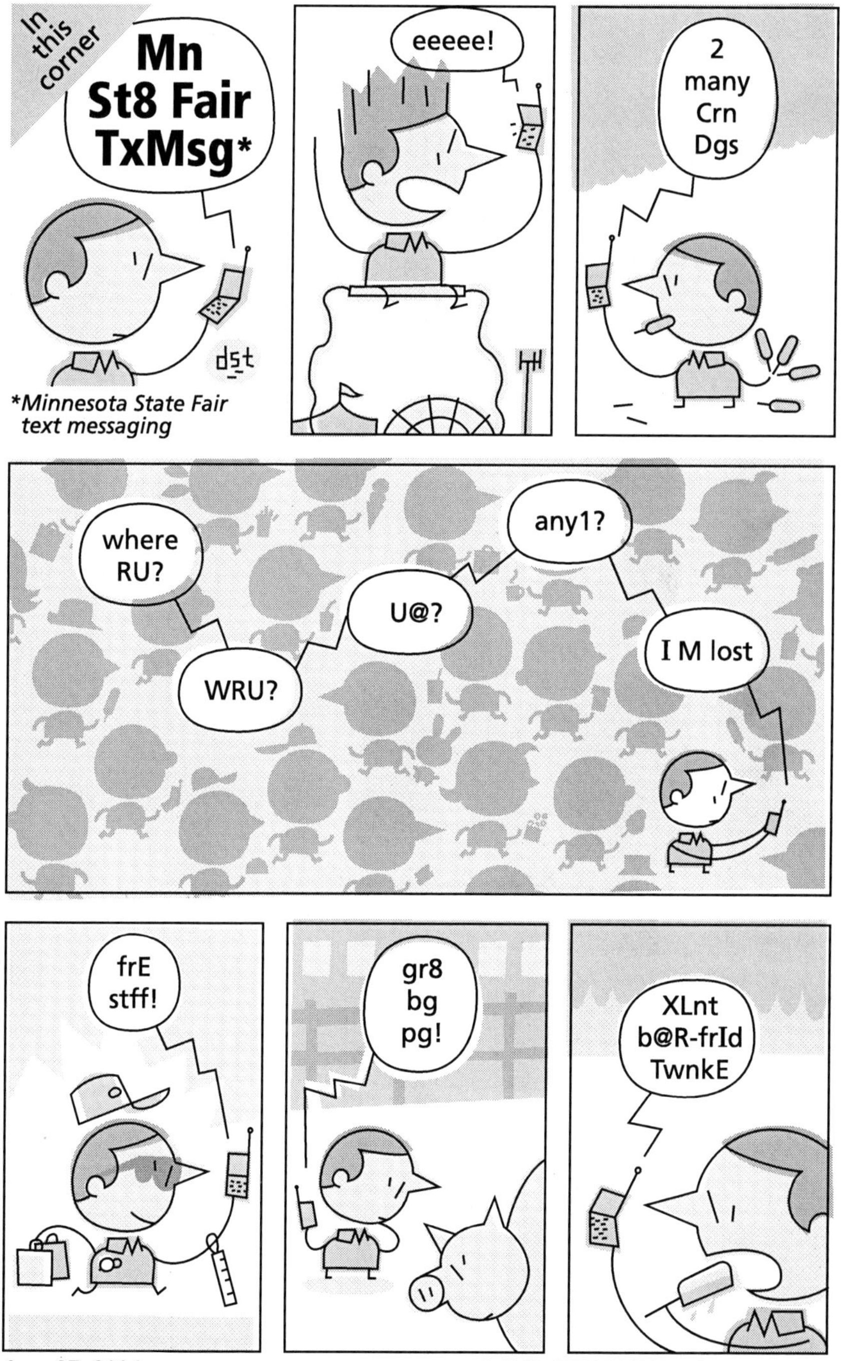
In this corner
Mn St8 Fair TxMsg*
dst
*Minnesota State Fair text messaging
eeeee!
2 many Crn Dgs
where RU?
WRU?
U@?
any1?
I M lost
frE stff!
gr8 bg pg!
XLnt b@R-frId TwnkE

Aug. 27, 2004

DAVID STEINLICHT, PIONEER PRESS

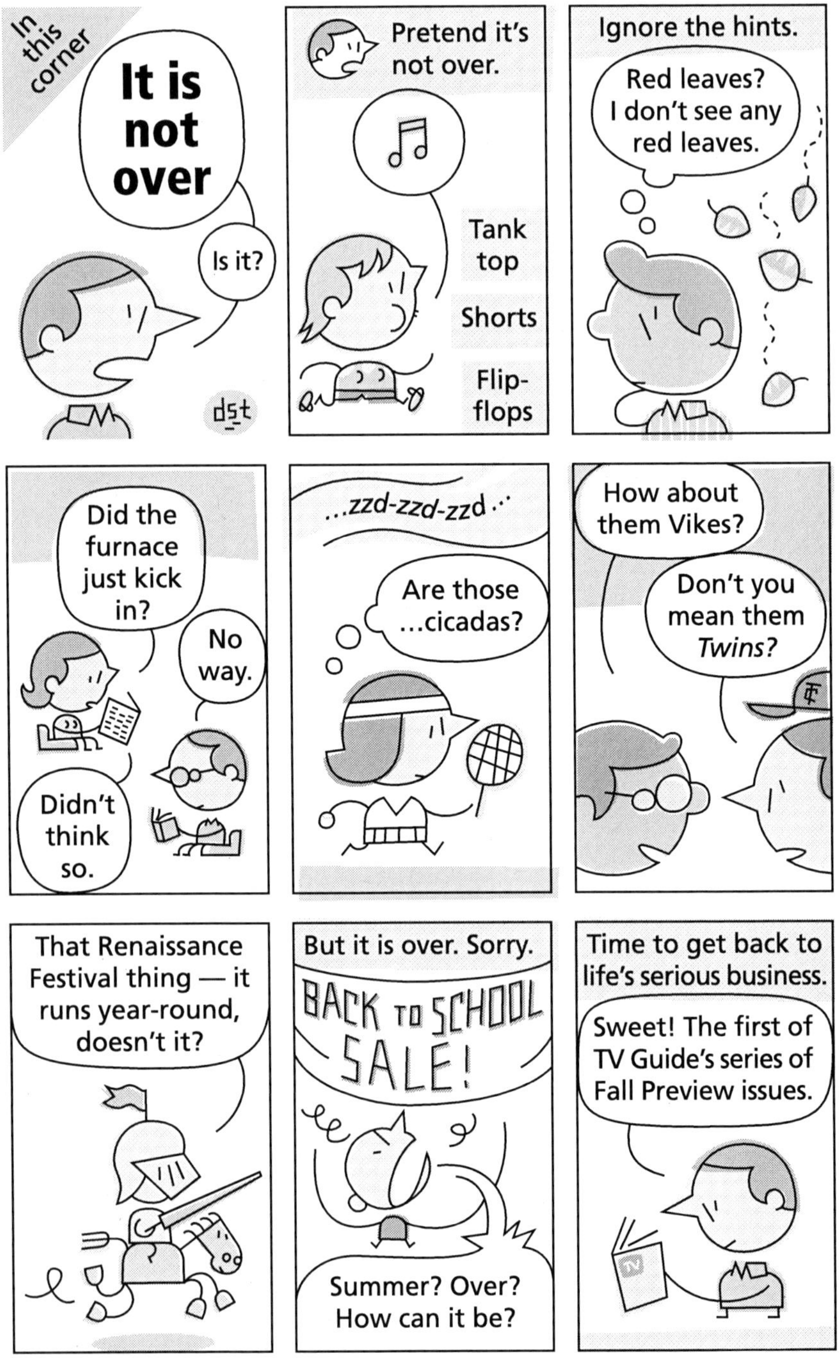
In this corner
It is not over
Is it?
dst
Pretend it's not over.
Tank top
Shorts
Flip-flops
Ignore the hints.
Red leaves? I don't see any red leaves.
Did the furnace just kick in?
No way.
Didn't think so.
...zzd-zzd-zzd...
Are those ...cicadas?
How about them Vikes?
Don't you mean them *Twins?*
That Renaissance Festival thing — it runs year-round, doesn't it?
But it is over. Sorry.
BACK TO SCHOOL SALE!
Summer? Over? How can it be?
Time to get back to life's serious business.
Sweet! The first of TV Guide's series of Fall Preview issues.
TV

Sept. 3, 2004

DAVID STEINLICHT, PIONEER PRESS

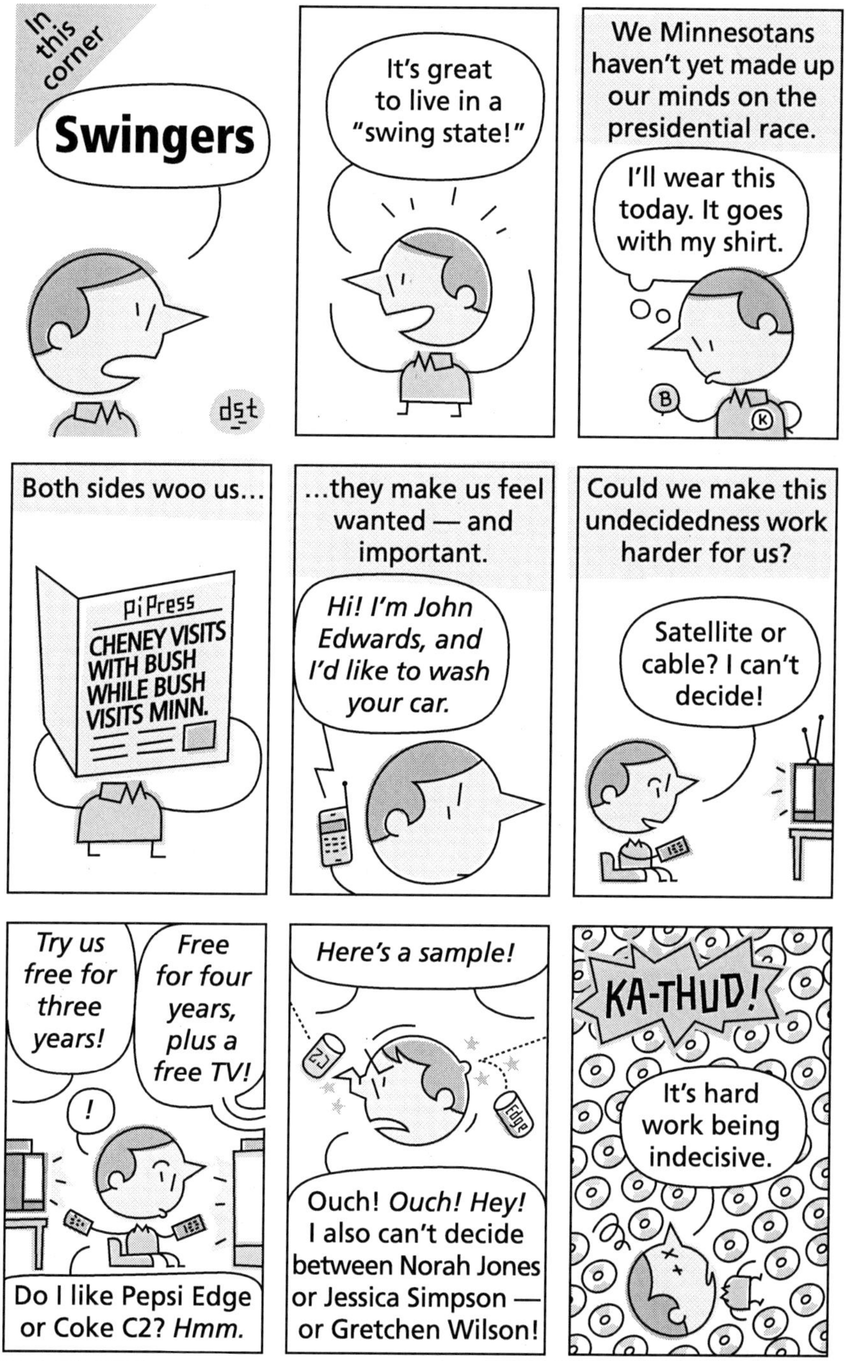
In this corner
Swingers
It's great to live in a "swing state!"
We Minnesotans haven't yet made up our minds on the presidential race.
I'll wear this today. It goes with my shirt.
B
K
Both sides woo us...
PiPress
CHENEY VISITS WITH BUSH WHILE BUSH VISITS MINN.
...they make us feel wanted — and important.
Hi! I'm John Edwards, and I'd like to wash your car.
Could we make this undecidedness work harder for us?
Satellite or cable? I can't decide!
Try us free for three years!
Free for four years, plus a free TV!
!
Do I like Pepsi Edge or Coke C2? Hmm.
Here's a sample!
C2
Edge
Ouch! Ouch! Hey! I also can't decide between Norah Jones or Jessica Simpson — or Gretchen Wilson!
KA-THUD!
It's hard work being indecisive.

Sept. 10, 2004

DAVID STEINLICHT, PIONEER PRESS

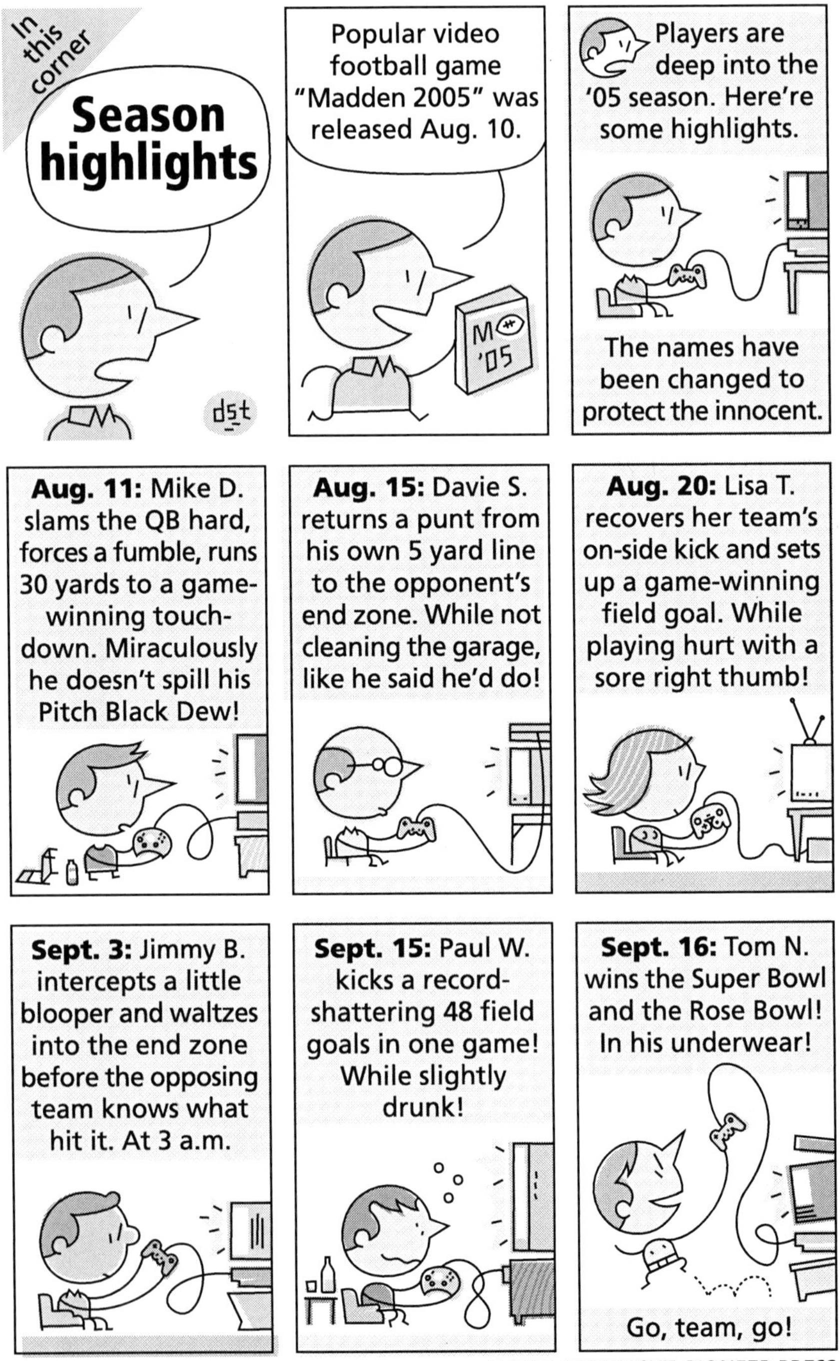
In this corner
Season highlights
dst
Popular video football game "Madden 2005" was released Aug. 10.
M '05
Players are deep into the '05 season. Here're some highlights.
The names have been changed to protect the innocent.
Aug. 11: Mike D. slams the QB hard, forces a fumble, runs 30 yards to a game-winning touchdown. Miraculously he doesn't spill his Pitch Black Dew!
Aug. 15: Davie S. returns a punt from his own 5 yard line to the opponent's end zone. While not cleaning the garage, like he said he'd do!
Aug. 20: Lisa T. recovers her team's on-side kick and sets up a game-winning field goal. While playing hurt with a sore right thumb!
Sept. 3: Jimmy B. intercepts a little blooper and waltzes into the end zone before the opposing team knows what hit it. At 3 a.m.
Sept. 15: Paul W. kicks a record-shattering 48 field goals in one game! While slightly drunk!
Sept. 16: Tom N. wins the Super Bowl and the Rose Bowl! In his underwear!
Go, team, go!

Sept. 17, 2004

DAVID STEINLICHT, PIONEER PRESS

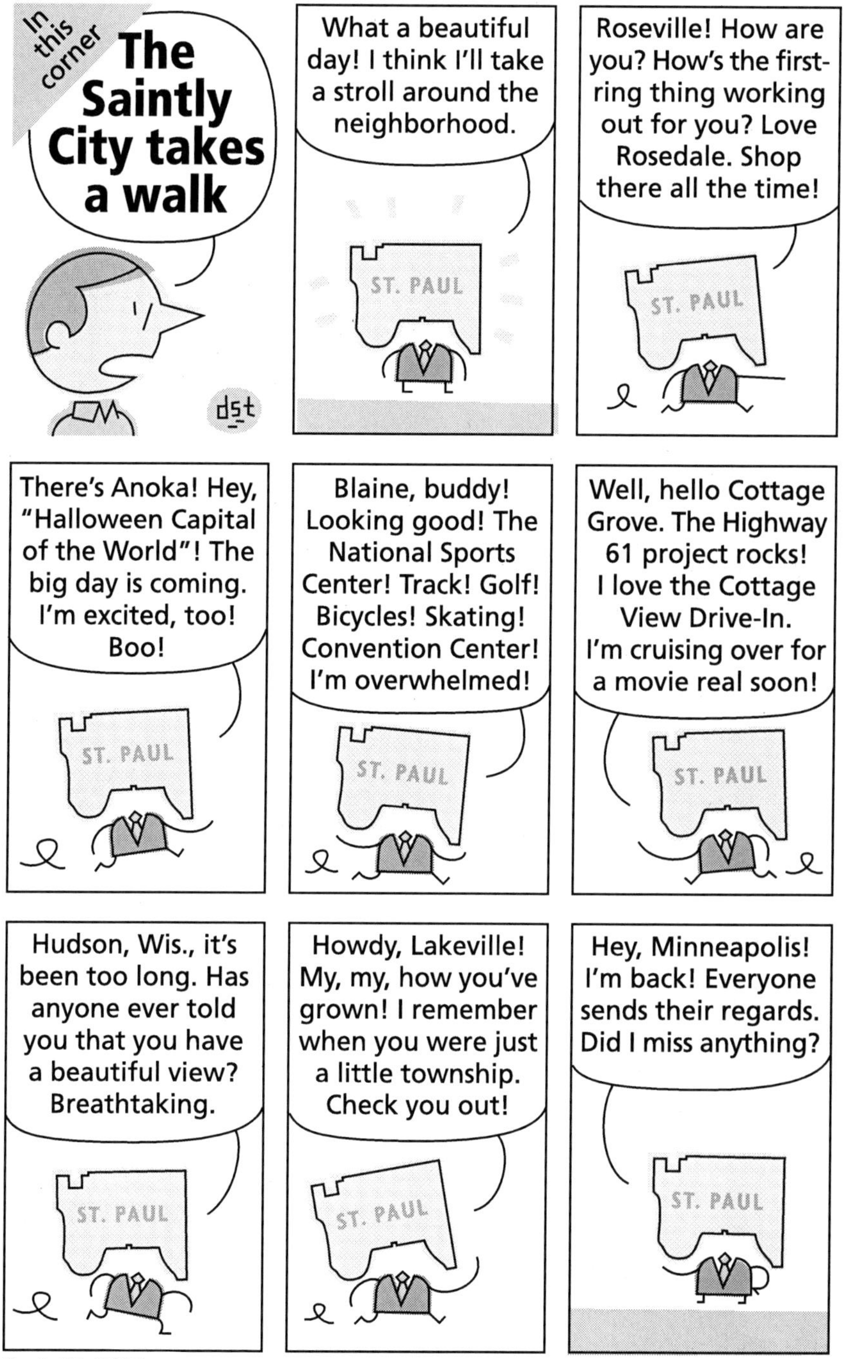
In this corner
The Saintly City takes a walk
dst
What a beautiful day! I think I'll take a stroll around the neighborhood.
ST. PAUL
Roseville! How are you? How's the first-ring thing working out for you? Love Rosedale. Shop there all the time!
There's Anoka! Hey, "Halloween Capital of the World"! The big day is coming. I'm excited, too! Boo!
Blaine, buddy! Looking good! The National Sports Center! Track! Golf! Bicycles! Skating! Convention Center! I'm overwhelmed!
Well, hello Cottage Grove. The Highway 61 project rocks! I love the Cottage View Drive-In. I'm cruising over for a movie real soon!
Hudson, Wis., it's been too long. Has anyone ever told you that you have a beautiful view? Breathtaking.
Howdy, Lakeville! My, my, how you've grown! I remember when you were just a little township. Check you out!
Hey, Minneapolis! I'm back! Everyone sends their regards. Did I miss anything?

Sept. 24, 2004

DAVID STEINLICHT, PIONEER PRESS

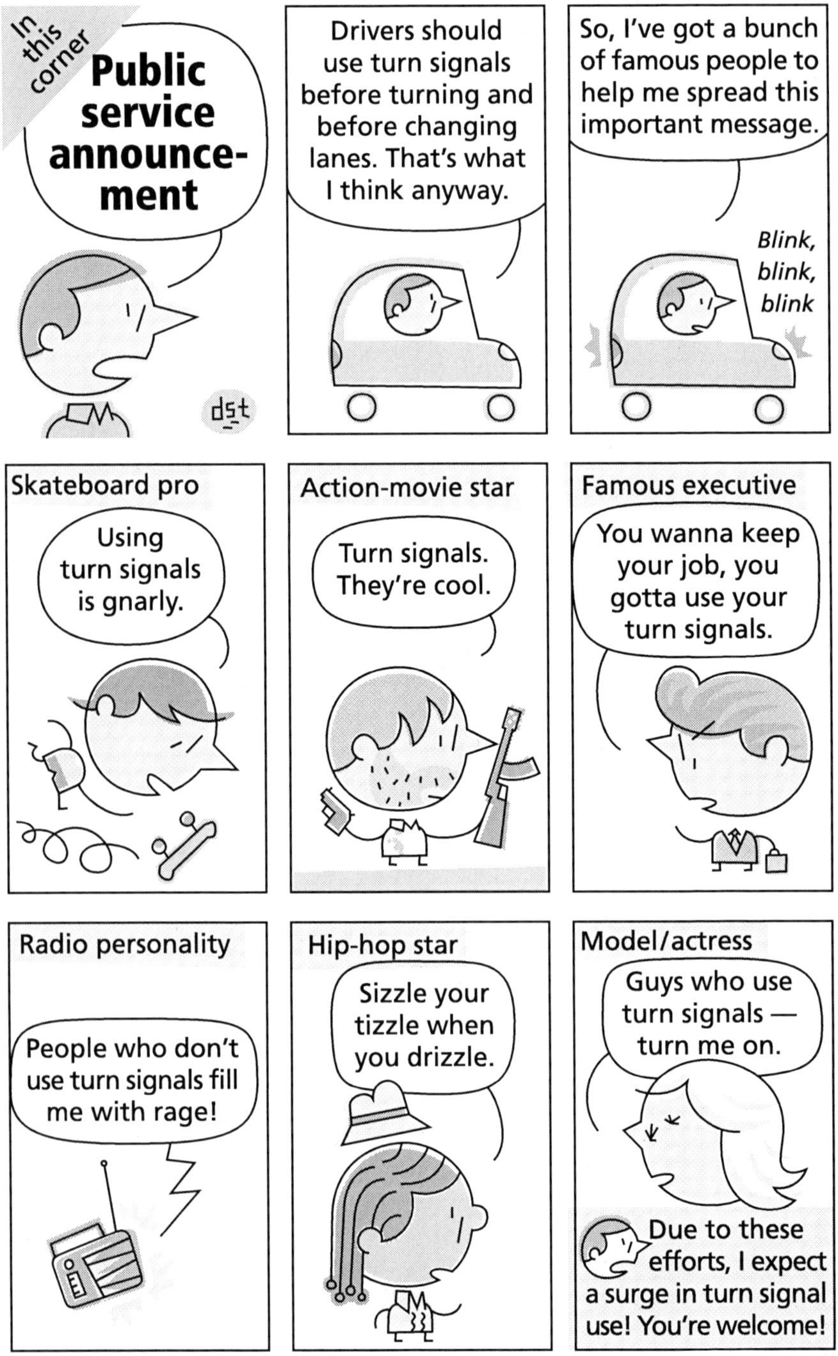
In this corner
Public service announcement
Drivers should use turn signals before turning and before changing lanes. That's what I think anyway.
So, I've got a bunch of famous people to help me spread this important message.
Blink, blink, blink
Skateboard pro
Using turn signals is gnarly.
Action-movie star
Turn signals. They're cool.
Famous executive
You wanna keep your job, you gotta use your turn signals.
Radio personality
People who don't use turn signals fill me with rage!
Hip-hop star
Sizzle your tizzle when you drizzle.
Model/actress
Guys who use turn signals — turn me on.
Due to these efforts, I expect a surge in turn signal use! You're welcome!

Oct. 1, 2004

DAVID STEINLICHT, PIONEER PRESS

Cycles

Saw an interesting motorcycle double feature.

"Interesting" is an interesting word.

"The Brown Bunny" featured a pro motorcycle racer...

Cool.

...he did more soul searching than racing.

Hmm.

Was there a bunny riding a motorcycle?

Oh.

Not that I noticed.

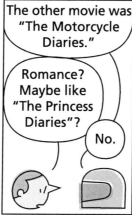

The other movie was "The Motorcycle Diaries."

Romance? Maybe like "The Princess Diaries"?

No.

A political coming-of-age film. In Spanish. Subtitles.

Hmm.

But with a good deal of motorcycle riding. That was a plus.

So, these movies were playing at the same theater on a double bill?

Close enough: At the Lagoon and the Uptown.

Just a block away from each other. A short hop.

Actually, I took a little jaunt to Wabasha between shows.

That's quite a trip. How fast did you go?

Don't ask.

Oct. 7, 2004

DAVID STEINLICHT, PIONEER PRESS

Note: This comic was inspired by some movies — and a story in the paper about a motorcycle rider given a ticket for going more than 100 mph.

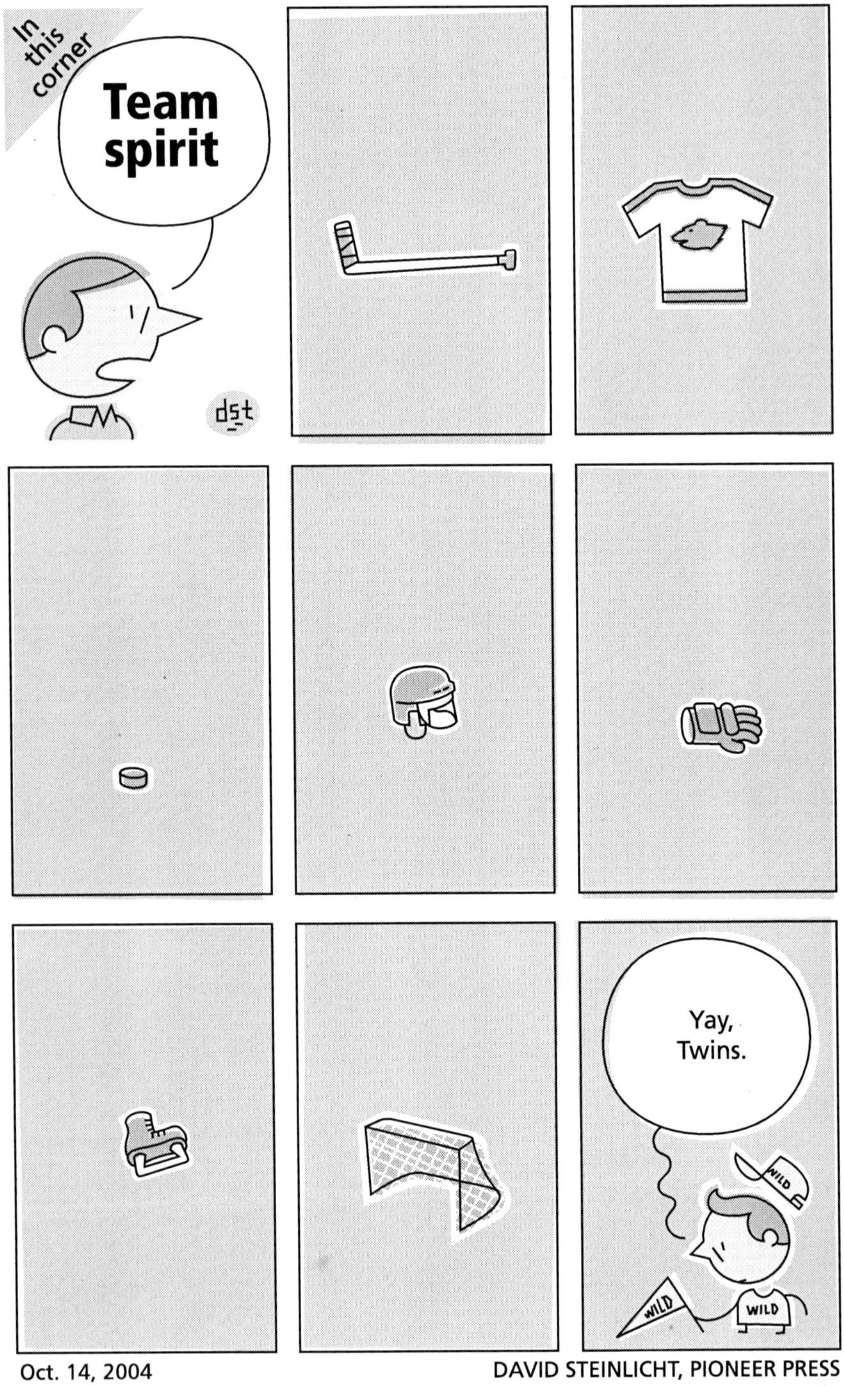
In this corner
Team spirit
dst
WILD
Yay, Twins.
WILD
WILD

Oct. 14, 2004

DAVID STEINLICHT, PIONEER PRESS

 Note: The heartbreak of a hockey strike in Minnesota.

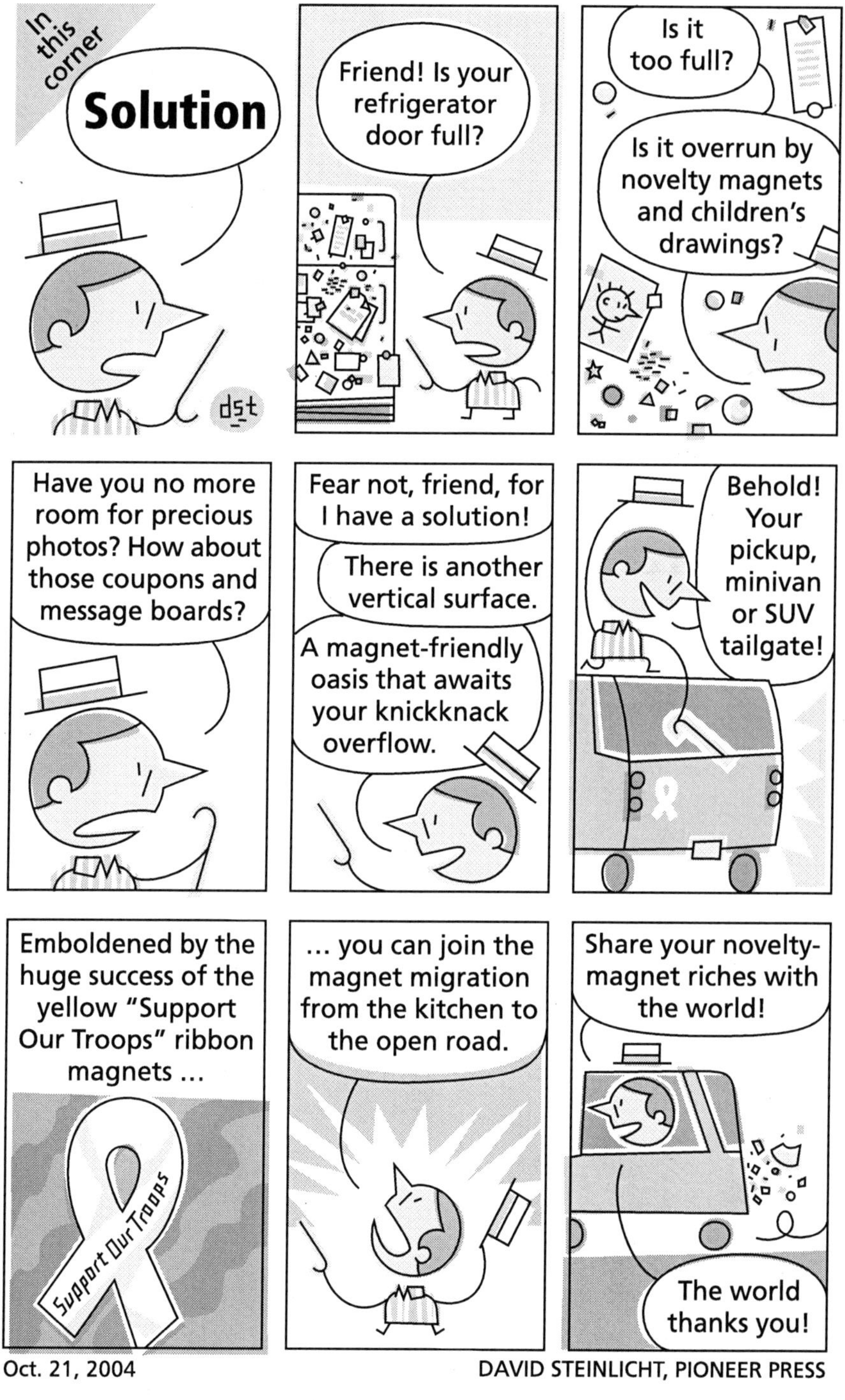
In this corner
Solution
dst
Friend! Is your refrigerator door full?
Is it too full?
Is it overrun by novelty magnets and children's drawings?
Have you no more room for precious photos? How about those coupons and message boards?
Fear not, friend, for I have a solution!
There is another vertical surface.
A magnet-friendly oasis that awaits your knickknack overflow.
Behold! Your pickup, minivan or SUV tailgate!
Emboldened by the huge success of the yellow "Support Our Troops" ribbon magnets ...
Support Our Troops
... you can join the magnet migration from the kitchen to the open road.
Share your novelty-magnet riches with the world!
The world thanks you!

Oct. 21, 2004

DAVID STEINLICHT, PIONEER PRESS

For a later DVD

There are a few things George Lucas wanted to put on the new "Star Wars" trilogy DVDs...

...but didn't 'cause he felt fans wouldn't approve.

It's all about the fans.

OK now, faster and more intense.

R2-D2 revealed to be a little guy in a little robot suit.

Dude, you're no robot!

Wookie musical number. On ice.

Rar-rr-rr!

Obi-Wan has trouble with his mind-clouding.

Those are the droids you're looking for. No, wait. I mean, they aren't.

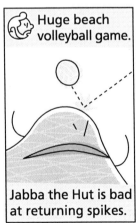

Huge beach volleyball game.

Jabba the Hut is bad at returning spikes.

Luke Skywalker loses a toe in a light saber mishap.

Anyone seen my...?

Oh.

Darth Vader is a woman. Played by Meryl Streep.

Luke, I am your evil stepmother!

!

Oct. 28, 2004

DAVID STEINLICHT, PIONEER PRESS

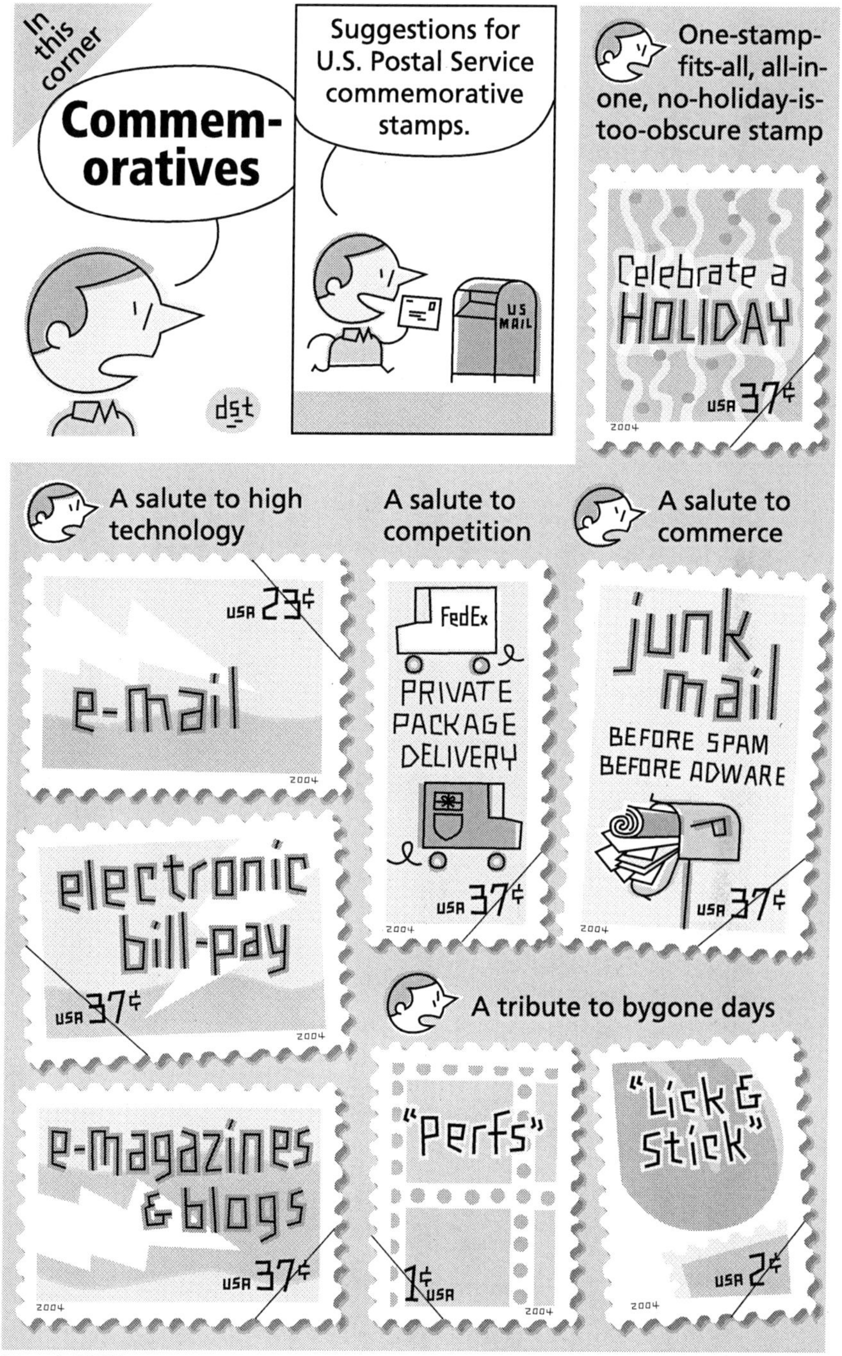

In this corner
Commem-oratives
dst
Suggestions for U.S. Postal Service commemorative stamps.
US MAIL
One-stamp-fits-all, all-in-one, no-holiday-is-too-obscure stamp
Celebrate a HOLIDAY
USA 37¢
2004
A salute to high technology
USA 23¢
e-mail
2004
electronic bill-pay
USA 37¢
2004
e-magazines & blogs
USA 37¢
2004
A salute to competition
FedEx
PRIVATE PACKAGE DELIVERY
USA 37¢
2004
A salute to commerce
junk mail
BEFORE SPAM
BEFORE ADWARE
USA 37¢
2004
A tribute to bygone days
"Perfs"
1¢ USA
2004
"Lick & Stick"
USA 2¢
2004

Nov. 4, 2004

DAVID STEINLICHT, PIONEER PRESS

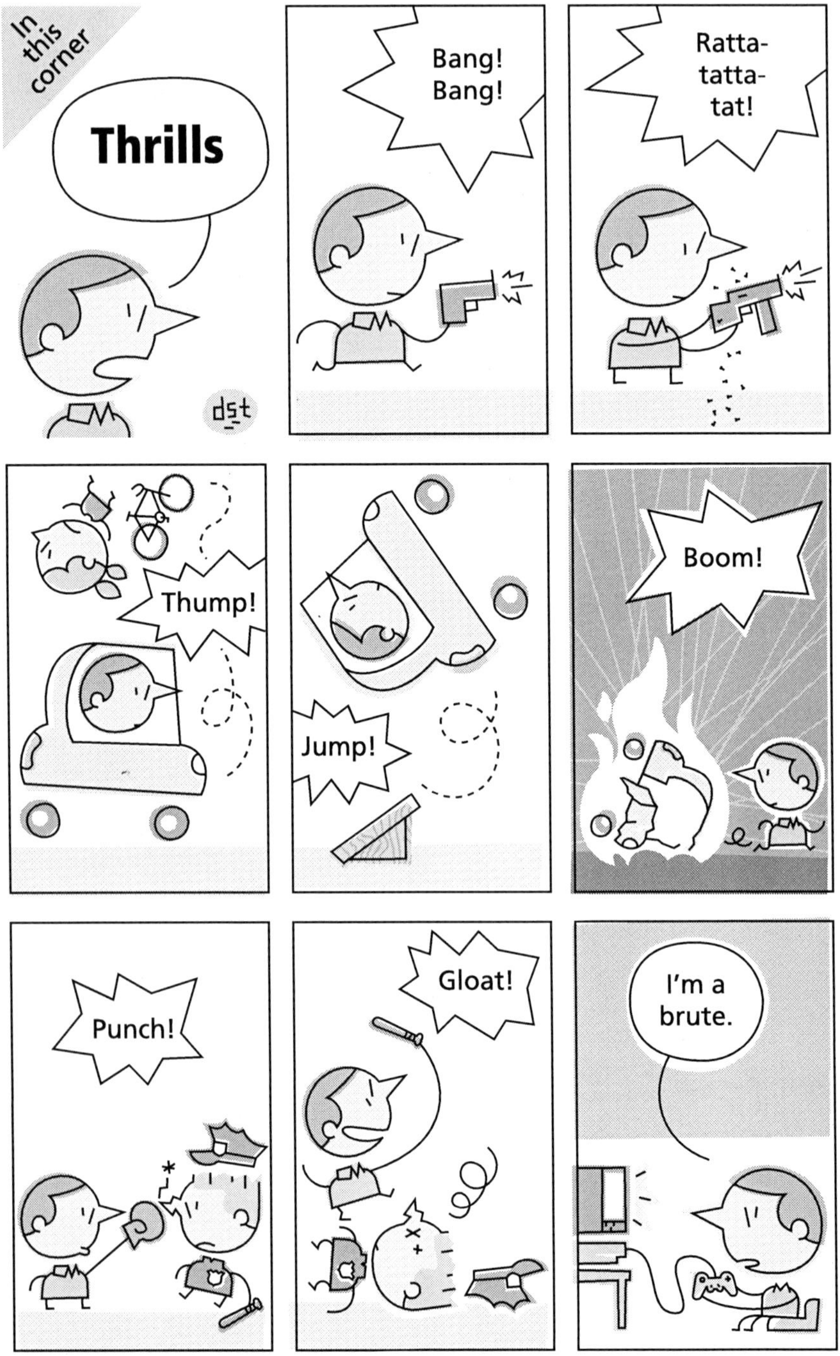
In this corner
Thrills
dst
Bang! Bang!
Ratta-tatta-tat!
Thump!
Jump!
Boom!
Punch!
Gloat!
I'm a brute.

Nov. 11, 2004

DAVID STEINLICHT, PIONEER PRESS

 Note: This won't be the last reference to *Grand Theft Auto* in these comics.

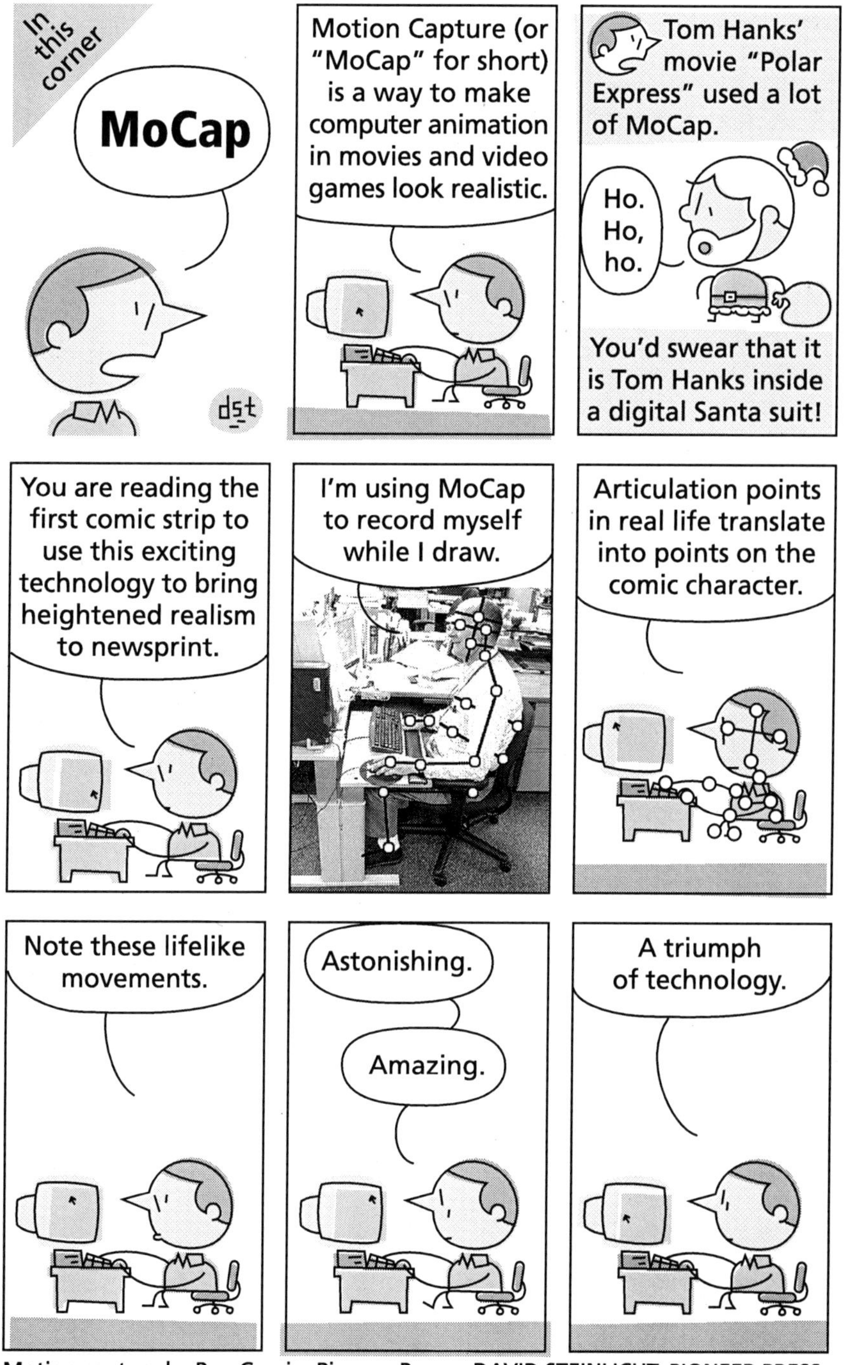
In this corner
MoCap
Motion Capture (or "MoCap" for short) is a way to make computer animation in movies and video games look realistic.
Tom Hanks' movie "Polar Express" used a lot of MoCap.
Ho. Ho, ho.
You'd swear that it is Tom Hanks inside a digital Santa suit!
dst
You are reading the first comic strip to use this exciting technology to bring heightened realism to newsprint.
I'm using MoCap to record myself while I draw.
Articulation points in real life translate into points on the comic character.
Note these lifelike movements.
Astonishing.
Amazing.
A triumph of technology.

Motion capture by Ben Garvin, Pioneer Press DAVID STEINLICHT, PIONEER PRESS
Nov. 18, 2004

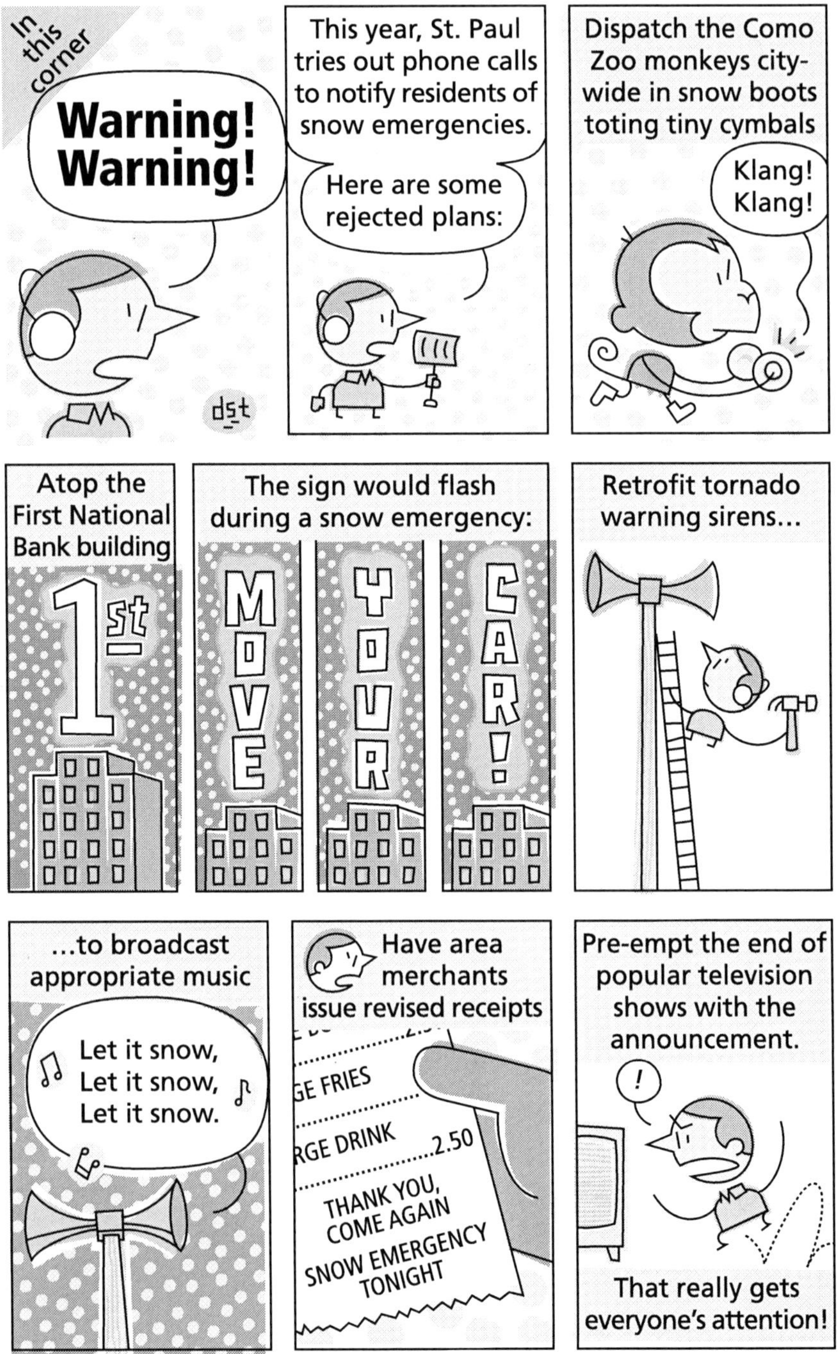
In this corner
Warning! Warning!
dst
This year, St. Paul tries out phone calls to notify residents of snow emergencies.
Here are some rejected plans:
Dispatch the Como Zoo monkeys city-wide in snow boots toting tiny cymbals
Klang! Klang!
Atop the First National Bank building
1st
The sign would flash during a snow emergency:
MOVE
YOUR
CAR!
Retrofit tornado warning sirens...
...to broadcast appropriate music
Let it snow, Let it snow, Let it snow.
Have area merchants issue revised receipts
GE FRIES
RGE DRINK 2.50
THANK YOU, COME AGAIN
SNOW EMERGENCY TONIGHT
Pre-empt the end of popular television shows with the announcement.
!
That really gets everyone's attention!

Nov. 25, 2004

DAVID STEINLICHT AND KRAIG ODDEN, PIONEER PRESS

In this corner
Remotes
dst
The remote for TiVo's TV recorder has a brightly colored Pause button right in the middle. You can't miss it. Could other specialized remotes be on the way?
A remote for teens
VOLUME
A remote for Mom
Off
A remote for the guy who says there's never anything good on
For the impatient
ON
The "Elvis" remote
TCB
Ruins the TV, but it's so, so satisfying
The "Values" remote
VIOLENCE
SEX
GENERAL NAUGHTINESS
A remote for when you can find the remote but you can't find the TV

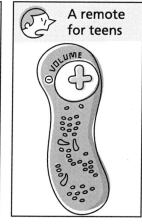

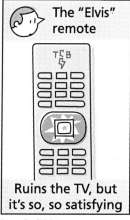

Dec. 2, 2004

DAVID STEINLICHT, PIONEER PRESS

In this corner

This season's not-hot gifts

dst

Frannie Flu doll

Coughs in your face!

Warm Wheels cars

They're warm!

"Xblocks" building block video game

How high can you stack the blocks?

Gag power strip

Sockets painted on!

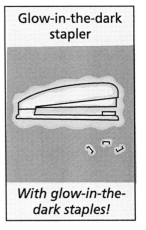

Glow-in-the-dark stapler

With glow-in-the-dark staples!

Rock, Scissors, Paper action figures

Let the battle begin!

"NBC Nightly News, the Brokaw Years, 1982-2004, the Complete Set" DVD

Whoopie cushion mouse pad (mouse not included)

Point, click, laugh!

Dec. 9. 2004

DAVID STEINLICHT, PIONEER PRESS

28

In this corner **Plants in the winter**

dst

Here's my guess as to what plants do during the long winter months.

I enjoy random selections from my DVD collection.

Today, "Little Shop of Horrors."

Knitting is comforting.

I read mysteries.

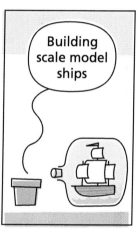

Building scale model ships

Researching my family history

I take cooking classes.

Yoga and meditation

Dec. 16, 2004

DAVID STEINLICHT, PIONEER PRESS

Gift skills

You've seen ads featuring a car with the big bow on it. Since you probably aren't getting a car, perhaps you should polish up your gift guessing skills.

What are these wrapped gifts? Answers are at the bottom of this comic.

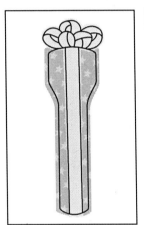

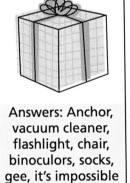

Answers: Anchor, vacuum cleaner, flashlight, chair, binoculors, socks, gee, it's impossible to know.

Dec. 23, 2004

DAVID STEINLICHT, PIONEER PRESS

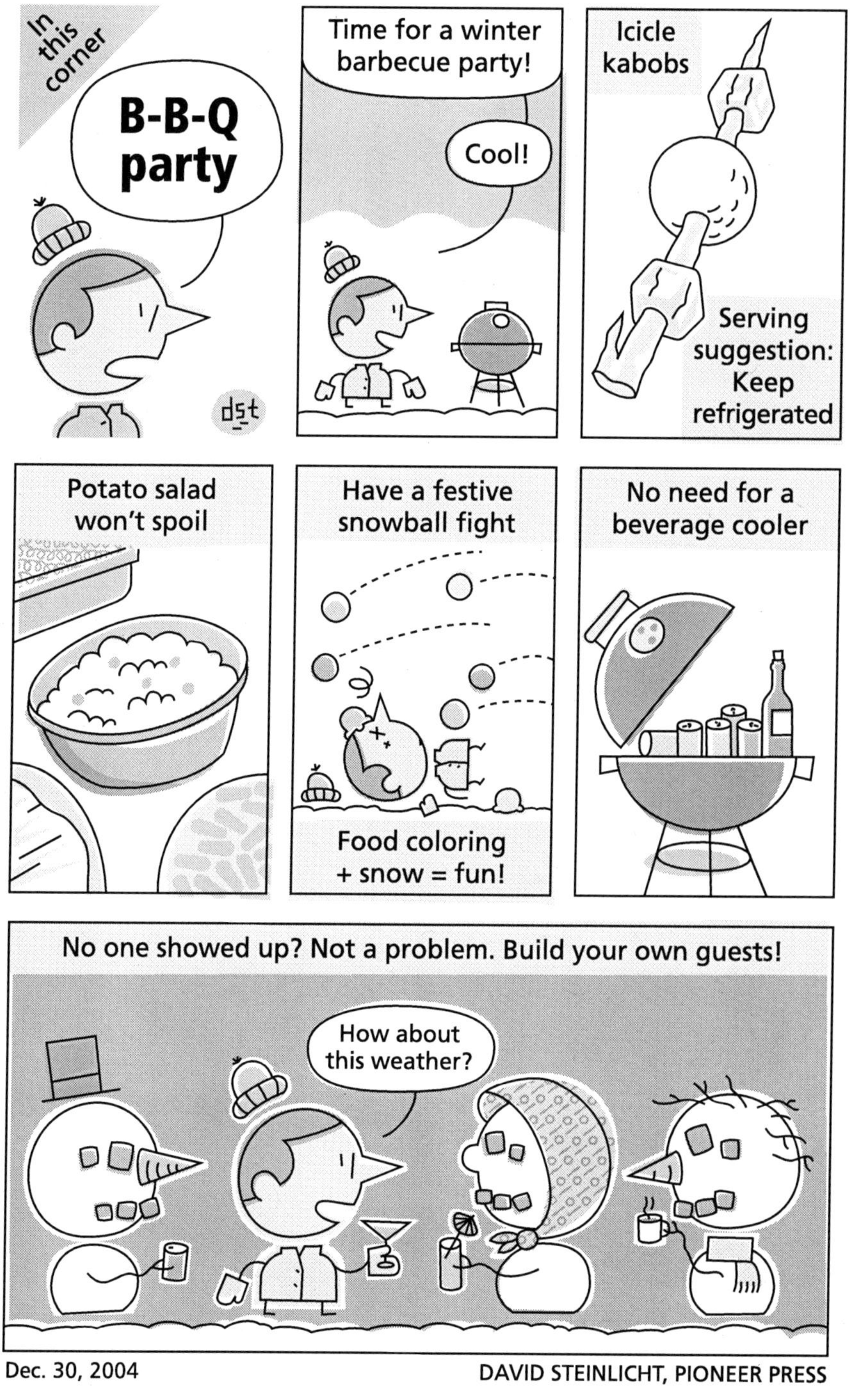
In this corner
B-B-Q party
dst
Time for a winter barbecue party!
Cool!
Icicle kabobs
Serving suggestion: Keep refrigerated
Potato salad won't spoil
Have a festive snowball fight
Food coloring + snow = fun!
No need for a beverage cooler
No one showed up? Not a problem. Build your own guests!
How about this weather?

Dec. 30, 2004

DAVID STEINLICHT, PIONEER PRESS

2004 | 2005 | 2006 | 2007 | 2008 | 2009

2005

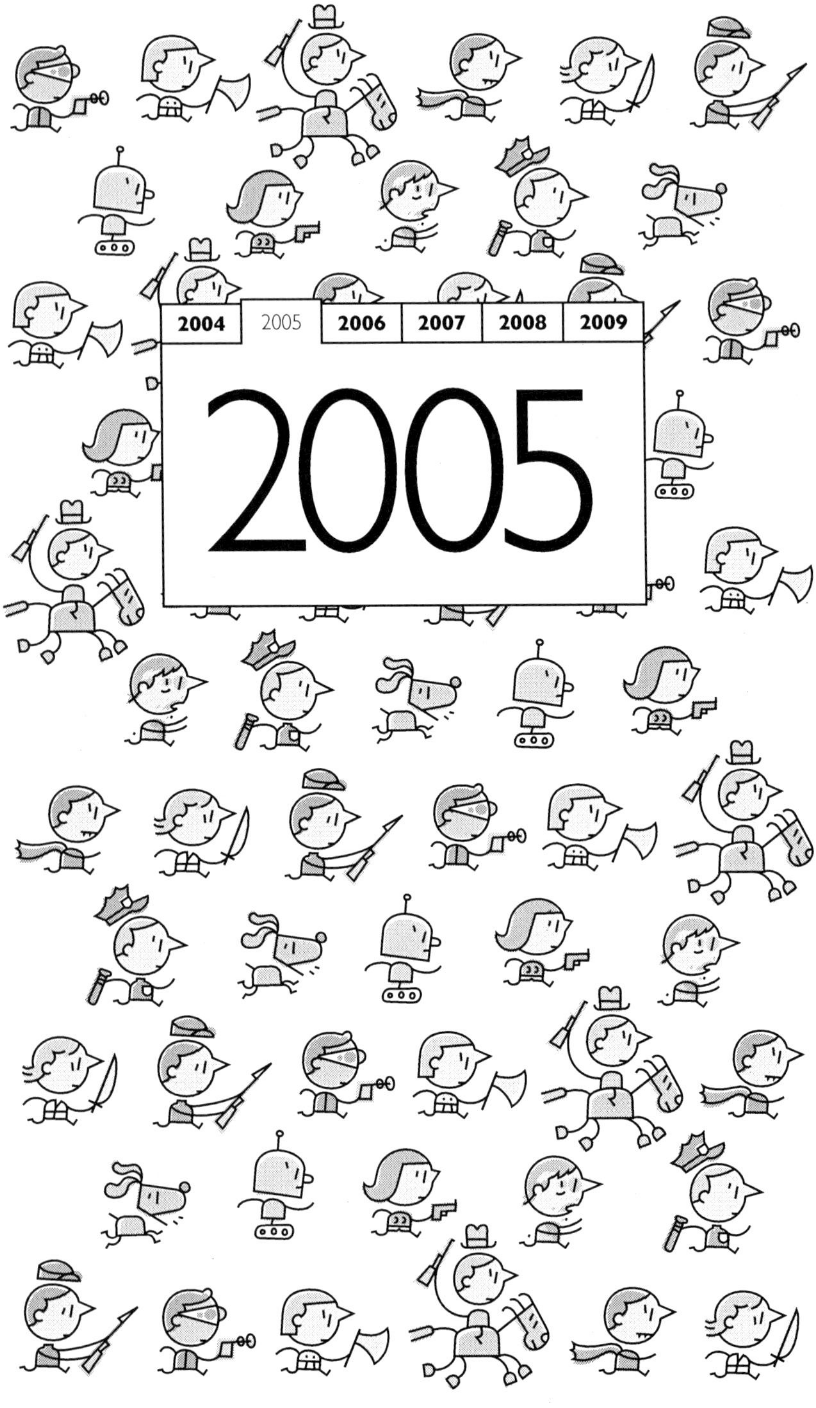

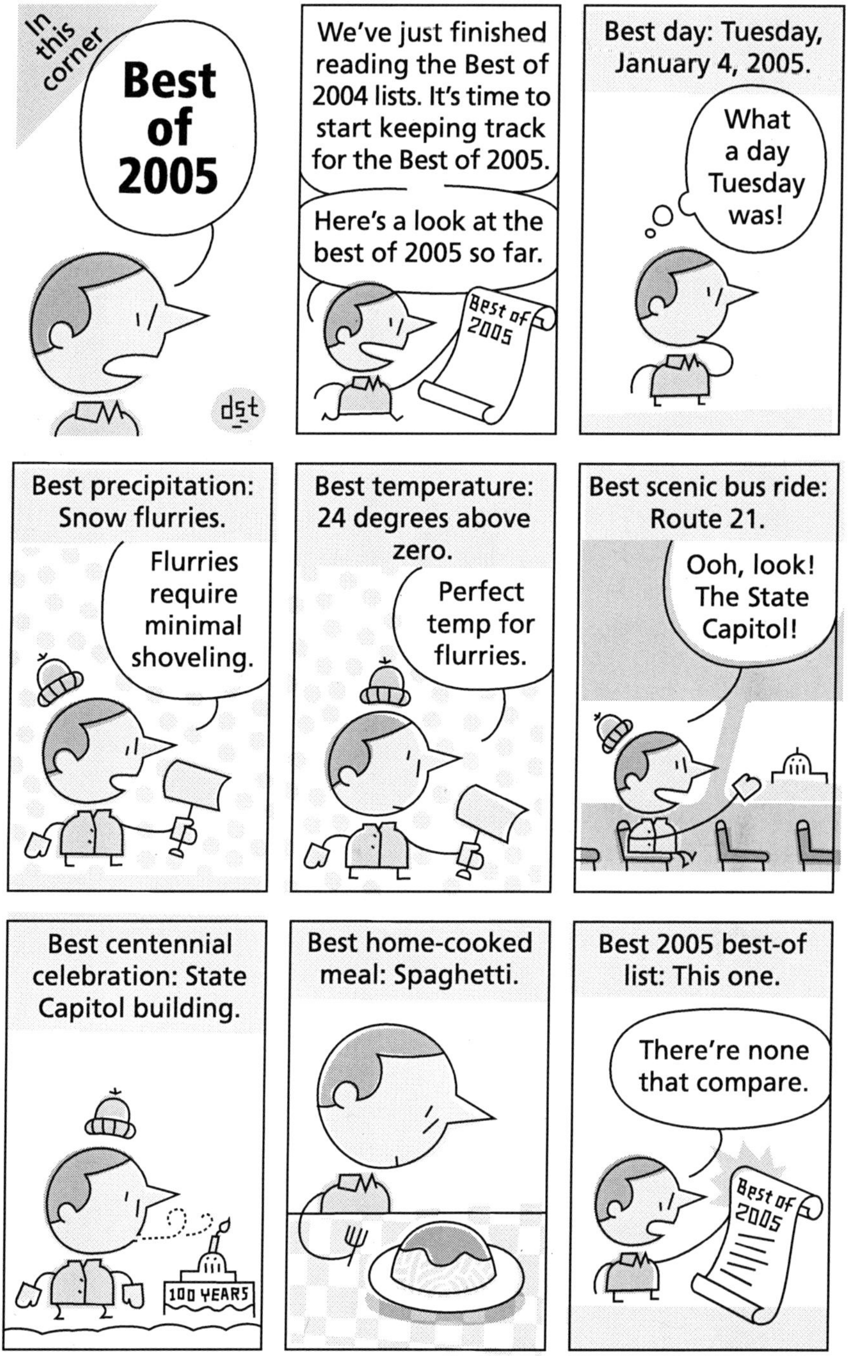

In this corner
Best of 2005
dst
We've just finished reading the Best of 2004 lists. It's time to start keeping track for the Best of 2005.
Here's a look at the best of 2005 so far.
Best of 2005
Best day: Tuesday, January 4, 2005.
What a day Tuesday was!
Best precipitation: Snow flurries.
Flurries require minimal shoveling.
Best temperature: 24 degrees above zero.
Perfect temp for flurries.
Best scenic bus ride: Route 21.
Ooh, look! The State Capitol!
Best centennial celebration: State Capitol building.
100 YEARS
Best home-cooked meal: Spaghetti.
Best 2005 best-of list: This one.
There're none that compare.
Best of 2005

Jan. 6, 2005

DAVID STEINLICHT, PIONEER PRESS

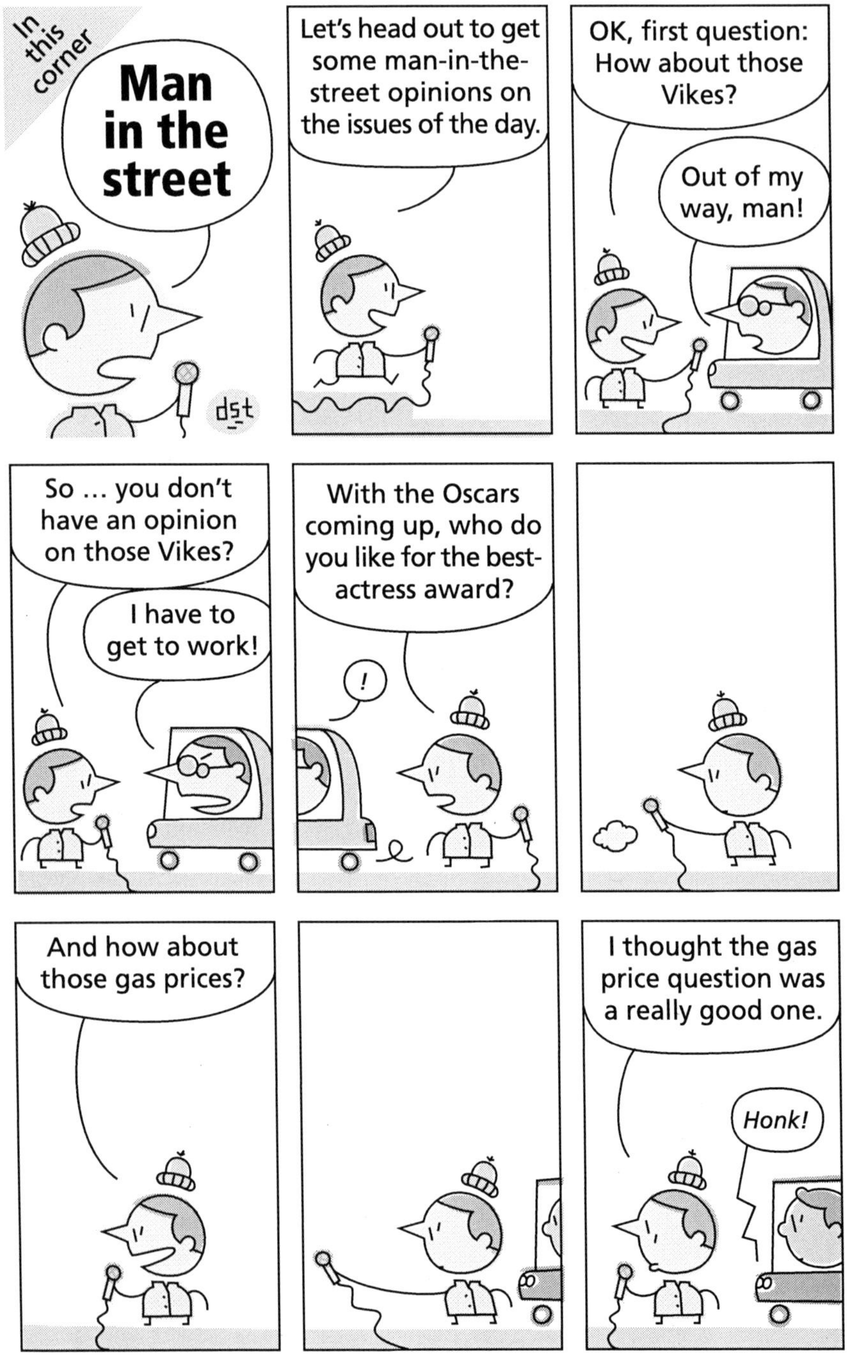
In this corner
Man in the street
dst
Let's head out to get some man-in-the-street opinions on the issues of the day.
OK, first question: How about those Vikes?
Out of my way, man!
So ... you don't have an opinion on those Vikes?
I have to get to work!
With the Oscars coming up, who do you like for the best-actress award?
!
And how about those gas prices?
I thought the gas price question was a really good one.
Honk!

Jan. 13, 2005

DAVID STEINLICHT, PIONEER PRESS

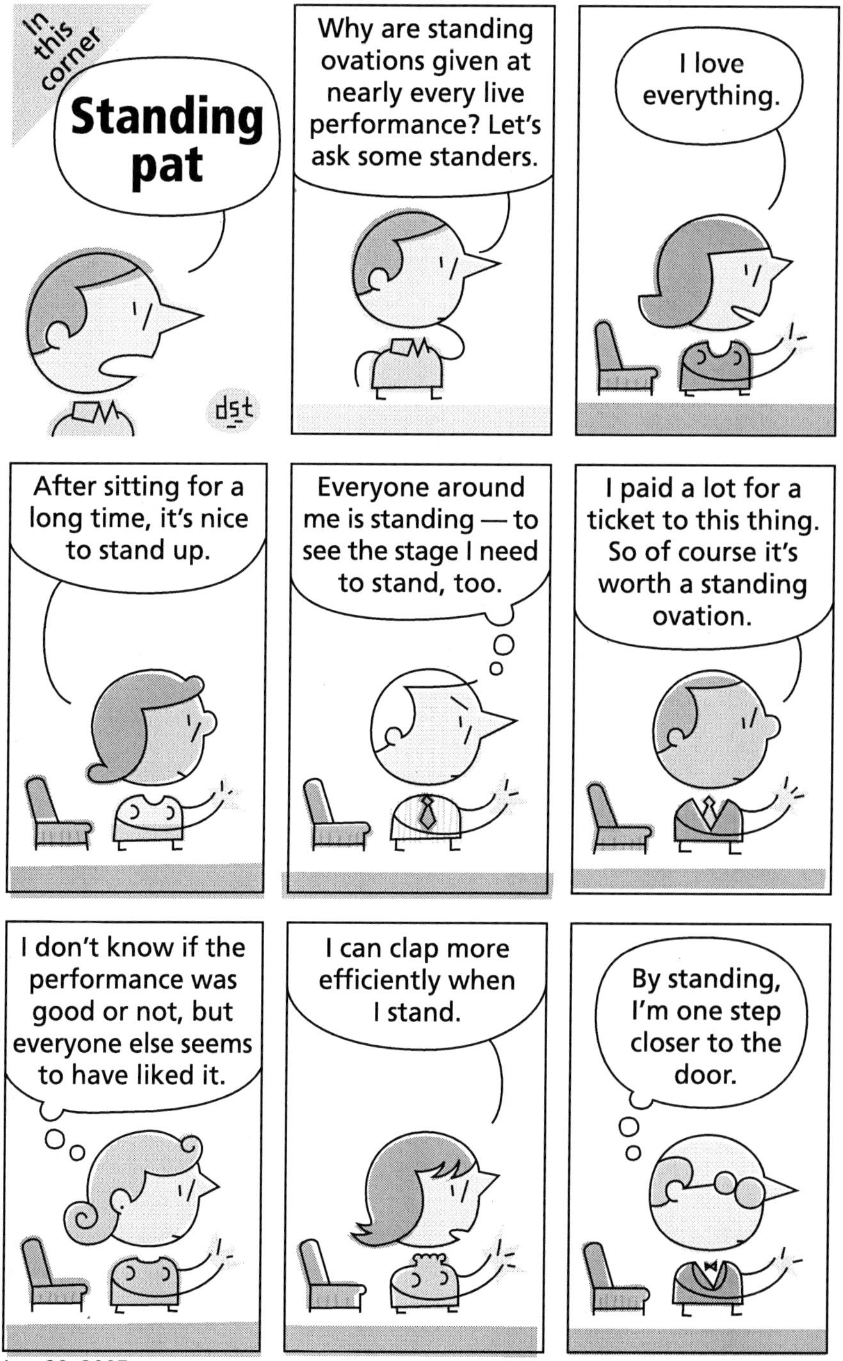
In this corner
Standing pat
dst
Why are standing ovations given at nearly every live performance? Let's ask some standers.
I love everything.
After sitting for a long time, it's nice to stand up.
Everyone around me is standing — to see the stage I need to stand, too.
I paid a lot for a ticket to this thing. So of course it's worth a standing ovation.
I don't know if the performance was good or not, but everyone else seems to have liked it.
I can clap more efficiently when I stand.
By standing, I'm one step closer to the door.

Jan. 20, 2005

DAVID STEINLICHT, PIONEER PRESS

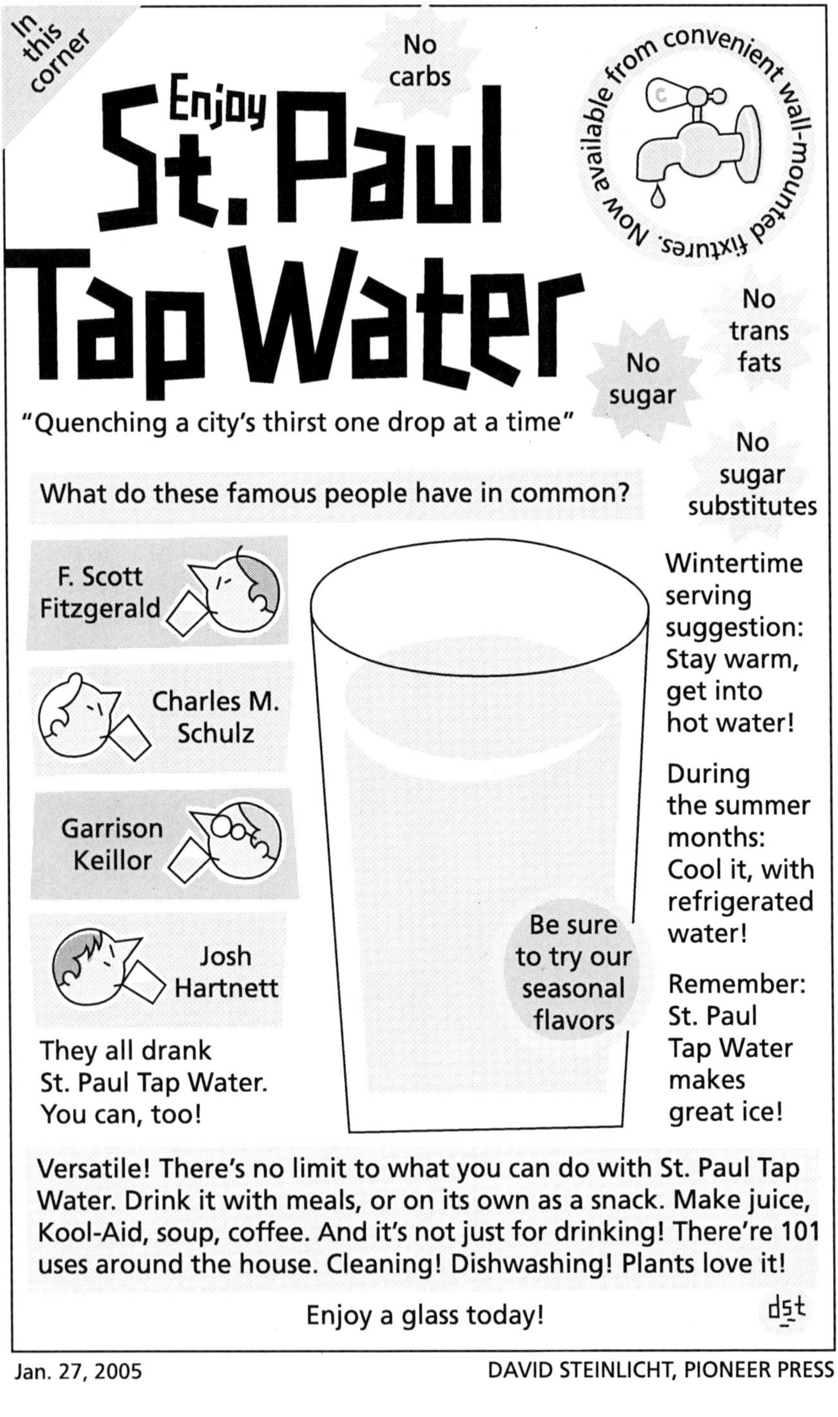

Enjoy St. Paul Tap Water

No carbs

Now available from convenient wall-mounted fixtures.

No sugar

No trans fats

No sugar substitutes

"Quenching a city's thirst one drop at a time"

What do these famous people have in common?

F. Scott Fitzgerald

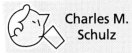

Charles M. Schulz

Garrison Keillor

Josh Hartnett

They all drank St. Paul Tap Water. You can, too!

Be sure to try our seasonal flavors

Wintertime serving suggestion: Stay warm, get into hot water!

During the summer months: Cool it, with refrigerated water!

Remember: St. Paul Tap Water makes great ice!

Versatile! There's no limit to what you can do with St. Paul Tap Water. Drink it with meals, or on its own as a snack. Make juice, Kool-Aid, soup, coffee. And it's not just for drinking! There're 101 uses around the house. Cleaning! Dishwashing! Plants love it!

Enjoy a glass today!

dst

Jan. 27, 2005

DAVID STEINLICHT, PIONEER PRESS

36 *Note:* It's a St. Paul thing … the water has a taste, okay?

Vulcan vs. Vulcan

Vulcanus Rex vs. Mr. Spock, a Vulcan.

Firehose	Phaser

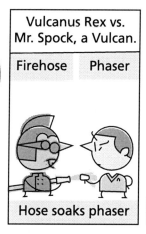

Hose soaks phaser

Frost-bit ears	Pointy ears

Cold blunts points

Beer	Logic

Beer confuses logic

Fire truck	Starship Enterprise

Starship toasts truck

Sidekick fight

Klondike Kate overpowers T'Pol

Mind meld	Snow melt

Wet?

Melt distracts meld

Live long and prosper

Community service and act silly

Spock's slogan is better

The winner? It's Vulcanus Rex!

Sorry, man. I win every year

Live long and party!

Feb. 3, 2005   DAVID STEINLICHT, PIONEER PRESS

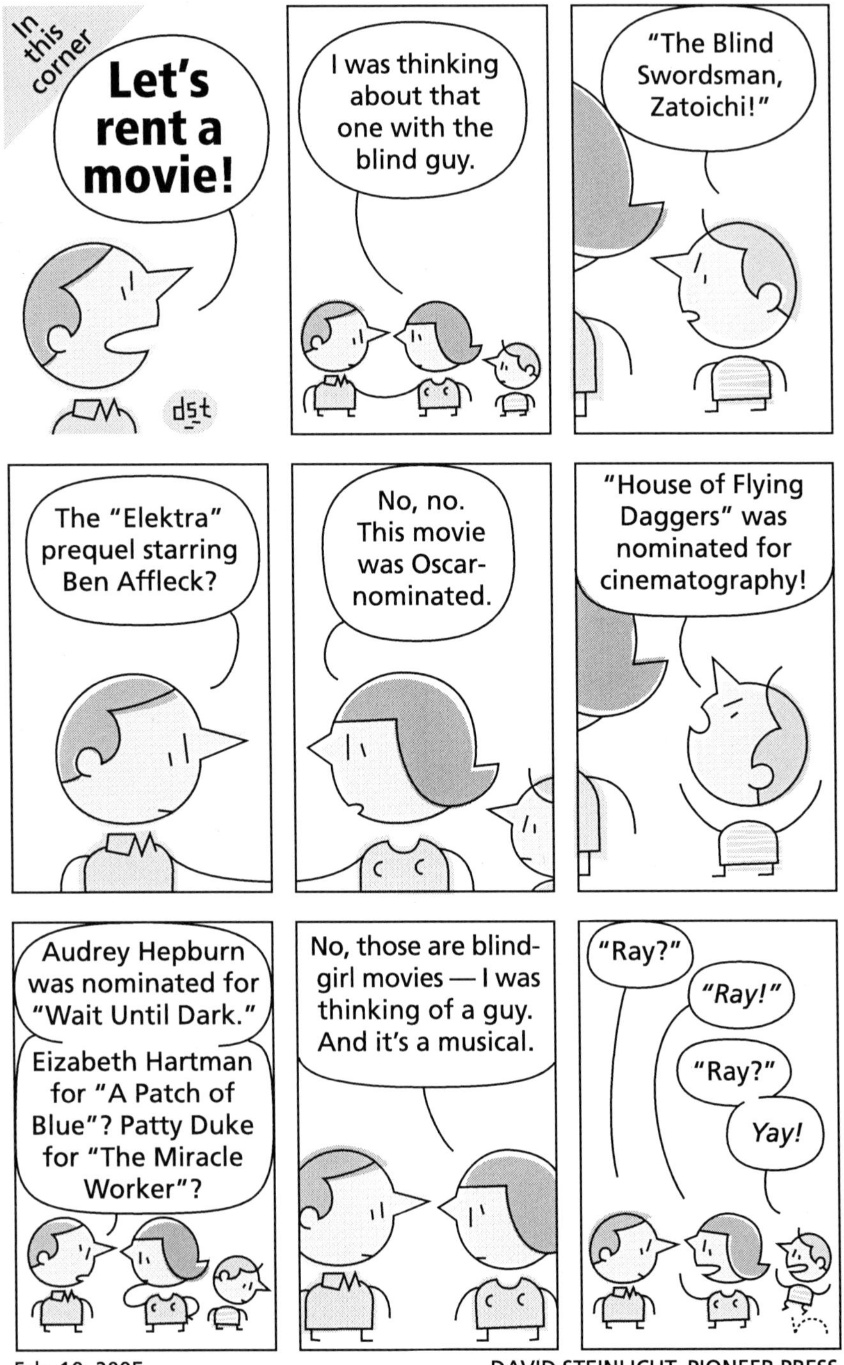
In this corner
Let's rent a movie!
dst
I was thinking about that one with the blind guy.
"The Blind Swordsman, Zatoichi!"
The "Elektra" prequel starring Ben Affleck?
No, no. This movie was Oscar-nominated.
"House of Flying Daggers" was nominated for cinematography!
Audrey Hepburn was nominated for "Wait Until Dark."
Eizabeth Hartman for "A Patch of Blue"? Patty Duke for "The Miracle Worker"?
No, those are blind-girl movies — I was thinking of a guy. And it's a musical.
"Ray?"
"Ray!"
"Ray?"
Yay!

Feb. 10, 2005

DAVID STEINLICHT, PIONEER PRESS

In this corner

Trend watch

dst

What's the next big thing?

Coughing.

Sniff!

Everyone's doing it.

Honk!

Sniffing

Snuffling

Hacking

Sneezing

Wheezing

It's a trend that couldn't be hotter.

As usual, kids are at the trend's forefront.

Erm!

Here's a Sick Fakie 360 — with cough.

However, businesses are catching up.

Where'd you get that cute cough?

Moviegoers and theatergoers're keeping the trend rolling along.

Ha, ha, ha, hack, hack, *hack, hack!*

And shoppers everywhere are clamoring to get in on the fun.

Cough! Cough! Cough! Cough! Cough! Cough! Cough! Cough! Cough! Cough!

So, get with it. Get coughing.

Feb. 17, 2005

DAVID STEINLICHT, PIONEER PRESS

Pluggerz

dst

Some pluggerz are direct while others are alternating.

AC stinks! DC rocks!

Maybe...

A few pluggerz just don't fit in.

Boo-hoo!

Many pluggerz are well-grounded.

I get a charge out of being dull.

There are pluggerz live wires.

You heard the one that starts, "A three-foot piece of Romex walks into a bar...?"

The pluggerz insurance plan.

If you get carried away, I'm there for you.

Occasionally, pluggerz have to adapt.

Three's a crowd? Not a problem.

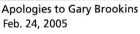

Pluggerz have a sense of community.

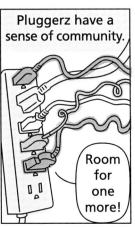

Room for one more!

Mostly, pluggerz keep on plugging.

Apologies to Gary Brookins
Feb. 24, 2005

DAVID STEINLICHT, PIONEER PRESS

40   Note: I happen to think inanimate objects are innately funny.

In this corner

The visitors

St. Paul is awash in visitors. High school sports tournaments are the reason. The Saintly City has advice for dealing with newcomers.

Sure thing, thanks for having me back in the comic. It's been awhile...

ST. PAUL

First off, visitors to St. Paul don't understand our street numbers. Heck, neither do I!

ST. PAUL

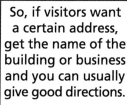

So, if visitors want a certain address, get the name of the building or business and you can usually give good directions.

ST. PAUL

Visitors are often looking for Xcel Energy Center, McDonald's, and Marshall Field's. And a nice fancy place to eat.

ST. PAUL

If you keep that in mind, you can usually direct visitors where they want to go.

ST. PAUL

Cool. So we shouldn't give them wrong directions just for fun?

Oh, no! If you want to have that kind of fun, go over to Minneapolis and give directions.

Hey!

ST. PAUL

MPLS.

Mar. 10, 2005

DAVID STEINLICHT, PIONEER PRESS

41

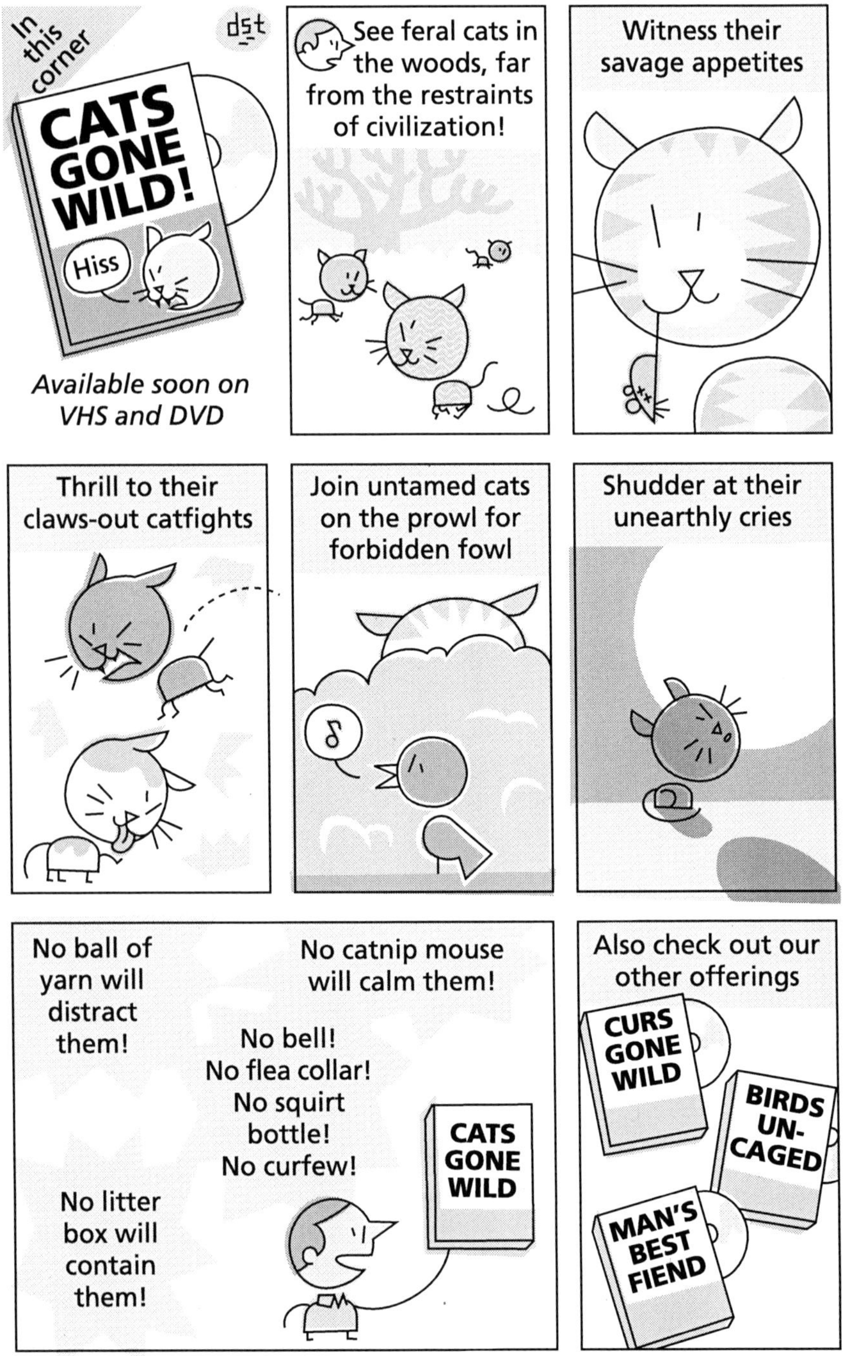
In this corner
dst
CATS GONE WILD!
Hiss
Available soon on VHS and DVD
See feral cats in the woods, far from the restraints of civilization!
Witness their savage appetites
Thrill to their claws-out catfights
Join untamed cats on the prowl for forbidden fowl
Shudder at their unearthly cries
No ball of yarn will distract them!
No catnip mouse will calm them!
No bell!
No flea collar!
No squirt bottle!
No curfew!
No litter box will contain them!
CATS GONE WILD
Also check out our other offerings
CURS GONE WILD
BIRDS UN-CAGED
MAN'S BEST FIEND

Mar. 17, 2005

DAVID STEINLICHT, PIONEER PRESS

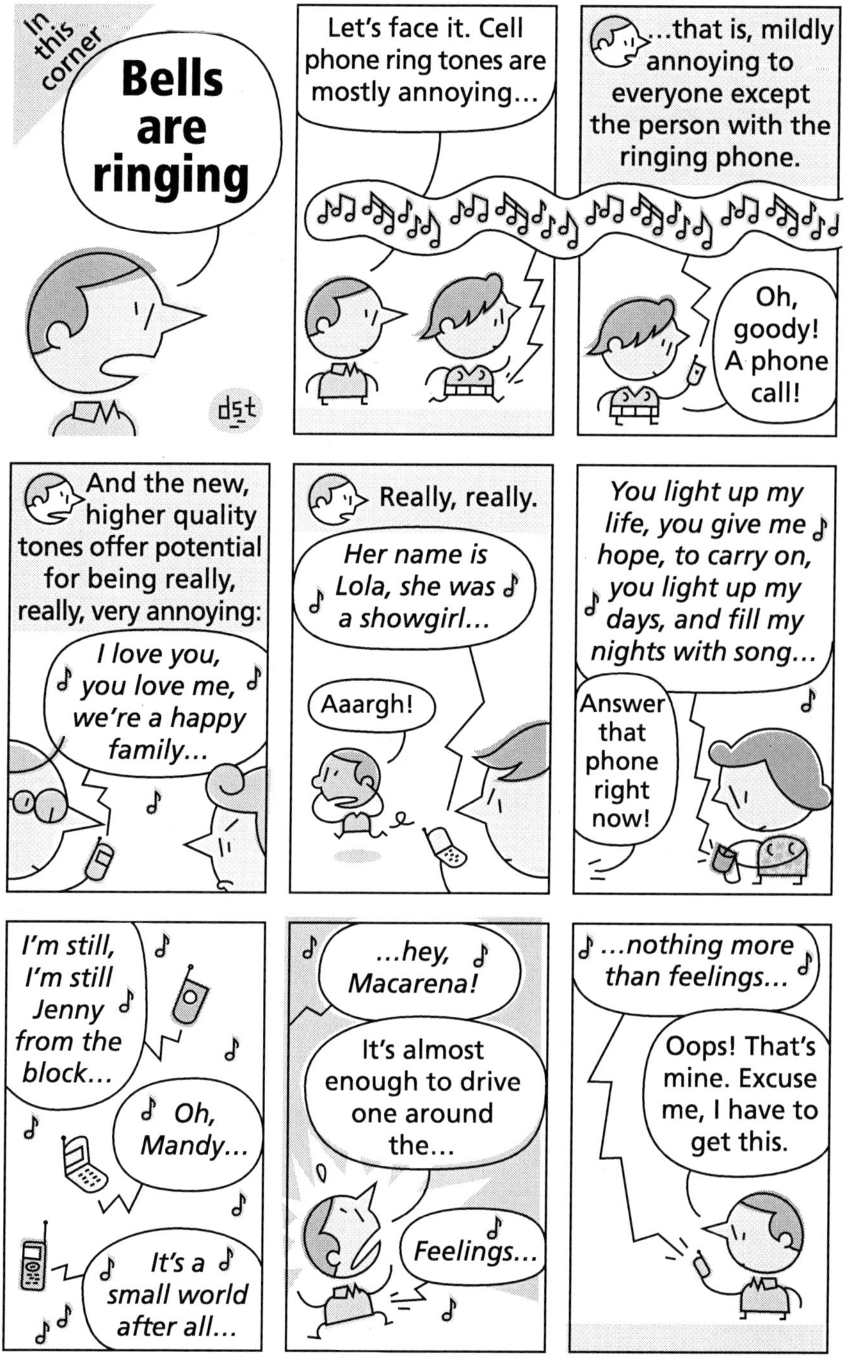

In this corner
Bells are ringing
dst
Let's face it. Cell phone ring tones are mostly annoying...
...that is, mildly annoying to everyone except the person with the ringing phone.
Oh, goody! A phone call!
And the new, higher quality tones offer potential for being really, really, very annoying:
I love you, you love me, we're a happy family...
Really, really.
Her name is Lola, she was a showgirl...
Aaargh!
You light up my life, you give me hope, to carry on, you light up my days, and fill my nights with song...
Answer that phone right now!
I'm still, I'm still Jenny from the block...
Oh, Mandy...
It's a small world after all...
...hey, Macarena!
It's almost enough to drive one around the...
Feelings...
...nothing more than feelings...
Oops! That's mine. Excuse me, I have to get this.

Mar. 24, 2005

DAVID STEINLICHT, PIONEER PRESS

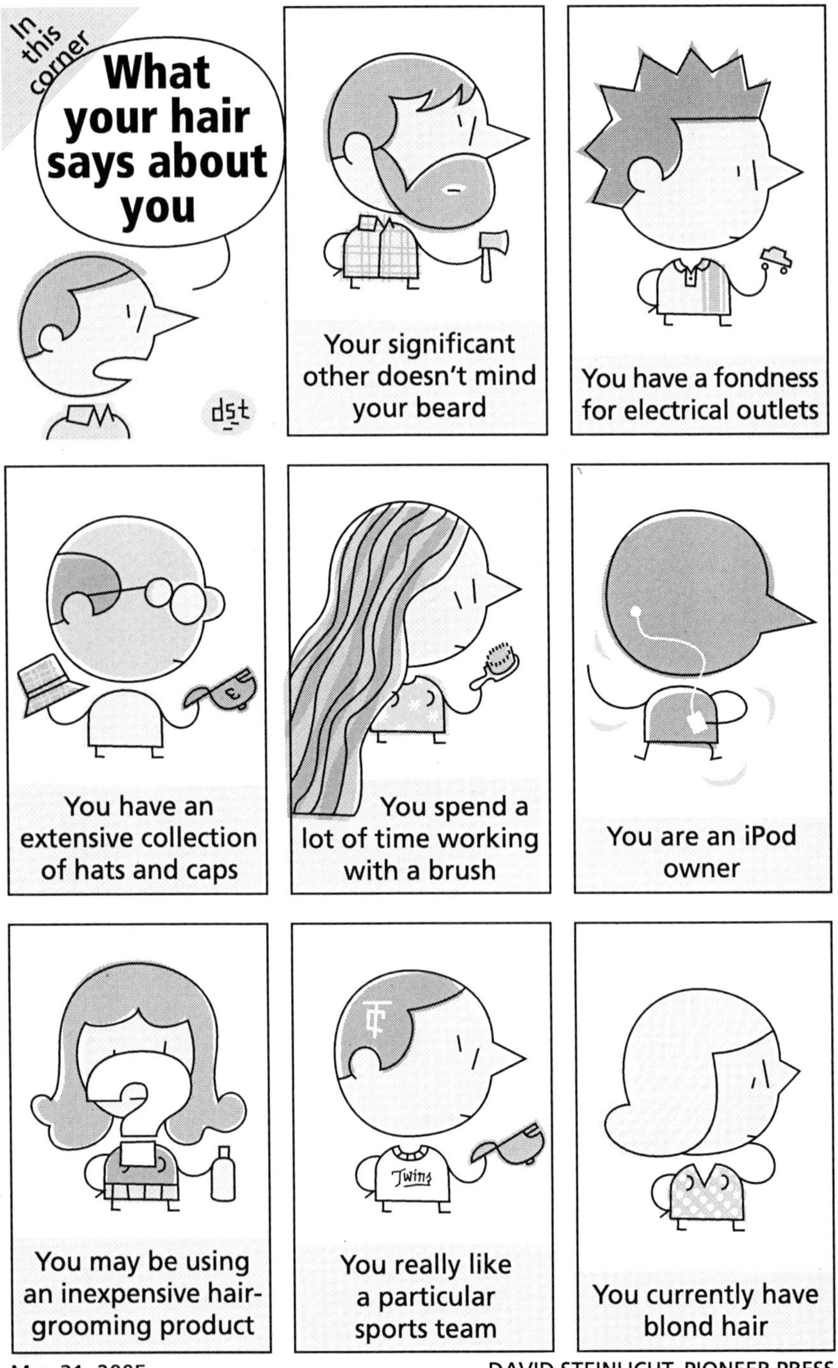
In this corner
What your hair says about you
dst
Your significant other doesn't mind your beard
You have a fondness for electrical outlets
You have an extensive collection of hats and caps
You spend a lot of time working with a brush
You are an iPod owner
You may be using an inexpensive hair-grooming product
You really like a particular sports team
Twins
You currently have blond hair

Mar. 31, 2005

DAVID STEINLICHT, PIONEER PRESS

Note: This comic was inspired by a series of bus stop posters featuring people with big question marks in front of their faces. Advertising a hair care product.

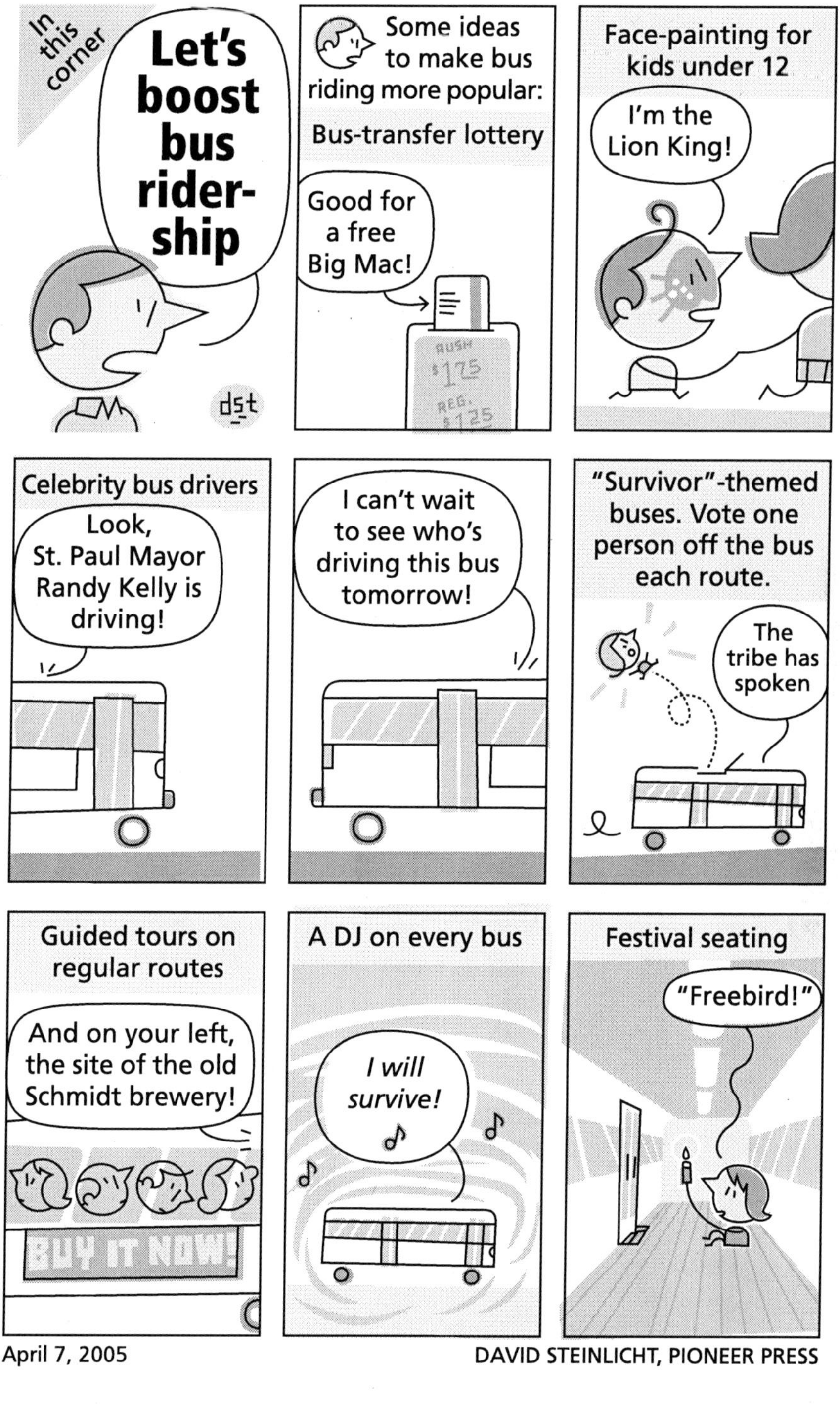
In this corner
Let's boost bus ridership
dst
Some ideas to make bus riding more popular:
Bus-transfer lottery
Good for a free Big Mac!
RUSH $1.75
REG. $1.25
Face-painting for kids under 12
I'm the Lion King!
Celebrity bus drivers
Look, St. Paul Mayor Randy Kelly is driving!
I can't wait to see who's driving this bus tomorrow!
"Survivor"-themed buses. Vote one person off the bus each route.
The tribe has spoken
Guided tours on regular routes
And on your left, the site of the old Schmidt brewery!
BUY IT NOW!
A DJ on every bus
I will survive!
Festival seating
"Freebird!"

April 7, 2005

DAVID STEINLICHT, PIONEER PRESS

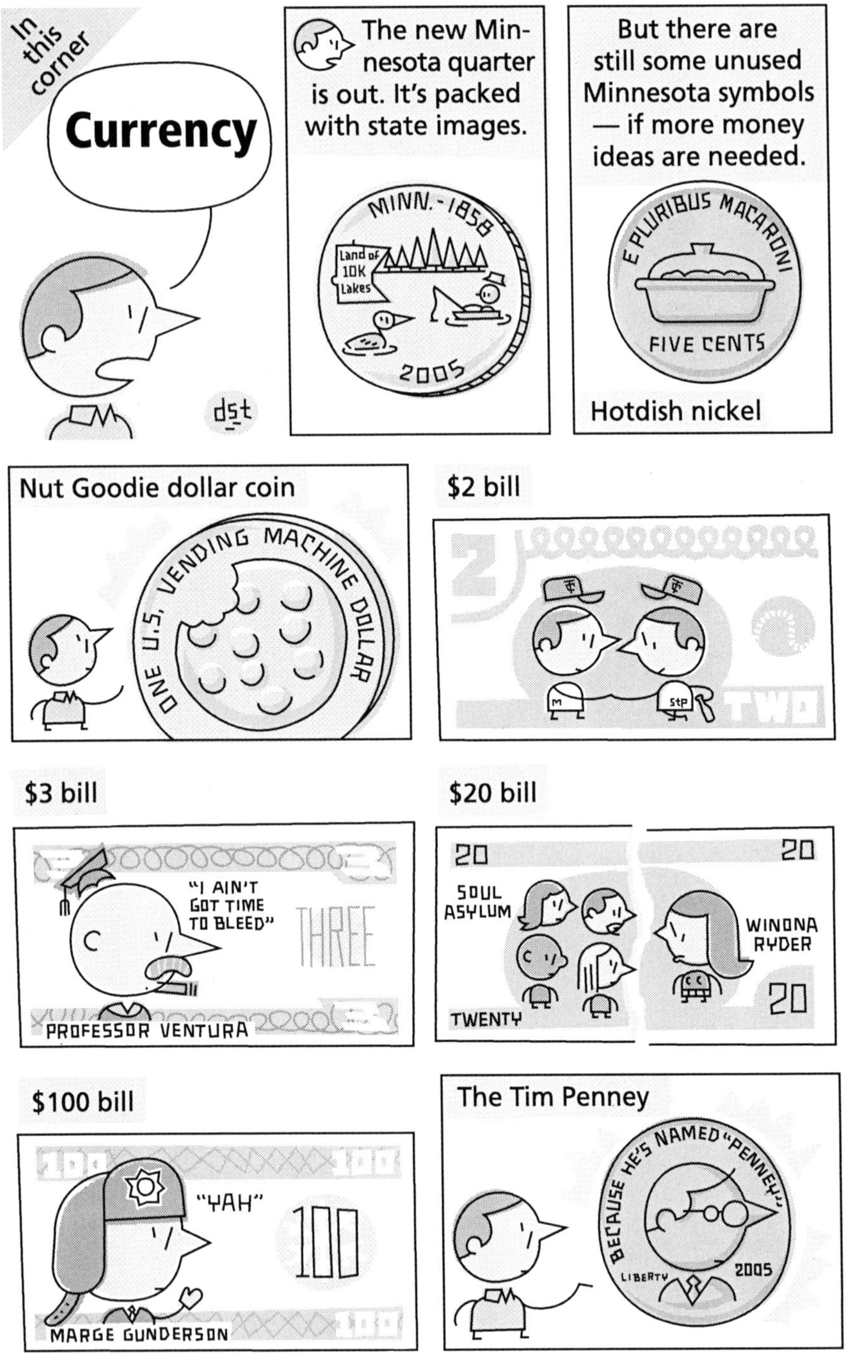

In this corner
Currency
dst
The new Minnesota quarter is out. It's packed with state images.
MINN.-1858
Land of 10K Lakes
2005
But there are still some unused Minnesota symbols — if more money ideas are needed.
E PLURIBUS MACARONI
FIVE CENTS
Hotdish nickel
Nut Goodie dollar coin
ONE U.S. VENDING MACHINE DOLLAR
$2 bill
TWO
$3 bill
"I AIN'T GOT TIME TO BLEED"
THREE
PROFESSOR VENTURA
$20 bill
20
SOUL ASYLUM
WINONA RYDER
TWENTY
$100 bill
"YAH"
100
MARGE GUNDERSON
The Tim Penney
BECAUSE HE'S NAMED "PENNEY"
LIBERTY
2005

April 21, 2005

DAVID STEINLICHT, PIONEER PRESS

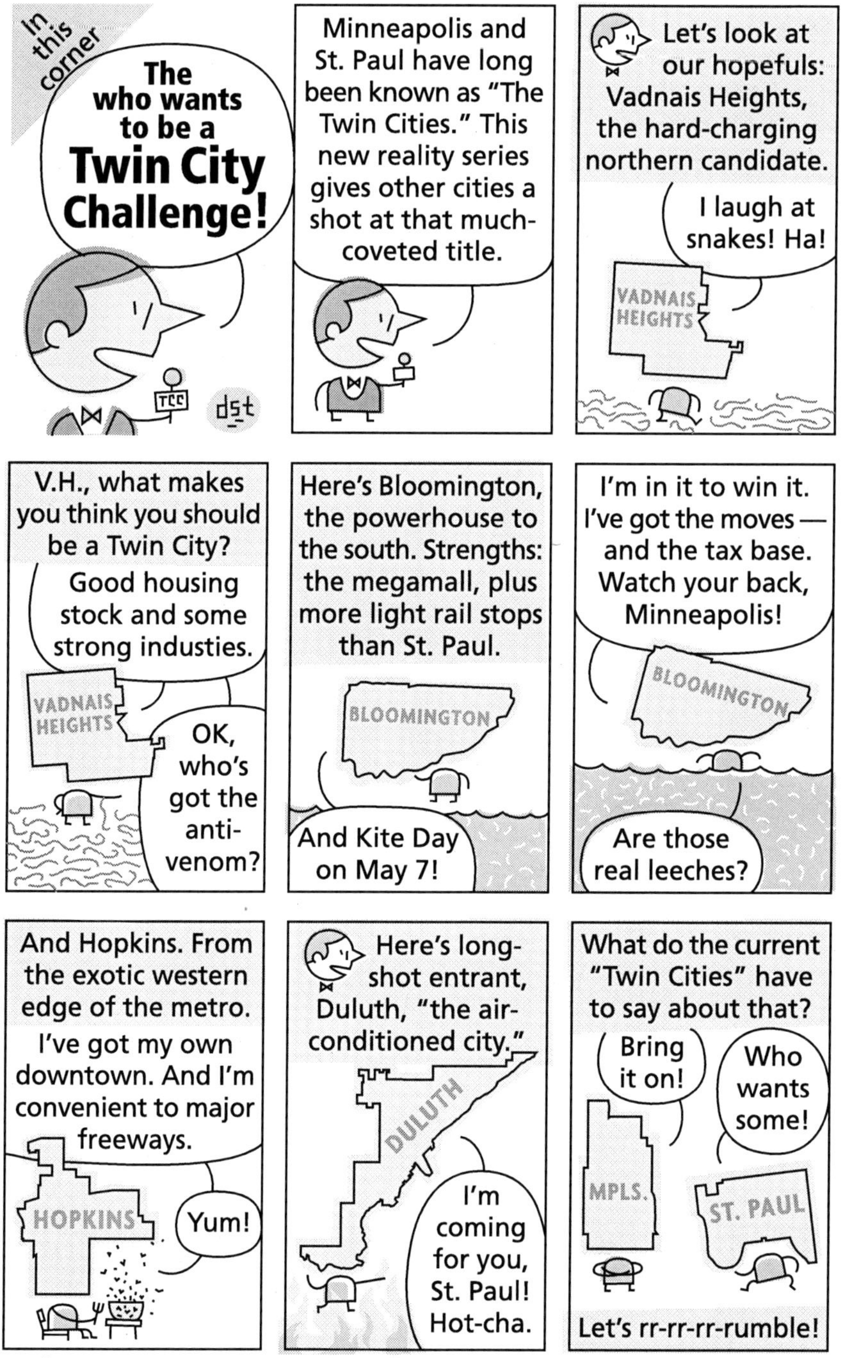
In this corner
The who wants to be a Twin City Challenge!
TCC
dst
Minneapolis and St. Paul have long been known as "The Twin Cities." This new reality series gives other cities a shot at that much-coveted title.
Let's look at our hopefuls: Vadnais Heights, the hard-charging northern candidate.
I laugh at snakes! Ha!
VADNAIS HEIGHTS
V.H., what makes you think you should be a Twin City?
Good housing stock and some strong industies.
VADNAIS HEIGHTS
OK, who's got the anti-venom?
Here's Bloomington, the powerhouse to the south. Strengths: the megamall, plus more light rail stops than St. Paul.
BLOOMINGTON
And Kite Day on May 7!
I'm in it to win it. I've got the moves — and the tax base. Watch your back, Minneapolis!
BLOOMINGTON
Are those real leeches?
And Hopkins. From the exotic western edge of the metro.
I've got my own downtown. And I'm convenient to major freeways.
HOPKINS
Yum!
Here's long-shot entrant, Duluth, "the air-conditioned city."
DULUTH
I'm coming for you, St. Paul! Hot-cha.
What do the current "Twin Cities" have to say about that?
Bring it on!
Who wants some!
MPLS.
ST. PAUL
Let's rr-rr-rr-rumble!

April 28, 2005

DAVID STEINLICHT, PIONEER PRESS

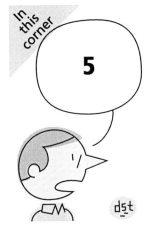

5

Did you notice today's date? May 5, 2005, can be abbreviated as 05/05/05. Wow, that's kinda cool!

Perhaps it's a day one should get excited about the fives that surround us in this world.

Five fingers on each hand...

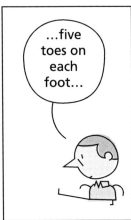

...five toes on each foot...

...five forward speeds on a gearshift...

Except when it's three or four or six.

...and, um, ah, lots of other instances...

...fives are absolutely everywhere...

...

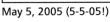

...how many can *you* name?

Later...
I think I got out of that one rather well.

You're telling me that "May 5, 2005" was the basis for the entire comic strip?

May 5, 2005 (5-5-05!)

DAVID STEINLICHT, PIONEER PRESS

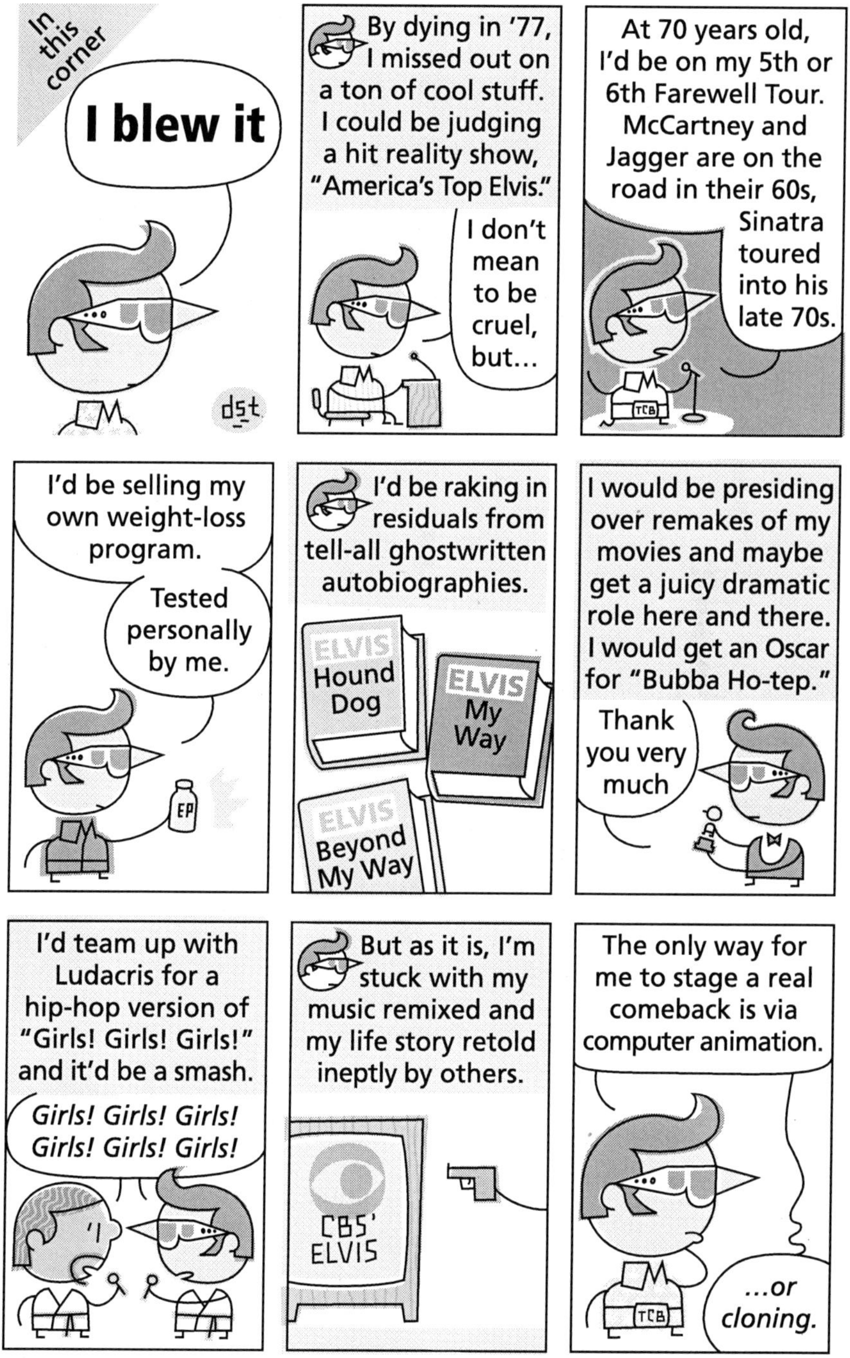
In this corner
I blew it
dst
By dying in '77, I missed out on a ton of cool stuff. I could be judging a hit reality show, "America's Top Elvis."
I don't mean to be cruel, but…
At 70 years old, I'd be on my 5th or 6th Farewell Tour. McCartney and Jagger are on the road in their 60s, Sinatra toured into his late 70s.
TCB
I'd be selling my own weight-loss program.
Tested personally by me.
EP
I'd be raking in residuals from tell-all ghostwritten autobiographies.
ELVIS Hound Dog
ELVIS My Way
ELVIS Beyond My Way
I would be presiding over remakes of my movies and maybe get a juicy dramatic role here and there. I would get an Oscar for "Bubba Ho-tep."
Thank you very much
I'd team up with Ludacris for a hip-hop version of "Girls! Girls! Girls!" and it'd be a smash.
Girls! Girls! Girls! Girls! Girls! Girls!
But as it is, I'm stuck with my music remixed and my life story retold ineptly by others.
CBS' ELVIS
The only way for me to stage a real comeback is via computer animation.
TCB
…or cloning.

May 12, 2005

DAVID STEINLICHT, PIONEER PRESS

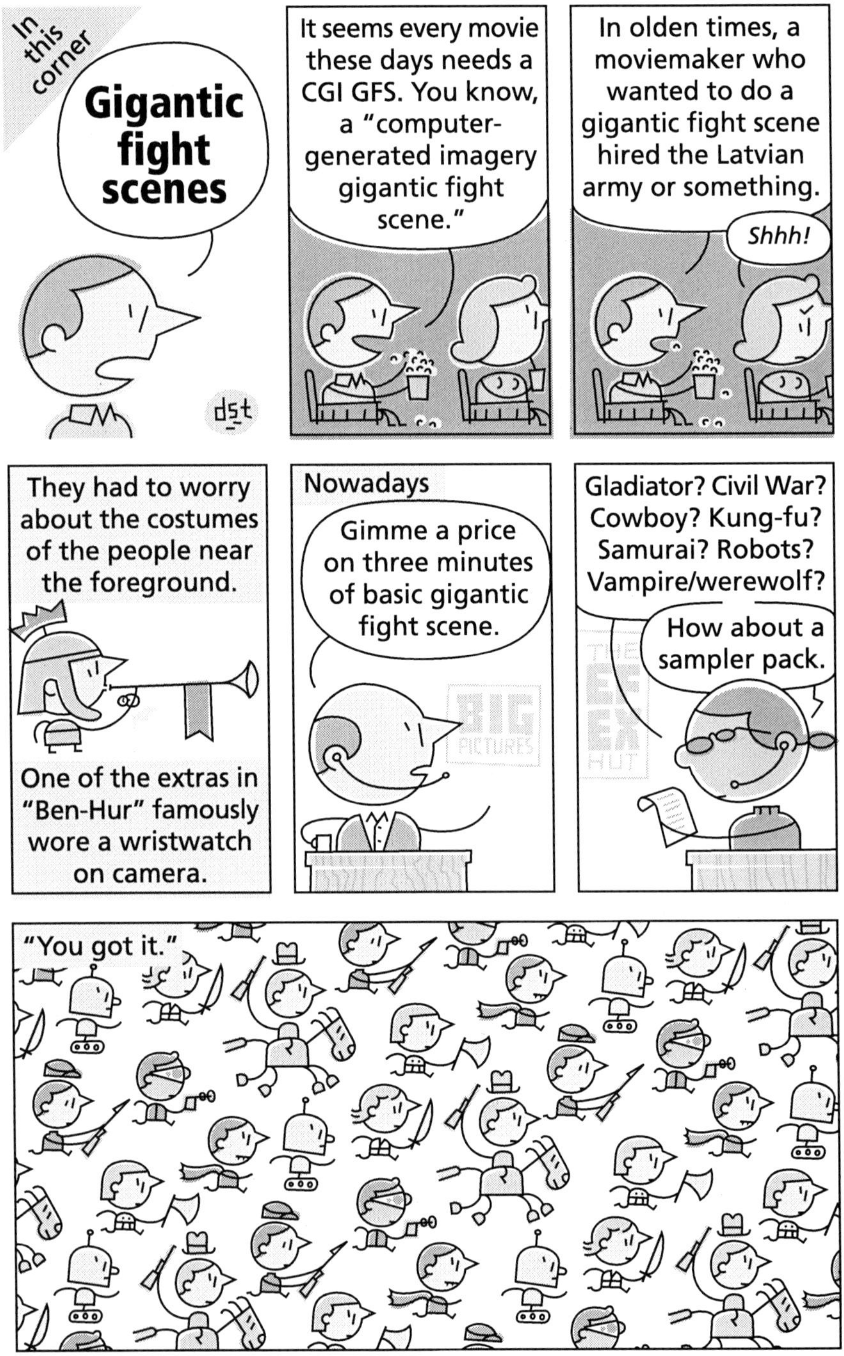
In this corner
Gigantic fight scenes
It seems every movie these days needs a CGI GFS. You know, a "computer-generated imagery gigantic fight scene."
In olden times, a moviemaker who wanted to do a gigantic fight scene hired the Latvian army or something.
Shhh!
They had to worry about the costumes of the people near the foreground.
One of the extras in "Ben-Hur" famously wore a wristwatch on camera.
Nowadays
Gimme a price on three minutes of basic gigantic fight scene.
BIG PICTURES
Gladiator? Civil War? Cowboy? Kung-fu? Samurai? Robots? Vampire/werewolf?
How about a sampler pack.
"You got it."

May 19, 2005 DAVID STEINLICHT, PIONEER PRESS

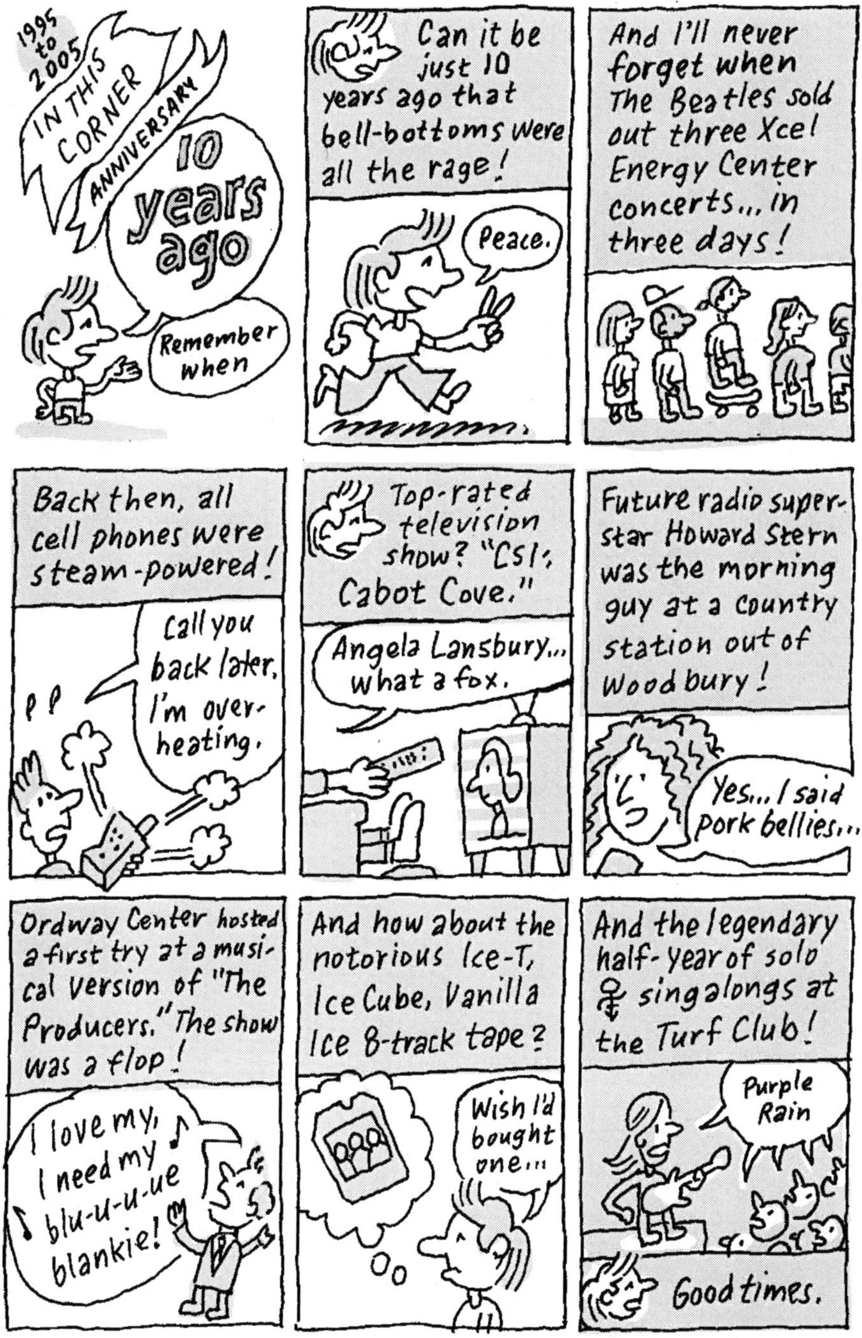
1995 to 2005
IN THIS CORNER
ANNIVERSARY
10 years ago
Remember when
Can it be just 10 years ago that bell-bottoms were all the rage!
Peace.
And I'll never forget when The Beatles sold out three Xcel Energy Center concerts... in three days!
Back then, all cell phones were steam-powered!
Call you back later. I'm over-heating.
Top-rated television show? "CSI: Cabot Cove."
Angela Lansbury... what a fox.
Future radio super-star Howard Stern was the morning guy at a country station out of Woodbury!
Yes... I said pork bellies...
Ordway Center hosted a first try at a musical version of "The Producers." The show was a flop!
I love my, I need my blu-u-u-ue blankie!
And how about the notorious Ice-T, Ice Cube, Vanilla Ice 8-track tape?
Wish I'd bought one...
And the legendary half-year of solo singalongs at the Turf Club!
Purple Rain
Good times.

May 26, 2005

DAVID STEINLICHT, PIONEER PRESS

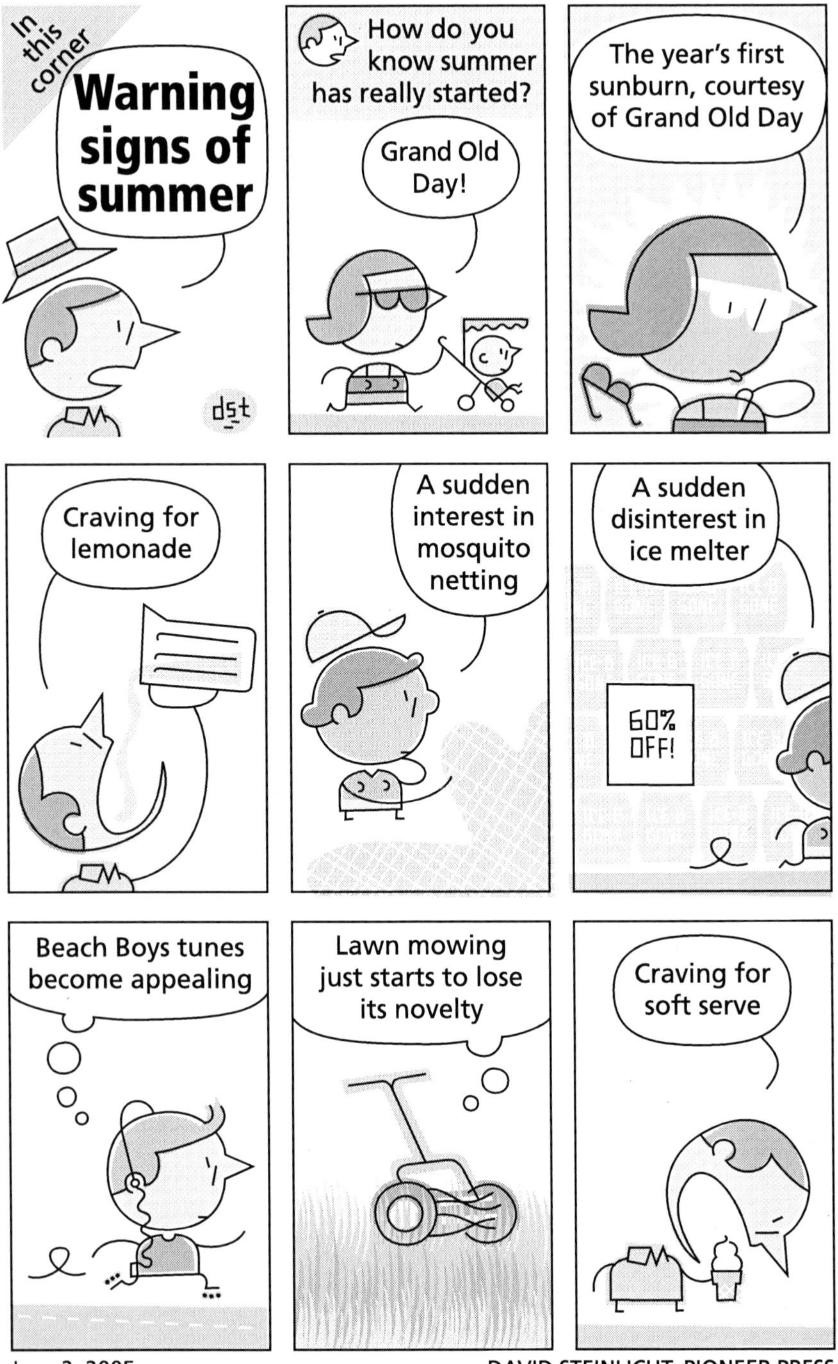
In this corner
Warning signs of summer
How do you know summer has really started?
Grand Old Day!
The year's first sunburn, courtesy of Grand Old Day
Craving for lemonade
A sudden interest in mosquito netting
A sudden disinterest in ice melter
60% OFF!
Beach Boys tunes become appealing
Lawn mowing just starts to lose its novelty
Craving for soft serve

June 2, 2005

DAVID STEINLICHT, PIONEER PRESS

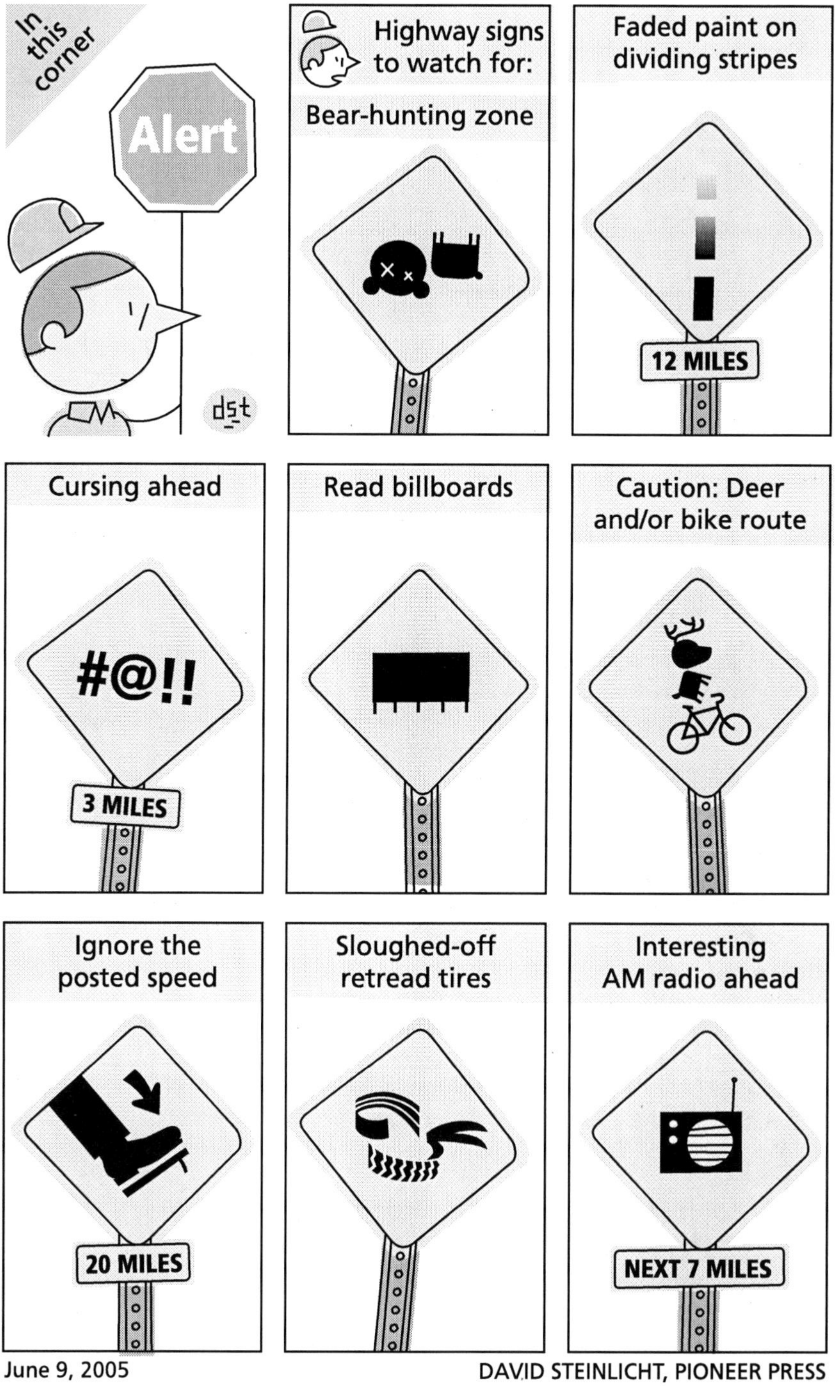
In this corner
Alert
dst
Highway signs to watch for:
Bear-hunting zone
Faded paint on dividing stripes
12 MILES
Cursing ahead
#@!!
3 MILES
Read billboards
Caution: Deer and/or bike route
Ignore the posted speed
20 MILES
Sloughed-off retread tires
Interesting AM radio ahead
NEXT 7 MILES

June 9, 2005

DAVID STEINLICHT, PIONEER PRESS

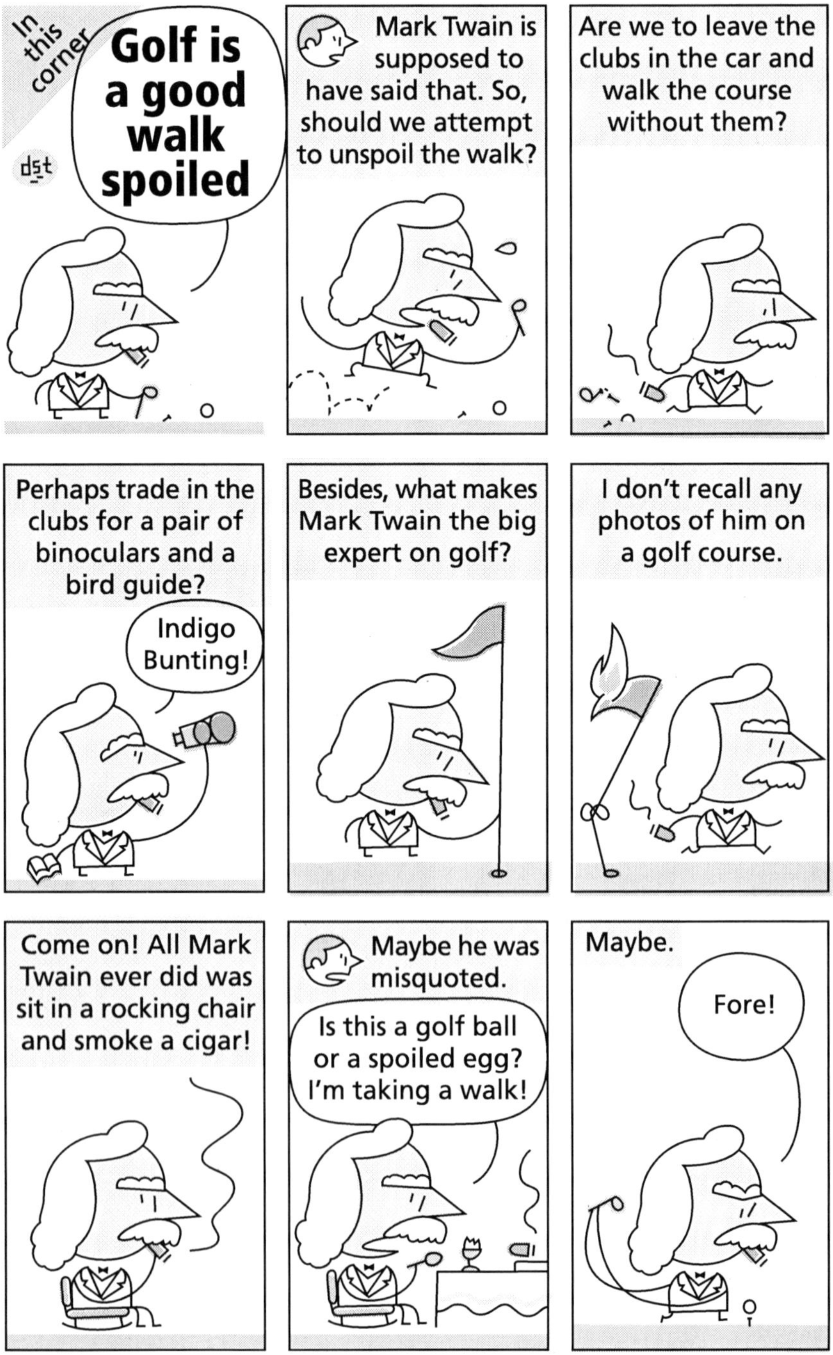
In this corner
dst
Golf is a good walk spoiled
Mark Twain is supposed to have said that. So, should we attempt to unspoil the walk?
Are we to leave the clubs in the car and walk the course without them?
Perhaps trade in the clubs for a pair of binoculars and a bird guide?
Indigo Bunting!
Besides, what makes Mark Twain the big expert on golf?
I don't recall any photos of him on a golf course.
Come on! All Mark Twain ever did was sit in a rocking chair and smoke a cigar!
Maybe he was misquoted.
Is this a golf ball or a spoiled egg? I'm taking a walk!
Maybe.
Fore!

June 16, 2005

DAVID STEINLICHT, PIONEER PRESS

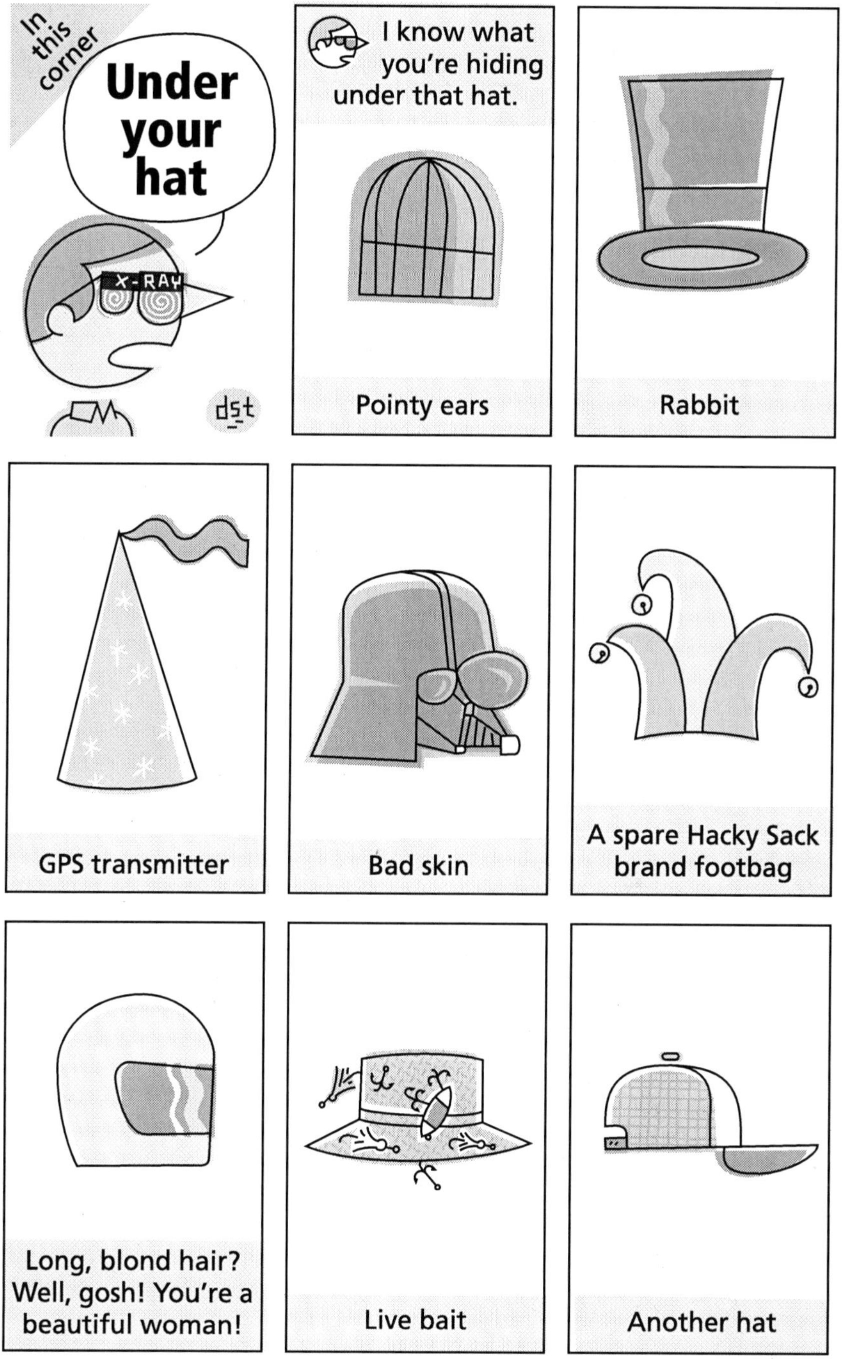
In this corner
Under your hat
X-RAY
dst
I know what you're hiding under that hat.
Pointy ears
Rabbit
GPS transmitter
Bad skin
A spare Hacky Sack brand footbag
Long, blond hair? Well, gosh! You're a beautiful woman!
Live bait
Another hat

June 23, 2005

DAVID STEINLICHT, PIONEER PRESS

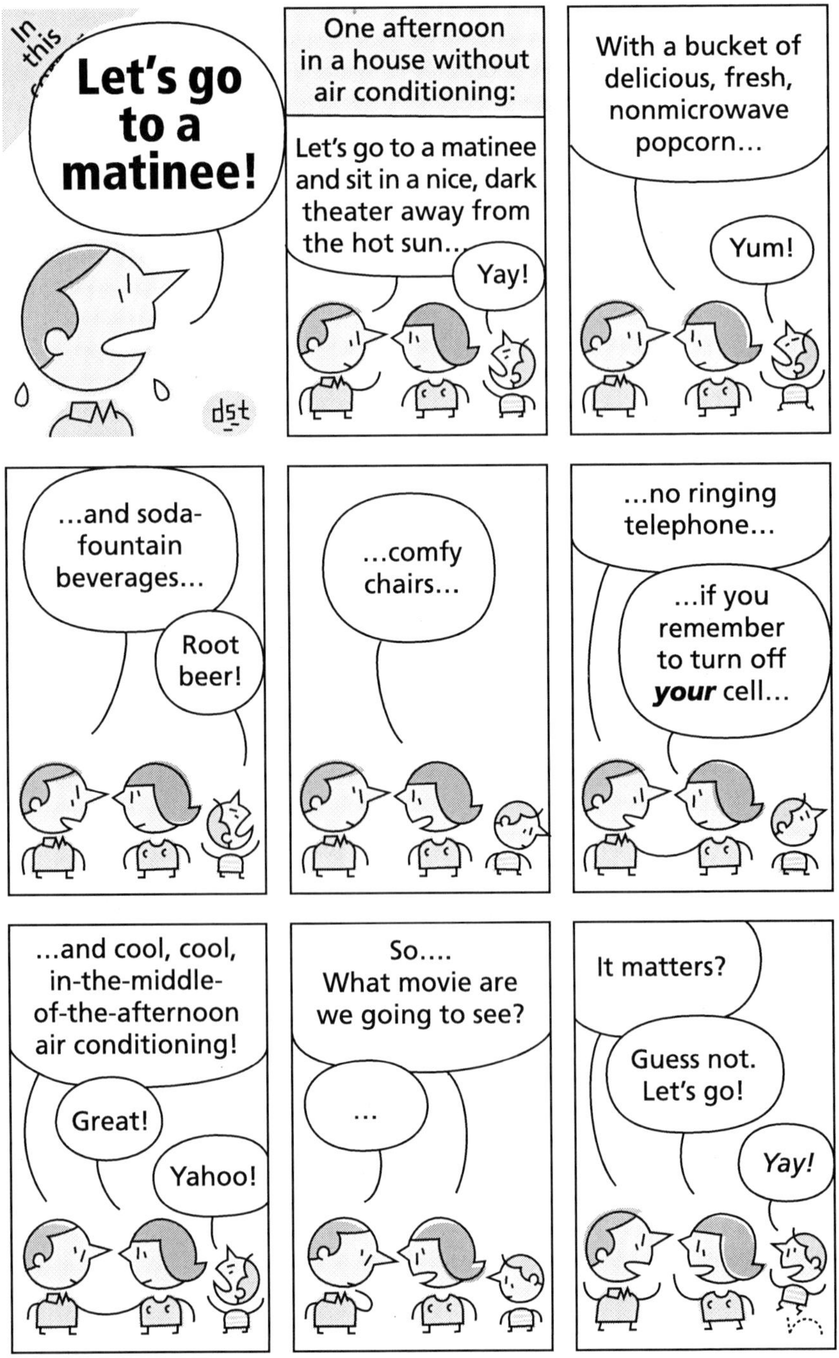
In this
Let's go to a matinee!
dst
One afternoon in a house without air conditioning:
Let's go to a matinee and sit in a nice, dark theater away from the hot sun…
Yay!
With a bucket of delicious, fresh, nonmicrowave popcorn…
Yum!
…and soda-fountain beverages…
Root beer!
…comfy chairs…
…no ringing telephone…
…if you remember to turn off *your* cell…
…and cool, cool, in-the-middle-of-the-afternoon air conditioning!
Great!
Yahoo!
So…. What movie are we going to see?
…
It matters?
Guess not. Let's go!
Yay!

June 30, 2005

DAVID STEINLICHT, PIONEER PRESS

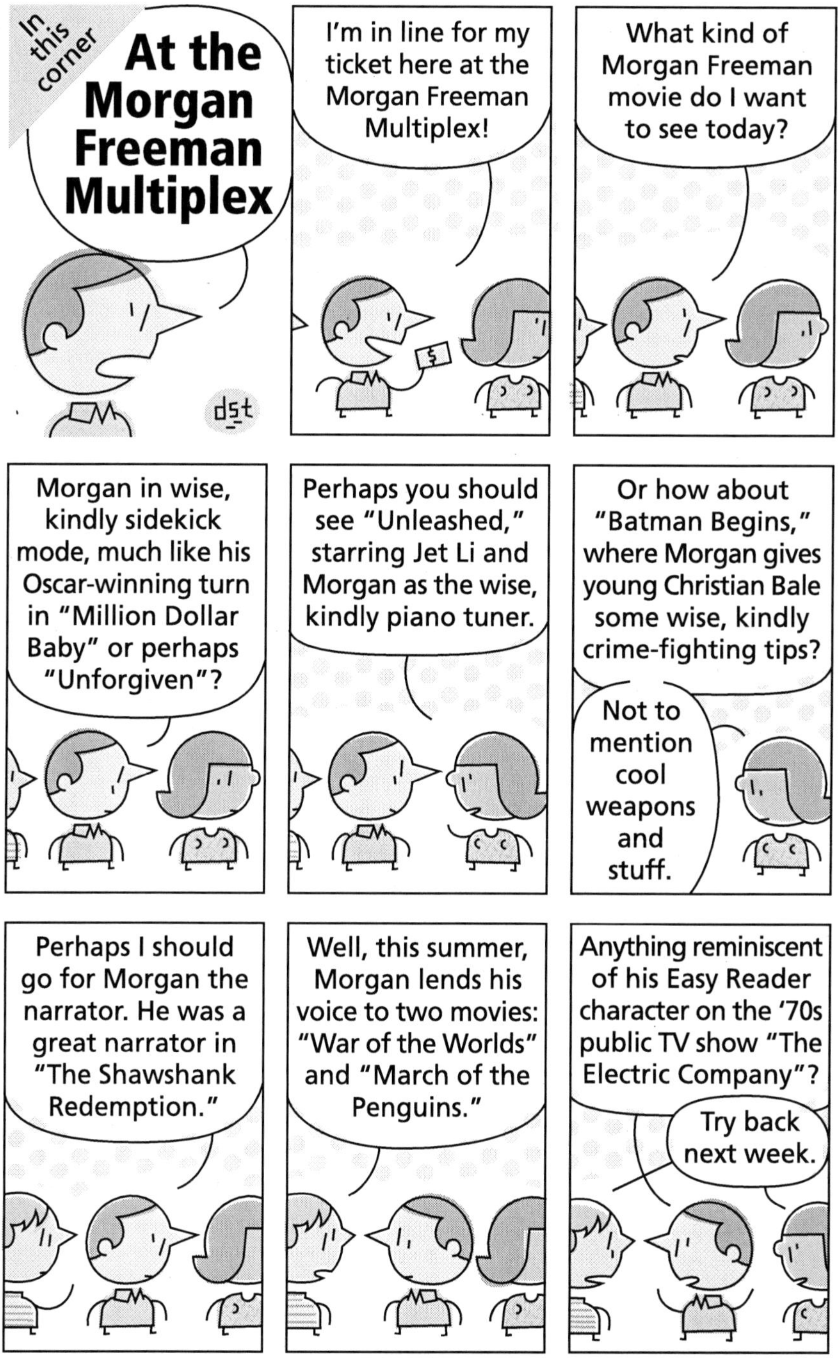
In this corner
At the Morgan Freeman Multiplex
dst
I'm in line for my ticket here at the Morgan Freeman Multiplex!
$
What kind of Morgan Freeman movie do I want to see today?
Morgan in wise, kindly sidekick mode, much like his Oscar-winning turn in "Million Dollar Baby" or perhaps "Unforgiven"?
Perhaps you should see "Unleashed," starring Jet Li and Morgan as the wise, kindly piano tuner.
Or how about "Batman Begins," where Morgan gives young Christian Bale some wise, kindly crime-fighting tips?
Not to mention cool weapons and stuff.
Perhaps I should go for Morgan the narrator. He was a great narrator in "The Shawshank Redemption."
Well, this summer, Morgan lends his voice to two movies: "War of the Worlds" and "March of the Penguins."
Anything reminiscent of his Easy Reader character on the '70s public TV show "The Electric Company"?
Try back next week.

July 7, 2005

DAVID STEINLICHT, PIONEER PRESS

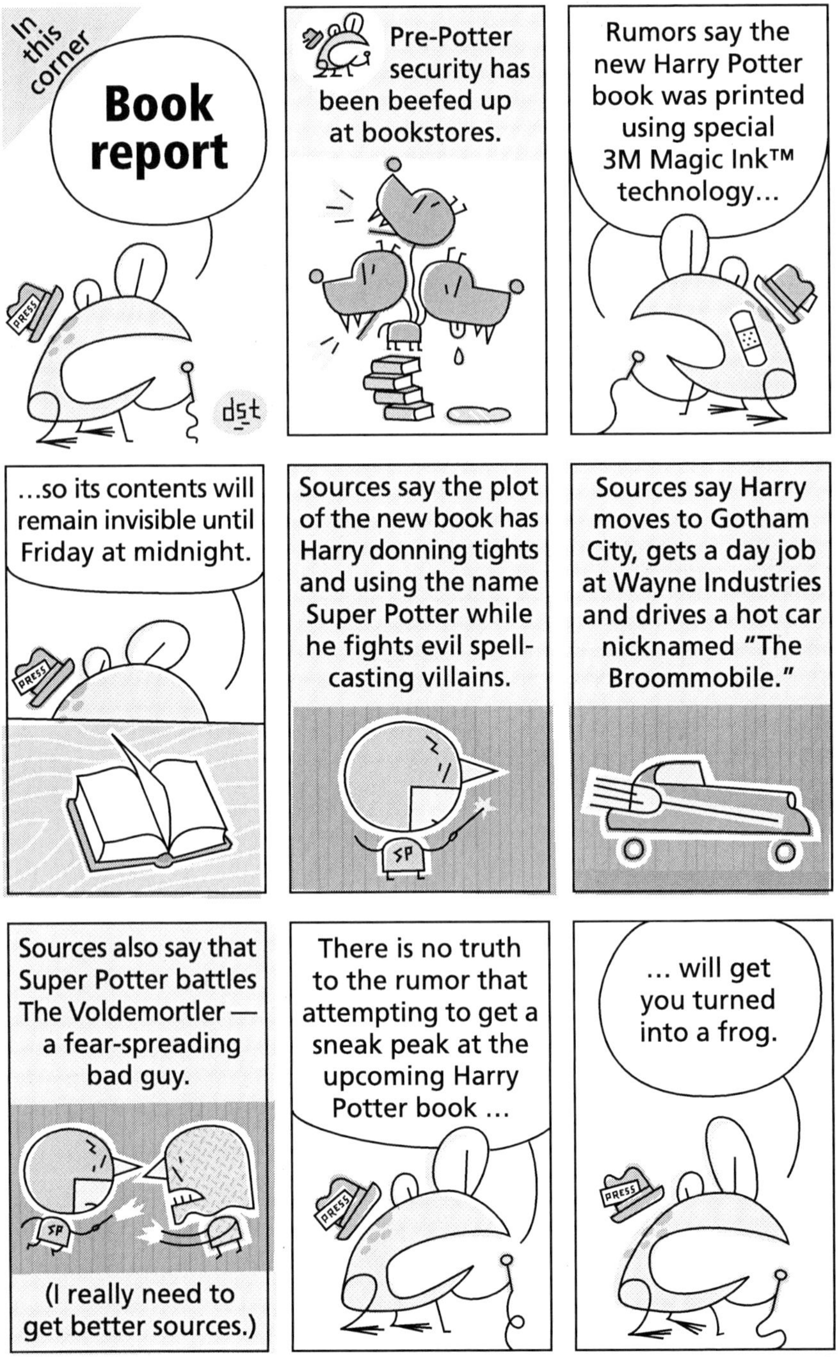
In this corner
Book report
dst
Pre-Potter security has been beefed up at bookstores.
Rumors say the new Harry Potter book was printed using special 3M Magic Ink™ technology…
…so its contents will remain invisible until Friday at midnight.
PRESS
Sources say the plot of the new book has Harry donning tights and using the name Super Potter while he fights evil spell-casting villains.
SP
Sources say Harry moves to Gotham City, gets a day job at Wayne Industries and drives a hot car nicknamed "The Broommobile."
Sources also say that Super Potter battles The Voldemortler — a fear-spreading bad guy.
(I really need to get better sources.)
There is no truth to the rumor that attempting to get a sneak peak at the upcoming Harry Potter book …
… will get you turned into a frog.

July 14, 2005

DAVID STEINLICHT, PIONEER PRESS

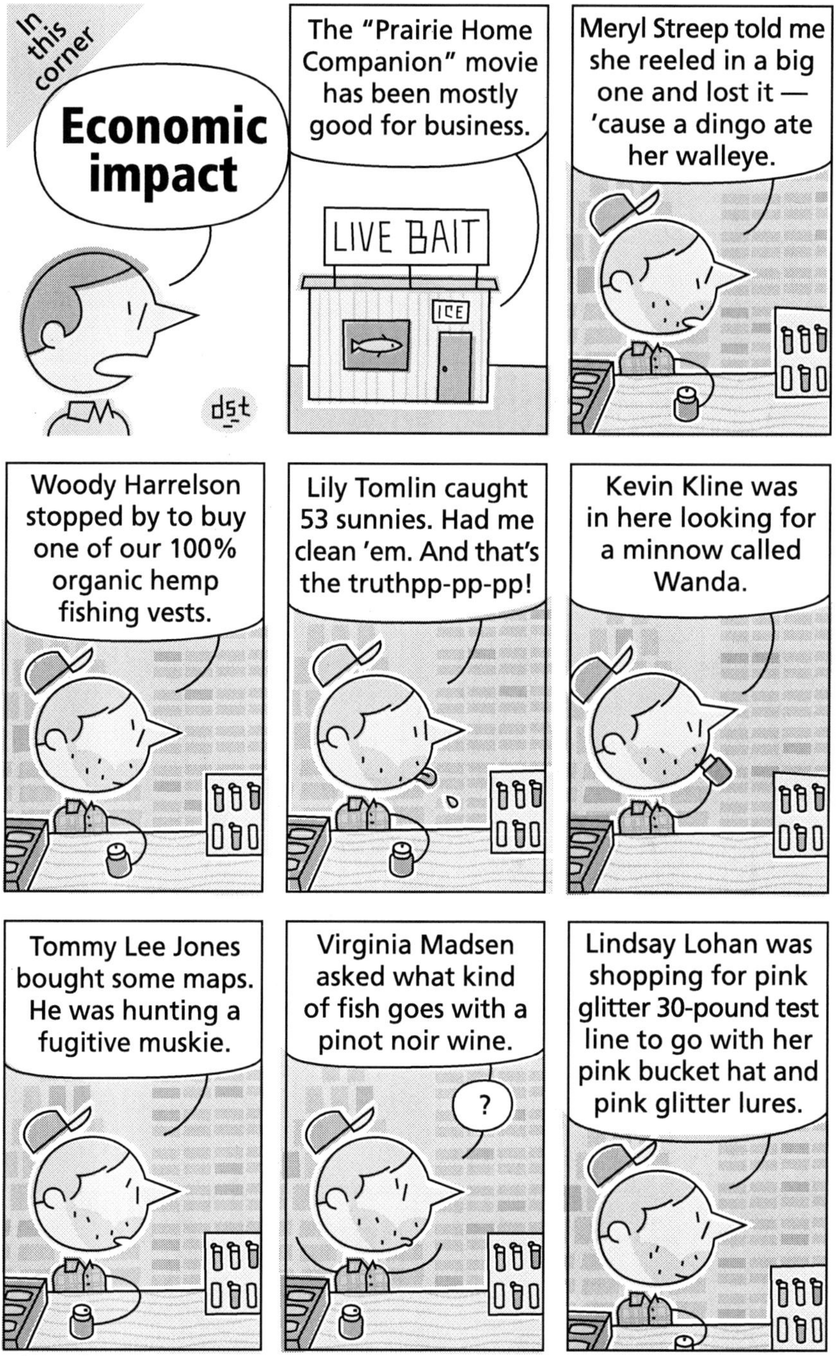
In this corner
Economic impact
The "Prairie Home Companion" movie has been mostly good for business.
LIVE BAIT
ICE
Meryl Streep told me she reeled in a big one and lost it — 'cause a dingo ate her walleye.
Woody Harrelson stopped by to buy one of our 100% organic hemp fishing vests.
Lily Tomlin caught 53 sunnies. Had me clean 'em. And that's the truthpp-pp-pp!
Kevin Kline was in here looking for a minnow called Wanda.
Tommy Lee Jones bought some maps. He was hunting a fugitive muskie.
Virginia Madsen asked what kind of fish goes with a pinot noir wine.
?
Lindsay Lohan was shopping for pink glitter 30-pound test line to go with her pink bucket hat and pink glitter lures.
dst

July 21, 2005

DAVID STEINLICHT, PIONEER PRESS

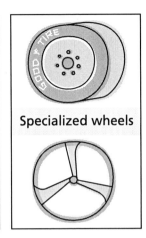

In this corner
The Tour de France is NASCAR
dst
Hmm. When you think about it, there are an awful lot of similarities...
GOOD TIRE
Specialized wheels
Sophisticated power plants
Pedals are involved
Participants sit
30
10
20
40
Spectacular crashes
BRAND
SERVICE
AD NETWORK
LOGO
Product names adorn every surface
SERVICE
LOGO
BRAND
BEVERAGE
50
NAME
ADV.
BUSINESS
47
SILVERADO
Sheryl Crow

July 28, 2005

DAVID STEINLICHT, PIONEER PRESS

 Note: I'm pretty sure Sheryl Crow used to be Lance Armstrong's girlfriend.

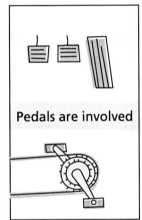

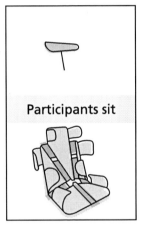

Alternative alternative festivals

dst

The Fringe Festival offers alternative theater entertainment.

But are there are other alternatives?

I'm glad you asked!

Cringe Festival!
Only really bad jokes

Fridge Festival!
It's too cool

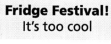

Fins Festival!
For fish fans

Flange Festival!
Celebrate the flange

Binge Festival!
Let's overdo it again

ROOT BEER

Midge Festival!
No-See-Ums in the spotlight

SLAP

Fringed Festival!
Only fringed clothing allowed

Aug. 4, 2005

DAVID STEINLICHT, PIONEER PRESS

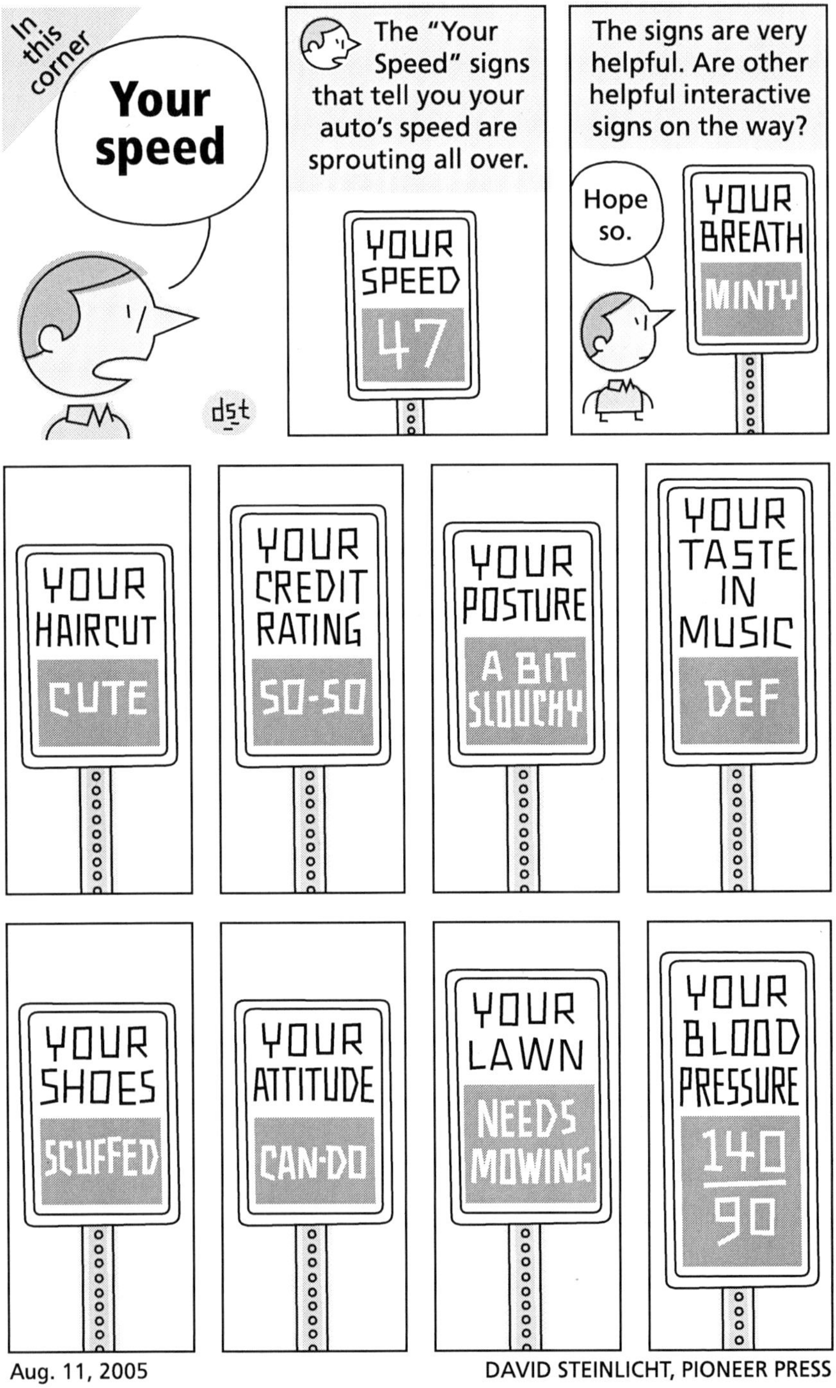
In this corner
Your speed
dst
The "Your Speed" signs that tell you your auto's speed are sprouting all over.
YOUR SPEED 47
The signs are very helpful. Are other helpful interactive signs on the way?
Hope so.
YOUR BREATH MINTY
YOUR HAIRCUT CUTE
YOUR CREDIT RATING SO-SO
YOUR POSTURE A BIT SLOUCHY
YOUR TASTE IN MUSIC DEF
YOUR SHOES SCUFFED
YOUR ATTITUDE CAN-DO
YOUR LAWN NEEDS MOWING
YOUR BLOOD PRESSURE 140/90

Aug. 11, 2005

DAVID STEINLICHT, PIONEER PRESS

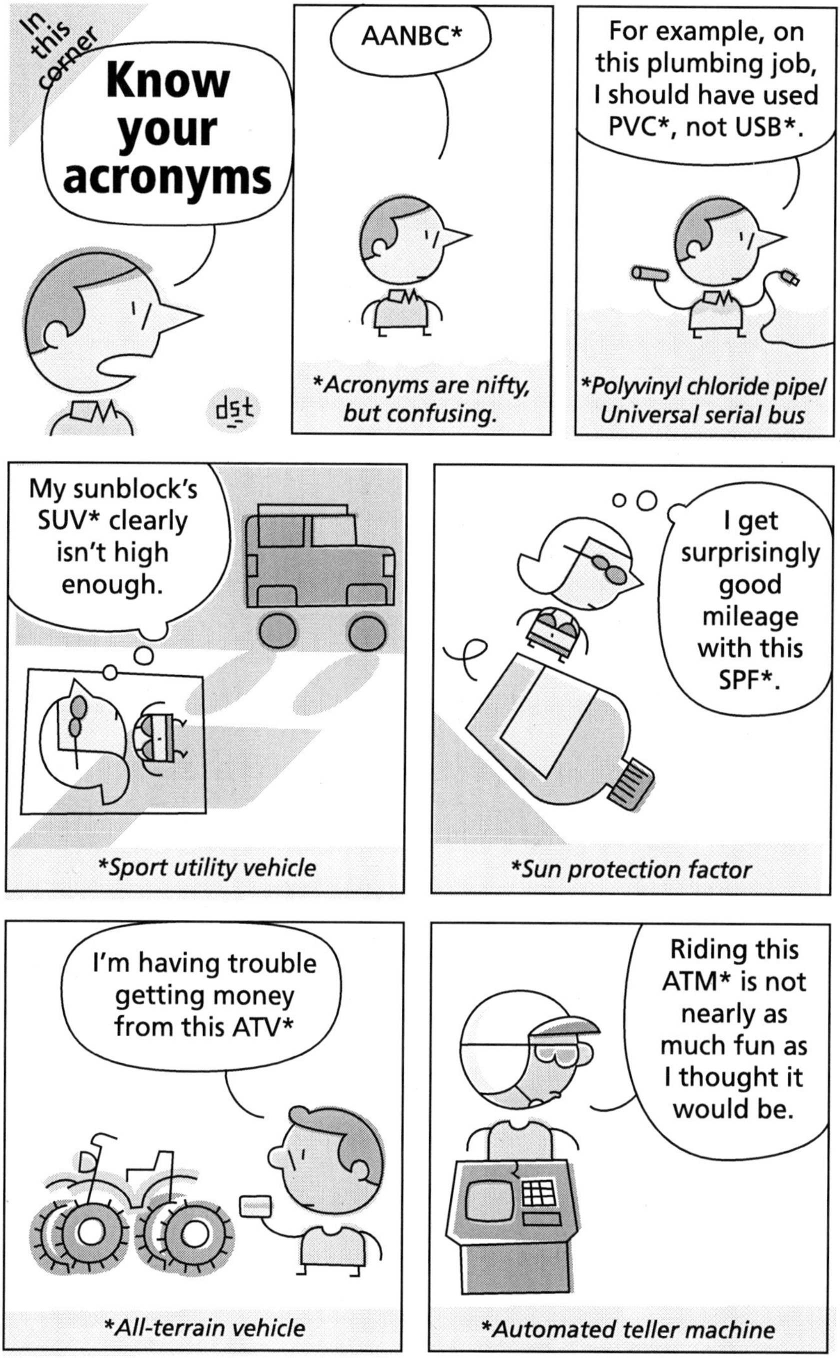
In this corner
Know your acronyms
dst
AANBC*
*Acronyms are nifty, but confusing.
For example, on this plumbing job, I should have used PVC*, not USB*.
*Polyvinyl chloride pipe/ Universal serial bus
My sunblock's SUV* clearly isn't high enough.
*Sport utility vehicle
I get surprisingly good mileage with this SPF*.
*Sun protection factor
I'm having trouble getting money from this ATV*
*All-terrain vehicle
Riding this ATM* is not nearly as much fun as I thought it would be.
*Automated teller machine

Aug. 18, 2005

DAVID STEINLICHT, PIONEER PRESS

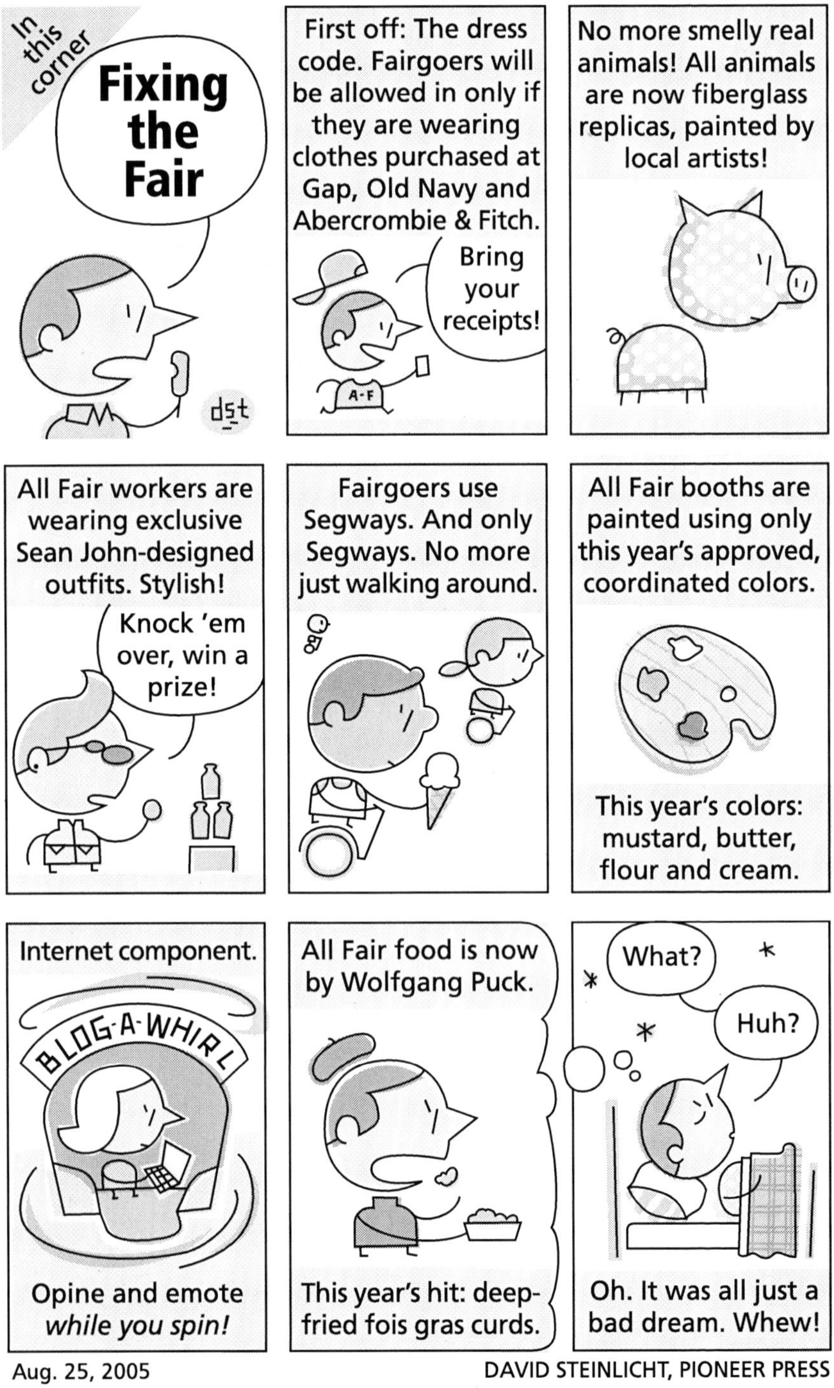
In this corner
Fixing the Fair
dst
First off: The dress code. Fairgoers will be allowed in only if they are wearing clothes purchased at Gap, Old Navy and Abercrombie & Fitch.
Bring your receipts!
A-F
No more smelly real animals! All animals are now fiberglass replicas, painted by local artists!
All Fair workers are wearing exclusive Sean John-designed outfits. Stylish!
Knock 'em over, win a prize!
Fairgoers use Segways. And only Segways. No more just walking around.
All Fair booths are painted using only this year's approved, coordinated colors.
This year's colors: mustard, butter, flour and cream.
Internet component.
BLOG-A-WHIRL
Opine and emote *while you spin!*
All Fair food is now by Wolfgang Puck.
This year's hit: deep-fried fois gras curds.
What?
Huh?
Oh. It was all just a bad dream. Whew!

Aug. 25, 2005

DAVID STEINLICHT, PIONEER PRESS

Thanks for taking part in our brief survey

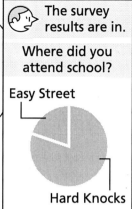

The survey results are in.

Where did you attend school?

Easy Street

Hard Knocks

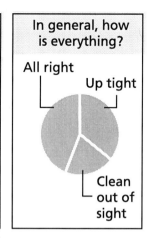

In general, how is everything?

All right

Up tight

Clean out of sight

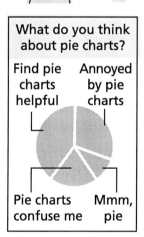

What do you think about pie charts?

Find pie charts helpful

Annoyed by pie charts

Pie charts confuse me

Mmm, pie

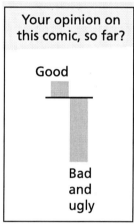

Your opinion on this comic, so far?

Good

Bad and ugly

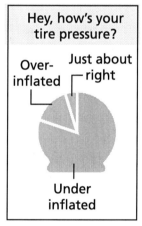

Hey, how's your tire pressure?

Over-inflated

Just about right

Under inflated

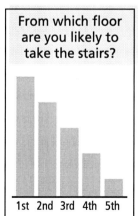

From which floor are you likely to take the stairs?

1st 2nd 3rd 4th 5th

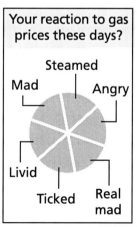

Your reaction to gas prices these days?

Steamed

Mad

Angry

Livid

Ticked

Real mad

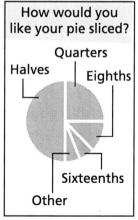

How would you like your pie sliced?

Quarters

Halves

Eighths

Sixteenths

Other

Sept. 1, 2005

DAVID STEINLICHT, PIONEER PRESS

65

In this corner

Wheel world

dst

Mobile ads are popular these days.

Energy drink pickup

Hot dog car

The Pioneer Press has a car with its columnists' pictures on the side.

Some rejected ideas for Pioneer Press promo vehicles:

PiPRESS

Newsprint car

Drawback: Had to be wrapped in plastic bag in bad weather.

Charley Walters' Shooter Scooter

Drawback: Dinged up in collision with the SidMobile.

Bulletin Board blimp

PIONEER PRESS

Drawback: Not so good in high winds.

The Joe Soucheray Joe-Cart

PiPr

Drawback: Fire hazard — fans keep trying to light cigar.

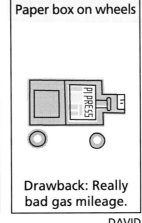

Paper box on wheels

Drawback: Really bad gas mileage.

Bulldog on wheels

PiPr

Drawback: Stops at all fire hydrants — and then there's the slobber problem.

Sept. 8, 2005

DAVID STEINLICHT, PIONEER PRESS

66 *Note:* A somewhat rare *Saint Paul Pioneer Press*-centric comic.

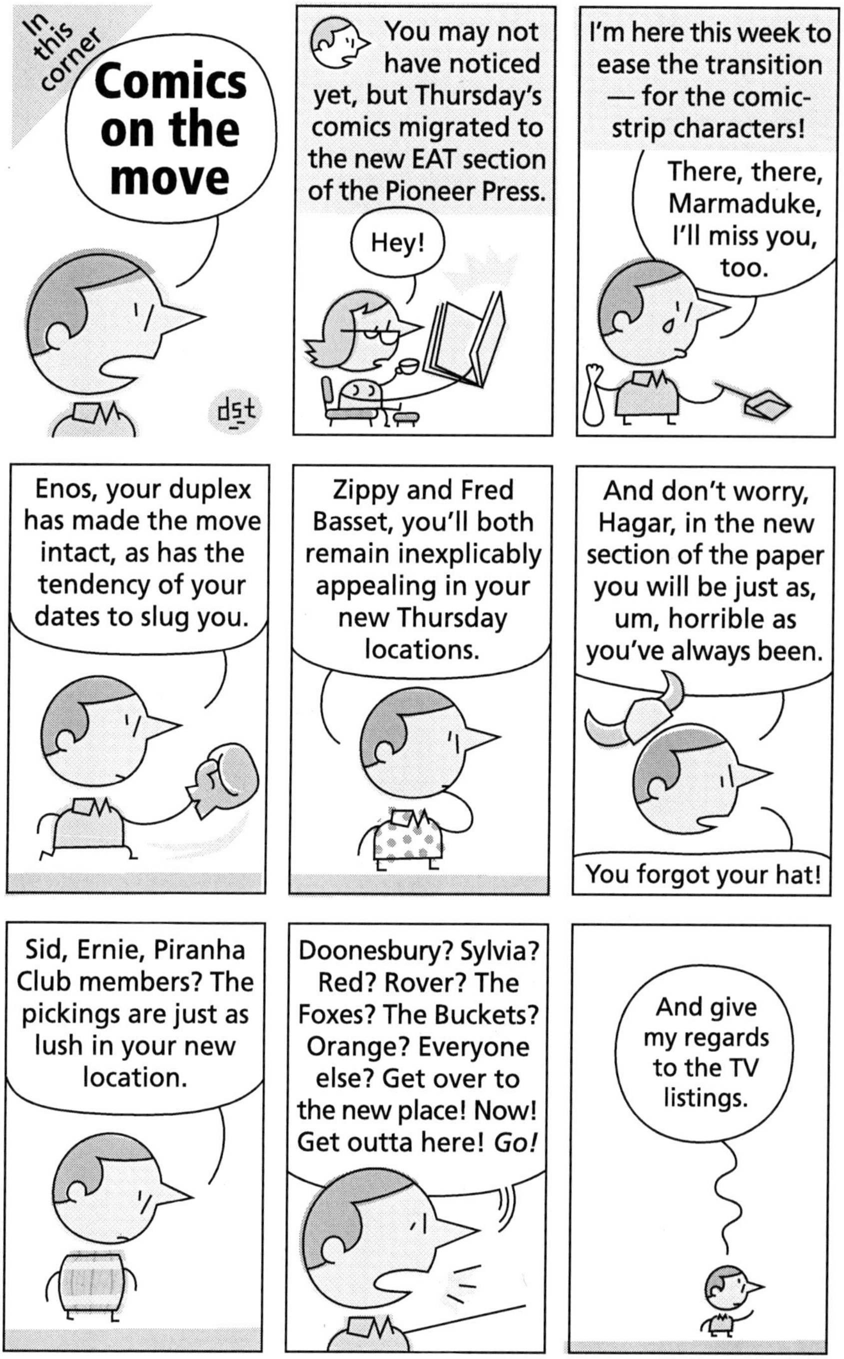
In this corner
Comics on the move
dst
You may not have noticed yet, but Thursday's comics migrated to the new EAT section of the Pioneer Press.
Hey!
I'm here this week to ease the transition — for the comic-strip characters!
There, there, Marmaduke, I'll miss you, too.
Enos, your duplex has made the move intact, as has the tendency of your dates to slug you.
Zippy and Fred Basset, you'll both remain inexplicably appealing in your new Thursday locations.
And don't worry, Hagar, in the new section of the paper you will be just as, um, horrible as you've always been.
You forgot your hat!
Sid, Ernie, Piranha Club members? The pickings are just as lush in your new location.
Doonesbury? Sylvia? Red? Rover? The Foxes? The Buckets? Orange? Everyone else? Get over to the new place! Now! Get outta here! *Go!*
And give my regards to the TV listings.

Sept. 15, 2005

DAVID STEINLICHT, PIONEER PRESS

Note: Okay, so, maybe *Pioneer Press*-centric comics aren't that rare.

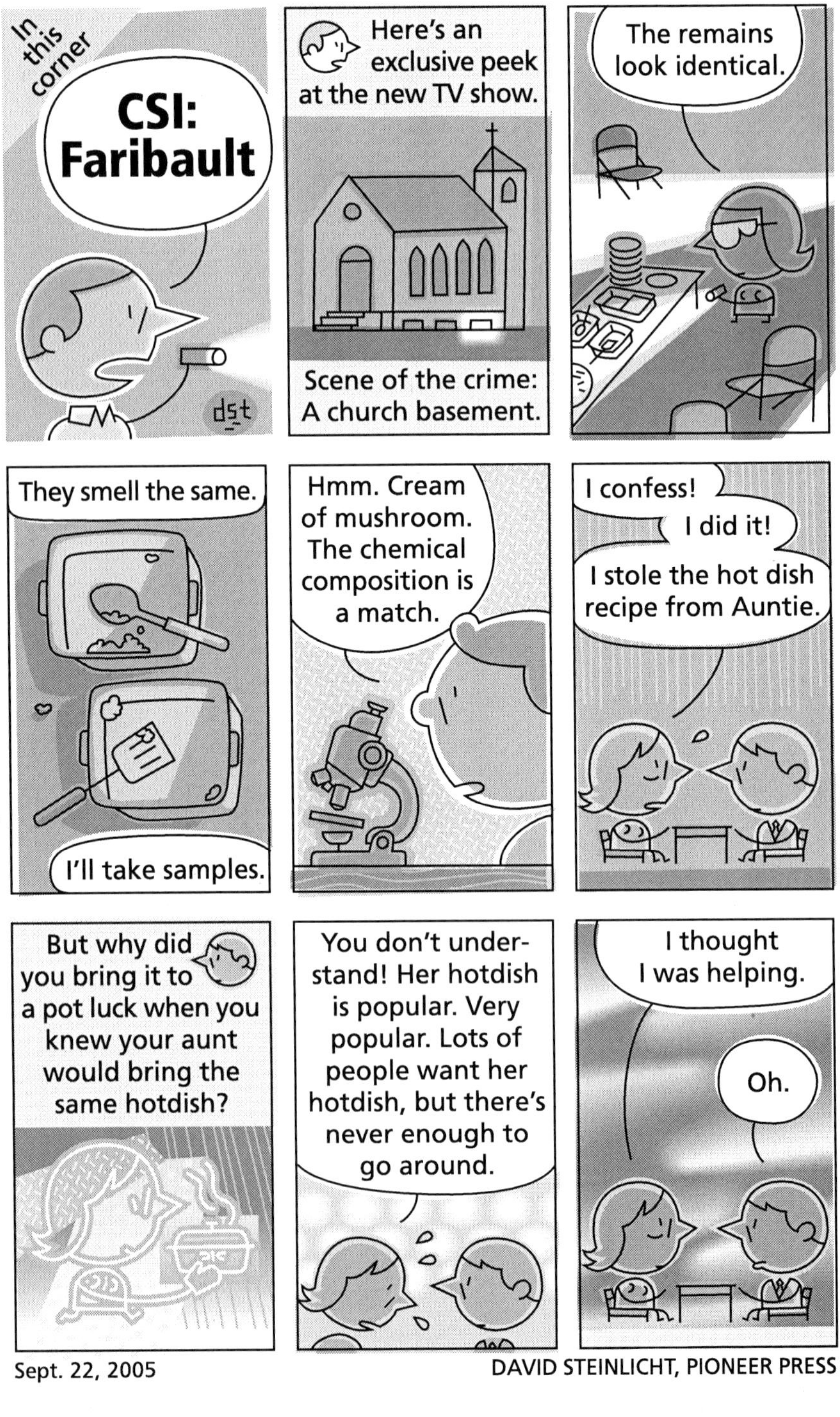
In this corner
CSI: Faribault
dst
Here's an exclusive peek at the new TV show.
Scene of the crime: A church basement.
The remains look identical.
They smell the same.
I'll take samples.
Hmm. Cream of mushroom. The chemical composition is a match.
I confess!
I did it!
I stole the hot dish recipe from Auntie.
But why did you bring it to a pot luck when you knew your aunt would bring the same hotdish?
You don't under-stand! Her hotdish is popular. Very popular. Lots of people want her hotdish, but there's never enough to go around.
I thought I was helping.
Oh.

Sept. 22, 2005

DAVID STEINLICHT, PIONEER PRESS

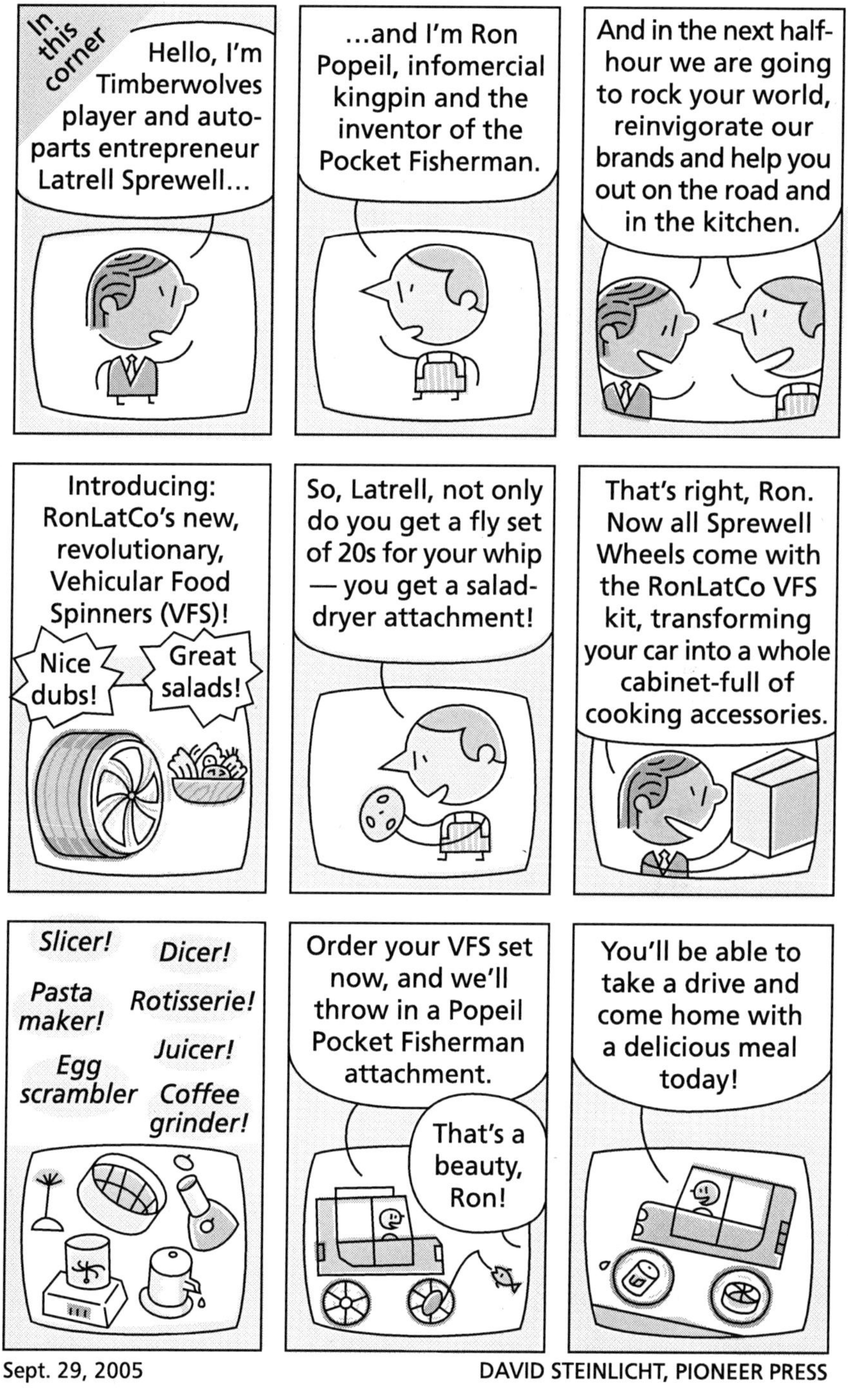
In this corner
Hello, I'm Timberwolves player and auto-parts entrepreneur Latrell Sprewell...
...and I'm Ron Popeil, infomercial kingpin and the inventor of the Pocket Fisherman.
And in the next half-hour we are going to rock your world, reinvigorate our brands and help you out on the road and in the kitchen.
Introducing: RonLatCo's new, revolutionary, Vehicular Food Spinners (VFS)!
Nice dubs!
Great salads!
So, Latrell, not only do you get a fly set of 20s for your whip — you get a salad-dryer attachment!
That's right, Ron. Now all Sprewell Wheels come with the RonLatCo VFS kit, transforming your car into a whole cabinet-full of cooking accessories.
Slicer!
Dicer!
Pasta maker!
Rotisserie!
Juicer!
Egg scrambler
Coffee grinder!
Order your VFS set now, and we'll throw in a Popeil Pocket Fisherman attachment.
That's a beauty, Ron!
You'll be able to take a drive and come home with a delicious meal today!

Sept. 29, 2005

DAVID STEINLICHT, PIONEER PRESS

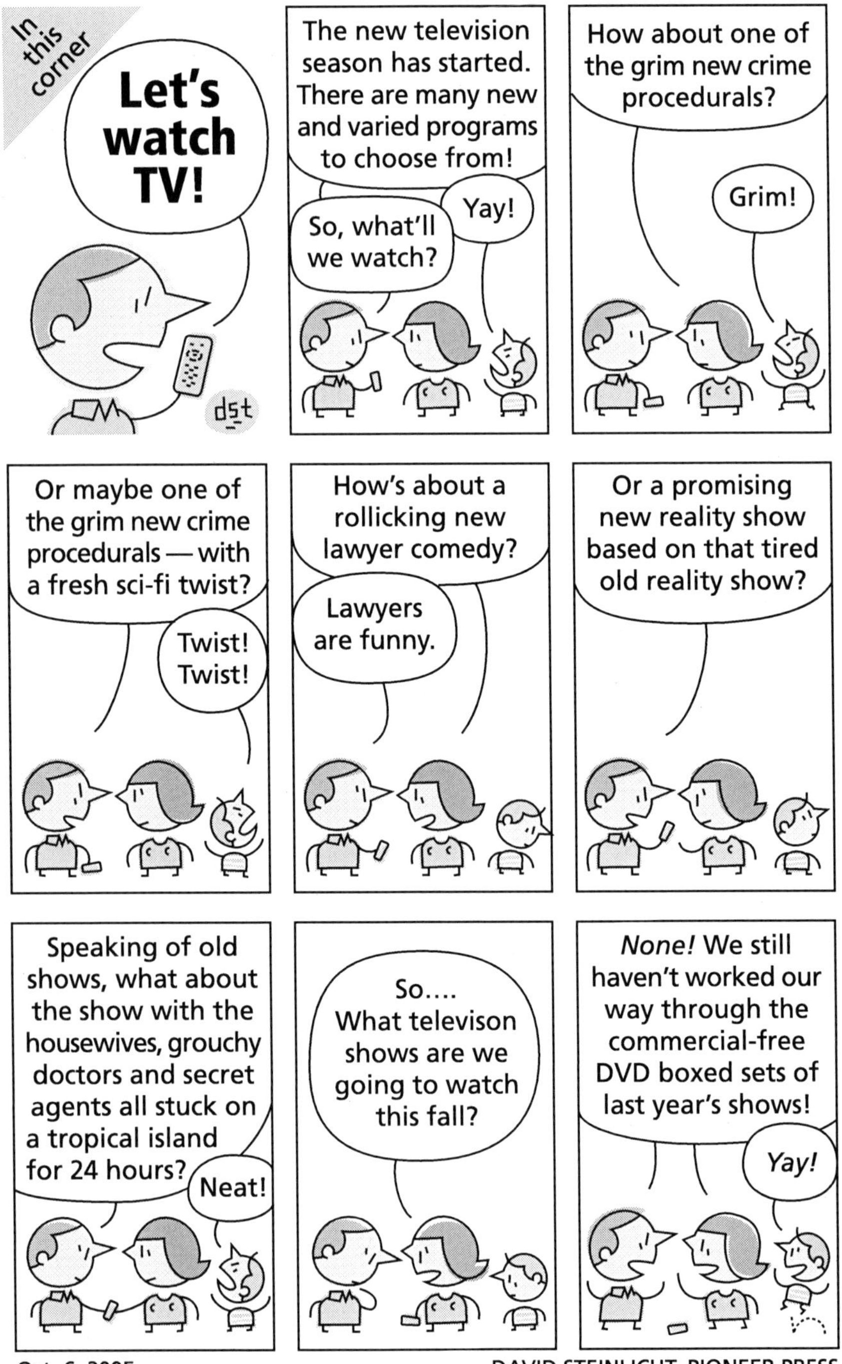
In this corner
Let's watch TV!
dst
The new television season has started. There are many new and varied programs to choose from!
So, what'll we watch?
Yay!
How about one of the grim new crime procedurals?
Grim!
Or maybe one of the grim new crime procedurals — with a fresh sci-fi twist?
Twist! Twist!
How's about a rollicking new lawyer comedy?
Lawyers are funny.
Or a promising new reality show based on that tired old reality show?
Speaking of old shows, what about the show with the housewives, grouchy doctors and secret agents all stuck on a tropical island for 24 hours?
Neat!
So.... What televison shows are we going to watch this fall?
None! We still haven't worked our way through the commercial-free DVD boxed sets of last year's shows!
Yay!

Oct. 6, 2005

DAVID STEINLICHT, PIONEER PRESS

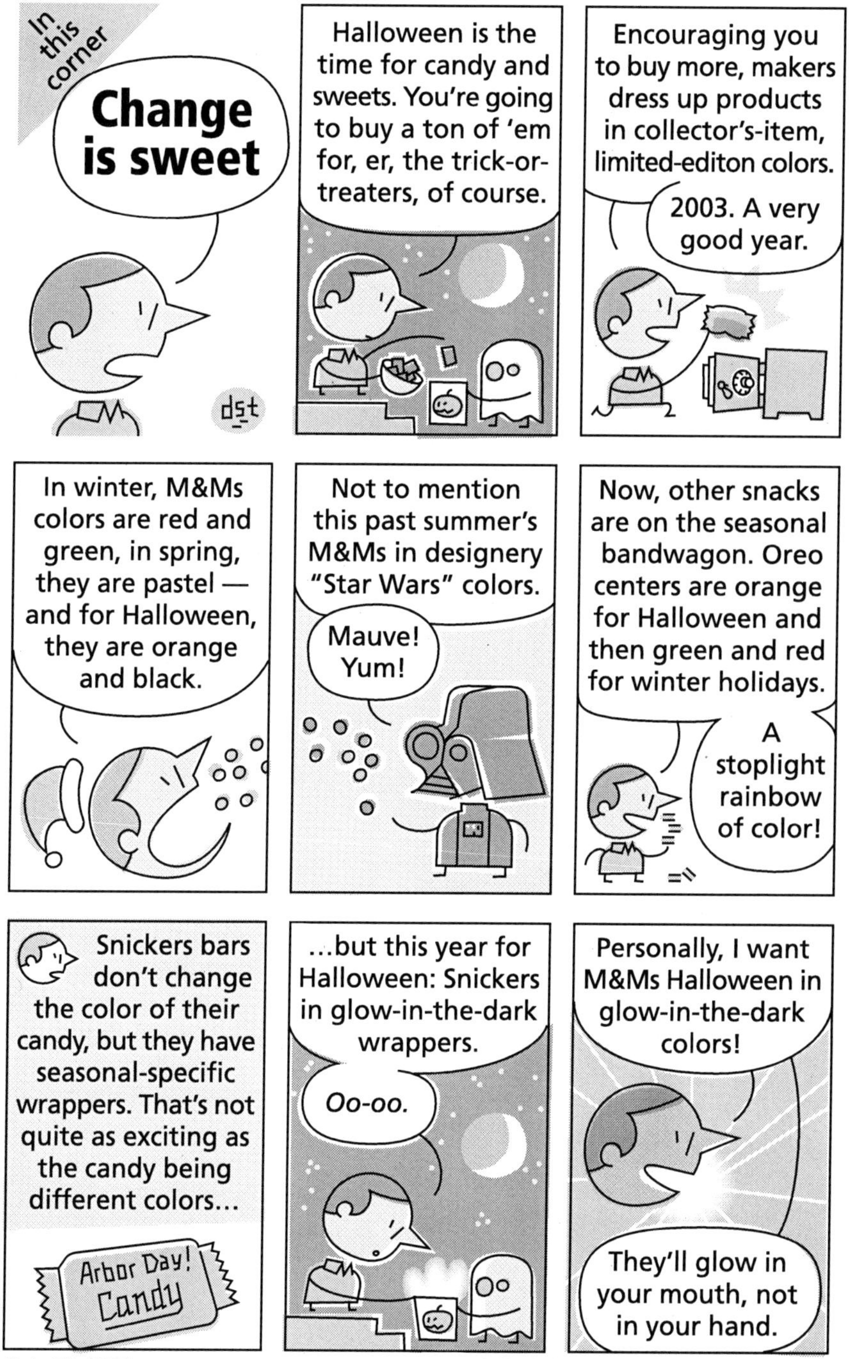
In this corner
Change is sweet
dst
Halloween is the time for candy and sweets. You're going to buy a ton of 'em for, er, the trick-or-treaters, of course.
Encouraging you to buy more, makers dress up products in collector's-item, limited-editon colors.
2003. A very good year.
In winter, M&Ms colors are red and green, in spring, they are pastel — and for Halloween, they are orange and black.
Not to mention this past summer's M&Ms in designery "Star Wars" colors.
Mauve! Yum!
Now, other snacks are on the seasonal bandwagon. Oreo centers are orange for Halloween and then green and red for winter holidays.
A stoplight rainbow of color!
Snickers bars don't change the color of their candy, but they have seasonal-specific wrappers. That's not quite as exciting as the candy being different colors...
Arbor Day! Candy
...but this year for Halloween: Snickers in glow-in-the-dark wrappers.
Oo-oo.
Personally, I want M&Ms Halloween in glow-in-the-dark colors!
They'll glow in your mouth, not in your hand.

Oct. 13, 2005

DAVID STEINLICHT, PIONEER PRESS

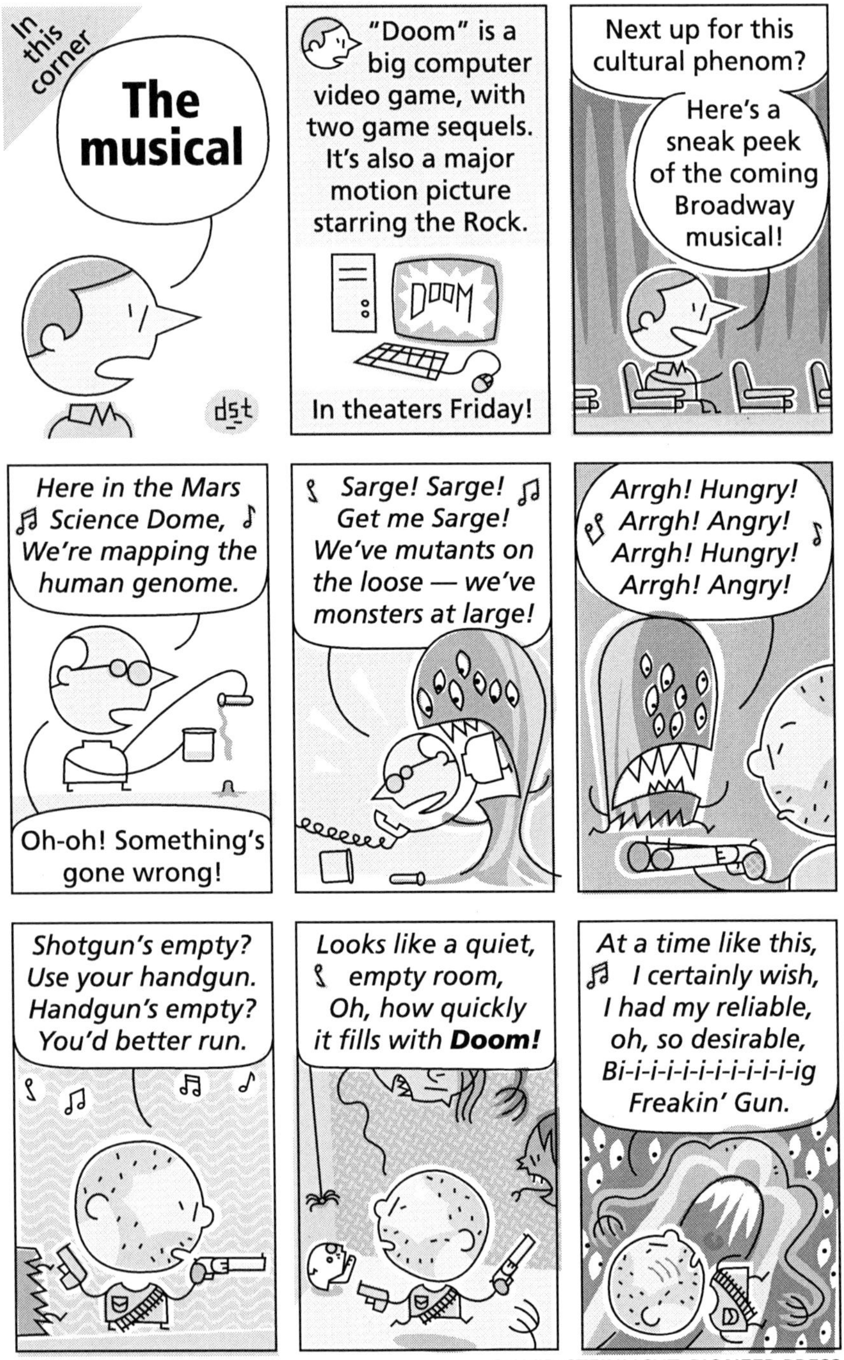
In this corner
The musical
dst
"Doom" is a big computer video game, with two game sequels. It's also a major motion picture starring the Rock.
DOOM
In theaters Friday!
Next up for this cultural phenom?
Here's a sneak peek of the coming Broadway musical!
Here in the Mars Science Dome, We're mapping the human genome.
Oh-oh! Something's gone wrong!
Sarge! Sarge! Get me Sarge! We've mutants on the loose — we've monsters at large!
Arrgh! Hungry! Arrgh! Angry! Arrgh! Hungry! Arrgh! Angry!
Shotgun's empty? Use your handgun. Handgun's empty? You'd better run.
Looks like a quiet, empty room, Oh, how quickly it fills with Doom!
At a time like this, I certainly wish, I had my reliable, oh, so desirable, Bi-i-i-i-i-i-i-i-i-i-ig Freakin' Gun.

Oct. 20, 2005

DAVID STEINLICHT, PIONEER PRESS

In this corner

This year, people are apparently dressing pets and electronic gizmos in Halloween costumes. Weird. But, rather than trying to discourage this dismaying development, I say, "If you can't beat 'em, join 'em." Have fun!

Special Halloween dress-up comic

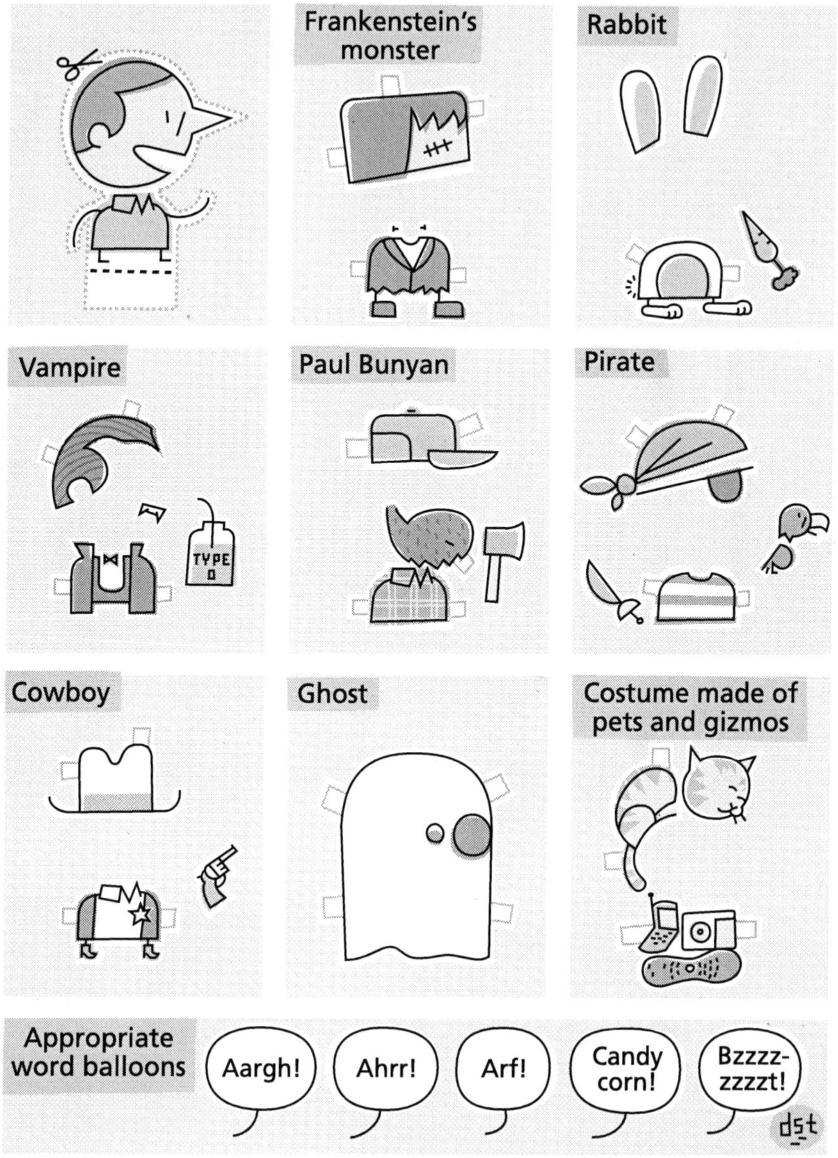

Frankenstein's monster
Rabbit
Vampire
TYPE O
Paul Bunyan
Pirate
Cowboy
Ghost
Costume made of pets and gizmos
Appropriate word balloons
Aargh!
Ahrr!
Arf!
Candy corn!
Bzzzz-zzzzt!
dst

Oct. 27, 2005

DAVID STEINLICHT, PIONEER PRESS

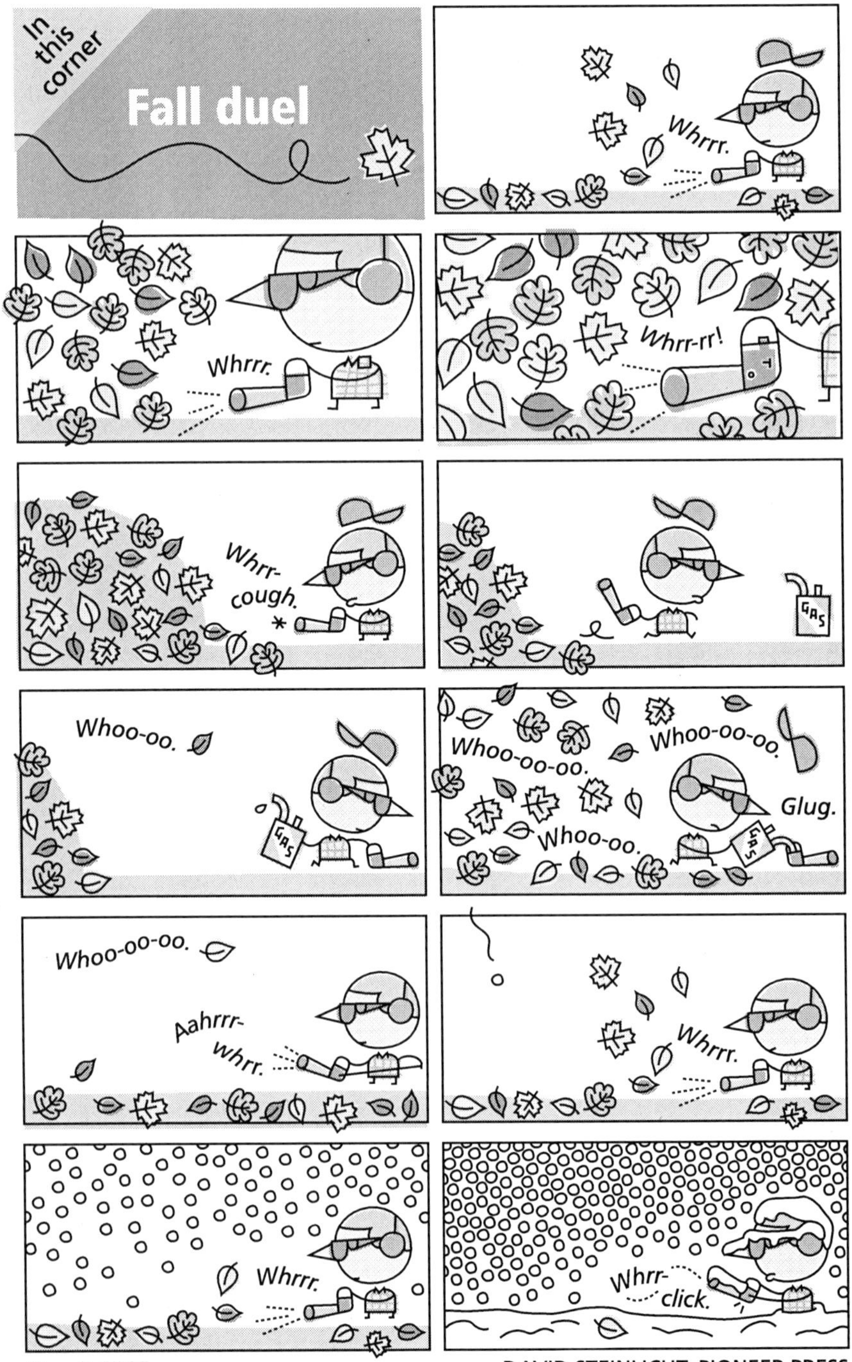
In this corner
Fall duel
Whrrr.
Whrrr.
Whrr-rr!
Whrr-cough.
*
GAS
Whoo-oo.
GAS
Whoo-oo-oo.
Whoo-oo-oo.
Whoo-oo.
Glug.
GAS
Whoo-oo-oo.
Aahrrr-whrr.
Whrrr.
Whrrr.
Whrr-click.

Nov. 3, 2005

DAVID STEINLICHT, PIONEER PRESS

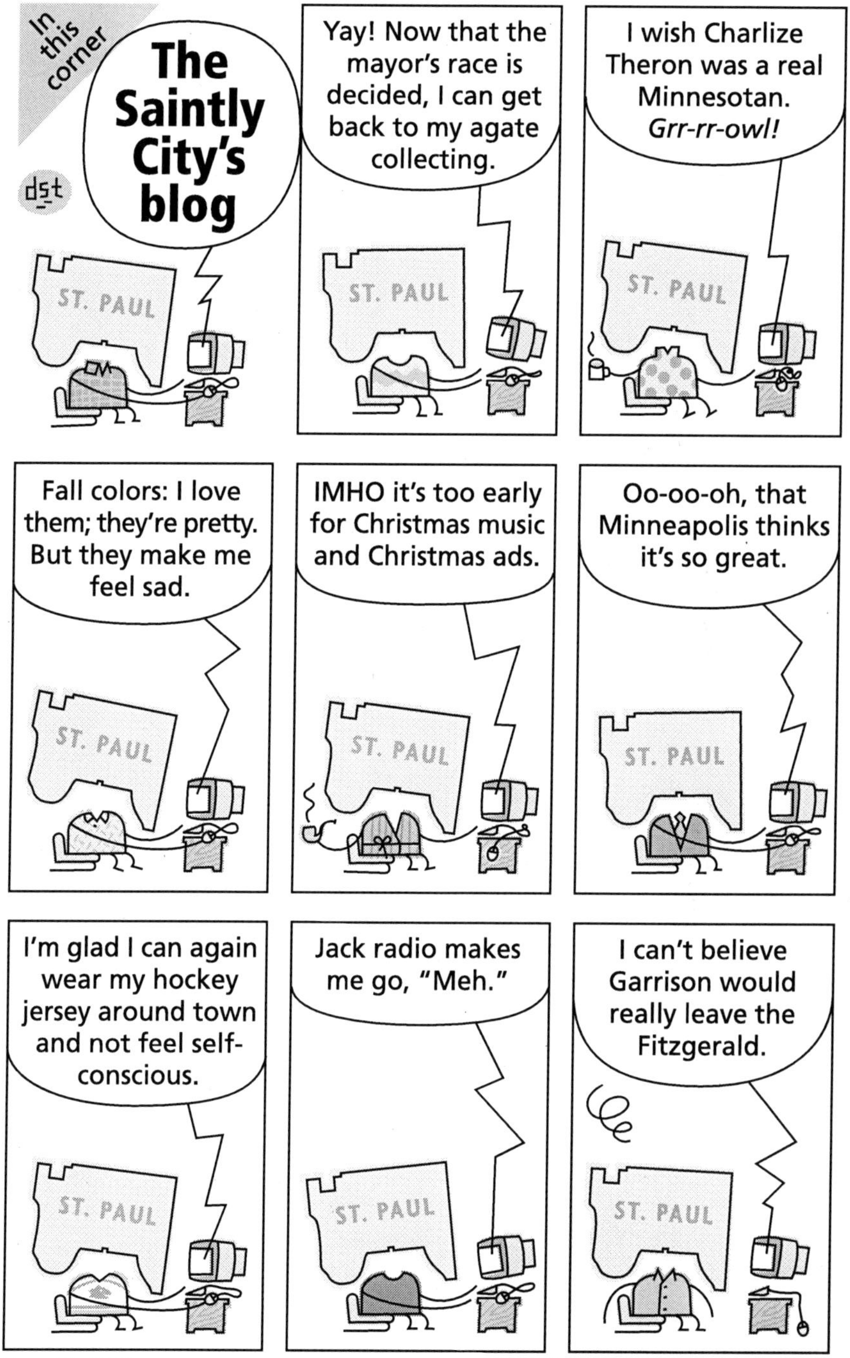
In this corner
The Saintly City's blog
dst
ST. PAUL
Yay! Now that the mayor's race is decided, I can get back to my agate collecting.
ST. PAUL
I wish Charlize Theron was a real Minnesotan. *Grr-rr-owl!*
ST. PAUL
Fall colors: I love them; they're pretty. But they make me feel sad.
ST. PAUL
IMHO it's too early for Christmas music and Christmas ads.
ST. PAUL
Oo-oo-oh, that Minneapolis thinks it's so great.
ST. PAUL
I'm glad I can again wear my hockey jersey around town and not feel self-conscious.
ST. PAUL
Jack radio makes me go, "Meh."
ST. PAUL
I can't believe Garrison would really leave the Fitzgerald.
ST. PAUL

Nov. 10, 2005 DAVID STEINLICHT, PIONEER PRESS

Note: South African-born and raised actor Charlize Theron acted like a Minnesotan in the 2005 movie *North Country.*

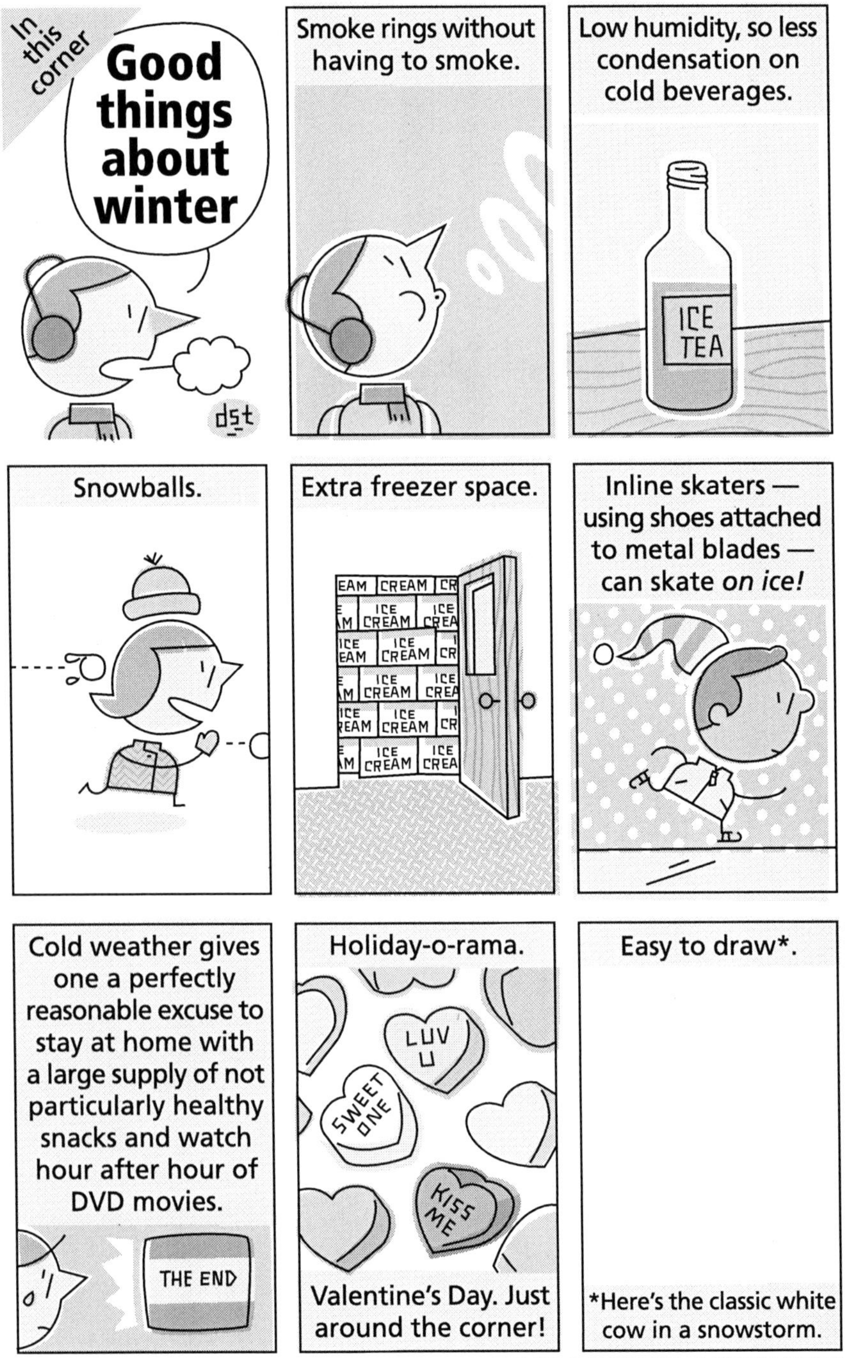
In this corner
Good things about winter
dst
Smoke rings without having to smoke.
Low humidity, so less condensation on cold beverages.
ICE TEA
Snowballs.
Extra freezer space.
ICE CREAM
Inline skaters — using shoes attached to metal blades — can skate *on ice!*
Cold weather gives one a perfectly reasonable excuse to stay at home with a large supply of not particularly healthy snacks and watch hour after hour of DVD movies.
THE END
Holiday-o-rama.
LUV U
SWEET ONE
KISS ME
Valentine's Day. Just around the corner!
Easy to draw*.
*Here's the classic white cow in a snowstorm.

Nov. 17, 2005

DAVID STEINLICHT, PIONEER PRESS

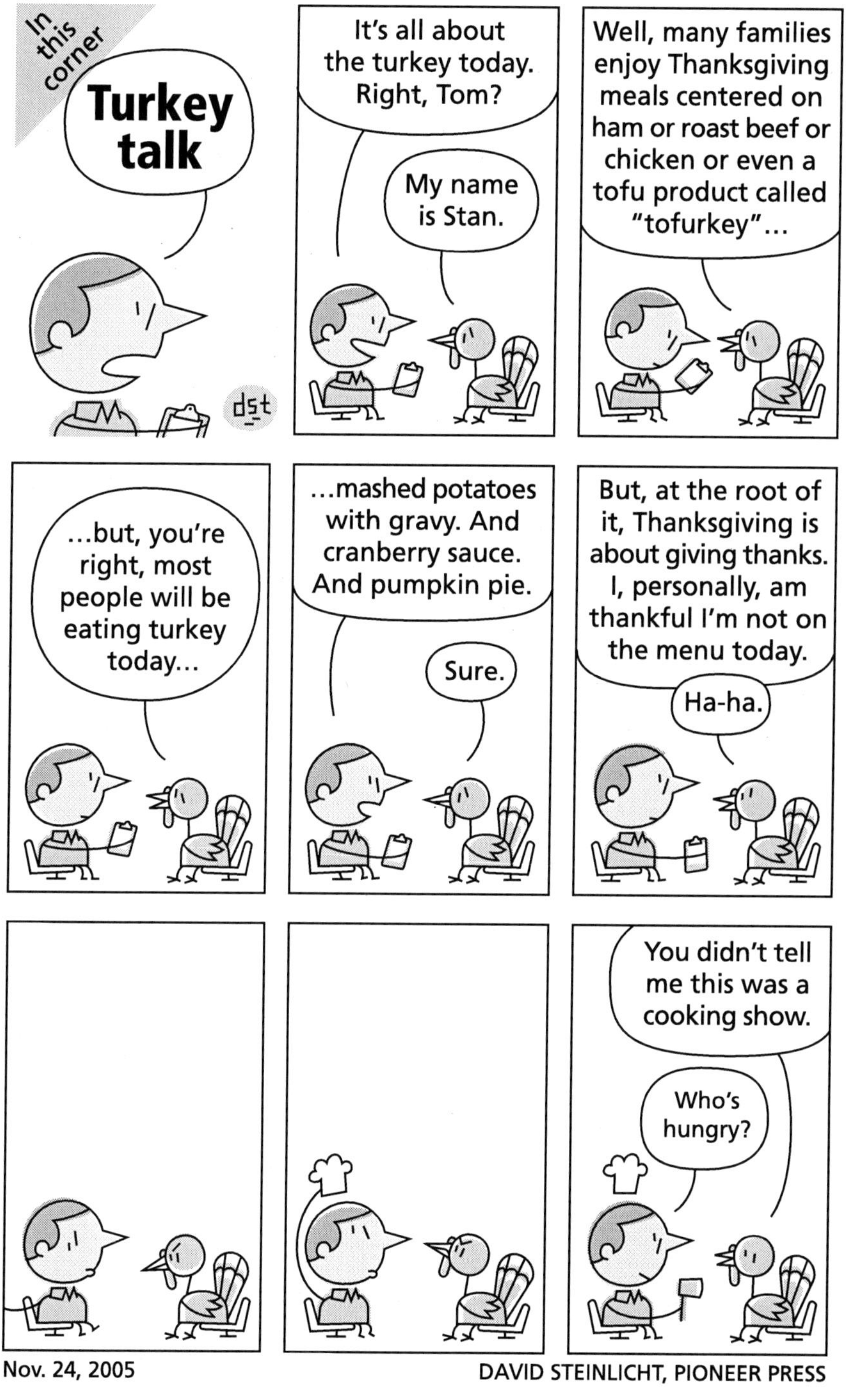
In this corner
Turkey talk
dst
It's all about the turkey today. Right, Tom?
My name is Stan.
Well, many families enjoy Thanksgiving meals centered on ham or roast beef or chicken or even a tofu product called "tofurkey"...
...but, you're right, most people will be eating turkey today...
...mashed potatoes with gravy. And cranberry sauce. And pumpkin pie.
Sure.
But, at the root of it, Thanksgiving is about giving thanks. I, personally, am thankful I'm not on the menu today.
Ha-ha.
You didn't tell me this was a cooking show.
Who's hungry?

Nov. 24, 2005

DAVID STEINLICHT, PIONEER PRESS

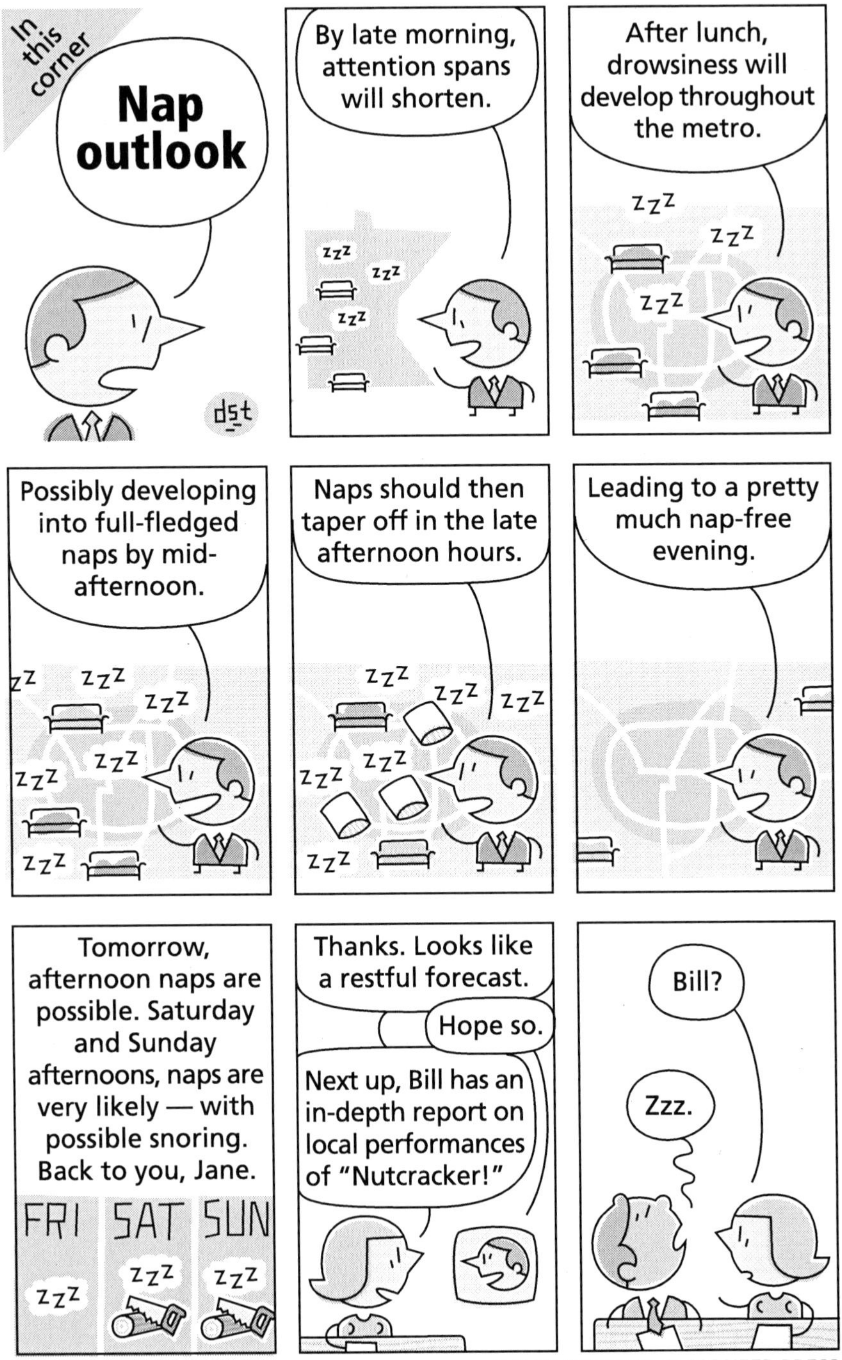
In this corner
Nap outlook
dst
By late morning, attention spans will shorten.
zzz
zzz
zzz
After lunch, drowsiness will develop throughout the metro.
zzz
zzz
zzz
Possibly developing into full-fledged naps by mid-afternoon.
zzz
zzz
zzz
zzz
zzz
Naps should then taper off in the late afternoon hours.
zzz
zzz
zzz
zzz
zzz
zzz
Leading to a pretty much nap-free evening.
Tomorrow, afternoon naps are possible. Saturday and Sunday afternoons, naps are very likely — with possible snoring. Back to you, Jane.
FRI
SAT
SUN
zzz
zzz
zzz
Thanks. Looks like a restful forecast.
Hope so.
Next up, Bill has an in-depth report on local performances of "Nutcracker!"
Bill?
Zzz.

Dec. 1, 2005

DAVID STEINLICHT, PIONEER PRESS

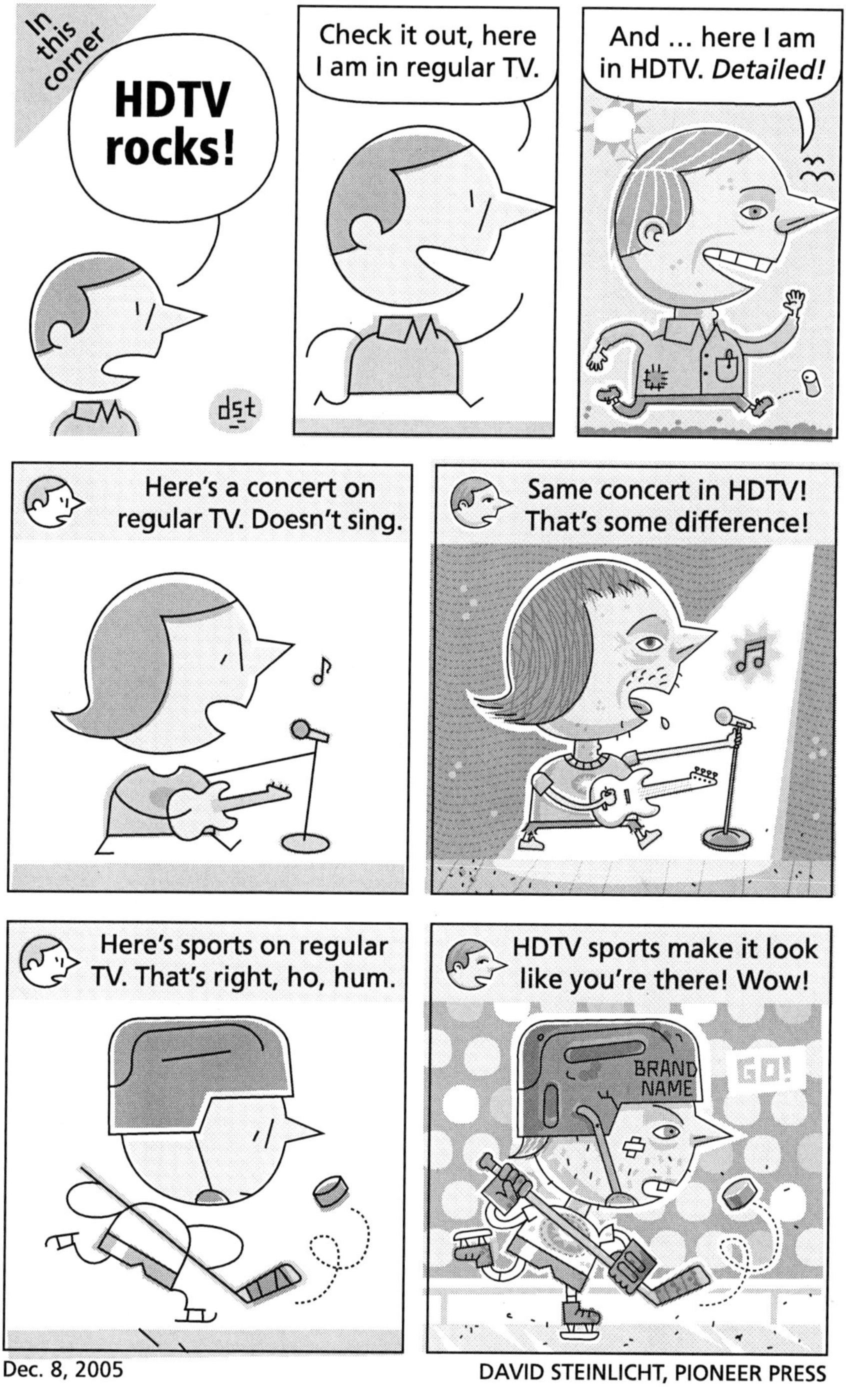

In this corner
HDTV rocks!
dst
Check it out, here I am in regular TV.
And ... here I am in HDTV. *Detailed!*
Here's a concert on regular TV. Doesn't sing.
Same concert in HDTV! That's some difference!
Here's sports on regular TV. That's right, ho, hum.
HDTV sports make it look like you're there! Wow!
BRAND NAME
GO!

Dec. 8, 2005

DAVID STEINLICHT, PIONEER PRESS

In this corner

Behind the scenes

Yeah, the big guy has a lot of fur to keep track of.

He was in the make-up chair for three hours each morning before filming.

Let me tell you, it takes some doing to handle a giant blow-dryer mounted on a backhoe.

Hair and fur conditioner? We'd buy it by the 55-gallon drum.

TANGLE B GONE

And then there was pest control. Whew! That guy is a nit magnet!

His natural jet-black fur photographs poorly. So we added silver highlights.

It's a shame his beautiful baby-blue eyes are hidden by brown contacts.

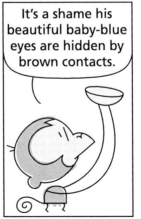

His nails — both hands and feet — had to be scuffed every day.

He's a real trouper.

Dec. 15, 2005

DAVID STEINLICHT, PIONEER PRESS

80

It's just what I wanted*

dst

*Or, anticipation's half the fun

It could be an iPod.

It probably is an Altoids tin filled with holiday Kleenex.

It could be a diamond bracelet from Tiffany's.

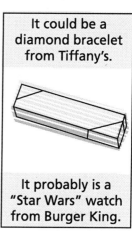

It probably is a "Star Wars" watch from Burger King.

It could be a remote-control helicopter.

It probably is a pair of snowpants.

It could be an Xbox 360.

It probably is a cardboard box with a $36 Target gift card taped to the inside.

It could be "The Da Vinci Code: The Illustrated Edition."

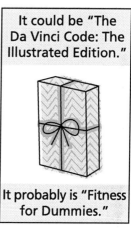

It probably is "Fitness for Dummies."

It could be a Motorola Razr cell phone.

It probably is a Gillette Mach 3 Turbo razor.

It could be a $1,000 bill.

It probably is a $5 bill.

It could be warm greetings from a friend.

It probably is warm greetings from a friend.

Dec. 22, 2005

DAVID STEINLICHT, PIONEER PRESS

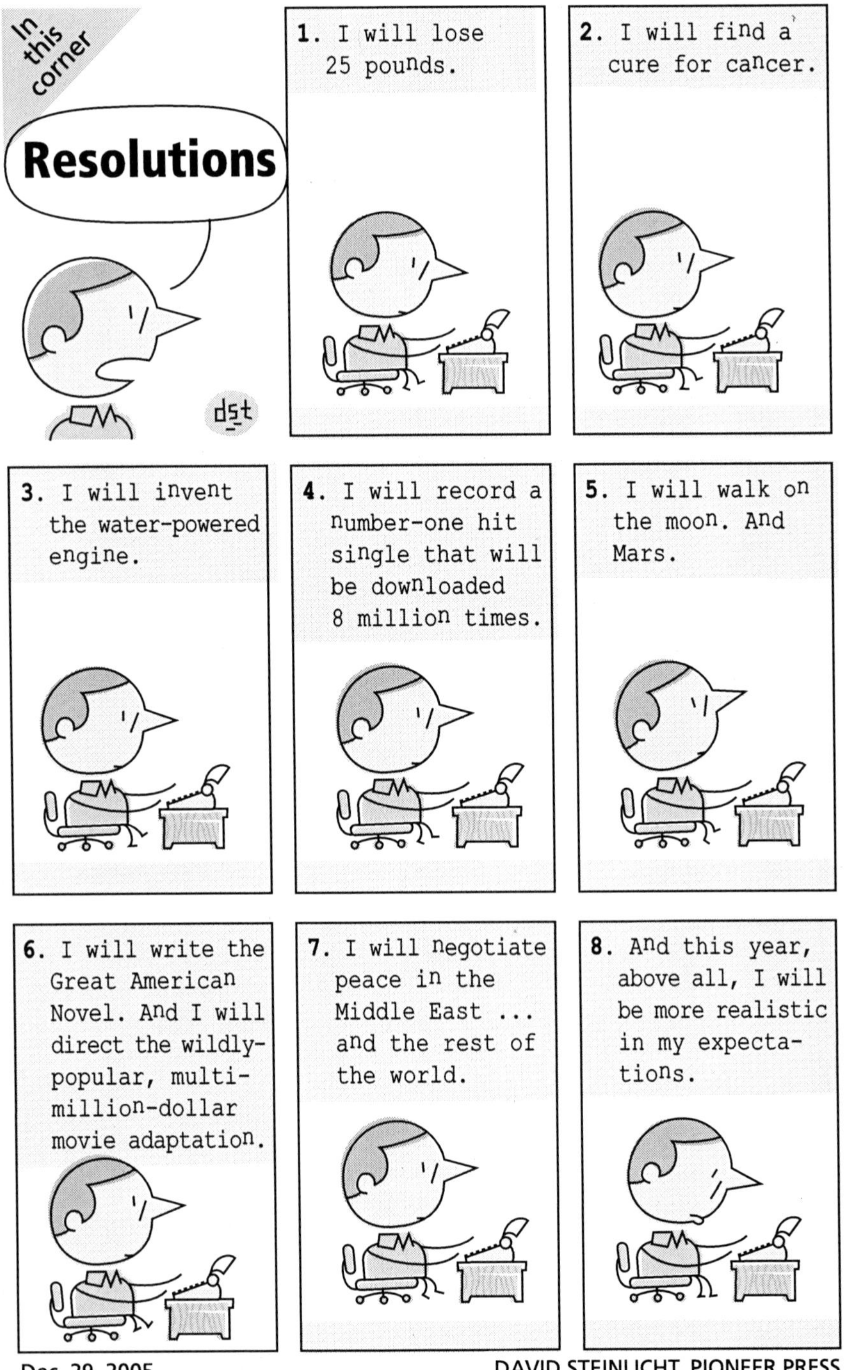
In this corner
Resolutions
dst
1. I will lose 25 pounds.
2. I will find a cure for cancer.
3. I will invent the water-powered engine.
4. I will record a number-one hit single that will be downloaded 8 million times.
5. I will walk on the moon. And Mars.
6. I will write the Great American Novel. And I will direct the wildly-popular, multi-million-dollar movie adaptation.
7. I will negotiate peace in the Middle East ... and the rest of the world.
8. And this year, above all, I will be more realistic in my expectations.

Dec. 29, 2005

DAVID STEINLICHT, PIONEER PRESS

2006

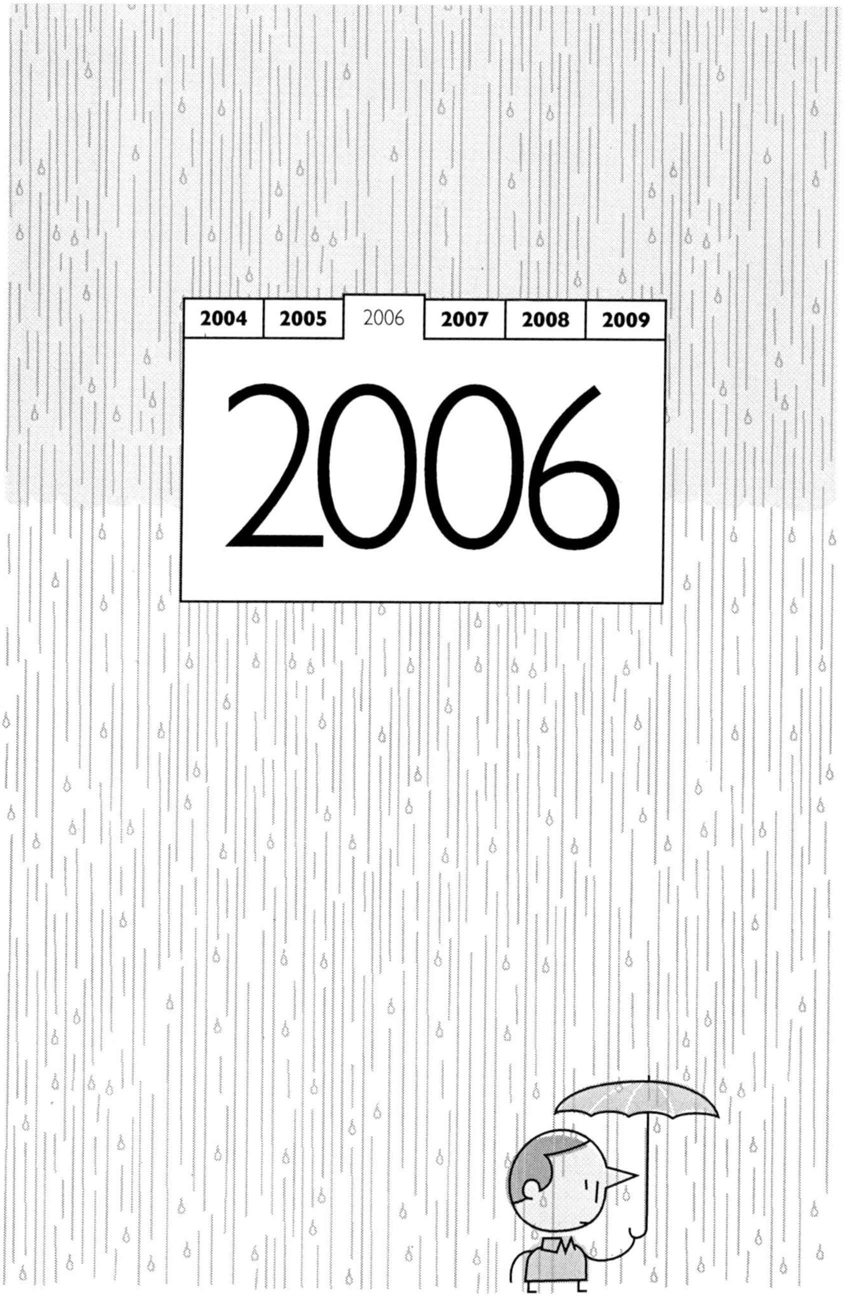
2004
2005
2006
2007
2008
2009

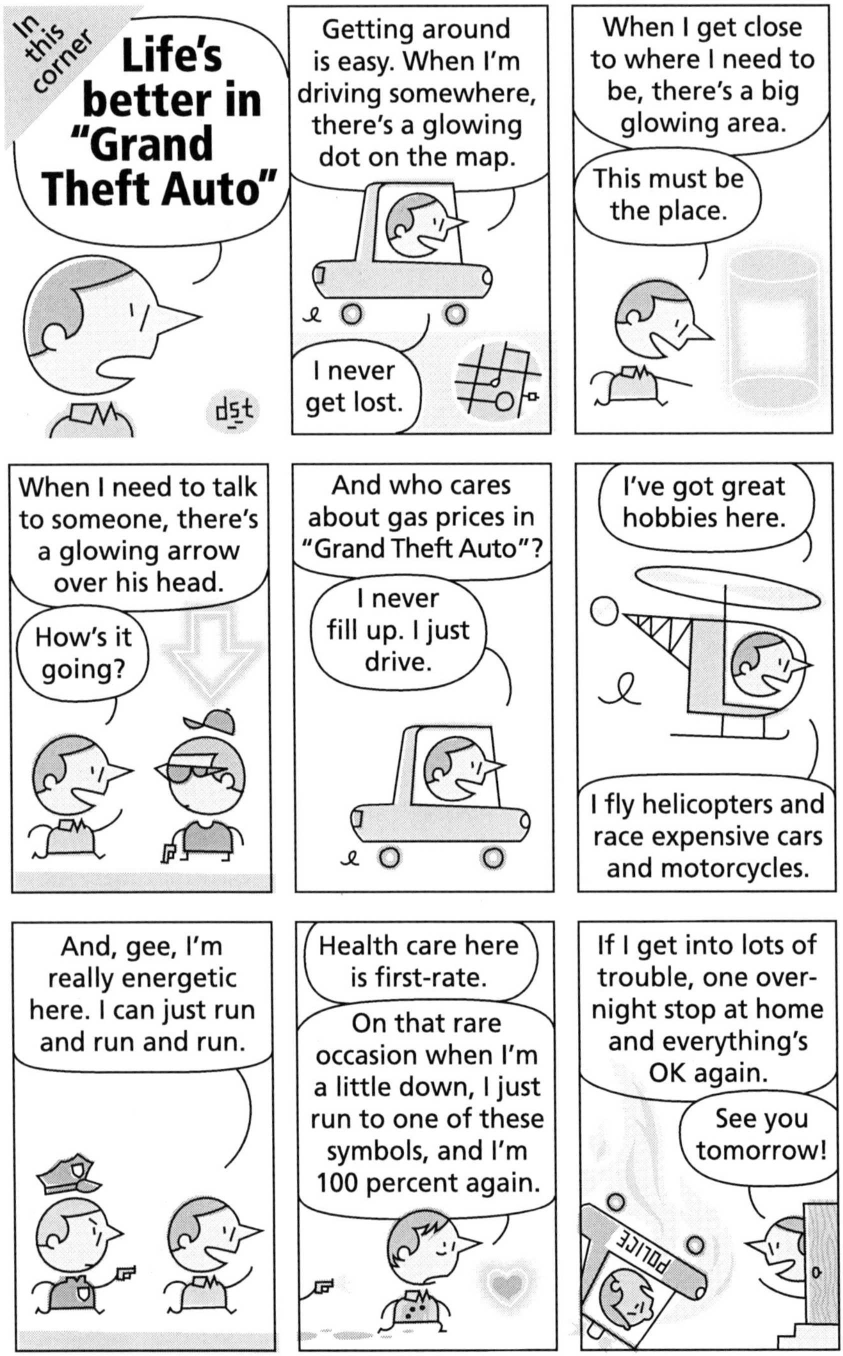
In this corner
Life's better in "Grand Theft Auto"
dst
Getting around is easy. When I'm driving somewhere, there's a glowing dot on the map.
I never get lost.
When I get close to where I need to be, there's a big glowing area.
This must be the place.
When I need to talk to someone, there's a glowing arrow over his head.
How's it going?
And who cares about gas prices in "Grand Theft Auto"?
I never fill up. I just drive.
I've got great hobbies here.
I fly helicopters and race expensive cars and motorcycles.
And, gee, I'm really energetic here. I can just run and run and run.
Health care here is first-rate.
On that rare occasion when I'm a little down, I just run to one of these symbols, and I'm 100 percent again.
If I get into lots of trouble, one over-night stop at home and everything's OK again.
See you tomorrow!
POLICE

Jan. 5, 2006

DAVID STEINLICHT, PIONEER PRESS

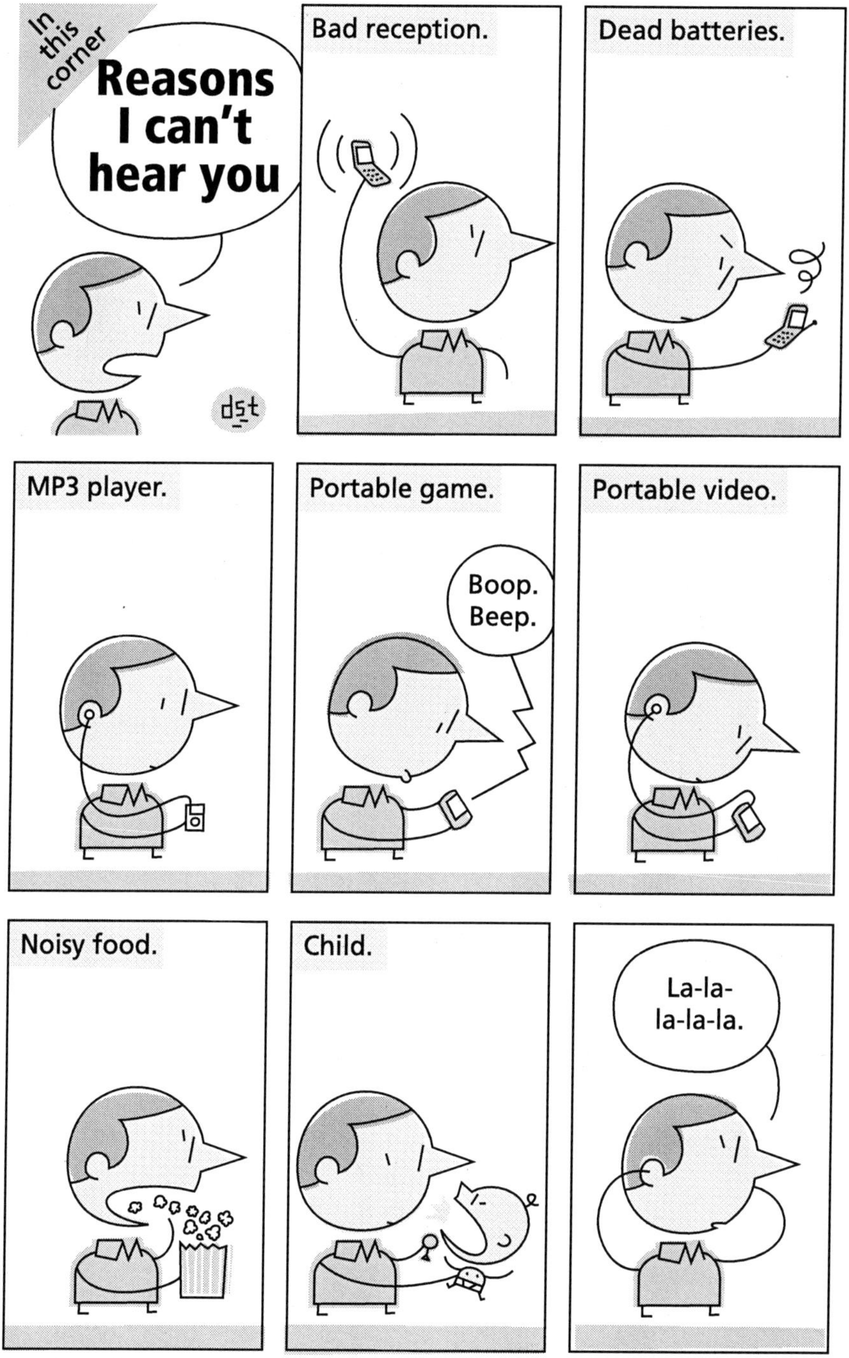
In this corner
Reasons I can't hear you
dst
Bad reception.
Dead batteries.
MP3 player.
Portable game.
Boop.
Beep.
Portable video.
Noisy food.
Child.
La-la-
la-la-la.

Jan. 12, 2006

DAVID STEINLICHT, PIONEER PRESS

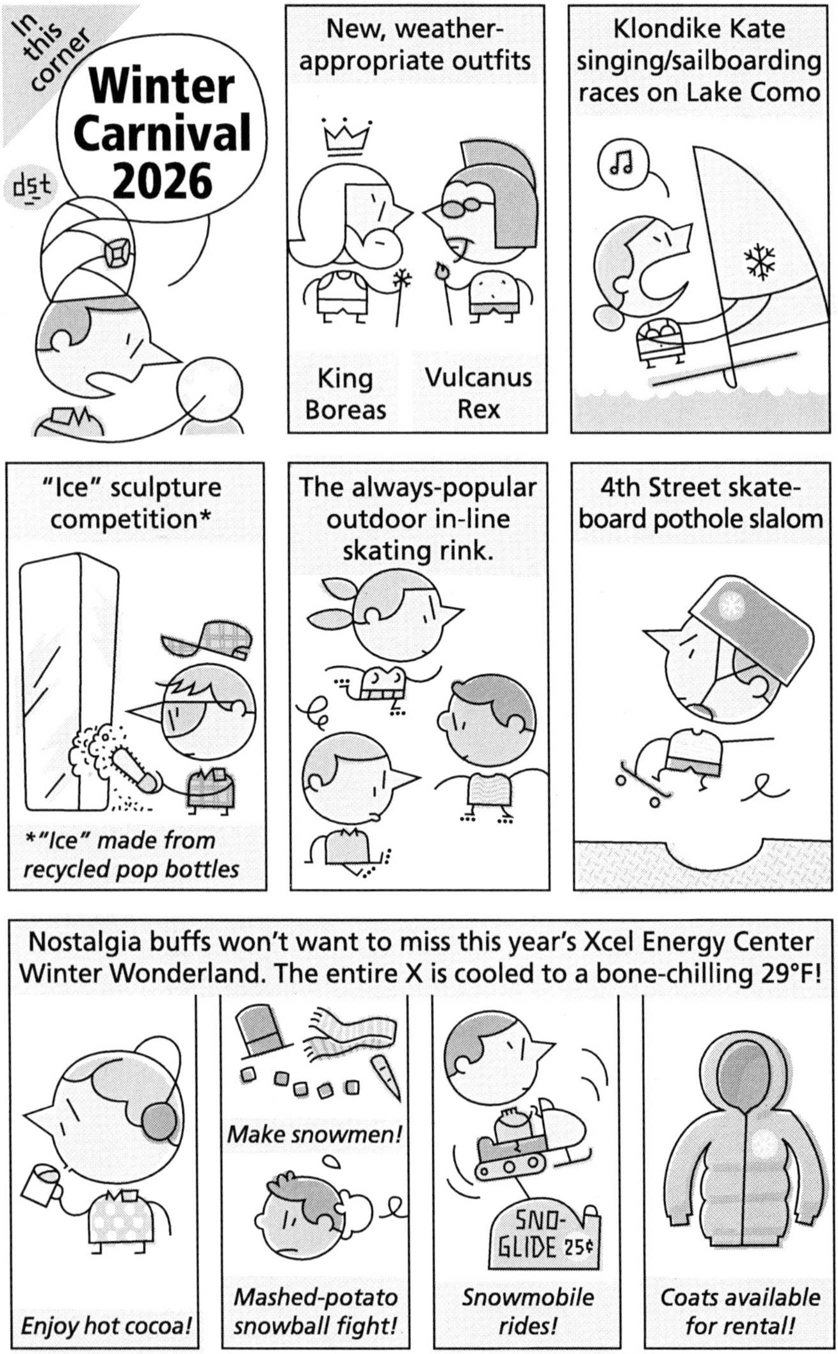
In this corner
Winter Carnival 2026
dst
New, weather-appropriate outfits
King Boreas
Vulcanus Rex
Klondike Kate singing/sailboarding races on Lake Como
"Ice" sculpture competition*
*"Ice" made from recycled pop bottles
The always-popular outdoor in-line skating rink.
4th Street skate-board pothole slalom
Nostalgia buffs won't want to miss this year's Xcel Energy Center Winter Wonderland. The entire X is cooled to a bone-chilling 29°F!
Enjoy hot cocoa!
Make snowmen!
Mashed-potato snowball fight!
SNO-GLIDE 25¢
Snowmobile rides!
Coats available for rental!

Jan. 19, 2006

DAVID STEINLICHT, PIONEER PRESS

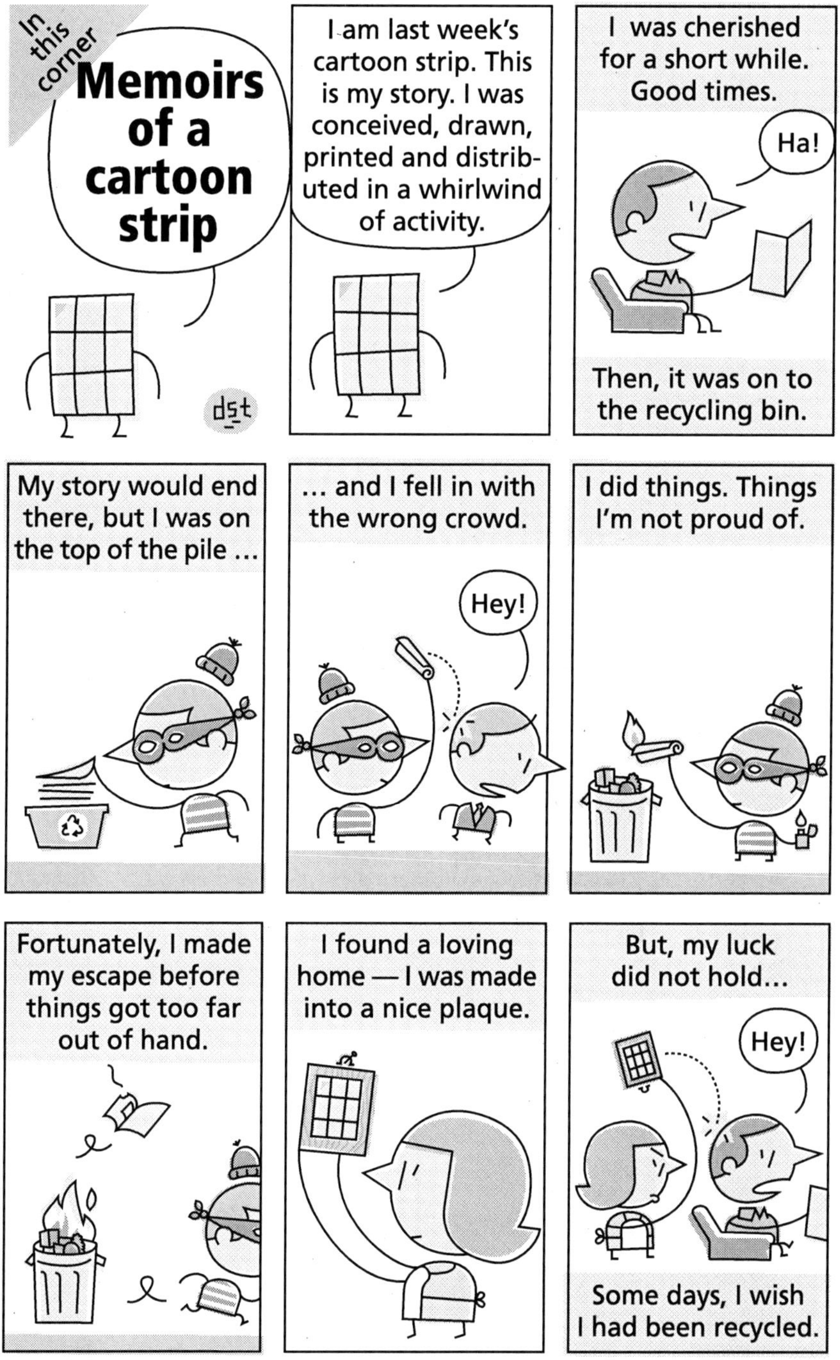
In this corner
Memoirs of a cartoon strip
dst
I am last week's cartoon strip. This is my story. I was conceived, drawn, printed and distributed in a whirlwind of activity.
I was cherished for a short while. Good times.
Ha!
Then, it was on to the recycling bin.
My story would end there, but I was on the top of the pile ...
... and I fell in with the wrong crowd.
Hey!
I did things. Things I'm not proud of.
Fortunately, I made my escape before things got too far out of hand.
I found a loving home — I was made into a nice plaque.
But, my luck did not hold...
Hey!
Some days, I wish I had been recycled.

Jan. 26, 2006 DAVID STEINLICHT, PIONEER PRESS

Note: The memoir, *A Million Little Pieces* was debunked on the "Oprah Winfrey" show, so I got in on the action and concocted another memoir.

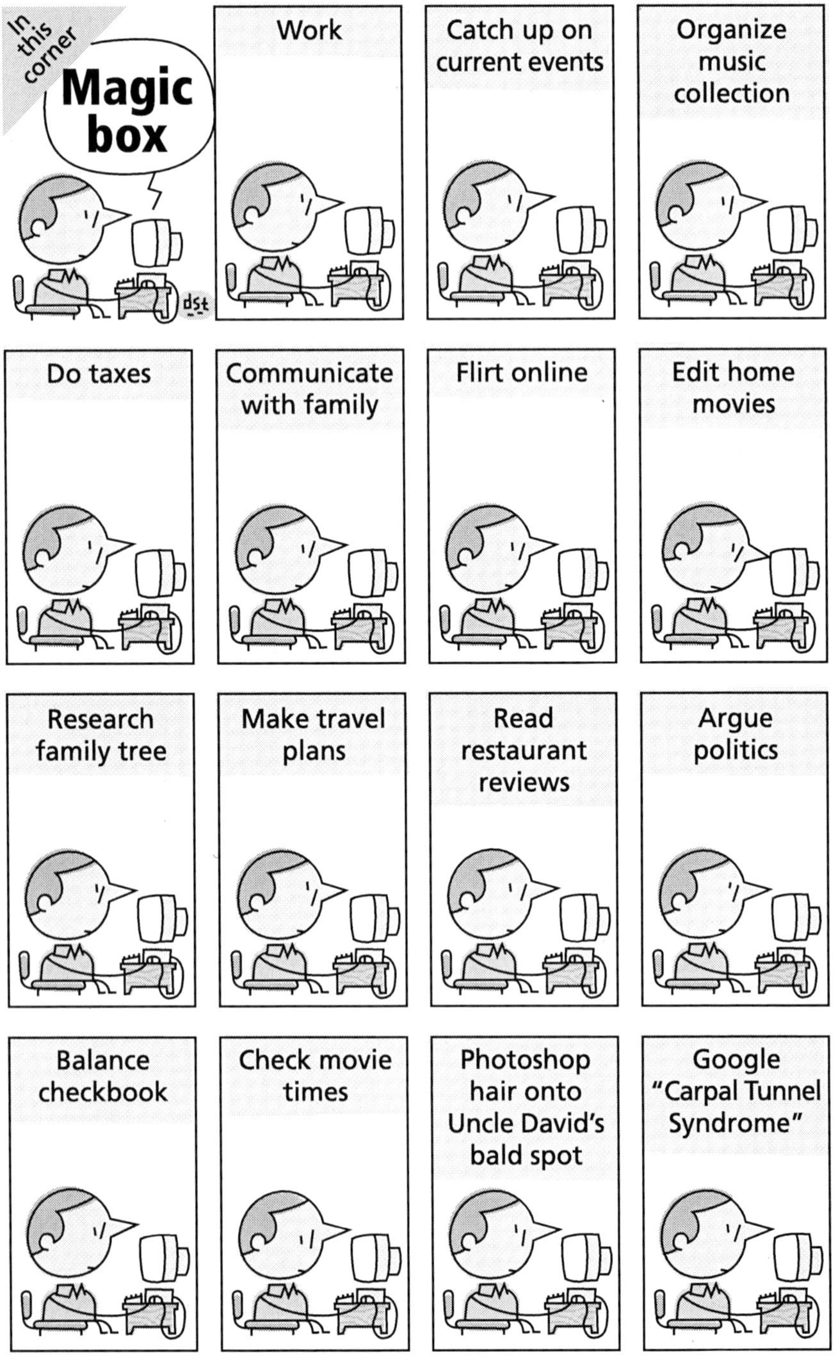
In this corner
Magic box
dst
Work
Catch up on current events
Organize music collection
Do taxes
Communicate with family
Flirt online
Edit home movies
Research family tree
Make travel plans
Read restaurant reviews
Argue politics
Balance checkbook
Check movie times
Photoshop hair onto Uncle David's bald spot
Google "Carpal Tunnel Syndrome"

Feb. 2, 2006

DAVID STEINLICHT, PIONEER PRESS

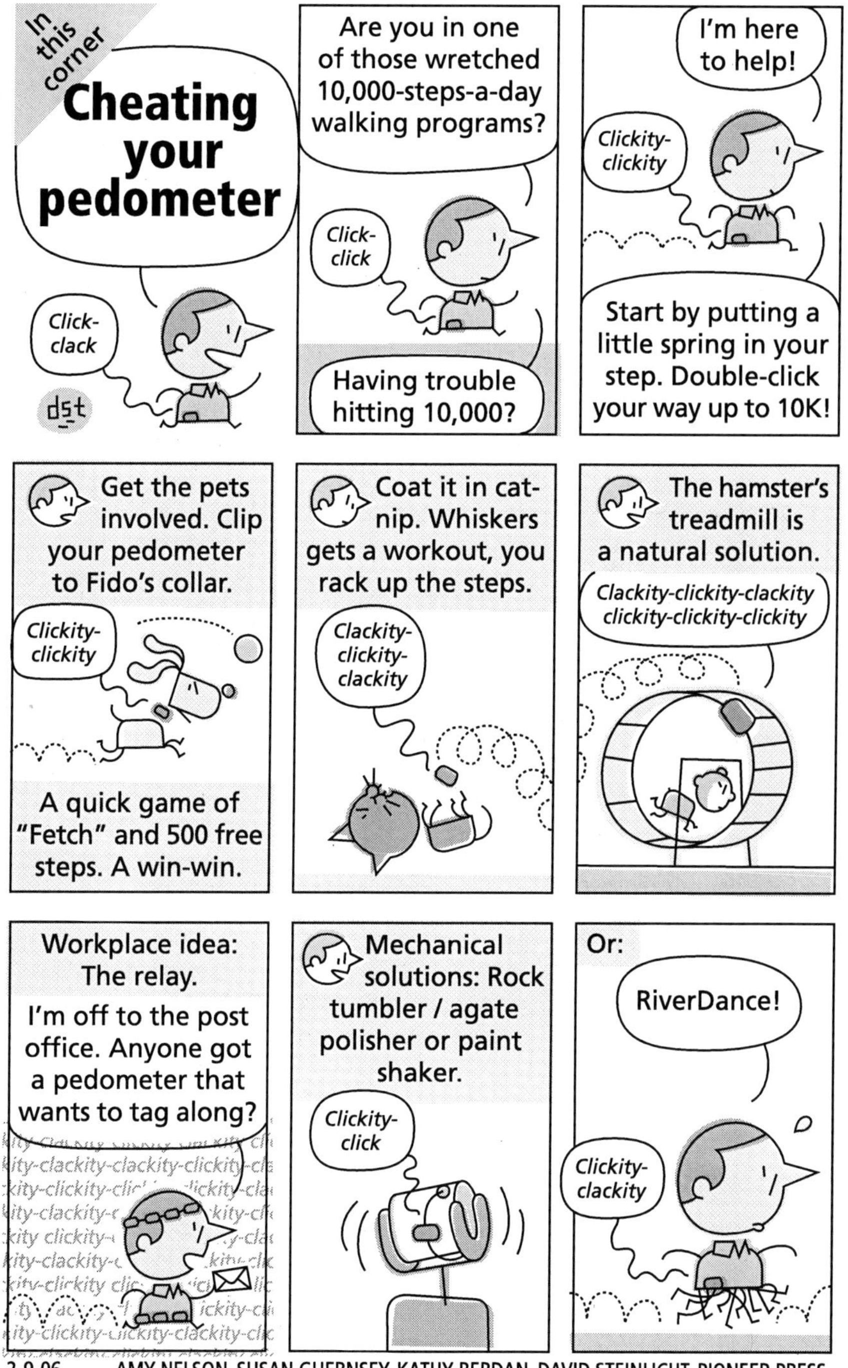
In this corner
Cheating your pedometer
Click-clack
dst
Are you in one of those wretched 10,000-steps-a-day walking programs?
Click-click
Having trouble hitting 10,000?
I'm here to help!
Clickity-clickity
Start by putting a little spring in your step. Double-click your way up to 10K!
Get the pets involved. Clip your pedometer to Fido's collar.
Clickity-clickity
A quick game of "Fetch" and 500 free steps. A win-win.
Coat it in cat-nip. Whiskers gets a workout, you rack up the steps.
Clackity-clickity-clackity
The hamster's treadmill is a natural solution.
Clackity-clickity-clackity clickity-clickity-clickity
Workplace idea: The relay.
I'm off to the post office. Anyone got a pedometer that wants to tag along?
Mechanical solutions: Rock tumbler / agate polisher or paint shaker.
Clickity-click
Or:
RiverDance!
Clickity-clackity

2-9-06 AMY NELSON, SUSAN GUERNSEY, KATHY BERDAN, DAVID STEINLICHT, PIONEER PRESS

Slapstick interlude

Thud!

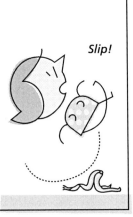

Slip!

Boink!

Zip!

Clunk!

Twack!

Whap!

Sometimes you have to stop and smell the coconut cream pie.

Feb. 17, 2006

DAVID STEINLICHT, PIONEER PRESS

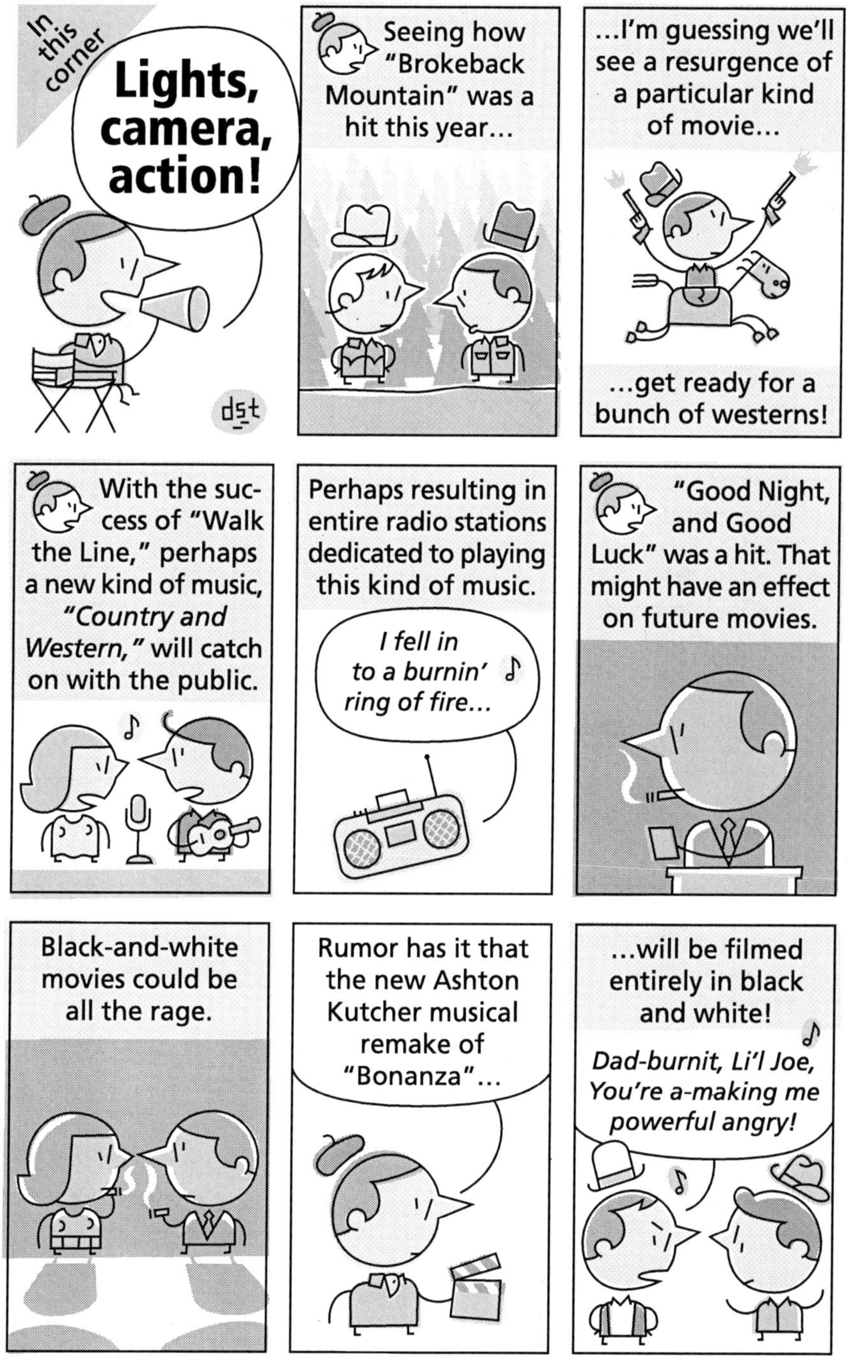
In this corner
Lights, camera, action!
dst
Seeing how "Brokeback Mountain" was a hit this year...
...I'm guessing we'll see a resurgence of a particular kind of movie...
...get ready for a bunch of westerns!
With the success of "Walk the Line," perhaps a new kind of music, "Country and Western," will catch on with the public.
Perhaps resulting in entire radio stations dedicated to playing this kind of music.
I fell in to a burnin' ring of fire...
"Good Night, and Good Luck" was a hit. That might have an effect on future movies.
Black-and-white movies could be all the rage.
Rumor has it that the new Ashton Kutcher musical remake of "Bonanza"...
...will be filmed entirely in black and white!
Dad-burnit, Li'l Joe, You're a-making me powerful angry!

Feb. 23, 2006

DAVID STEINLICHT, PIONEER PRESS

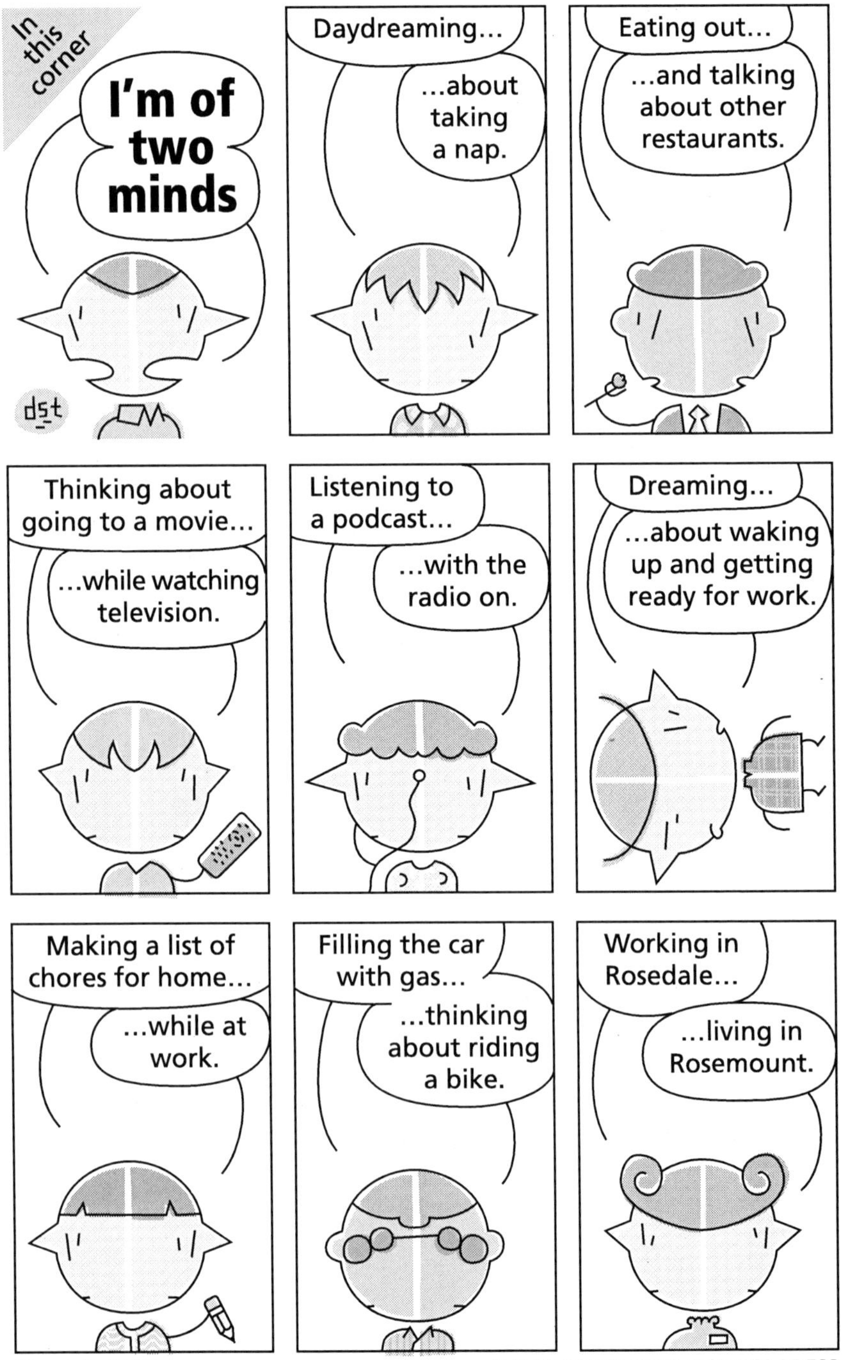
In this corner
I'm of two minds
dst
Daydreaming...
...about taking a nap.
Eating out...
...and talking about other restaurants.
Thinking about going to a movie...
...while watching television.
Listening to a podcast...
...with the radio on.
Dreaming...
...about waking up and getting ready for work.
Making a list of chores for home...
...while at work.
Filling the car with gas...
...thinking about riding a bike.
Working in Rosedale...
...living in Rosemount.

March 2, 2006 DAVID STEINLICHT, PIONEER PRESS

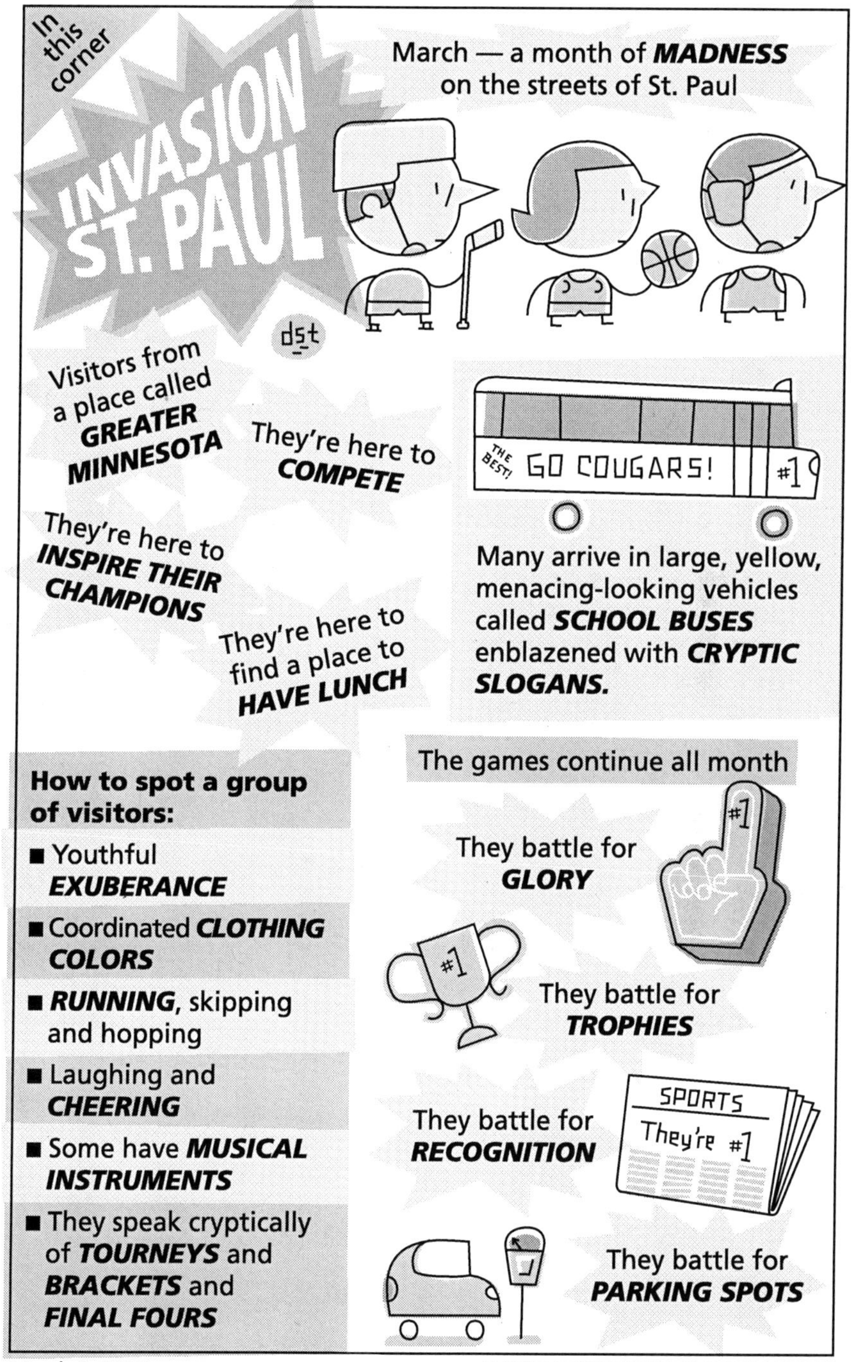
In this corner
INVASION ST. PAUL
March — a month of MADNESS on the streets of St. Paul
dst
Visitors from a place called GREATER MINNESOTA
They're here to COMPETE
They're here to INSPIRE THEIR CHAMPIONS
They're here to find a place to HAVE LUNCH
THE BEST! GO COUGARS! #1
Many arrive in large, yellow, menacing-looking vehicles called SCHOOL BUSES enblazened with CRYPTIC SLOGANS.
How to spot a group of visitors:
■ Youthful EXUBERANCE
■ Coordinated CLOTHING COLORS
■ RUNNING, skipping and hopping
■ Laughing and CHEERING
■ Some have MUSICAL INSTRUMENTS
■ They speak cryptically of TOURNEYS and BRACKETS and FINAL FOURS
The games continue all month
#1
They battle for GLORY
#1
They battle for TROPHIES
SPORTS
They're #1
They battle for RECOGNITION
They battle for PARKING SPOTS

March 9, 2006

DAVID STEINLICHT, PIONEER PRESS

The iPod economy

Cashing in on that exciting device

dst

Pre-stressing
Much like stone-washed jeans, pre-stressed iPods have that appealing lived-in look.

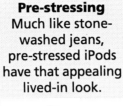

List coolification
"Coolifiers" can purge all noncool songs from your iPod. For a premium, your uncool songs can be renamed...

... so while the playlist says you're listening to critic-approved Lucinda Williams, you are actually listening to not-cool REO Speedwagon.

Designer earbud covers
A rainbow of colors, wacky shapes.

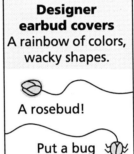

A rosebud!

Put a bug in your ear!

A carrot!

Wire covers
You have covers for the iPod, why not covers for the wires?

Looks like a rose stem!

Spaghetti with sauce!

Worm!

iSpinner
Waterproof case that doubles as a fishing lure.

?

BeltDock
Make sure your iPod is securely strapped in when you drive.

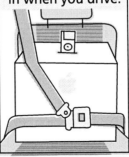

ChiaPod
Seed-embedded ceramic cover gives the device a high-tech natural look.

March 16, 2006

DAVID STEINLICHT, PIONEER PRESS

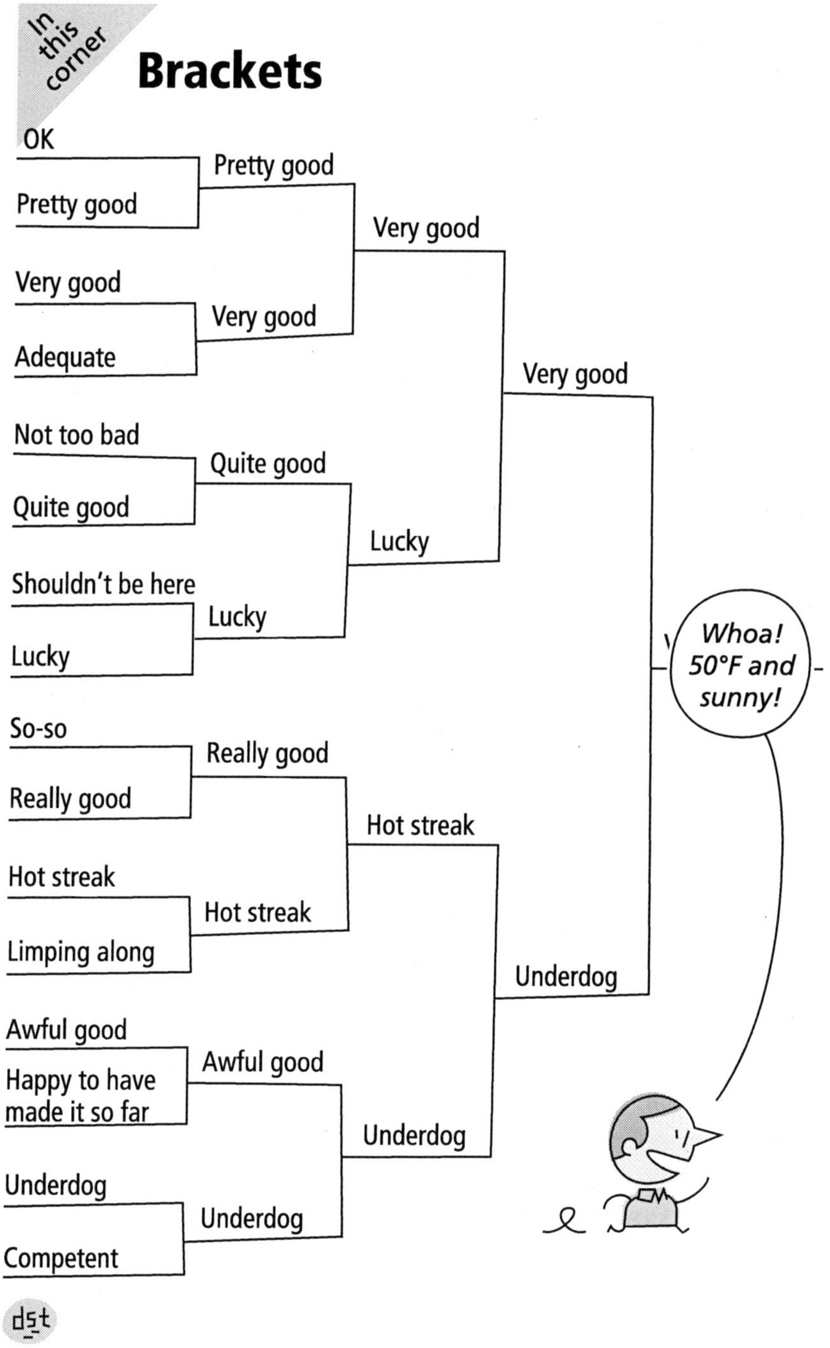
In this corner
Brackets
OK
Pretty good
Very good
Adequate
Not too bad
Quite good
Shouldn't be here
Lucky
So-so
Really good
Hot streak
Limping along
Awful good
Happy to have made it so far
Underdog
Competent
Pretty good
Very good
Quite good
Lucky
Really good
Hot streak
Awful good
Underdog
Very good
Lucky
Hot streak
Underdog
Very good
Underdog
Whoa! 50°F and sunny!
dst

March 23, 2006

DAVID STEINLICHT, PIONEER PRESS

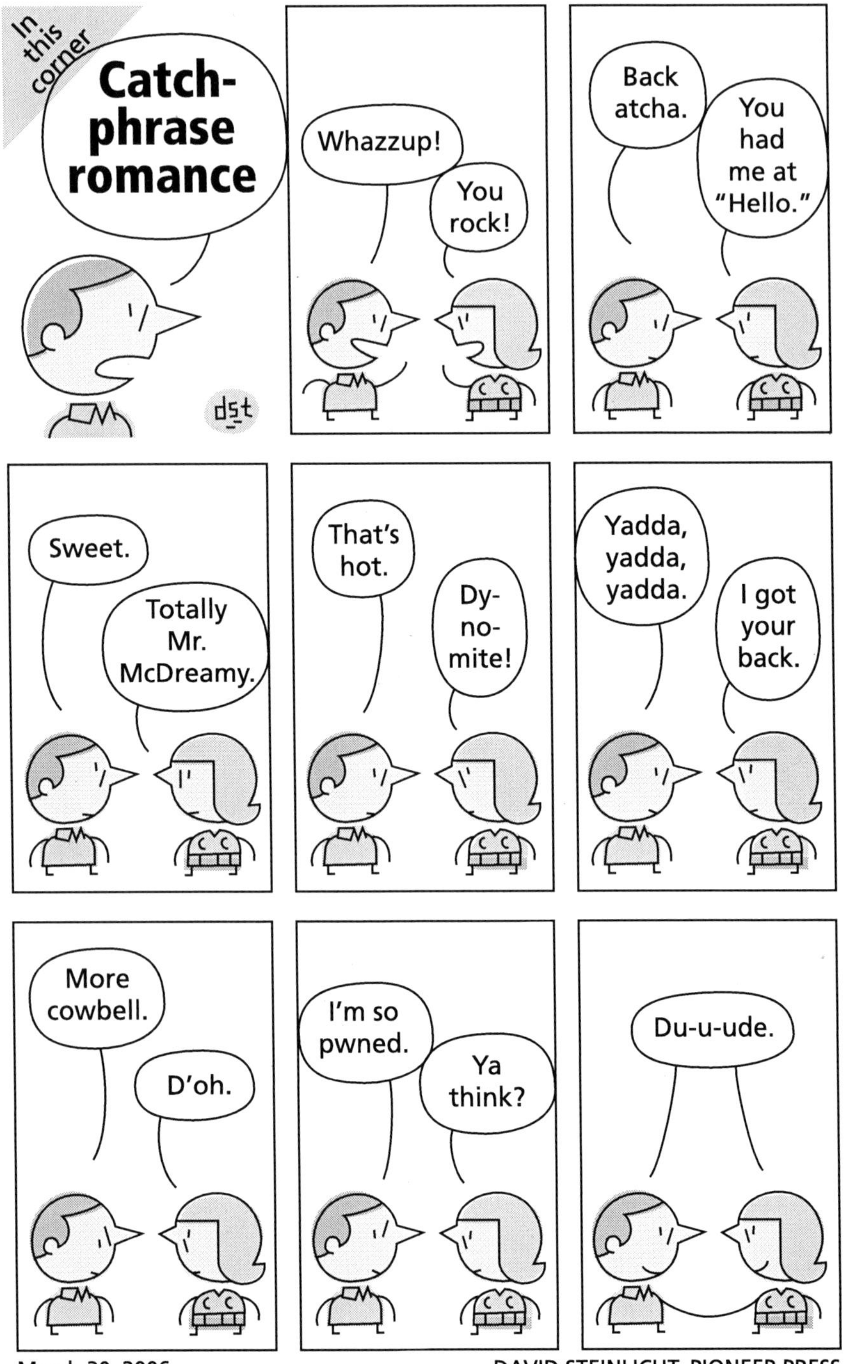
In this corner
Catch-phrase romance
dst
Whazzup!
You rock!
Back atcha.
You had me at "Hello."
Sweet.
Totally Mr. McDreamy.
That's hot.
Dy-no-mite!
Yadda, yadda, yadda.
I got your back.
More cowbell.
D'oh.
I'm so pwned.
Ya think?
Du-u-ude.
March 30, 2006

DAVID STEINLICHT, PIONEER PRESS

In this corner
New uses for bar ashtrays
dst
What can be done with all these now-obsolete ashtrays?
Slightly fragile glass shuffleboard pucks.
10
8
8
Game pieces for oversized checkers matches.
King me.
Novelty eyeglasses.
The metal ashtrays could double as lousy frisbees …
… or lousy ninja discs.
Stick a couple on your shoes for tap dancing.
Tappity-tap-tap!
Containers for new novelty drinks.
This one's called "A Squat Shot."
Here's the recipe for "The Smoky Bar":
1 part gin
1 part scotch
1/2 inch cig. ash
(produced off-site)
Serve shaken, over-the-rocks or blended.

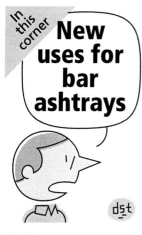

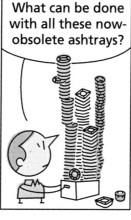

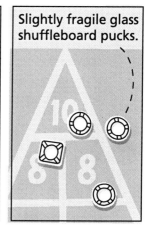

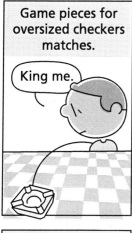

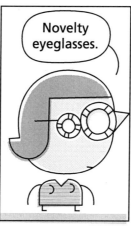

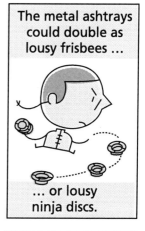

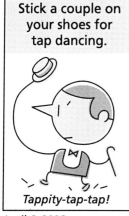

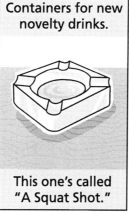

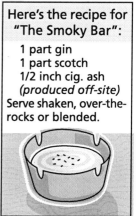

April 6, 2006

DAVID STEINLICHT, PIONEER PRESS

Note: Smoking in bars was banned in St. Paul.

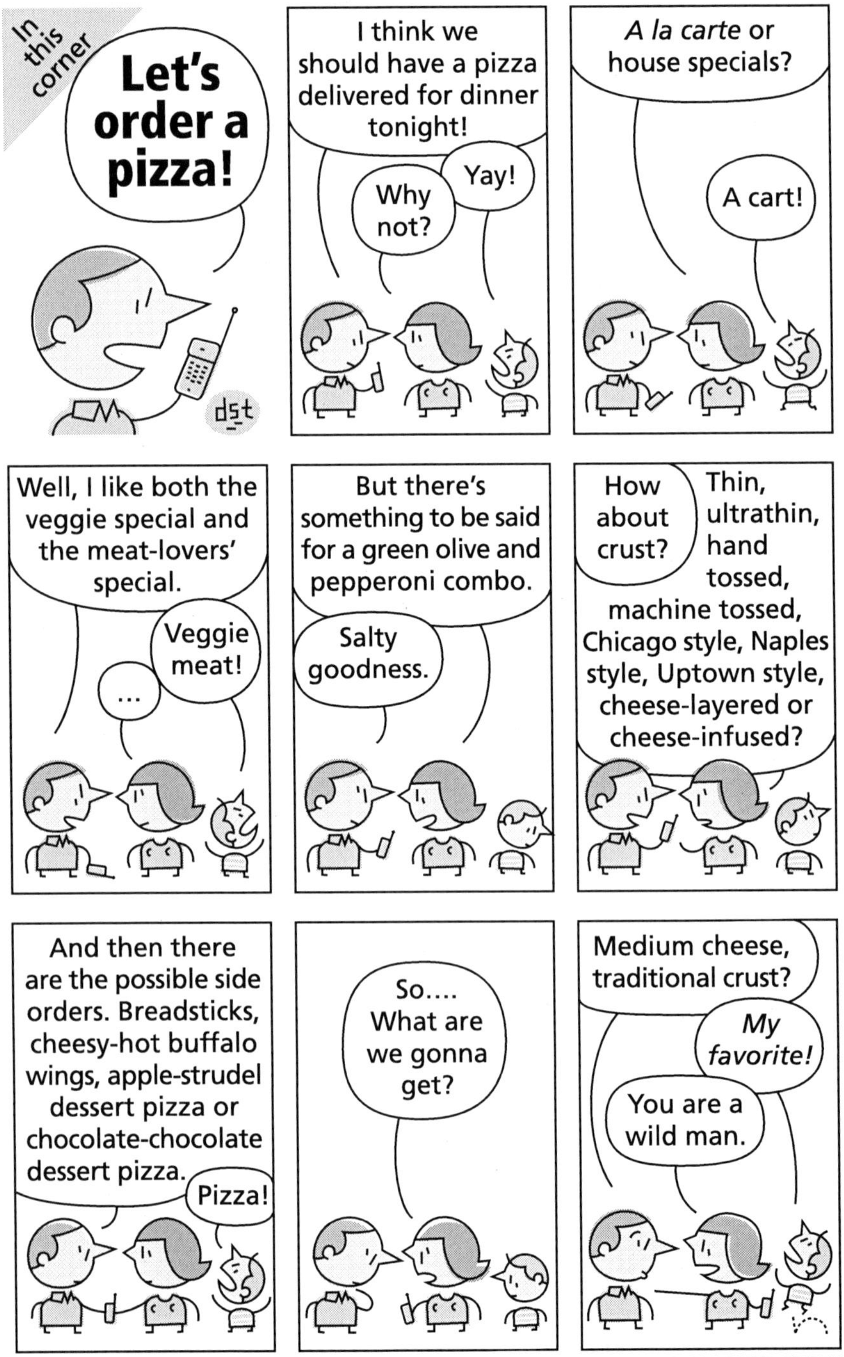
In this corner
Let's order a pizza!
dst
I think we should have a pizza delivered for dinner tonight!
Why not?
Yay!
A la carte or house specials?
A cart!
Well, I like both the veggie special and the meat-lovers' special.
...
Veggie meat!
But there's something to be said for a green olive and pepperoni combo.
Salty goodness.
How about crust?
Thin, ultrathin, hand tossed, machine tossed, Chicago style, Naples style, Uptown style, cheese-layered or cheese-infused?
And then there are the possible side orders. Breadsticks, cheesy-hot buffalo wings, apple-strudel dessert pizza or chocolate-chocolate dessert pizza.
Pizza!
So.... What are we gonna get?
Medium cheese, traditional crust?
My favorite!
You are a wild man.

April 13, 2006

DAVID STEINLICHT, PIONEER PRESS

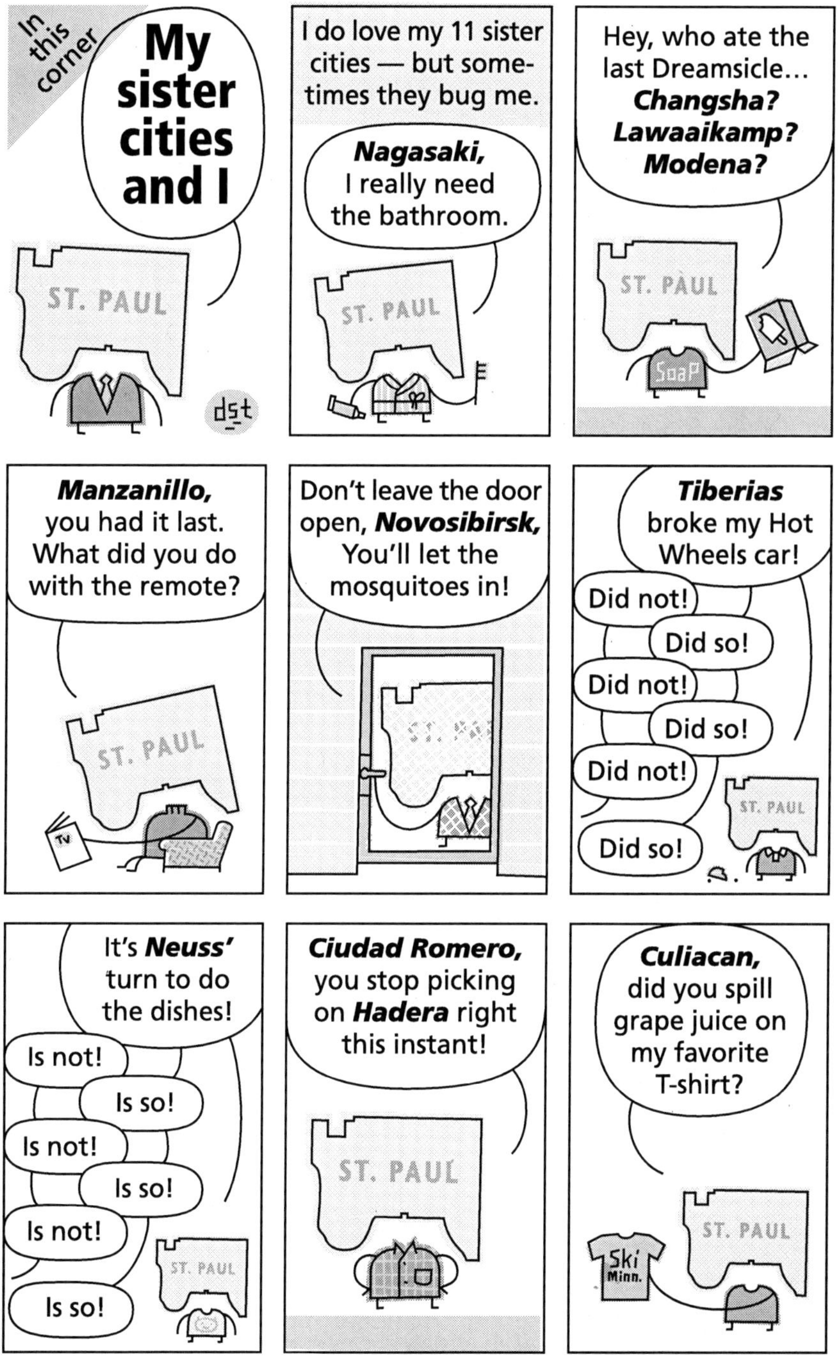
In this corner
My sister cities and I
ST. PAUL
dst
I do love my 11 sister cities — but sometimes they bug me.
Nagasaki, I really need the bathroom.
ST. PAUL
Hey, who ate the last Dreamsicle... Changsha? Lawaaikamp? Modena?
ST. PAUL
SoaP
Manzanillo, you had it last. What did you do with the remote?
ST. PAUL
TV
Don't leave the door open, Novosibirsk, You'll let the mosquitoes in!
Tiberias broke my Hot Wheels car!
Did not!
Did so!
Did not!
Did so!
Did not!
Did so!
ST. PAUL
It's Neuss' turn to do the dishes!
Is not!
Is so!
Is not!
Is so!
Is not!
Is so!
ST. PAUL
Ciudad Romero, you stop picking on Hadera right this instant!
ST. PAUL
Culiacan, did you spill grape juice on my favorite T-shirt?
Ski Minn.
ST. PAUL

April 20, 2006

DAVID STEINLICHT, PIONEER PRESS

Note: These are real sister cities.

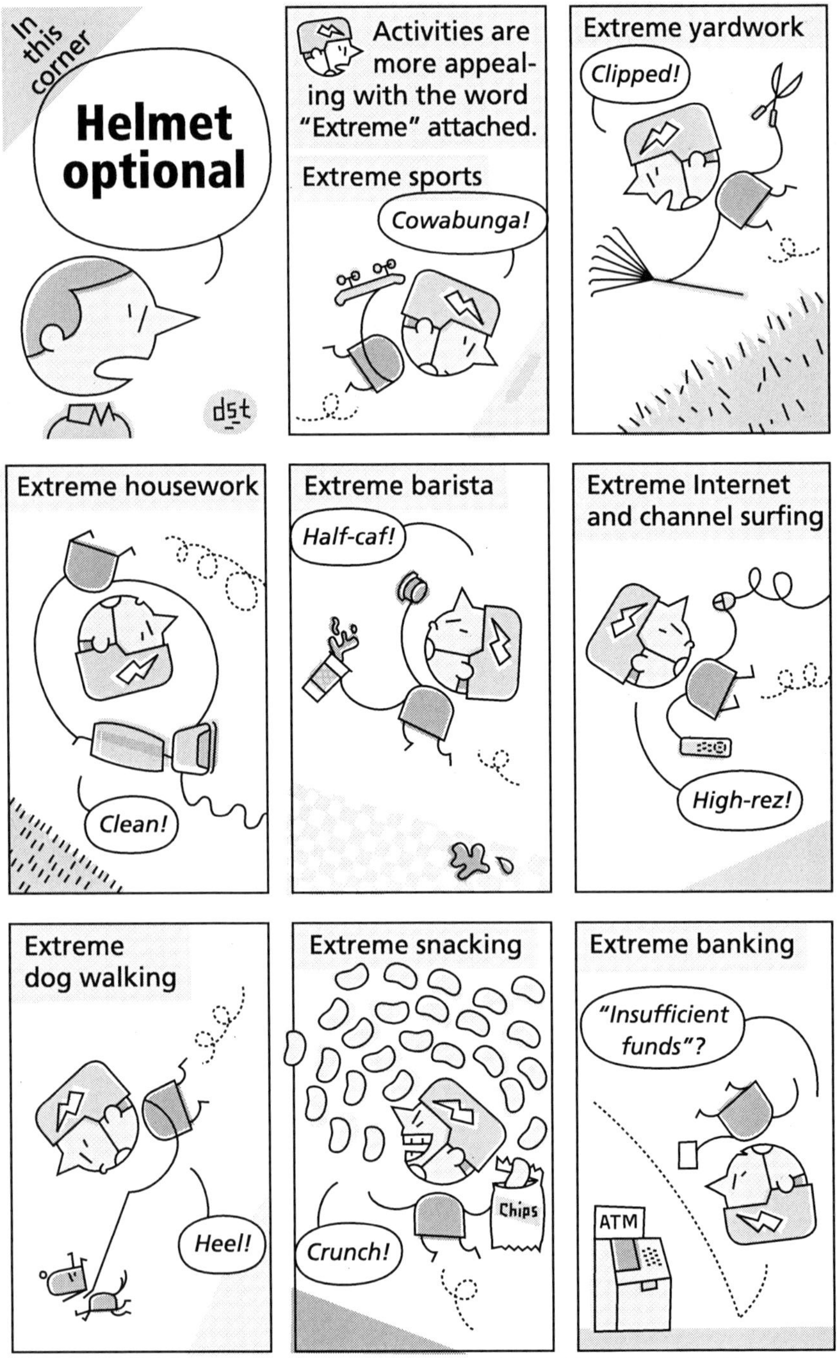
In this corner
Helmet optional
dst
Activities are more appealing with the word "Extreme" attached.
Extreme sports
Cowabunga!
Extreme yardwork
Clipped!
Extreme housework
Clean!
Extreme barista
Half-caf!
Extreme Internet and channel surfing
High-rez!
Extreme dog walking
Heel!
Extreme snacking
Chips
Crunch!
Extreme banking
"Insufficient funds"?
ATM

April 27, 2006

DAVID STEINLICHT, PIONEER PRESS

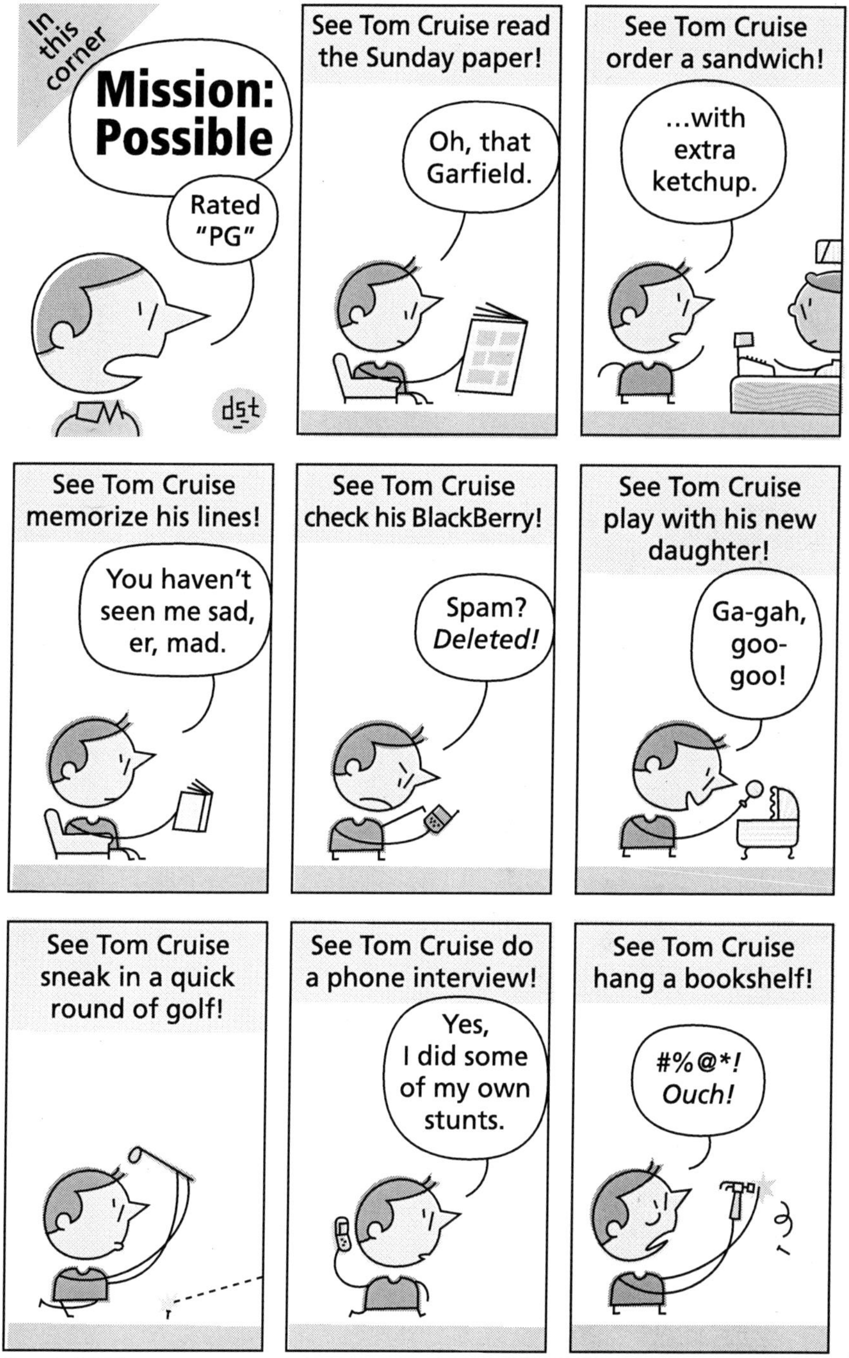
In this corner
Mission: Possible
Rated "PG"
dst
See Tom Cruise read the Sunday paper!
Oh, that Garfield.
See Tom Cruise order a sandwich!
...with extra ketchup.
See Tom Cruise memorize his lines!
You haven't seen me sad, er, mad.
See Tom Cruise check his BlackBerry!
Spam? *Deleted!*
See Tom Cruise play with his new daughter!
Ga-gah, goo-goo!
See Tom Cruise sneak in a quick round of golf!
See Tom Cruise do a phone interview!
Yes, I did some of my own stunts.
See Tom Cruise hang a bookshelf!
#%@*! *Ouch!*

May 4, 2006

DAVID STEINLICHT, PIONEER PRESS

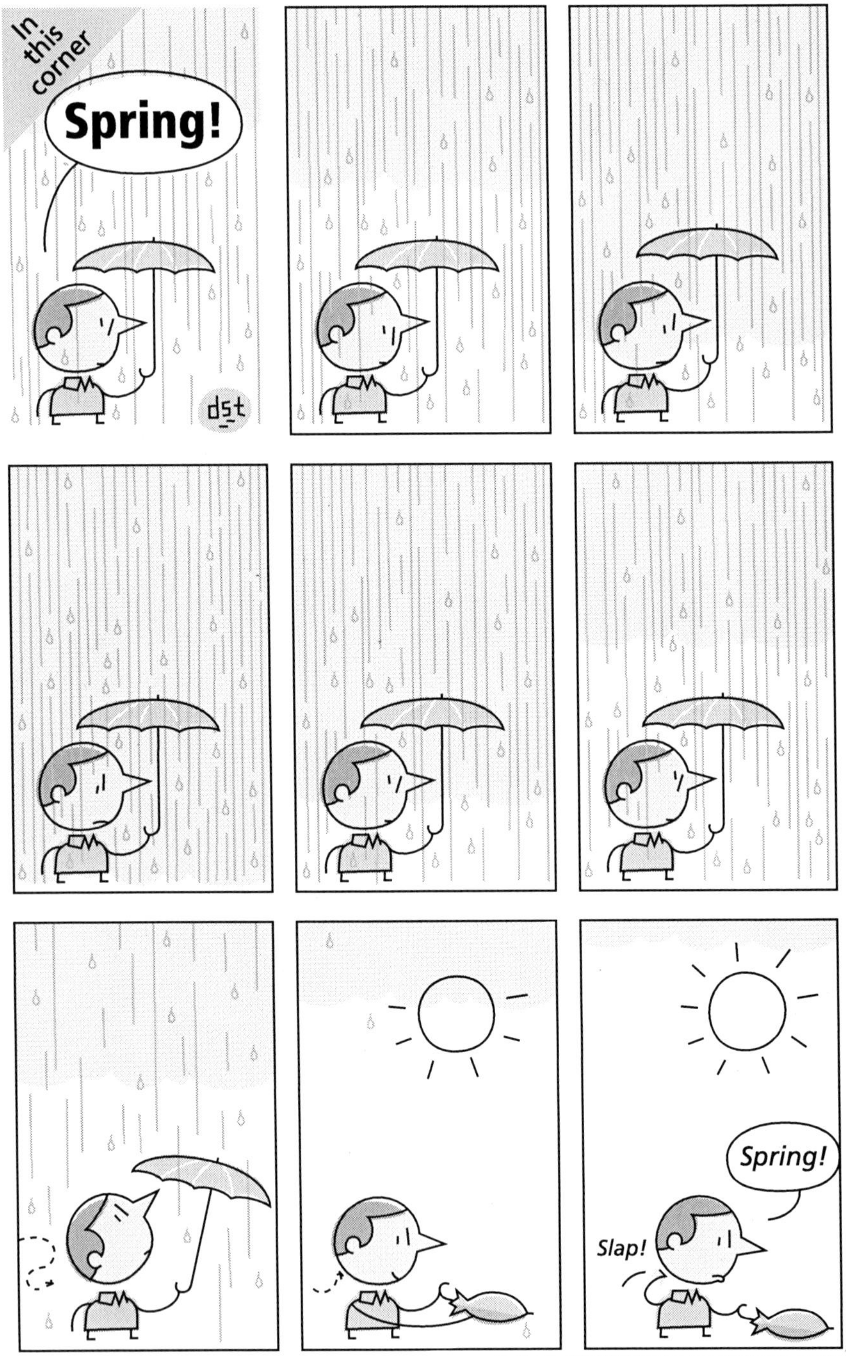

In this corner
Spring!
dst
Slap!
Spring!

May 11, 2006

DAVID STEINLICHT, PIONEER PRESS

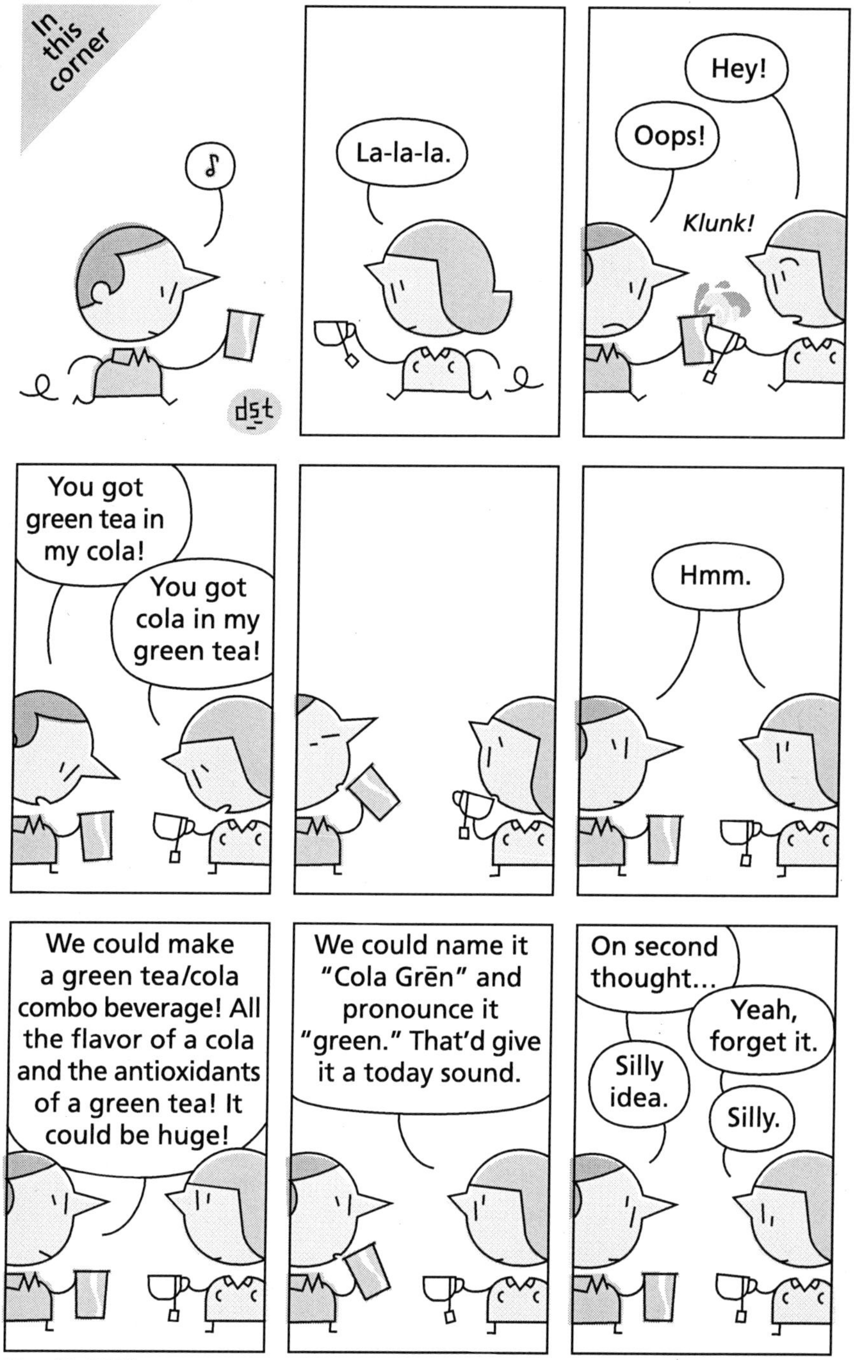
In this corner
La-la-la.
Oops!
Hey!
Klunk!
You got green tea in my cola!
You got cola in my green tea!
Hmm.
We could make a green tea/cola combo beverage! All the flavor of a cola and the antioxidants of a green tea! It could be huge!
We could name it "Cola Grēn" and pronounce it "green." That'd give it a today sound.
On second thought…
Silly idea.
Yeah, forget it.
Silly.

May 18, 2006

DAVID STEINLICHT, PIONEER PRESS

Note: A mash-up of the old Reese's Peanut Butter Cup commercial and the failed product introduction of coffee/cola combo Coca-Cola Blāk (*pronounced "black"*).

Tech whiz quiz

Do you know these symbols?

1

A. GameCube
B. PlayStation
C. Xbox
D. Atari 2600

2

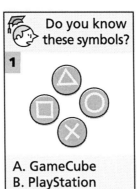

A. GameCube
B. PlayStation
C. Xbox
D. Saturn

3

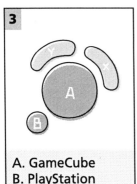

A. GameCube
B. PlayStation
C. Xbox
D. 3dO

4

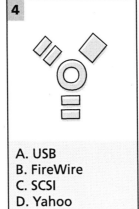

A. USB
B. FireWire
C. SCSI
D. Yahoo

5

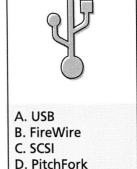

A. USB
B. FireWire
C. SCSI
D. PitchFork

6

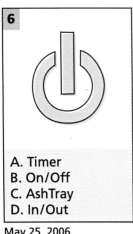

A. Timer
B. On/Off
C. AshTray
D. In/Out

7

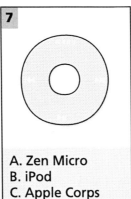

A. Zen Micro
B. iPod
C. Apple Corps
D. :-)

Answers:
1B, 2C, 3A, 4B, 5A, 6B, 7B

If you got:

None-2 correct
You're a normal person

3-6 correct
You are nerdish

7 correct
You are probably a copyright lawyer

May 25, 2006

DAVID STEINLICHT, PIONEER PRESS

In this corner

Bunny/ Squirrel Exchange

dst

Something is going on. I don't know what. *But, maybe it's this:*

We saw the great success of the Lake Elmo Deer/Squirrel Switch program.

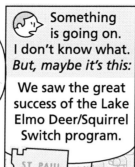

ST. PAUL

And the Racoon/ Squirrel Replacement went well in Elk River. So we thought we'd try our own program.

ST. PAUL

And, so far, our Bunny/Squirrel Exchange program is going well.

ST. PAUL

People like bunnies almost as much as they dislike squirrels.

Ooo, those fuzzy little bunnies!

Sure, there have been complaints from gardeners.

My lettuce! Gone!

Ooo, those fuzzy little bunnies!

Besides added civic cuteness, there are other advantages.

No more acorns dropping on my car.

The kids have stopped pestering me for a pet rabbit.

Plus, it's a straight rodent-for-rodent swap, so the environmental impact should be minimal.

ST. PAUL

June 1, 2006

DAVID STEINLICHT, PIONEER PRESS

105

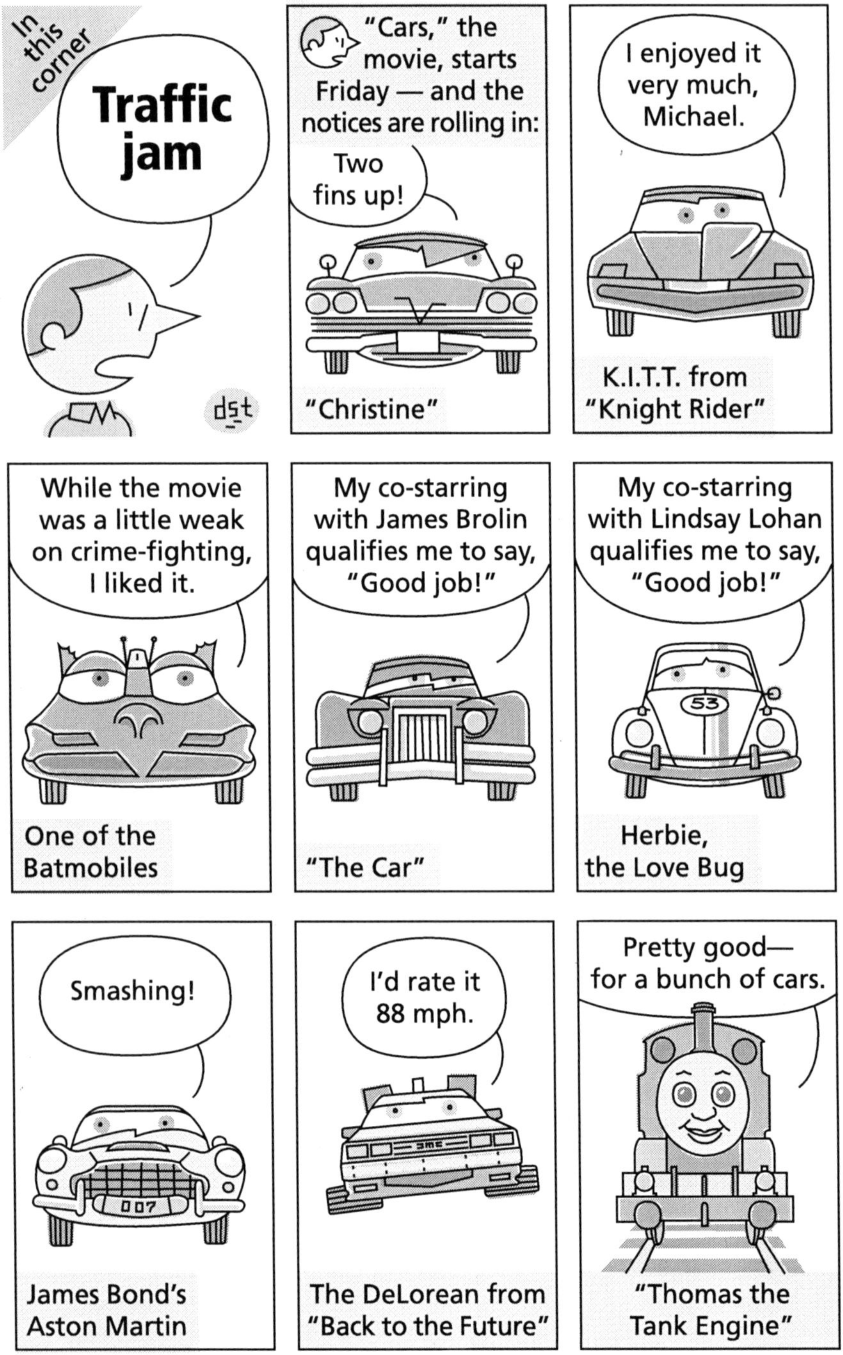
In this corner
Traffic jam
dst
"Cars," the movie, starts Friday — and the notices are rolling in:
Two fins up!
"Christine"
I enjoyed it very much, Michael.
K.I.T.T. from "Knight Rider"
While the movie was a little weak on crime-fighting, I liked it.
One of the Batmobiles
My co-starring with James Brolin qualifies me to say, "Good job!"
"The Car"
My co-starring with Lindsay Lohan qualifies me to say, "Good job!"
53
Herbie, the Love Bug
Smashing!
007
James Bond's Aston Martin
I'd rate it 88 mph.
DMC
The DeLorean from "Back to the Future"
Pretty good— for a bunch of cars.
"Thomas the Tank Engine"

June 8, 2006

DAVID STEINLICHT, PIONEER PRESS

 Note: Any excuse to draw the star of 1977's *The Car* (no, not James Brolin).

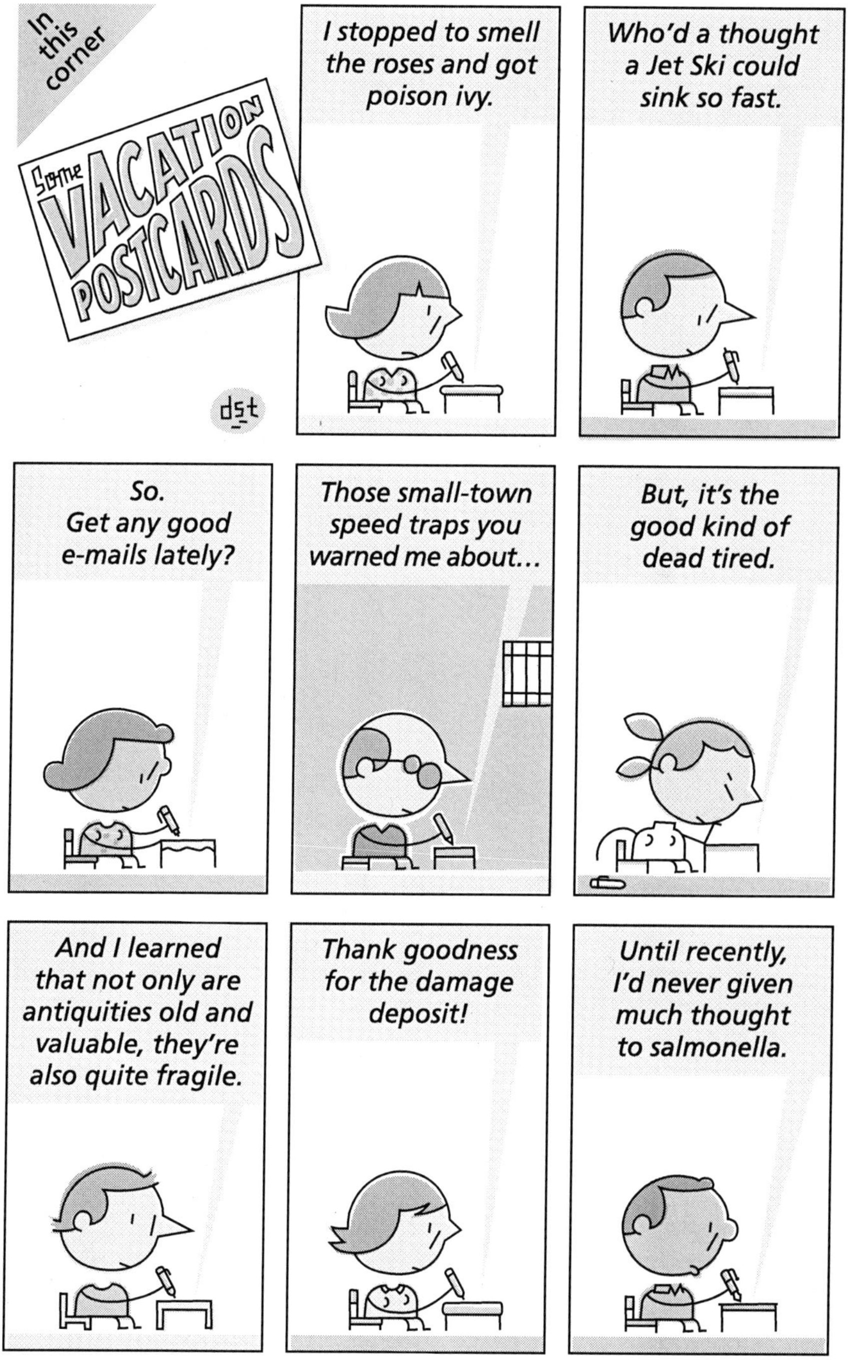

In this corner
Some VACATION POSTCARDS
dst
I stopped to smell the roses and got poison ivy.
Who'd a thought a Jet Ski could sink so fast.
So. Get any good e-mails lately?
Those small-town speed traps you warned me about…
But, it's the good kind of dead tired.
And I learned that not only are antiquities old and valuable, they're also quite fragile.
Thank goodness for the damage deposit!
Until recently, I'd never given much thought to salmonella.

June 15, 2006

DAVID STEINLICHT, PIONEER PRESS

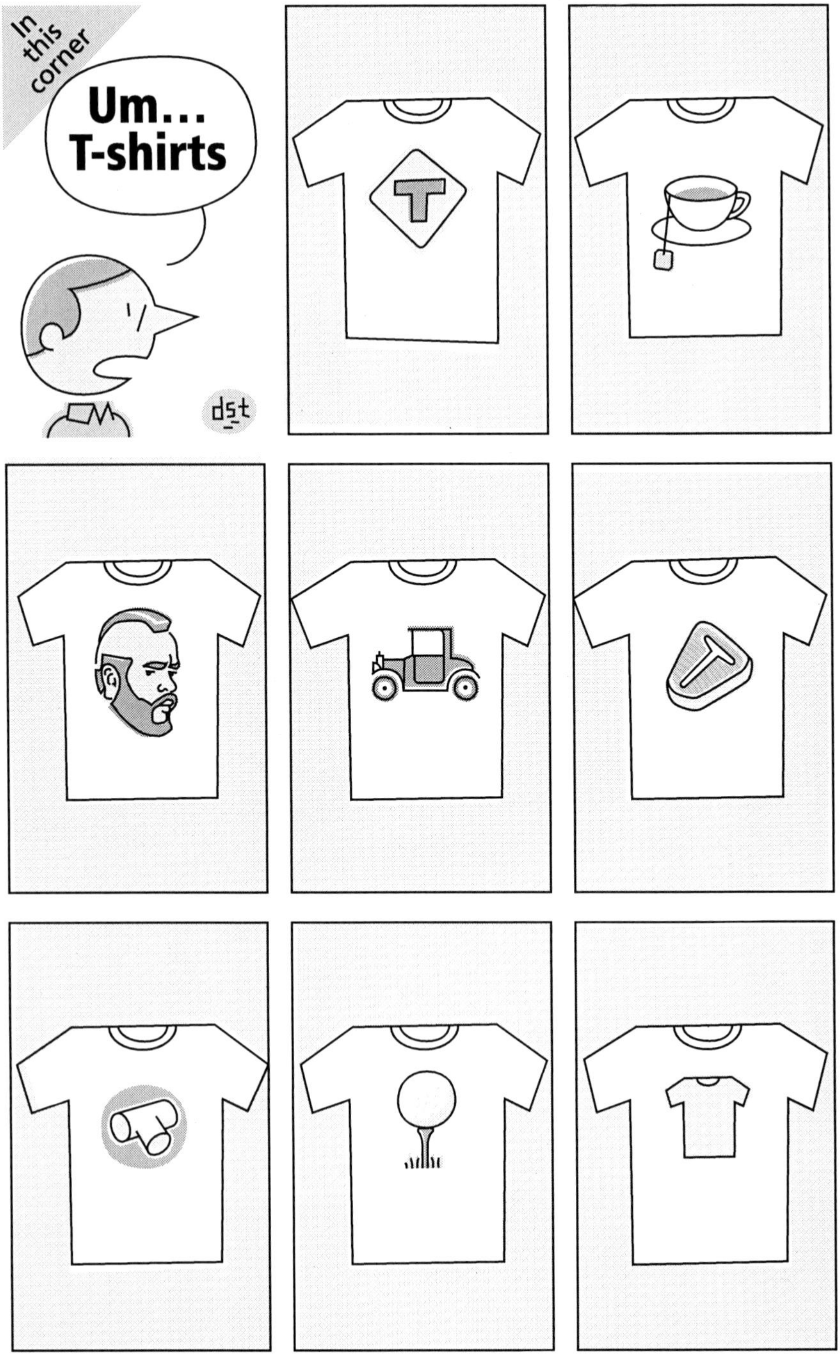
In this corner
Um... T-shirts
dst

June 22, 2006

DAVID STEINLICHT, PIONEER PRESS

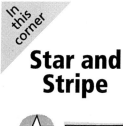

In this corner
Star and Stripe
"Star"
"Stripe"
dst
Big day coming up.
Bigger than Flag Day?
Oh, yeah.
July 4.
That is big.
Independence Day.
Parades. Picnics. Pageantry. Patriotism.
Rockets' red glare.
Oh, say!
Pledges of allegiance.
Baseball!
Hot dogs!
Apple pie!
Mom!
Stock cars!
Broad stripes?
Check.
Bright stars?
Check.
How proudly do we wave?
Way proudly!
When do we wave?
Now!
No need to get all pointy. That's my job.
Sorry, I just get so excited.

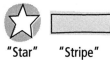

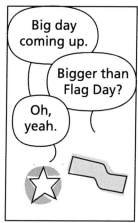

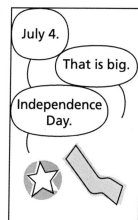

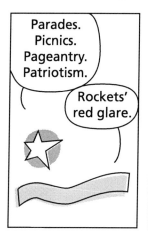

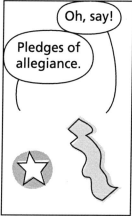

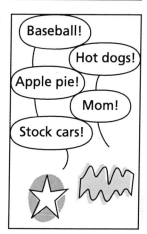

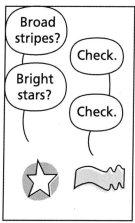

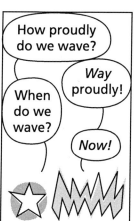

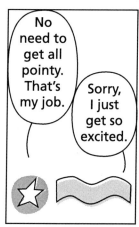

June 29, 2006

DAVID STEINLICHT, PIONEER PRESS

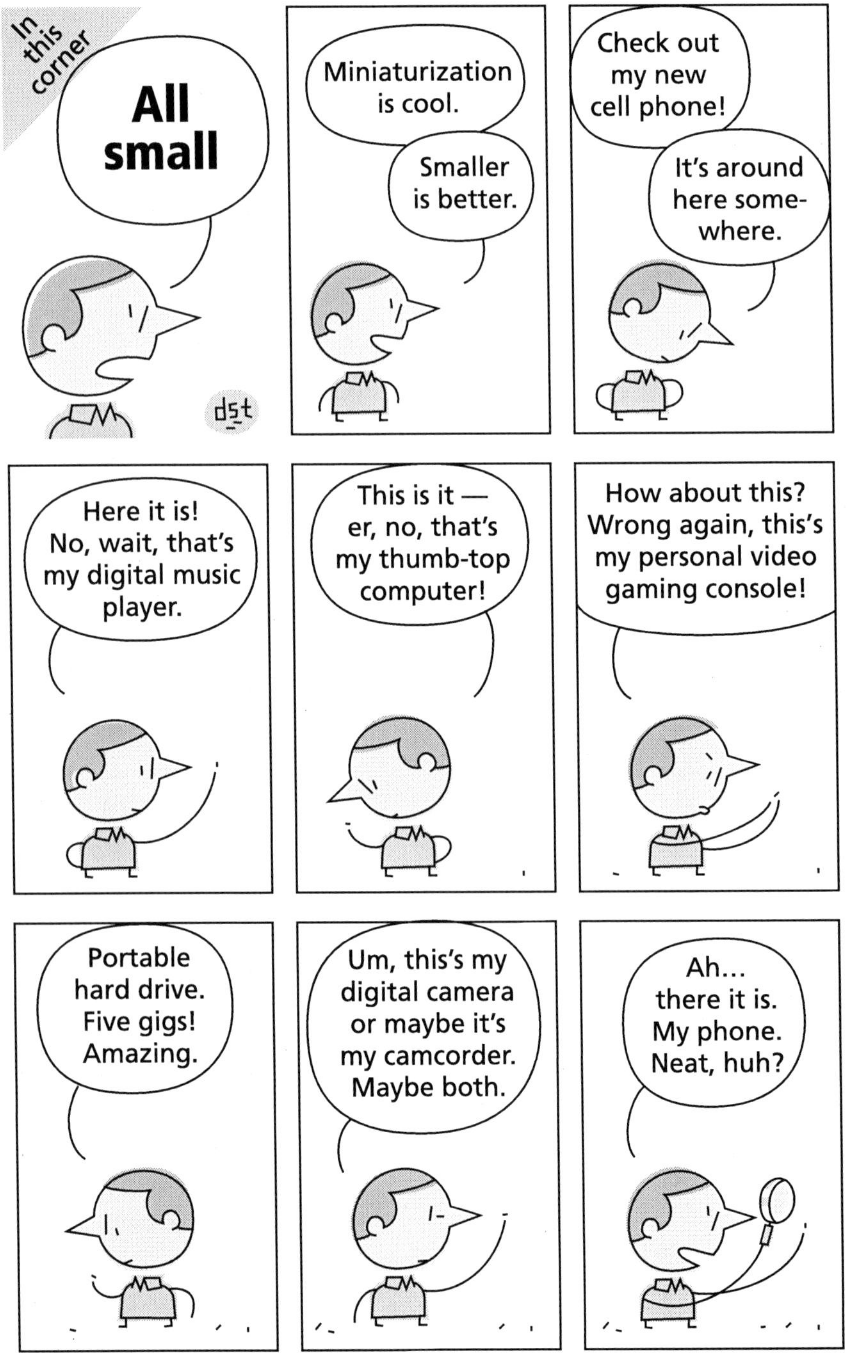
In this corner
All small
Miniaturization is cool.
Smaller is better.
Check out my new cell phone!
It's around here some-where.
Here it is! No, wait, that's my digital music player.
This is it — er, no, that's my thumb-top computer!
How about this? Wrong again, this's my personal video gaming console!
Portable hard drive. Five gigs! Amazing.
Um, this's my digital camera or maybe it's my camcorder. Maybe both.
Ah... there it is. My phone. Neat, huh?

July 6, 2006

DAVID STEINLICHT, PIONEER PRESS

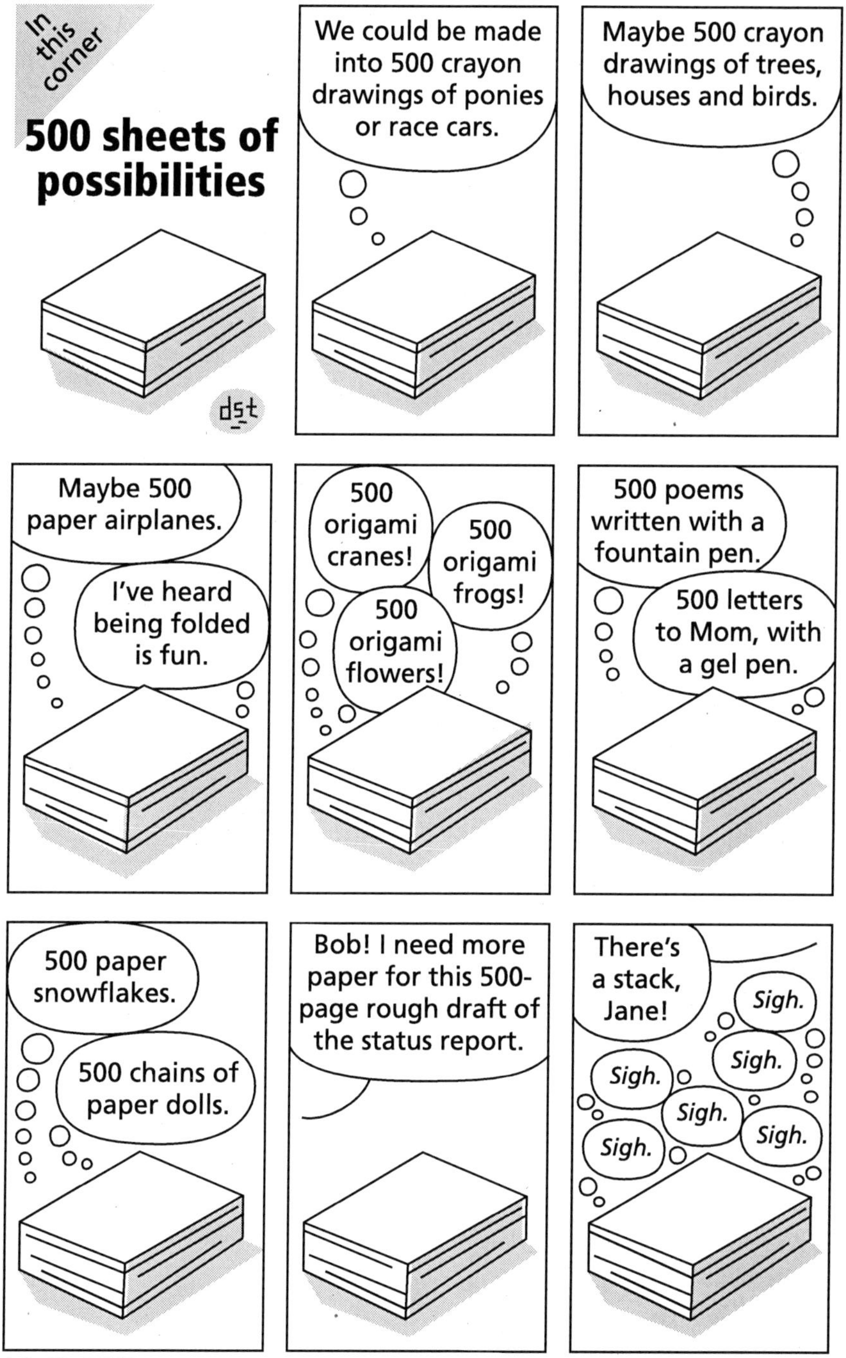
In this corner
500 sheets of possibilities
dst
We could be made into 500 crayon drawings of ponies or race cars.
Maybe 500 crayon drawings of trees, houses and birds.
Maybe 500 paper airplanes.
I've heard being folded is fun.
500 origami cranes!
500 origami frogs!
500 origami flowers!
500 poems written with a fountain pen.
500 letters to Mom, with a gel pen.
500 paper snowflakes.
500 chains of paper dolls.
Bob! I need more paper for this 500-page rough draft of the status report.
There's a stack, Jane!
Sigh.
Sigh.
Sigh.
Sigh.
Sigh.
Sigh.

July 13, 2006

DAVID STEINLICHT, PIONEER PRESS

Note: This comic was reprinted in the Bulletin Board section of the paper.

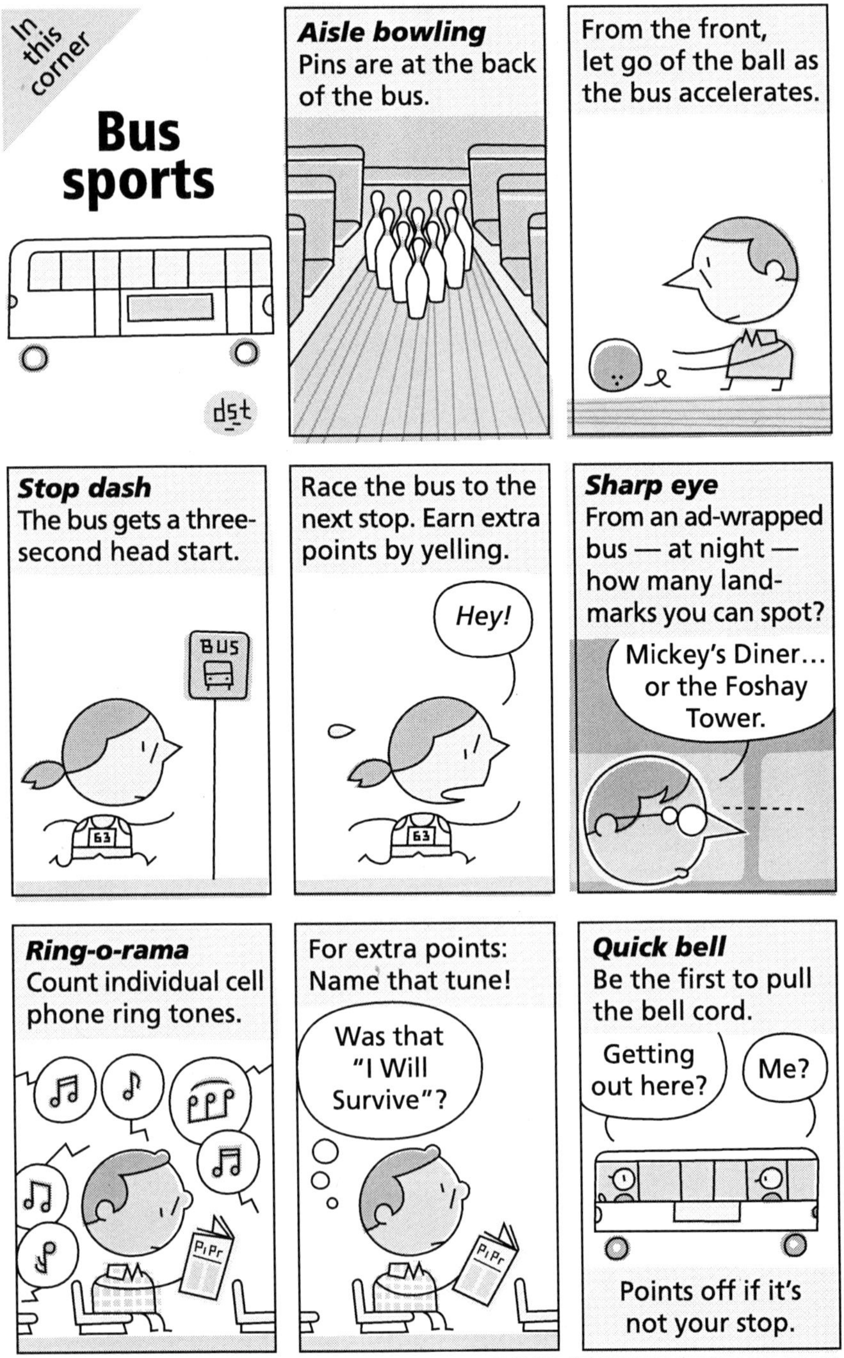
In this corner
Bus sports
dst
Aisle bowling
Pins are at the back of the bus.
From the front, let go of the ball as the bus accelerates.
Stop dash
The bus gets a three-second head start.
BUS
63
Race the bus to the next stop. Earn extra points by yelling.
Hey!
63
Sharp eye
From an ad-wrapped bus — at night — how many land-marks you can spot?
Mickey's Diner… or the Foshay Tower.
Ring-o-rama
Count individual cell phone ring tones.
PiPr
For extra points: Name that tune!
Was that "I Will Survive"?
PiPr
Quick bell
Be the first to pull the bell cord.
Getting out here?
Me?
Points off if it's not your stop.

July 20, 2006

DAVID STEINLICHT, PIONEER PRESS

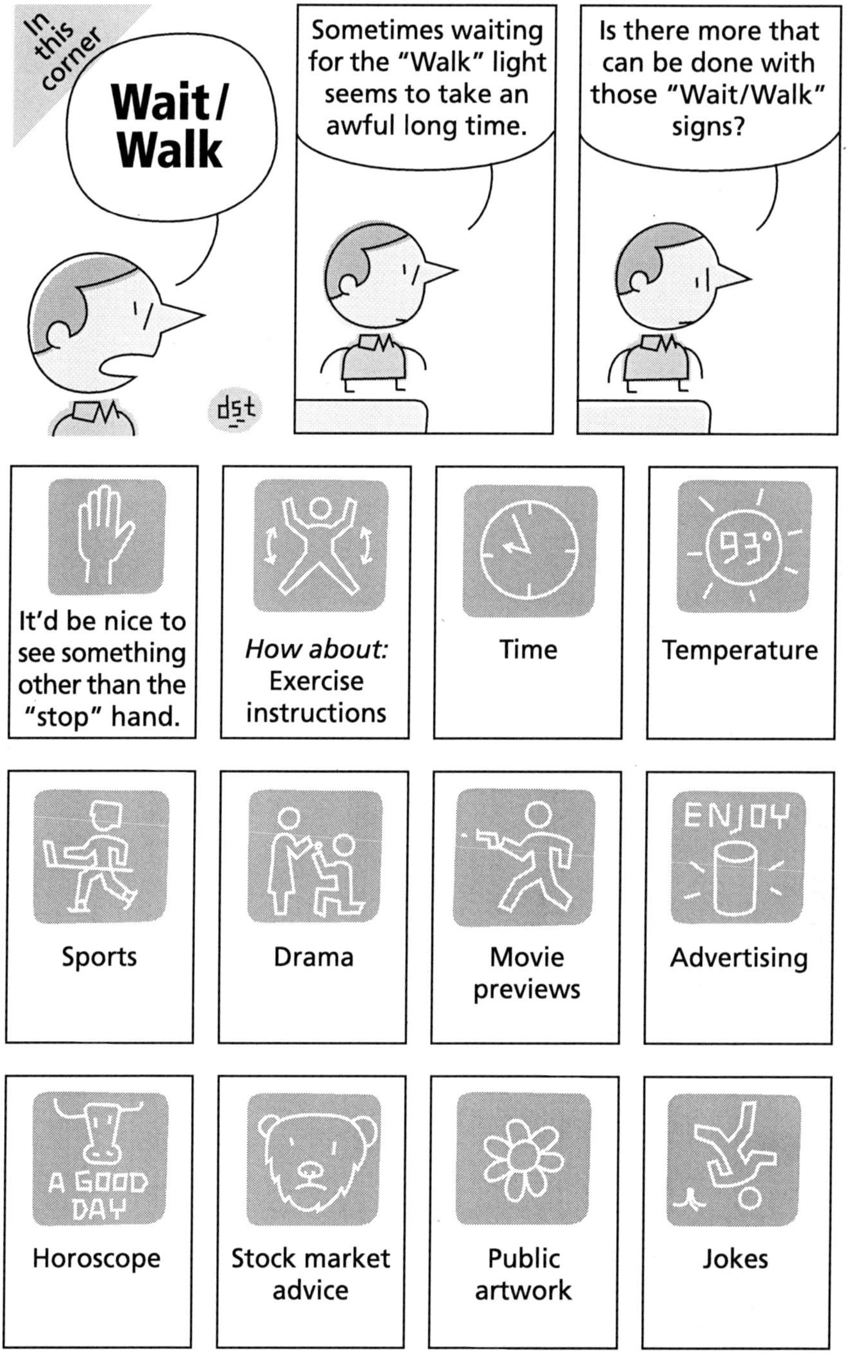
In this corner
Wait/ Walk
dst
Sometimes waiting for the "Walk" light seems to take an awful long time.
Is there more that can be done with those "Wait/Walk" signs?
It'd be nice to see something other than the "stop" hand.
How about: Exercise instructions
Time
93°
Temperature
Sports
Drama
Movie previews
ENJOY
Advertising
A GOOD DAY
Horoscope
Stock market advice
Public artwork
Jokes

July 27, 2006

DAVID STEINLICHT, PIONEER PRESS

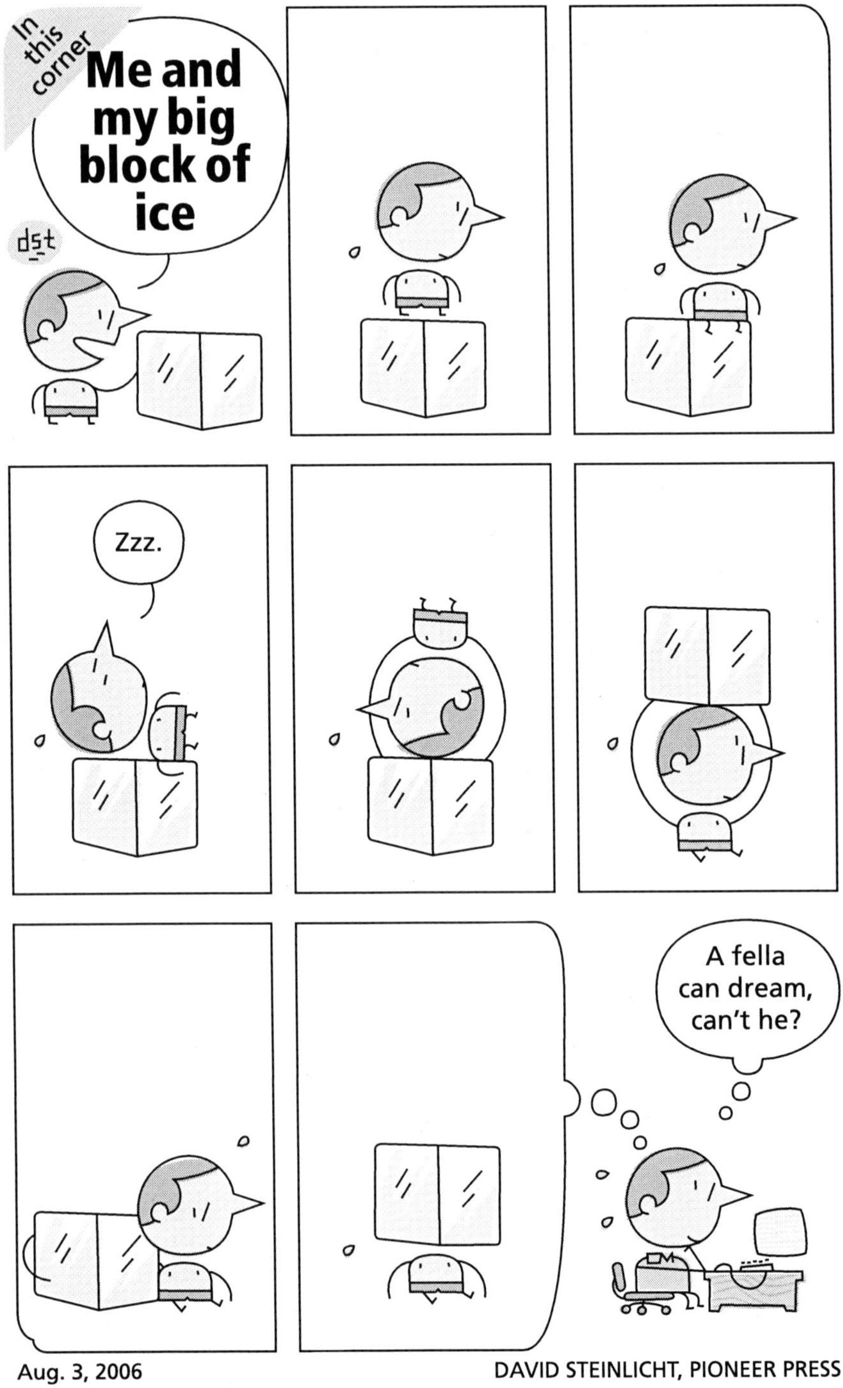
In this corner
Me and my big block of ice
dst
Zzz.
A fella can dream, can't he?

Aug. 3, 2006

DAVID STEINLICHT, PIONEER PRESS

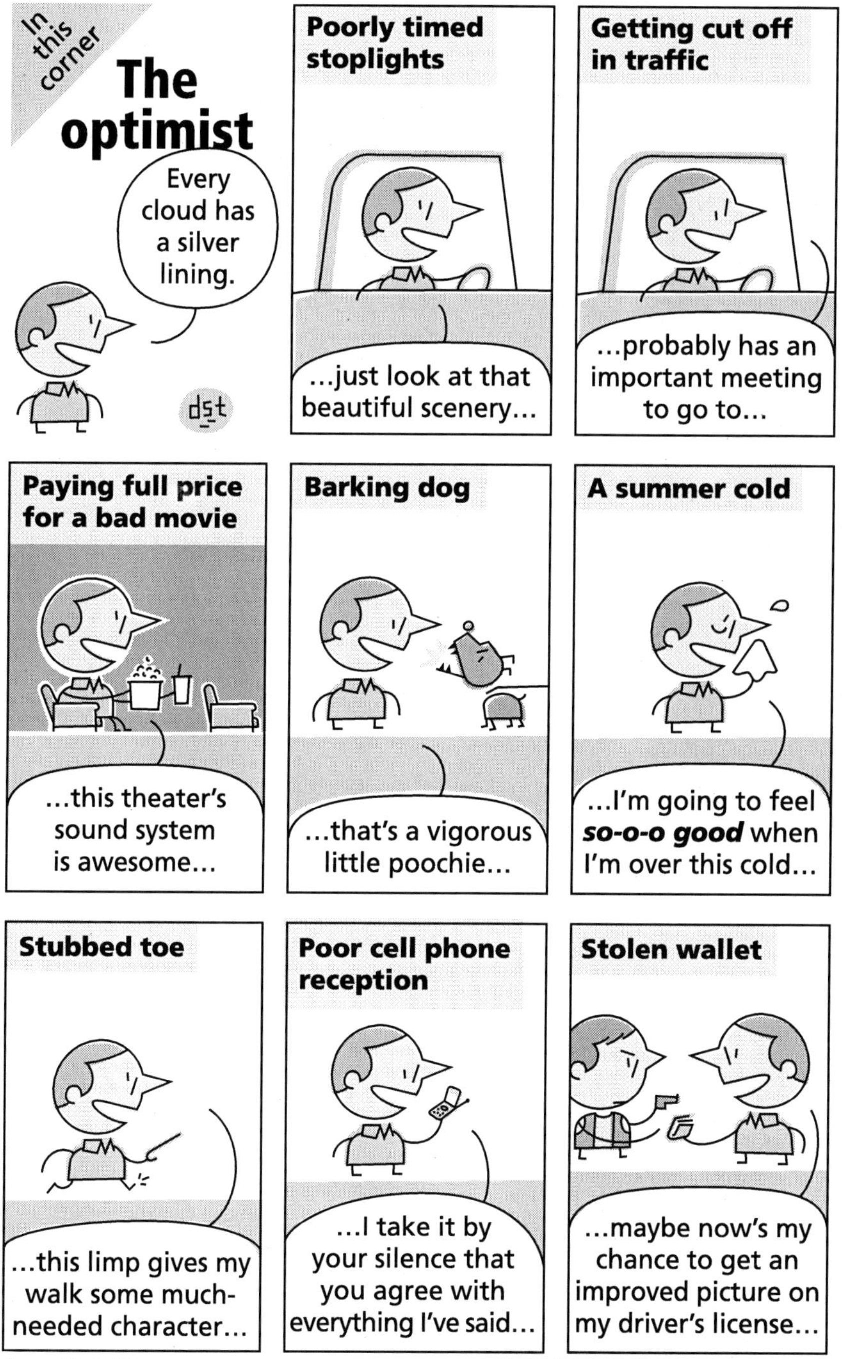

In this corner
The optimist
Every cloud has a silver lining.
dst
Poorly timed stoplights
...just look at that beautiful scenery...
Getting cut off in traffic
...probably has an important meeting to go to...
Paying full price for a bad movie
...this theater's sound system is awesome...
Barking dog
...that's a vigorous little poochie...
A summer cold
...I'm going to feel ***so-o-o good*** when I'm over this cold...
Stubbed toe
...this limp gives my walk some much-needed character...
Poor cell phone reception
...I take it by your silence that you agree with everything I've said...
Stolen wallet
...maybe now's my chance to get an improved picture on my driver's license...

Aug. 10, 2006

DAVID STEINLICHT, PIONEER PRESS

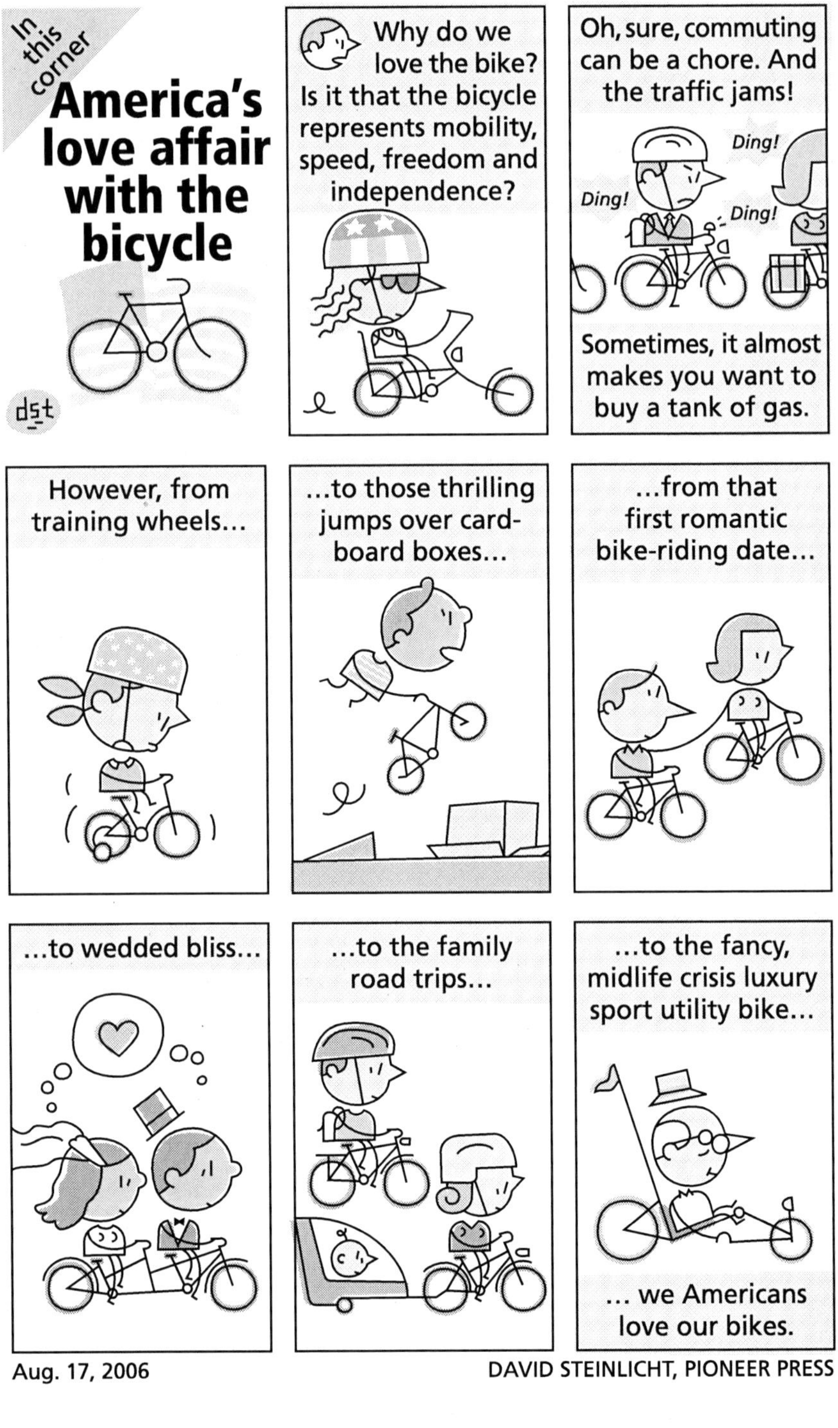
In this corner
America's love affair with the bicycle
dst
Why do we love the bike? Is it that the bicycle represents mobility, speed, freedom and independence?
Oh, sure, commuting can be a chore. And the traffic jams!
Ding!
Ding!
Ding!
Sometimes, it almost makes you want to buy a tank of gas.
However, from training wheels...
...to those thrilling jumps over card-board boxes...
...from that first romantic bike-riding date...
...to wedded bliss...
...to the family road trips...
...to the fancy, midlife crisis luxury sport utility bike...
... we Americans love our bikes.

Aug. 17, 2006

DAVID STEINLICHT, PIONEER PRESS

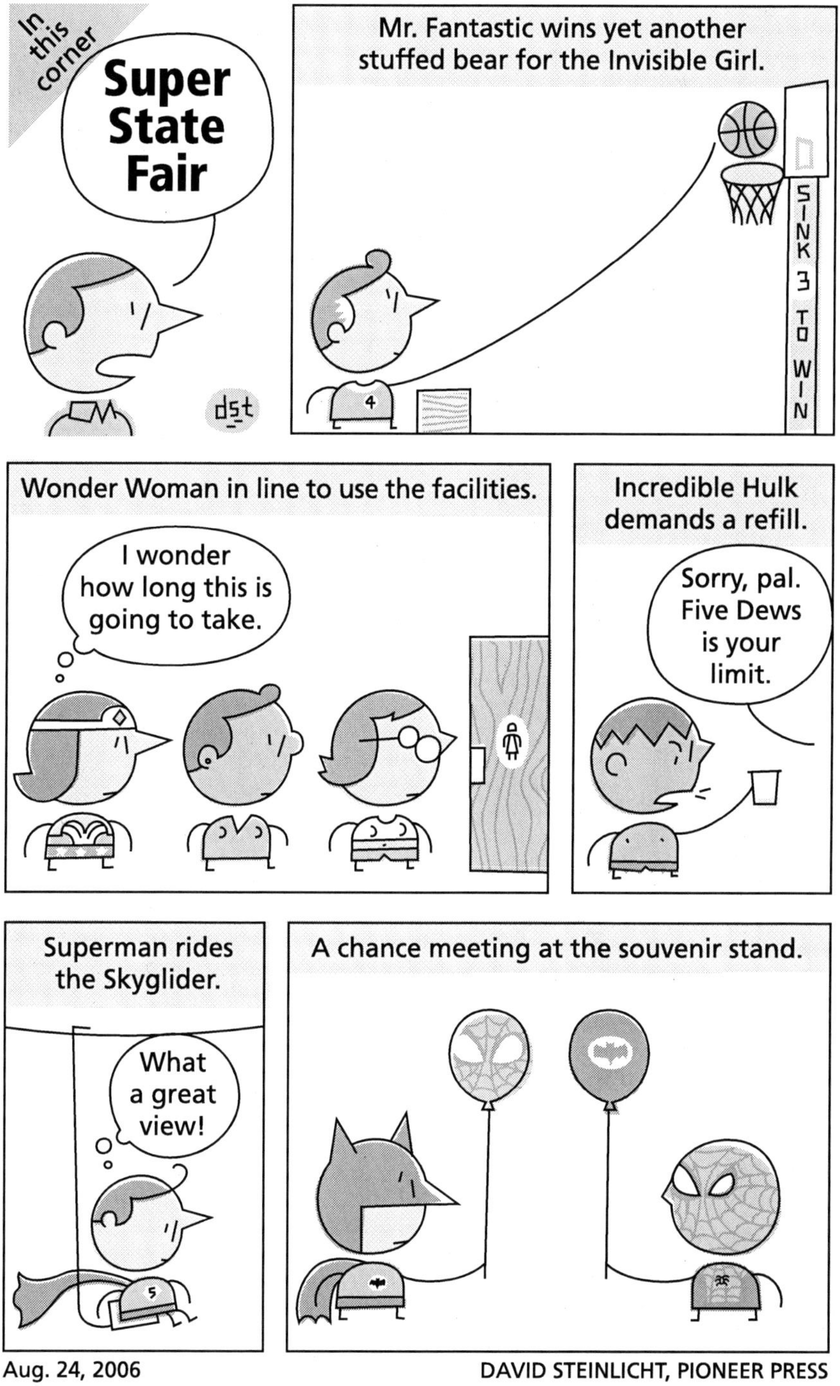
In this corner
Super State Fair
dst
Mr. Fantastic wins yet another stuffed bear for the Invisible Girl.
4
SINK 3 TO WIN
Wonder Woman in line to use the facilities.
I wonder how long this is going to take.
Incredible Hulk demands a refill.
Sorry, pal. Five Dews is your limit.
Superman rides the Skyglider.
What a great view!
5
A chance meeting at the souvenir stand.

Aug. 24, 2006

DAVID STEINLICHT, PIONEER PRESS

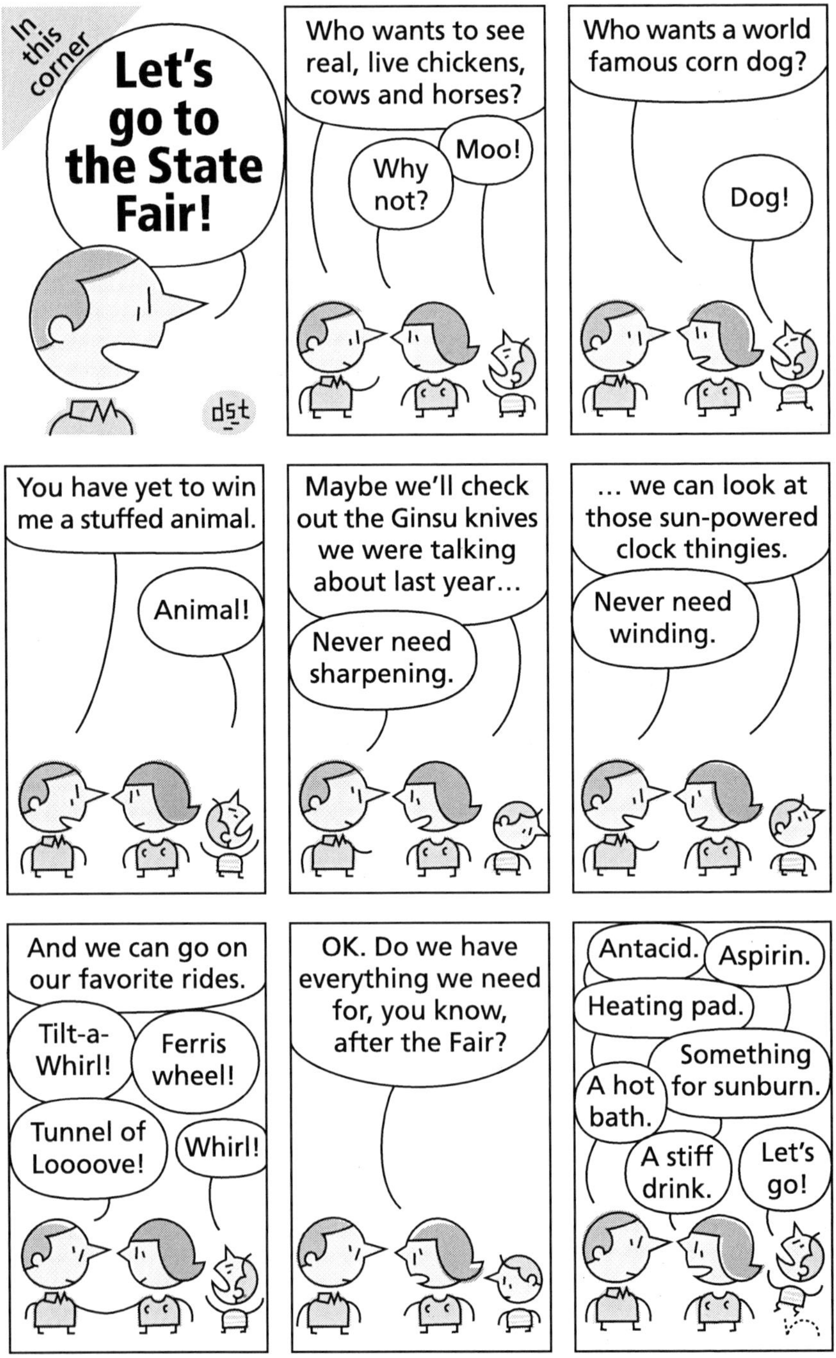
In this corner
Let's go to the State Fair!
dst
Who wants to see real, live chickens, cows and horses?
Why not?
Moo!
Who wants a world famous corn dog?
Dog!
You have yet to win me a stuffed animal.
Animal!
Maybe we'll check out the Ginsu knives we were talking about last year…
Never need sharpening.
… we can look at those sun-powered clock thingies.
Never need winding.
And we can go on our favorite rides.
Tilt-a-Whirl!
Ferris wheel!
Tunnel of Loooove!
Whirl!
OK. Do we have everything we need for, you know, after the Fair?
Antacid.
Aspirin.
Heating pad.
Something for sunburn.
A hot bath.
A stiff drink.
Let's go!

Aug. 31, 2006

DAVID STEINLICHT, PIONEER PRESS

In this corner
Checklist
dst
Memorial Day
Cookout
Fishing
Kite
Sun hat
Creeping Charlie
Mosquito
No Bug
Water ski
Maybe next year
Tourist trap
THE DANCING WATERS
Big, dumb summer movie
BUCKET O' CORN
Fireworks
Drenched
Tomatoes
Labor Day
That was easy.

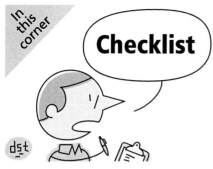

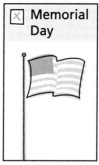

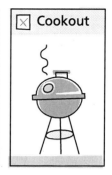

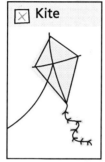

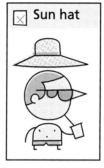

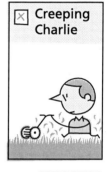

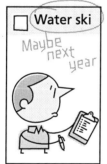

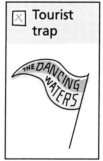

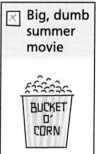

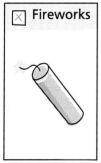

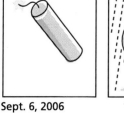

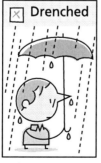

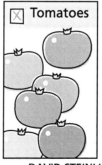

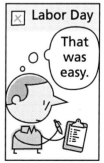

Sept. 6, 2006

DAVID STEINLICHT, PIONEER PRESS

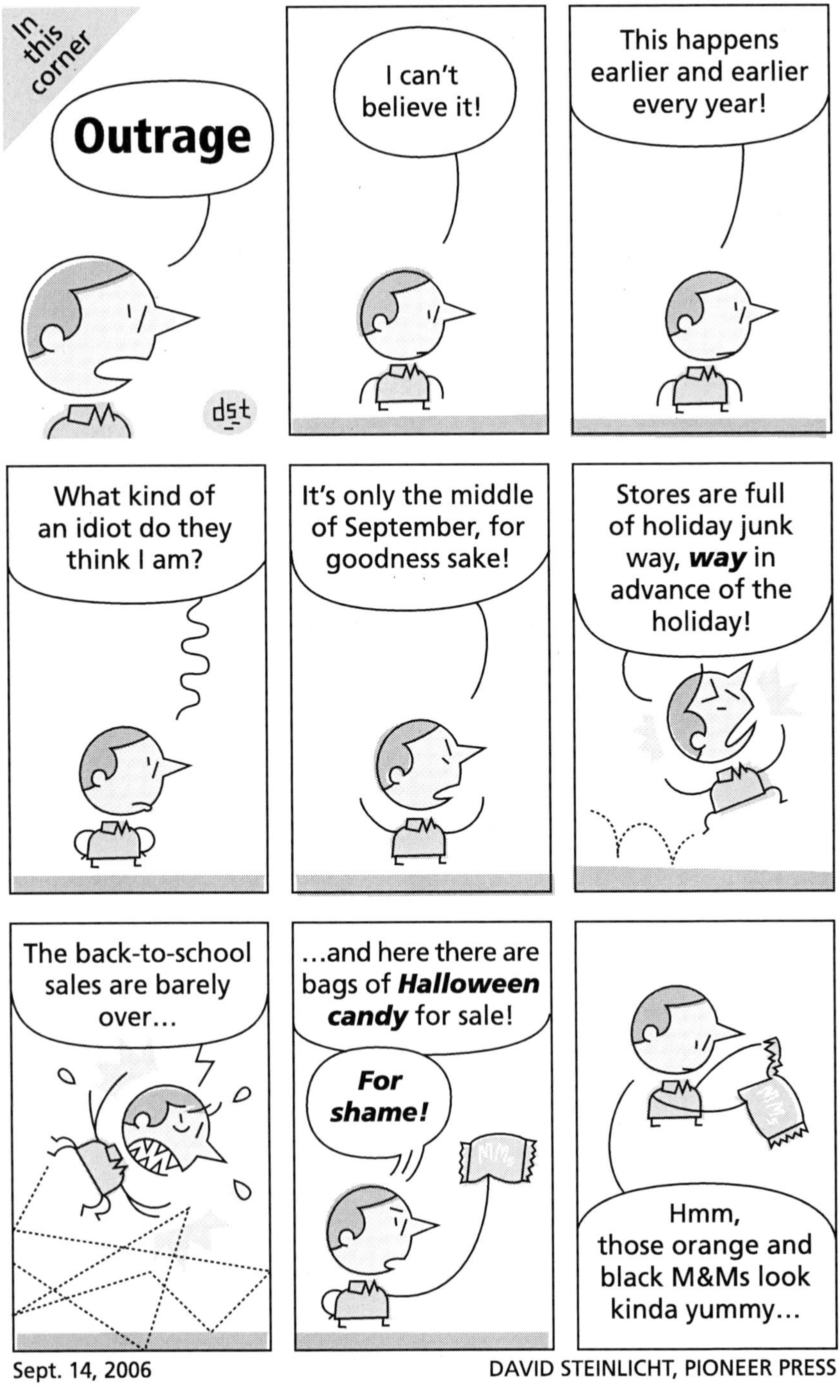
In this corner
Outrage
dst
I can't believe it!
This happens earlier and earlier every year!
What kind of an idiot do they think I am?
It's only the middle of September, for goodness sake!
Stores are full of holiday junk way, ***way*** in advance of the holiday!
The back-to-school sales are barely over…
…and here there are bags of ***Halloween candy*** for sale!
For shame!
Hmm, those orange and black M&Ms look kinda yummy…

Sept. 14, 2006

DAVID STEINLICHT, PIONEER PRESS

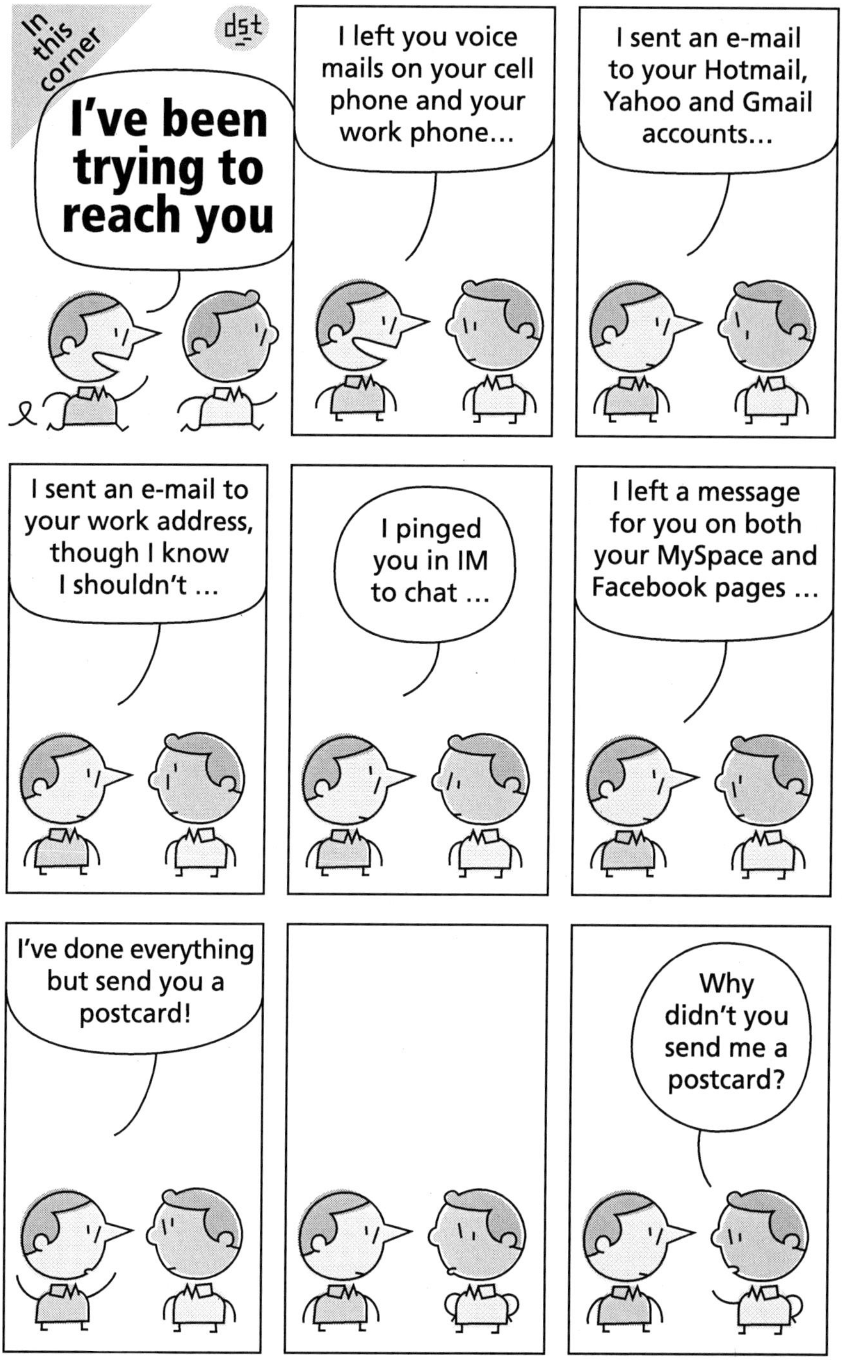
In this corner
dst
I've been trying to reach you
I left you voice mails on your cell phone and your work phone...
I sent an e-mail to your Hotmail, Yahoo and Gmail accounts...
I sent an e-mail to your work address, though I know I shouldn't ...
I pinged you in IM to chat ...
I left a message for you on both your MySpace and Facebook pages ...
I've done everything but send you a postcard!
Why didn't you send me a postcard?

Sept. 21, 2006

DAVID STEINLICHT, PIONEER PRESS

In this corner
Meet the Utensils
dst
I could never eat roast beef. I love vegetables. Maybe a tuna salad.
If you haven't stirred coffee, you haven't lived.
I go for chicken noodle soup, myself.
I'm sure I could handle steak! I'm serrated…
Stick with PB&J, pal. Believe me, you'll be happier.
There's an upside to being a plastic disposable fork. I'm ready for anything. Picnics, takeout, birthday parties…
Huh?
I do solids as well as liquids. I only need a chance to prove myself.
Boo-hoo! I don't fit in!
Here we go again.

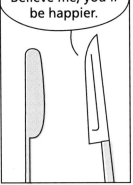

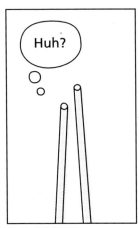

Sept. 28, 2006 DAVID STEINLICHT, PIONEER PRESS

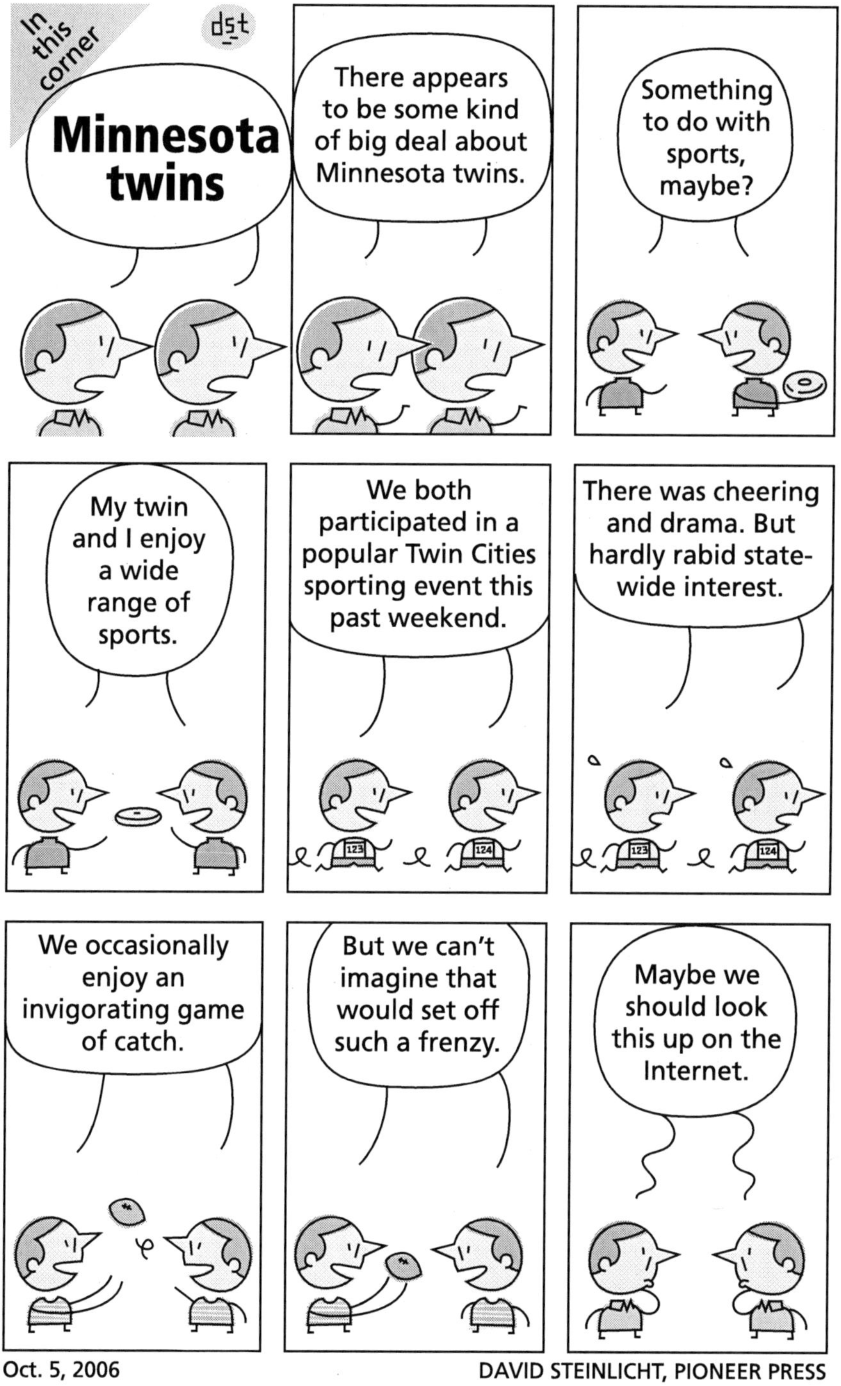
In this corner
dst
Minnesota twins
There appears to be some kind of big deal about Minnesota twins.
Something to do with sports, maybe?
My twin and I enjoy a wide range of sports.
We both participated in a popular Twin Cities sporting event this past weekend.
123
124
There was cheering and drama. But hardly rabid state-wide interest.
123
124
We occasionally enjoy an invigorating game of catch.
But we can't imagine that would set off such a frenzy.
Maybe we should look this up on the Internet.

Oct. 5, 2006

DAVID STEINLICHT, PIONEER PRESS

In this corner
Getting ready
dst
Now… where did I put those Science Museum tickets?

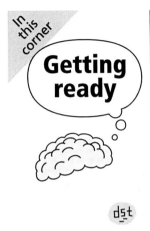

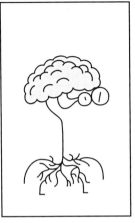

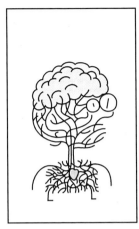

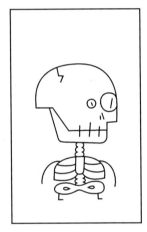

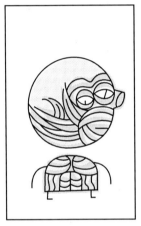

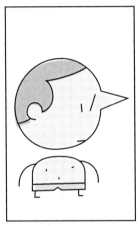

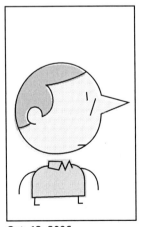

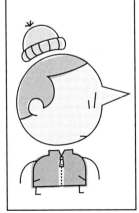

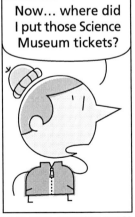

Oct. 12, 2006

DAVID STEINLICHT, PIONEER PRESS

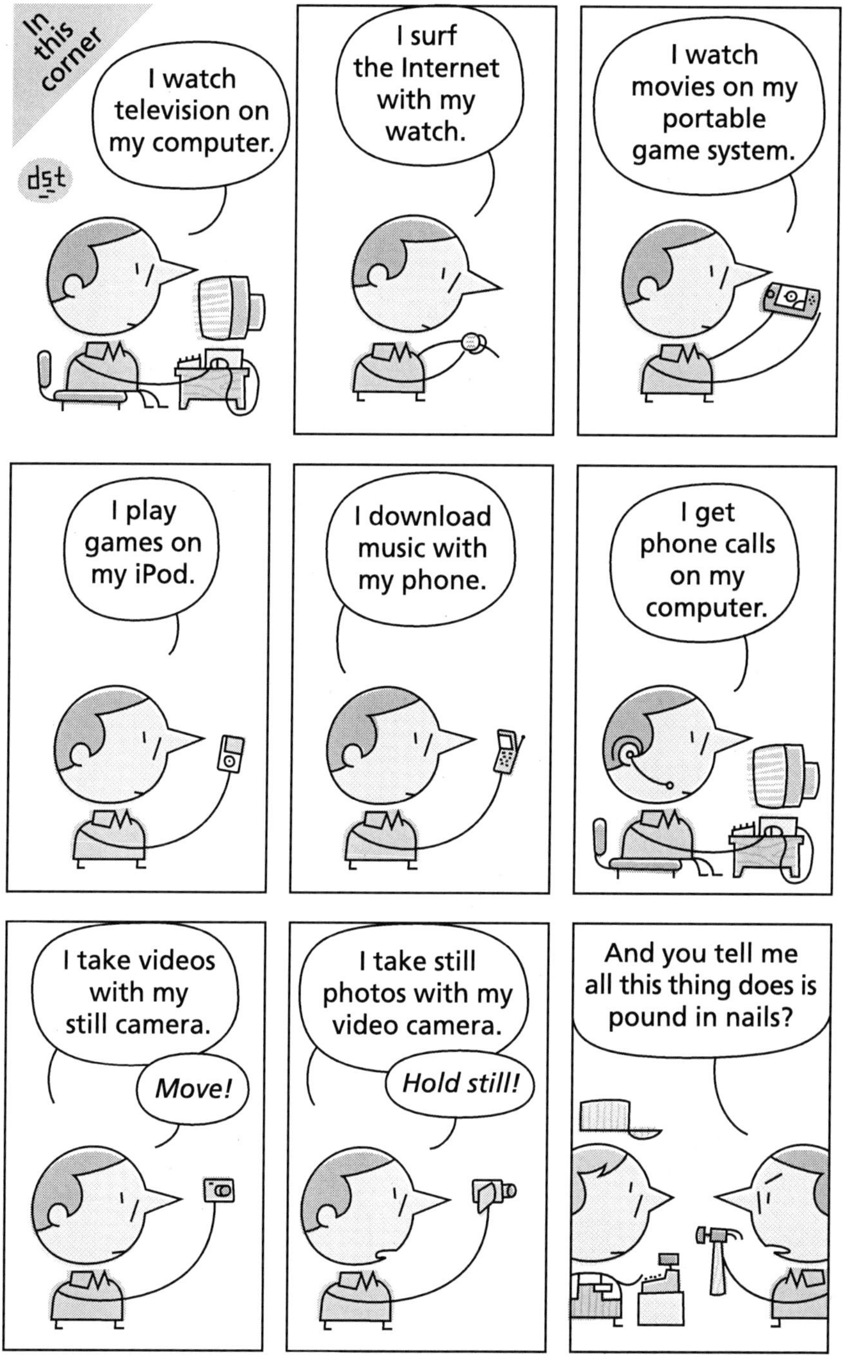
In this corner
dst
I watch television on my computer.
I surf the Internet with my watch.
I watch movies on my portable game system.
I play games on my iPod.
I download music with my phone.
I get phone calls on my computer.
I take videos with my still camera.
Move!
I take still photos with my video camera.
Hold still!
And you tell me all this thing does is pound in nails?

Oct. 26, 2006

DAVID STEINLICHT, PIONEER PRESS

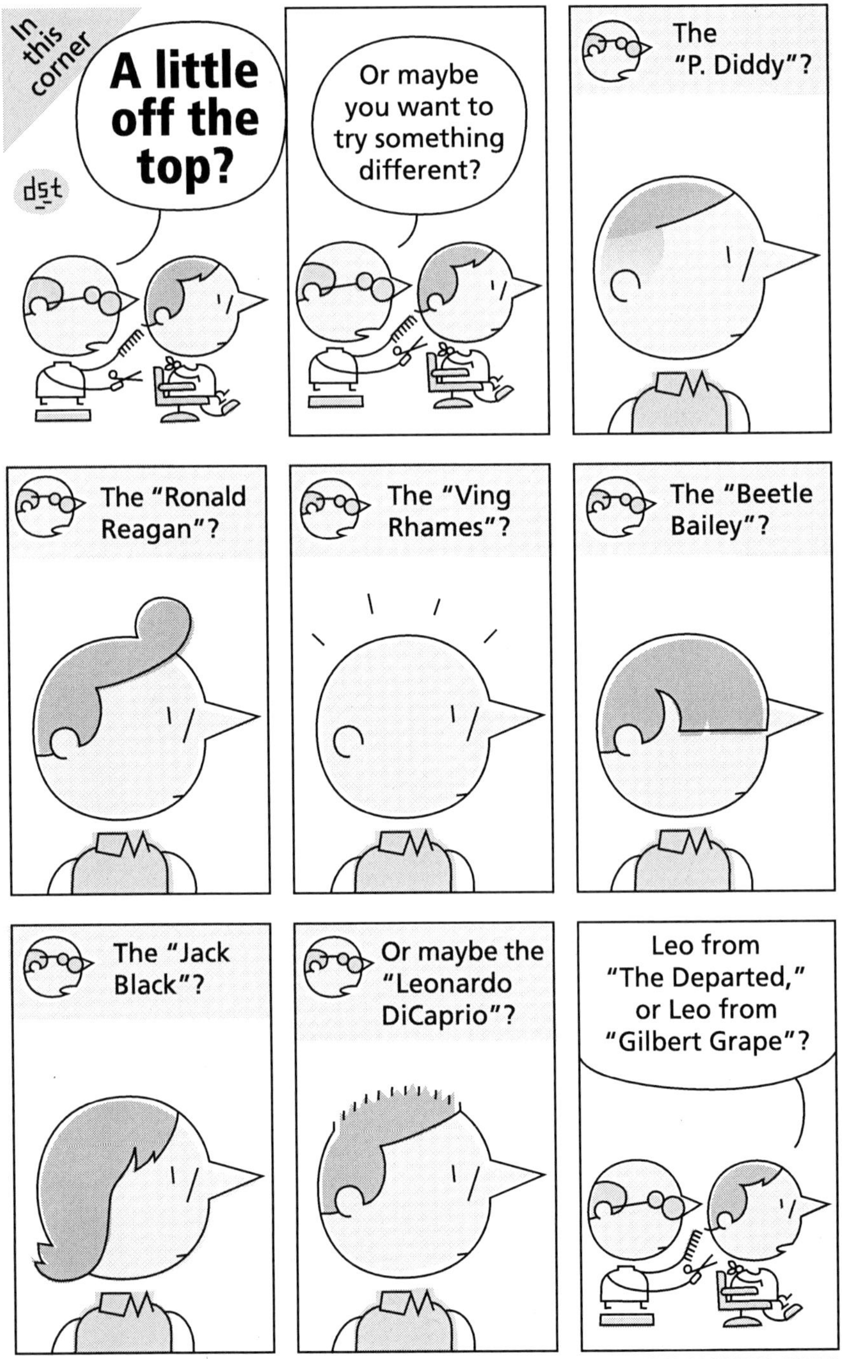

In this corner
dst
A little off the top?
Or maybe you want to try something different?
The "P. Diddy"?
The "Ronald Reagan"?
The "Ving Rhames"?
The "Beetle Bailey"?
The "Jack Black"?
Or maybe the "Leonardo DiCaprio"?
Leo from "The Departed," or Leo from "Gilbert Grape"?

Nov. 2, 2006

DAVID STEINLICHT, PIONEER PRESS

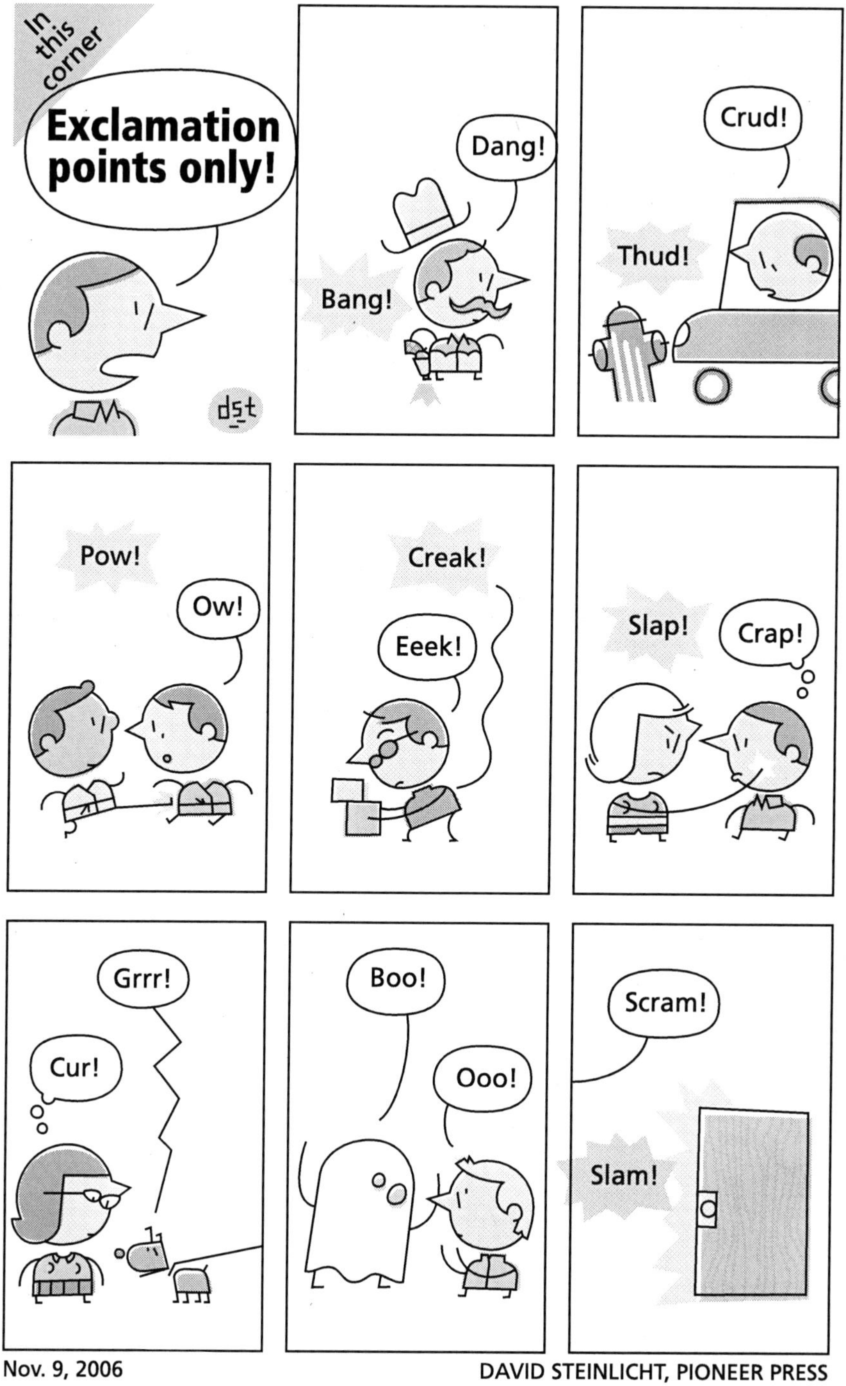
In this corner
Exclamation points only!
dst
Bang!
Dang!
Thud!
Crud!
Pow!
Ow!
Creak!
Eeek!
Slap!
Crap!
Grrr!
Cur!
Boo!
Ooo!
Scram!
Slam!

Nov. 9, 2006

DAVID STEINLICHT, PIONEER PRESS

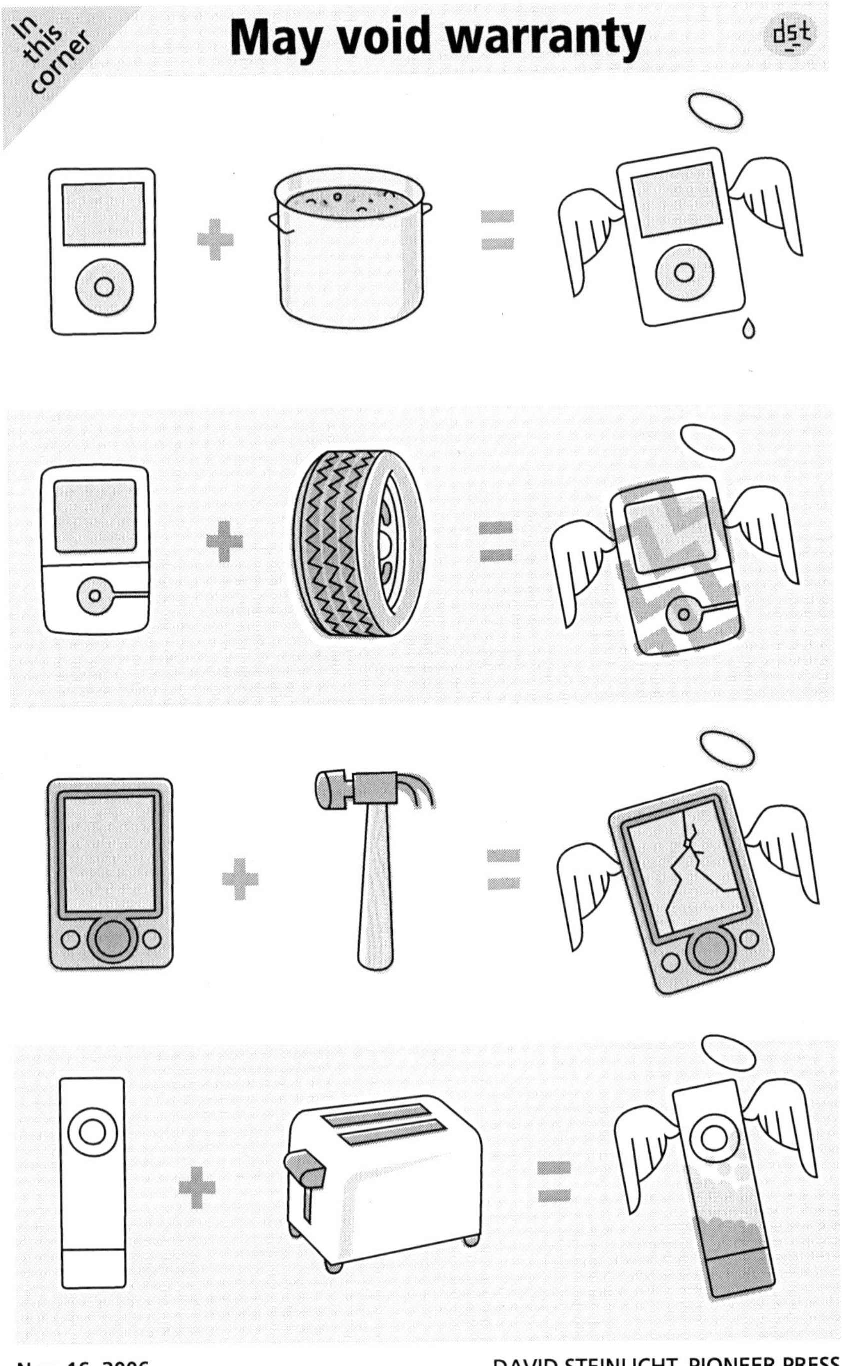
In this corner
May void warranty
dst

Nov. 16, 2006

DAVID STEINLICHT, PIONEER PRESS

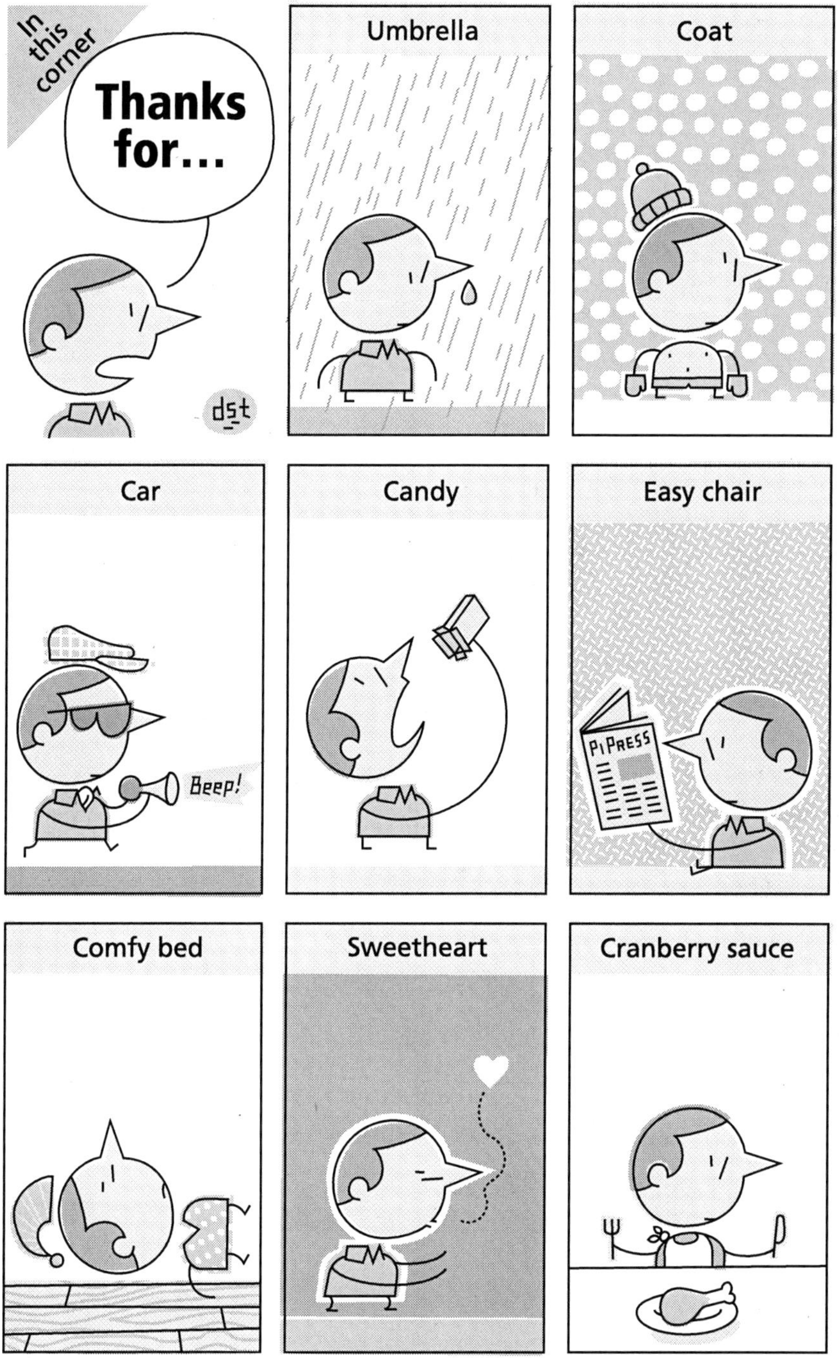
In this corner
Thanks for…
dst
Umbrella
Coat
Car
Beep!
Candy
Easy chair
PiPRESS
Comfy bed
Sweetheart
Cranberry sauce

Nov. 23, 2006

DAVID STEINLICHT, PIONEER PRESS

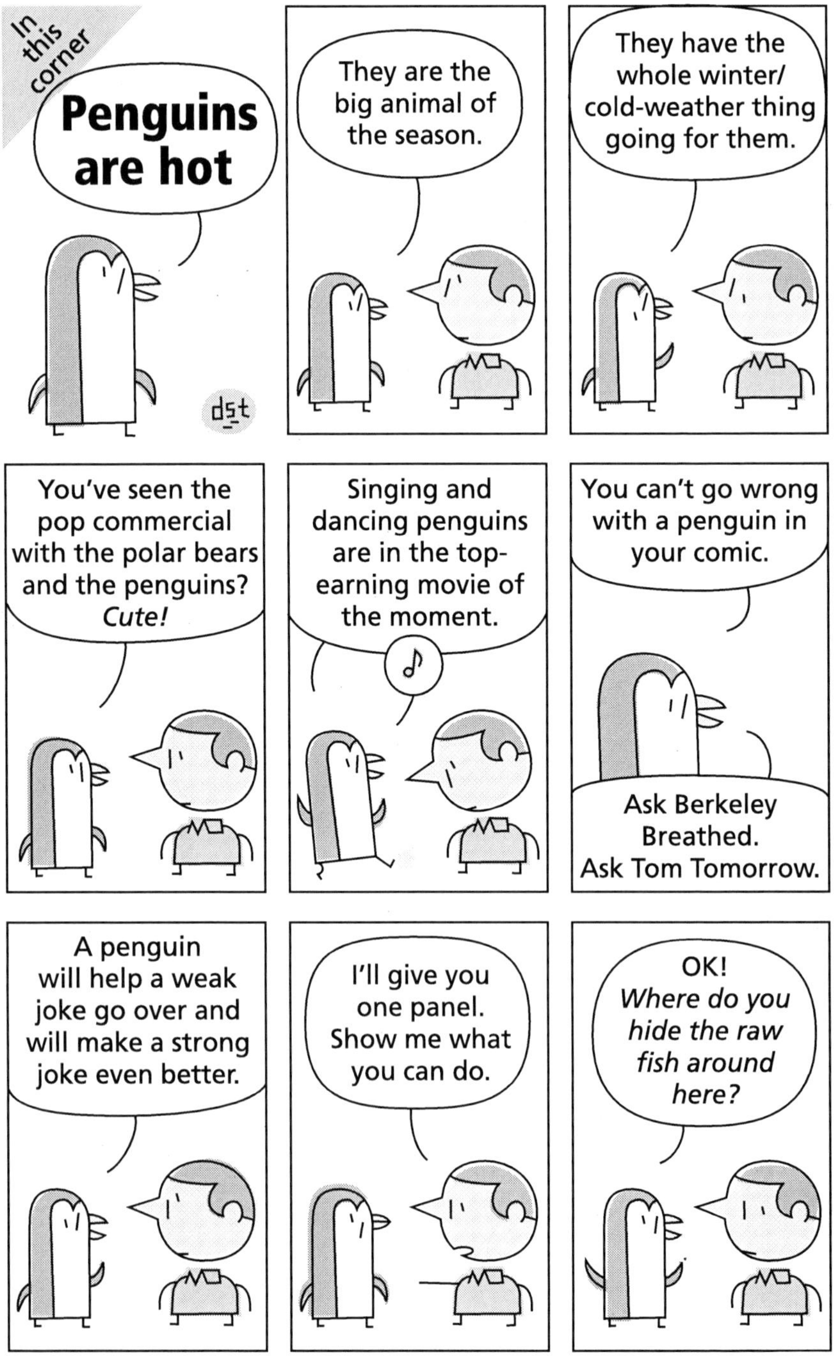
In this corner
Penguins are hot
dst
They are the big animal of the season.
They have the whole winter/ cold-weather thing going for them.
You've seen the pop commercial with the polar bears and the penguins? *Cute!*
Singing and dancing penguins are in the top-earning movie of the moment.
♪
You can't go wrong with a penguin in your comic.
Ask Berkeley Breathed. Ask Tom Tomorrow.
A penguin will help a weak joke go over and will make a strong joke even better.
I'll give you one panel. Show me what you can do.
OK! *Where do you hide the raw fish around here?*

Nov. 30, 2006

DAVID STEINLICHT, PIONEER PRESS

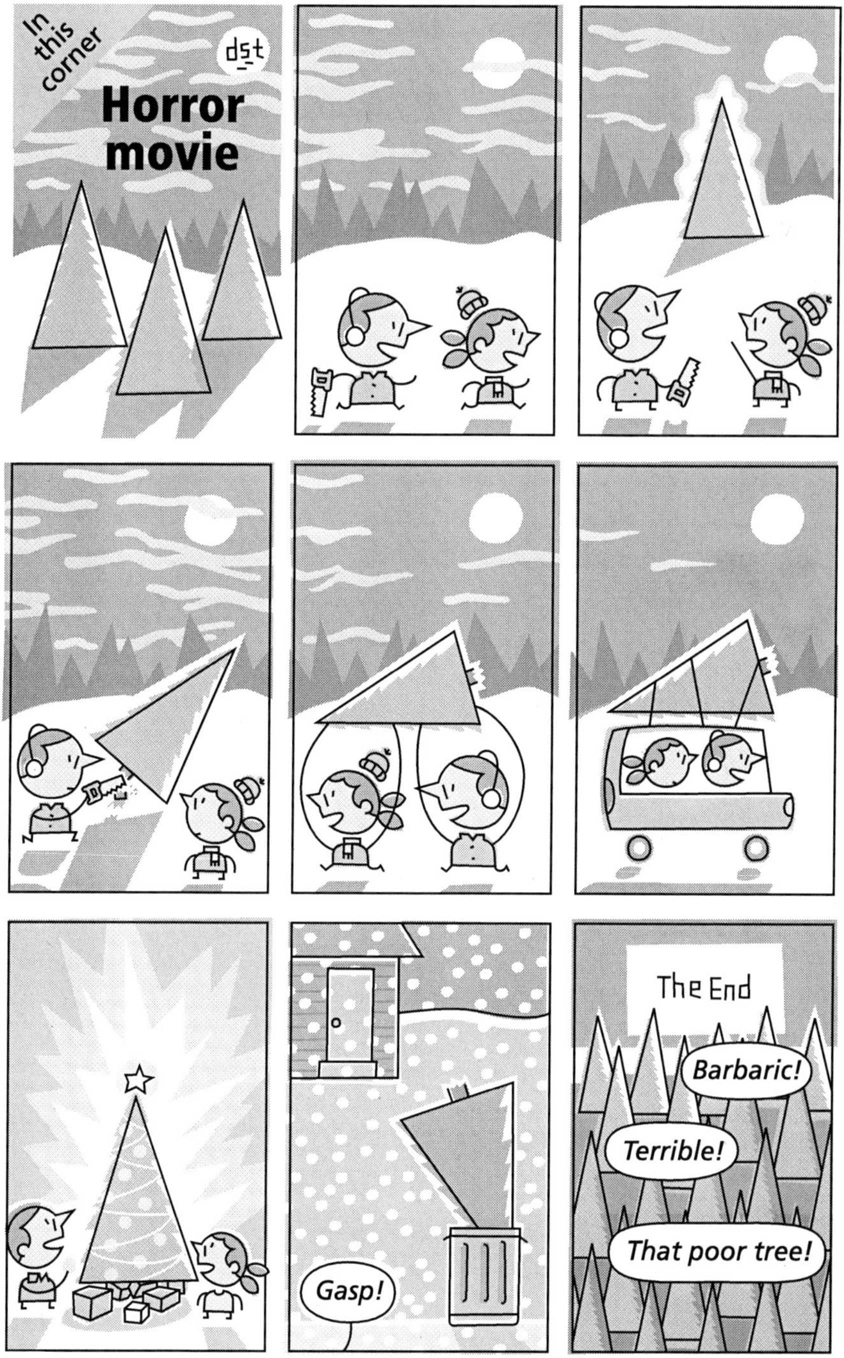
In this corner
dst
Horror movie
The End
Barbaric!
Terrible!
That poor tree!
Gasp!

Dec. 7, 2006

DAVID STEINLICHT, PIONEER PRESS

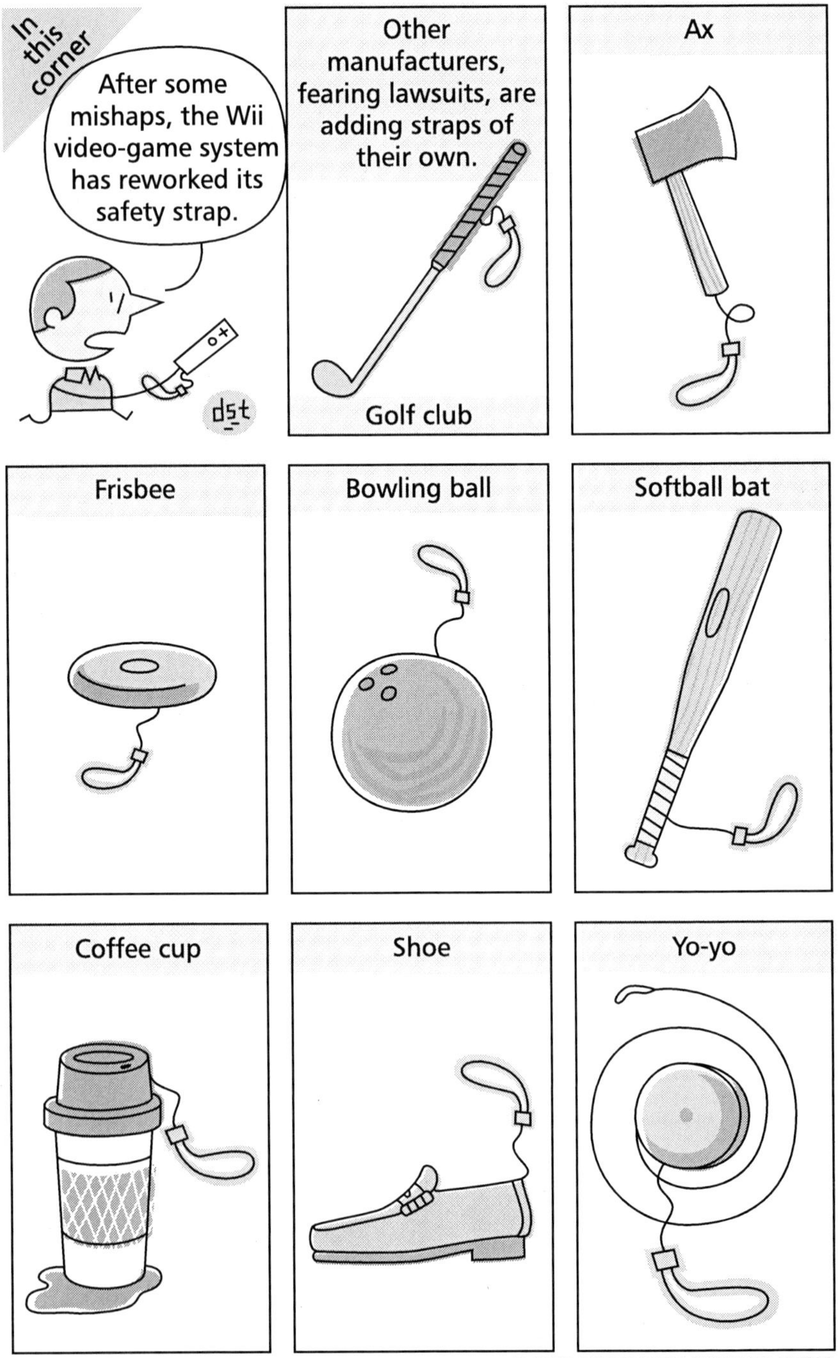
In this corner
After some mishaps, the Wii video-game system has reworked its safety strap.
dst
Other manufacturers, fearing lawsuits, are adding straps of their own.
Golf club
Ax
Frisbee
Bowling ball
Softball bat
Coffee cup
Shoe
Yo-yo

Dec. 21, 2006

DAVID STEINLICHT, PIONEER PRESS

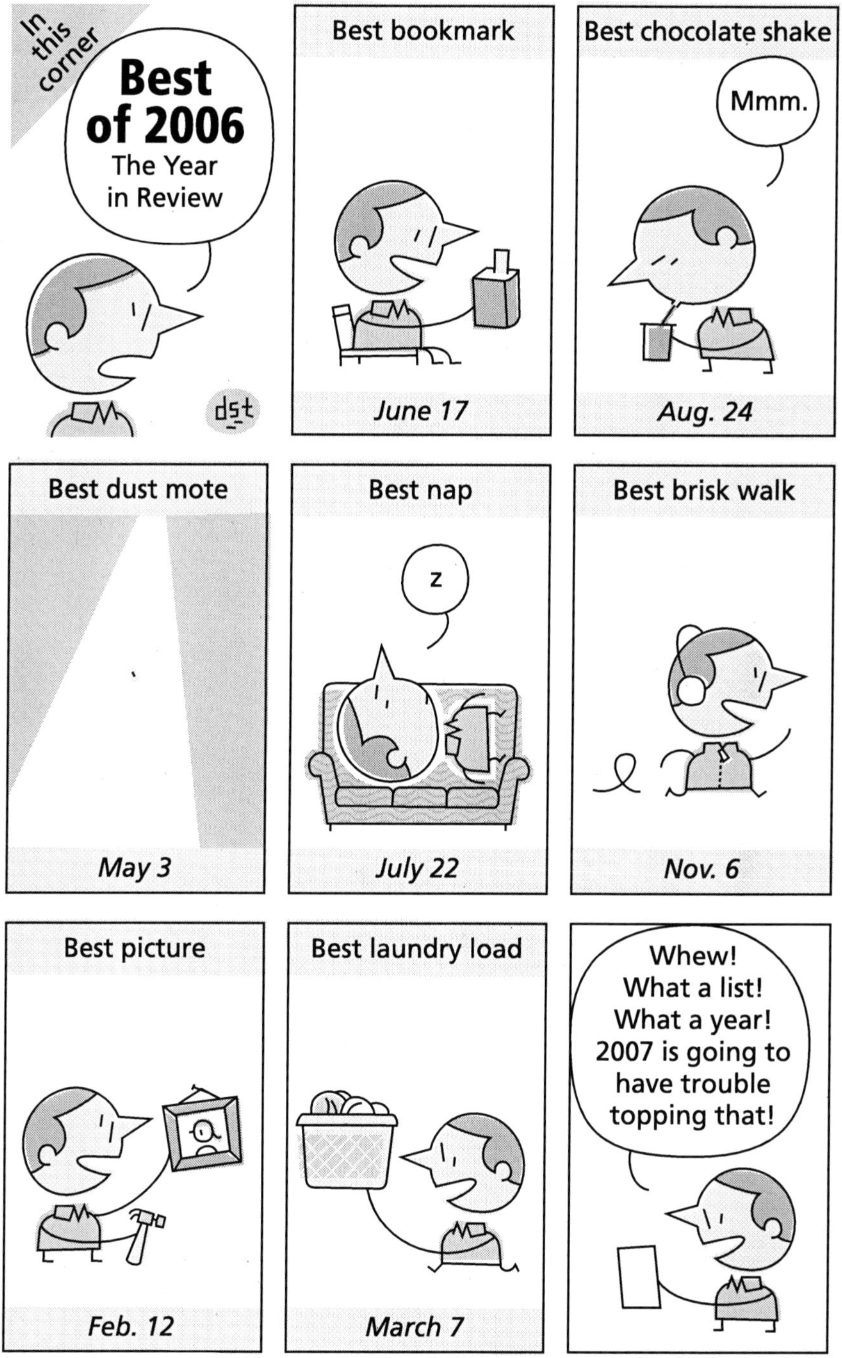
In this corner
Best of 2006
The Year in Review
dst
Best bookmark
June 17
Best chocolate shake
Mmm.
Aug. 24
Best dust mote
May 3
Best nap
z
July 22
Best brisk walk
Nov. 6
Best picture
Feb. 12
Best laundry load
March 7
Whew!
What a list!
What a year!
2007 is going to have trouble topping that!

Dec. 28, 2006

DAVID STEINLICHT, PIONEER PRESS

In this corner
The anvil
dst
I could gaze into your eyes all day long.
It does tingle a bit.
Later
Glad it didn't land on anything important.
Ha-ha.
Later
Do that anvil thing again.
...
I was kidding.
Ha-ha.
I could gaze into your eyes all day long.

Jan. 4, 2007

DAVID STEINLICHT, PIONEER PRESS

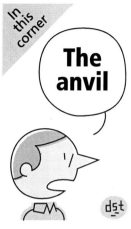

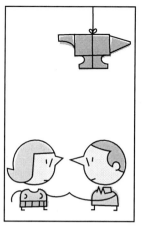

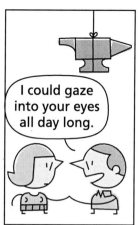

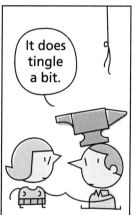

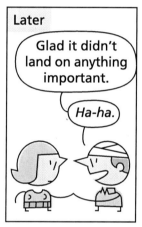

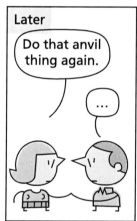

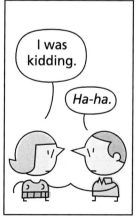

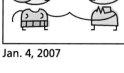

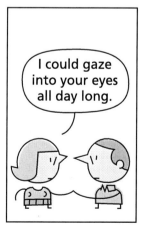

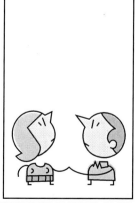

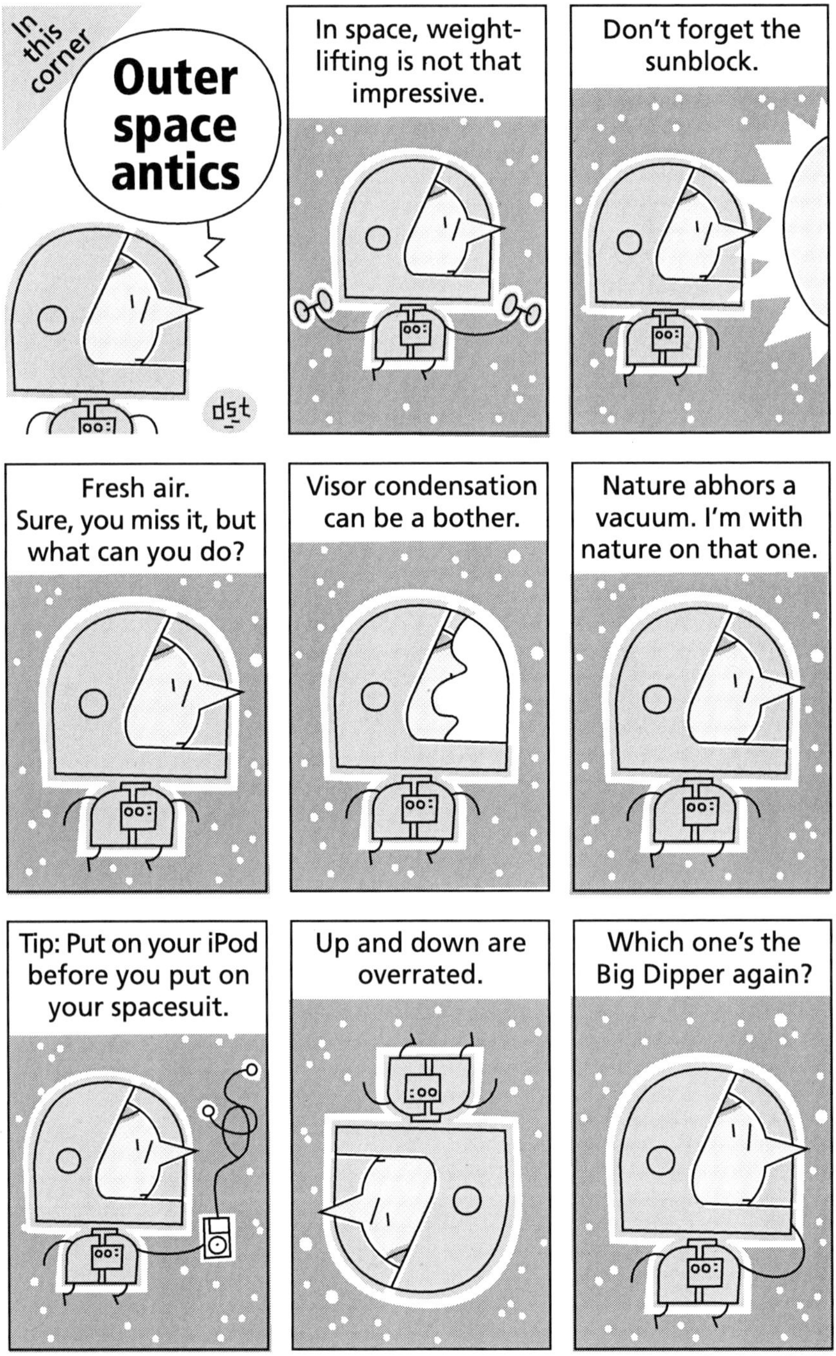
In this corner
Outer space antics
dst
In space, weight-lifting is not that impressive.
Don't forget the sunblock.
Fresh air. Sure, you miss it, but what can you do?
Visor condensation can be a bother.
Nature abhors a vacuum. I'm with nature on that one.
Tip: Put on your iPod before you put on your spacesuit.
Up and down are overrated.
Which one's the Big Dipper again?

Jan. 11, 2007

DAVID STEINLICHT, PIONEER PRESS

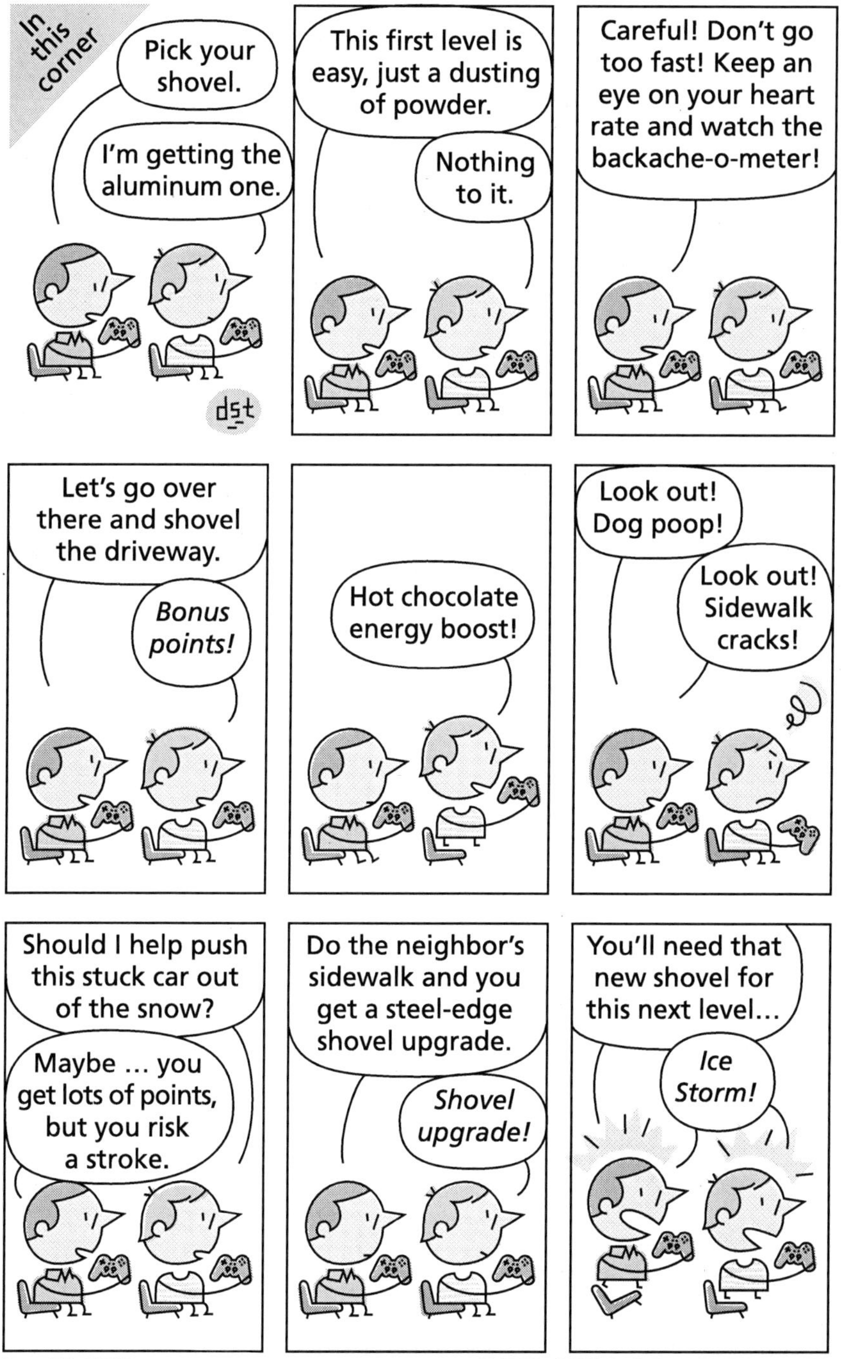
In this corner
Pick your shovel.
I'm getting the aluminum one.
dst
This first level is easy, just a dusting of powder.
Nothing to it.
Careful! Don't go too fast! Keep an eye on your heart rate and watch the backache-o-meter!
Let's go over there and shovel the driveway.
Bonus points!
Hot chocolate energy boost!
Look out! Dog poop!
Look out! Sidewalk cracks!
Should I help push this stuck car out of the snow?
Maybe … you get lots of points, but you risk a stroke.
Do the neighbor's sidewalk and you get a steel-edge shovel upgrade.
Shovel upgrade!
You'll need that new shovel for this next level…
Ice Storm!

Jan. 18, 2007

DAVID STEINLICHT, PIONEER PRESS

King of the kitchen

In this corner

Used to be: You want to cook something, you work with me.

SOUP

You want a refreshing beverage? You work with me.

There was always a can or bottle to be opened. I opened them all ...

... except wine. Old Screwy over there took care of that.

Then, along came foil-packed coffee. And those doggone juice boxes!

Premium Blend

Juice

Seems like now every bottle has a twist-off top, every can has a pull tab.

I go for days without people looking for me in the drawer.

But every once in a while, there's a can of beans — without a pull top — that needs opening.

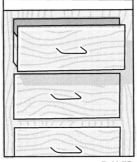

I'm the guy to do it.

Jan. 25, 2007

DAVID STEINLICHT, PIONEER PRESS

138

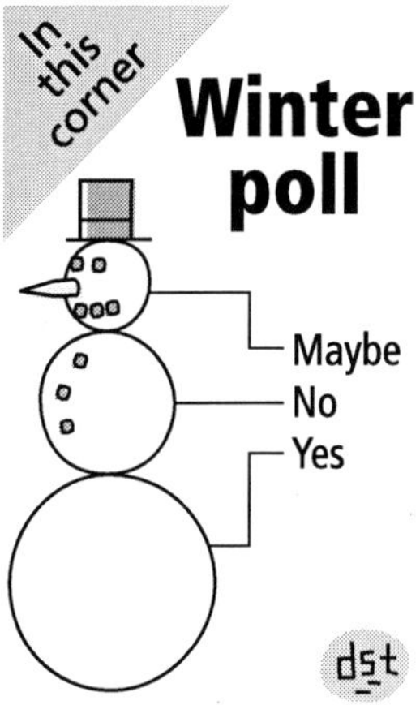
In this corner
Winter poll
Maybe
No
Yes
dst

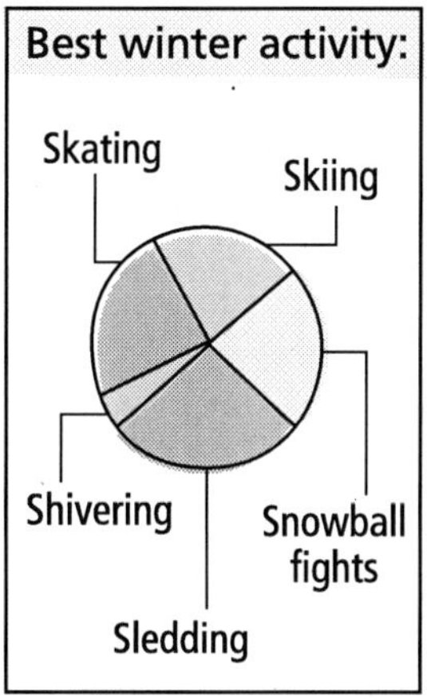
Best winter activity:
Skating
Skiing
Shivering
Snowball fights
Sledding

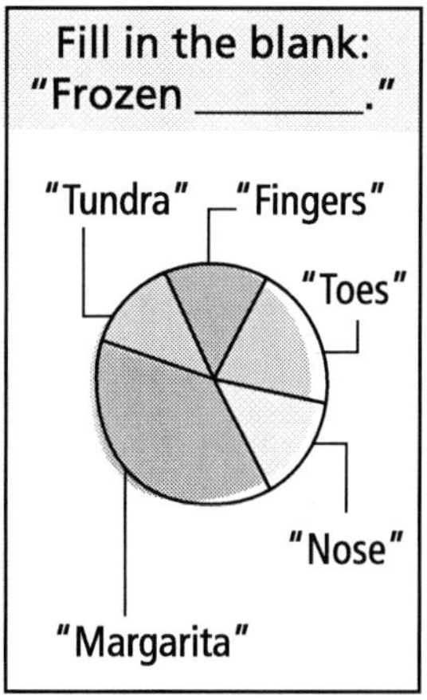
Fill in the blank: "Frozen ________."
"Tundra"
"Fingers"
"Toes"
"Nose"
"Margarita"

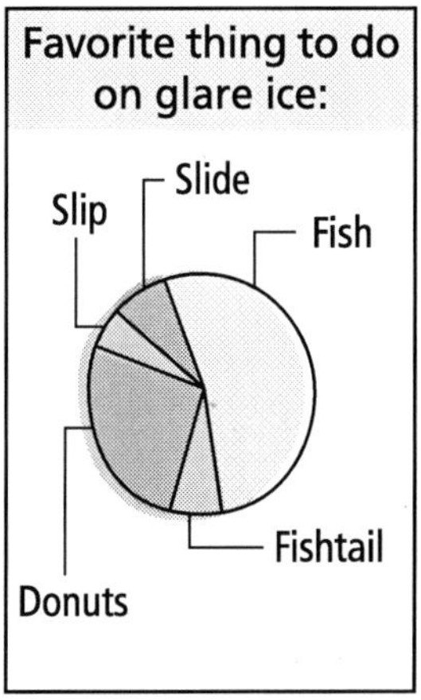
Favorite thing to do on glare ice:
Slip
Slide
Fish
Fishtail
Donuts

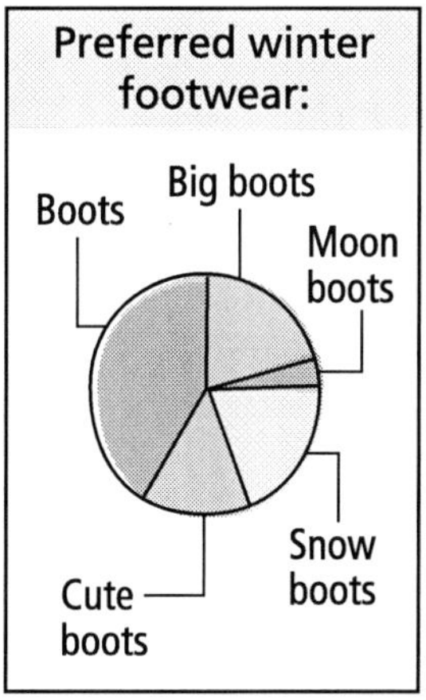
Preferred winter footwear:
Boots
Big boots
Moon boots
Snow boots
Cute boots

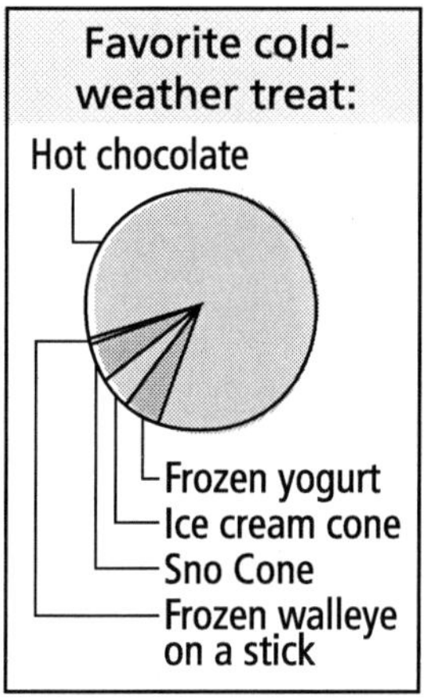
Favorite cold-weather treat:
Hot chocolate
Frozen yogurt
Ice cream cone
Sno Cone
Frozen walleye on a stick

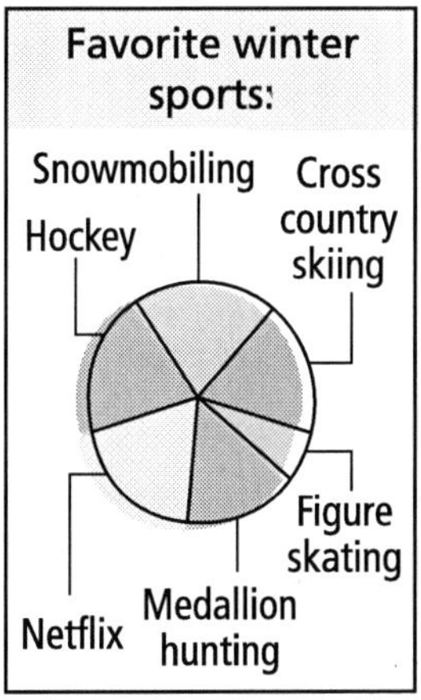
Favorite winter sports:
Snowmobiling
Cross country skiing
Hockey
Figure skating
Medallion hunting
Netflix

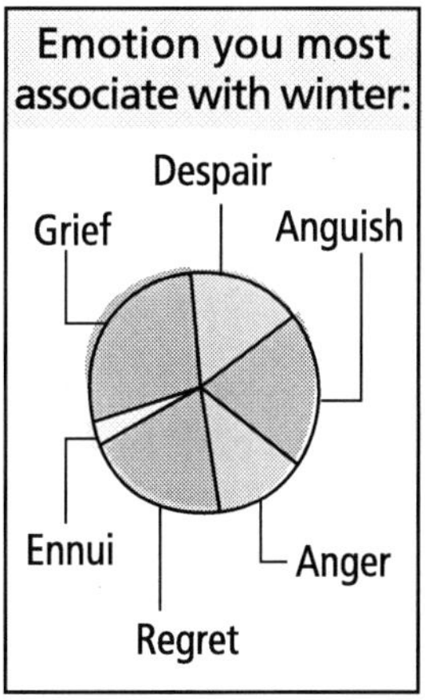
Emotion you most associate with winter:
Despair
Grief
Anguish
Ennui
Anger
Regret

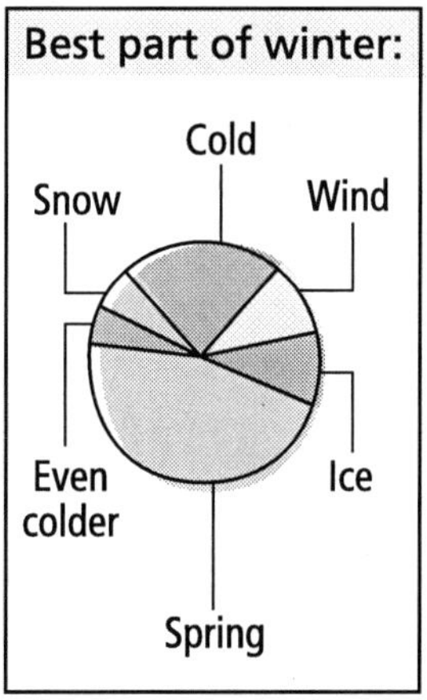
Best part of winter:
Cold
Snow
Wind
Even colder
Ice
Spring

Feb. 1, 2007

DAVID STEINLICHT, PIONEER PRESS

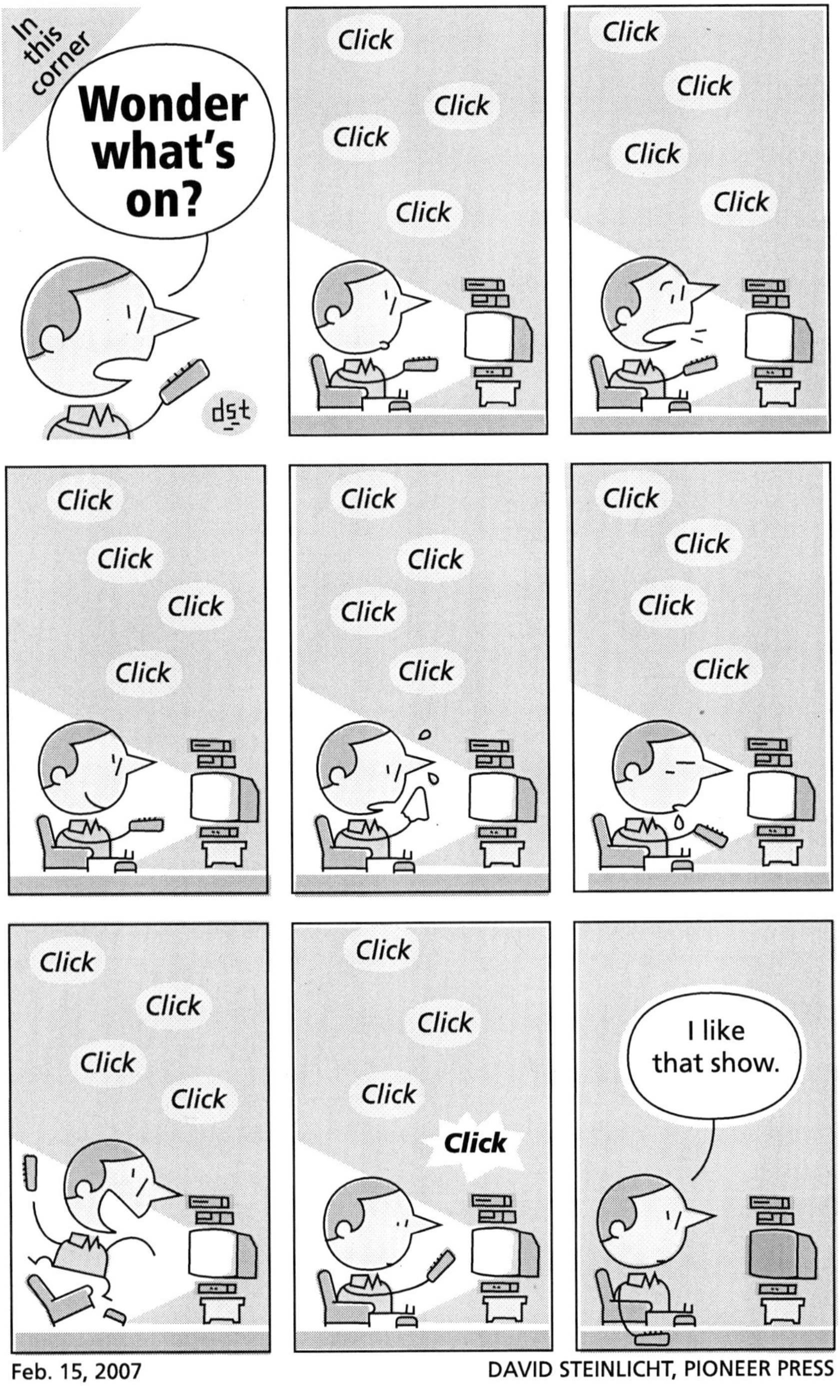
In this corner
Wonder what's on?
dst
Click
Click
Click
Click
Click
Click
Click
Click
Click
Click
Click
Click
Click
Click
Click
Click
Click
Click
Click
Click
Click
Click
Click
Click
Click
Click
Click
Click
I like that show.

Feb. 15, 2007

DAVID STEINLICHT, PIONEER PRESS

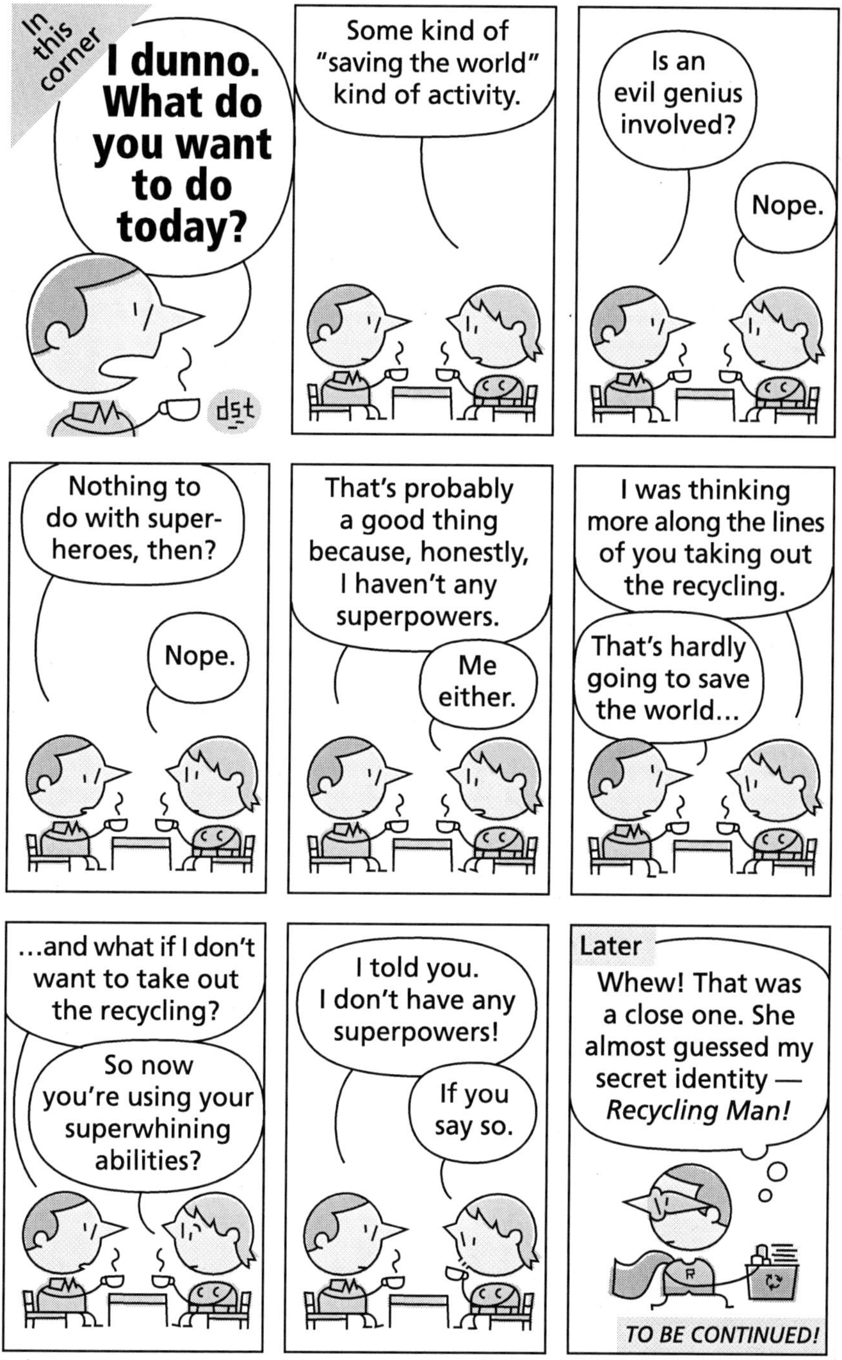
In this corner
I dunno. What do you want to do today?
dst
Some kind of "saving the world" kind of activity.
Is an evil genius involved?
Nope.
Nothing to do with super-heroes, then?
Nope.
That's probably a good thing because, honestly, I haven't any superpowers.
Me either.
I was thinking more along the lines of you taking out the recycling.
That's hardly going to save the world...
...and what if I don't want to take out the recycling?
So now you're using your superwhining abilities?
I told you. I don't have any superpowers!
If you say so.
Later
Whew! That was a close one. She almost guessed my secret identity — *Recycling Man!*
TO BE CONTINUED!

Feb. 22, 2007

DAVID STEINLICHT, PIONEER PRESS

Note: The only two-parter.

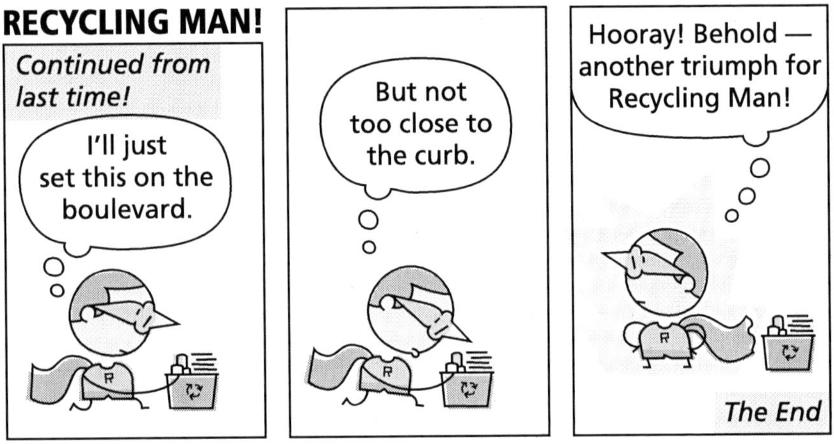
RECYCLING MAN!
Continued from last time!
I'll just set this on the boulevard.
But not too close to the curb.
Hooray! Behold — another triumph for Recycling Man!
The End

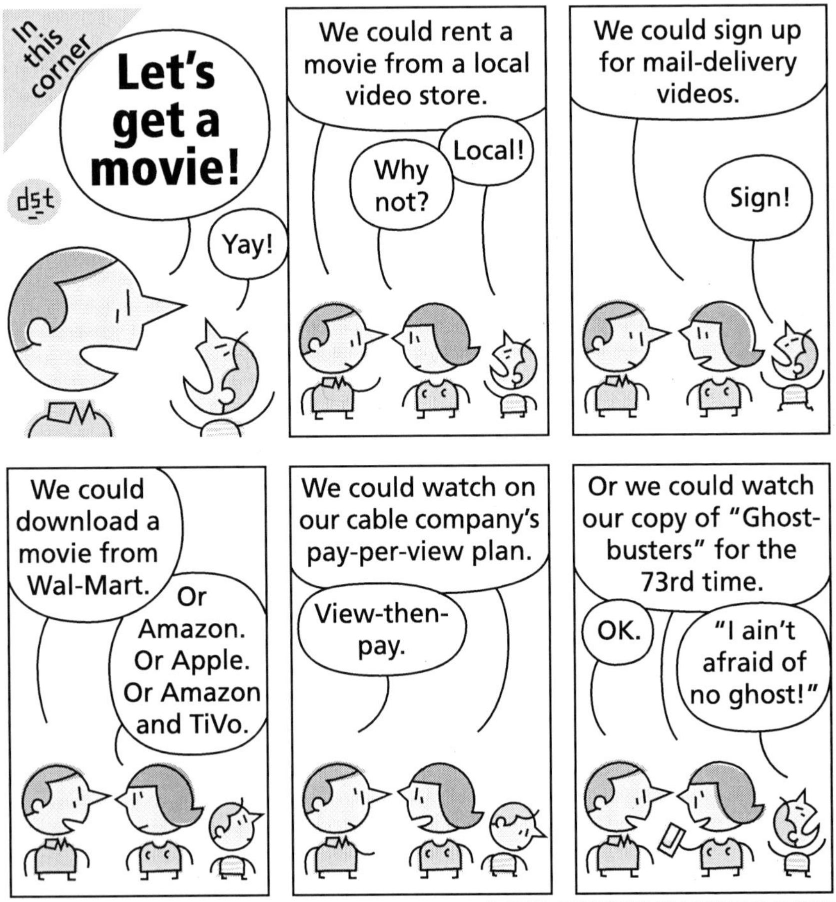
In this corner
dst
Let's get a movie!
Yay!
We could rent a movie from a local video store.
Why not?
Local!
We could sign up for mail-delivery videos.
Sign!
We could download a movie from Wal-Mart.
Or Amazon. Or Apple. Or Amazon and TiVo.
We could watch on our cable company's pay-per-view plan.
View-then-pay.
Or we could watch our copy of "Ghost-busters" for the 73rd time.
OK.
"I ain't afraid of no ghost!"

March 1, 2007

DAVID STEINLICHT, PIONEER PRESS

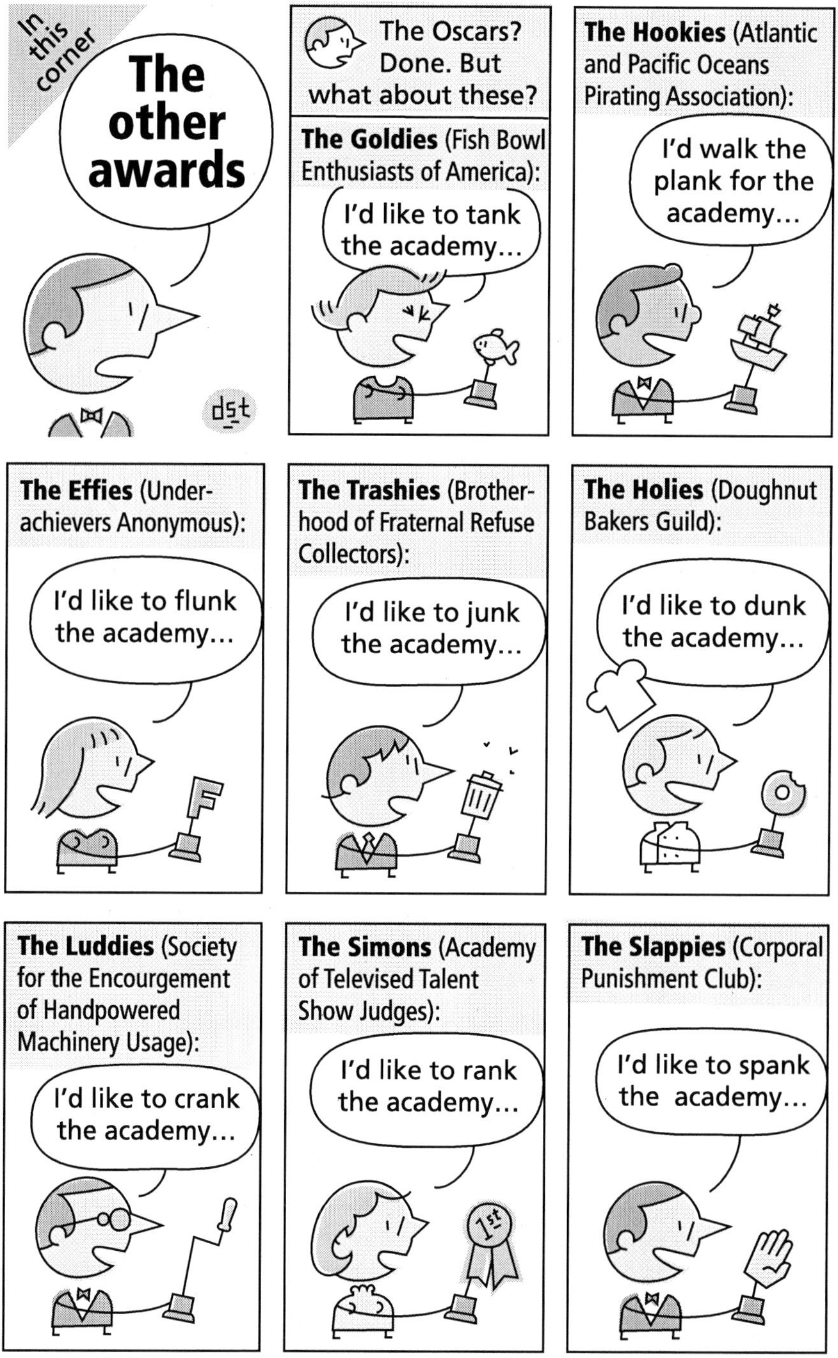
In this corner
The other awards
dst
The Oscars? Done. But what about these?
The Goldies (Fish Bowl Enthusiasts of America):
I'd like to tank the academy...
The Hookies (Atlantic and Pacific Oceans Pirating Association):
I'd walk the plank for the academy...
The Effies (Under-achievers Anonymous):
I'd like to flunk the academy...
F
The Trashies (Brotherhood of Fraternal Refuse Collectors):
I'd like to junk the academy...
The Holies (Doughnut Bakers Guild):
I'd like to dunk the academy...
The Luddies (Society for the Encourgement of Handpowered Machinery Usage):
I'd like to crank the academy...
The Simons (Academy of Televised Talent Show Judges):
I'd like to rank the academy...
1st
The Slappies (Corporal Punishment Club):
I'd like to spank the academy...

March 8, 2007

DAVID STEINLICHT, PIONEER PRESS

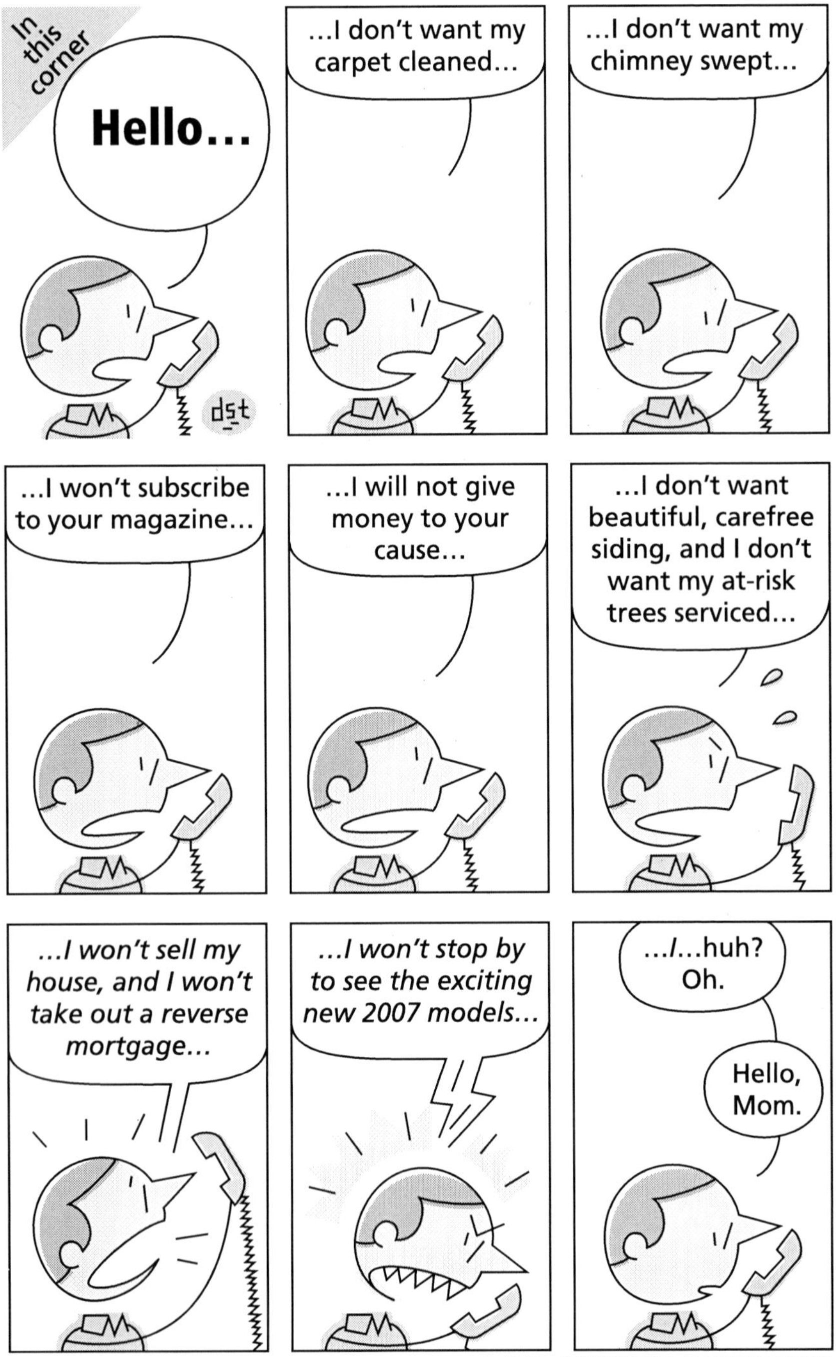
In this corner
Hello...
...I don't want my carpet cleaned...
...I don't want my chimney swept...
...I won't subscribe to your magazine...
...I will not give money to your cause...
...I don't want beautiful, carefree siding, and I don't want my at-risk trees serviced...
...I won't sell my house, and I won't take out a reverse mortgage...
...I won't stop by to see the exciting new 2007 models...
...I...huh? Oh.
Hello, Mom.

March 15, 2007

DAVID STEINLICHT, PIONEER PRESS

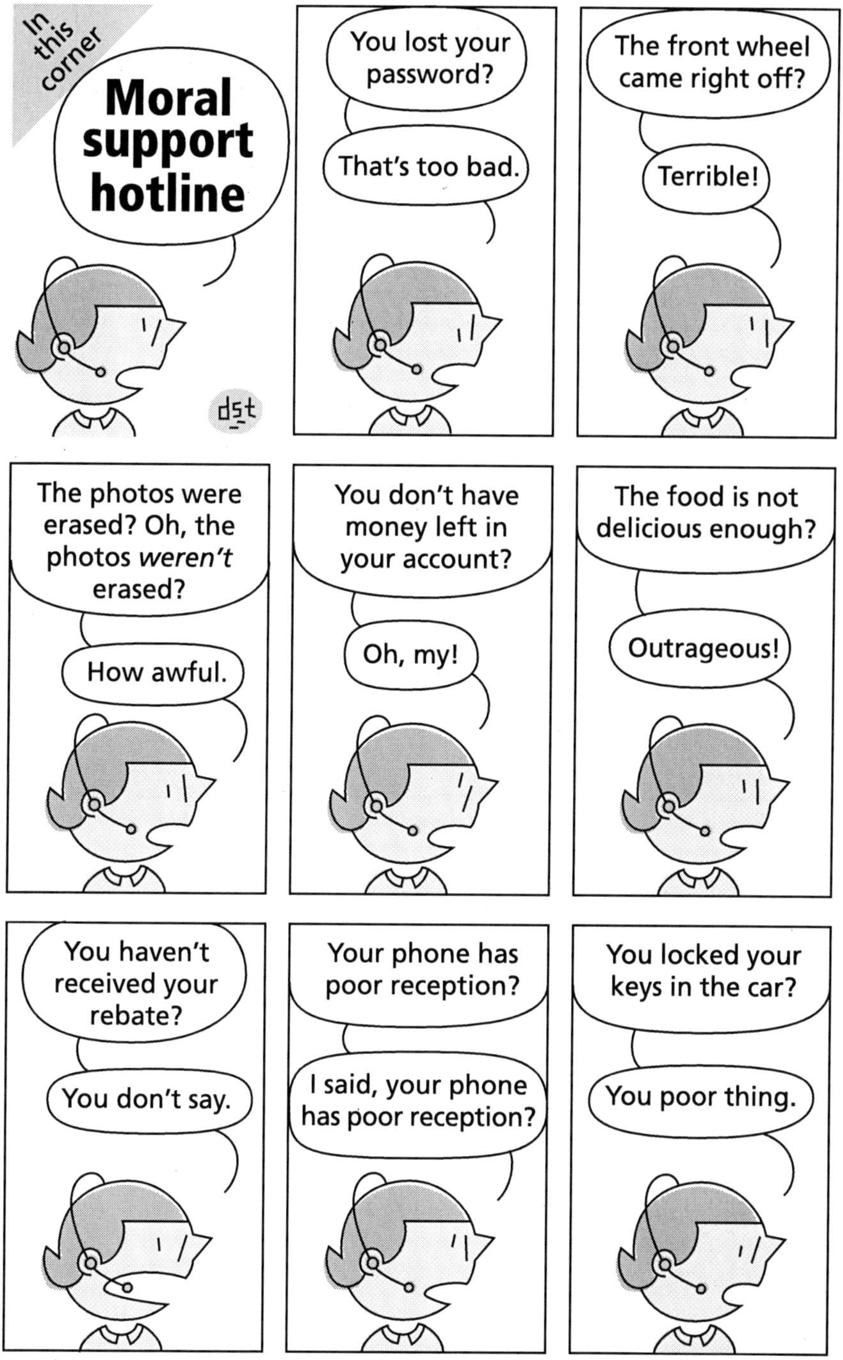
In this corner
Moral support hotline
dst
You lost your password?
That's too bad.
The front wheel came right off?
Terrible!
The photos were erased? Oh, the photos *weren't* erased?
How awful.
You don't have money left in your account?
Oh, my!
The food is not delicious enough?
Outrageous!
You haven't received your rebate?
You don't say.
Your phone has poor reception?
I said, your phone has poor reception?
You locked your keys in the car?
You poor thing.

March 29, 2007

DAVID STEINLICHT, PIONEER PRESS

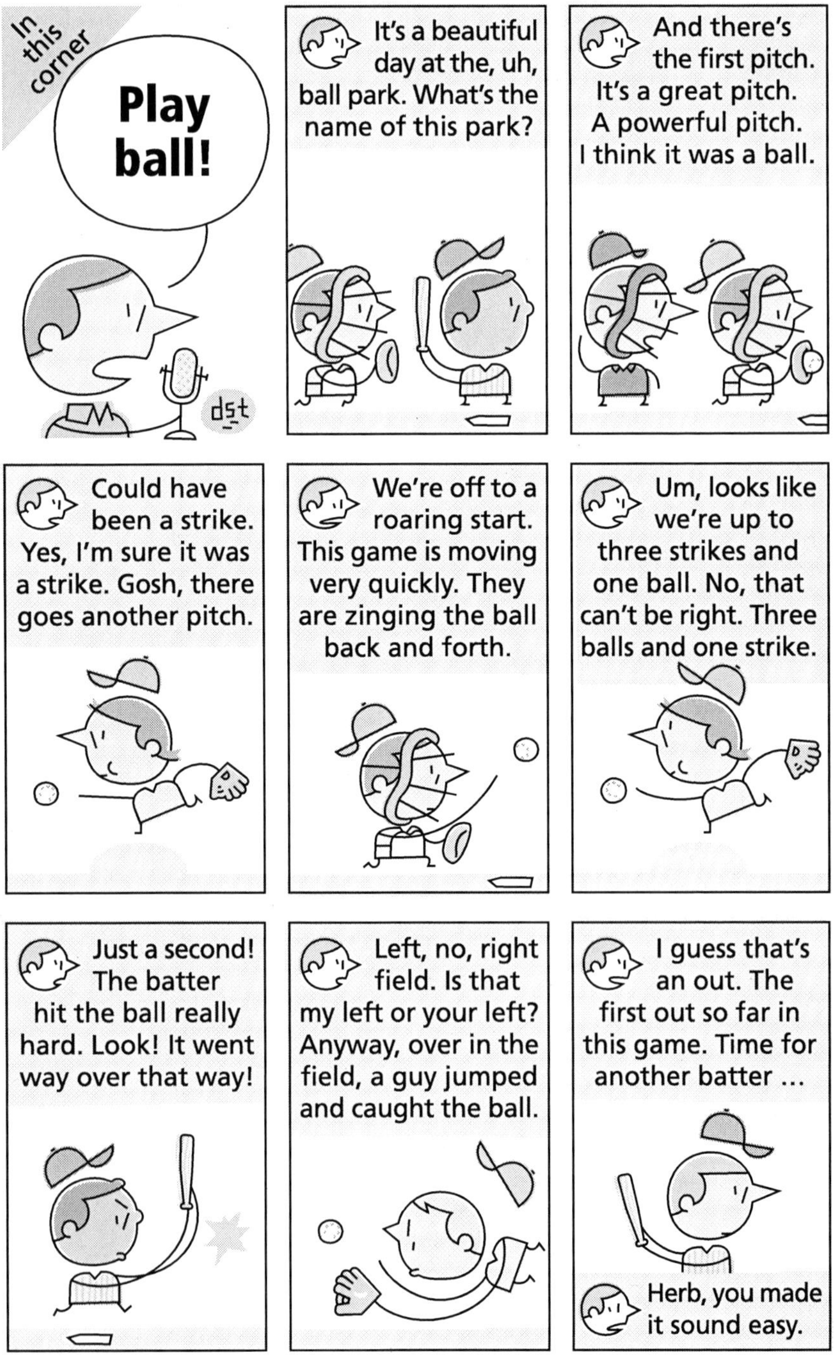
In this corner
Play ball!
dst
It's a beautiful day at the, uh, ball park. What's the name of this park?
And there's the first pitch. It's a great pitch. A powerful pitch. I think it was a ball.
Could have been a strike. Yes, I'm sure it was a strike. Gosh, there goes another pitch.
We're off to a roaring start. This game is moving very quickly. They are zinging the ball back and forth.
Um, looks like we're up to three strikes and one ball. No, that can't be right. Three balls and one strike.
Just a second! The batter hit the ball really hard. Look! It went way over that way!
Left, no, right field. Is that my left or your left? Anyway, over in the field, a guy jumped and caught the ball.
I guess that's an out. The first out so far in this game. Time for another batter ...
Herb, you made it sound easy.

April 4, 2007 DAVID STEINLICHT, PIONEER PRESS

 Note: Herb Carneal died. He was the long-time Minnesota Twins announcer.

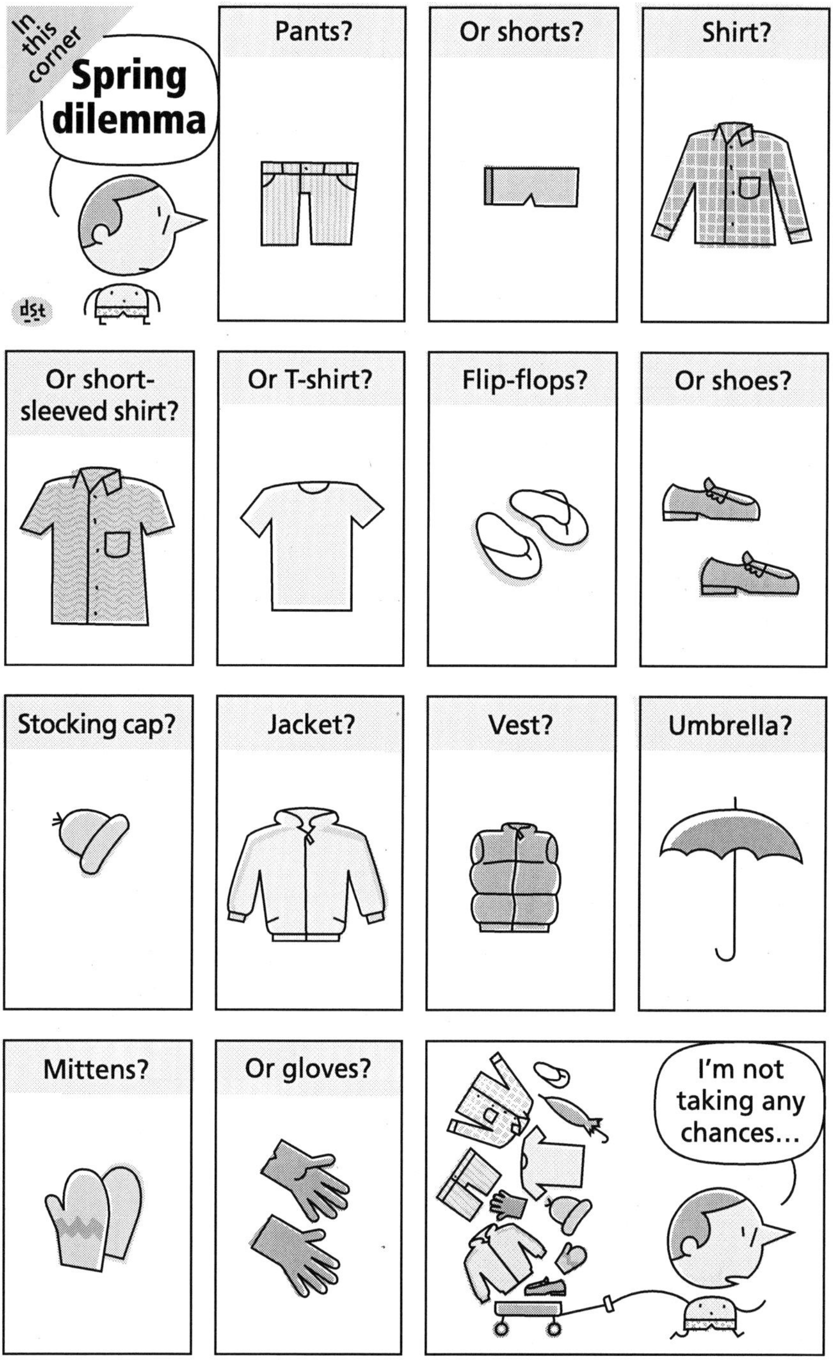
In this corner
Spring dilemma
dst
Pants?
Or shorts?
Shirt?
Or short-sleeved shirt?
Or T-shirt?
Flip-flops?
Or shoes?
Stocking cap?
Jacket?
Vest?
Umbrella?
Mittens?
Or gloves?
I'm not taking any chances…

April 19, 2007

DAVID STEINLICHT, PIONEER PRESS

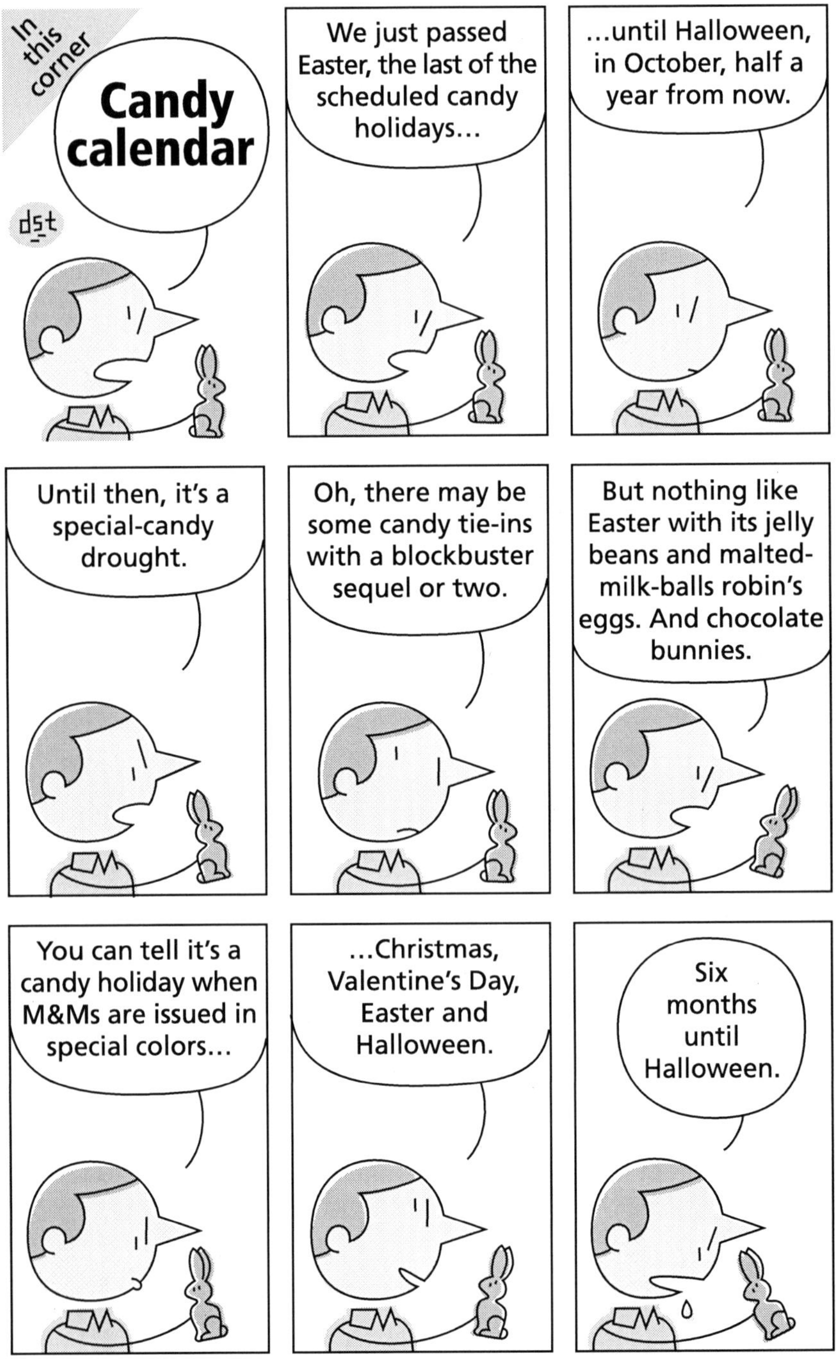
In this corner
Candy calendar
dst
We just passed Easter, the last of the scheduled candy holidays...
...until Halloween, in October, half a year from now.
Until then, it's a special-candy drought.
Oh, there may be some candy tie-ins with a blockbuster sequel or two.
But nothing like Easter with its jelly beans and malted-milk-balls robin's eggs. And chocolate bunnies.
You can tell it's a candy holiday when M&Ms are issued in special colors...
...Christmas, Valentine's Day, Easter and Halloween.
Six months until Halloween.

April 26, 2007

DAVID STEINLICHT, PIONEER PRESS

 Note: Christmastime brings mint M&Ms — the highlight of my candy calendar.

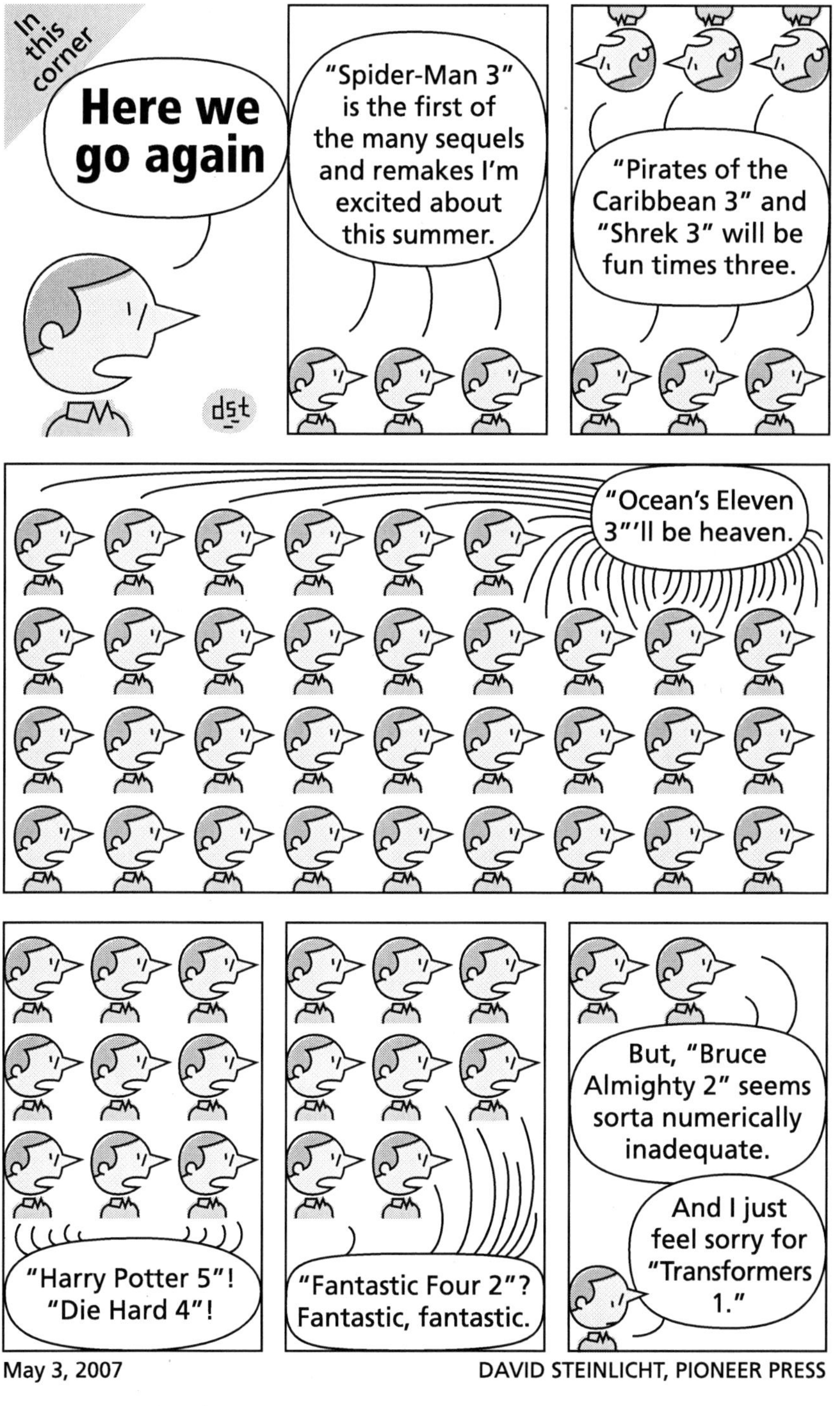
In this corner
Here we go again
"Spider-Man 3" is the first of the many sequels and remakes I'm excited about this summer.
"Pirates of the Caribbean 3" and "Shrek 3" will be fun times three.
"Ocean's Eleven 3"'ll be heaven.
"Harry Potter 5"! "Die Hard 4"!
"Fantastic Four 2"? Fantastic, fantastic.
But, "Bruce Almighty 2" seems sorta numerically inadequate.
And I just feel sorry for "Transformers 1."

May 3, 2007

DAVID STEINLICHT, PIONEER PRESS

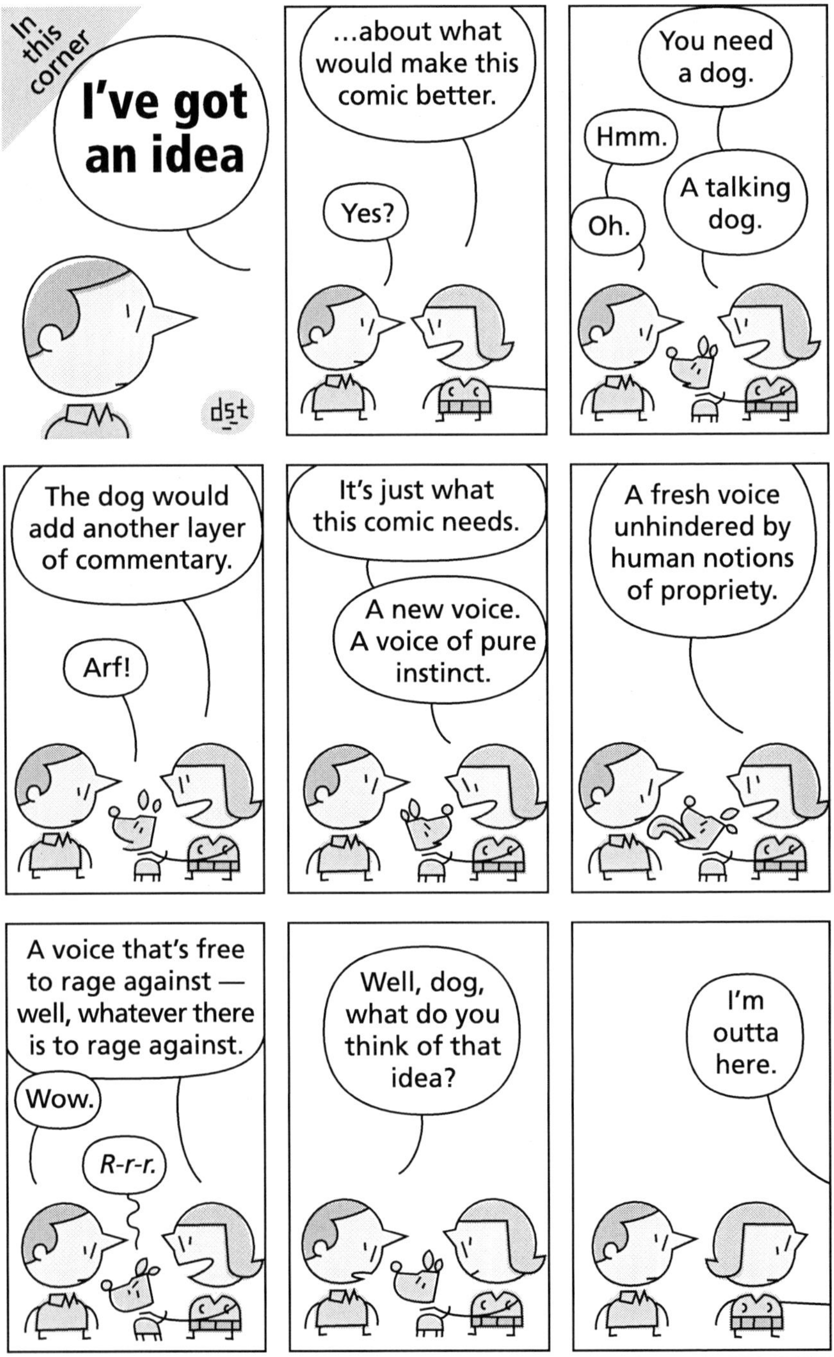
In this corner
I've got an idea
dst
...about what would make this comic better.
Yes?
You need a dog.
Hmm.
A talking dog.
Oh.
The dog would add another layer of commentary.
Arf!
It's just what this comic needs.
A new voice. A voice of pure instinct.
A fresh voice unhindered by human notions of propriety.
A voice that's free to rage against — well, whatever there is to rage against.
Wow.
R-r-r.
Well, dog, what do you think of that idea?
I'm outta here.

May 10, 2007 DAVID STEINLICHT, PIONEER PRESS

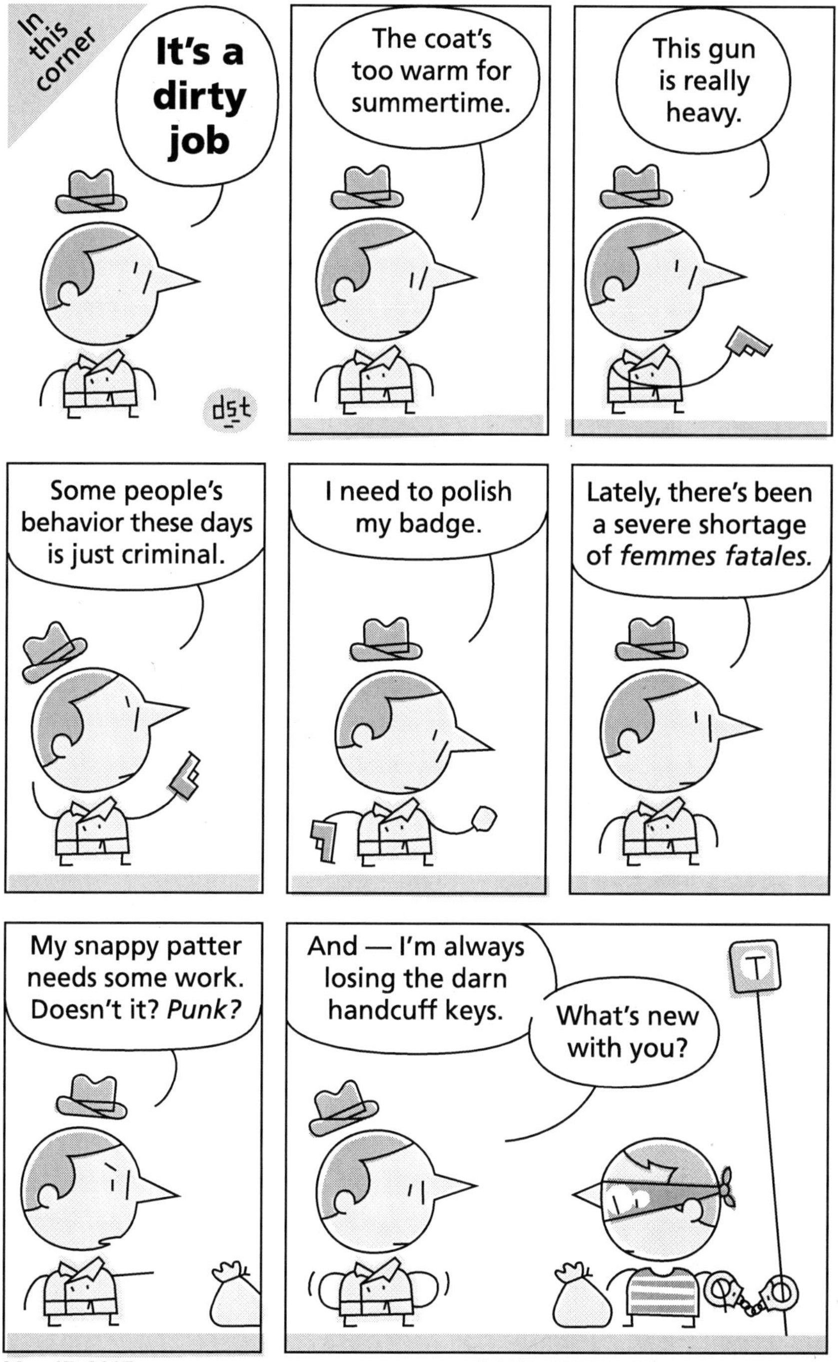
In this corner
It's a dirty job
The coat's too warm for summertime.
This gun is really heavy.
Some people's behavior these days is just criminal.
I need to polish my badge.
Lately, there's been a severe shortage of *femmes fatales.*
My snappy patter needs some work. Doesn't it? *Punk?*
And — I'm always losing the darn handcuff keys.
What's new with you?

May 17, 2007

DAVID STEINLICHT, PIONEER PRESS

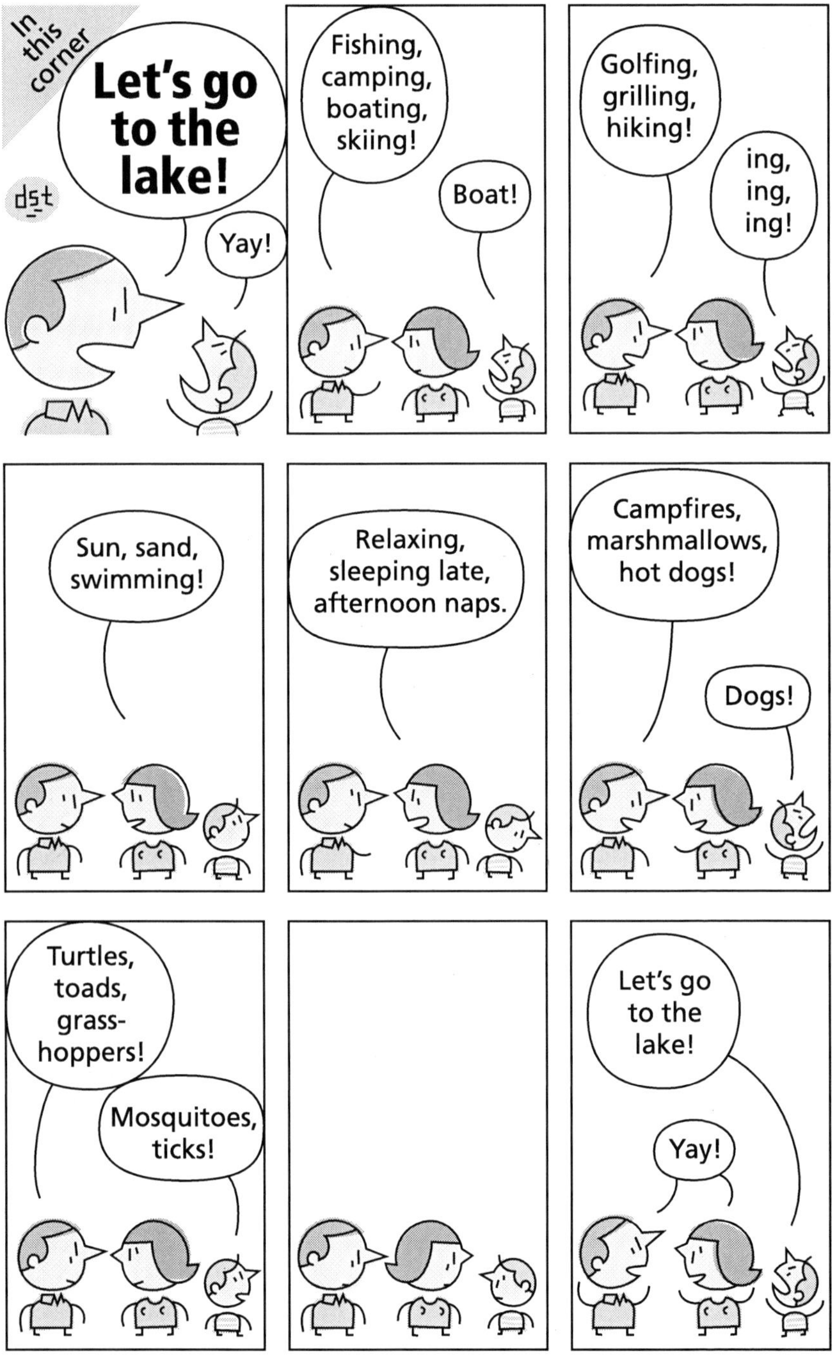
In this corner
dst
Let's go to the lake!
Yay!
Fishing, camping, boating, skiing!
Boat!
Golfing, grilling, hiking!
ing, ing, ing!
Sun, sand, swimming!
Relaxing, sleeping late, afternoon naps.
Campfires, marshmallows, hot dogs!
Dogs!
Turtles, toads, grass-hoppers!
Mosquitoes, ticks!
Let's go to the lake!
Yay!

May 24, 2007

DAVID STEINLICHT, PIONEER PRESS

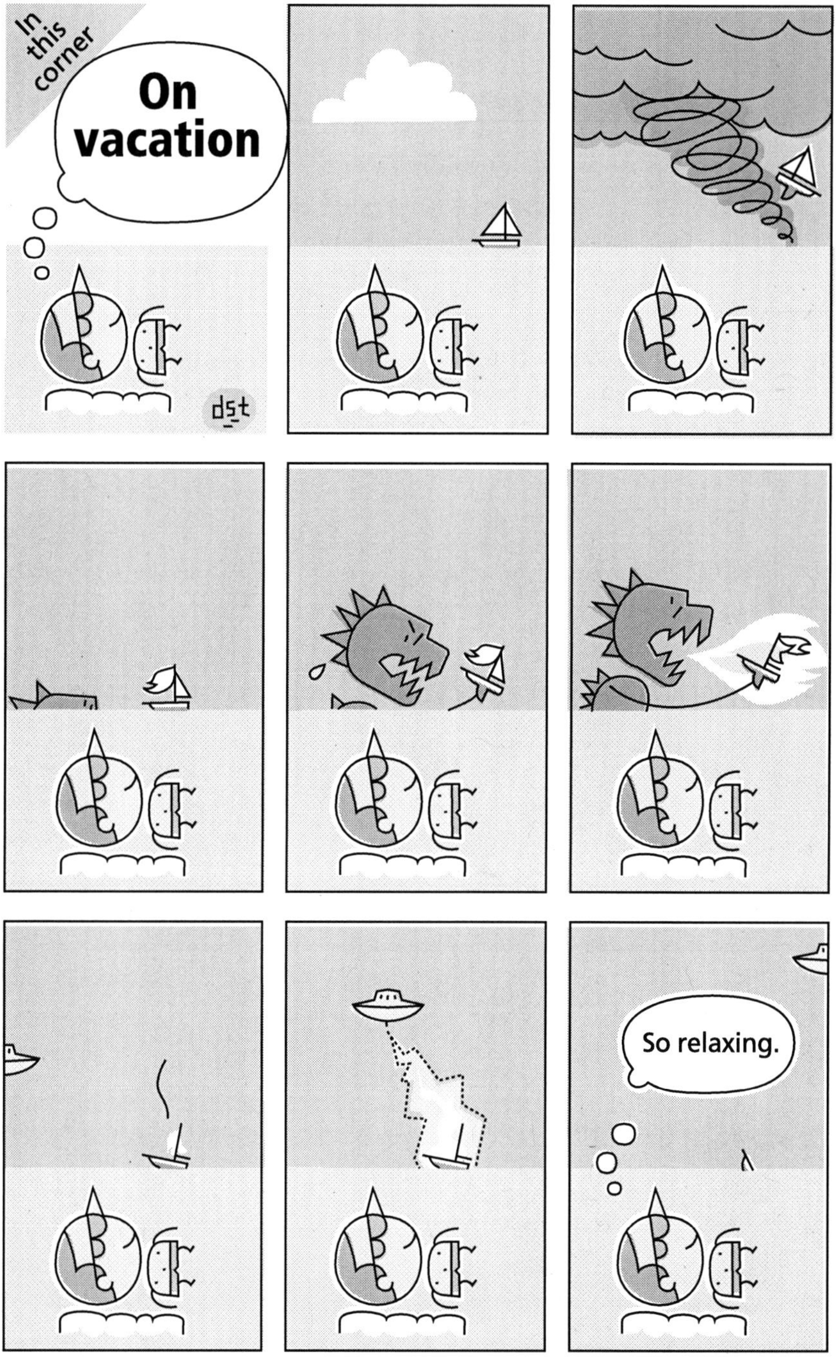
In this corner
On vacation
dst
So relaxing.

May 31, 2007 DAVID STEINLICHT, PIONEER PRESS

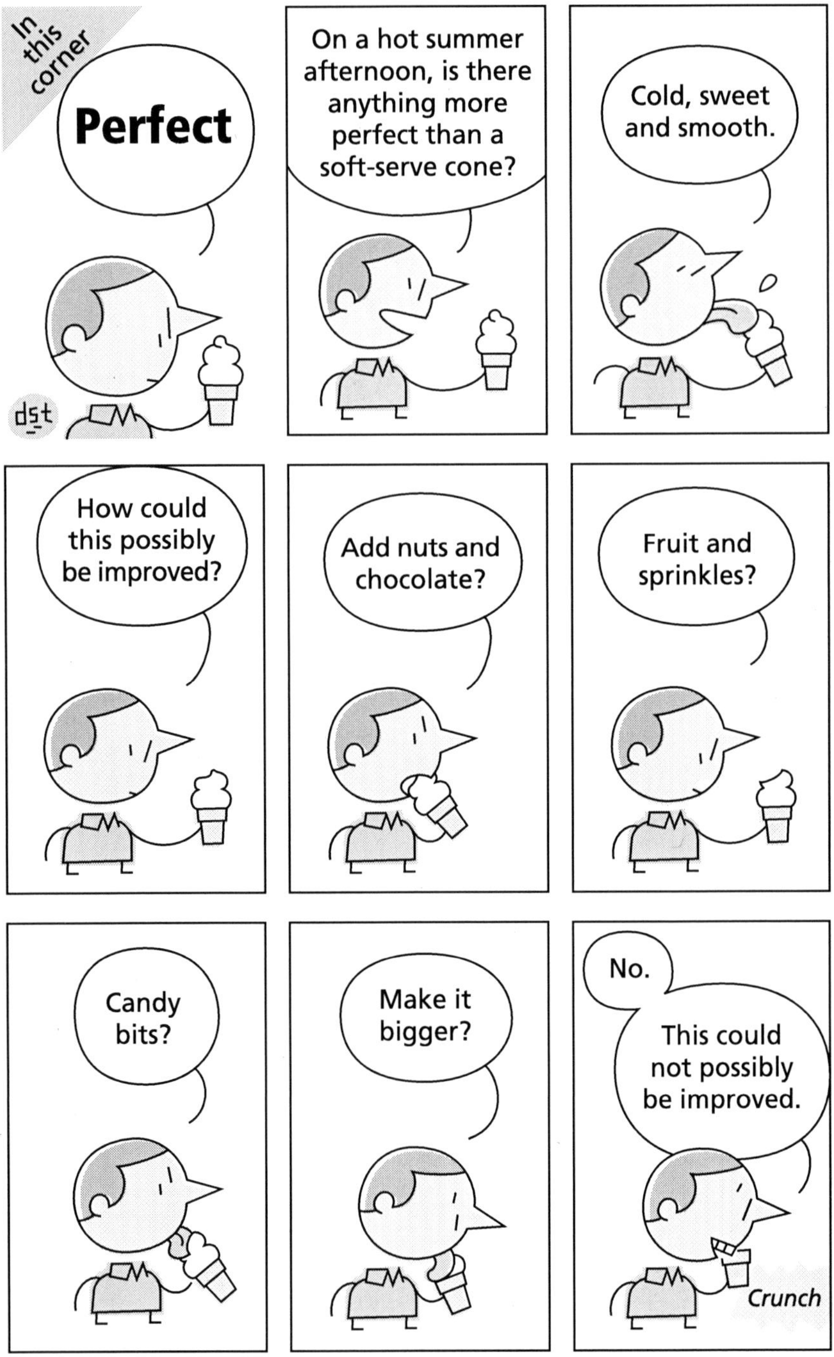
In this corner
Perfect
On a hot summer afternoon, is there anything more perfect than a soft-serve cone?
Cold, sweet and smooth.
How could this possibly be improved?
Add nuts and chocolate?
Fruit and sprinkles?
Candy bits?
Make it bigger?
No.
This could not possibly be improved.
Crunch

June 7, 2007

DAVID STEINLICHT, PIONEER PRESS

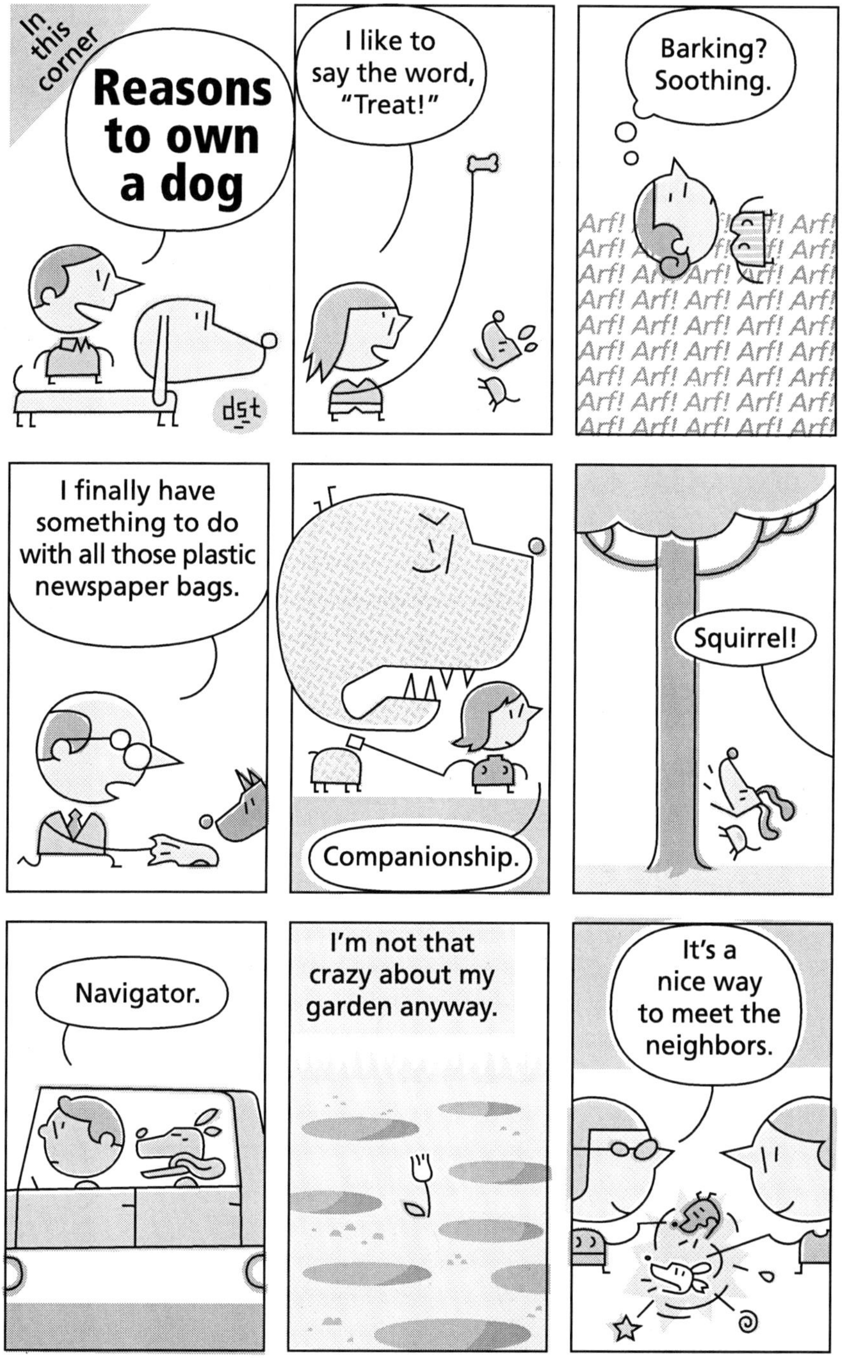
In this corner
Reasons to own a dog
dst
I like to say the word, "Treat!"
Barking? Soothing.
Arf! Arf! Arf! Arf! Arf!
Arf! Arf! Arf! Arf! Arf!
Arf! Arf! Arf! Arf! Arf!
Arf! Arf! Arf! Arf! Arf!
Arf! Arf! Arf! Arf! Arf!
I finally have something to do with all those plastic newspaper bags.
Companionship.
Squirrel!
Navigator.
I'm not that crazy about my garden anyway.
It's a nice way to meet the neighbors.

June 14, 2007

DAVID STEINLICHT, PIONEER PRESS

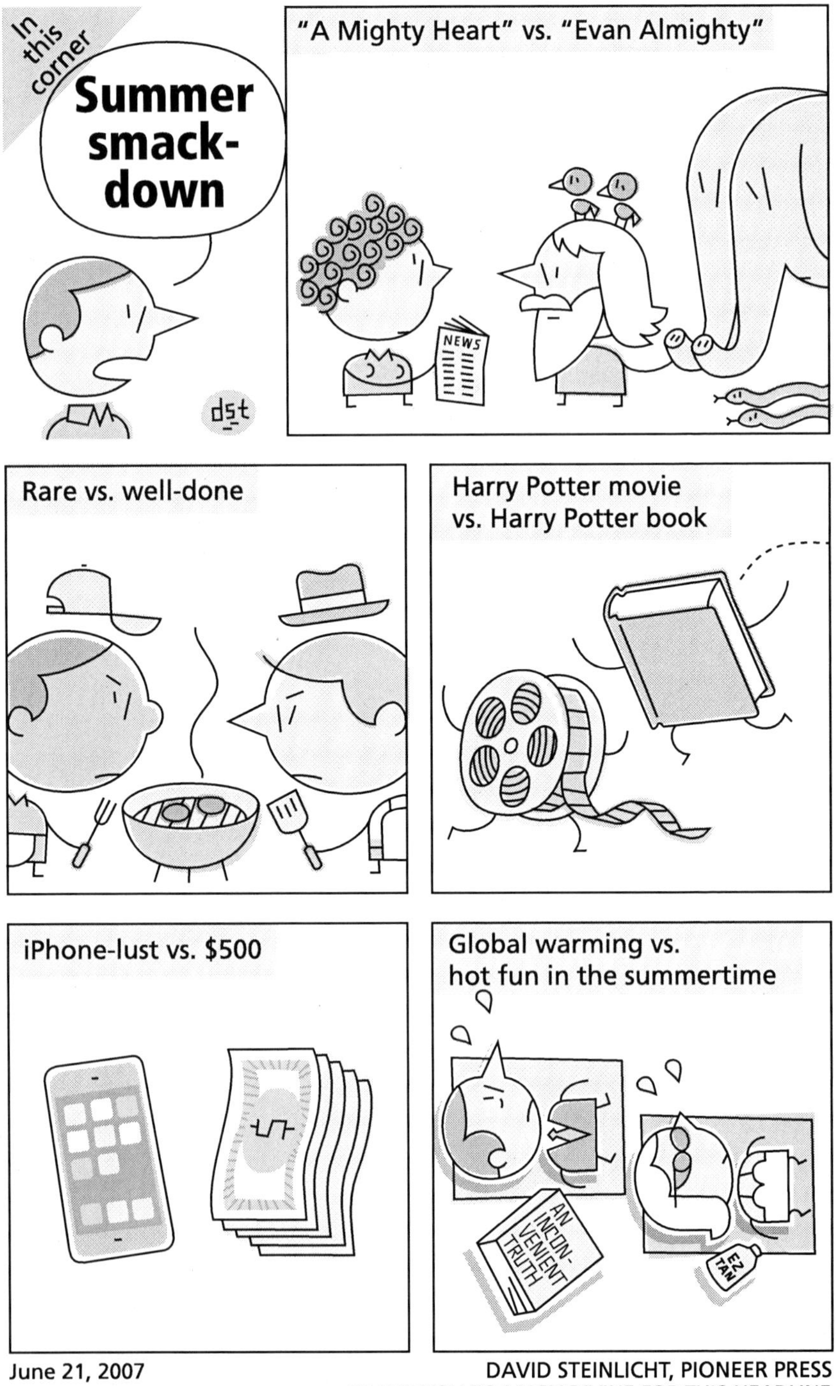
In this corner
Summer smack-down
dst
"A Mighty Heart" vs. "Evan Almighty"
NEWS
Rare vs. well-done
Harry Potter movie vs. Harry Potter book
iPhone-lust vs. $500
Global warming vs. hot fun in the summertime
AN INCON-VENIENT TRUTH
EZ TAN

June 21, 2007

DAVID STEINLICHT, PIONEER PRESS
THANK YOU TO MARY DIVINE FOR THIS HEADLINE

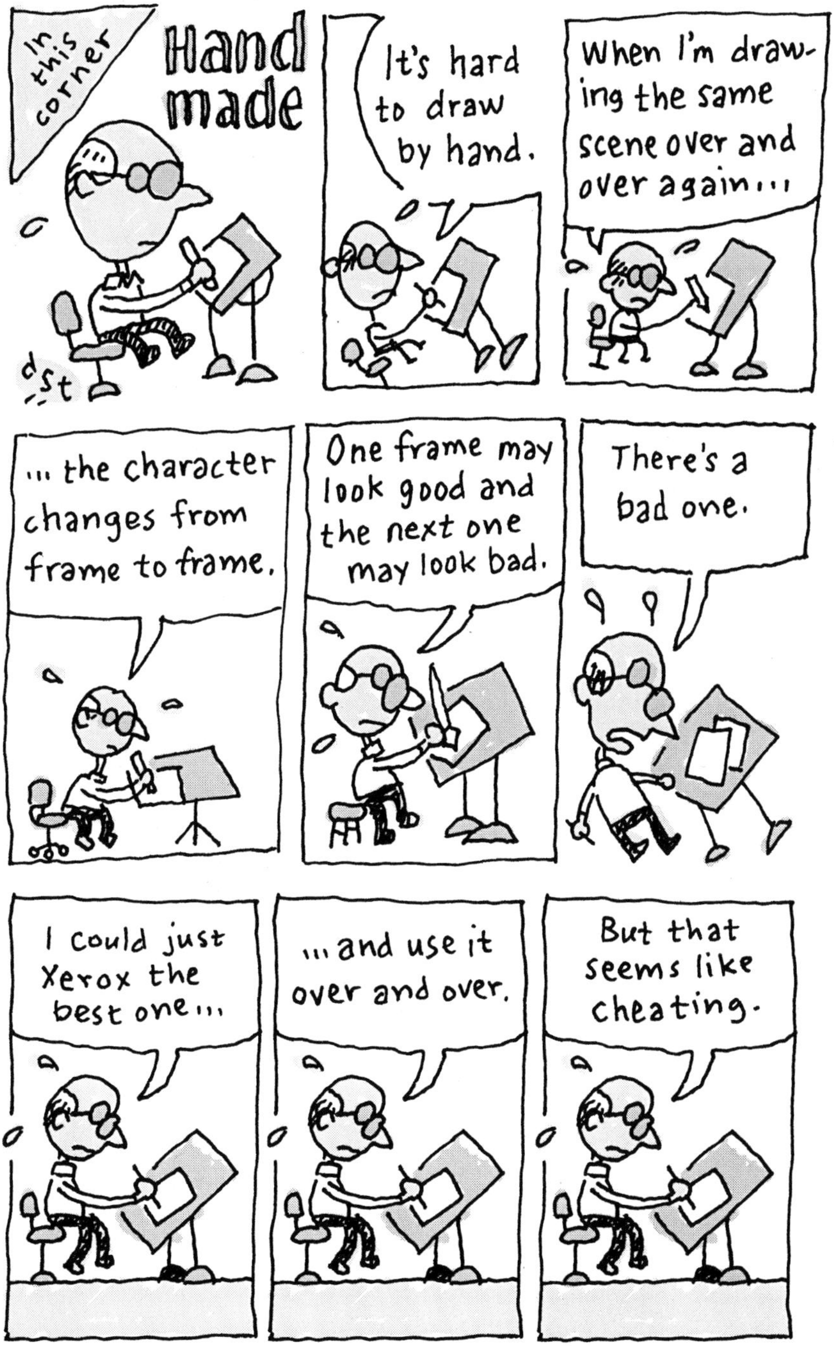

In this corner
Hand made
It's hard to draw by hand.
When I'm drawing the same scene over and over again...
... the character changes from frame to frame.
One frame may look good and the next one may look bad.
There's a bad one.
I could just Xerox the best one...
... and use it over and over.
But that seems like cheating.

June 28, 2007

David Steinlicht, Pioneer Press

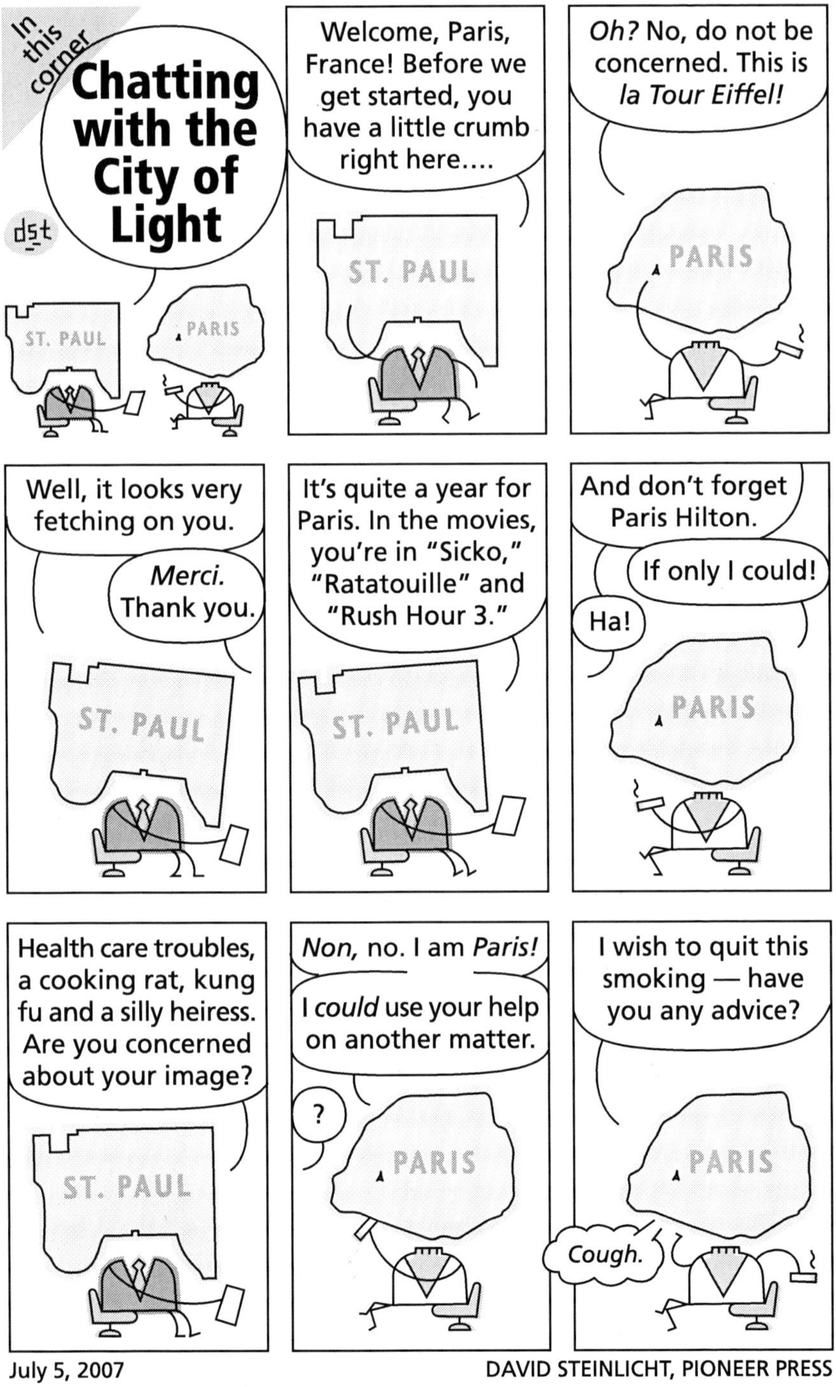
In this corner
Chatting with the City of Light
dst
ST. PAUL
PARIS
Welcome, Paris, France! Before we get started, you have a little crumb right here....
ST. PAUL
Oh? No, do not be concerned. This is la Tour Eiffel!
PARIS
Well, it looks very fetching on you.
Merci. Thank you.
ST. PAUL
It's quite a year for Paris. In the movies, you're in "Sicko," "Ratatouille" and "Rush Hour 3."
ST. PAUL
And don't forget Paris Hilton.
If only I could!
Ha!
PARIS
Health care troubles, a cooking rat, kung fu and a silly heiress. Are you concerned about your image?
ST. PAUL
Non, no. I am Paris!
I could use your help on another matter.
?
PARIS
I wish to quit this smoking — have you any advice?
PARIS
Cough.

July 5, 2007

DAVID STEINLICHT, PIONEER PRESS

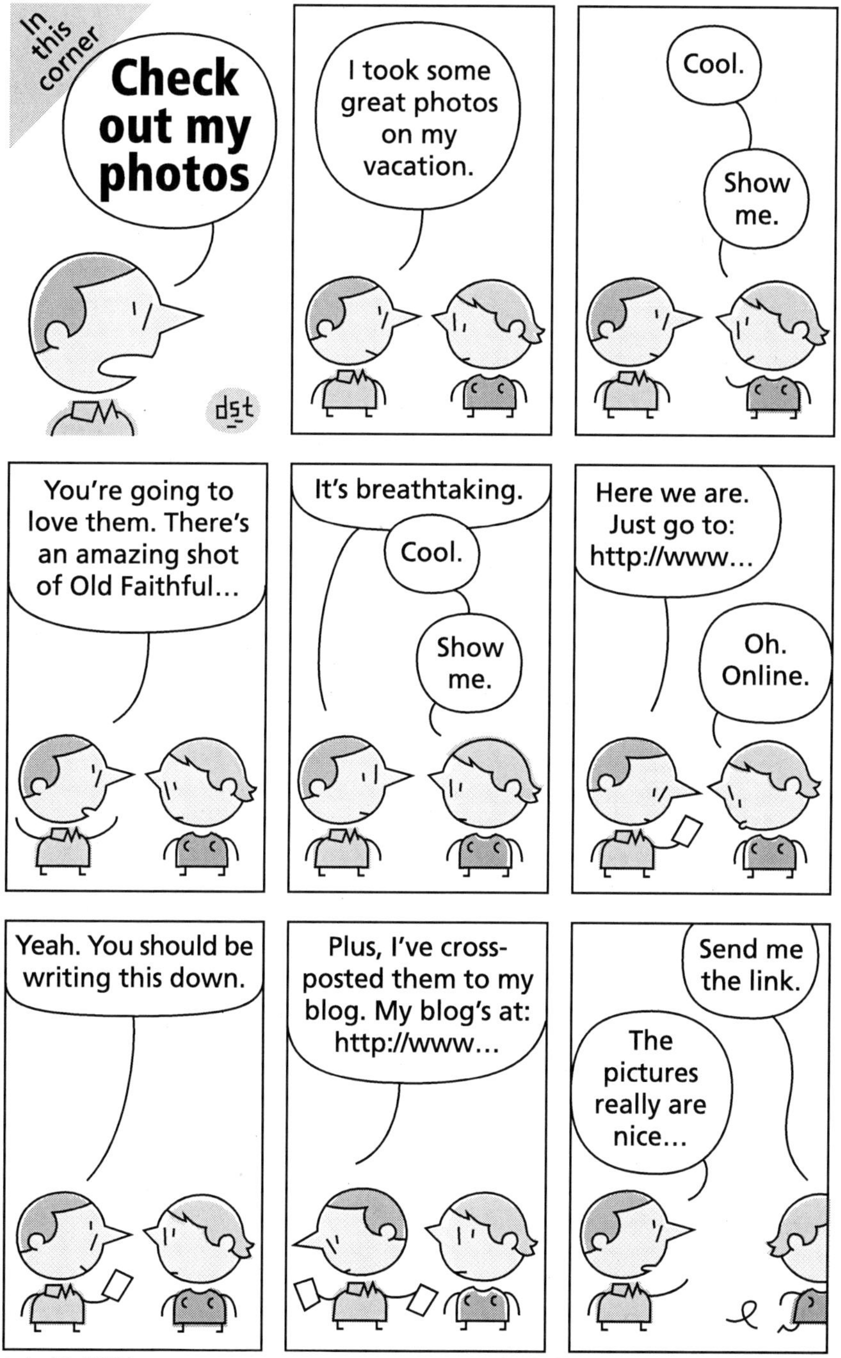

In this corner
Check out my photos
dst
I took some great photos on my vacation.
Cool.
Show me.
You're going to love them. There's an amazing shot of Old Faithful...
It's breathtaking.
Cool.
Show me.
Here we are. Just go to: http://www...
Oh. Online.
Yeah. You should be writing this down.
Plus, I've cross-posted them to my blog. My blog's at: http://www...
Send me the link.
The pictures really are nice...

July 12, 2007

DAVID STEINLICHT, PIONEER PRESS

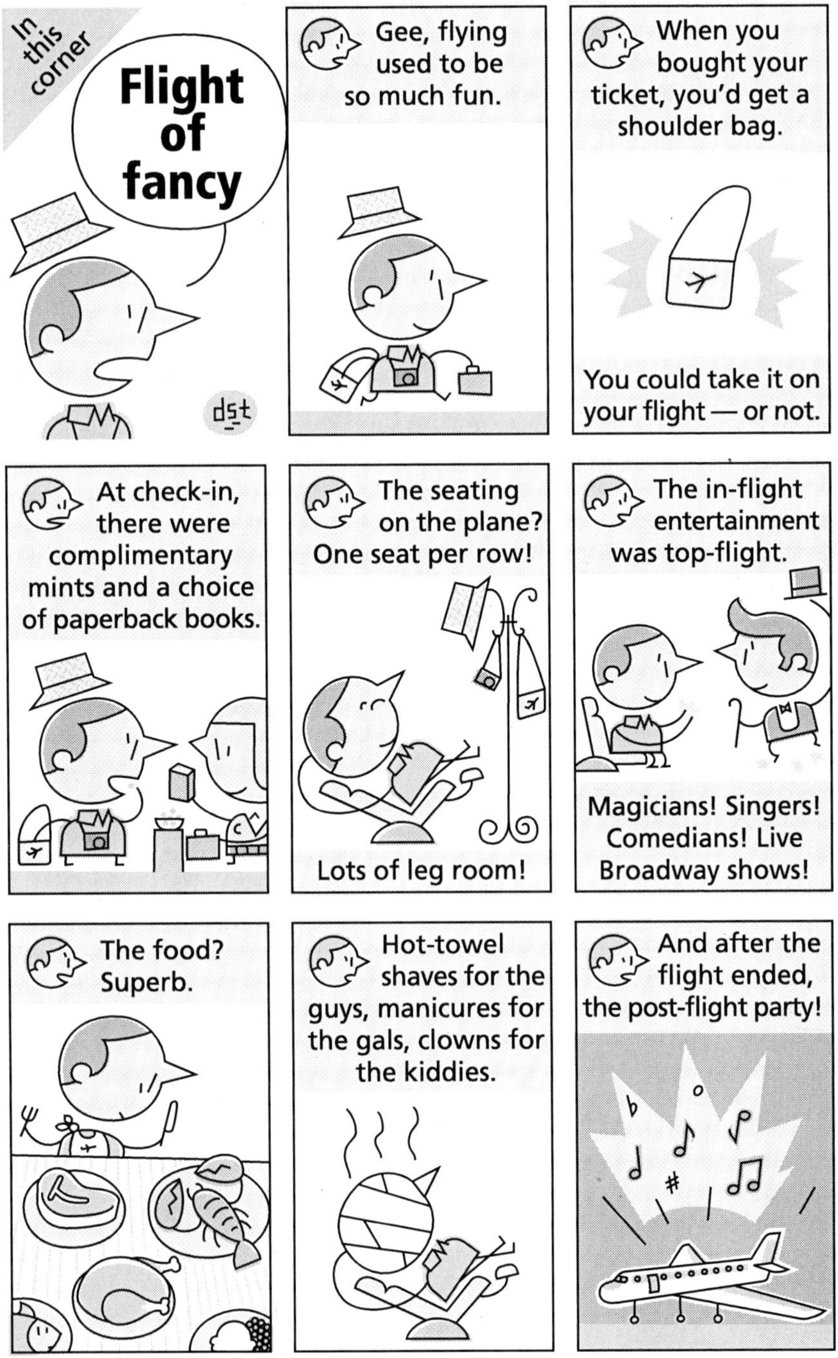
In this corner
Flight of fancy
dst
Gee, flying used to be so much fun.
When you bought your ticket, you'd get a shoulder bag.
You could take it on your flight — or not.
At check-in, there were complimentary mints and a choice of paperback books.
The seating on the plane? One seat per row!
Lots of leg room!
The in-flight entertainment was top-flight.
Magicians! Singers! Comedians! Live Broadway shows!
The food? Superb.
Hot-towel shaves for the guys, manicures for the gals, clowns for the kiddies.
And after the flight ended, the post-flight party!

July 19, 2007

DAVID STEINLICHT, PIONEER PRESS

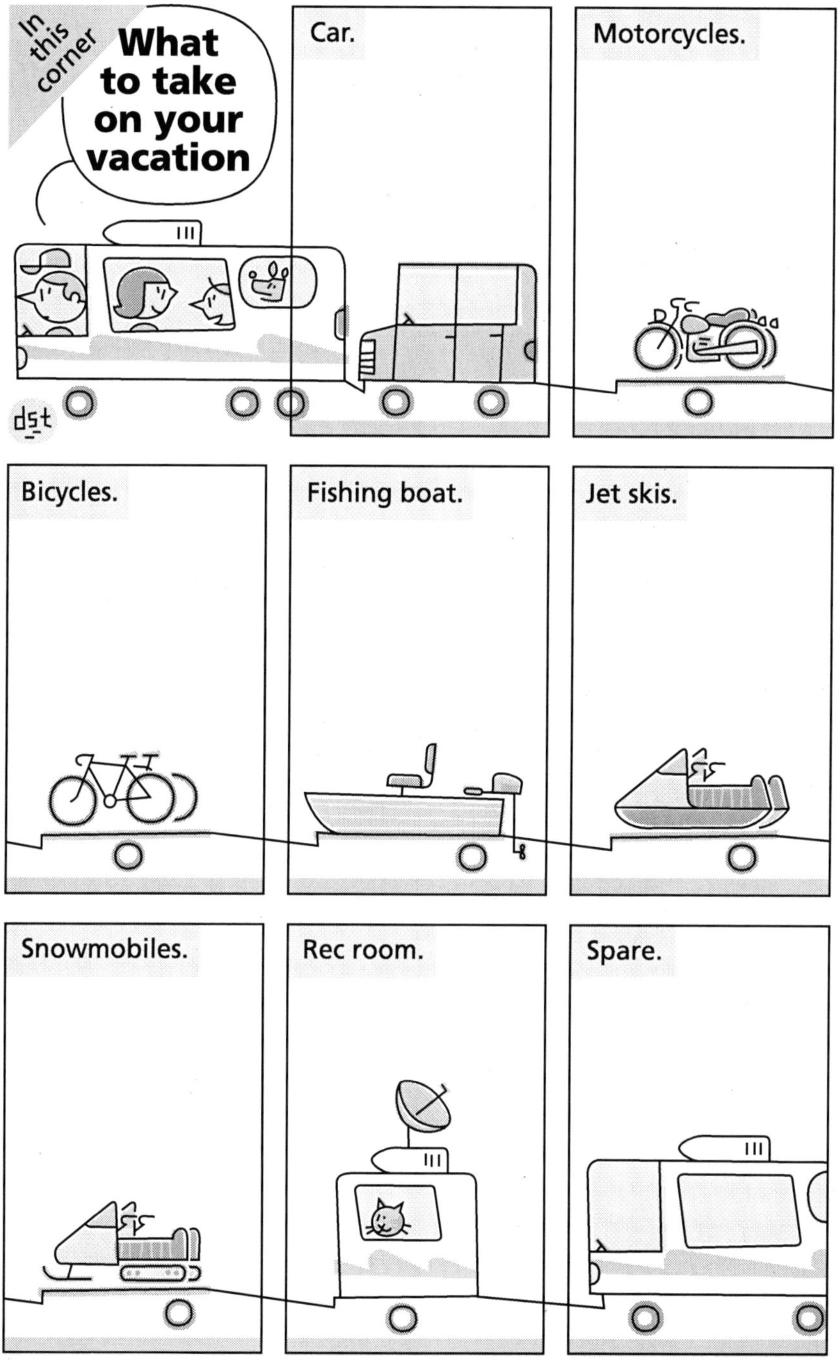
In this corner
What to take on your vacation
Car.
Motorcycles.
Bicycles.
Fishing boat.
Jet skis.
Snowmobiles.
Rec room.
Spare.

July 26, 2007

DAVID STEINLICHT, PIONEER PRESS

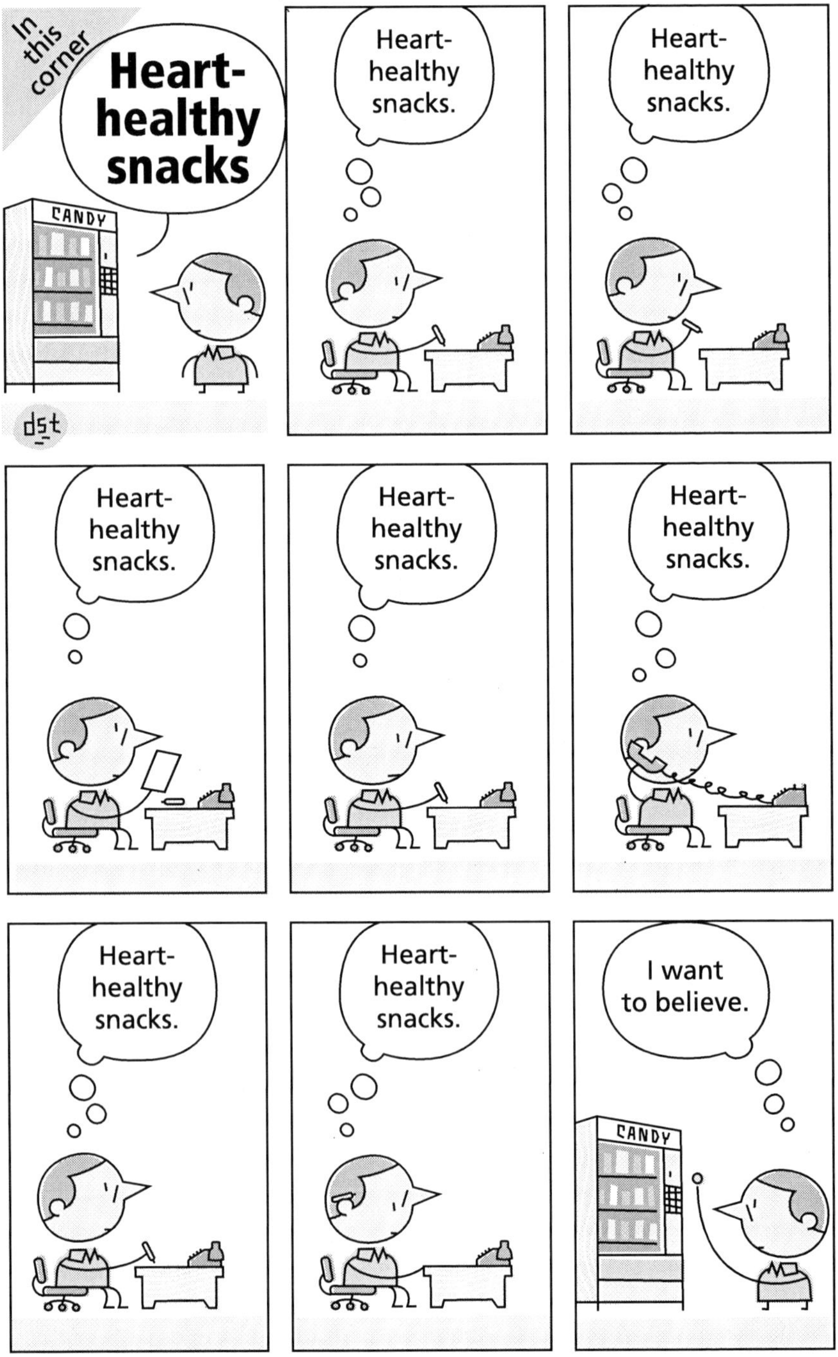
In this corner
Heart-healthy snacks
CANDY
Heart-healthy snacks.
Heart-healthy snacks.
Heart-healthy snacks.
Heart-healthy snacks.
Heart-healthy snacks.
Heart-healthy snacks.
Heart-healthy snacks.
I want to believe.
CANDY

Aug. 2, 2007

DAVID STEINLICHT, PIONEER PRESS

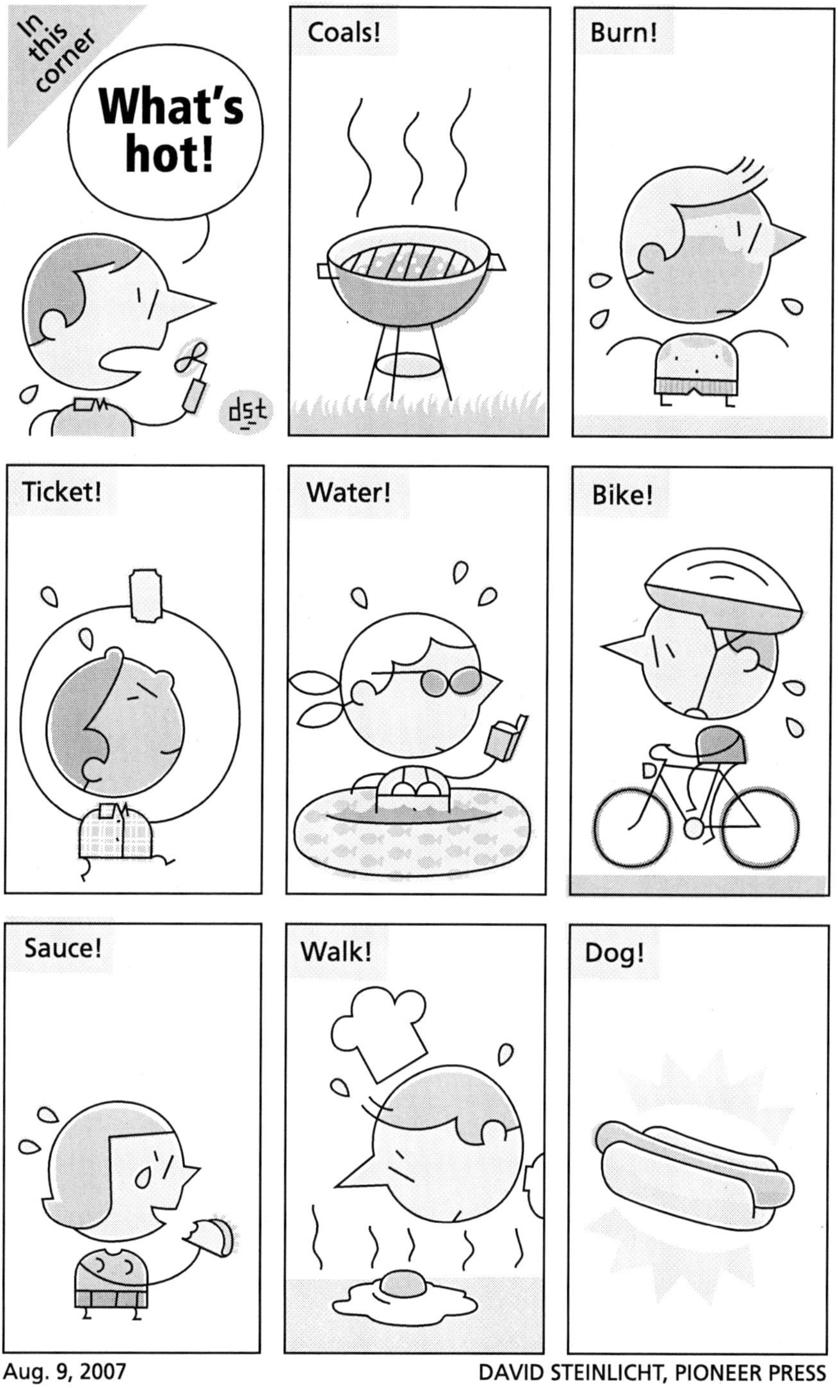
In this corner
What's hot!
dst
Coals!
Burn!
Ticket!
Water!
Bike!
Sauce!
Walk!
Dog!

Aug. 9, 2007

DAVID STEINLICHT, PIONEER PRESS

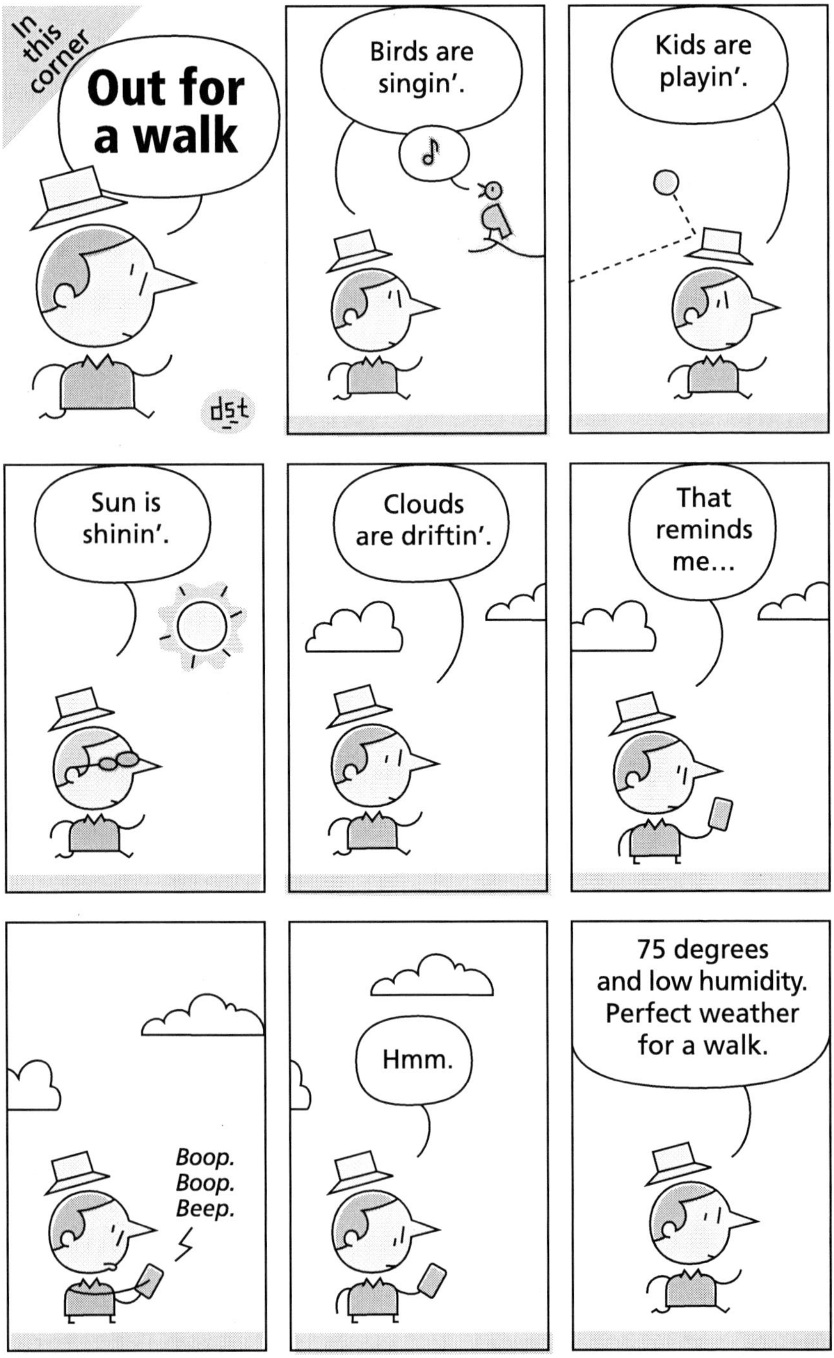
In this corner
Out for a walk
dst
Birds are singin'.
Kids are playin'.
Sun is shinin'.
Clouds are driftin'.
That reminds me…
Boop. Boop. Beep.
Hmm.
75 degrees and low humidity. Perfect weather for a walk.

Aug. 16, 2007

DAVID STEINLICHT, PIONEER PRESS

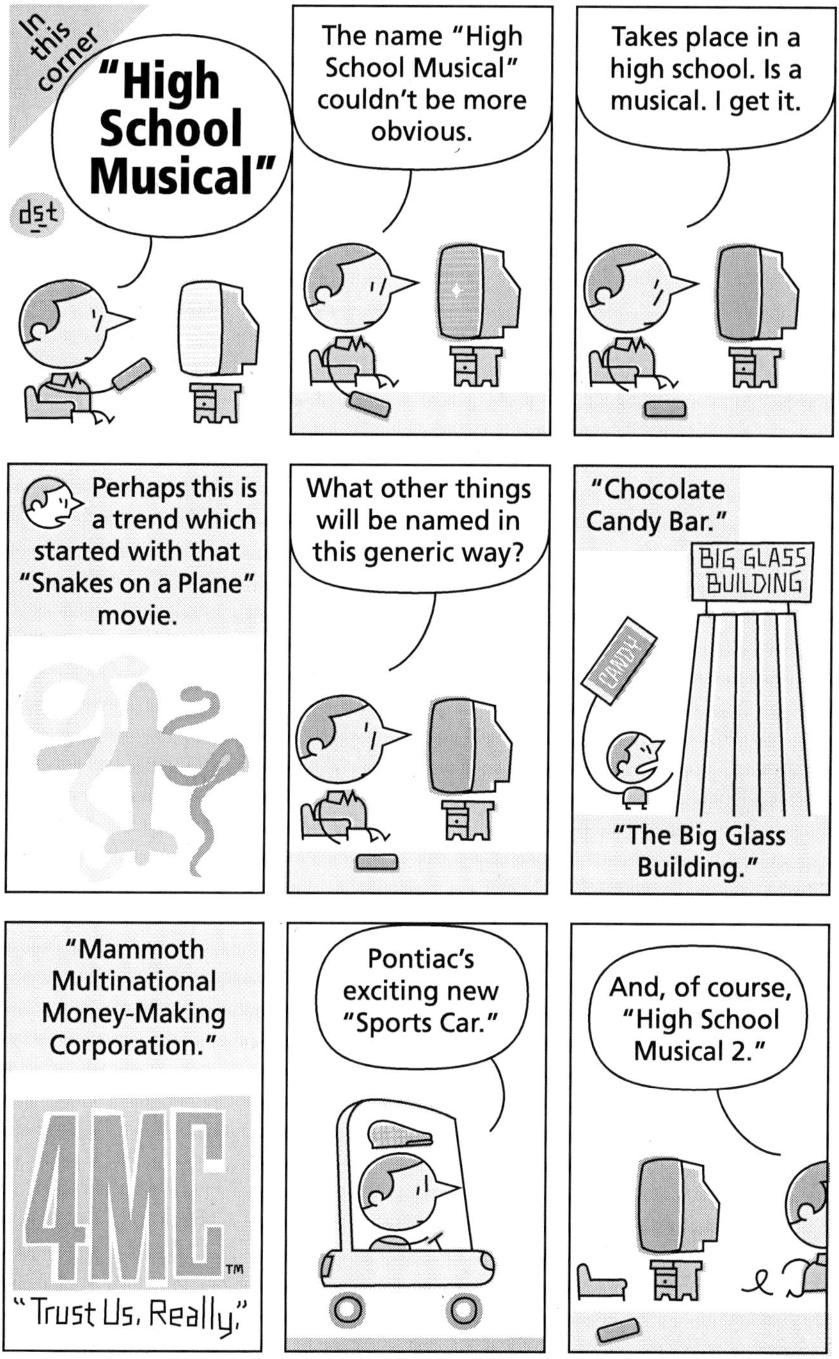
In this corner
"High School Musical"
dst
The name "High School Musical" couldn't be more obvious.
Takes place in a high school. Is a musical. I get it.
Perhaps this is a trend which started with that "Snakes on a Plane" movie.
What other things will be named in this generic way?
"Chocolate Candy Bar."
CANDY
BIG GLASS BUILDING
"The Big Glass Building."
"Mammoth Multinational Money-Making Corporation."
4MC™
"Trust Us, Really."
Pontiac's exciting new "Sports Car."
And, of course, "High School Musical 2."

Aug. 24, 2007

DAVID STEINLICHT, PIONEER PRESS

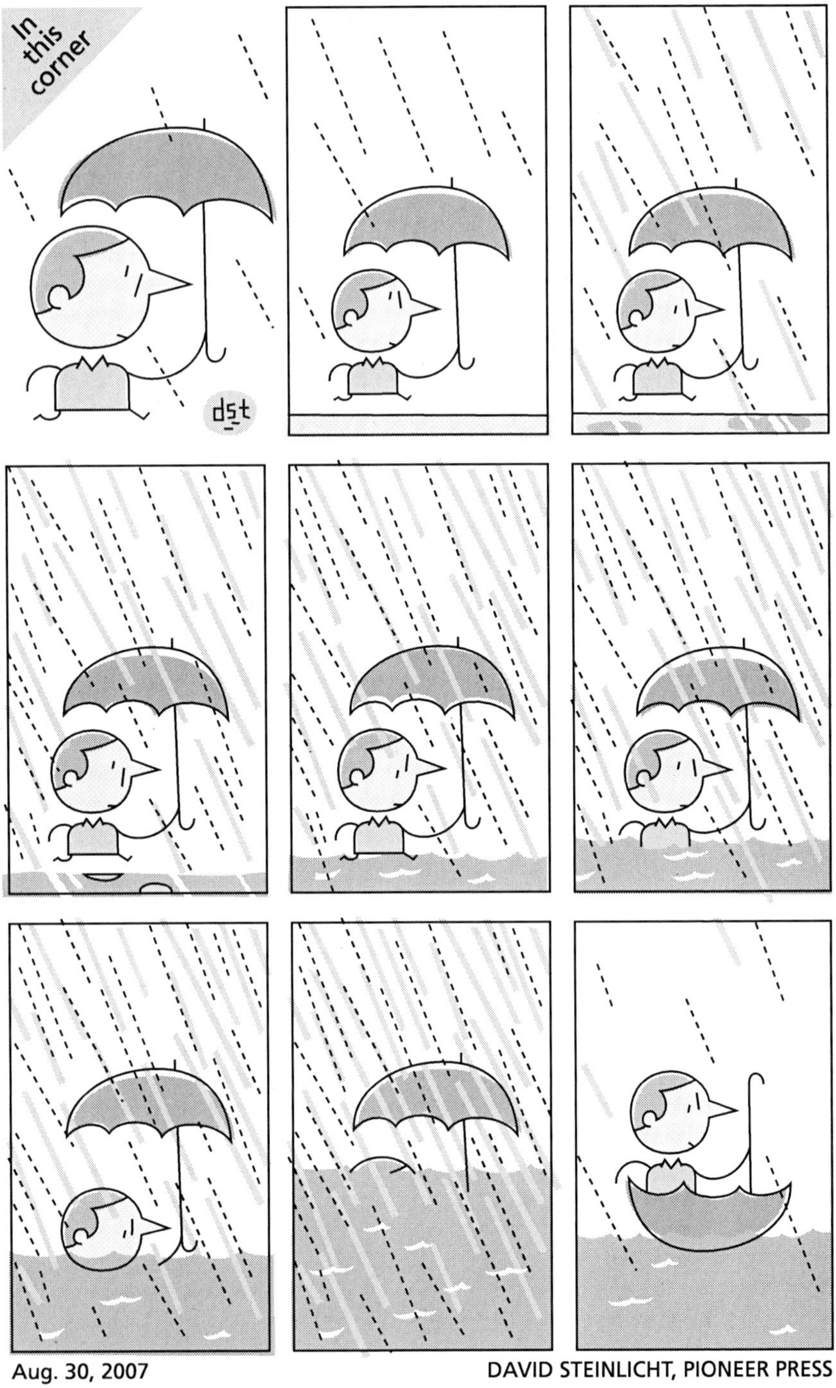
In this corner
dst

Aug. 30, 2007

DAVID STEINLICHT, PIONEER PRESS

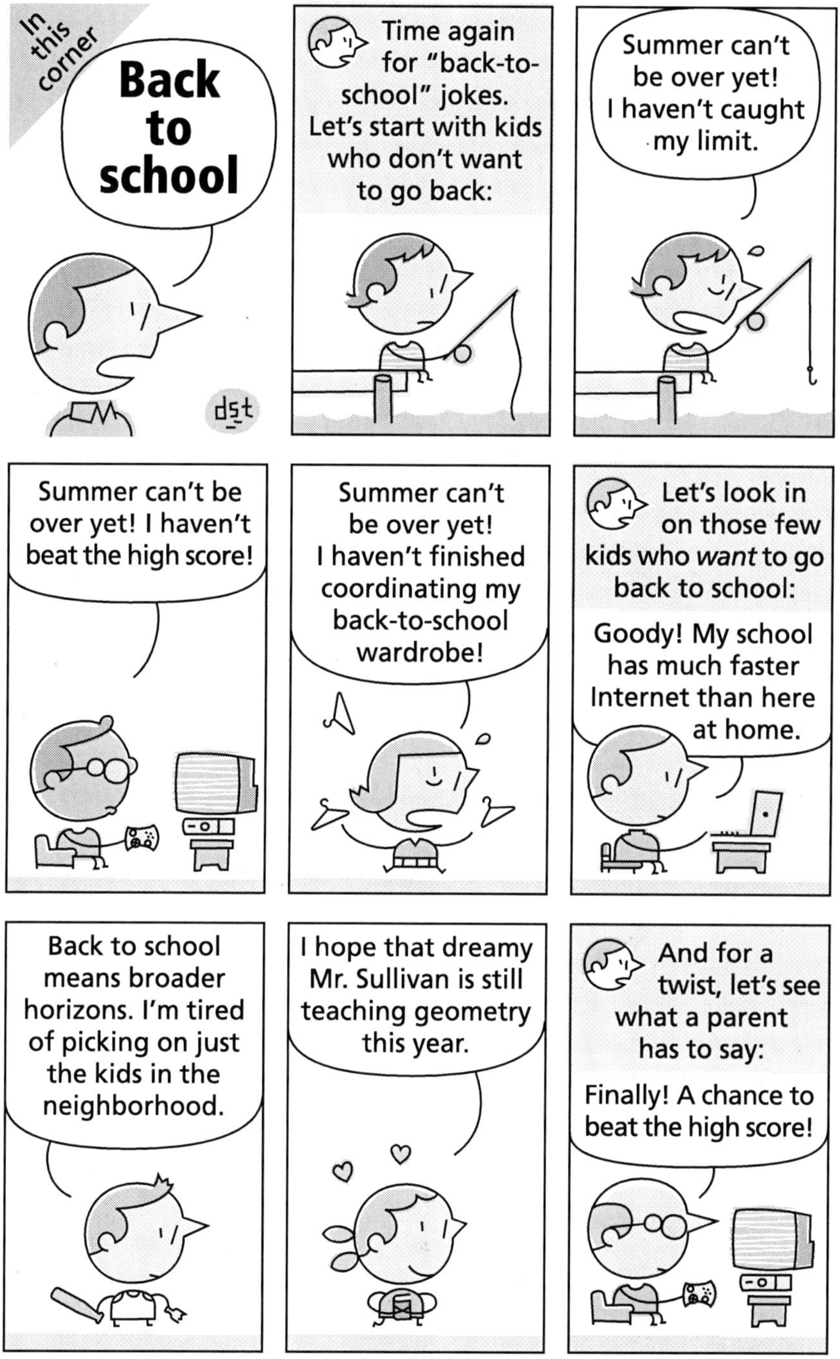
In this corner
Back to school
dst
Time again for "back-to-school" jokes. Let's start with kids who don't want to go back:
Summer can't be over yet! I haven't caught my limit.
Summer can't be over yet! I haven't beat the high score!
Summer can't be over yet! I haven't finished coordinating my back-to-school wardrobe!
Let's look in on those few kids who *want* to go back to school:
Goody! My school has much faster Internet than here at home.
Back to school means broader horizons. I'm tired of picking on just the kids in the neighborhood.
I hope that dreamy Mr. Sullivan is still teaching geometry this year.
And for a twist, let's see what a parent has to say:
Finally! A chance to beat the high score!

Sept. 7, 2007

DAVID STEINLICHT, PIONEER PRESS

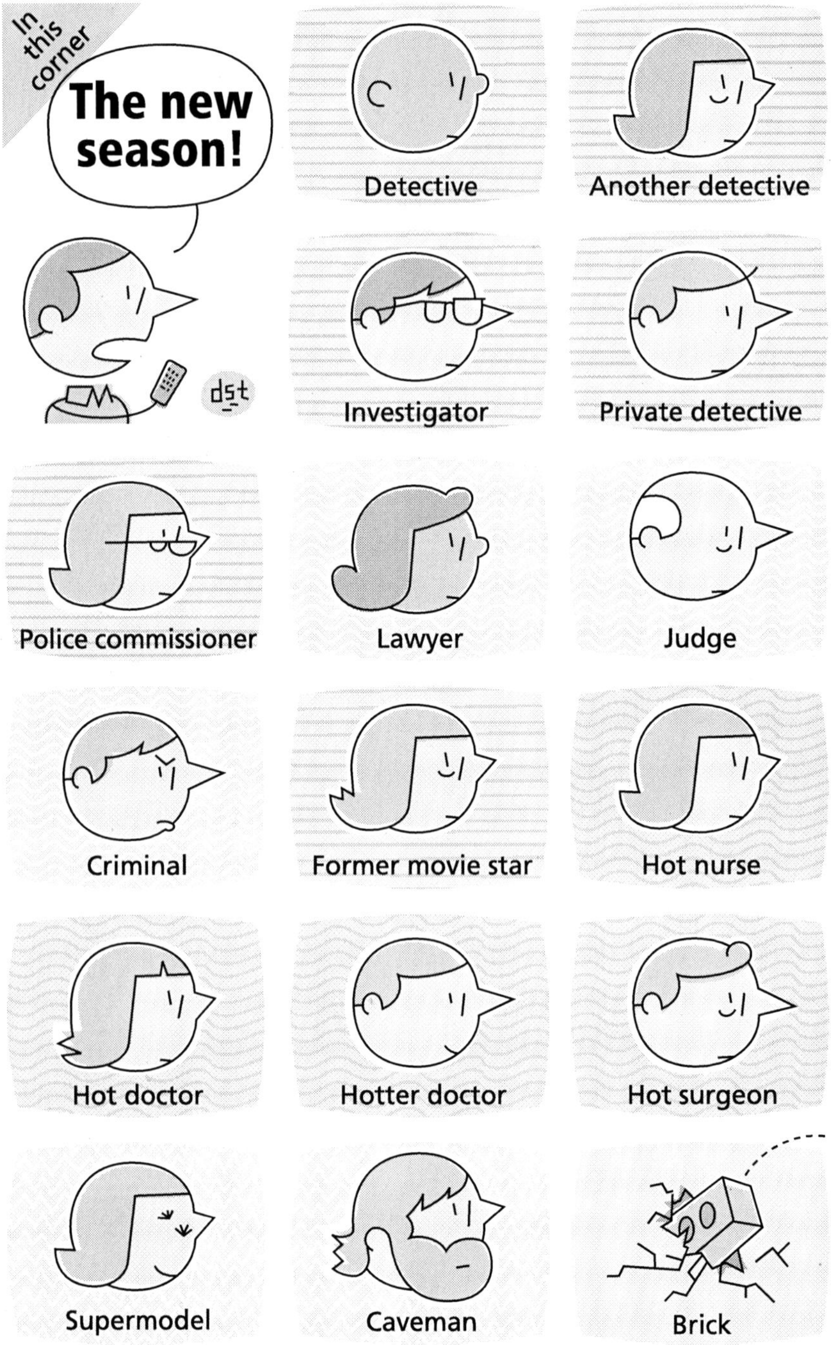
In this corner
The new season!
dst
Detective
Another detective
Investigator
Private detective
Police commissioner
Lawyer
Judge
Criminal
Former movie star
Hot nurse
Hot doctor
Hotter doctor
Hot surgeon
Supermodel
Caveman
Brick

Sept. 14, 2007

DAVID STEINLICHT, PIONEER PRESS

 Note: Anyone remember the *Caveman* television show? Me neither.

In this corner

Nifty features of new $5 bill

A few of the hard-to-copy printing techniques incorporated into official United States currency. Look for them!

dst

Very nice portrait of Abraham Lincoln. He was one of the presidents of the United States.

Bald eagles. Make certain they are bald and not just "balding." Many counterfeiters don't know the difference.

Make certain it says "5" in all four corners of the bill. If one of the numbers is "6," you may have a phony bill!

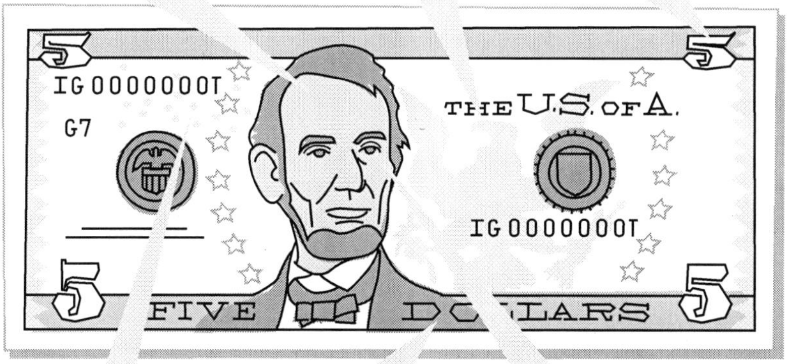

IG 00000000T
G7
THE U.S. OF A.
IG 00000000T
FIVE

There's a smattering of golden "5s" that look like someone sneezed all over the left side of the bill. Eeew!

Run your fingernail lightly across the bottom of the bill where it says "Five Dollars." Listen carefully. Do you hear, "Oh, say, can you see..."? You don't? Neither do I. Wouldn't it be cool if we did?

Look at Lincoln's eyes. They're focused slightly to your right. What's *that* all about?

Hold the bill up to the light. Does light pass through it? Is it printed on plastic? If the bill is printed on plastic — beware.

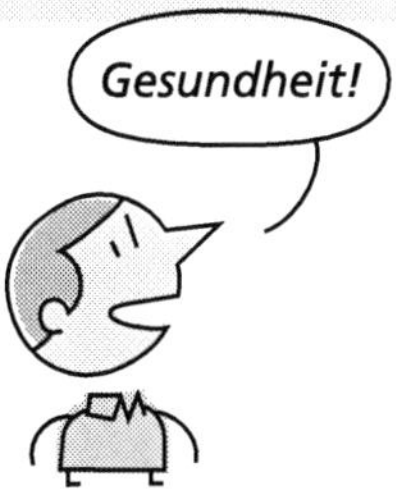

Gesundheit!

When held under a black light, the entire bill looks really weird. All the light areas turn this really bright purple color! Whoa!

Sept. 28, 2007

DAVID STEINLICHT, PIONEER PRESS

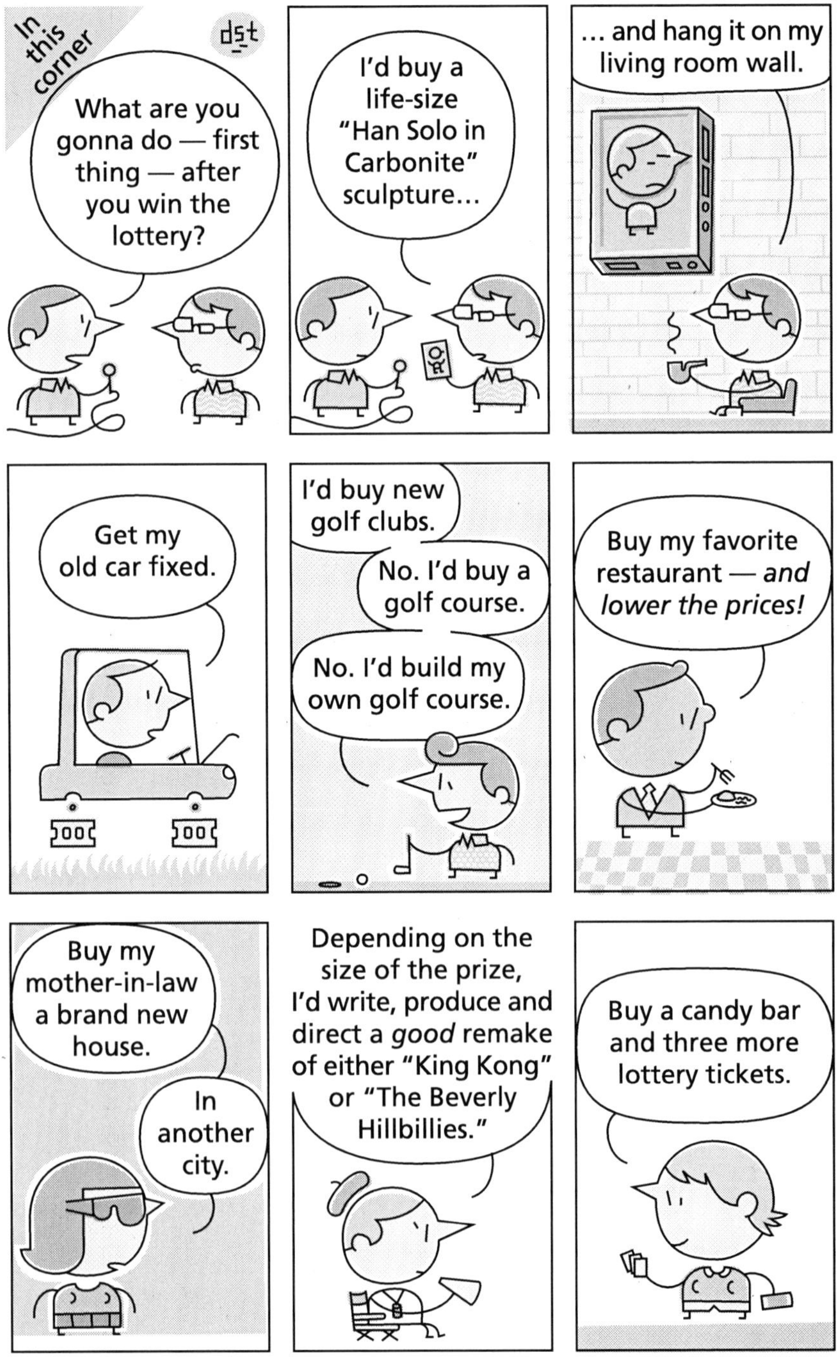
In this corner
dst
What are you gonna do — first thing — after you win the lottery?
I'd buy a life-size "Han Solo in Carbonite" sculpture...
... and hang it on my living room wall.
Get my old car fixed.
I'd buy new golf clubs.
No. I'd buy a golf course.
No. I'd build my own golf course.
Buy my favorite restaurant — *and lower the prices!*
Buy my mother-in-law a brand new house.
In another city.
Depending on the size of the prize, I'd write, produce and direct a *good* remake of either "King Kong" or "The Beverly Hillbillies."
Buy a candy bar and three more lottery tickets.

Oct. 5, 2007 DAVID STEINLICHT, PIONEER PRESS

Note: That's Julio Ojeda-Zapata who's getting the life-sized Han Solo in carbonite, Dennis Lien with the old car and Dan Kelly with the golf course. Good luck, fellas!

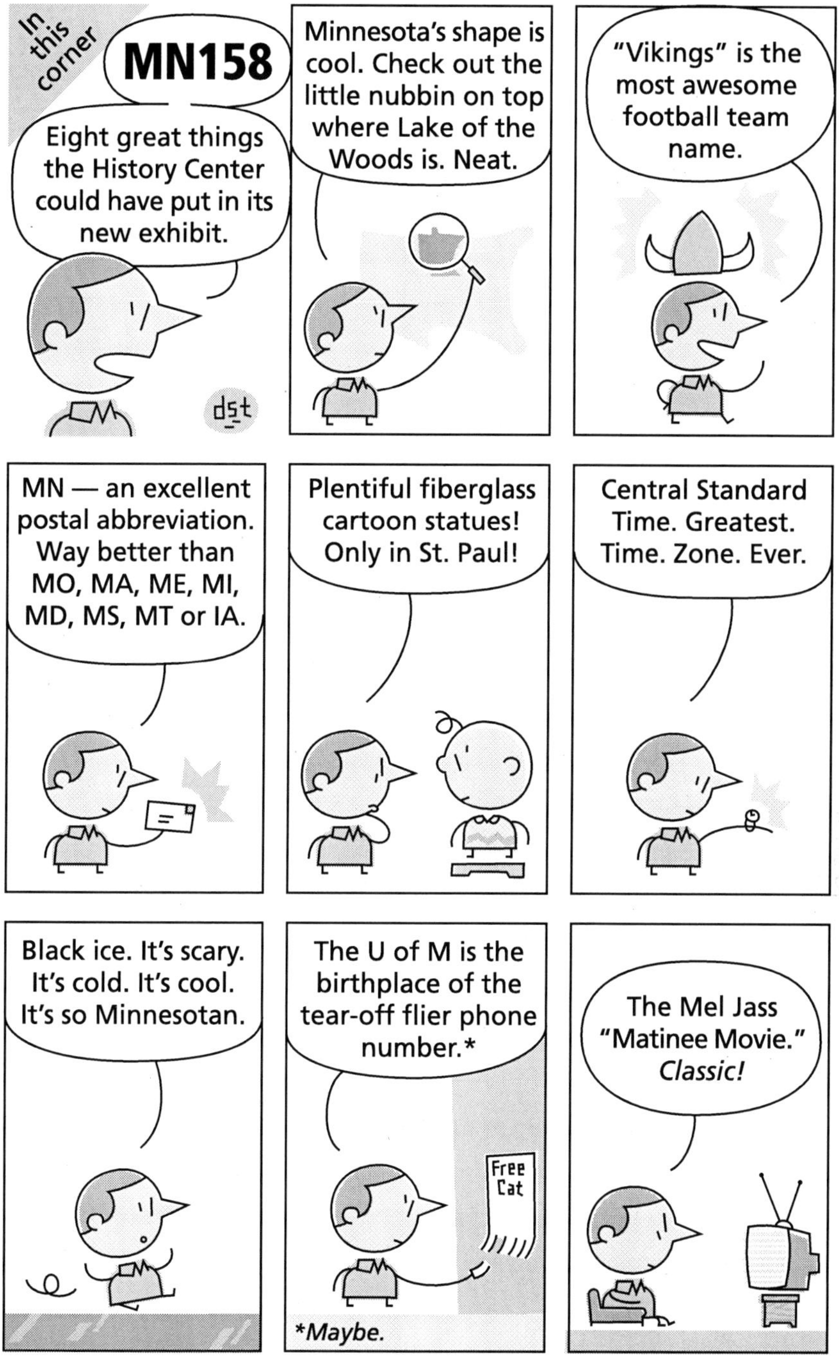
In this corner
MN158
Eight great things the History Center could have put in its new exhibit.
dst
Minnesota's shape is cool. Check out the little nubbin on top where Lake of the Woods is. Neat.
"Vikings" is the most awesome football team name.
MN — an excellent postal abbreviation. Way better than MO, MA, ME, MI, MD, MS, MT or IA.
Plentiful fiberglass cartoon statues! Only in St. Paul!
Central Standard Time. Greatest. Time. Zone. Ever.
Black ice. It's scary. It's cold. It's cool. It's so Minnesotan.
The U of M is the birthplace of the tear-off flier phone number.*
Free Cat
*Maybe.
The Mel Jass "Matinee Movie." *Classic!*

Oct. 12, 2007

DAVID STEINLICHT, PIONEER PRESS

Note: To celebrate Minnesota's whatchama-tennial (150 years) the Minnesota History Center picked 150 great things about the state. I picked eight more.

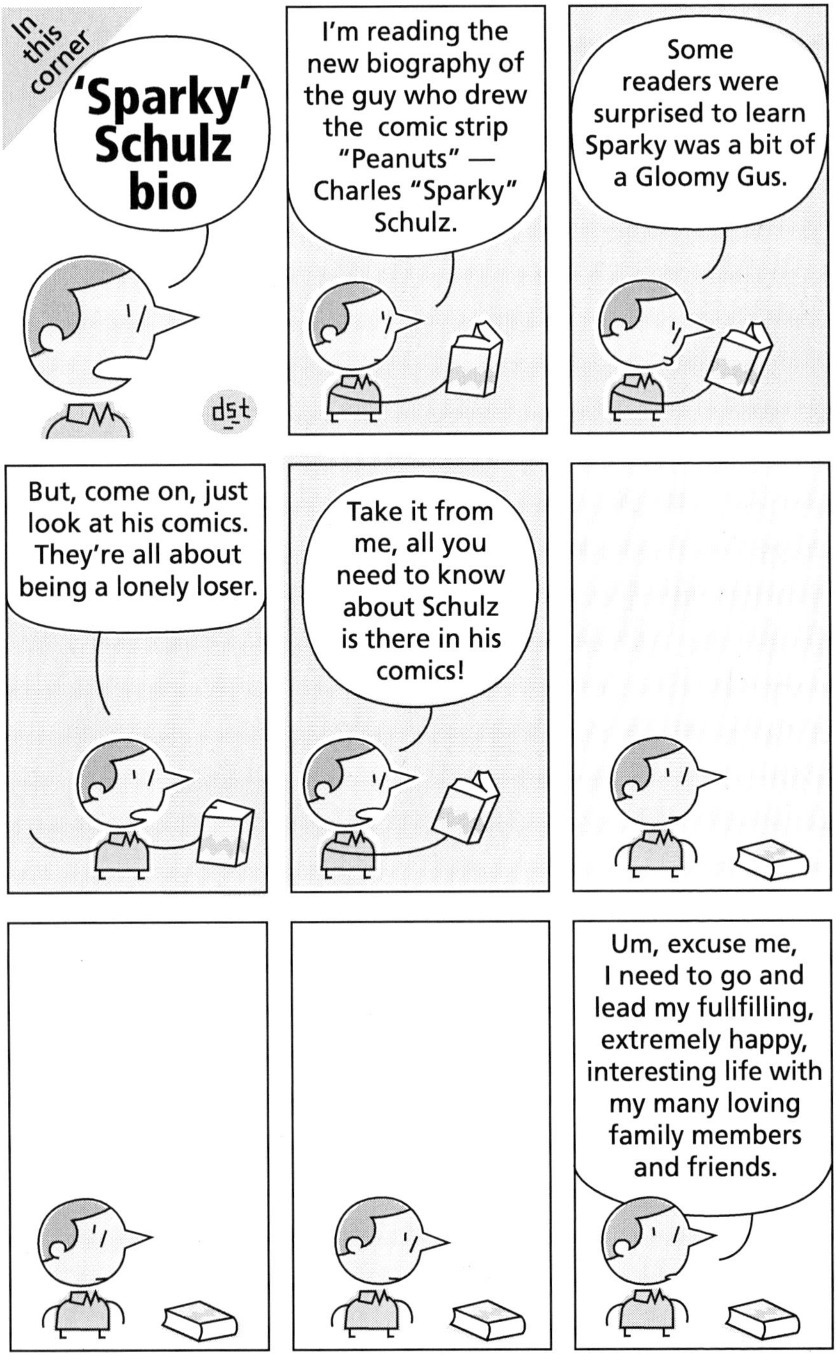
In this corner
'Sparky' Schulz bio
dst
I'm reading the new biography of the guy who drew the comic strip "Peanuts" — Charles "Sparky" Schulz.
Some readers were surprised to learn Sparky was a bit of a Gloomy Gus.
But, come on, just look at his comics. They're all about being a lonely loser.
Take it from me, all you need to know about Schulz is there in his comics!
Um, excuse me, I need to go and lead my fullfilling, extremely happy, interesting life with my many loving family members and friends.

Oct. 19, 2007

DAVID STEINLICHT, PIONEER PRESS

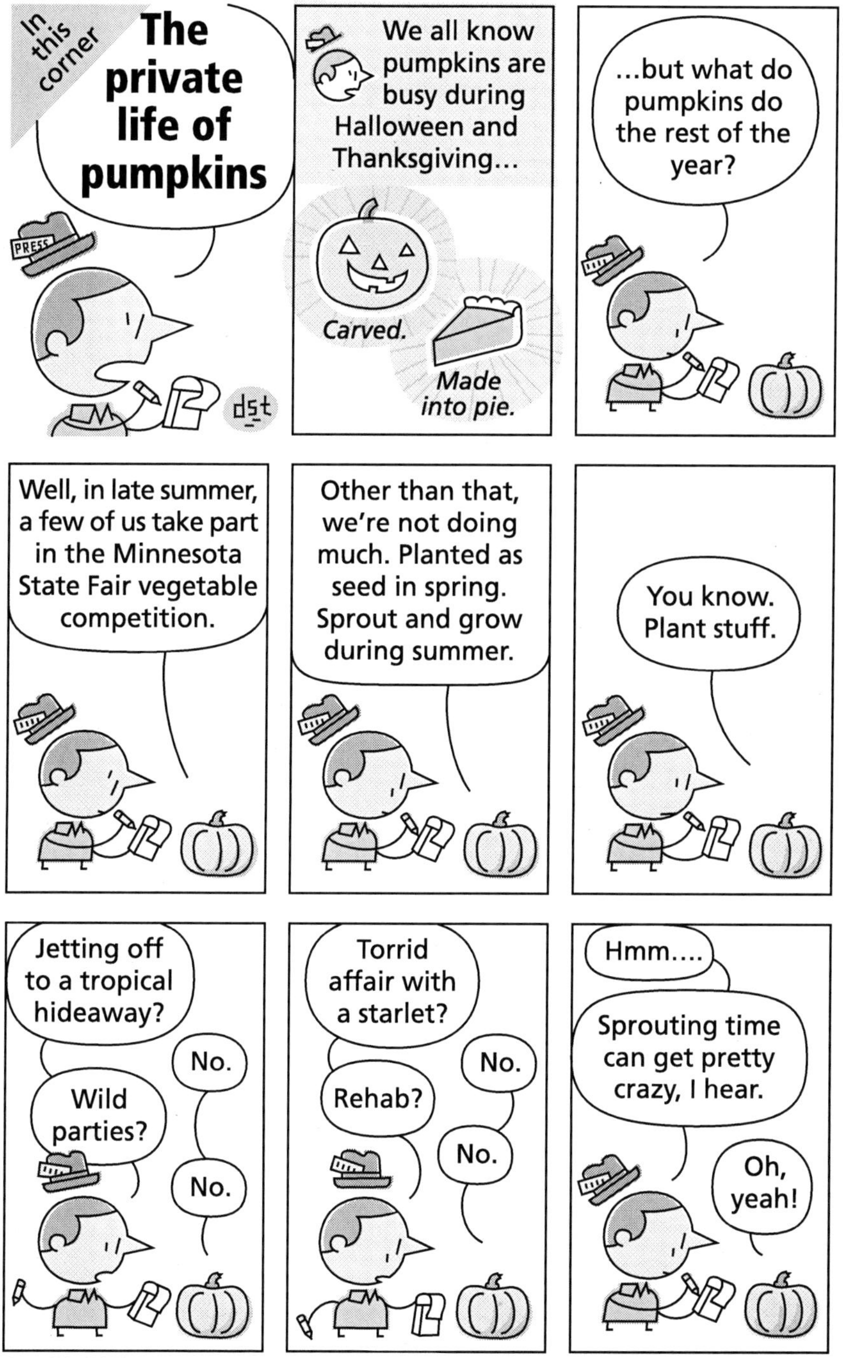
In this corner
The private life of pumpkins
PRESS
dst
We all know pumpkins are busy during Halloween and Thanksgiving...
Carved.
Made into pie.
...but what do pumpkins do the rest of the year?
Well, in late summer, a few of us take part in the Minnesota State Fair vegetable competition.
Other than that, we're not doing much. Planted as seed in spring. Sprout and grow during summer.
You know. Plant stuff.
Jetting off to a tropical hideaway?
No.
Wild parties?
No.
Torrid affair with a starlet?
No.
Rehab?
No.
Hmm....
Sprouting time can get pretty crazy, I hear.
Oh, yeah!

Oct. 31, 2007

DAVID STEINLICHT, PIONEER PRESS

Note: Reporters sometimes go after a story that doesn't really turn out to be the story it promised to be. But, they come back with a story anyway!

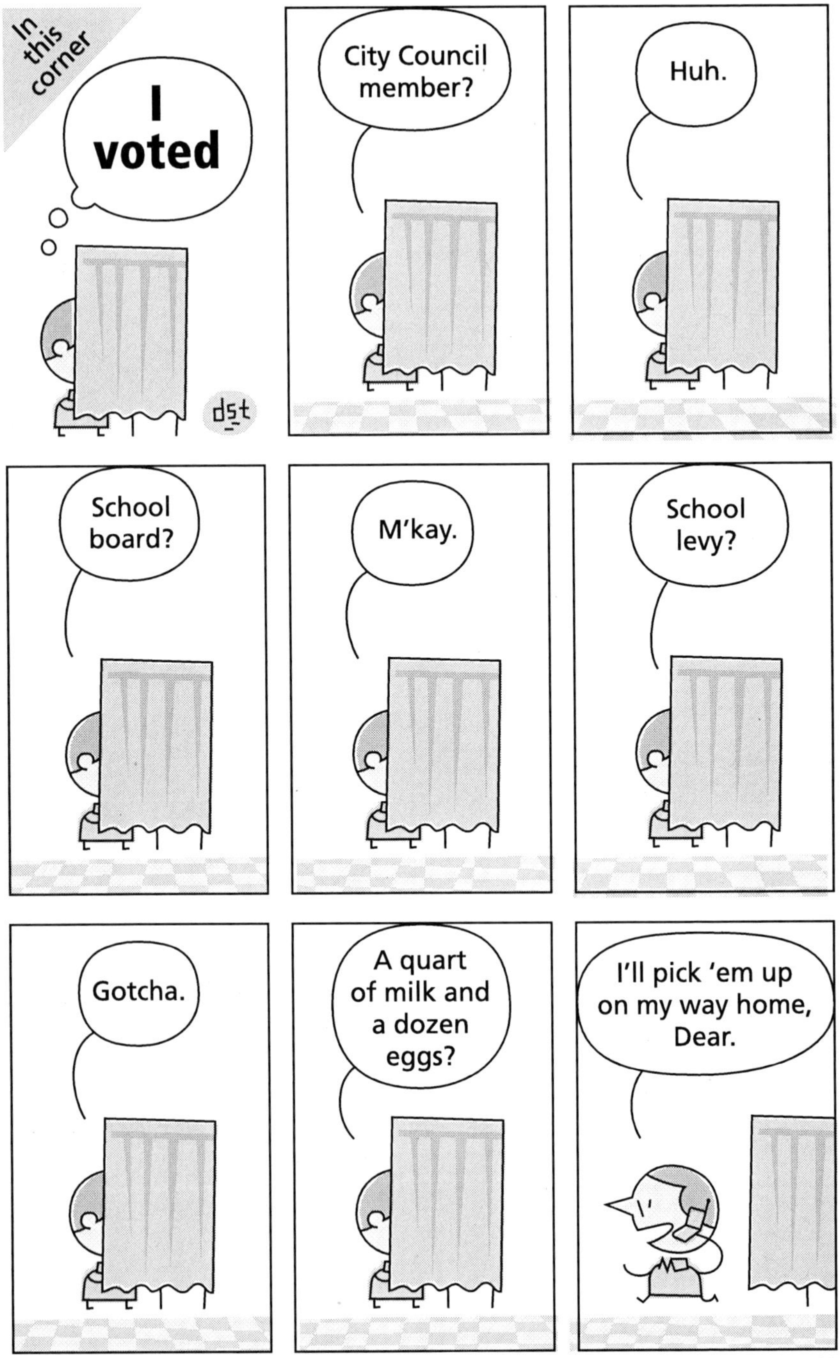
In this corner
I voted
dst
City Council member?
Huh.
School board?
M'kay.
School levy?
Gotcha.
A quart of milk and a dozen eggs?
I'll pick 'em up on my way home, Dear.

Nov. 2, 2007

DAVID STEINLICHT, PIONEER PRESS

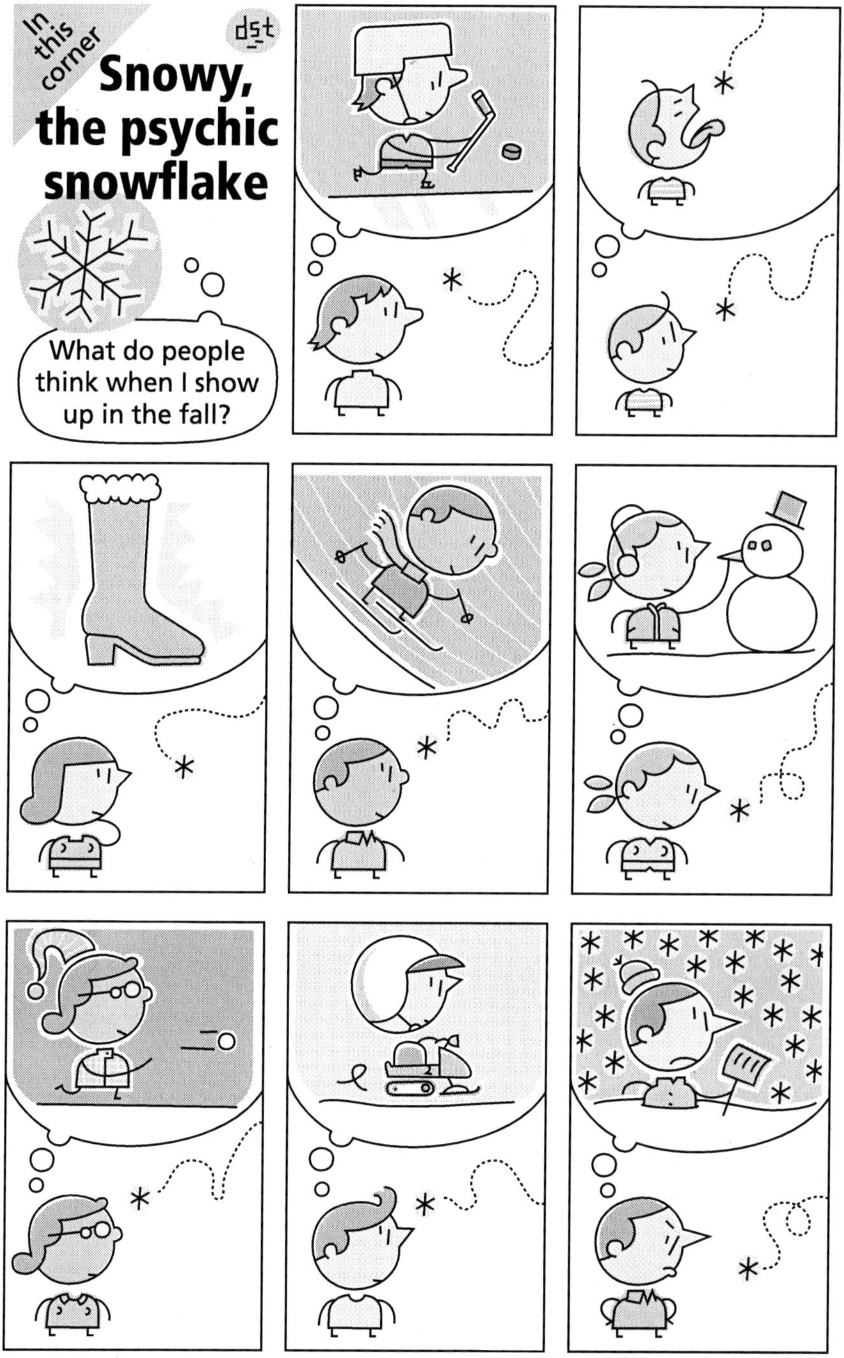

In this corner
dst
Snowy, the psychic snowflake
What do people think when I show up in the fall?

Nov. 9, 2007

DAVID STEINLICHT, PIONEER PRESS

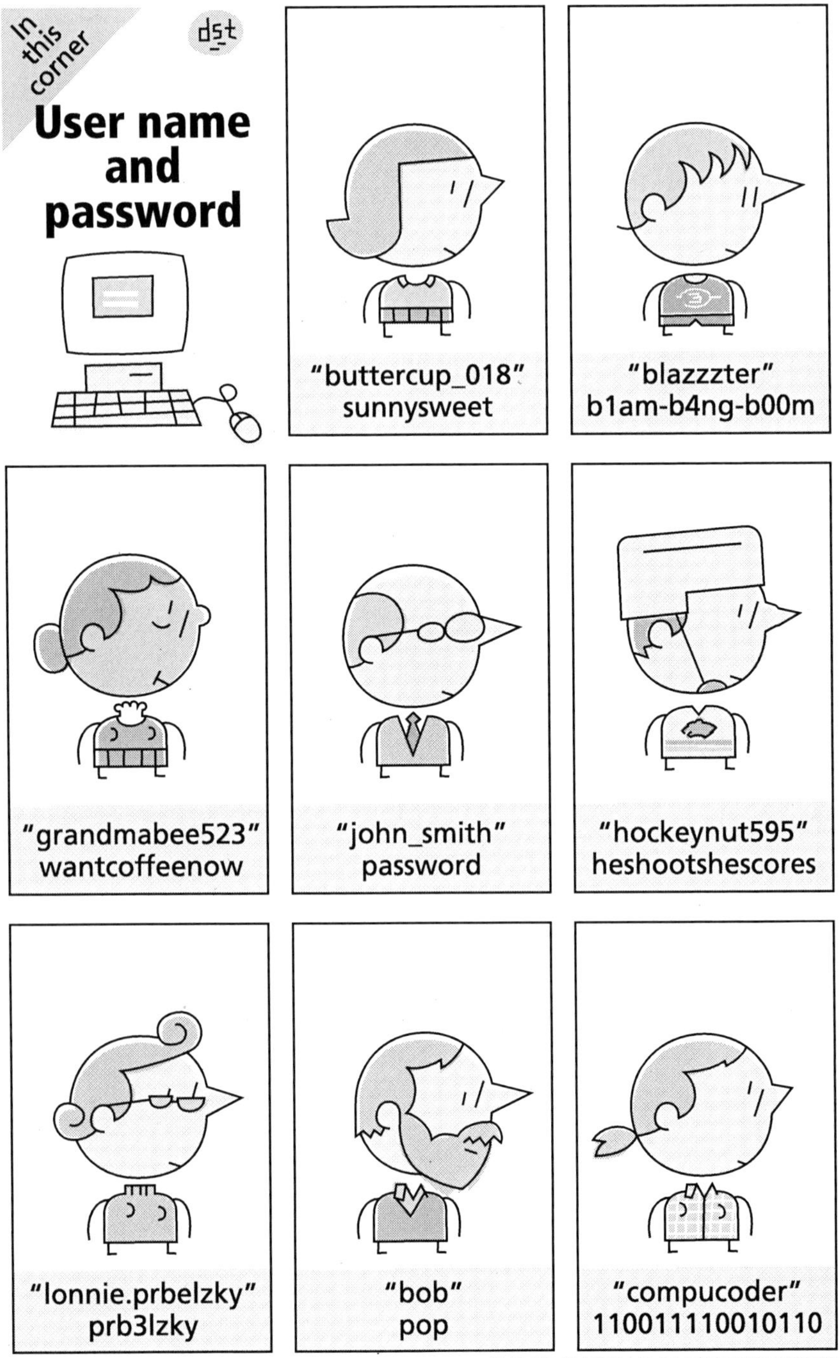
In this corner
dst
User name and password
"buttercup_018"
sunnysweet
"blazzzter"
b1am-b4ng-b00m
"grandmabee523"
wantcoffeenow
"john_smith"
password
"hockeynut595"
heshootshescores
"lonnie.prbelzky"
prb3lzky
"bob"
pop
"compucoder"
110011110010110

Nov. 16, 2007

DAVID STEINLICHT, PIONEER PRESS

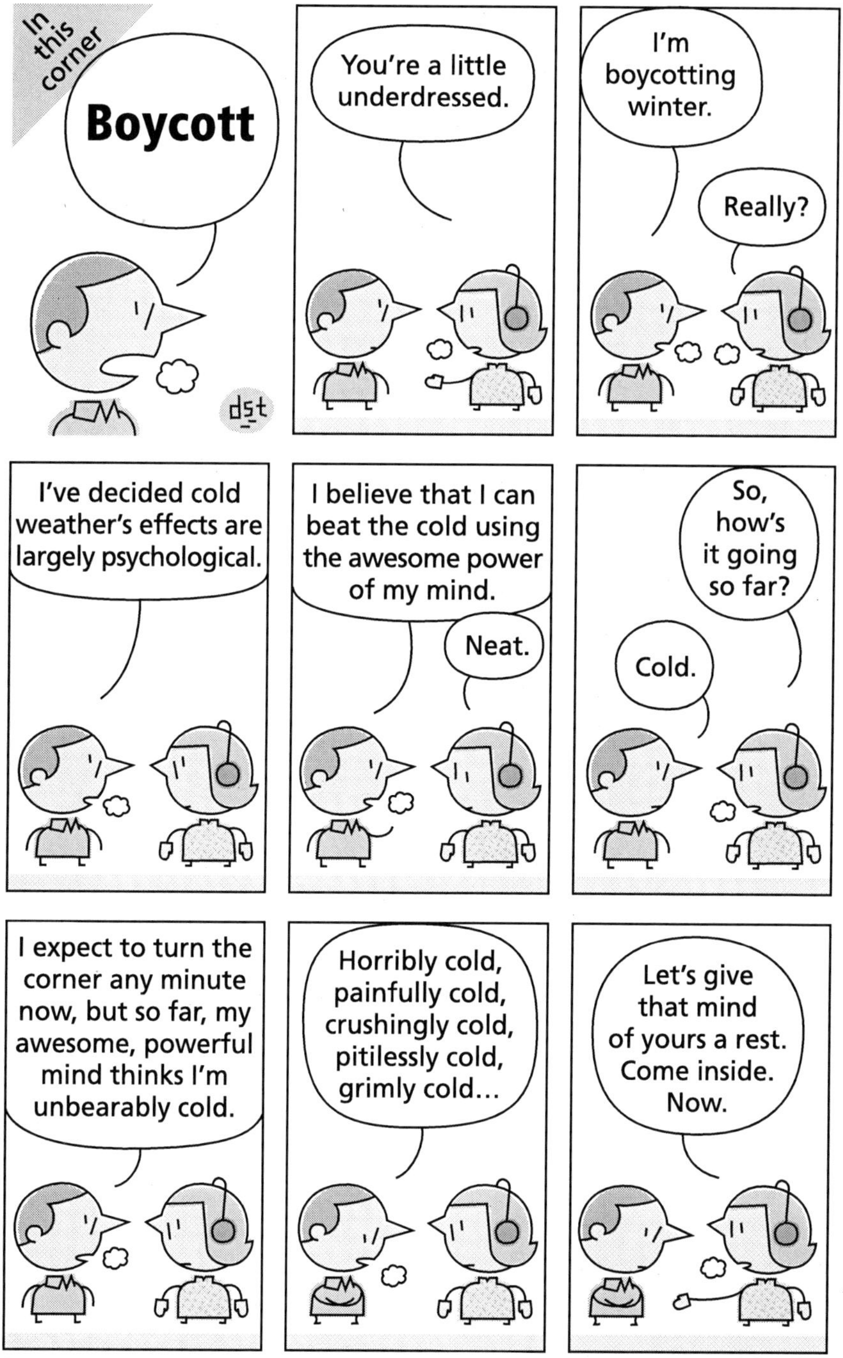

In this corner
Boycott
dst
You're a little underdressed.
I'm boycotting winter.
Really?
I've decided cold weather's effects are largely psychological.
I believe that I can beat the cold using the awesome power of my mind.
Neat.
So, how's it going so far?
Cold.
I expect to turn the corner any minute now, but so far, my awesome, powerful mind thinks I'm unbearably cold.
Horribly cold, painfully cold, crushingly cold, pitilessly cold, grimly cold…
Let's give that mind of yours a rest. Come inside. Now.

Nov. 23, 2007

DAVID STEINLICHT, PIONEER PRESS

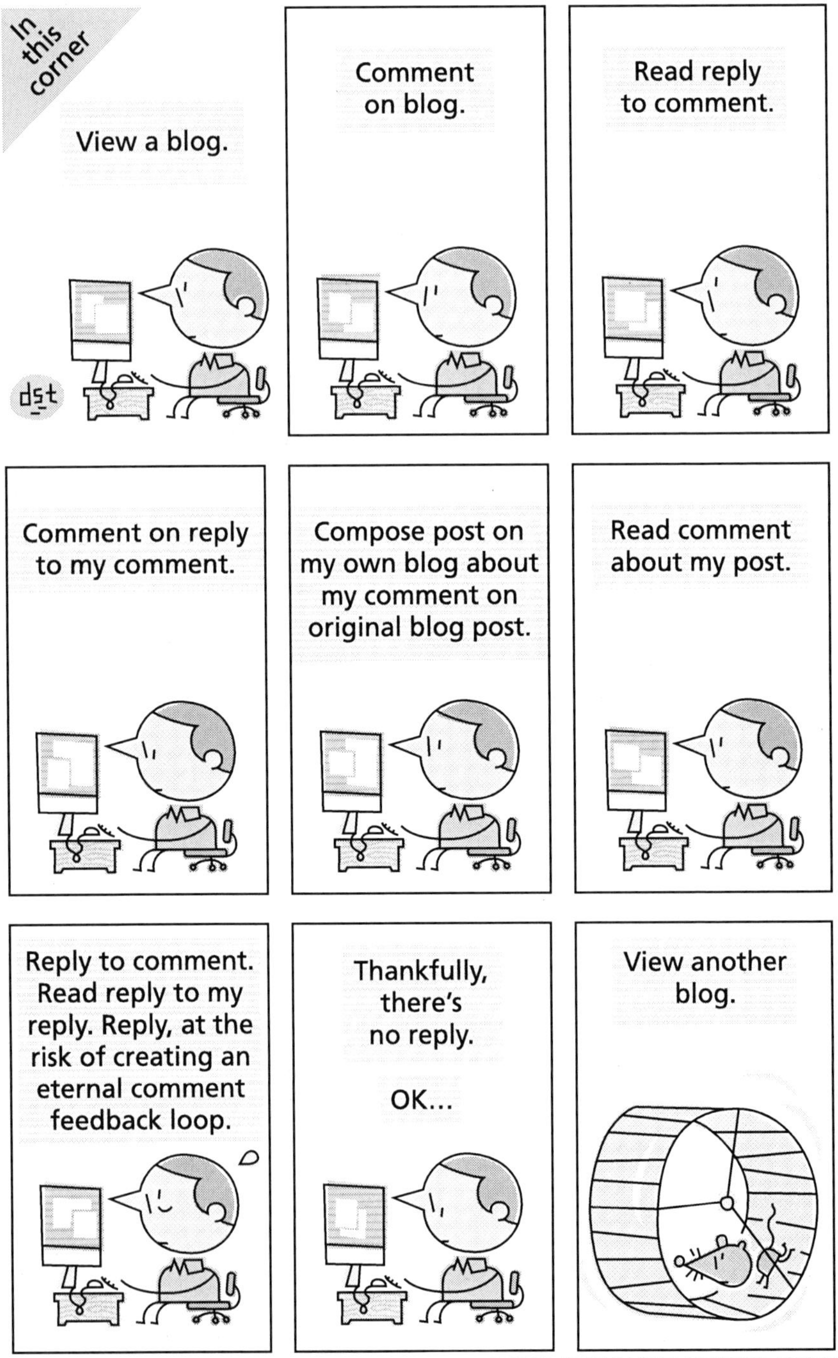
In this corner
View a blog.
dst
Comment on blog.
Read reply to comment.
Comment on reply to my comment.
Compose post on my own blog about my comment on original blog post.
Read comment about my post.
Reply to comment. Read reply to my reply. Reply, at the risk of creating an eternal comment feedback loop.
Thankfully, there's no reply.
OK...
View another blog.

Nov. 30, 2007

DAVID STEINLICHT, PIONEER PRESS

 Note: I don't do this. Not at all.

In this corner **dst**

More versions of "Blade Runner"

Shocking new ending: Harrison Ford is a replicant — and a robot coffeepot!

Decaf?

3-D version. Watch out for the flying frozen eyeballs!

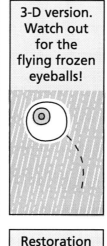

New soundtrack by Jay-Z.

♫ That old blade-runner magic that you weave so well. ♫

Jackie Chan brought in to spice up the kung fu in fight scenes.

A "Mystery Science Theater 3000" version.

Look at the size of that blimp!

OFF WORLD

Restoration of car chase scene.

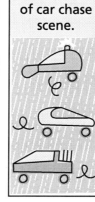

Computer used to recast lead roles with Bogart, Monroe and John Wayne.

The things I've seen, Pilgrim.

Deckard gets a smart-mouthed teen sidekick.

Ya think maybe it's a fake snake, Deck?

Theme park ride.

Very dystopian!

Free version with real advertising on all in-movie billboards and info screens.

BRAWNY PAPER TOWELING presents BLADE RUNNER

Rain-free version.

Before.

After.

Dec. 7, 2007

DAVID STEINLICHT, PIONEER PRESS

Cookie decorating tips

dst

Classic

Pirate

Convict

Vampire

Mummy

Cowboy

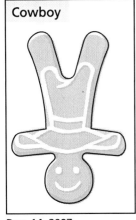

Businessman

Geek

Dec. 14, 2007

DAVID STEINLICHT, PIONEER PRESS

180

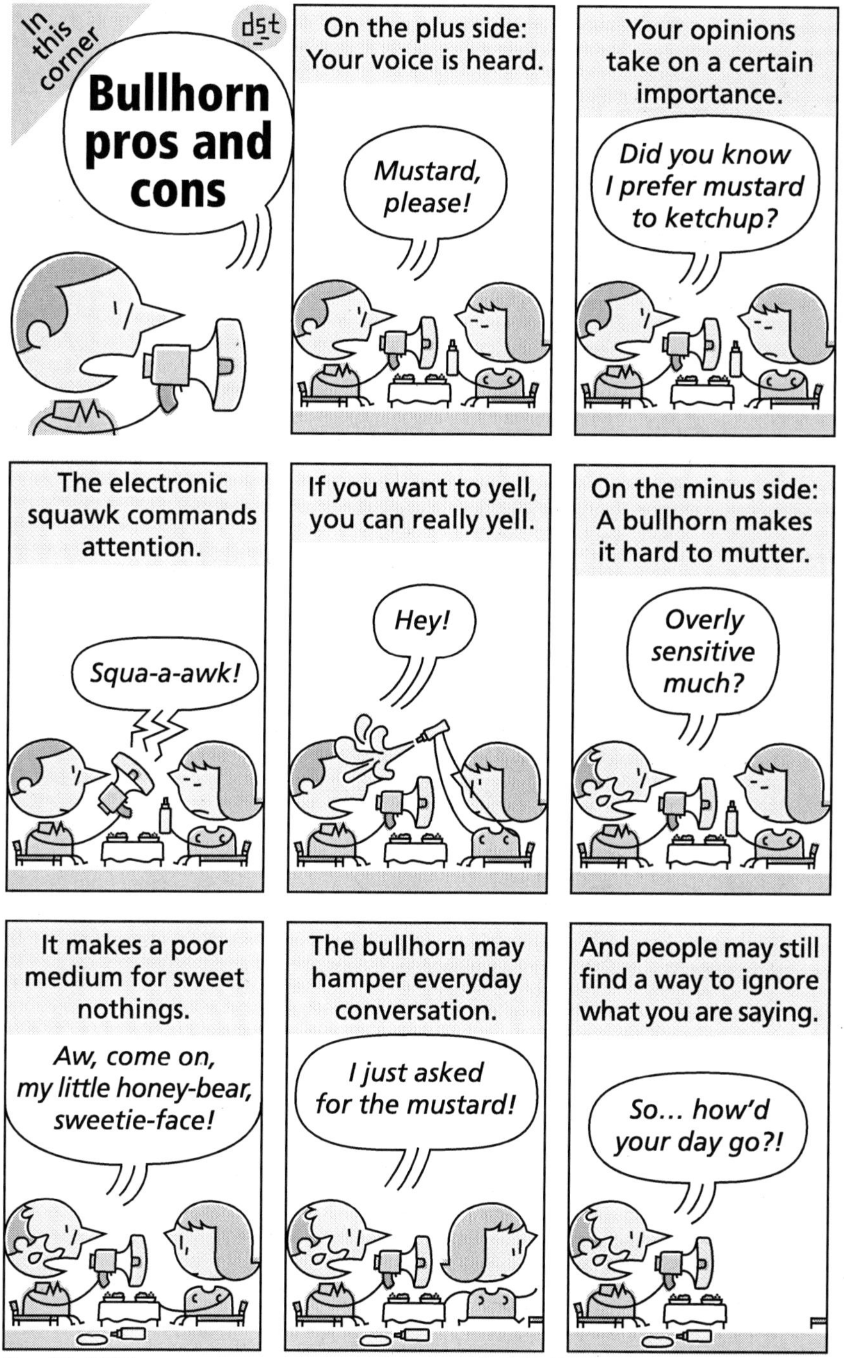
In this corner
dst
Bullhorn pros and cons
On the plus side: Your voice is heard.
Mustard, please!
Your opinions take on a certain importance.
Did you know I prefer mustard to ketchup?
The electronic squawk commands attention.
Squa-a-awk!
If you want to yell, you can really yell.
Hey!
On the minus side: A bullhorn makes it hard to mutter.
Overly sensitive much?
It makes a poor medium for sweet nothings.
Aw, come on, my little honey-bear, sweetie-face!
The bullhorn may hamper everyday conversation.
I just asked for the mustard!
And people may still find a way to ignore what you are saying.
So… how'd your day go?!

Dec. 21, 2007

DAVID STEINLICHT, PIONEER PRESS

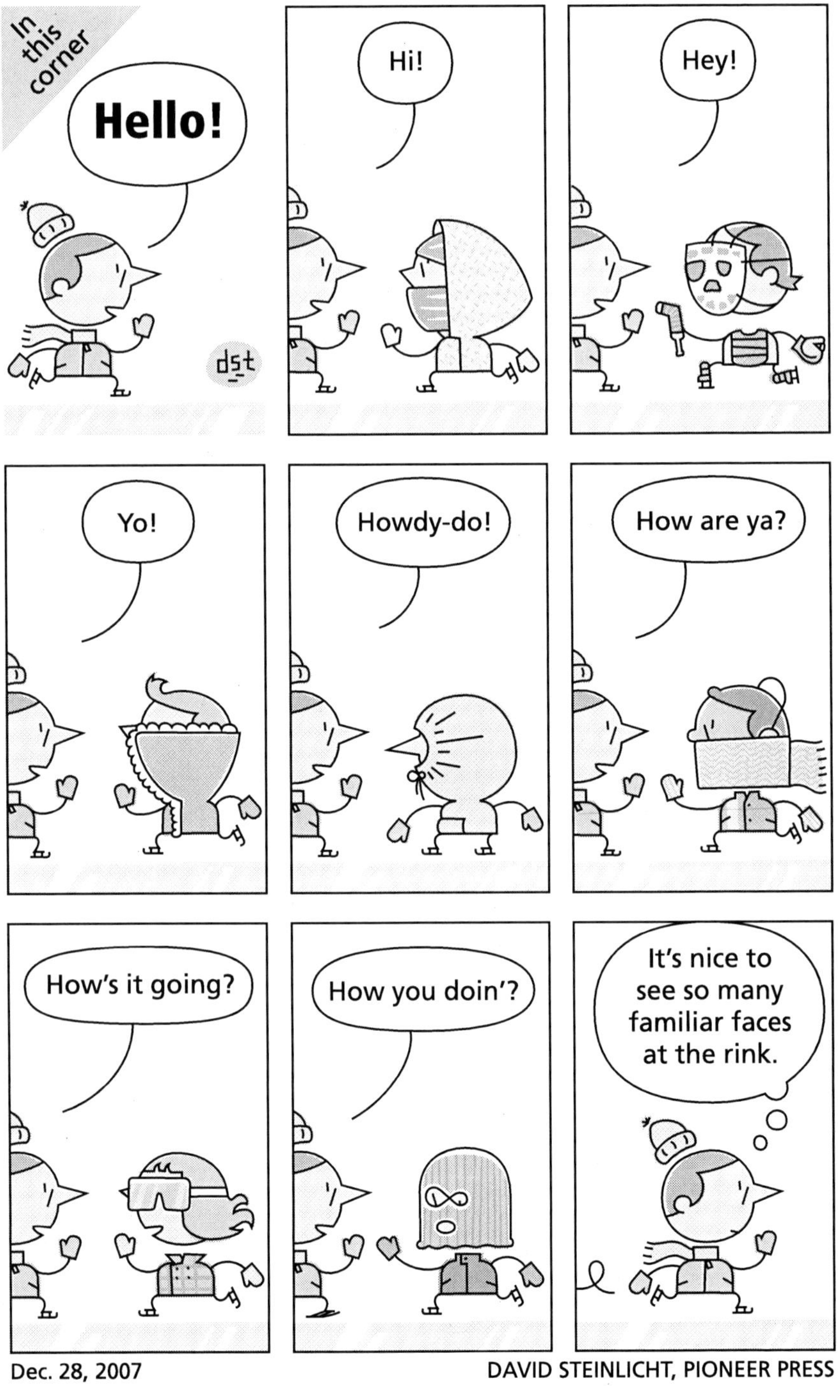
In this corner
Hello!
dst
Hi!
Hey!
Yo!
Howdy-do!
How are ya?
How's it going?
How you doin'?
It's nice to see so many familiar faces at the rink.

Dec. 28, 2007

DAVID STEINLICHT, PIONEER PRESS

2004	2005	2006	2007	2008	2009

2008

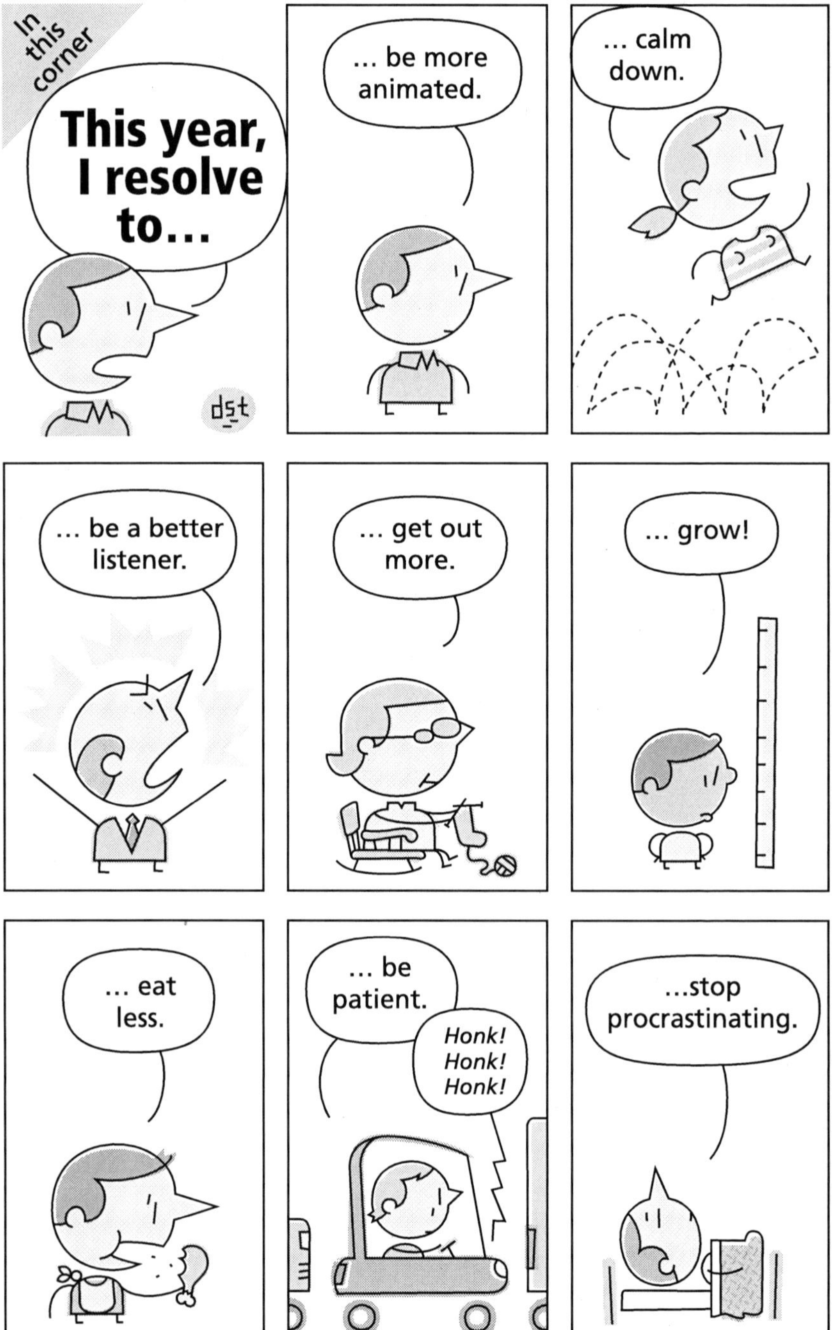
In this corner
This year, I resolve to...
dst
... be more animated.
... calm down.
... be a better listener.
... get out more.
... grow!
... eat less.
... be patient.
Honk! Honk! Honk!
...stop procrastinating.

Jan. 4, 2008

DAVID STEINLICHT, PIONEER PRESS

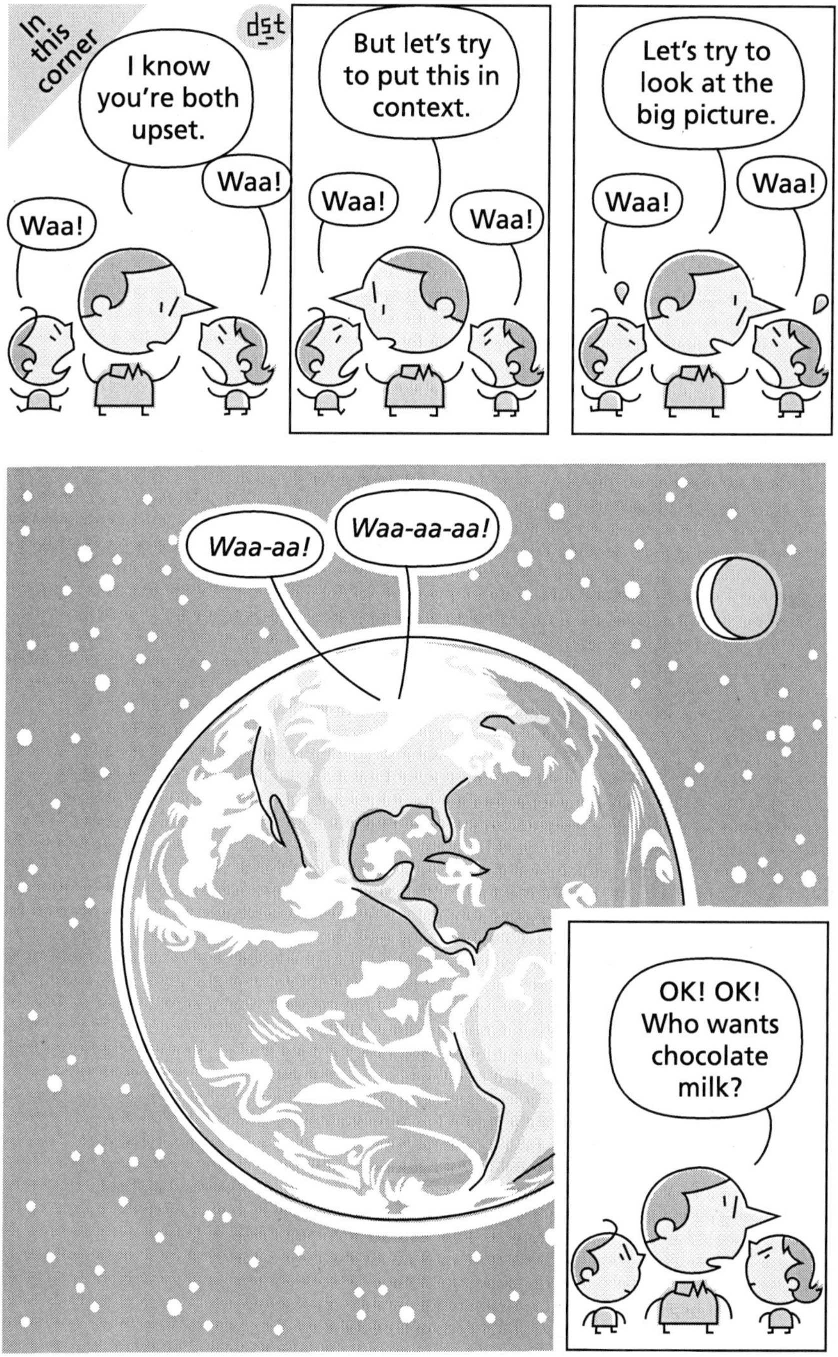
In this corner
dst
I know you're both upset.
Waa!
Waa!
But let's try to put this in context.
Waa!
Waa!
Let's try to look at the big picture.
Waa!
Waa!
Waa-aa!
Waa-aa-aa!
OK! OK! Who wants chocolate milk?

Jan. 11, 2008

DAVID STEINLICHT, PIONEER PRESS

Bucket list

In this corner

dst

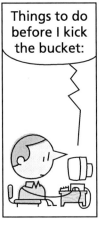

Things to do before I kick the bucket:

1) Get pair of bucket-kicking shoes, preferably steel-toed.

2) Investigate possibility of using plastic bucket.

3) Make sure bucket isn't filled with anything too heavy...

... be on the lookout for cement, rocks and sand.

4) If bucket's filled with water, kick it where there's good drainage.

5) Might be better to use bucket with hole in it.

6) Does accuracy of kick count?

7) Height?
8) Distance?

9) Run to kick, or just stand and kick?

10) Use soccer-style kick. Easier on the shoe — and foot!

Jan. 18, 2008

DAVID STEINLICHT, PIONEER PRESS

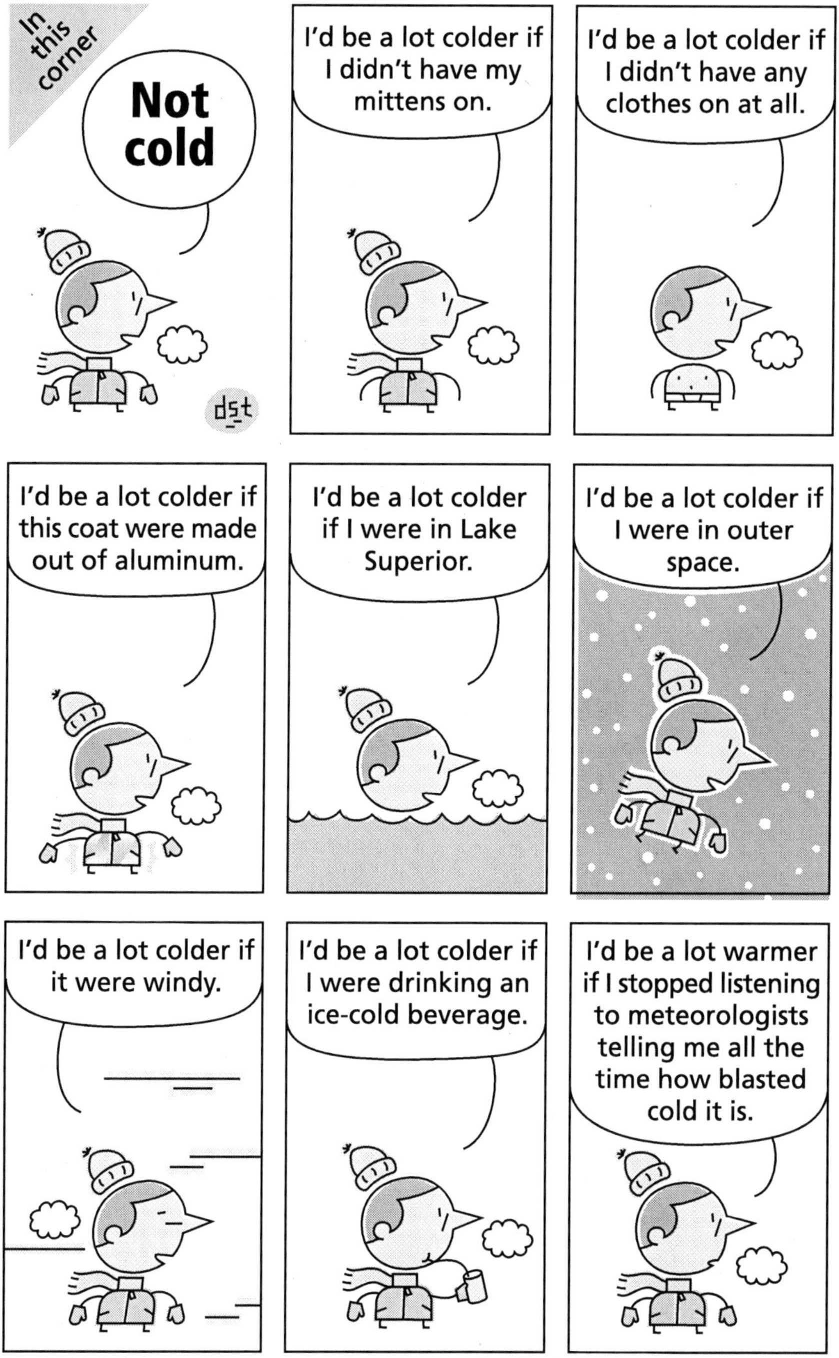
In this corner
Not cold
dst
I'd be a lot colder if I didn't have my mittens on.
I'd be a lot colder if I didn't have any clothes on at all.
I'd be a lot colder if this coat were made out of aluminum.
I'd be a lot colder if I were in Lake Superior.
I'd be a lot colder if I were in outer space.
I'd be a lot colder if it were windy.
I'd be a lot colder if I were drinking an ice-cold beverage.
I'd be a lot warmer if I stopped listening to meteorologists telling me all the time how blasted cold it is.

Jan. 25, 2008

DAVID STEINLICHT, PIONEER PRESS

In this corner

Mitten fashion

The all-together. A warmer hand, fingers and thumb together.

Switcher. There's no wrong way to wear this mitt, also great for Texas fans.

Glotten. When you have to use your fingertips.

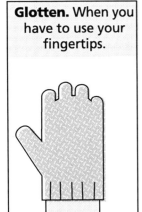

Peekaboo. Show knuckle cleavage for a sexy winter look.

Midi-mitt. For when a full mitten is just too much.

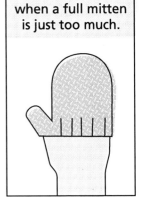

Criticmitten. Sewn into a permanent thumbs up or down.

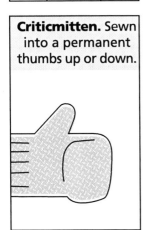

Mittips. Keep your fingernails warm.

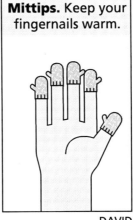

Chatten. Includes a pouch for your cell.

Feb. 1, 2008   DAVID STEINLICHT, PIONEER PRESS

Note: It was suggested to me that I could make a lot of money selling "Switcher" mittens. Attention venture capitalists! My e-mail is in the front of this book.

188

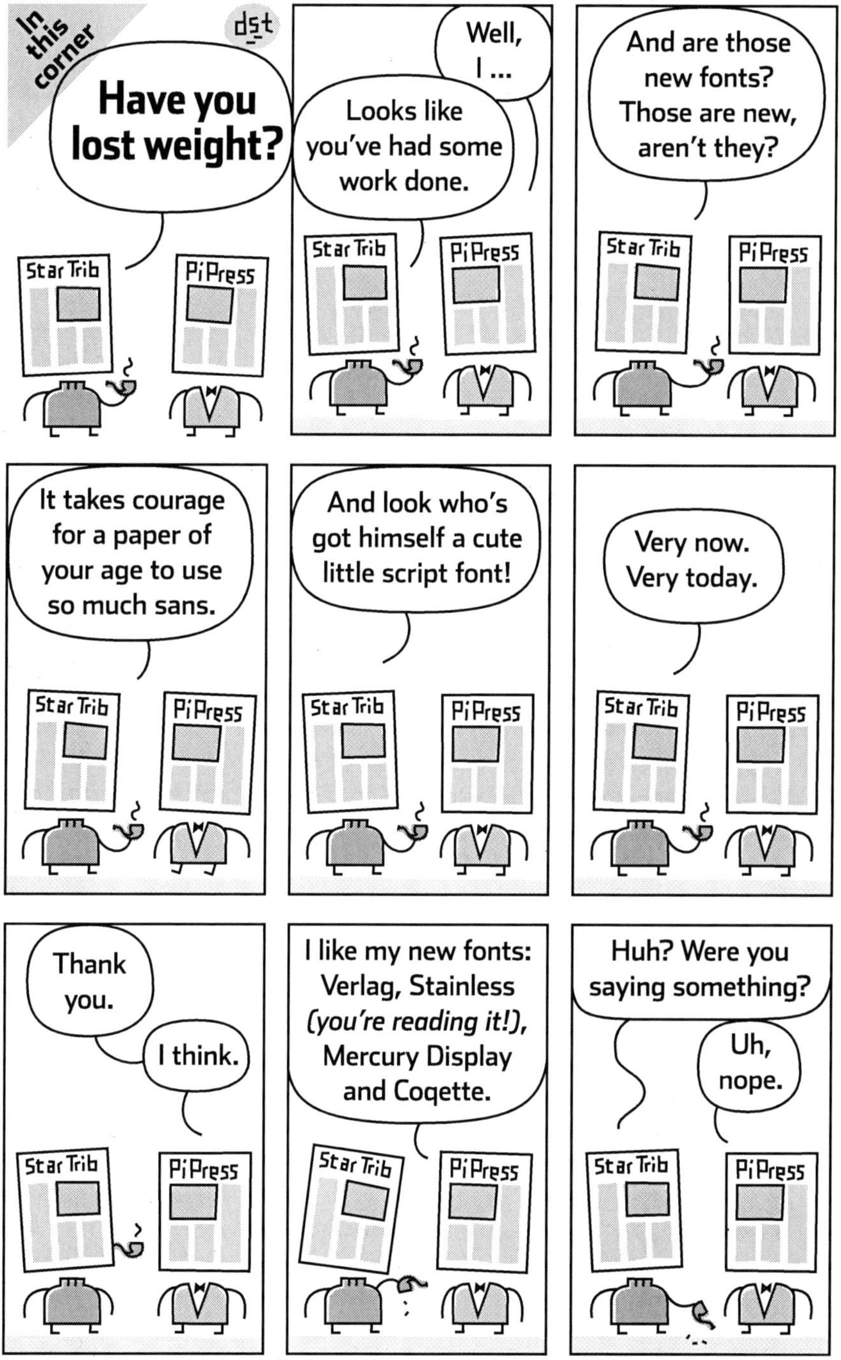
In this corner
dst
Have you lost weight?
Star Trib
Pi Press
Well, I ...
Looks like you've had some work done.
And are those new fonts? Those are new, aren't they?
It takes courage for a paper of your age to use so much sans.
And look who's got himself a cute little script font!
Very now. Very today.
Thank you.
I think.
I like my new fonts: Verlag, Stainless (you're reading it!), Mercury Display and Coqette.
Huh? Were you saying something?
Uh, nope.

Feb. 22, 2008 PIONEER PRESS: DAVID STEINLICHT

Note: A redesign for the paper means I get to use new fonts, too.

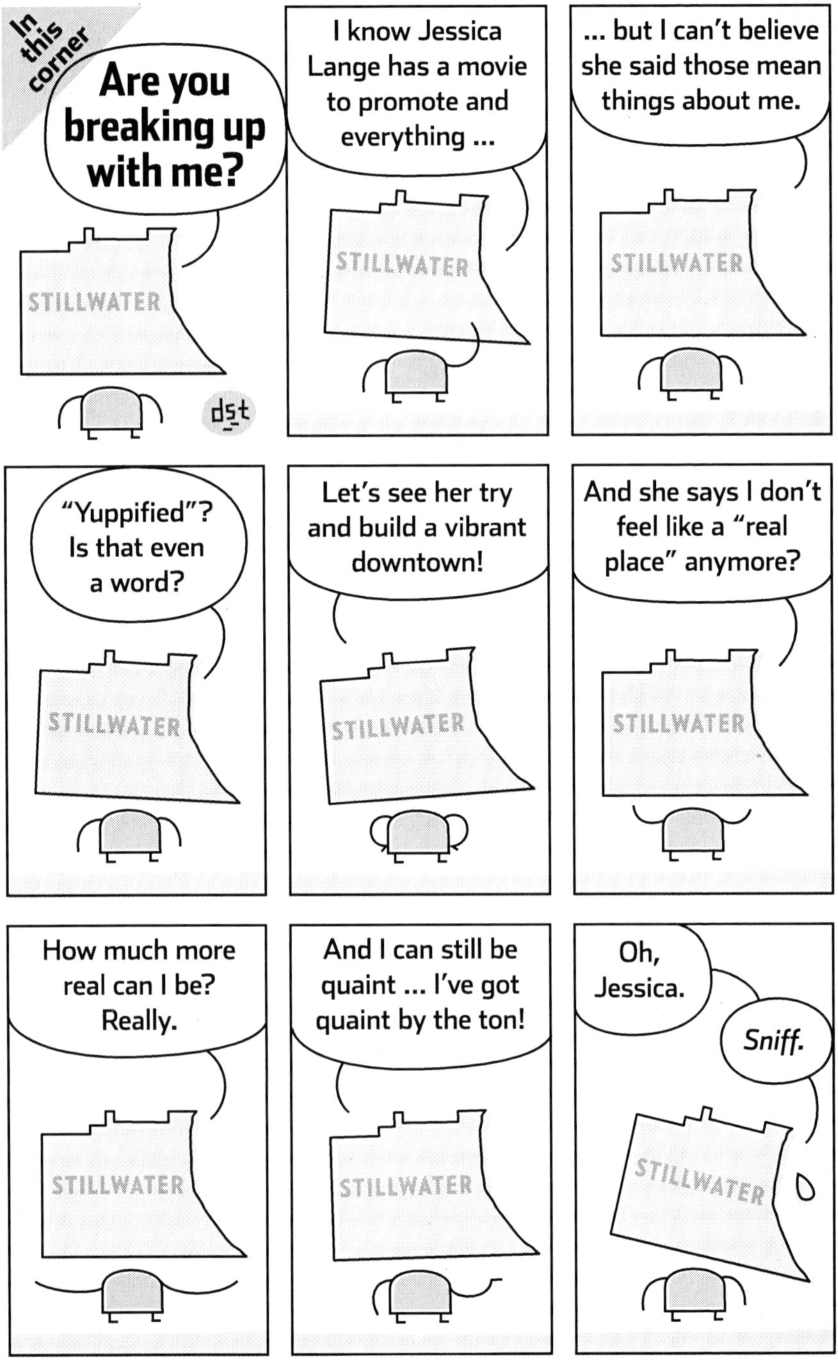
In this corner
Are you breaking up with me?
STILLWATER
dst
I know Jessica Lange has a movie to promote and everything ...
STILLWATER
... but I can't believe she said those mean things about me.
STILLWATER
"Yuppified"? Is that even a word?
STILLWATER
Let's see her try and build a vibrant downtown!
STILLWATER
And she says I don't feel like a "real place" anymore?
STILLWATER
How much more real can I be? Really.
STILLWATER
And I can still be quaint ... I've got quaint by the ton!
STILLWATER
Oh, Jessica.
Sniff.
STILLWATER

Feb. 29, 2008 PIONEER PRESS: DAVID STEINLICHT

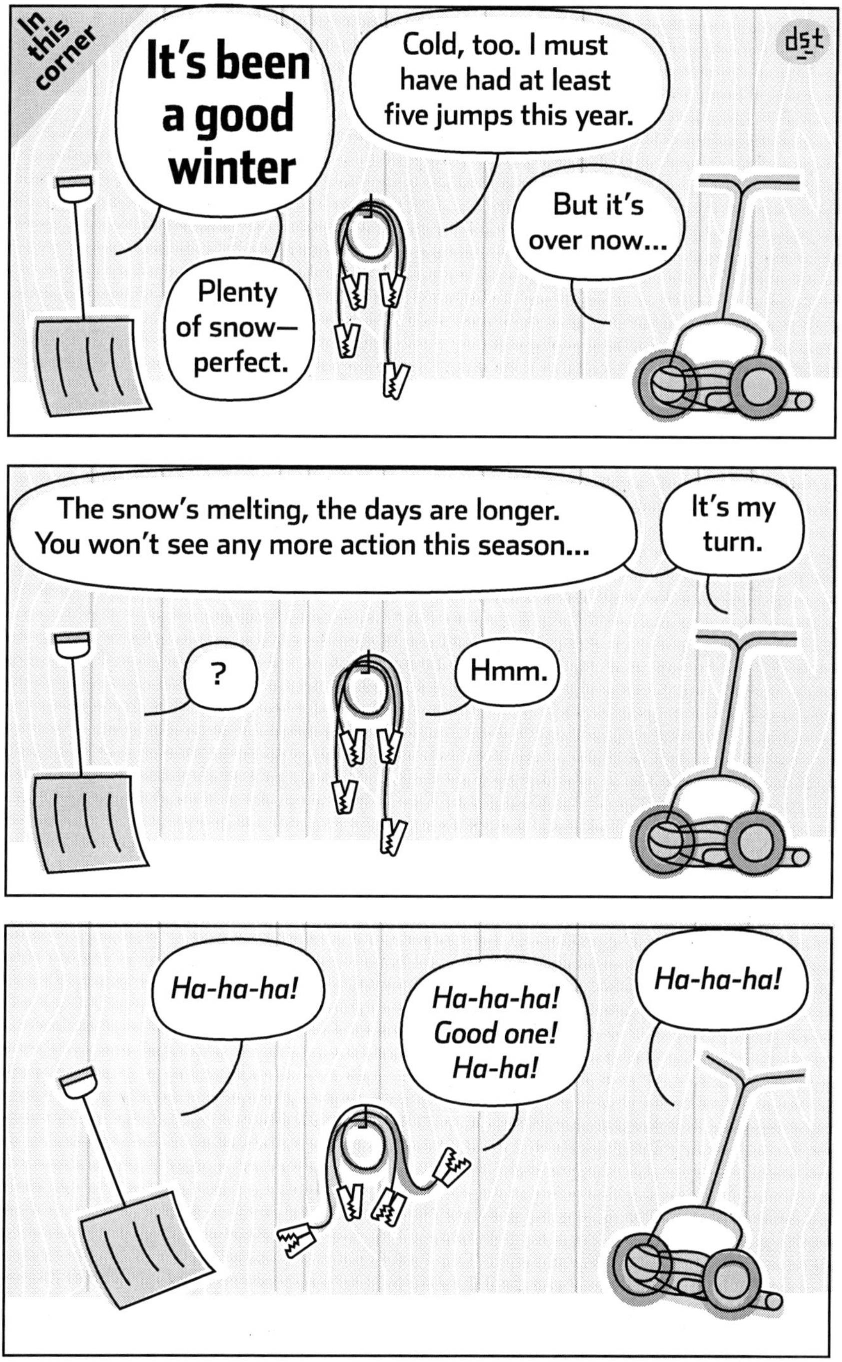
In this corner
dst
It's been a good winter
Plenty of snow—perfect.
Cold, too. I must have had at least five jumps this year.
But it's over now...
The snow's melting, the days are longer. You won't see any more action this season...
It's my turn.
?
Hmm.
Ha-ha-ha!
Ha-ha-ha! Good one! Ha-ha!
Ha-ha-ha!

March 14, 2008

PIONEER PRESS: DAVID STEINLICHT

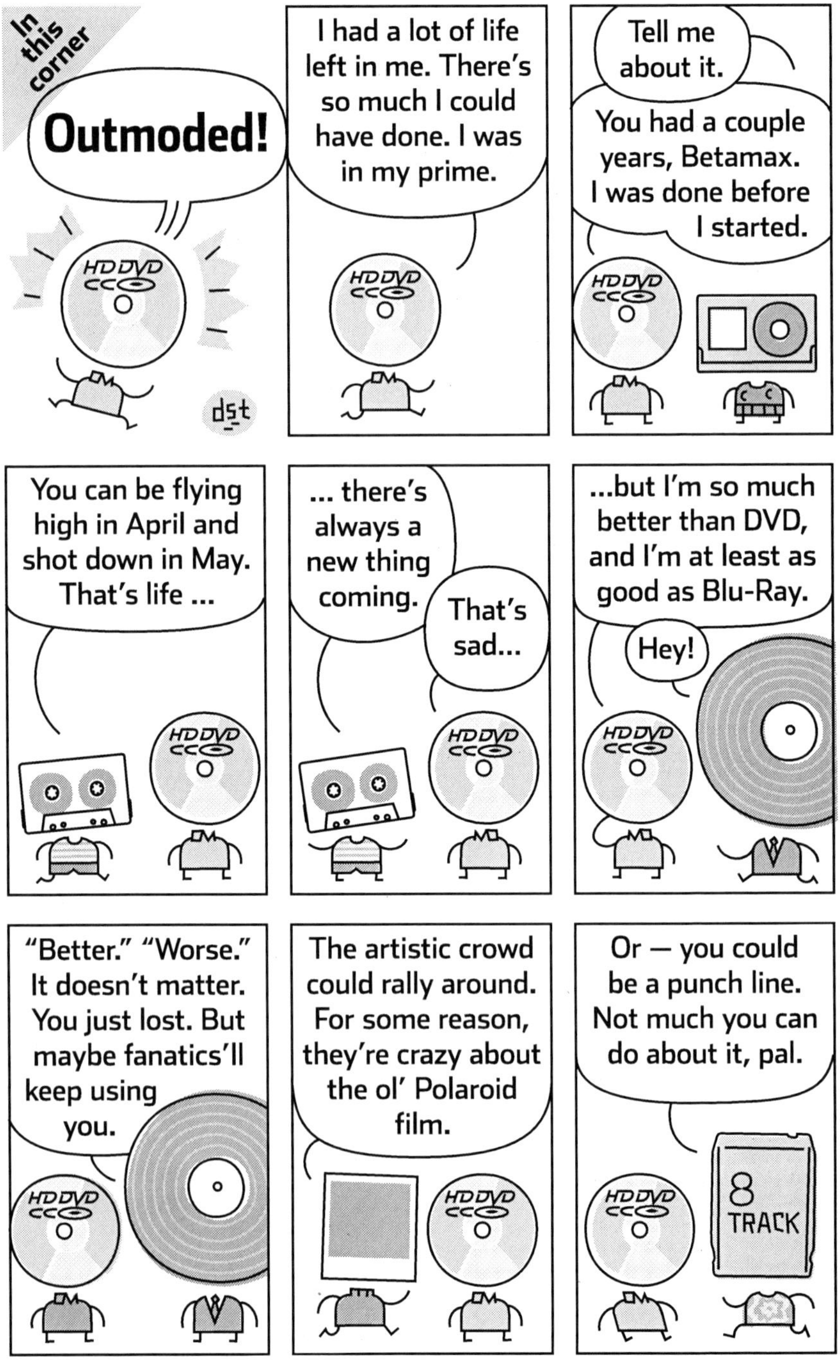

In this corner
Outmoded!
dst
HD DVD
I had a lot of life left in me. There's so much I could have done. I was in my prime.
Tell me about it.
You had a couple years, Betamax. I was done before I started.
You can be flying high in April and shot down in May. That's life ...
... there's always a new thing coming.
That's sad...
...but I'm so much better than DVD, and I'm at least as good as Blu-Ray.
Hey!
"Better." "Worse." It doesn't matter. You just lost. But maybe fanatics'll keep using you.
The artistic crowd could rally around. For some reason, they're crazy about the ol' Polaroid film.
Or — you could be a punch line. Not much you can do about it, pal.
8 TRACK

March 21, 2008 PIONEER PRESS: DAVID STEINLICHT

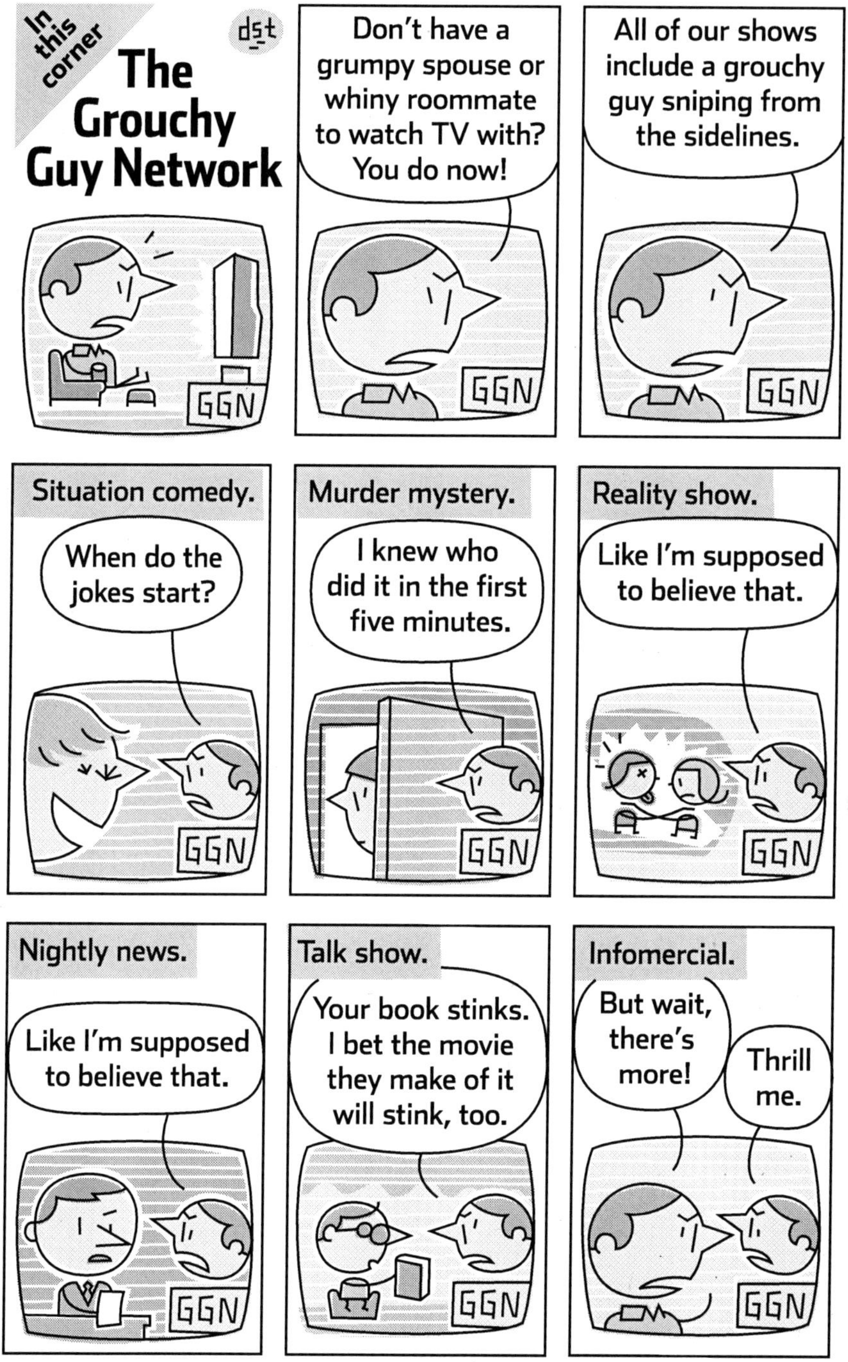
In this corner
The Grouchy Guy Network
dst
GGN
Don't have a grumpy spouse or whiny roommate to watch TV with? You do now!
GGN
All of our shows include a grouchy guy sniping from the sidelines.
GGN
Situation comedy.
When do the jokes start?
GGN
Murder mystery.
I knew who did it in the first five minutes.
GGN
Reality show.
Like I'm supposed to believe that.
GGN
Nightly news.
Like I'm supposed to believe that.
GGN
Talk show.
Your book stinks. I bet the movie they make of it will stink, too.
GGN
Infomercial.
But wait, there's more!
Thrill me.
GGN

April 4, 2008

PIONEER PRESS: DAVID STEINLICHT

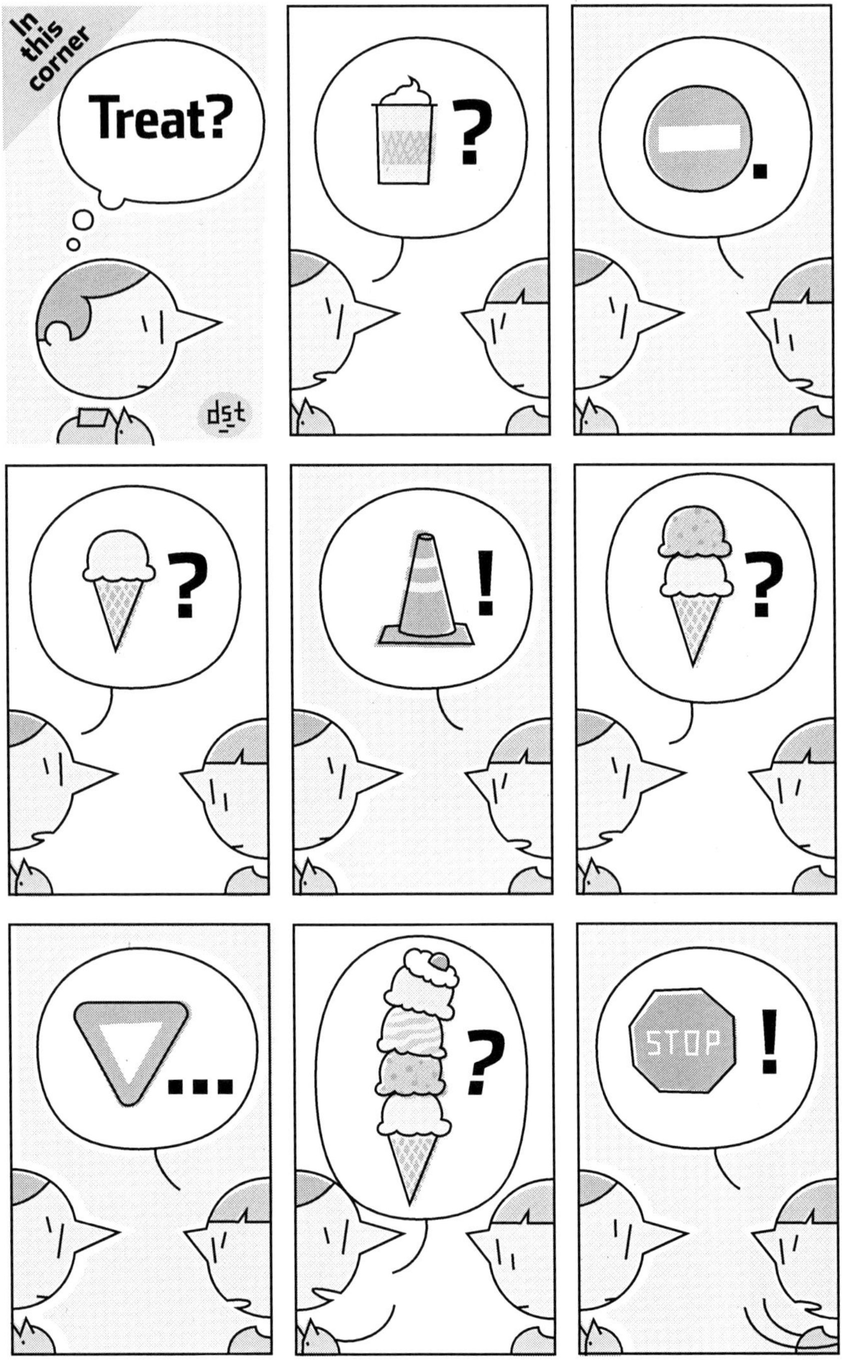
In this corner
Treat?
dst
?
.
?
!
?
...
?
STOP
!

April 11, 2008

PIONEER PRESS: DAVID STEINLICHT

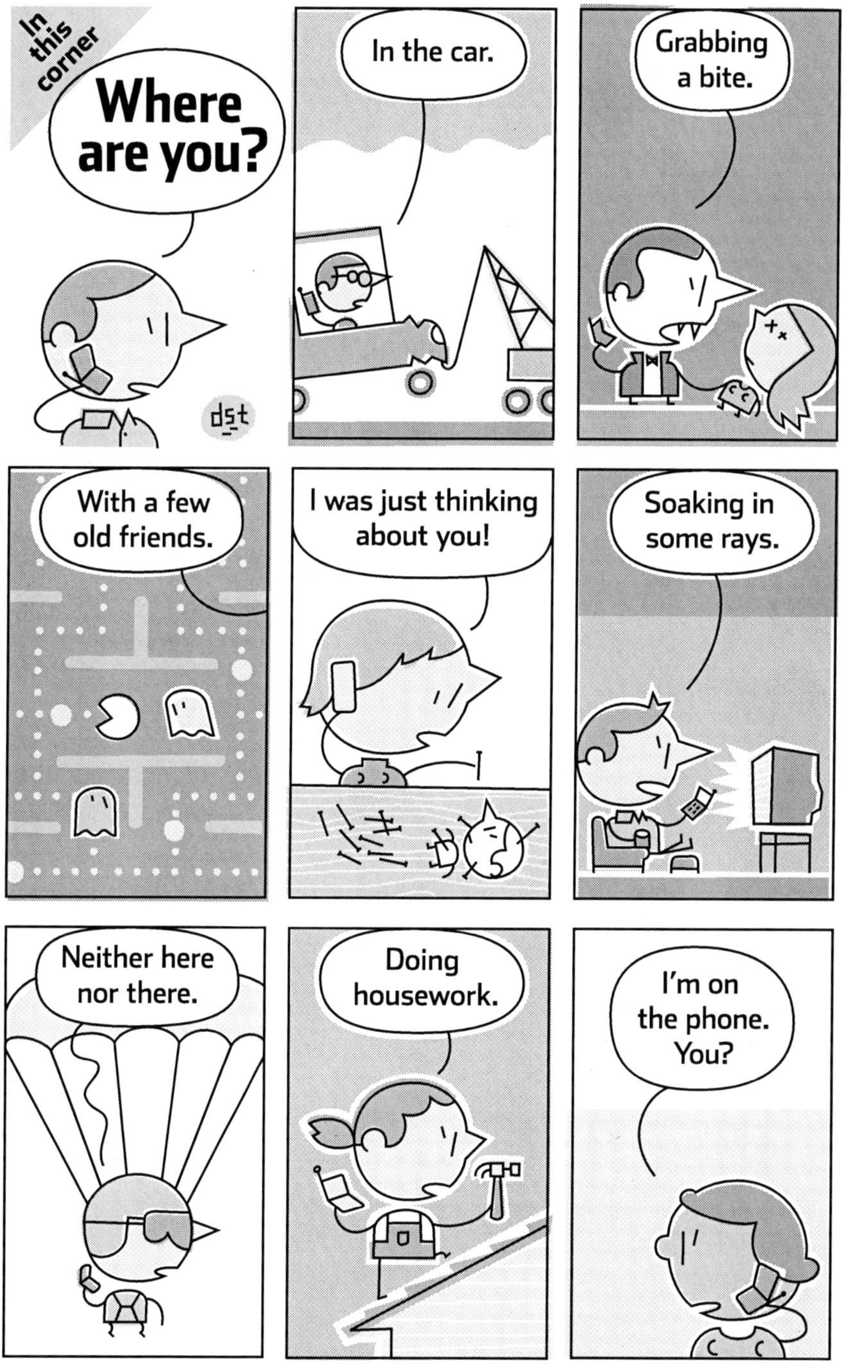
In this corner
Where are you?
In the car.
Grabbing a bite.
With a few old friends.
I was just thinking about you!
Soaking in some rays.
Neither here nor there.
Doing housework.
I'm on the phone. You?
dst

April 18, 2008

PIONEER PRESS: DAVID STEINLICHT

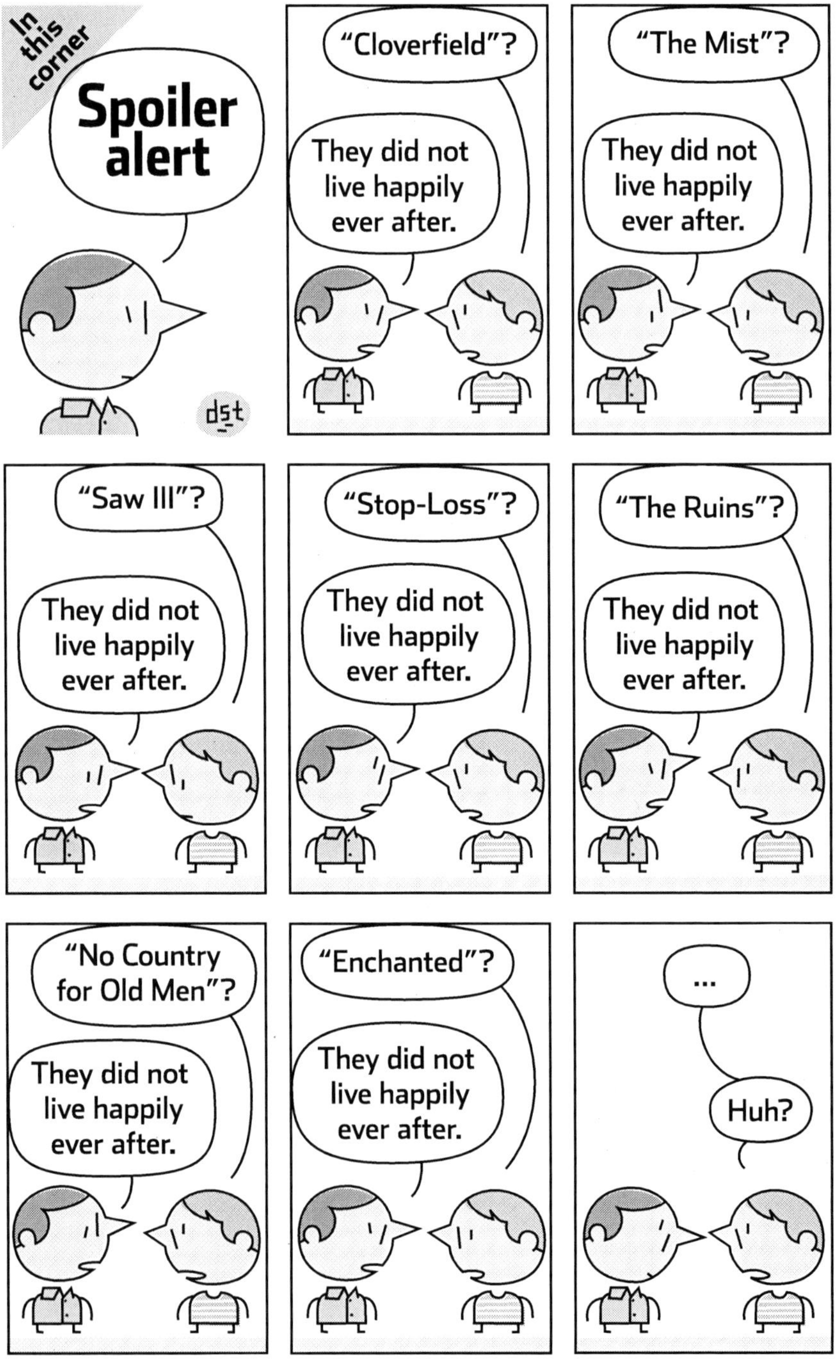
In this corner
Spoiler alert
dst
"Cloverfield"?
They did not live happily ever after.
"The Mist"?
They did not live happily ever after.
"Saw III"?
They did not live happily ever after.
"Stop-Loss"?
They did not live happily ever after.
"The Ruins"?
They did not live happily ever after.
"No Country for Old Men"?
They did not live happily ever after.
"Enchanted"?
They did not live happily ever after.
...
Huh?

April 25, 2008

PIONEER PRESS: DAVID STEINLICHT

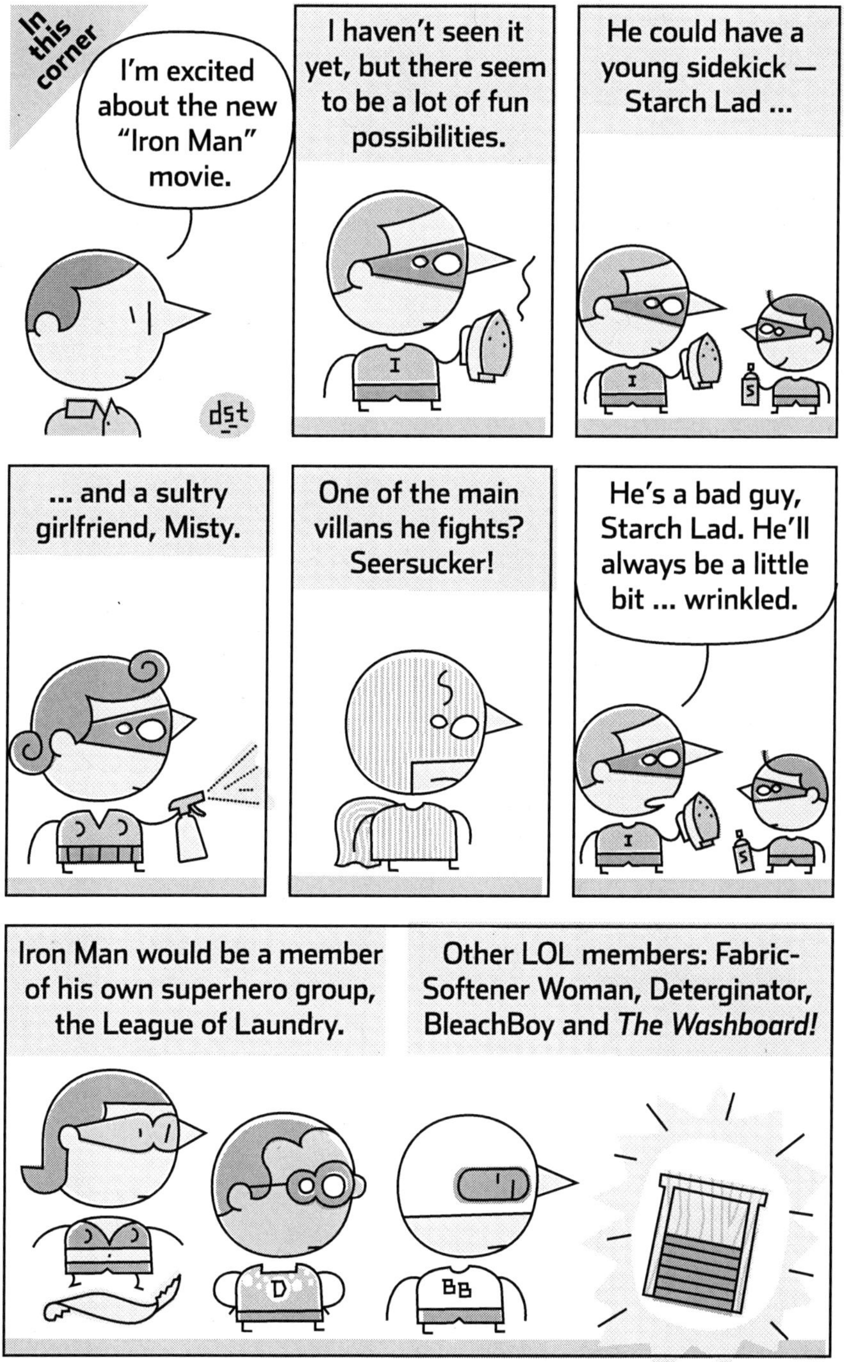
In this corner
I'm excited about the new "Iron Man" movie.
dst
I haven't seen it yet, but there seem to be a lot of fun possibilities.
He could have a young sidekick — Starch Lad ...
S
... and a sultry girlfriend, Misty.
One of the main villans he fights? Seersucker!
He's a bad guy, Starch Lad. He'll always be a little bit ... wrinkled.
Iron Man would be a member of his own superhero group, the League of Laundry.
Other LOL members: Fabric-Softener Woman, Deterginator, BleachBoy and *The Washboard!*
D
BB

May 2, 2008

PIONEER PRESS: DAVID STEINLICHT

Note: I did finally see the *Iron Man* movie — it was nothing like this.

In this corner
dst

Inanimate Objects Playhouse
The upcoming season

Pen Vs. Pencil
This time it's permanent!

The Broom's Tale
A brush with greatness.

Wrench In The Works
Circling the drain

Deck Chair Story
"Personally, I like the new arrangement."

An Economic Stimulus Check
Spending time at the mall

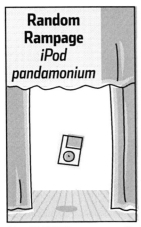

Random Rampage
iPod pandamonium

ATM Monologues
When "$20 quick cash" means "I love you."

Paperback Thriller
Run for hardcover

May 16, 2008 TwinCities.com PIONEER PRESS: DAVID STEINLICHT

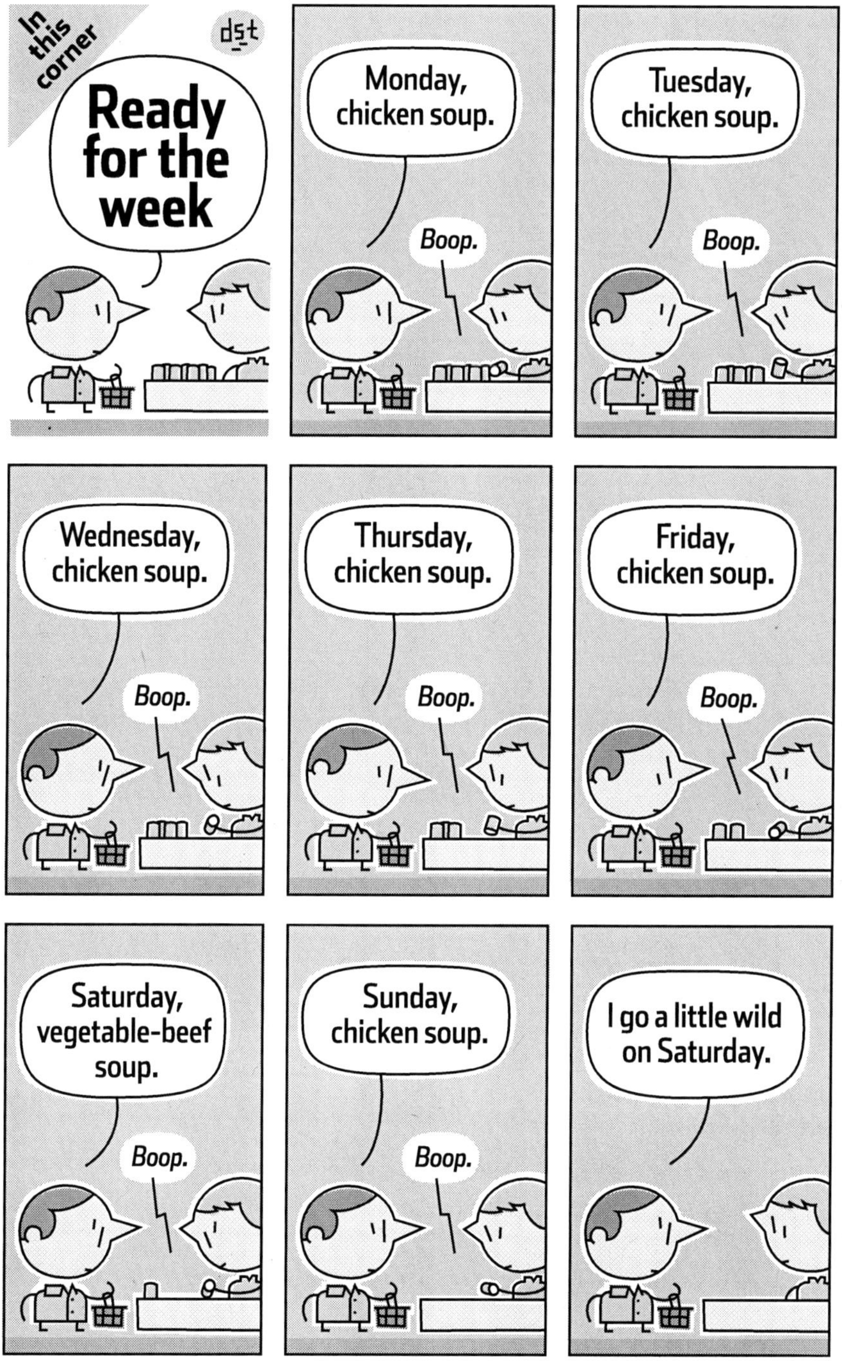
In this corner
dst
Ready for the week
Monday, chicken soup.
Boop.
Tuesday, chicken soup.
Boop.
Wednesday, chicken soup.
Boop.
Thursday, chicken soup.
Boop.
Friday, chicken soup.
Boop.
Saturday, vegetable-beef soup.
Boop.
Sunday, chicken soup.
Boop.
I go a little wild on Saturday.

May 23, 2008

PIONEER PRESS: DAVID STEINLICHT

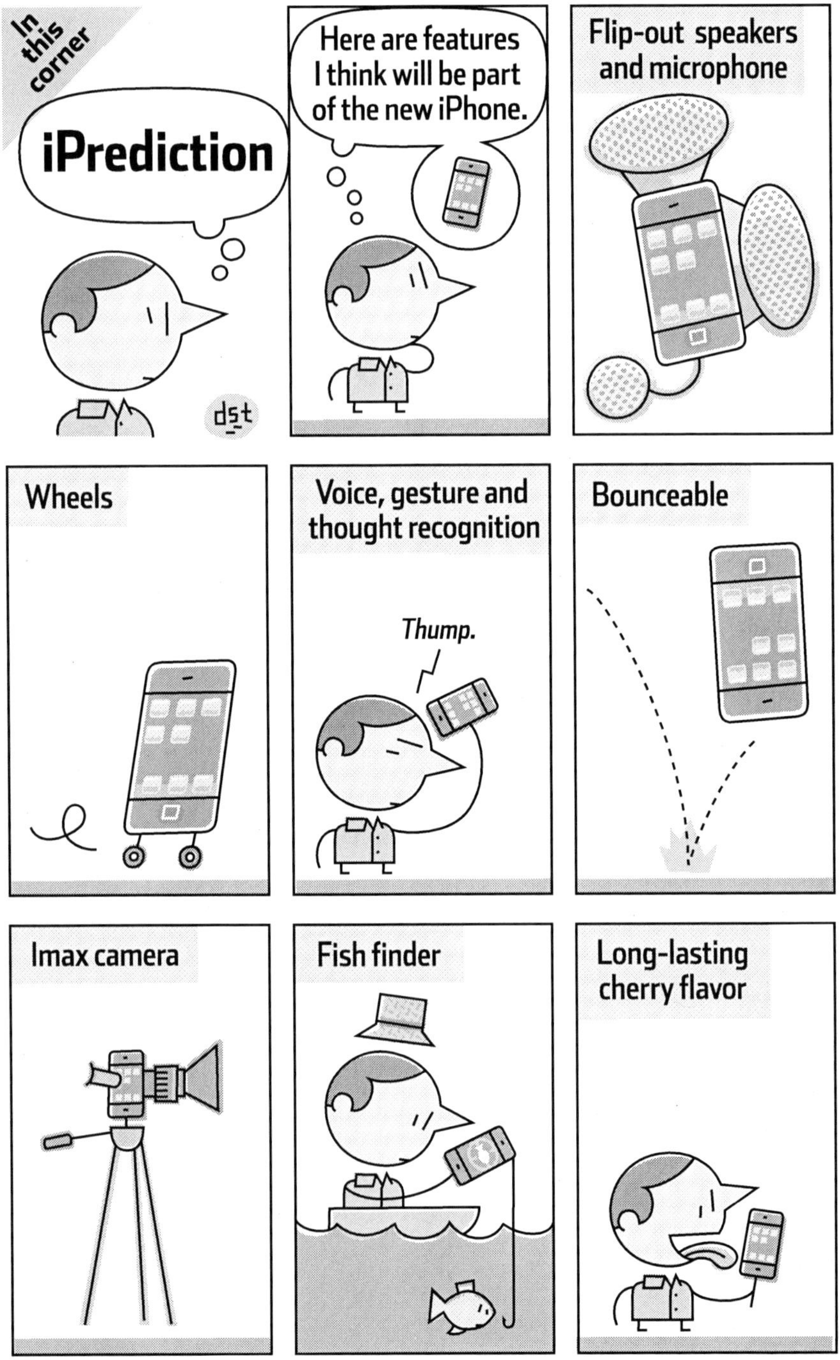
In this corner
iPrediction
dst
Here are features I think will be part of the new iPhone.
Flip-out speakers and microphone
Wheels
Voice, gesture and thought recognition
Thump.
Bounceable
Imax camera
Fish finder
Long-lasting cherry flavor

May 30, 2008

PIONEER PRESS: DAVID STEINLICHT

 Note: Remember when we all cared about new iPhone features? Me neither.

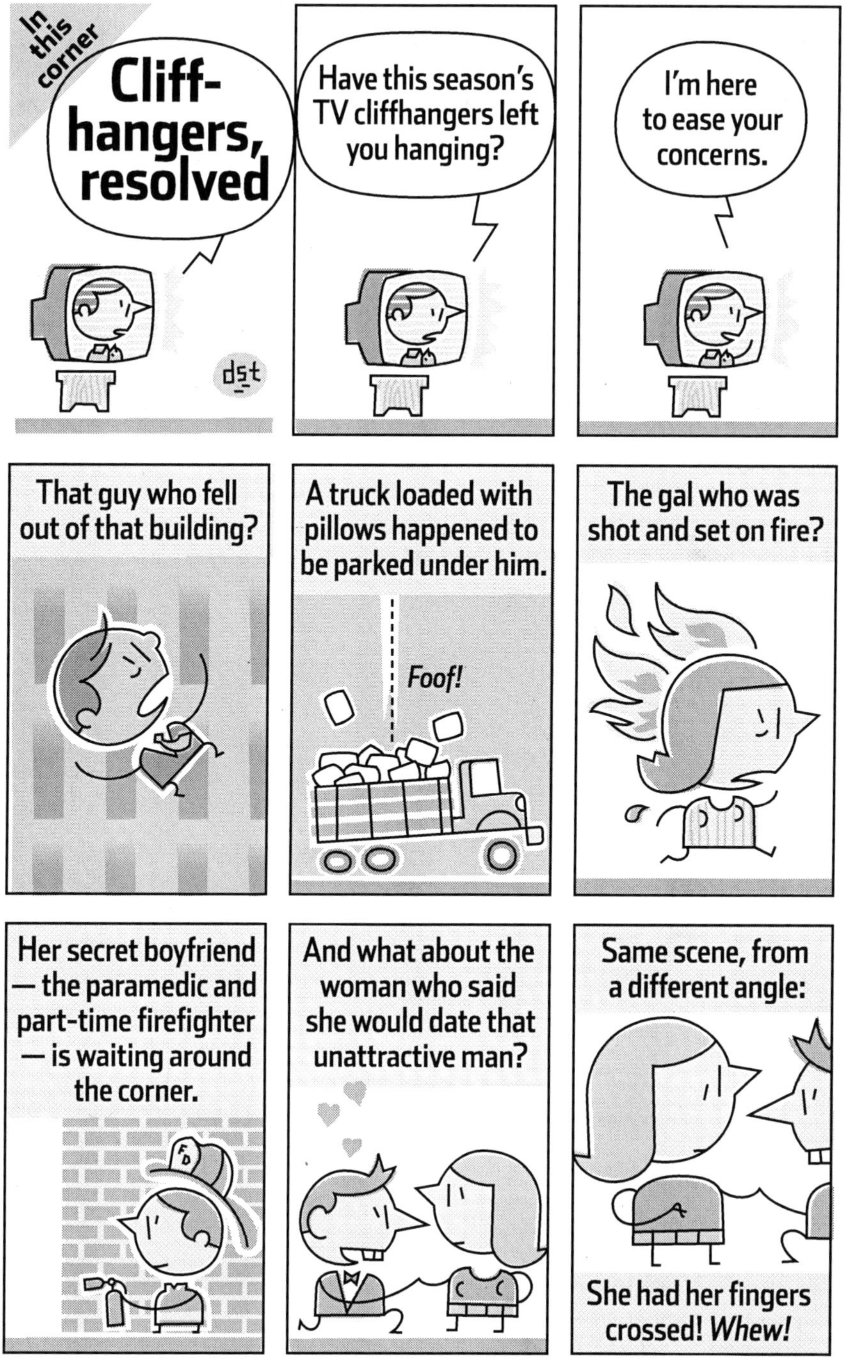
In this corner
Cliff-hangers, resolved
dst
Have this season's TV cliffhangers left you hanging?
I'm here to ease your concerns.
That guy who fell out of that building?
A truck loaded with pillows happened to be parked under him.
Foof!
The gal who was shot and set on fire?
Her secret boyfriend — the paramedic and part-time firefighter — is waiting around the corner.
FD
And what about the woman who said she would date that unattractive man?
Same scene, from a different angle:
She had her fingers crossed! *Whew!*

June 6, 2008

PIONEER PRESS: DAVID STEINLICHT

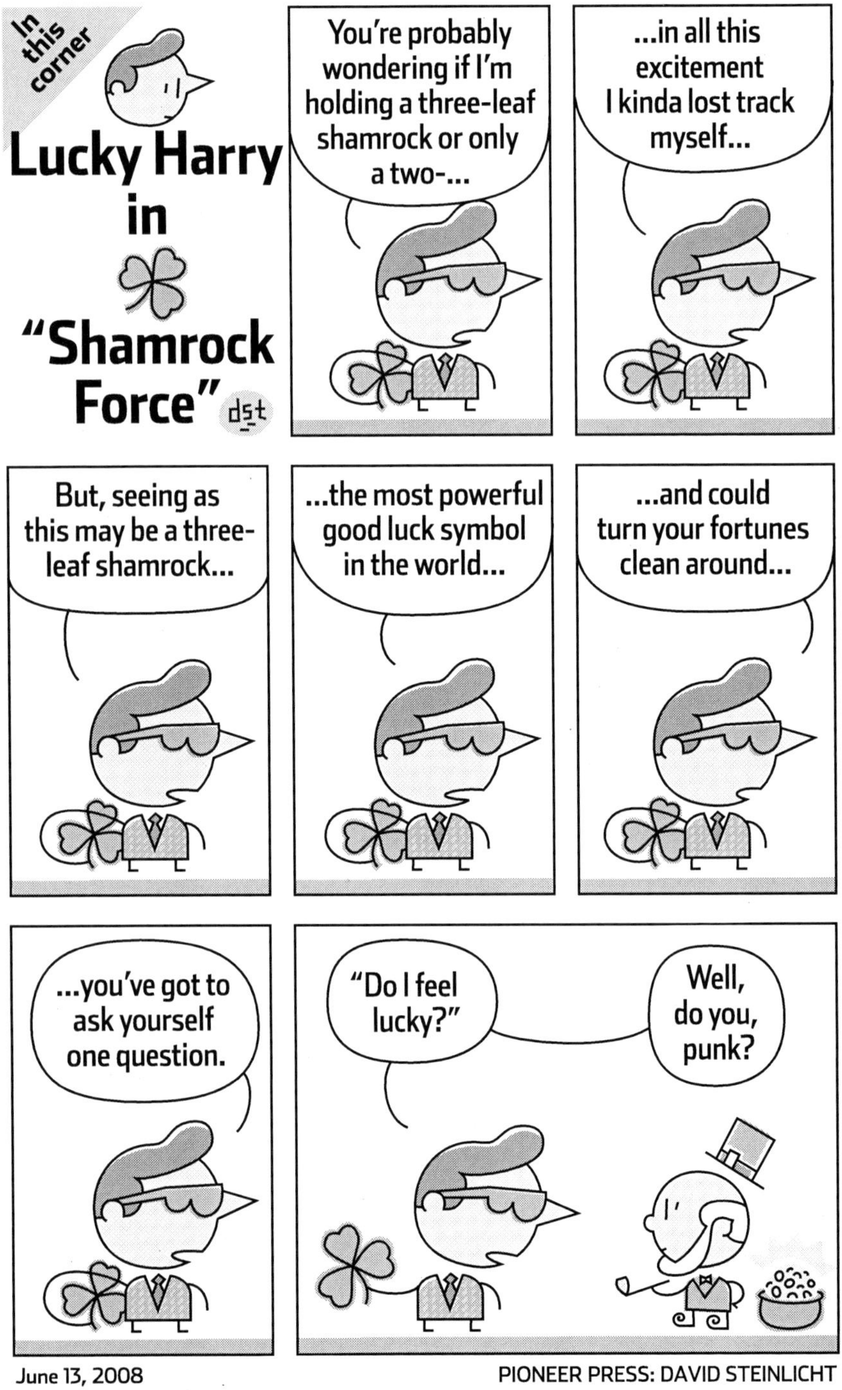

In this corner
Lucky Harry in "Shamrock Force"
dst
You're probably wondering if I'm holding a three-leaf shamrock or only a two-...
...in all this excitement I kinda lost track myself...
But, seeing as this may be a three-leaf shamrock...
...the most powerful good luck symbol in the world...
...and could turn your fortunes clean around...
...you've got to ask yourself one question.
"Do I feel lucky?"
Well, do you, punk?

June 13, 2008

PIONEER PRESS: DAVID STEINLICHT

 Note: I admit I'm a fan of the first *Dirty Harry* movie.

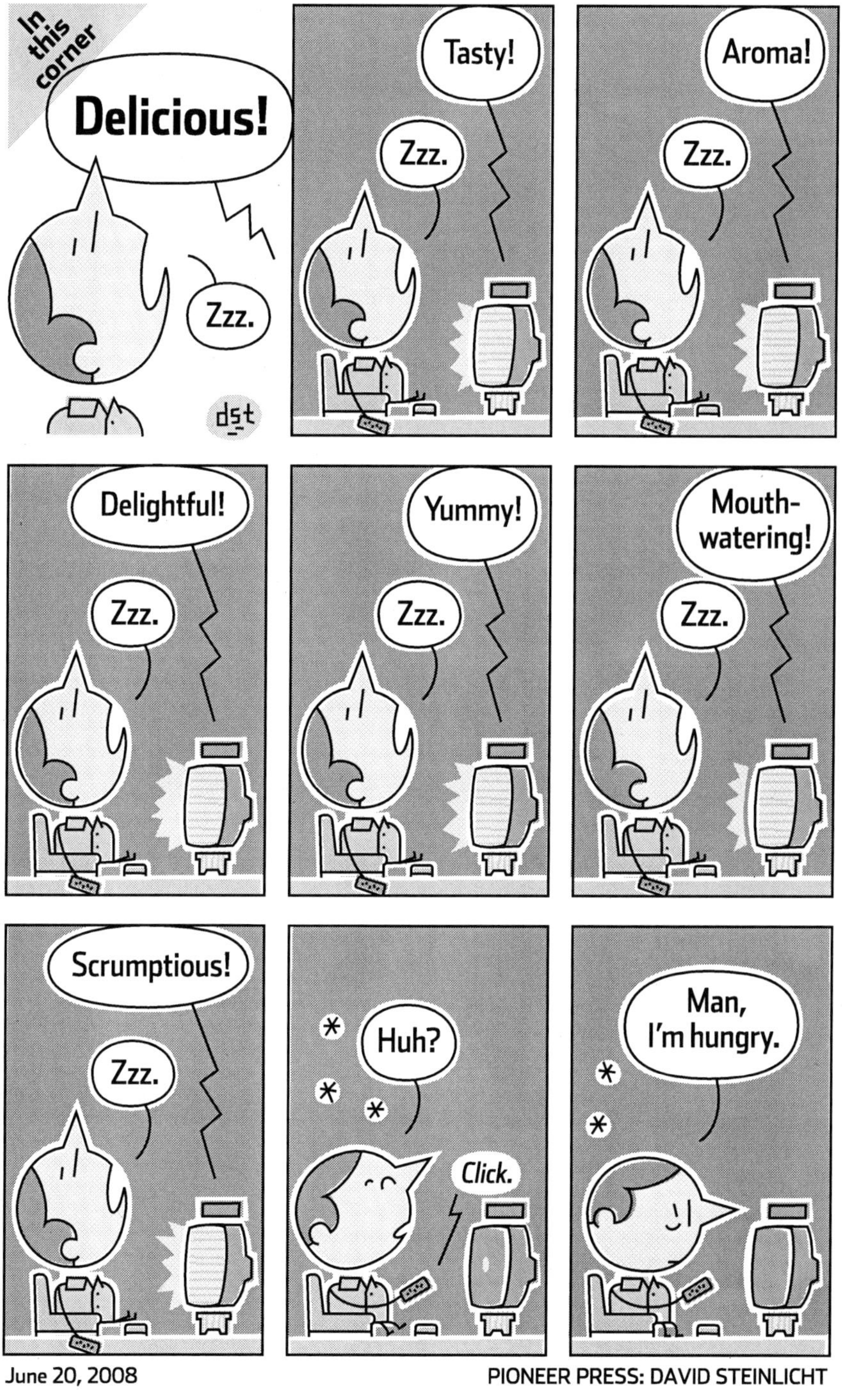
In this corner
Delicious!
Zzz.
dst
Tasty!
Zzz.
Aroma!
Zzz.
Delightful!
Zzz.
Yummy!
Zzz.
Mouth-watering!
Zzz.
Scrumptious!
Zzz.
Huh?
Click.
Man, I'm hungry.

June 20, 2008

PIONEER PRESS: DAVID STEINLICHT

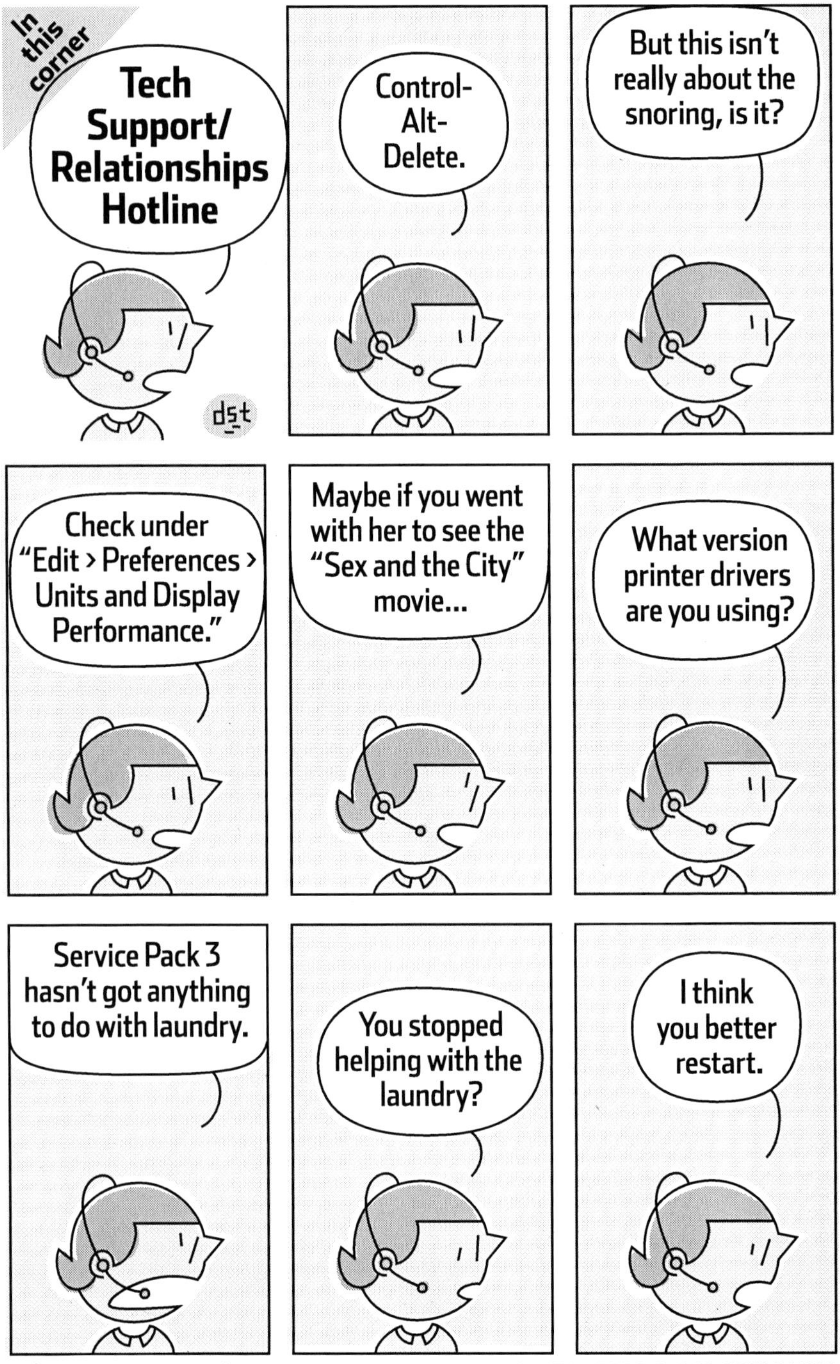
In this corner
Tech Support/ Relationships Hotline
dst
Control- Alt- Delete.
But this isn't really about the snoring, is it?
Check under "Edit > Preferences > Units and Display Performance."
Maybe if you went with her to see the "Sex and the City" movie...
What version printer drivers are you using?
Service Pack 3 hasn't got anything to do with laundry.
You stopped helping with the laundry?
I think you better restart.

June 27, 2008

PIONEER PRESS: DAVID STEINLICHT

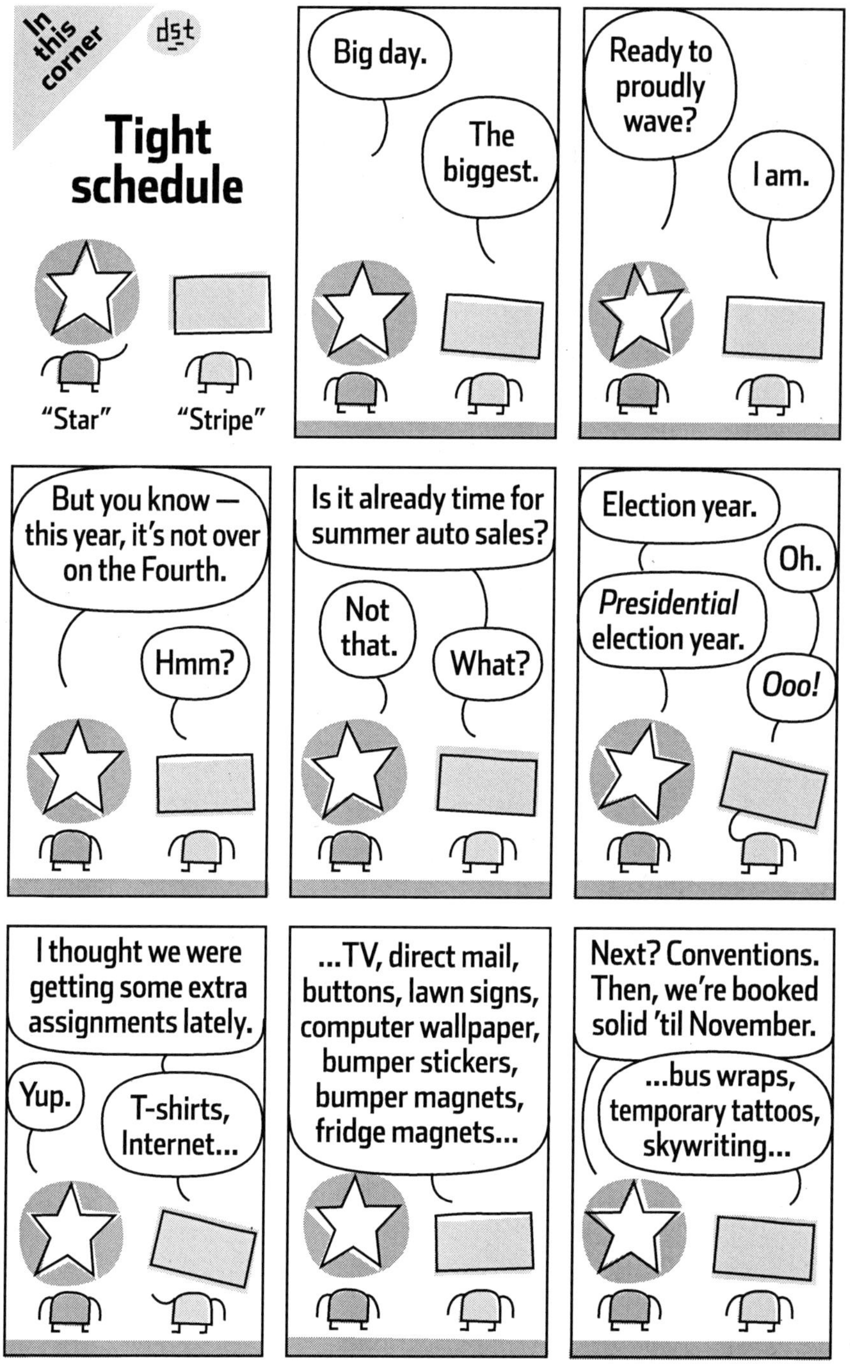
In this corner
dst
Tight schedule
"Star"
"Stripe"
Big day.
The biggest.
Ready to proudly wave?
I am.
But you know — this year, it's not over on the Fourth.
Hmm?
Is it already time for summer auto sales?
Not that.
What?
Election year.
Oh.
Presidential election year.
Ooo!
I thought we were getting some extra assignments lately.
Yup.
T-shirts, Internet...
...TV, direct mail, buttons, lawn signs, computer wallpaper, bumper stickers, bumper magnets, fridge magnets...
Next? Conventions. Then, we're booked solid 'til November.
...bus wraps, temporary tattoos, skywriting...

July 4, 2008

PIONEER PRESS: DAVID STEINLICHT

Note: The first appearance of Star and Stripe is on page 109.

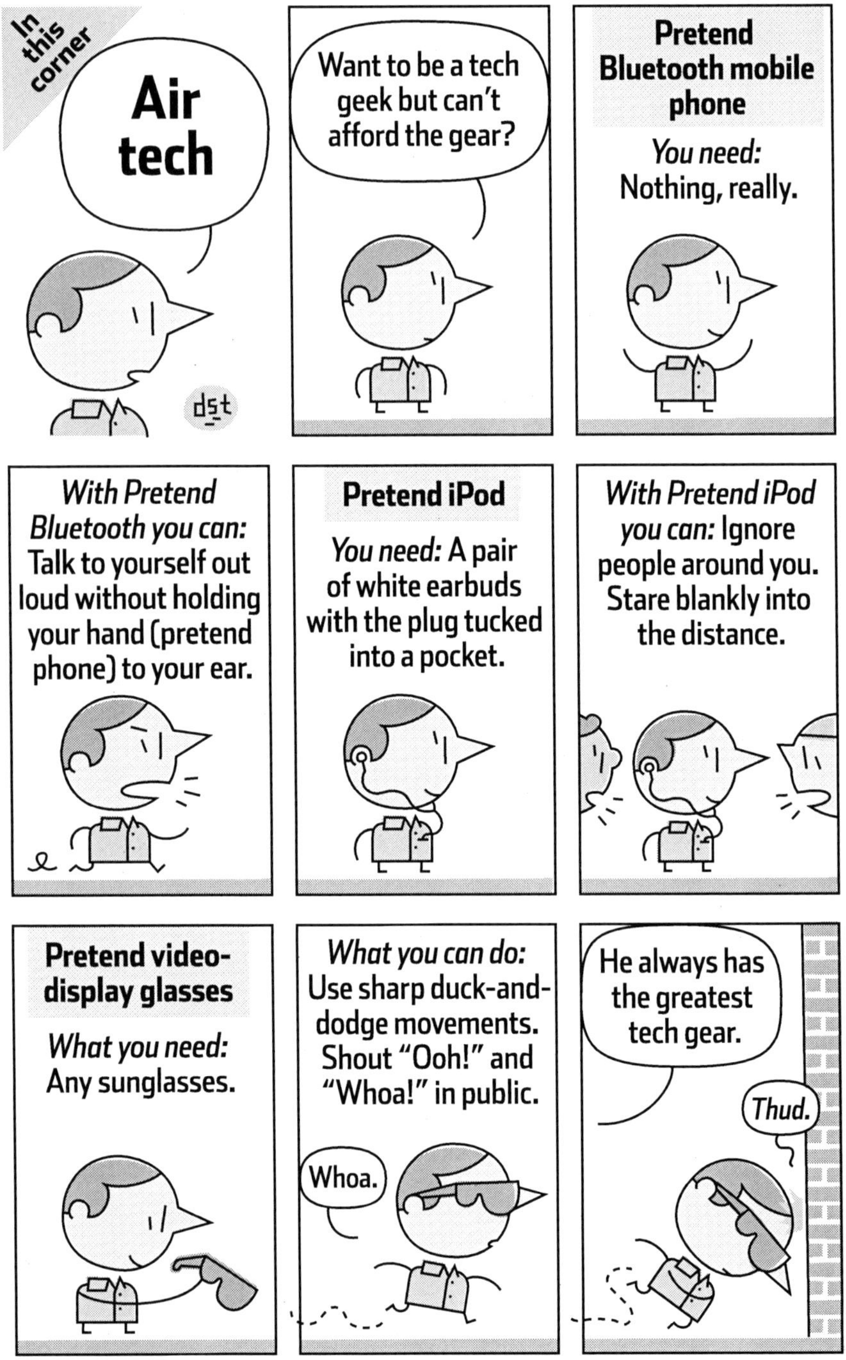

In this corner
Air tech
Want to be a tech geek but can't afford the gear?
Pretend Bluetooth mobile phone
You need: Nothing, really.
With Pretend Bluetooth you can: Talk to yourself out loud without holding your hand (pretend phone) to your ear.
Pretend iPod
You need: A pair of white earbuds with the plug tucked into a pocket.
With Pretend iPod you can: Ignore people around you. Stare blankly into the distance.
Pretend video-display glasses
What you need: Any sunglasses.
What you can do: Use sharp duck-and-dodge movements. Shout "Ooh!" and "Whoa!" in public.
Whoa.
He always has the greatest tech gear.
Thud.

July 11, 2008

PIONEER PRESS: DAVID STEINLICHT

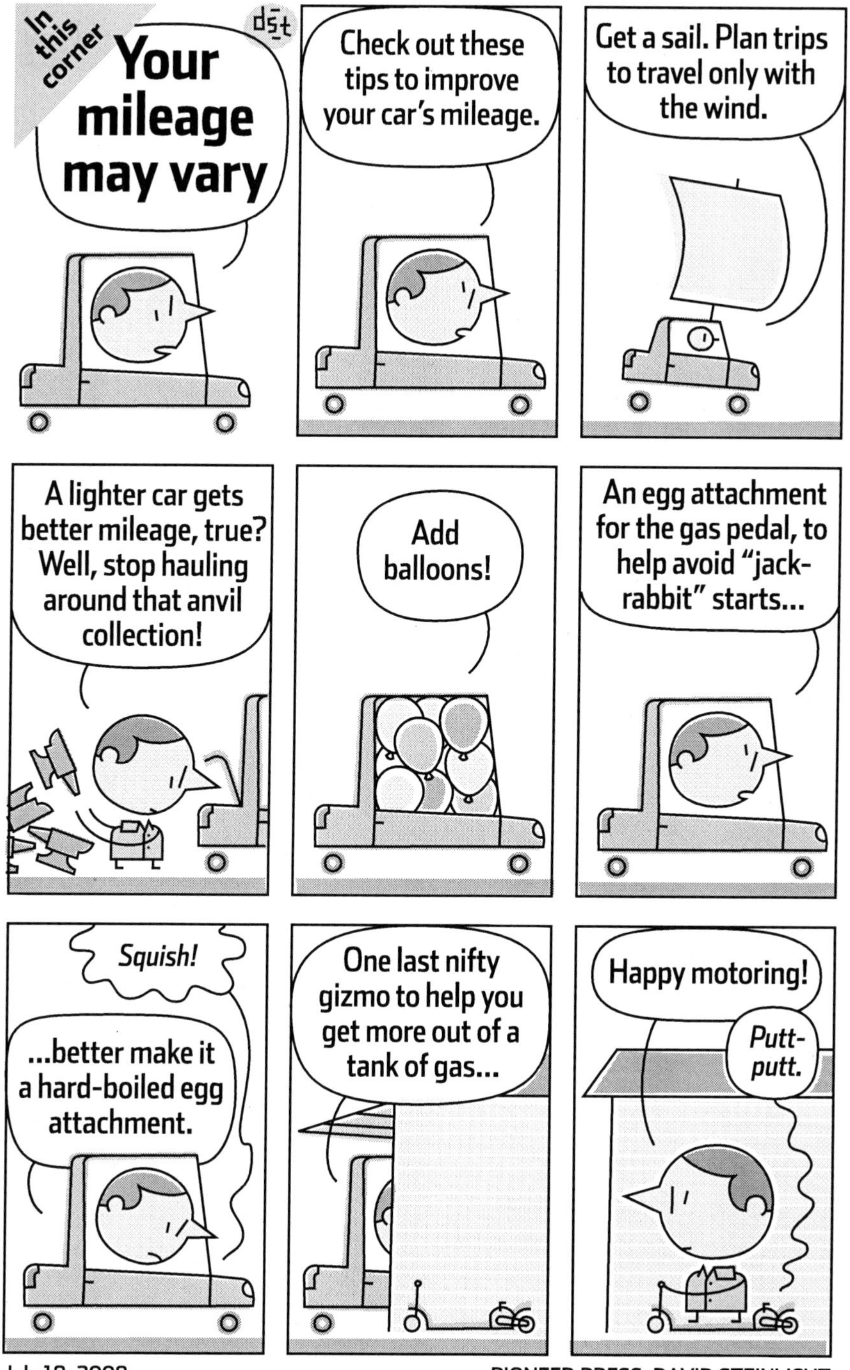
In this corner
Your mileage may vary
dst
Check out these tips to improve your car's mileage.
Get a sail. Plan trips to travel only with the wind.
A lighter car gets better mileage, true? Well, stop hauling around that anvil collection!
Add balloons!
An egg attachment for the gas pedal, to help avoid "jack-rabbit" starts...
Squish!
...better make it a hard-boiled egg attachment.
One last nifty gizmo to help you get more out of a tank of gas...
Happy motoring!
Putt-putt.

July 18, 2008

PIONEER PRESS: DAVID STEINLICHT

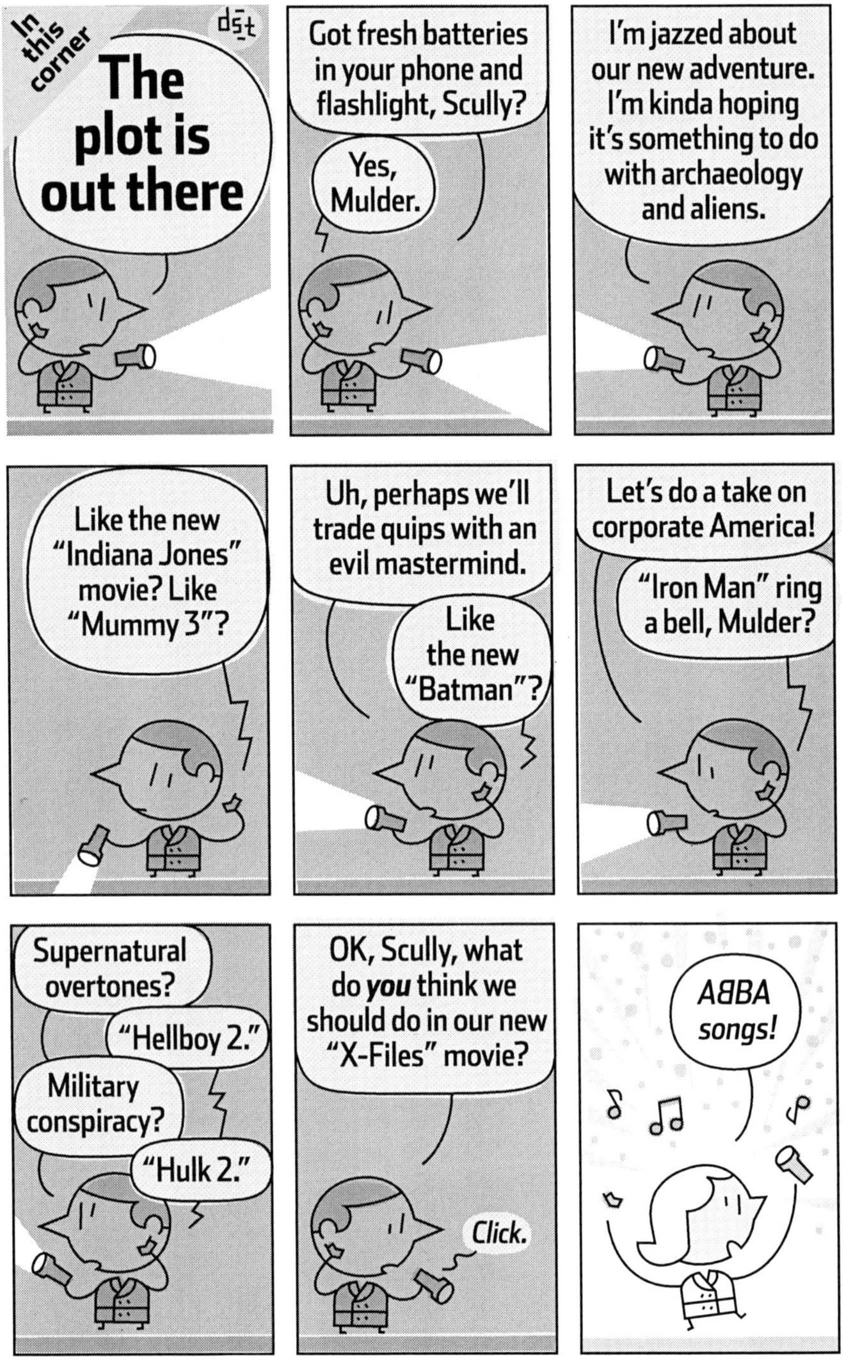
In this corner
dst
The plot is out there
Got fresh batteries in your phone and flashlight, Scully?
Yes, Mulder.
I'm jazzed about our new adventure. I'm kinda hoping it's something to do with archaeology and aliens.
Like the new "Indiana Jones" movie? Like "Mummy 3"?
Uh, perhaps we'll trade quips with an evil mastermind.
Like the new "Batman"?
Let's do a take on corporate America!
"Iron Man" ring a bell, Mulder?
Supernatural overtones?
"Hellboy 2."
Military conspiracy?
"Hulk 2."
OK, Scully, what do *you* think we should do in our new "X-Files" movie?
Click.
ABBA songs!

July 25, 2008

PIONEER PRESS: DAVID STEINLICHT

St. Paul checklist

You're hosting the Republican National Convention. Please provide these items.

× Straw

× 24-hour calliope music

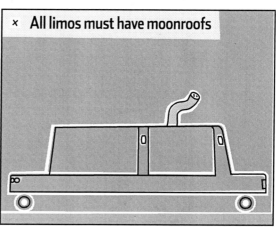

× All limos must have moonroofs

× Ready supply of fresh water

× Lots of peanuts

× Mouse-free environment

Aug. 1, 2008

PIONEER PRESS: DAVID STEINLICHT

Note: Sadly, during the actual RNC convention, there were very few real elephants being chauffeured around in limousines.

In this corner

Why not?

Well ... I didn't see the new Batman movie 'cause Katie Holmes isn't in it.

dst

I didn't see the new Batman movie because the title misspells "Night."

I didn't see the new Batman movie 'cause the new Joker doesn't seem to be particularly funny.

I didn't see the new Batman movie 'cause I'm allergic to brooding.

I didn't see the new Batman movie 'cause I have all the action figures and my adventures are better than any old movie.

I didn't see the new Batman movie 'cause it seems to endorse reckless driving.

I didn't see the new Batman movie 'cause I'm waiting for the one with the Penguin in it.

I did't see it because I don't want to relive the frighteningly deep, emotional experience that was "Batman Returns."

Sniffle.

I didn't see the new Batman movie 'cause only Adam West is Batman.

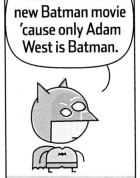

Aug. 8, 2008

PIONEER PRESS: DAVID STEINLICHT

210

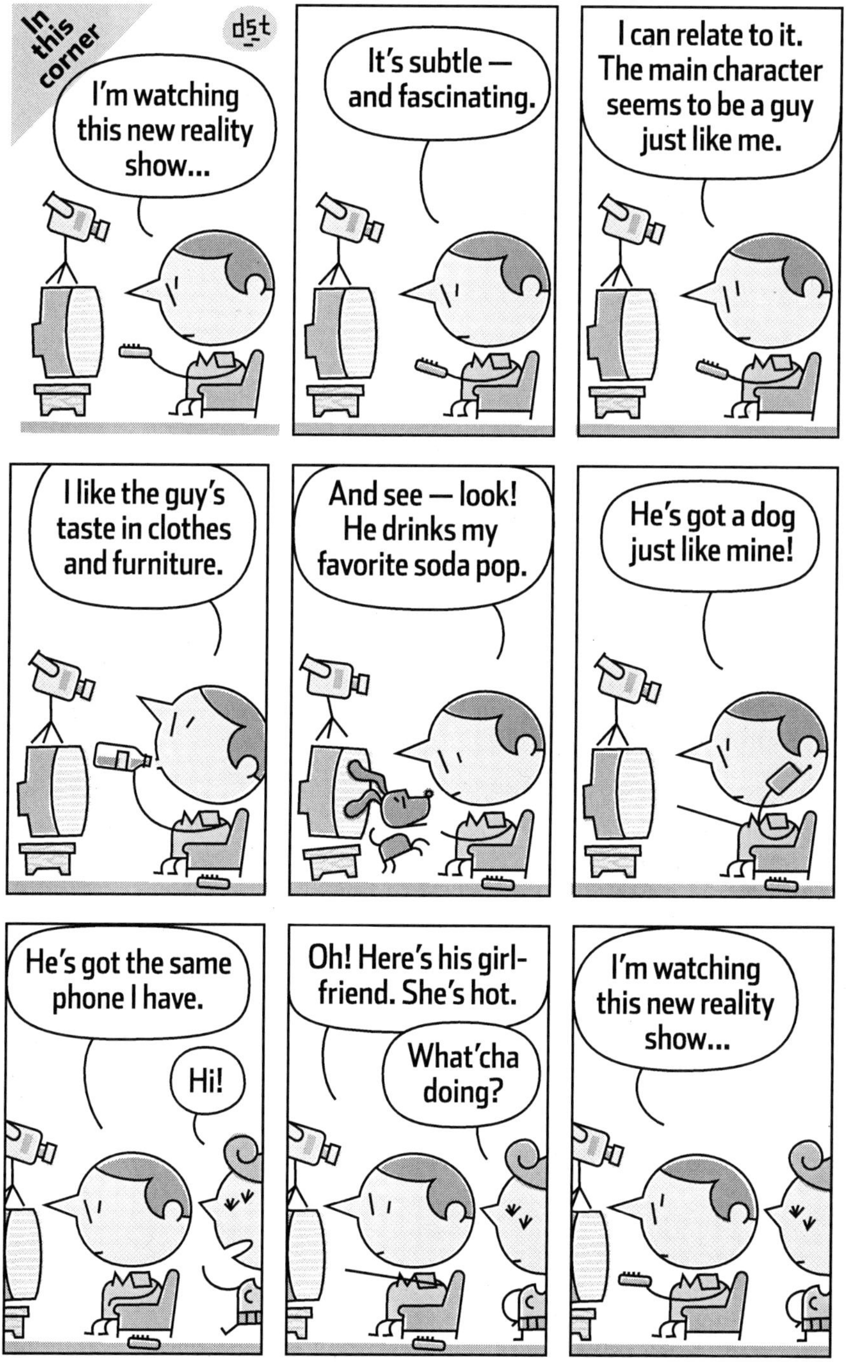
In this corner
dst
I'm watching this new reality show...
It's subtle — and fascinating.
I can relate to it. The main character seems to be a guy just like me.
I like the guy's taste in clothes and furniture.
And see — look! He drinks my favorite soda pop.
He's got a dog just like mine!
He's got the same phone I have.
Hi!
Oh! Here's his girl-friend. She's hot.
What'cha doing?
I'm watching this new reality show...

Aug. 15, 2008

PIONEER PRESS: DAVID STEINLICHT

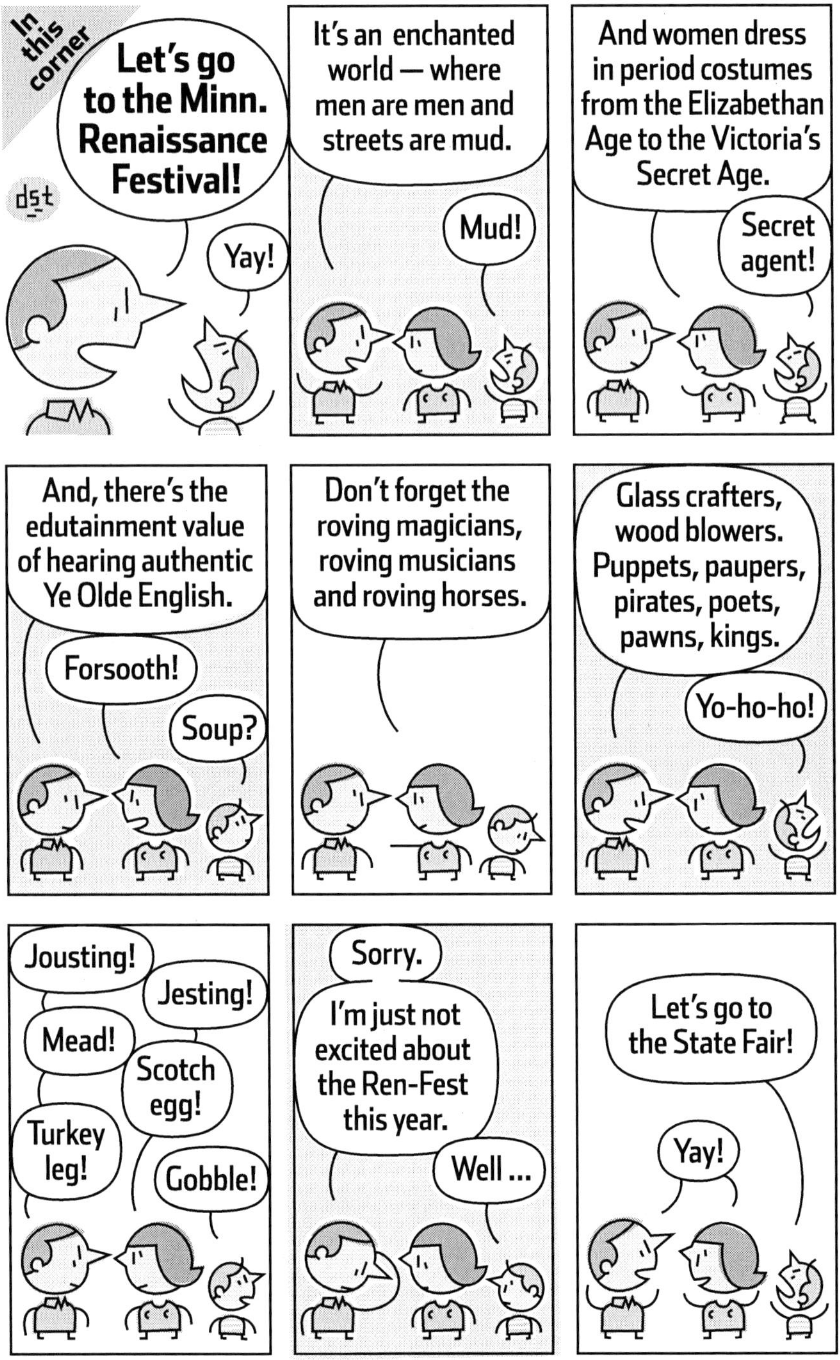
In this corner
dst
Let's go to the Minn. Renaissance Festival!
Yay!
It's an enchanted world — where men are men and streets are mud.
Mud!
And women dress in period costumes from the Elizabethan Age to the Victoria's Secret Age.
Secret agent!
And, there's the edutainment value of hearing authentic Ye Olde English.
Forsooth!
Soup?
Don't forget the roving magicians, roving musicians and roving horses.
Glass crafters, wood blowers. Puppets, paupers, pirates, poets, pawns, kings.
Yo-ho-ho!
Jousting!
Jesting!
Mead!
Scotch egg!
Turkey leg!
Gobble!
Sorry.
I'm just not excited about the Ren-Fest this year.
Well ...
Let's go to the State Fair!
Yay!

Aug. 22, 2008

PIONEER PRESS: DAVID STEINLICHT

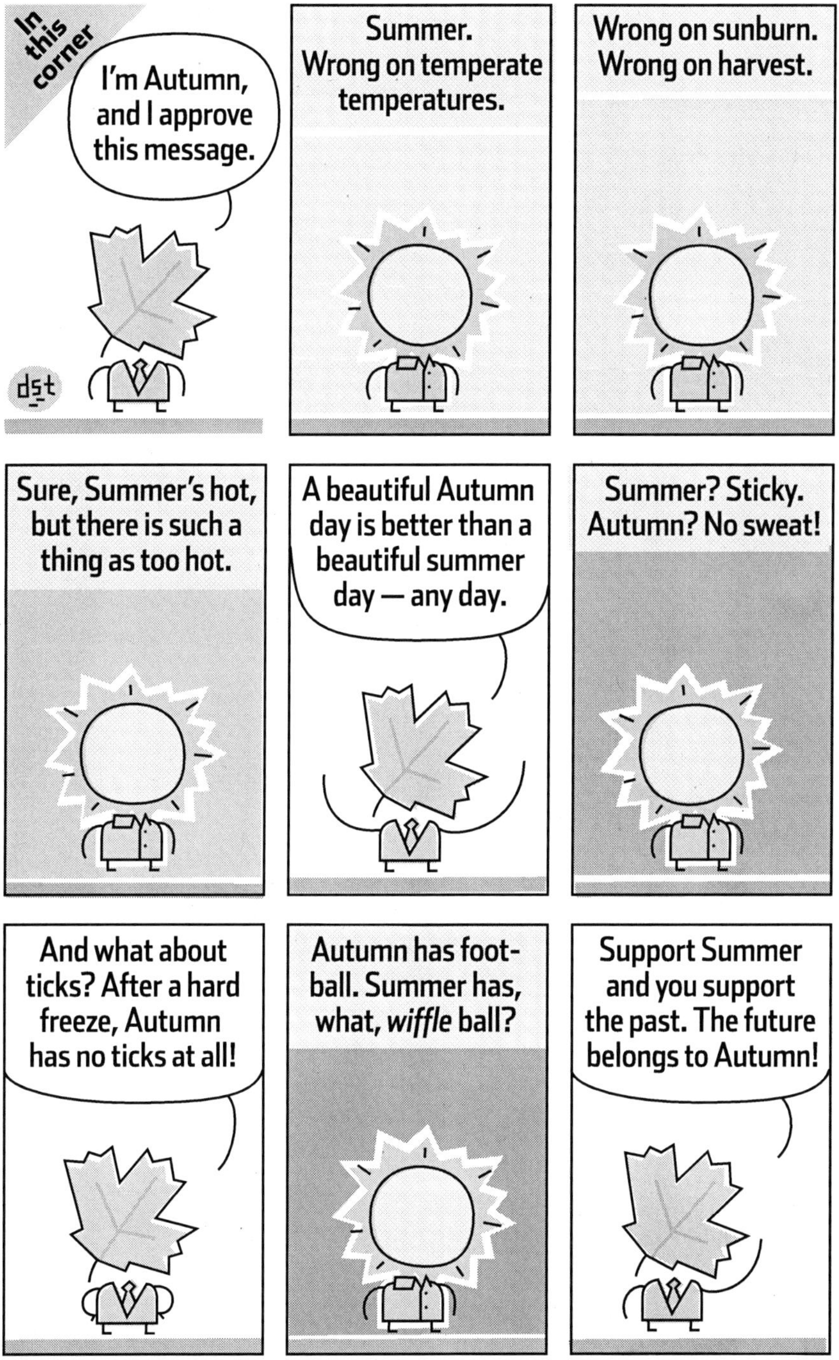
In this corner
I'm Autumn, and I approve this message.
dst
Summer. Wrong on temperate temperatures.
Wrong on sunburn. Wrong on harvest.
Sure, Summer's hot, but there is such a thing as too hot.
A beautiful Autumn day is better than a beautiful summer day — any day.
Summer? Sticky. Autumn? No sweat!
And what about ticks? After a hard freeze, Autumn has no ticks at all!
Autumn has football. Summer has, what, *wiffle* ball?
Support Summer and you support the past. The future belongs to Autumn!

Aug. 29, 2008

PIONEER PRESS: DAVID STEINLICHT

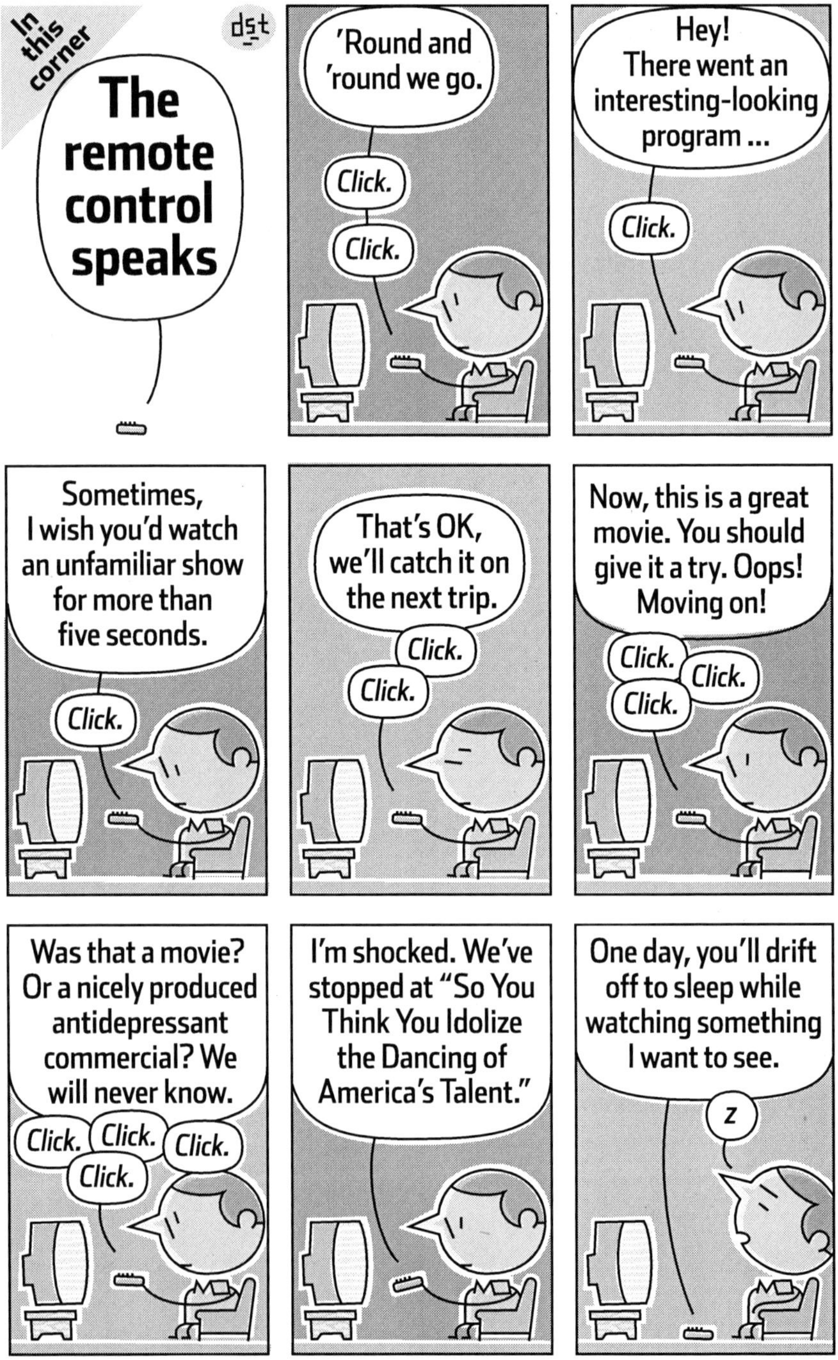
In this corner
dst
The remote control speaks
'Round and 'round we go.
Click.
Click.
Hey! There went an interesting-looking program ...
Click.
Sometimes, I wish you'd watch an unfamiliar show for more than five seconds.
Click.
That's OK, we'll catch it on the next trip.
Click.
Click.
Now, this is a great movie. You should give it a try. Oops! Moving on!
Click.
Click.
Click.
Was that a movie? Or a nicely produced antidepressant commercial? We will never know.
Click.
Click.
Click.
Click.
I'm shocked. We've stopped at "So You Think You Idolize the Dancing of America's Talent."
One day, you'll drift off to sleep while watching something I want to see.
z

Sept. 5, 2008

PIONEER PRESS: DAVID STEINLICHT

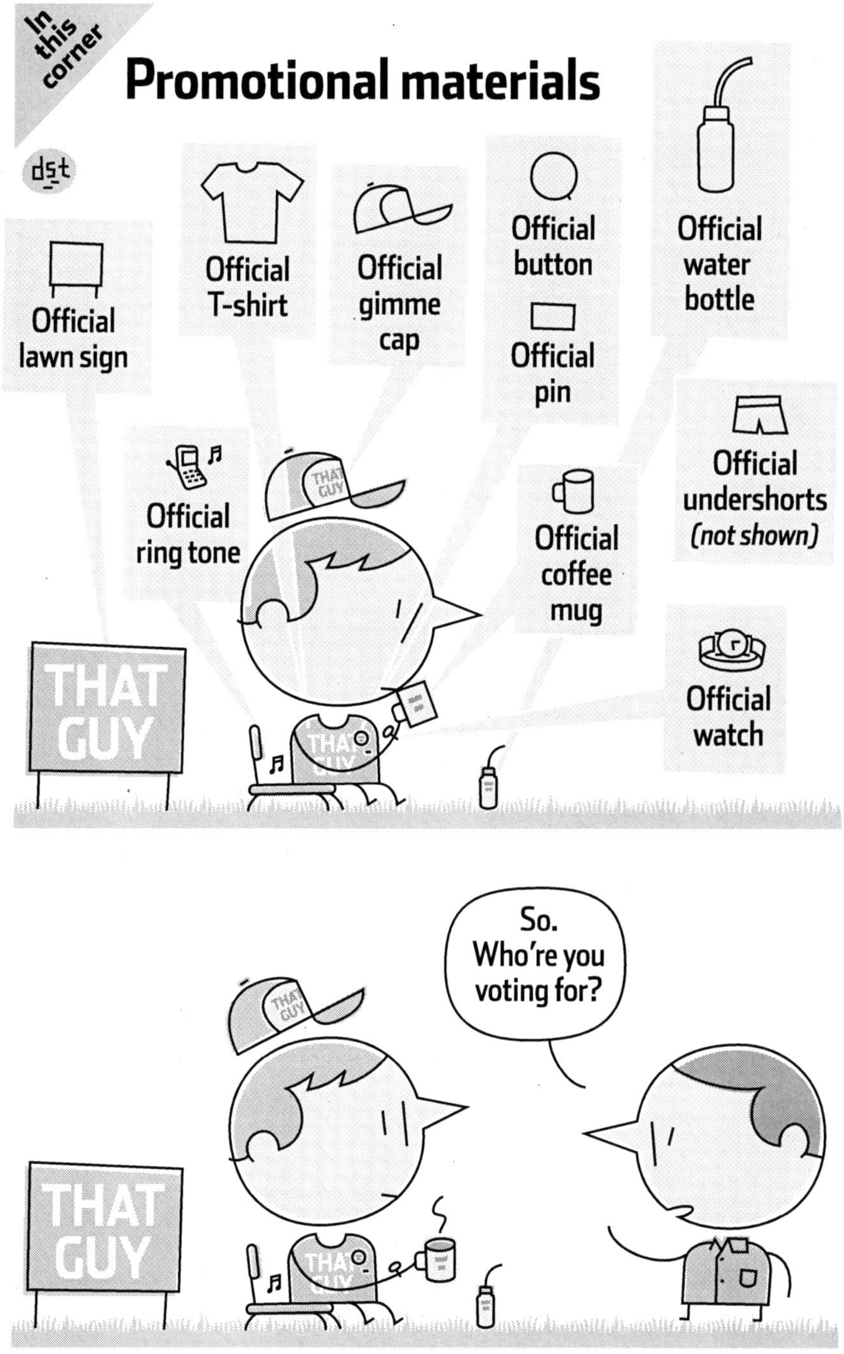
In this corner
Promotional materials
dst
Official lawn sign
Official T-shirt
Official gimme cap
Official button
Official pin
Official water bottle
Official ring tone
Official coffee mug
Official undershorts *(not shown)*
Official watch
THAT GUY
So. Who're you voting for?
THAT GUY

Sept. 12, 2008

PIONEER PRESS: DAVID STEINLICHT

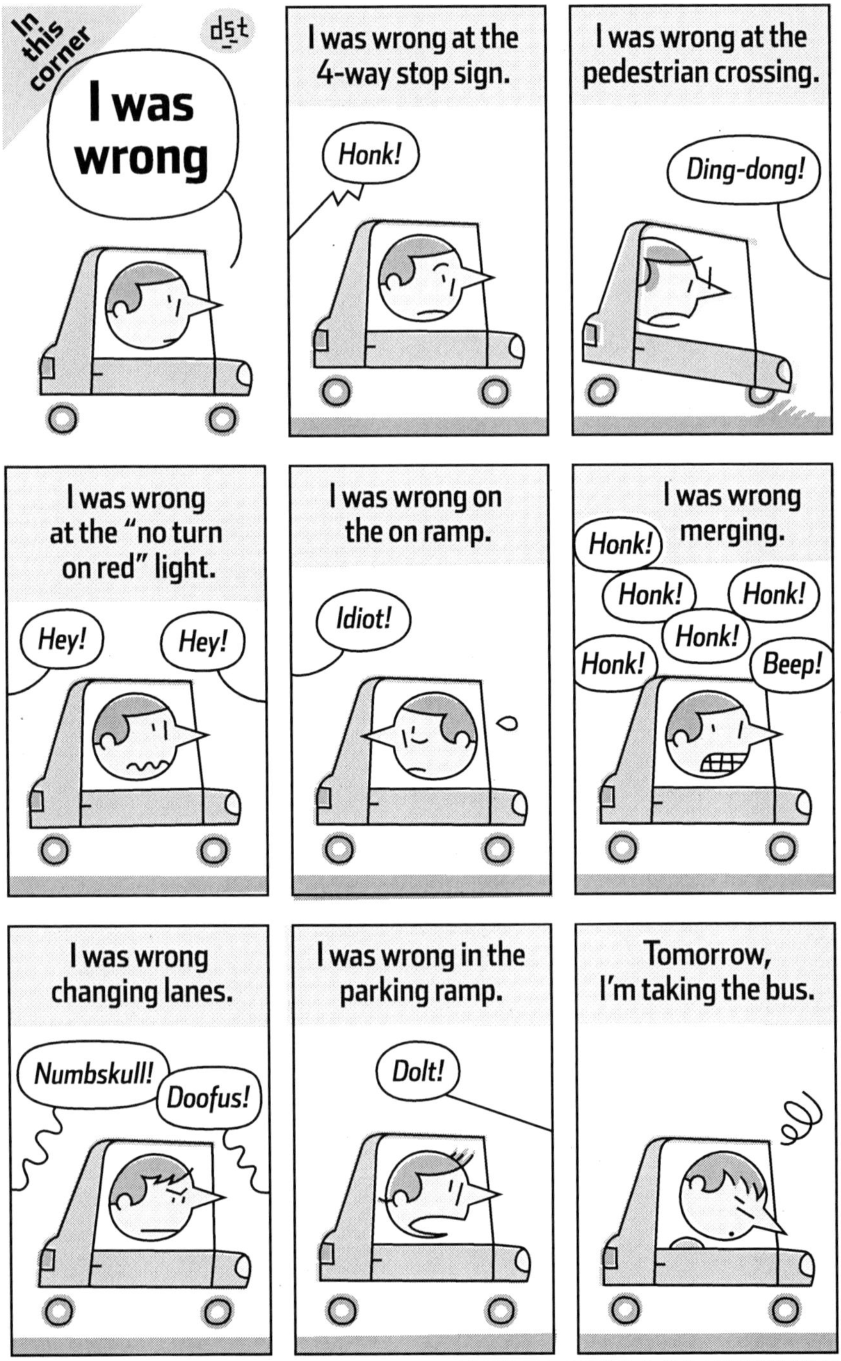
In this corner
dst
I was wrong
I was wrong at the 4-way stop sign.
Honk!
I was wrong at the pedestrian crossing.
Ding-dong!
I was wrong at the "no turn on red" light.
Hey!
Hey!
I was wrong on the on ramp.
Idiot!
I was wrong merging.
Honk!
Honk!
Honk!
Honk!
Honk!
Beep!
I was wrong changing lanes.
Numbskull!
Doofus!
I was wrong in the parking ramp.
Dolt!
Tomorrow, I'm taking the bus.

Sept. 19, 2008

PIONEER PRESS: DAVID STEINLICHT

Some to-do lists

1. Play GTA III
2. Sleep
3. Play GTA IV

1. Check BlackBerry
2. *Sell!*
3. Check BlackBerry
4. *Buy!*

1. Loot
2. Pillage
3. Burn
4. Say "Arr."

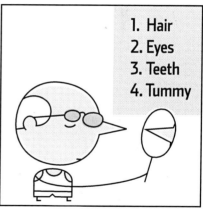

1. Hair
2. Eyes
3. Teeth
4. Tummy

1. Rinse
2. Lather
3. Repeat

1. Must...
2. Consume...
3. Human...
4. Brains!

Sept. 26, 2008

PIONEER PRESS: DAVID STEINLICHT

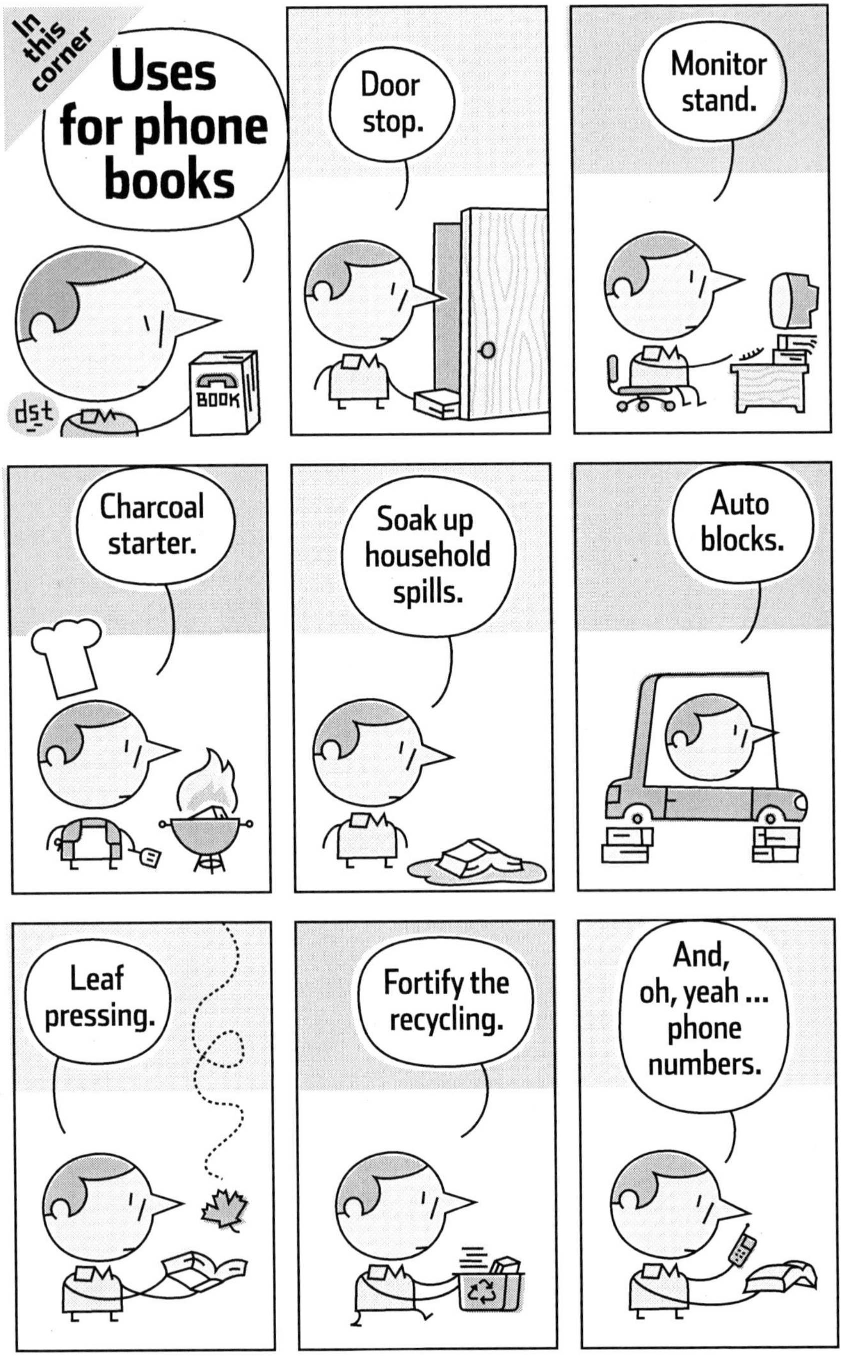
In this corner
Uses for phone books
BOOK
dst
Door stop.
Monitor stand.
Charcoal starter.
Soak up household spills.
Auto blocks.
Leaf pressing.
Fortify the recycling.
And, oh, yeah ... phone numbers.

Oct. 3, 2008

PIONEER PRESS: DAVID STEINLICHT

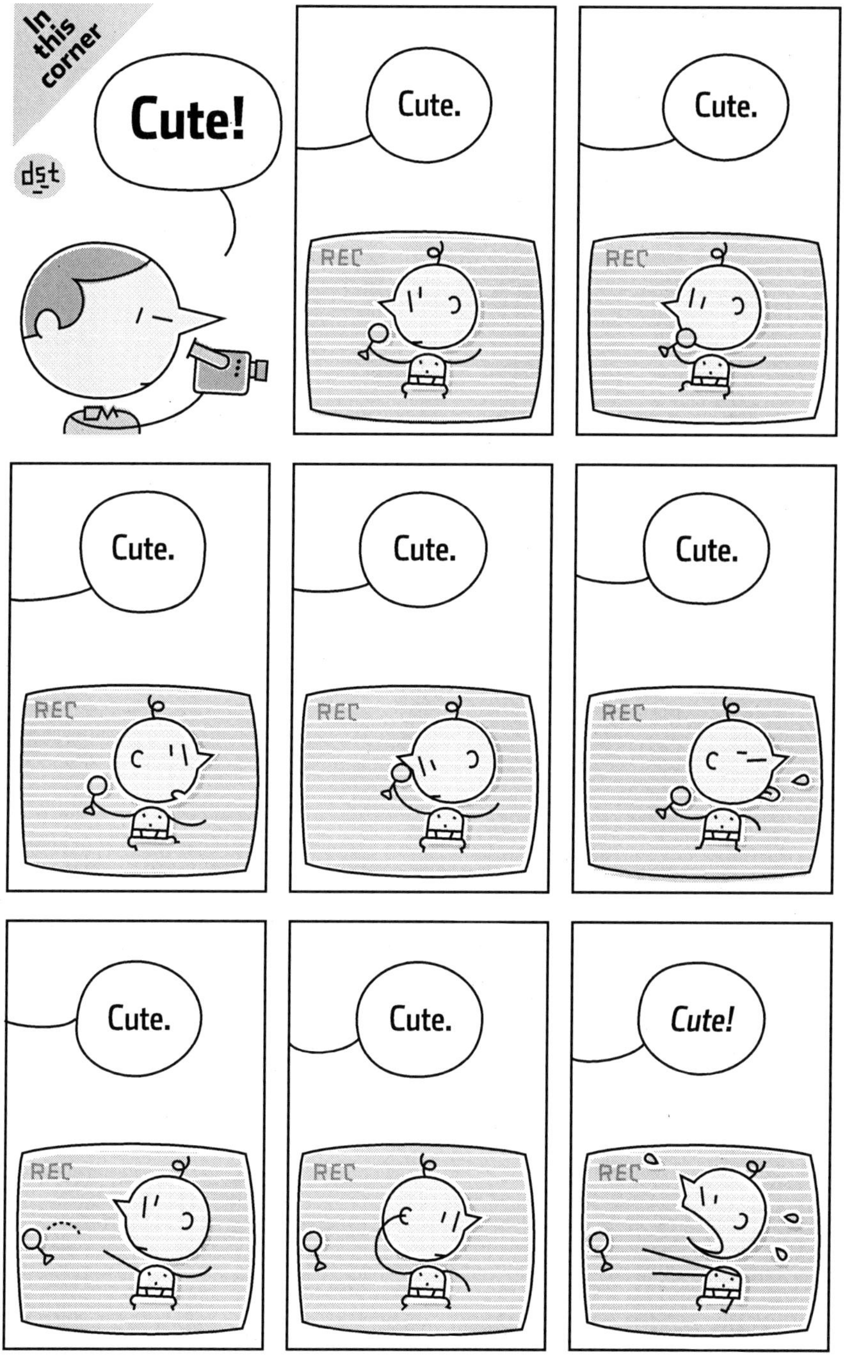
In this corner
dst
Cute!
REC
Cute.
REC
Cute.
REC
Cute.
REC
Cute.
REC
Cute.
REC
Cute.
REC
Cute.
REC
Cute!
REC

Oct. 10, 2008

PIONEER PRESS: DAVID STEINLICHT

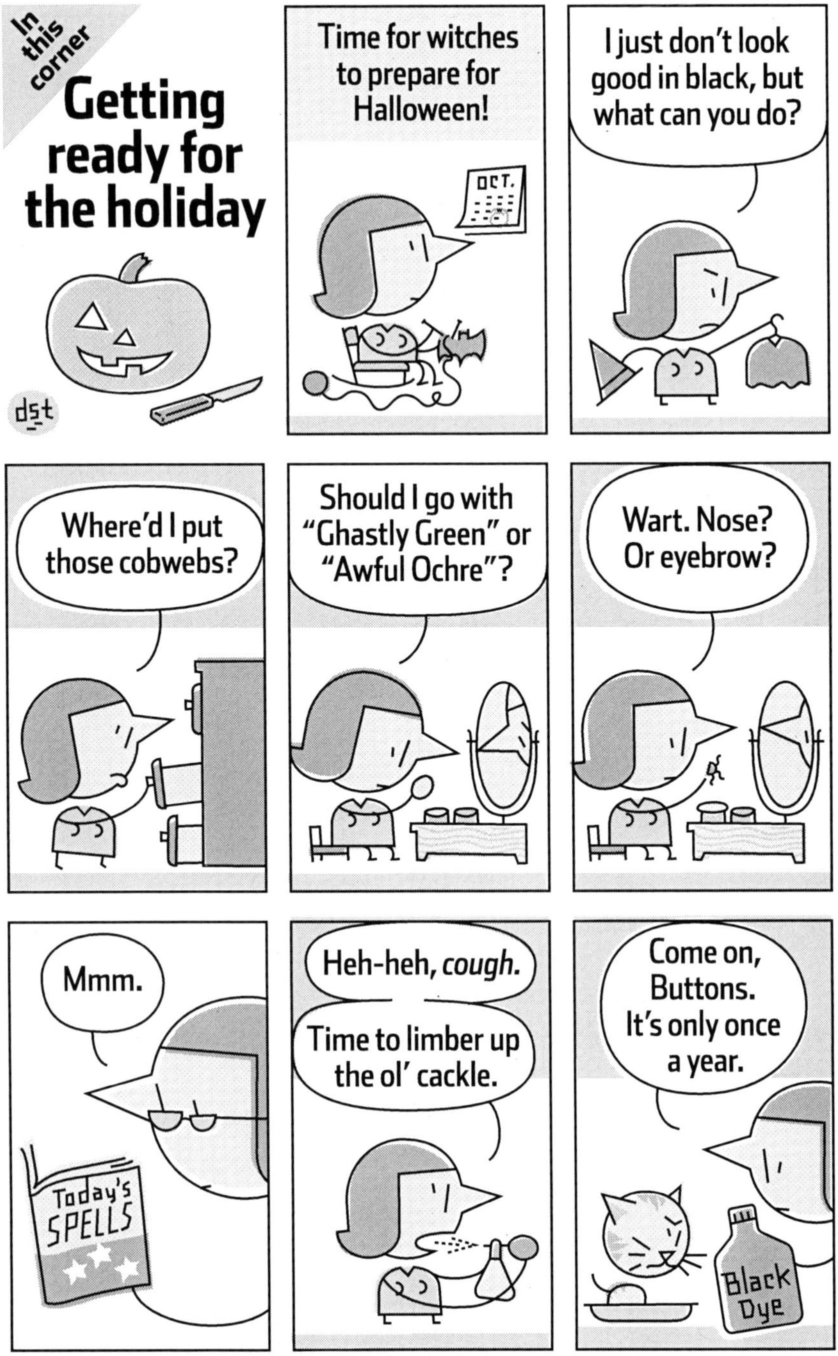
In this corner
Getting ready for the holiday
dst
Time for witches to prepare for Halloween!
OCT.
I just don't look good in black, but what can you do?
Where'd I put those cobwebs?
Should I go with "Ghastly Green" or "Awful Ochre"?
Wart. Nose? Or eyebrow?
Mmm.
Today's SPELLS
Heh-heh, *cough.*
Time to limber up the ol' cackle.
Come on, Buttons. It's only once a year.
Black Dye

Oct. 17, 2008

PIONEER PRESS: DAVID STEINLICHT

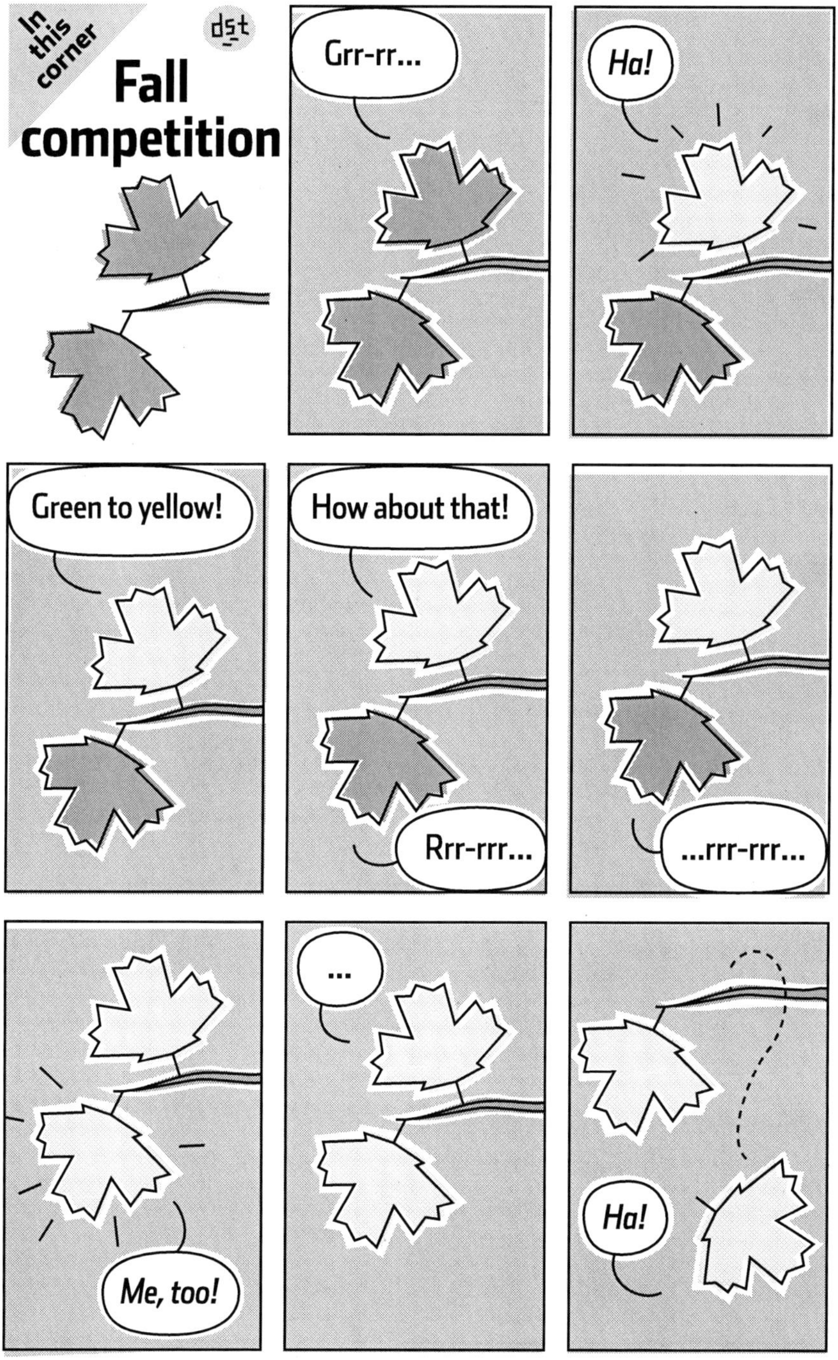
In this corner
dst
Fall competition
Grr-rr...
Ha!
Green to yellow!
How about that!
Rrr-rrr...
...rrr-rrr...
Me, too!
...
Ha!

Oct. 24, 2008

PIONEER PRESS: DAVID STEINLICHT

Tattoo guidelines

In this corner

dst

If you are going to get a tattoo, get a tattoo of something that is important to you.

zzz.

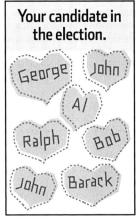

Your candidate in the election.

George
John
Al
Ralph
Bob
John
Barack

The mortgage rate on your home loan.

5.3%

The combination of your bike lock.

R10
L20
R33

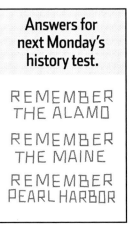

Answers for next Monday's history test.

REMEMBER THE ALAMO

REMEMBER THE MAINE

REMEMBER PEARL HARBOR

Your credit card numbers and ATM PIN numbers.

CREDIT CARD

Signature

A map for the treasure you buried on a Caribbean island.

A unicorn.

Nov. 7, 2008

PIONEER PRESS: DAVID STEINLICHT

222

In this corner

Mix your own 007 movie

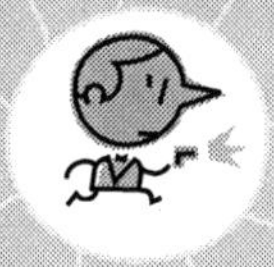

You know there's a James Bond movie formula. Why don't you mix your own?

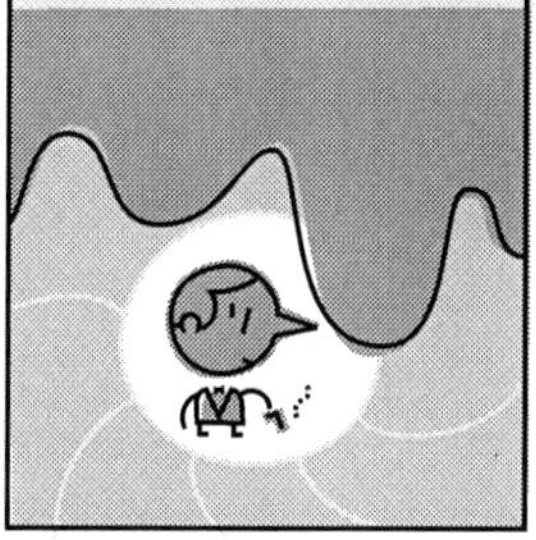

Bond's new car

- ☐ Aston Martin
- ☐ BMW
- ☐ Tesla
- ☐ Chrysler

Doomed Bond girl

- ☐ Dumb blonde
- ☐ Dumb brunette
- ☐ Dumb redhead
- ☐ Lindsay Lohan

Bond girl

- ☐ Blonde
- ☐ Brunette
- ☐ Redhead
- ☐ Blond highlights

Villain

- ☐ Evil genius
- ☐ Psycho genius
- ☐ Genius psycho
- ☐ Grouchy genius

Villain's scheme

- ☐ Control money
- ☐ Control food
- ☐ Control oil
- ☐ Control oily food

Exotic locales

- ☐ Third World
- ☐ China
- ☐ Paris
- ☐ Schenectady, N.Y.

Theme song by

- ☐ Blondie
- ☐ Pink
- ☐ David Archuleta
- ☐ Judi Dench

Nov. 14, 2008

PIONEER PRESS: DAVID STEINLICHT

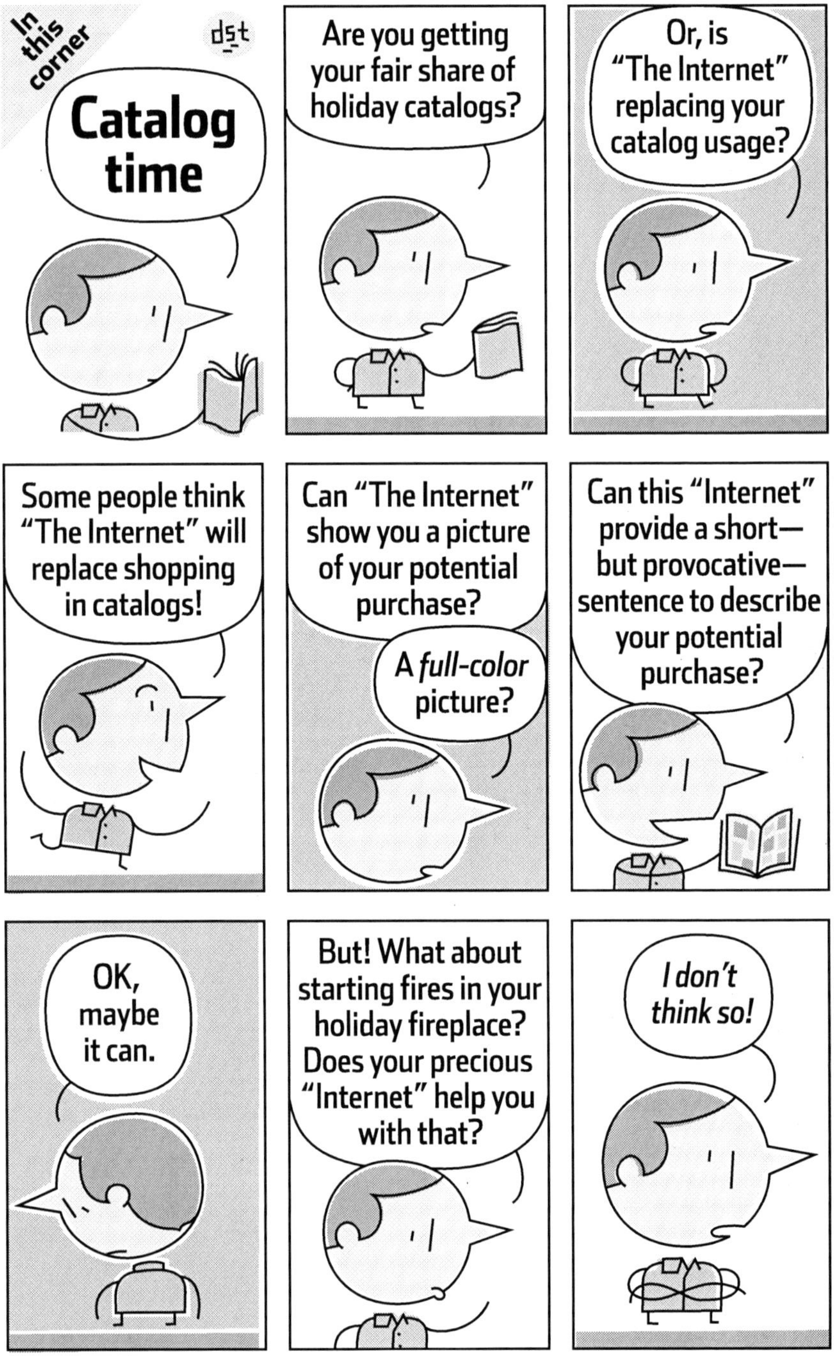
In this corner
dst
Catalog time
Are you getting your fair share of holiday catalogs?
Or, is "The Internet" replacing your catalog usage?
Some people think "The Internet" will replace shopping in catalogs!
Can "The Internet" show you a picture of your potential purchase?
A *full-color* picture?
Can this "Internet" provide a short—but provocative—sentence to describe your potential purchase?
OK, maybe it can.
But! What about starting fires in your holiday fireplace? Does your precious "Internet" help you with that?
I don't think so!

Nov. 21, 2008

PIONEER PRESS: DAVID STEINLICHT

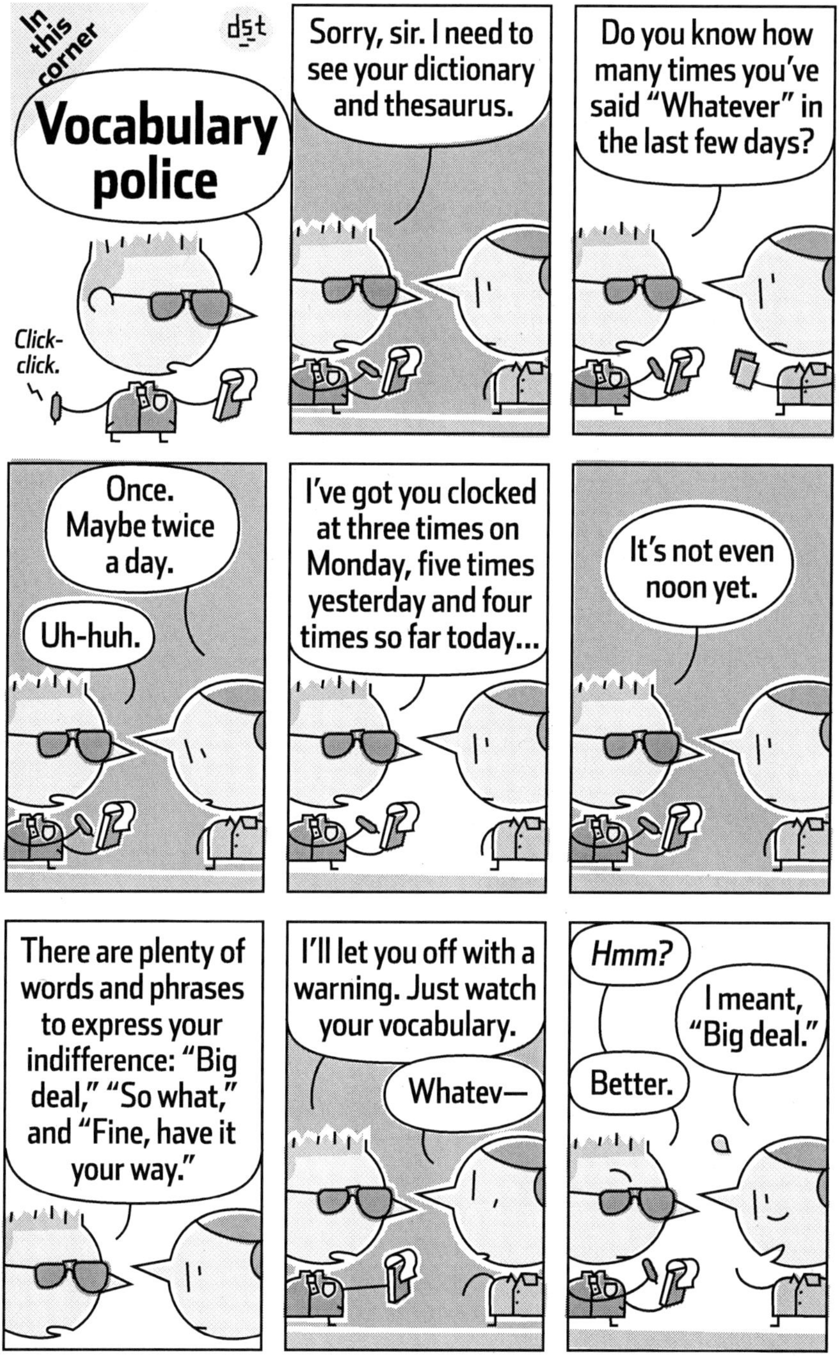
In this corner
dst
Vocabulary police
Click-click.
Sorry, sir. I need to see your dictionary and thesaurus.
Do you know how many times you've said "Whatever" in the last few days?
Once. Maybe twice a day.
Uh-huh.
I've got you clocked at three times on Monday, five times yesterday and four times so far today...
It's not even noon yet.
There are plenty of words and phrases to express your indifference: "Big deal," "So what," and "Fine, have it your way."
I'll let you off with a warning. Just watch your vocabulary.
Whatev—
Hmm?
I meant, "Big deal."
Better.

Nov. 28, 2008 PIONEER PRESS: DAVID STEINLICHT

Note: The police officer is based on Simon Pegg's character in the movie *Hot Fuzz.*

Hey, kids! **New toys** for the new economy!

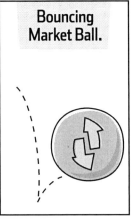

Bouncing Market Ball.

Shrinking Work Force.

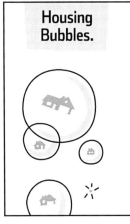

Housing Bubbles.

Collapsible Bank.

Sliding Profits.

Recessionary Spiral.

Soft Dollar.

Bernanke Bear.

Dec. 5, 2008

PIONEER PRESS: DAVID STEINLICHT

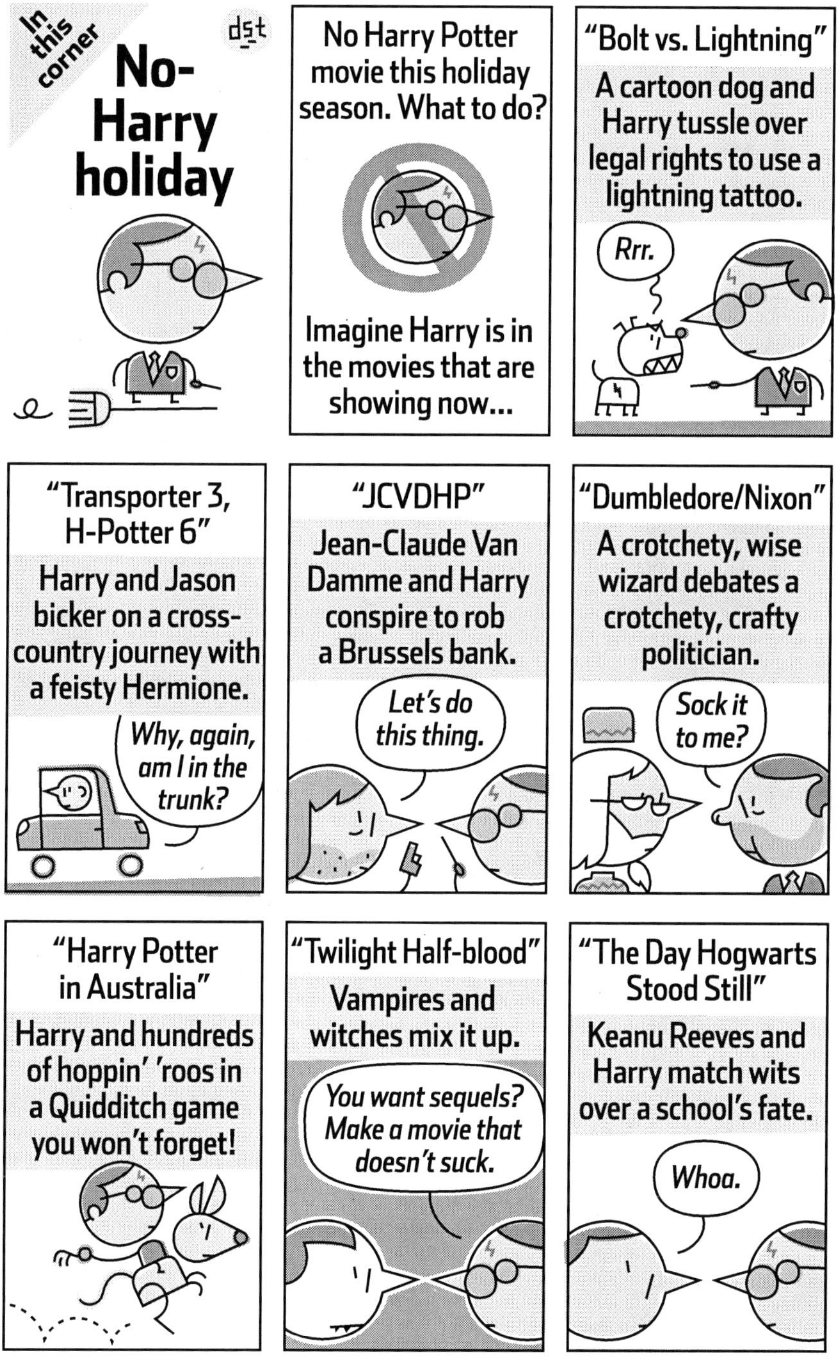

In this corner
No-Harry holiday
dst
No Harry Potter movie this holiday season. What to do?
Imagine Harry is in the movies that are showing now...
"Bolt vs. Lightning"
A cartoon dog and Harry tussle over legal rights to use a lightning tattoo.
Rrr.
"Transporter 3, H-Potter 6"
Harry and Jason bicker on a cross-country journey with a feisty Hermione.
Why, again, am I in the trunk?
"JCVDHP"
Jean-Claude Van Damme and Harry conspire to rob a Brussels bank.
Let's do this thing.
"Dumbledore/Nixon"
A crotchety, wise wizard debates a crotchety, crafty politician.
Sock it to me?
"Harry Potter in Australia"
Harry and hundreds of hoppin' 'roos in a Quidditch game you won't forget!
"Twilight Half-blood"
Vampires and witches mix it up.
You want sequels? Make a movie that doesn't suck.
"The Day Hogwarts Stood Still"
Keanu Reeves and Harry match wits over a school's fate.
Whoa.

Dec. 12, 2008

PIONEER PRESS: DAVID STEINLICHT

Note: A Harry Potter/Jean-Claude Van Damme team-up would be so great.

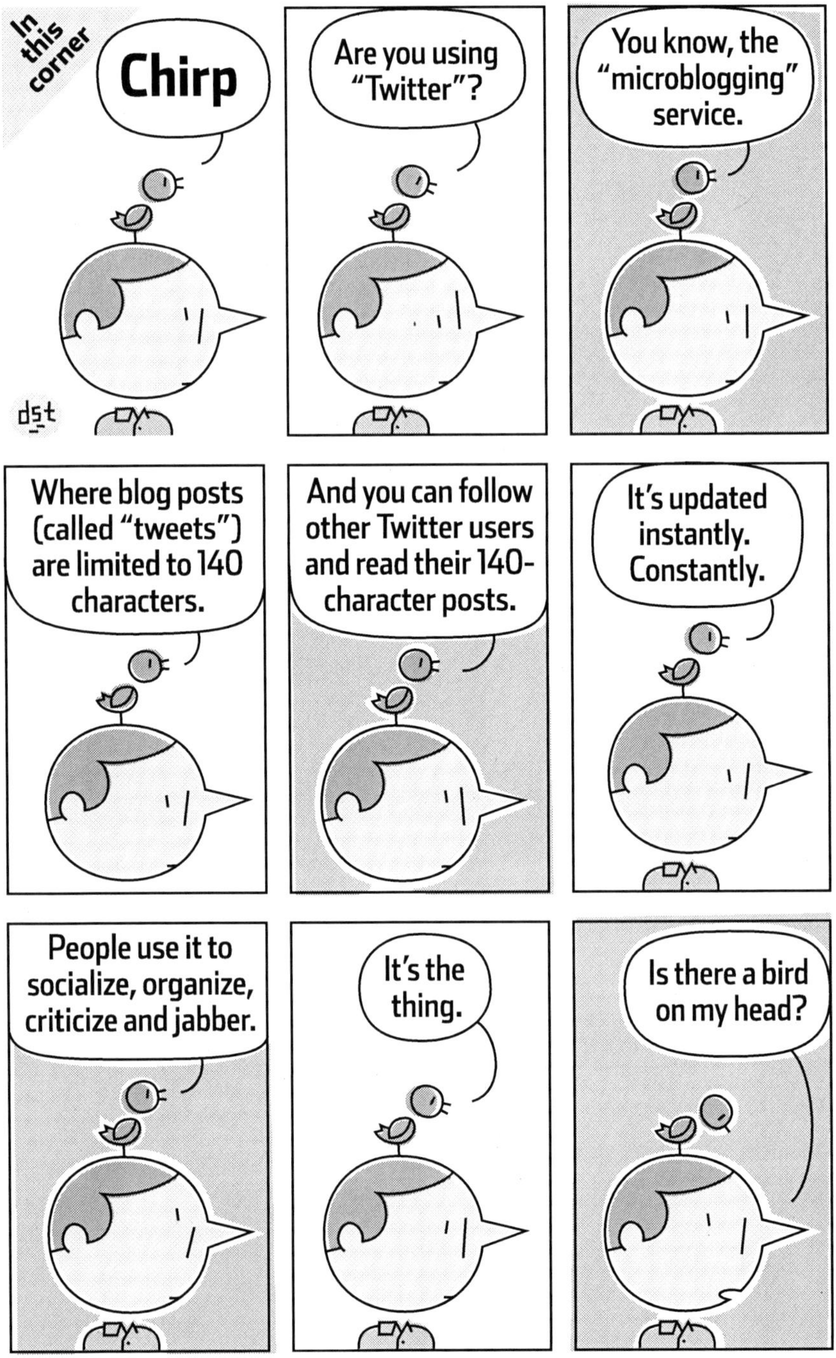
In this corner
Chirp
Are you using "Twitter"?
You know, the "microblogging" service.
Where blog posts (called "tweets") are limited to 140 characters.
And you can follow other Twitter users and read their 140-character posts.
It's updated instantly. Constantly.
People use it to socialize, organize, criticize and jabber.
It's the thing.
Is there a bird on my head?

Dec. 19, 2008

PIONEER PRESS: DAVID STEINLICHT

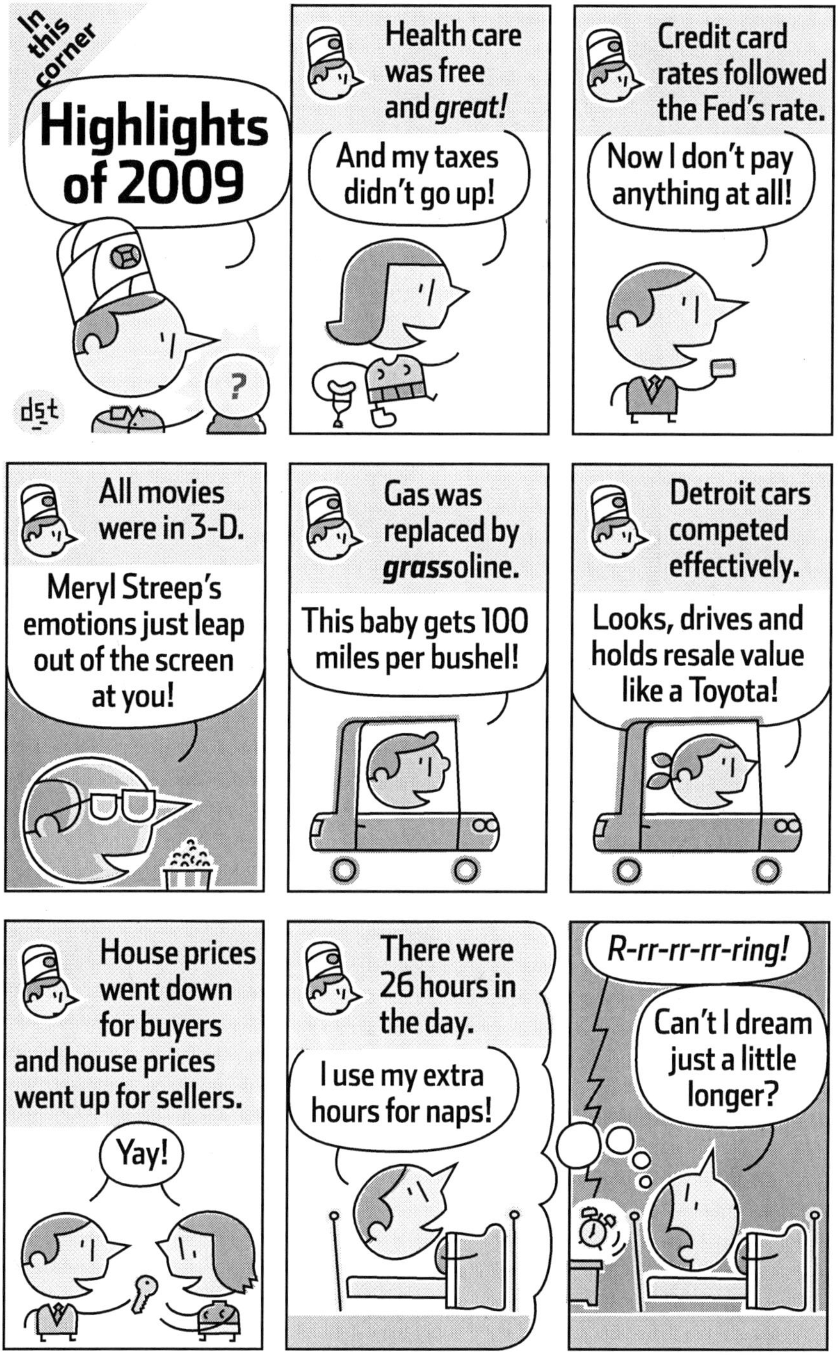
In this corner
Highlights of 2009
Health care was free and *great!*
And my taxes didn't go up!
Credit card rates followed the Fed's rate.
Now I don't pay anything at all!
All movies were in 3-D.
Meryl Streep's emotions just leap out of the screen at you!
Gas was replaced by ***grass***oline.
This baby gets 100 miles per bushel!
Detroit cars competed effectively.
Looks, drives and holds resale value like a Toyota!
House prices went down for buyers and house prices went up for sellers.
Yay!
There were 26 hours in the day.
I use my extra hours for naps!
R-rr-rr-rr-ring!
Can't I dream just a little longer?

Dec. 26, 2008

PIONEER PRESS: DAVID STEINLICHT

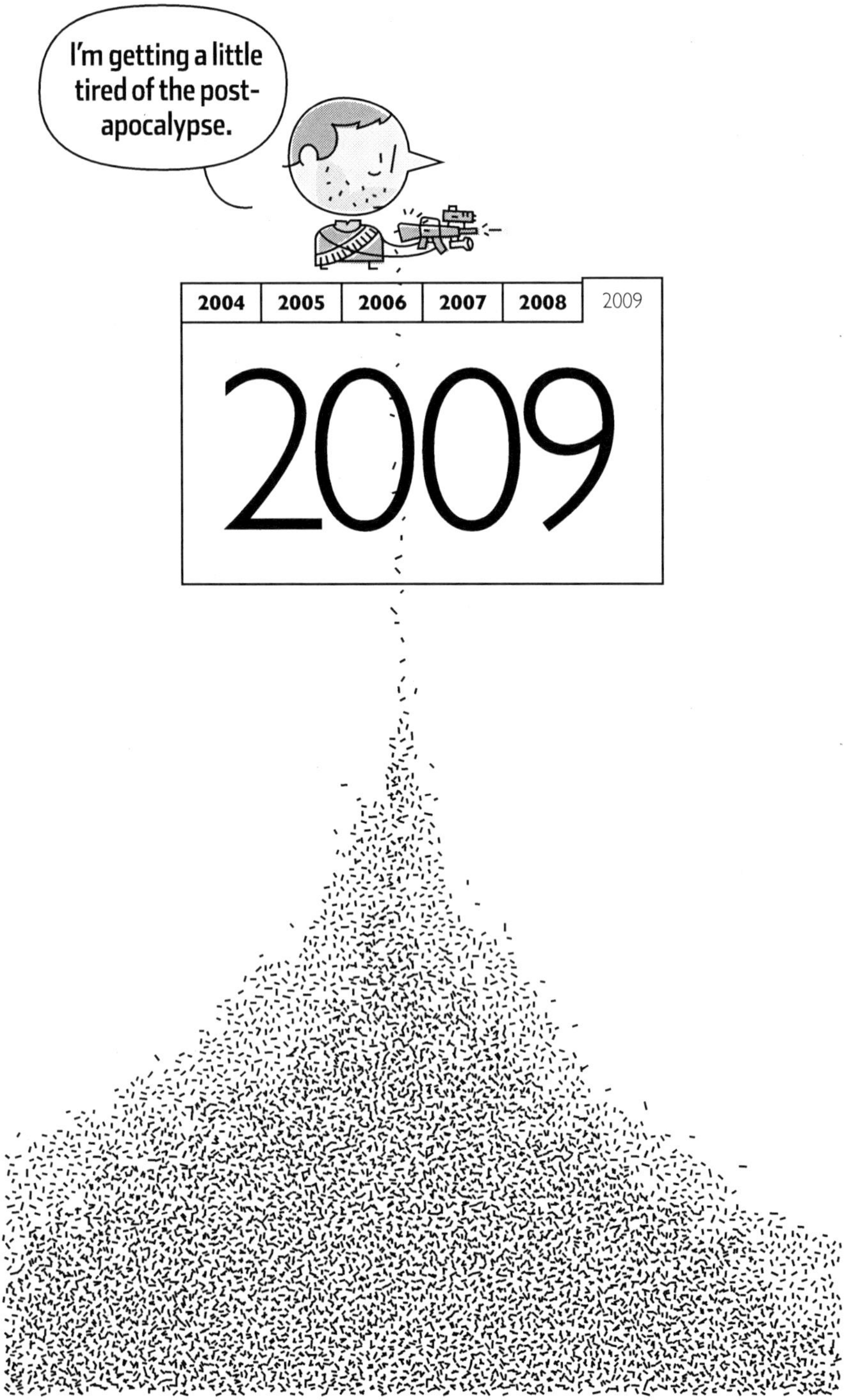
I'm getting a little tired of the post-apocalypse.
2004
2005
2006
2007
2008
2009
2009

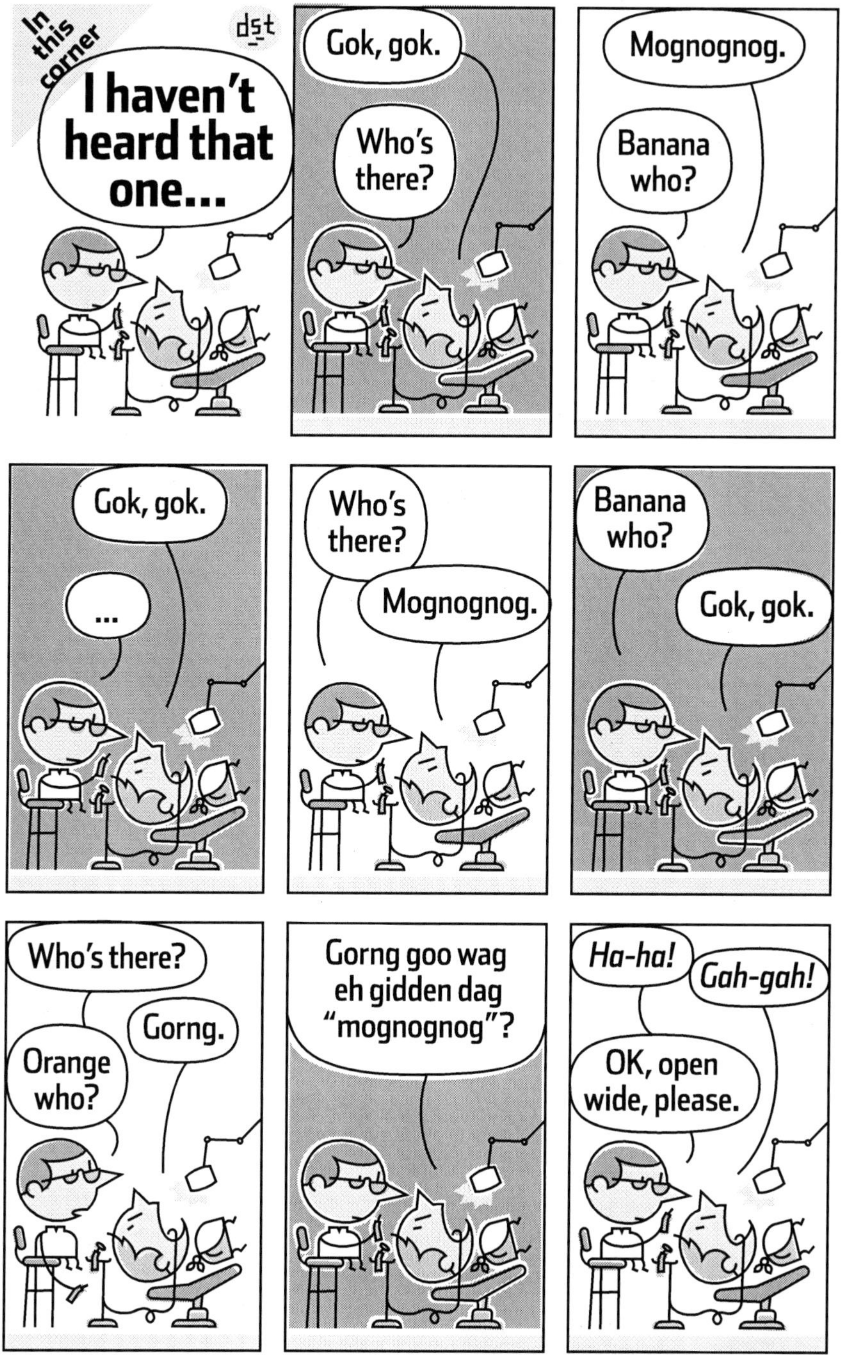
In this corner
dst
I haven't heard that one...
Gok, gok.
Who's there?
Mognognog.
Banana who?
Gok, gok.
...
Who's there?
Mognognog.
Banana who?
Gok, gok.
Who's there?
Gorng.
Orange who?
Gorng goo wag eh gidden dag "mognognog"?
Ha-ha!
Gah-gah!
OK, open wide, please.

Jan. 2, 2009

PIONEER PRESS: DAVID STEINLICHT

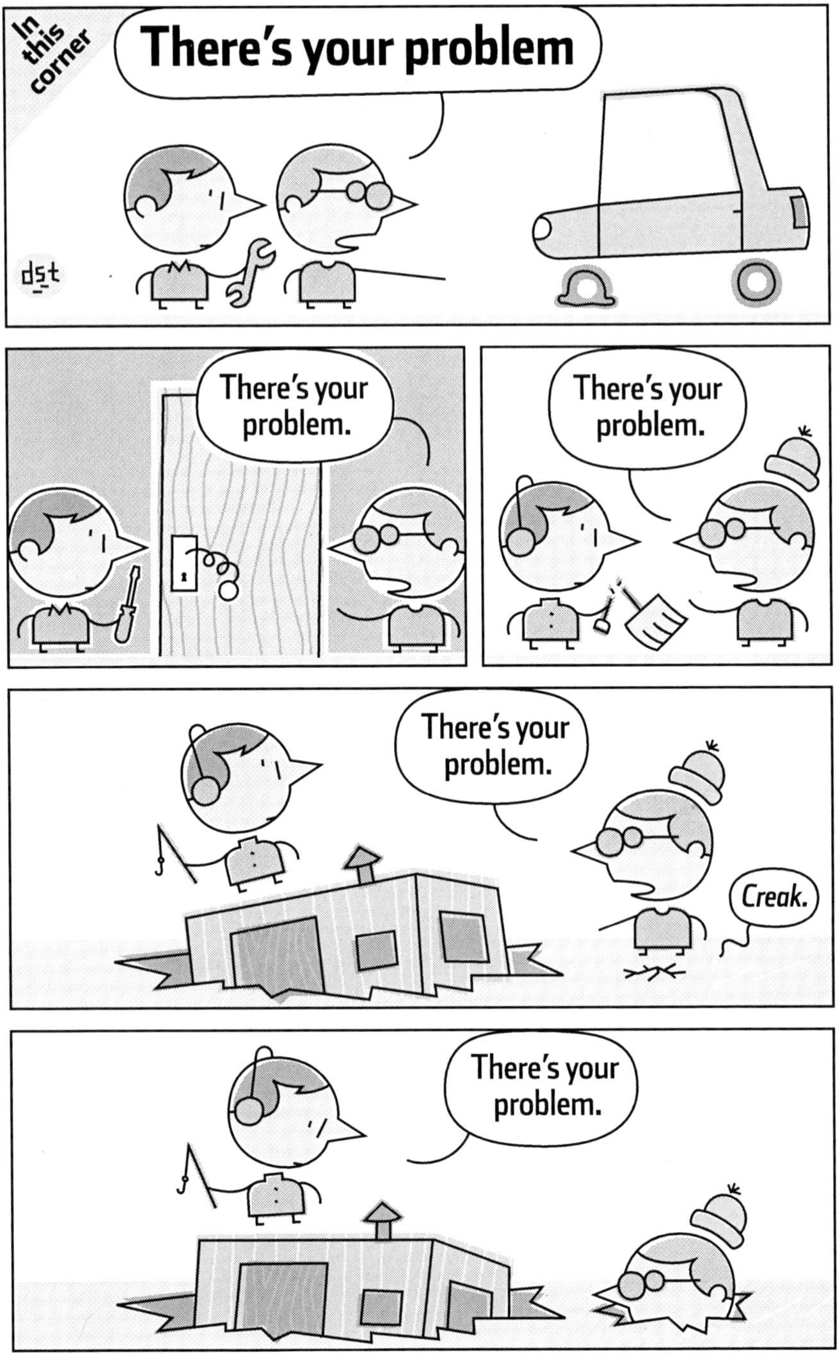
In this corner
There's your problem
dst
There's your problem.
There's your problem.
There's your problem.
Creak.
There's your problem.

Jan. 9, 2009 PIONEER PRESS: DAVID STEINLICHT

Ideas for Winter Carnival events

King Boreas vs. Vulcanus Rex paint-balloon fight.

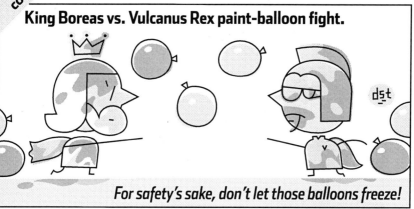

For safety's sake, don't let those balloons freeze!

King Boreas vs. Vulcanus Rex chili vs. smoothie cookoff.

Rumor has it, King Boreas' chili is smoking hot.

Marching bands on ice skates.

Flood and freeze
Fourth Street from Rice Park to Lowertown — add
skates, drums and trombones, and you've got an exciting parade.

Jan. 16, 2009   PIONEER PRESS: DAVID STEINLICHT

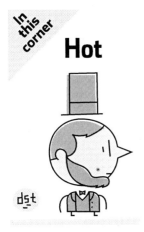

In this corner

Hot

Abraham Lincoln is suddenly everywhere.

Is it the stovepipe hat?

Is it the beard?

The bow tie?

The way with words?

Four score...

The fascinating wife?

The Madonna / Marilyn Monroe beauty mark?

The awesome skateboard skills?

Jan. 30, 2009

PIONEER PRESS: DAVID STEINLICHT

234 *Note:* Around inauguration time, mentions of Abe started turning up everywhere.

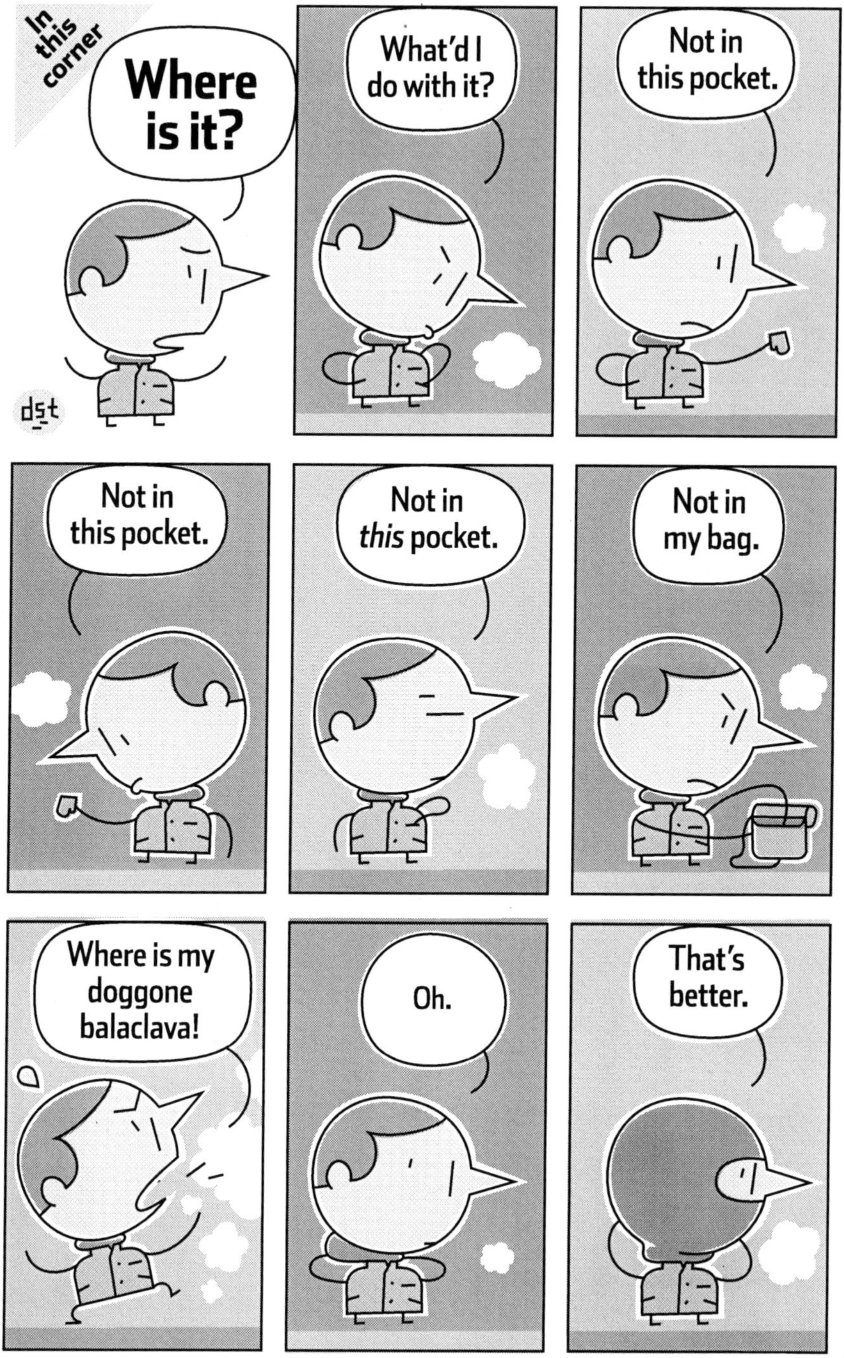
In this corner
Where is it?
dst
What'd I do with it?
Not in this pocket.
Not in this pocket.
Not in *this* pocket.
Not in my bag.
Where is my doggone balaclava!
Oh.
That's better.

Feb. 6, 2009

PIONEER PRESS: DAVID STEINLICHT

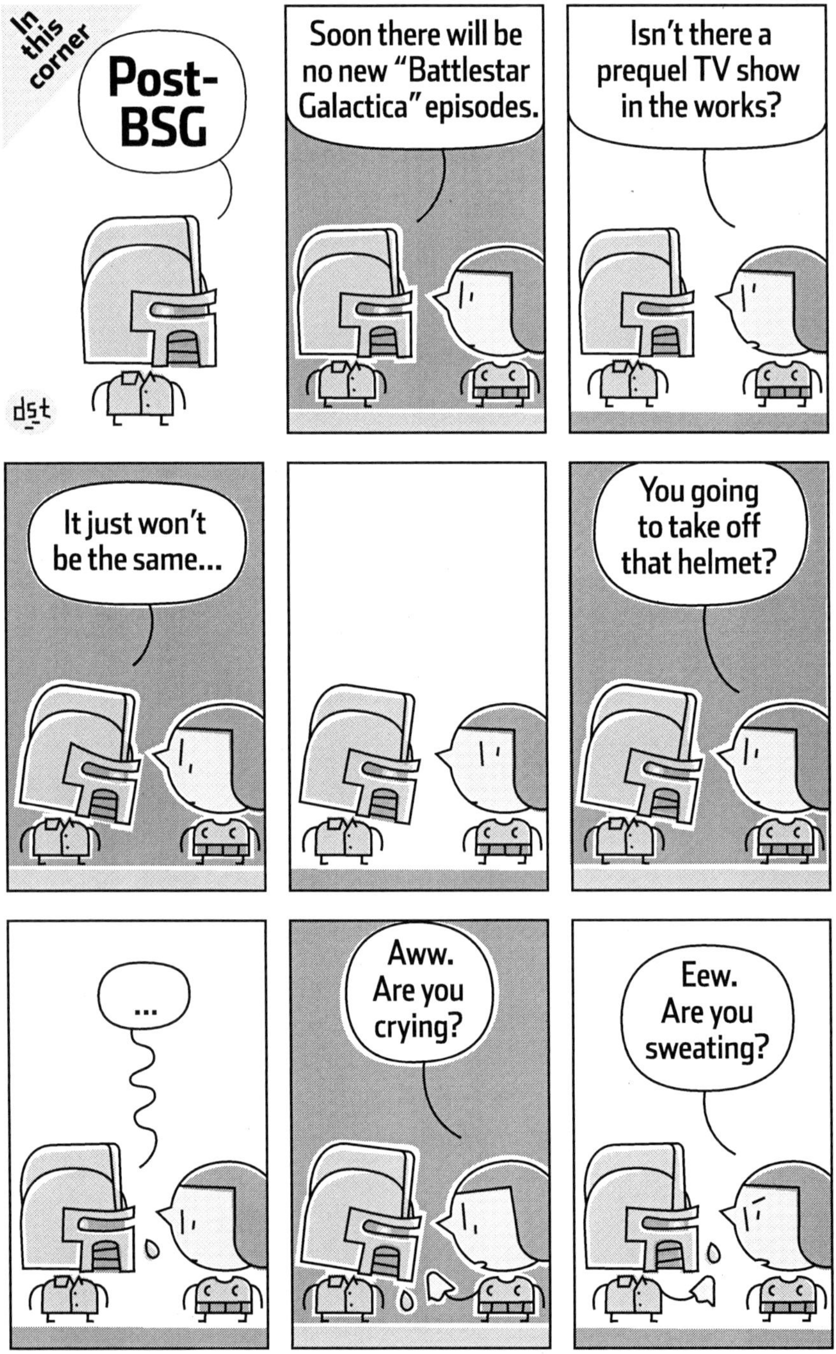

In this corner
Post-BSG
dst
Soon there will be no new "Battlestar Galactica" episodes.
Isn't there a prequel TV show in the works?
It just won't be the same...
You going to take off that helmet?
...
Aww. Are you crying?
Eew. Are you sweating?

Feb. 20, 2009

PIONEER PRESS: DAVID STEINLICHT

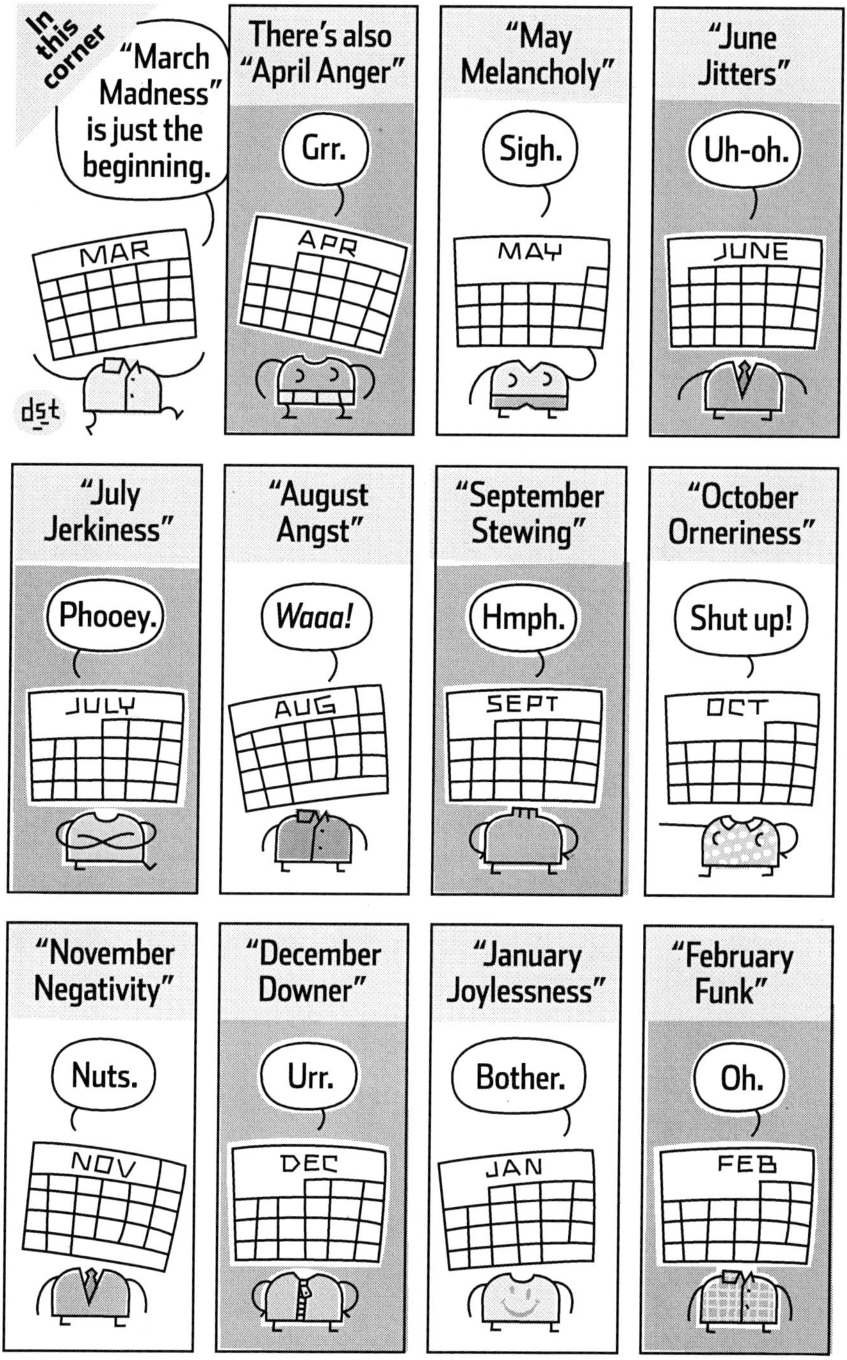
In this corner
"March Madness" is just the beginning.
MAR
dst
There's also "April Anger"
Grr.
APR
"May Melancholy"
Sigh.
MAY
"June Jitters"
Uh-oh.
JUNE
"July Jerkiness"
Phooey.
JULY
"August Angst"
Waaa!
AUG
"September Stewing"
Hmph.
SEPT
"October Orneriness"
Shut up!
OCT
"November Negativity"
Nuts.
NOV
"December Downer"
Urr.
DEC
"January Joylessness"
Bother.
JAN
"February Funk"
Oh.
FEB

Mar. 6, 2009

PIONEER PRESS: DAVID STEINLICHT

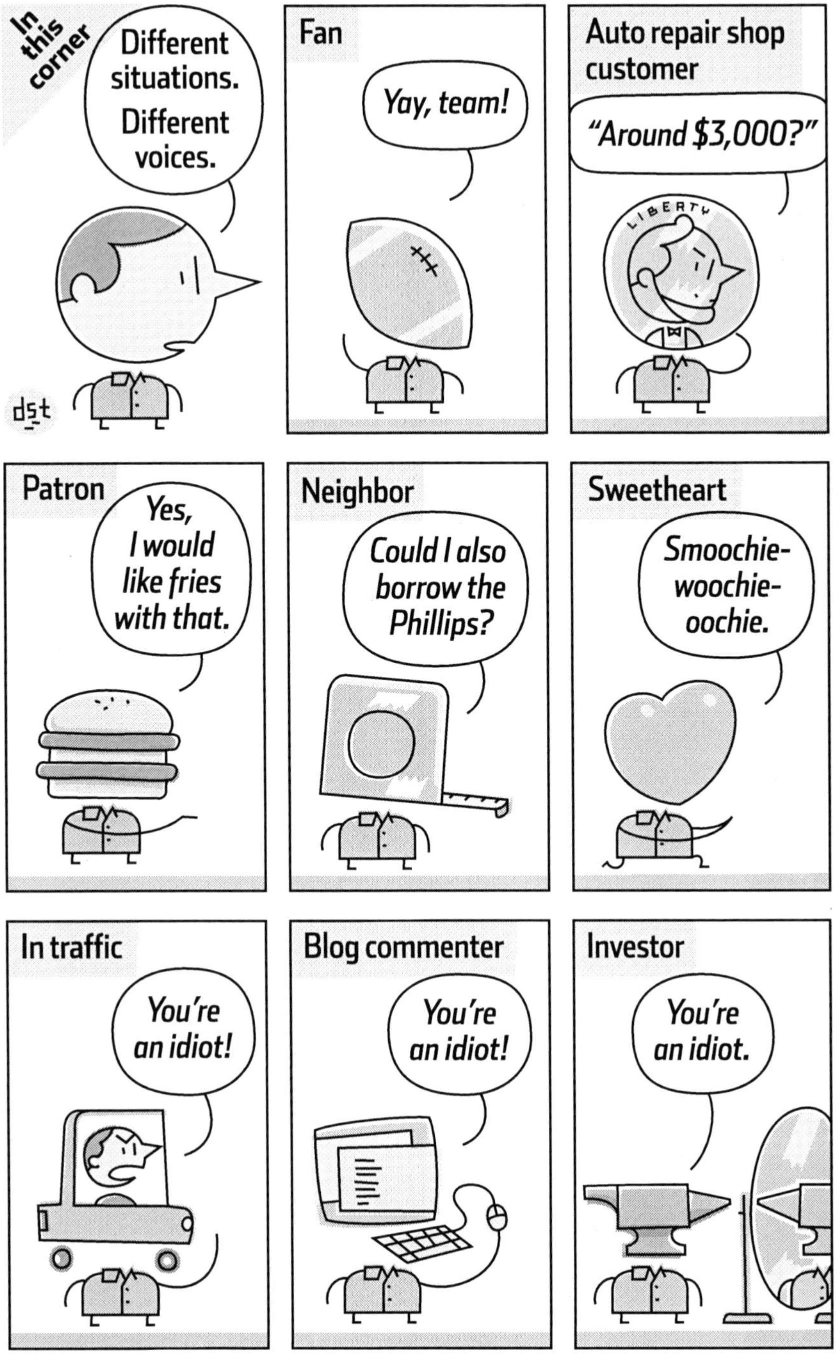
In this corner
Different situations. Different voices.
dst
Fan
Yay, team!
Auto repair shop customer
"Around $3,000?"
LIBERTY
Patron
Yes, I would like fries with that.
Neighbor
Could I also borrow the Phillips?
Sweetheart
Smoochie-woochie-oochie.
In traffic
You're an idiot!
Blog commenter
You're an idiot!
Investor
You're an idiot.

Mar. 13, 2009

PIONEER PRESS: DAVID STEINLICHT

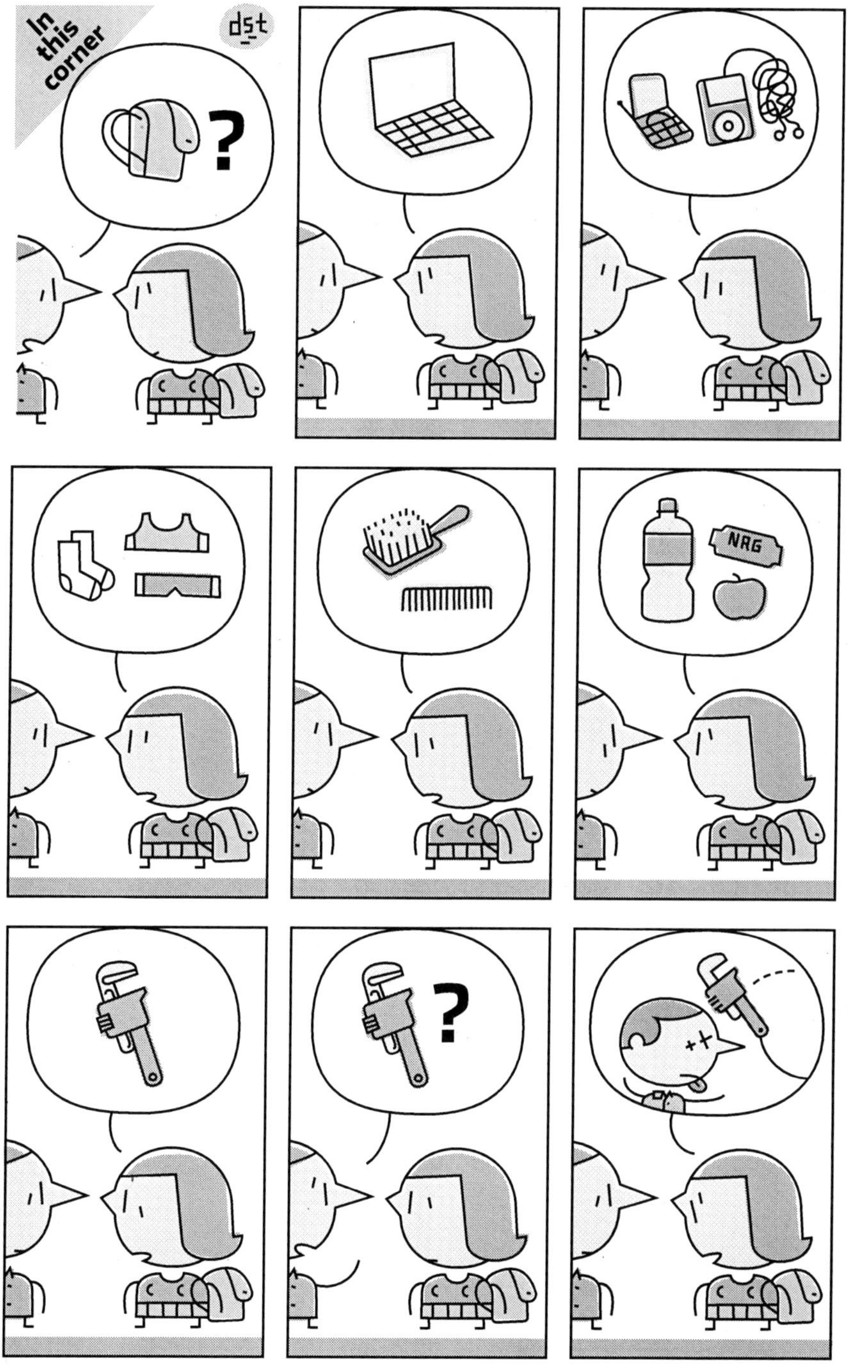
In this corner
dst
?
NRG
?

Mar. 20, 2009

PIONEER PRESS: DAVID STEINLICHT

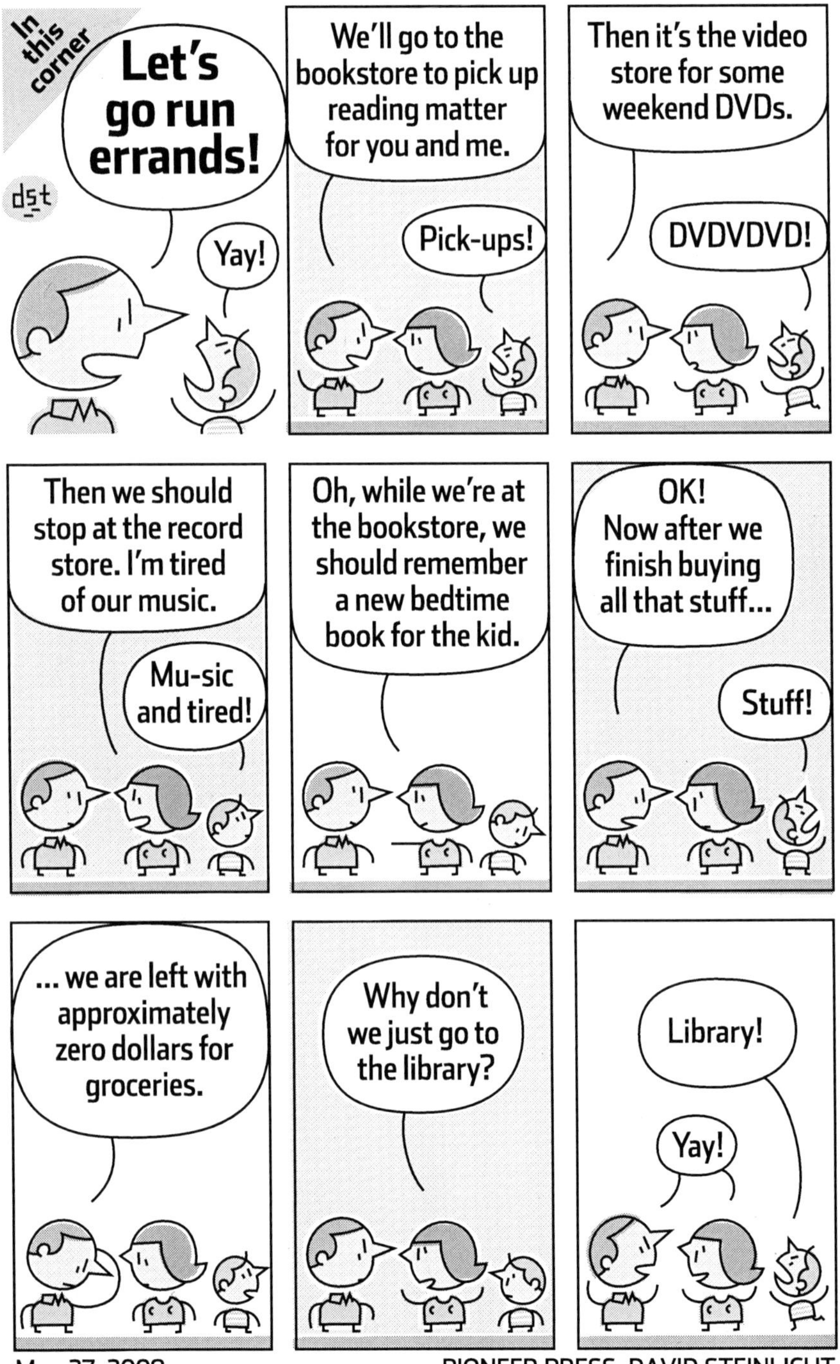
In this corner
Let's go run errands!
dst
Yay!
We'll go to the bookstore to pick up reading matter for you and me.
Pick-ups!
Then it's the video store for some weekend DVDs.
DVDVDVD!
Then we should stop at the record store. I'm tired of our music.
Mu-sic and tired!
Oh, while we're at the bookstore, we should remember a new bedtime book for the kid.
OK! Now after we finish buying all that stuff...
Stuff!
... we are left with approximately zero dollars for groceries.
Why don't we just go to the library?
Library!
Yay!

Mar. 27, 2009 PIONEER PRESS: DAVID STEINLICHT

 Note: The public library — *yay!*

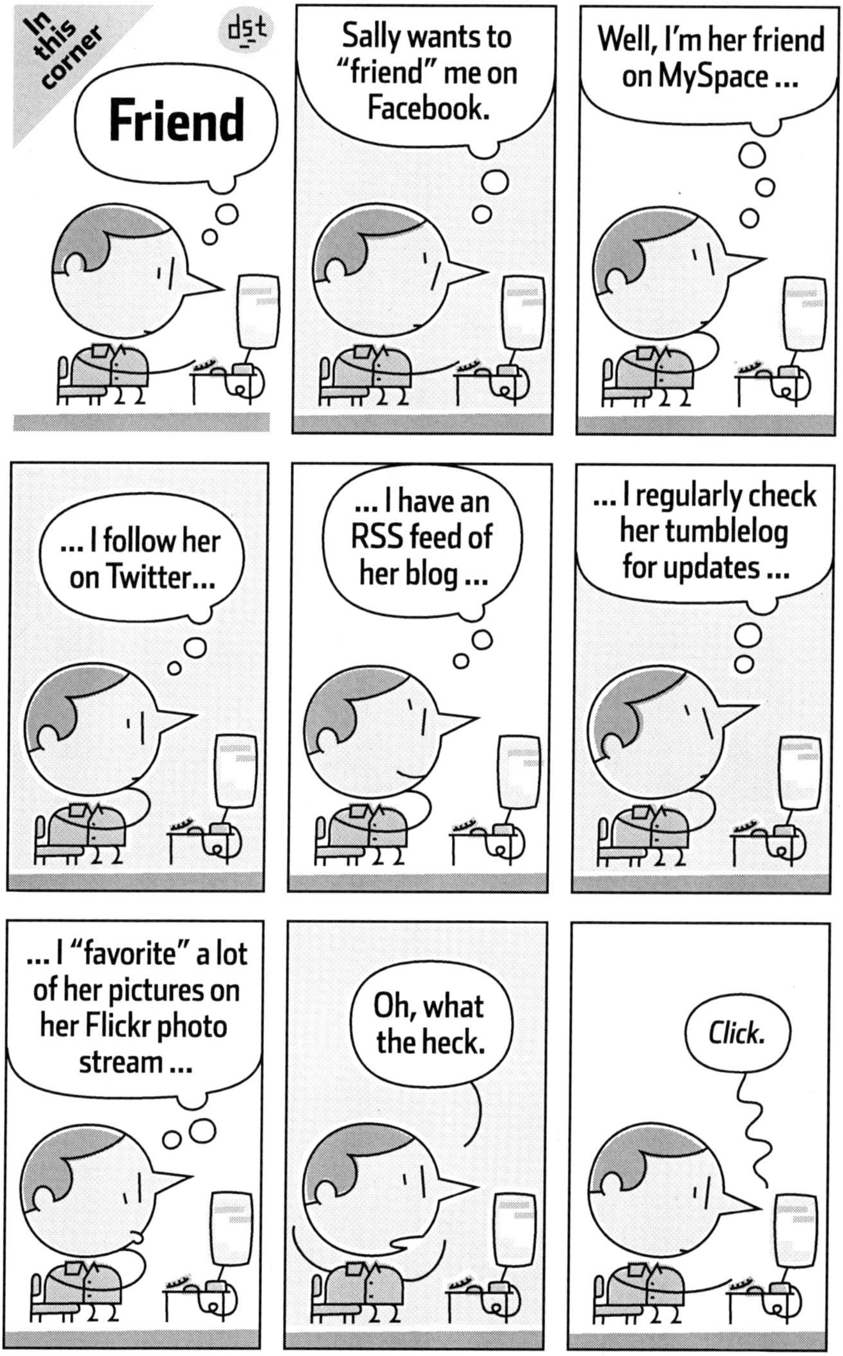
In this corner
dst
Friend
Sally wants to "friend" me on Facebook.
Well, I'm her friend on MySpace ...
... I follow her on Twitter...
... I have an RSS feed of her blog ...
... I regularly check her tumblelog for updates ...
... I "favorite" a lot of her pictures on her Flickr photo stream ...
Oh, what the heck.
Click.

April 2, 2009 PIONEER PRESS: DAVID STEINLICHT

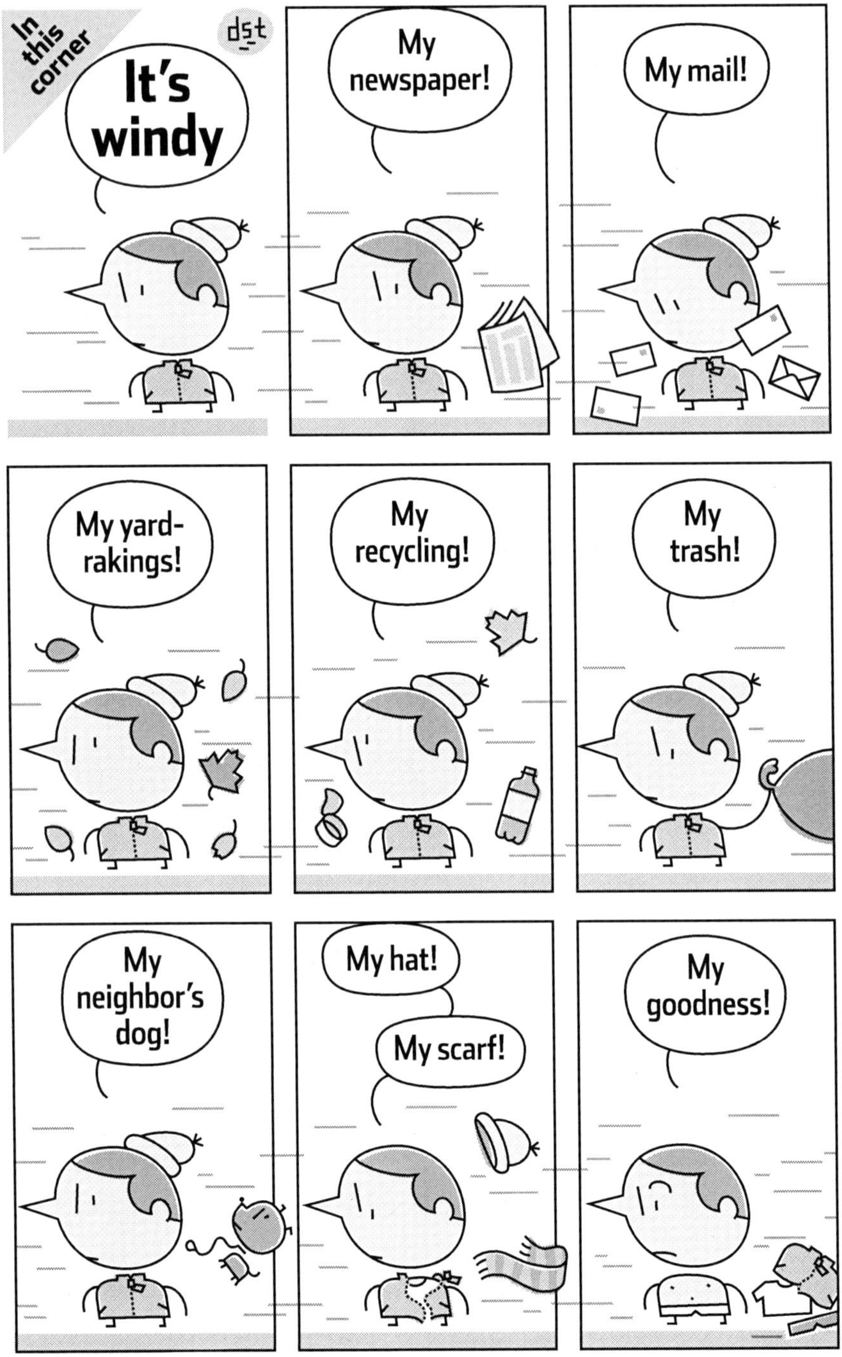
In this corner
dst
It's windy
My newspaper!
My mail!
My yard-rakings!
My recycling!
My trash!
My neighbor's dog!
My hat!
My scarf!
My goodness!

April 10, 2009

PIONEER PRESS: DAVID STEINLICHT

In this corner
dst
Numbers
Wages
Expenses
Deductions
Interest
Mileage
Credit/Debit
Federal/State/Local
Form 1040

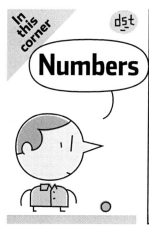

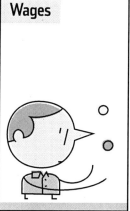

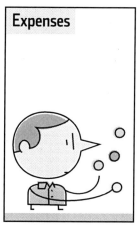

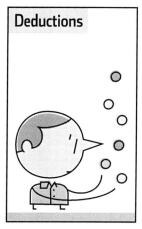

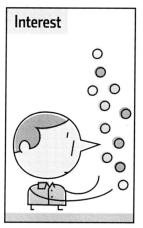

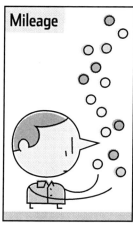

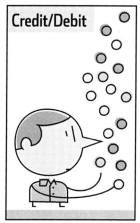

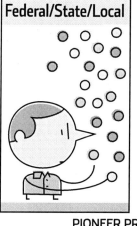

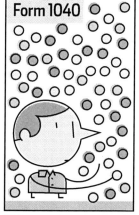

April 17, 2009

PIONEER PRESS: DAVID STEINLICHT

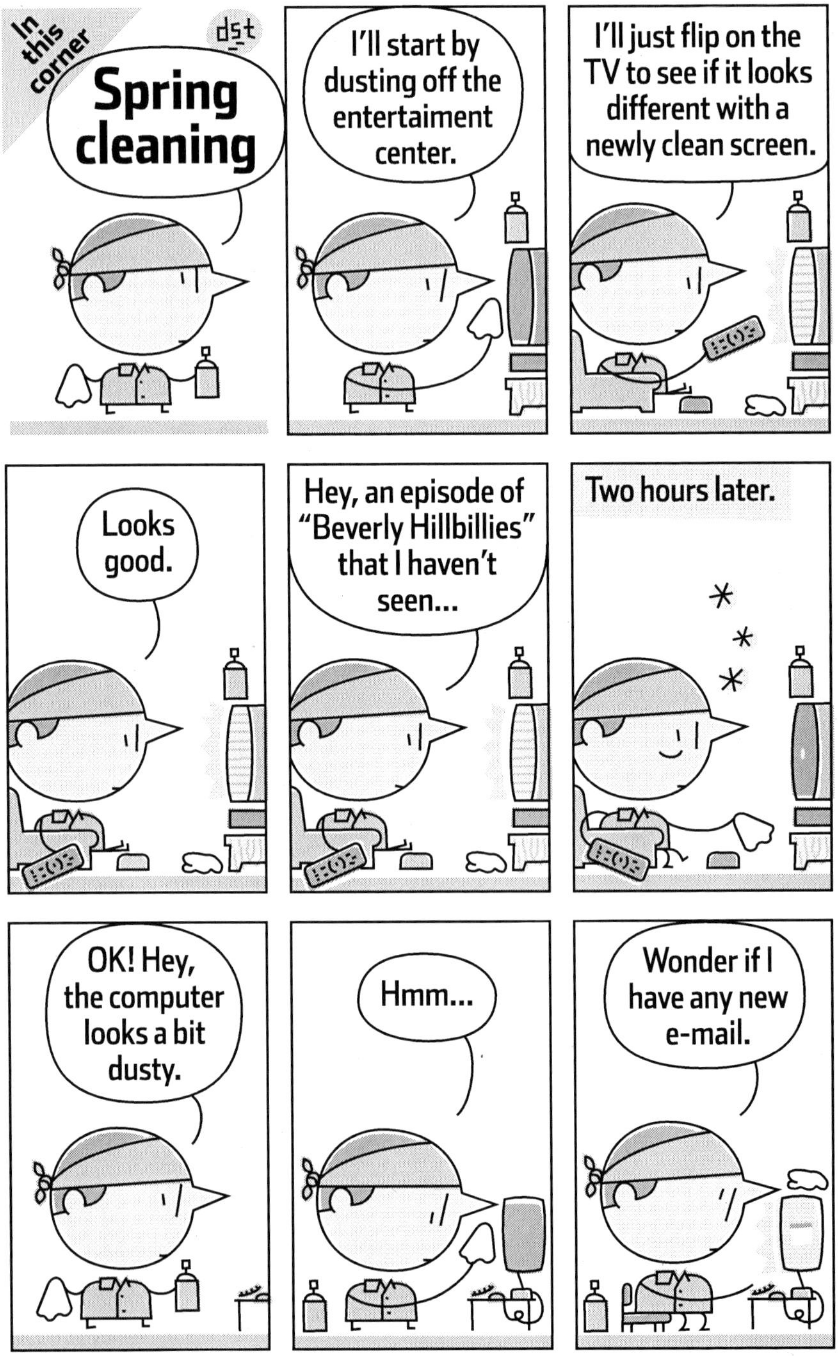
In this corner
dst
Spring cleaning
I'll start by dusting off the entertaiment center.
I'll just flip on the TV to see if it looks different with a newly clean screen.
Looks good.
Hey, an episode of "Beverly Hillbillies" that I haven't seen...
Two hours later.
OK! Hey, the computer looks a bit dusty.
Hmm...
Wonder if I have any new e-mail.

April 24, 2009

PIONEER PRESS: DAVID STEINLICHT

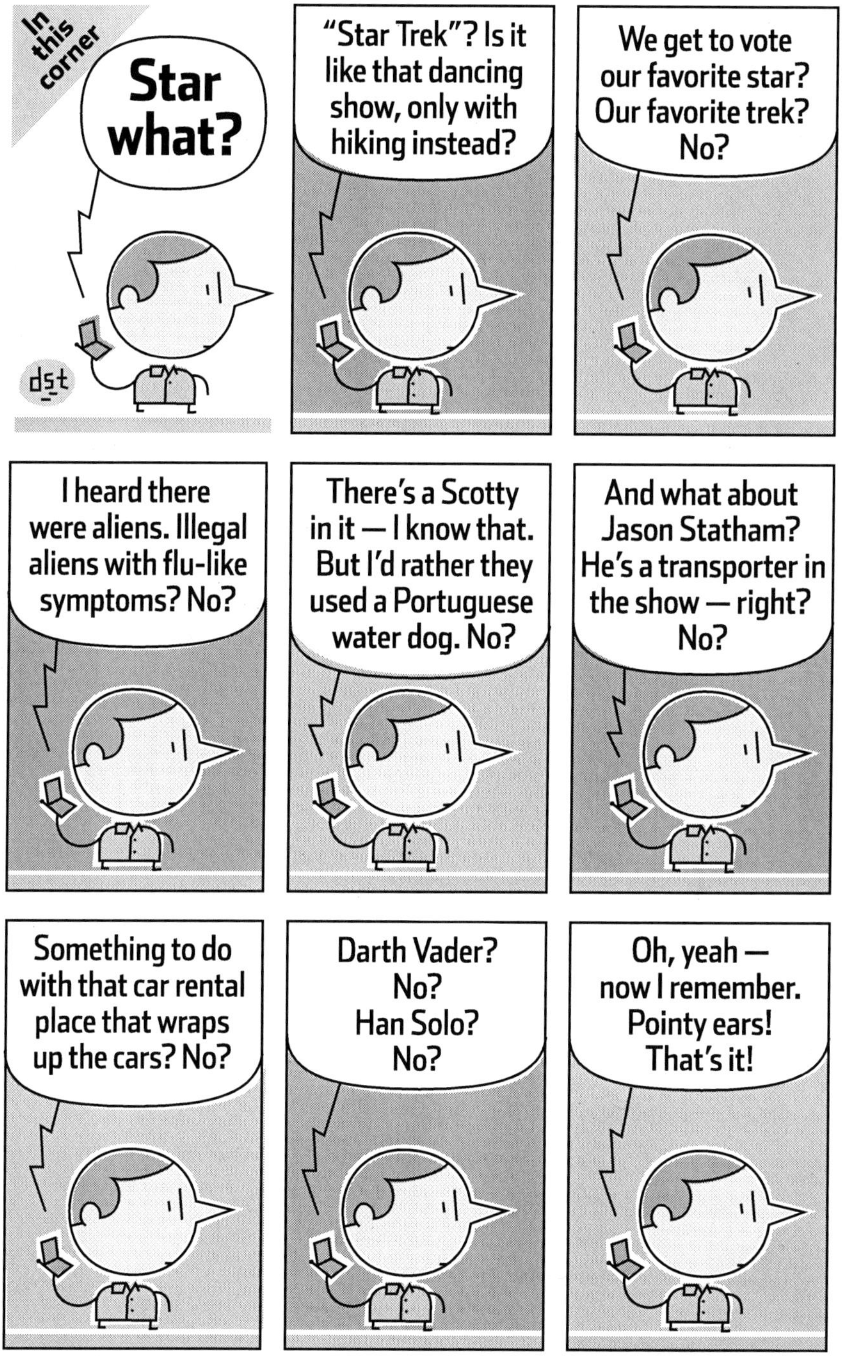
In this corner
Star what?
dst
"Star Trek"? Is it like that dancing show, only with hiking instead?
We get to vote our favorite star? Our favorite trek? No?
I heard there were aliens. Illegal aliens with flu-like symptoms? No?
There's a Scotty in it — I know that. But I'd rather they used a Portuguese water dog. No?
And what about Jason Statham? He's a transporter in the show — right? No?
Something to do with that car rental place that wraps up the cars? No?
Darth Vader? No? Han Solo? No?
Oh, yeah — now I remember. Pointy ears! That's it!

May 1, 2009

PIONEER PRESS: DAVID STEINLICHT

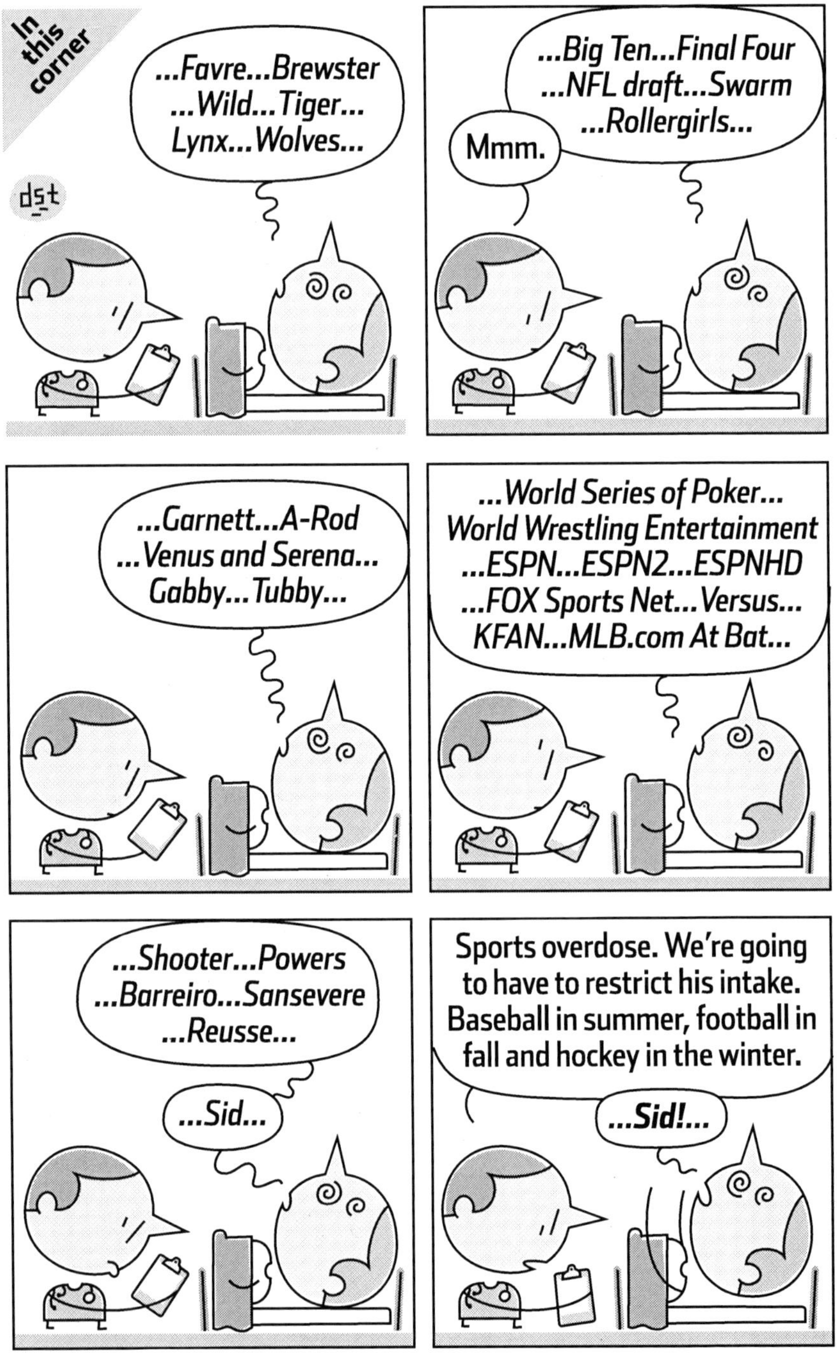
In this corner
dst
...Favre...Brewster ...Wild...Tiger... Lynx...Wolves...
...Big Ten...Final Four ...NFL draft...Swarm ...Rollergirls...
Mmm.
...Garnett...A-Rod ...Venus and Serena... Gabby...Tubby...
...World Series of Poker... World Wrestling Entertainment ...ESPN...ESPN2...ESPNHD ...FOX Sports Net...Versus... KFAN...MLB.com At Bat...
...Shooter...Powers ...Barreiro...Sansevere ...Reusse...
...Sid...
Sports overdose. We're going to have to restrict his intake. Baseball in summer, football in fall and hockey in the winter.
...Sid!...

May 8, 2009 PIONEER PRESS: DAVID STEINLICHT *(Thank you, Kevin C.!)*

 Note: Kevin Cusick helped me look like I know about sports.

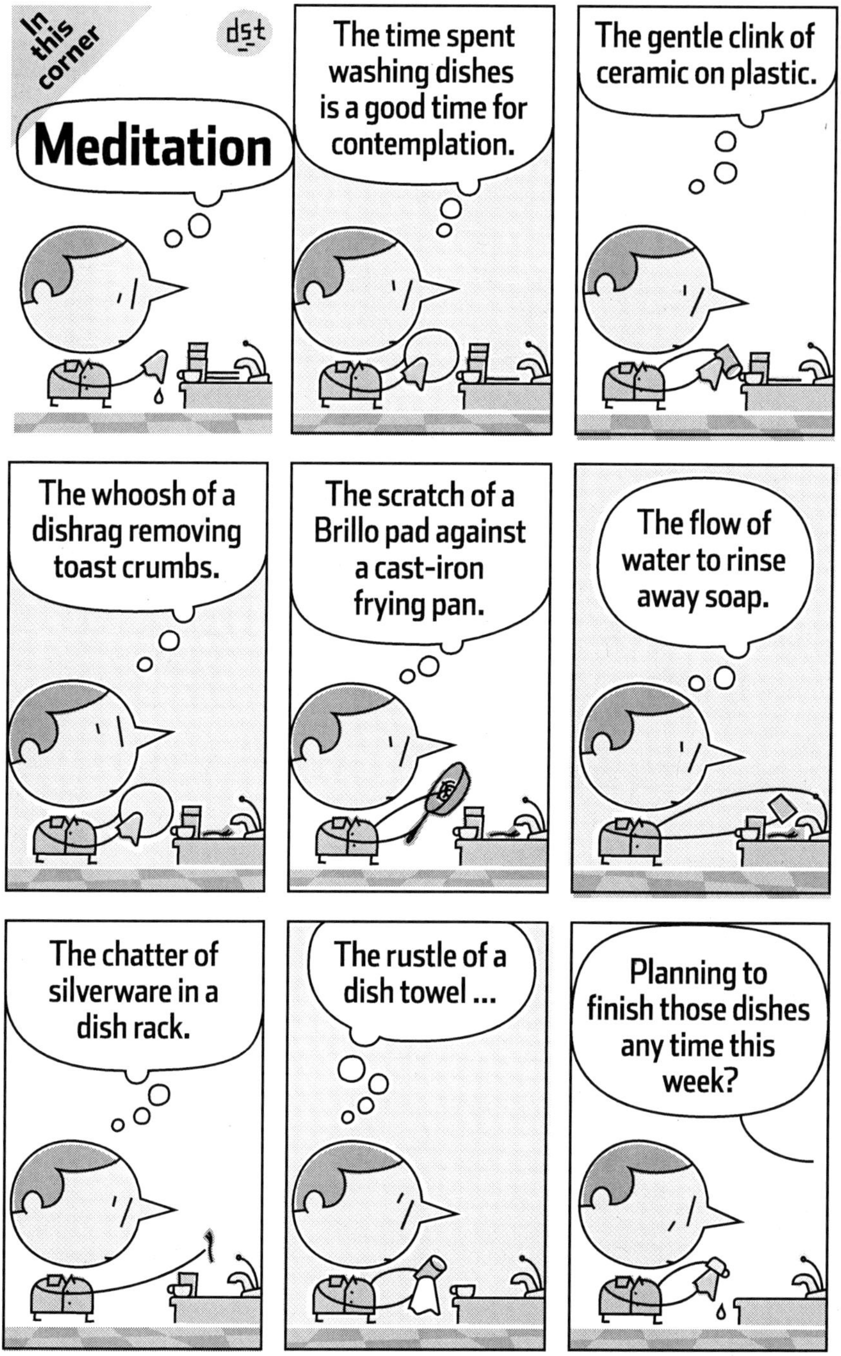
In this corner
dst
Meditation
The time spent washing dishes is a good time for contemplation.
The gentle clink of ceramic on plastic.
The whoosh of a dishrag removing toast crumbs.
The scratch of a Brillo pad against a cast-iron frying pan.
The flow of water to rinse away soap.
The chatter of silverware in a dish rack.
The rustle of a dish towel ...
Planning to finish those dishes any time this week?

May 15, 2009

PIONEER PRESS: DAVID STEINLICHT

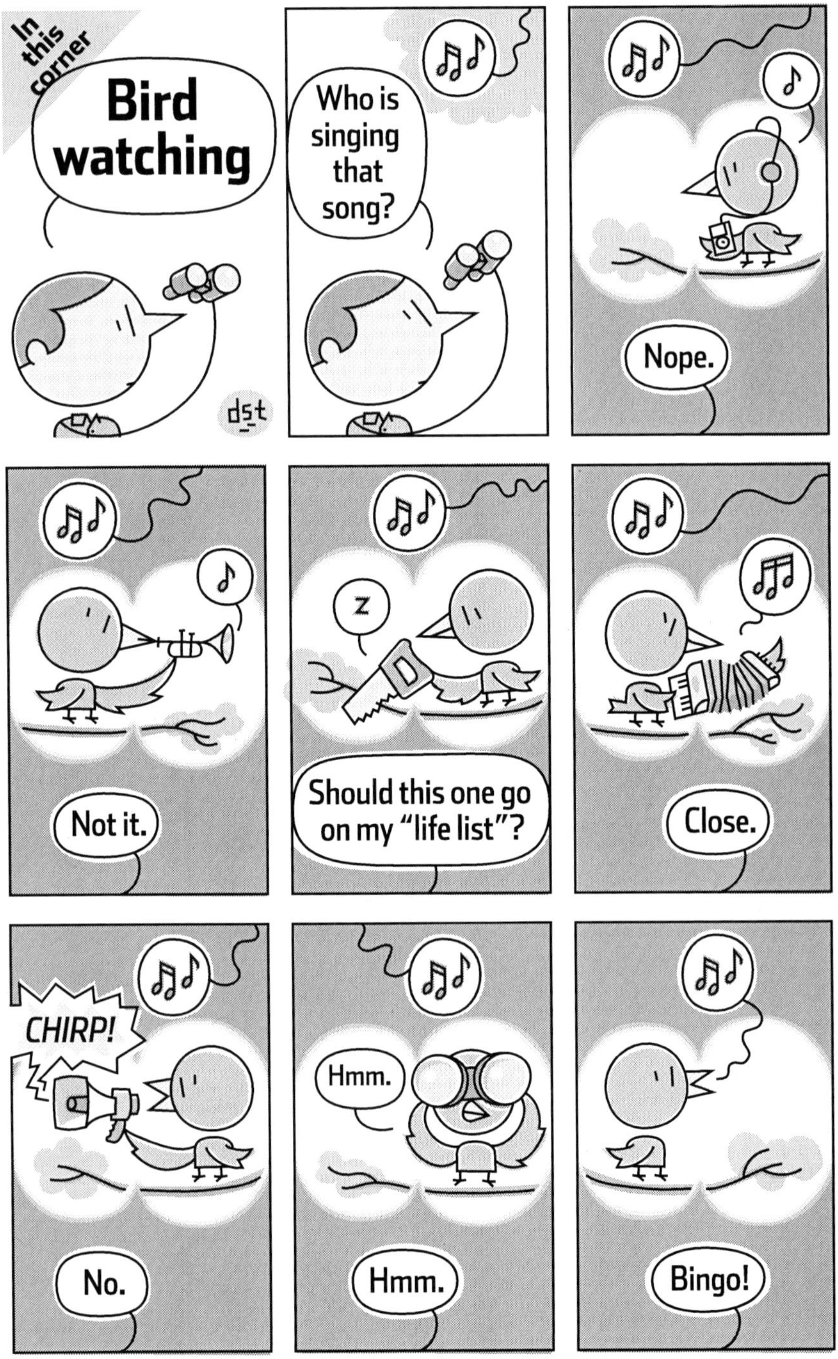
In this corner
Bird watching
Who is singing that song?
Nope.
Not it.
Z
Should this one go on my "life list"?
Close.
CHIRP!
No.
Hmm.
Hmm.
Bingo!

May 22, 2009 PIONEER PRESS: DAVID STEINLICHT

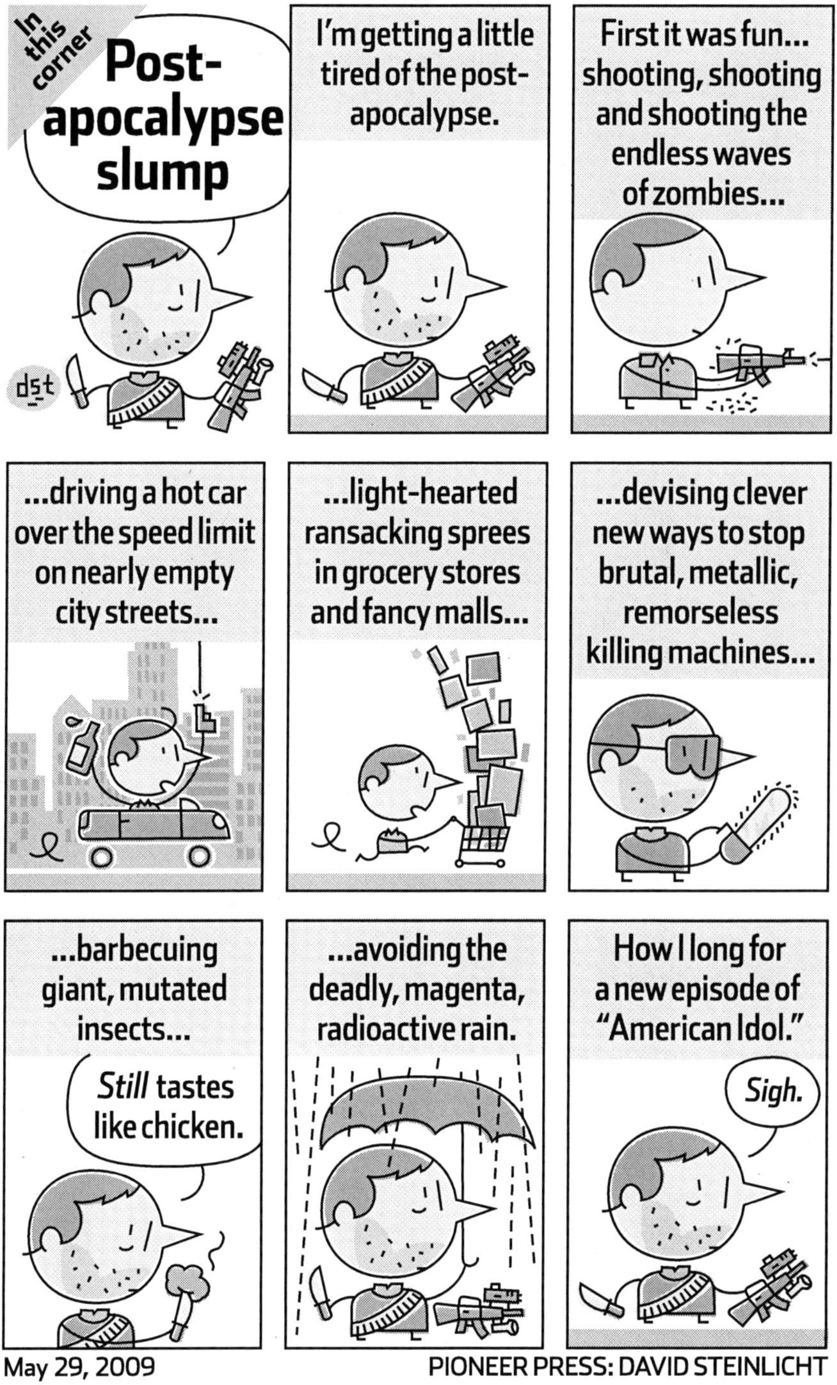
In this corner
Post-apocalypse slump
dst
I'm getting a little tired of the post-apocalypse.
First it was fun... shooting, shooting and shooting the endless waves of zombies...
...driving a hot car over the speed limit on nearly empty city streets...
...light-hearted ransacking sprees in grocery stores and fancy malls...
...devising clever new ways to stop brutal, metallic, remorseless killing machines...
...barbecuing giant, mutated insects...
Still tastes like chicken.
...avoiding the deadly, magenta, radioactive rain.
How I long for a new episode of "American Idol."
Sigh.

May 29, 2009

PIONEER PRESS: DAVID STEINLICHT

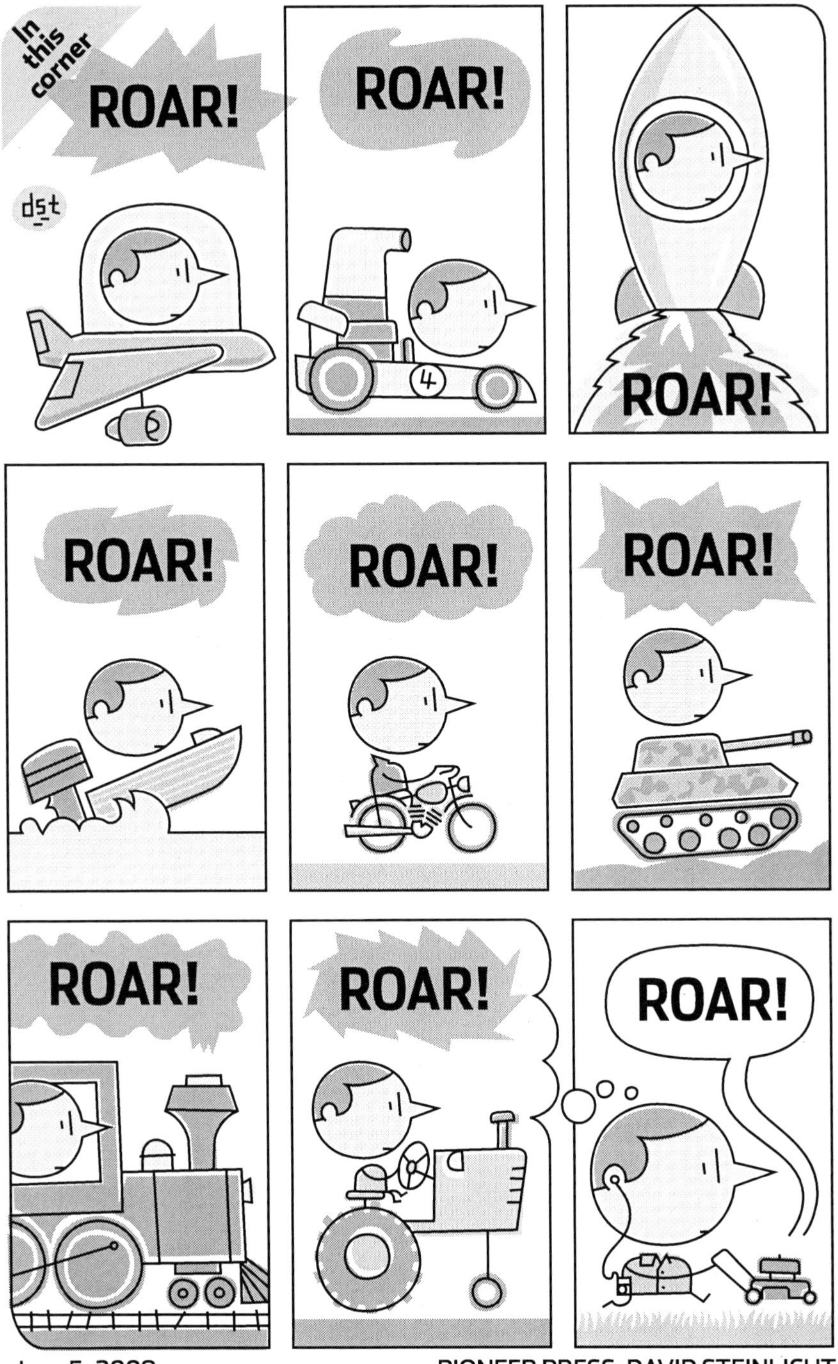
In this corner
ROAR!
dst
ROAR!
4
ROAR!
ROAR!
ROAR!
ROAR!
ROAR!
ROAR!
ROAR!

June 5, 2009 PIONEER PRESS: DAVID STEINLICHT

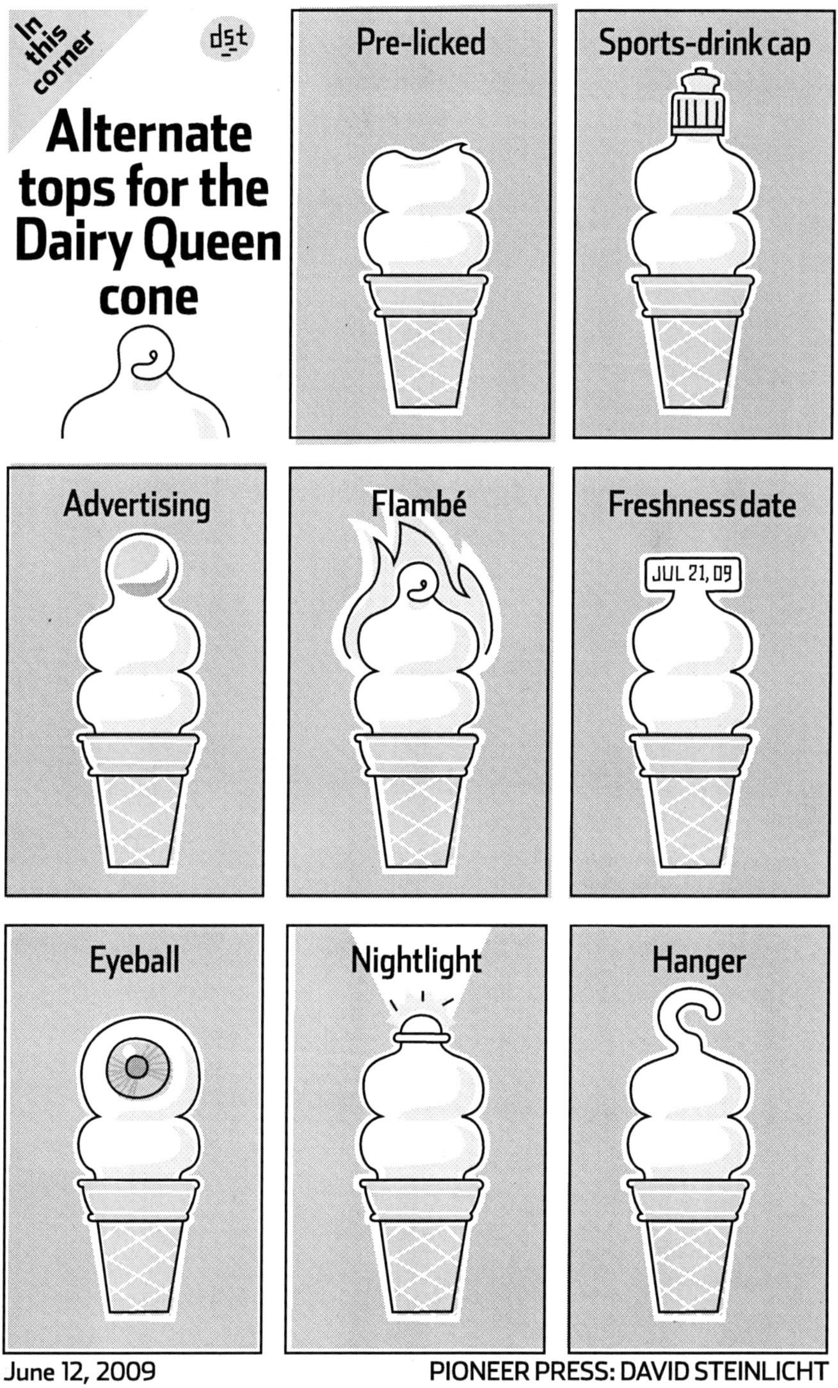
In this corner
dst
Alternate tops for the Dairy Queen cone
Pre-licked
Sports-drink cap
Advertising
Flambé
Freshness date
JUL 21, 09
Eyeball
Nightlight
Hanger

June 12, 2009

PIONEER PRESS: DAVID STEINLICHT

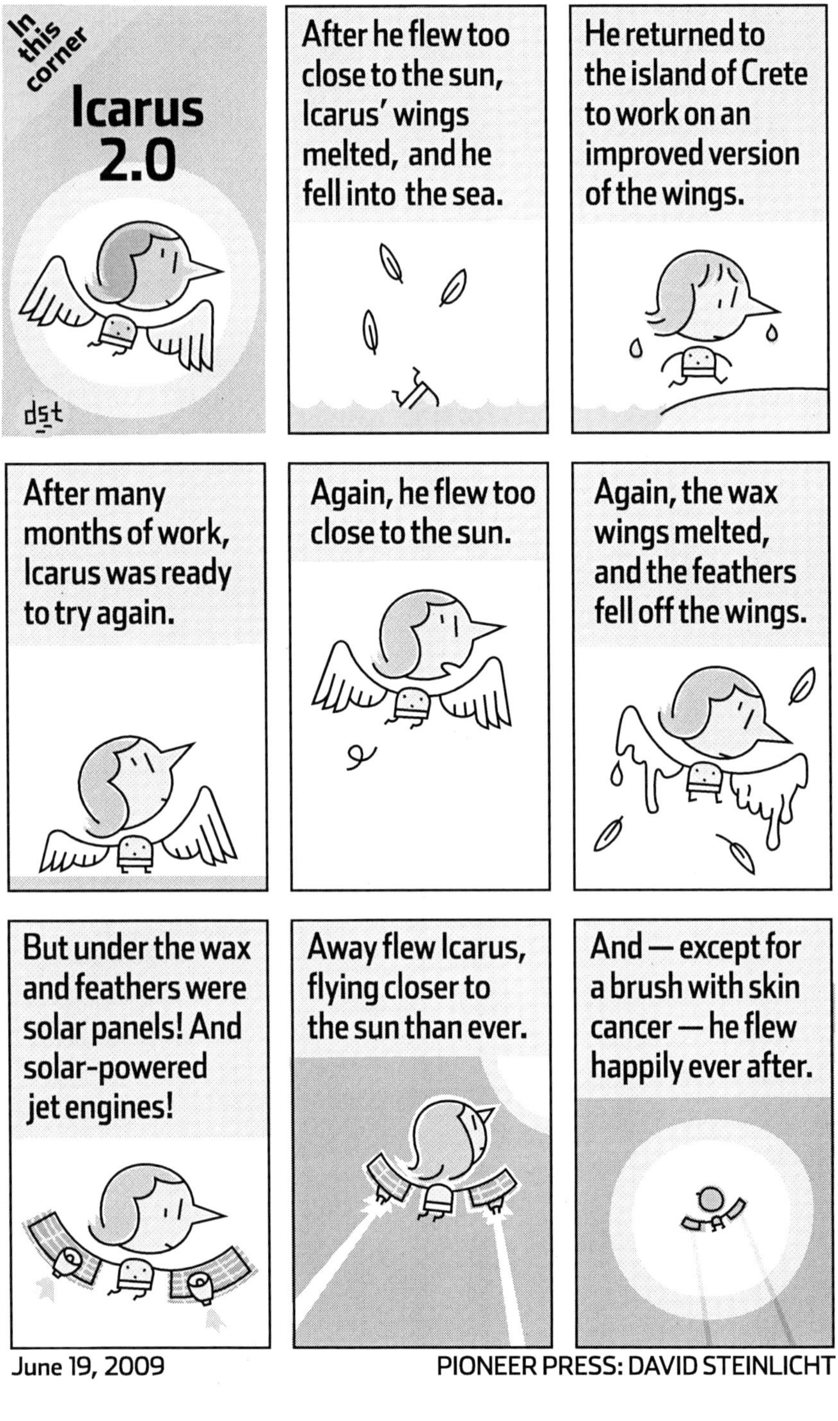
In this corner
Icarus 2.0
dst
After he flew too close to the sun, Icarus' wings melted, and he fell into the sea.
He returned to the island of Crete to work on an improved version of the wings.
After many months of work, Icarus was ready to try again.
Again, he flew too close to the sun.
Again, the wax wings melted, and the feathers fell off the wings.
But under the wax and feathers were solar panels! And solar-powered jet engines!
Away flew Icarus, flying closer to the sun than ever.
And — except for a brush with skin cancer — he flew happily ever after.

June 19, 2009

PIONEER PRESS: DAVID STEINLICHT

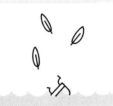

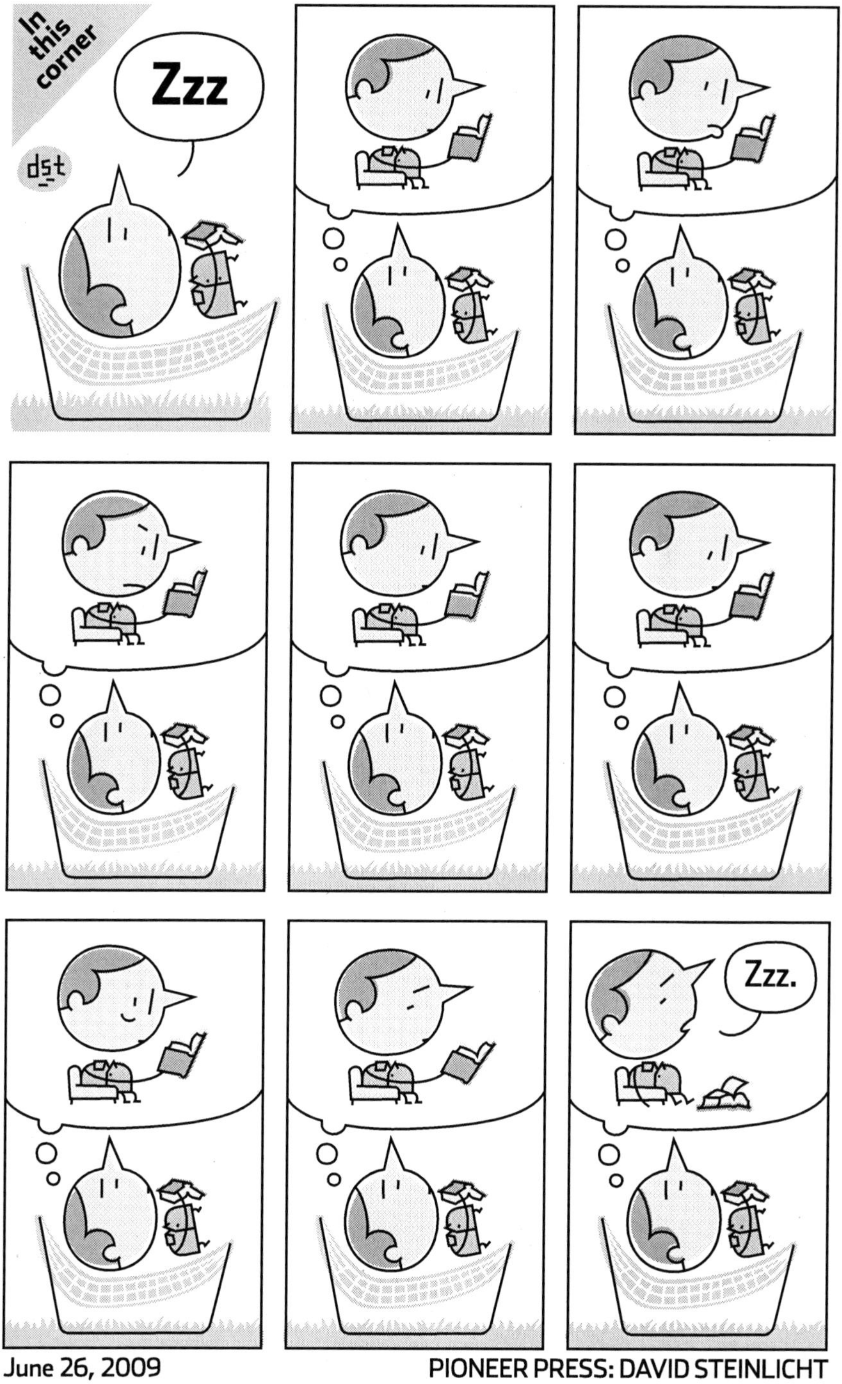
In this corner
dst
Zzz
Zzz.

June 26, 2009

PIONEER PRESS: DAVID STEINLICHT

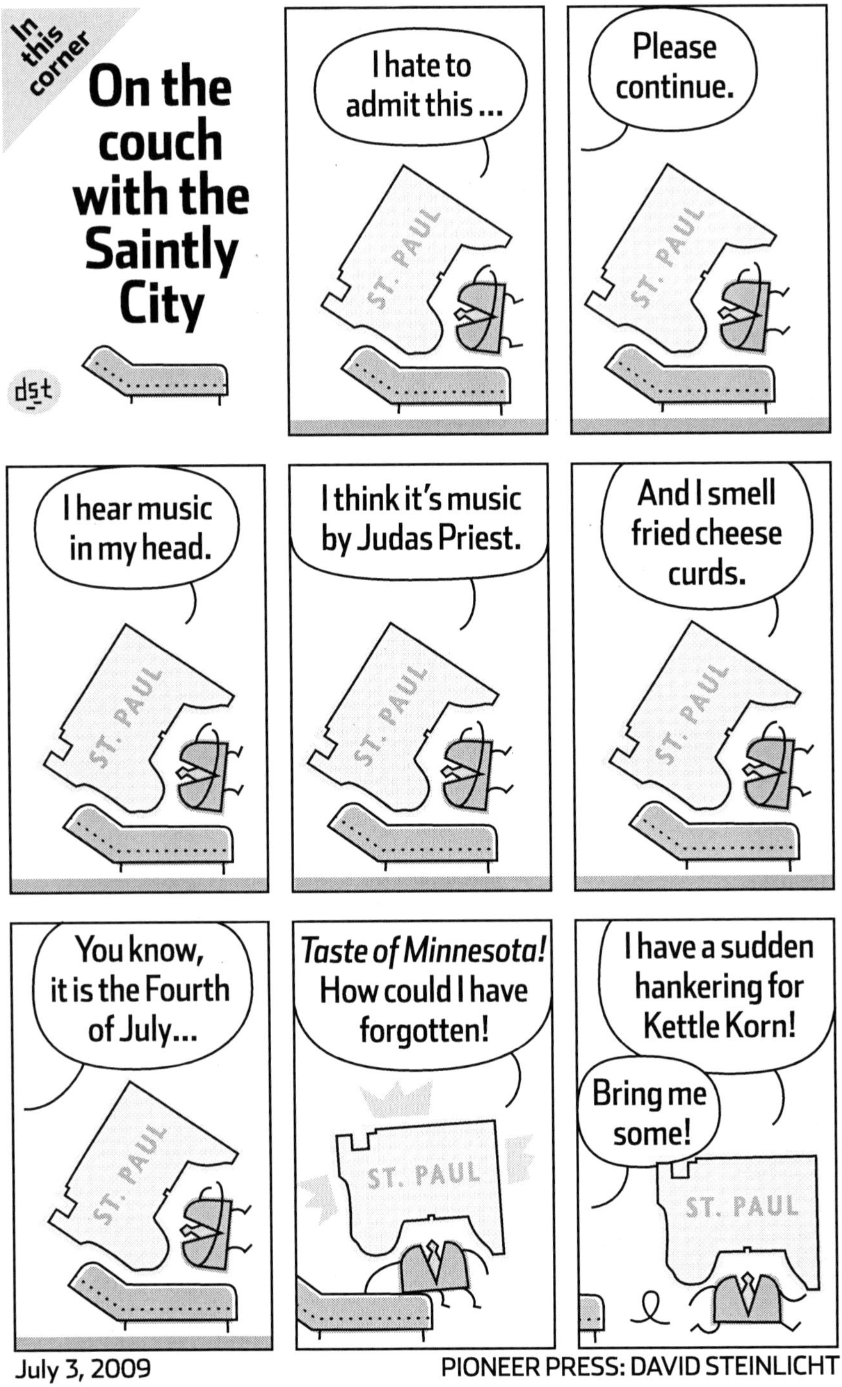
In this corner
On the couch with the Saintly City
dst
I hate to admit this ...
Please continue.
I hear music in my head.
I think it's music by Judas Priest.
And I smell fried cheese curds.
You know, it is the Fourth of July...
Taste of Minnesota! How could I have forgotten!
I have a sudden hankering for Kettle Korn!
Bring me some!
ST. PAUL

July 3, 2009

PIONEER PRESS: DAVID STEINLICHT

In this corner

Coming next summer!

Transformers 3: Rampage in the Kitchenette!

It's just a harmless microwave oven.

Or is it?

Clunk-clack-click!

Oh, my goodness! It has transformed into a toaster oven!

Mini-fridge?

Clunk-clack-click!

Or cooler!

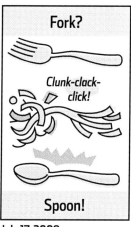

Fork?

Clunk-clack-click!

Spoon!

Frosted corn flakes?

Clunk-clack-click!

Raisin bran!

With astonishing transformations like these, the battle for the kitchenette has truly begun!

PIONEER PRESS: DAVID STEINLICHT

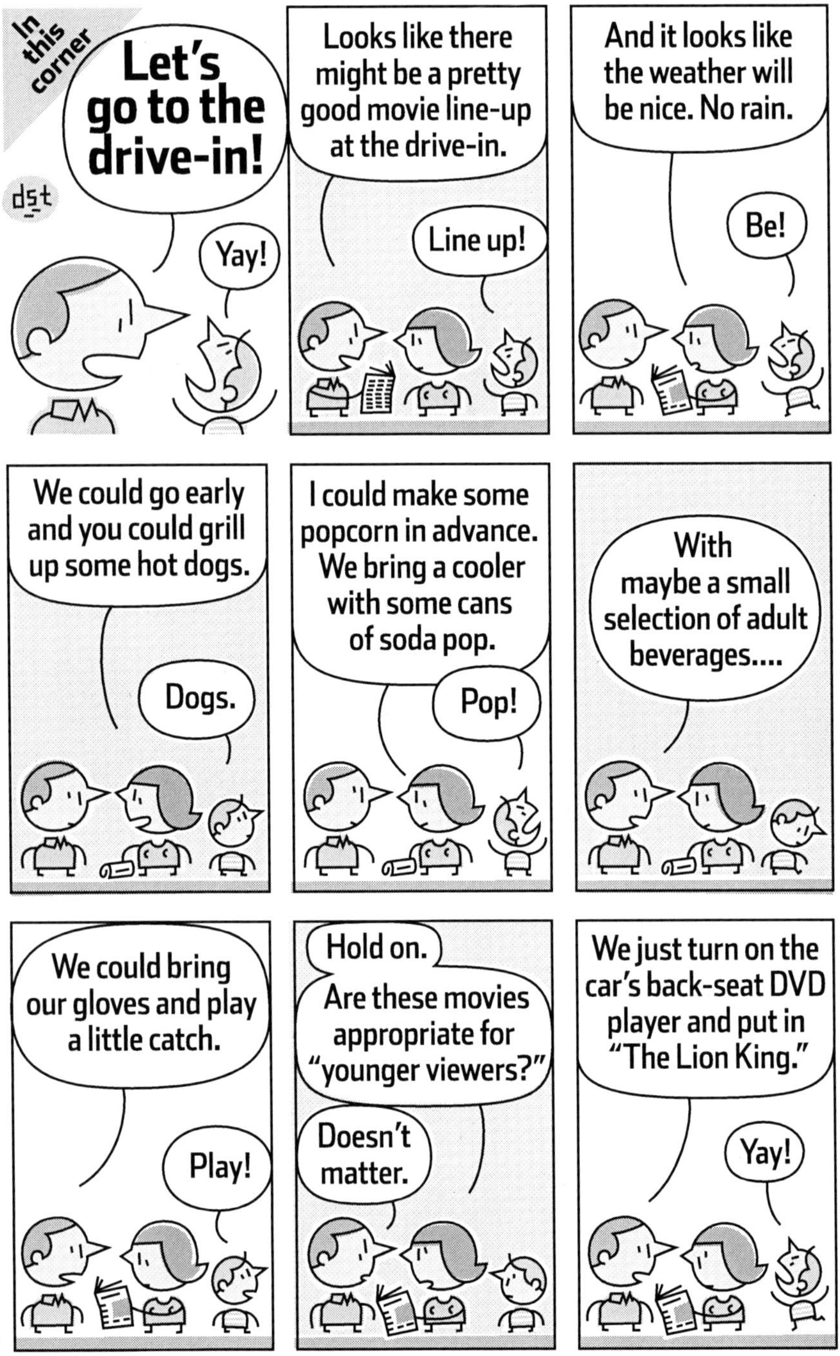
In this corner
dst
Let's go to the drive-in!
Yay!
Looks like there might be a pretty good movie line-up at the drive-in.
Line up!
And it looks like the weather will be nice. No rain.
Be!
We could go early and you could grill up some hot dogs.
Dogs.
I could make some popcorn in advance. We bring a cooler with some cans of soda pop.
Pop!
With maybe a small selection of adult beverages....
We could bring our gloves and play a little catch.
Play!
Hold on.
Are these movies appropriate for "younger viewers?"
Doesn't matter.
We just turn on the car's back-seat DVD player and put in "The Lion King."
Yay!

July 31, 2009

PIONEER PRESS: DAVID STEINLICHT

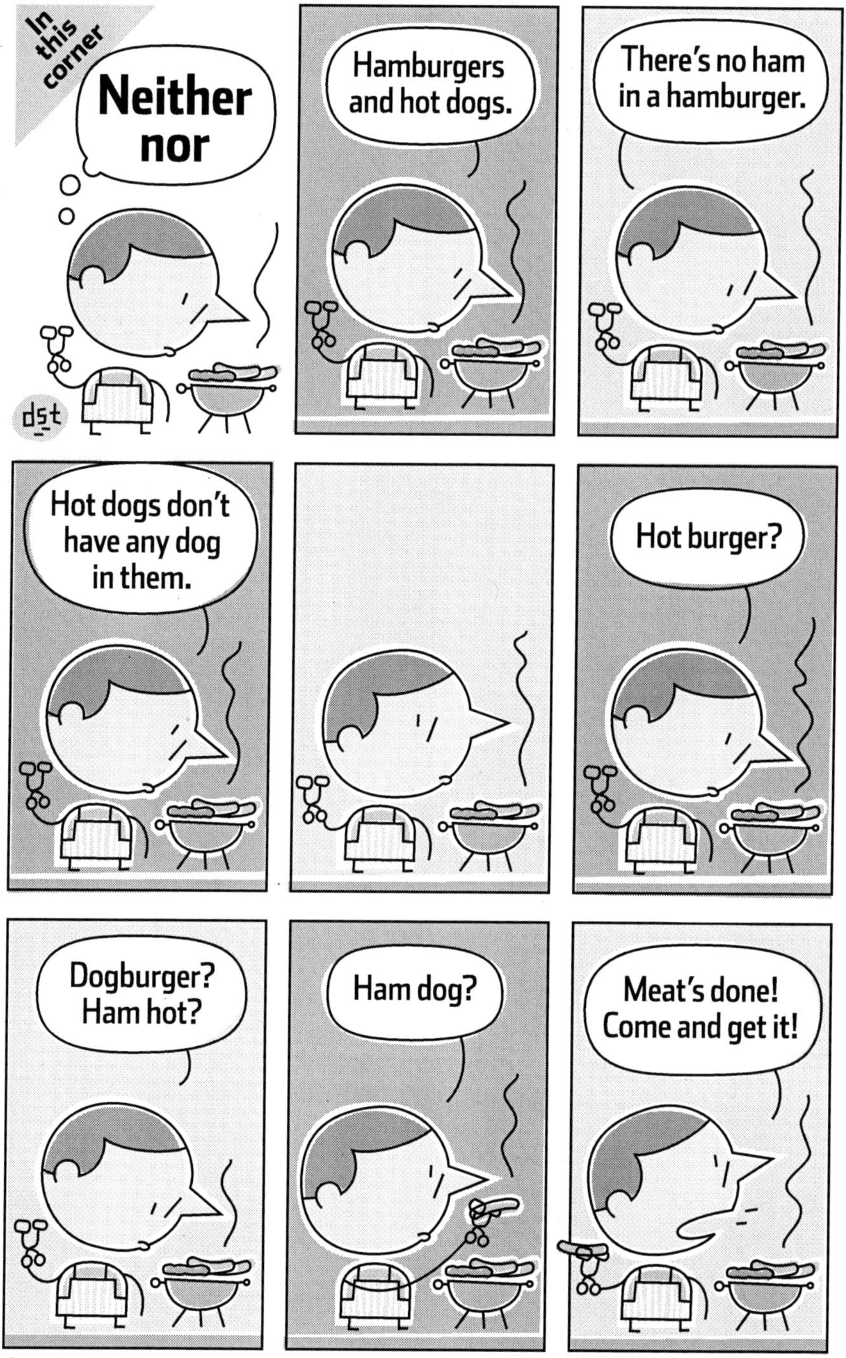
In this corner
dst
Neither nor
Hamburgers and hot dogs.
There's no ham in a hamburger.
Hot dogs don't have any dog in them.
Hot burger?
Dogburger? Ham hot?
Ham dog?
Meat's done! Come and get it!

Aug. 7, 2009

PIONEER PRESS: DAVID STEINLICHT

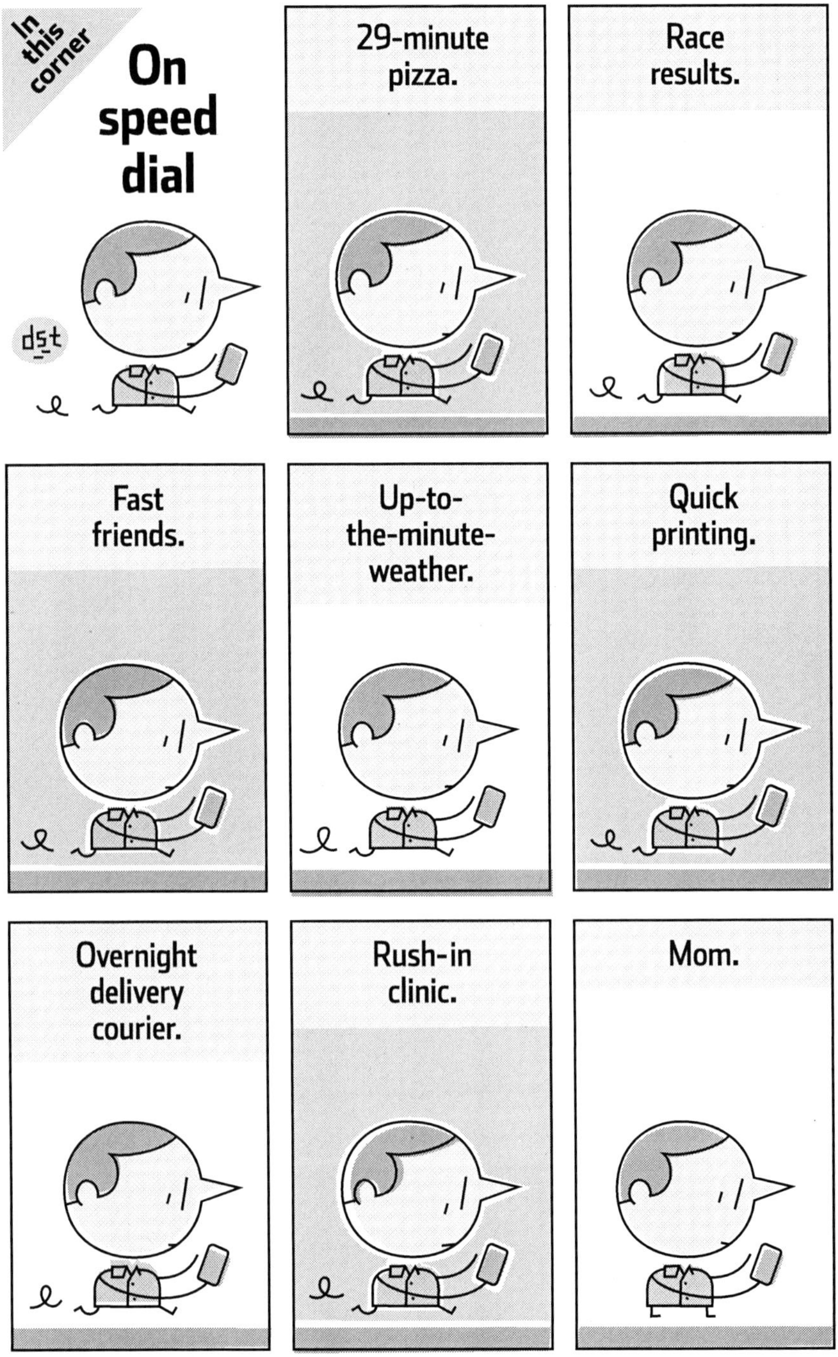
In this corner
On speed dial
dst
29-minute pizza.
Race results.
Fast friends.
Up-to- the-minute- weather.
Quick printing.
Overnight delivery courier.
Rush-in clinic.
Mom.

Aug. 14, 2009

PIONEER PRESS: DAVID STEINLICHT

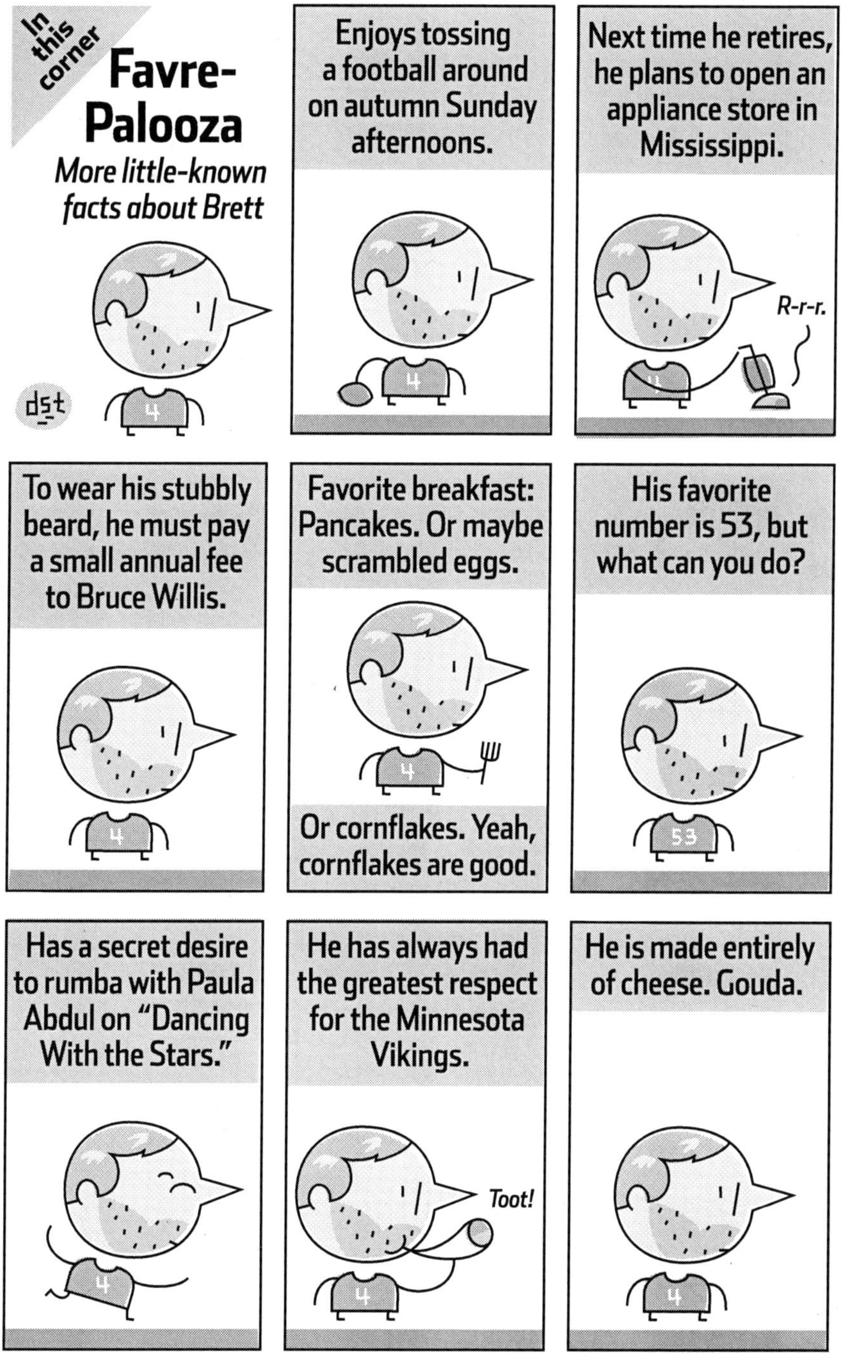
In this corner
Favre-Palooza
More little-known facts about Brett
dst
Enjoys tossing a football around on autumn Sunday afternoons.
Next time he retires, he plans to open an appliance store in Mississippi.
R-r-r.
To wear his stubbly beard, he must pay a small annual fee to Bruce Willis.
Favorite breakfast: Pancakes. Or maybe scrambled eggs.
Or cornflakes. Yeah, cornflakes are good.
His favorite number is 53, but what can you do?
53
Has a secret desire to rumba with Paula Abdul on "Dancing With the Stars."
He has always had the greatest respect for the Minnesota Vikings.
Toot!
He is made entirely of cheese. Gouda.

Aug. 21, 2009

PIONEER PRESS: DAVID STEINLICHT

Corn dog

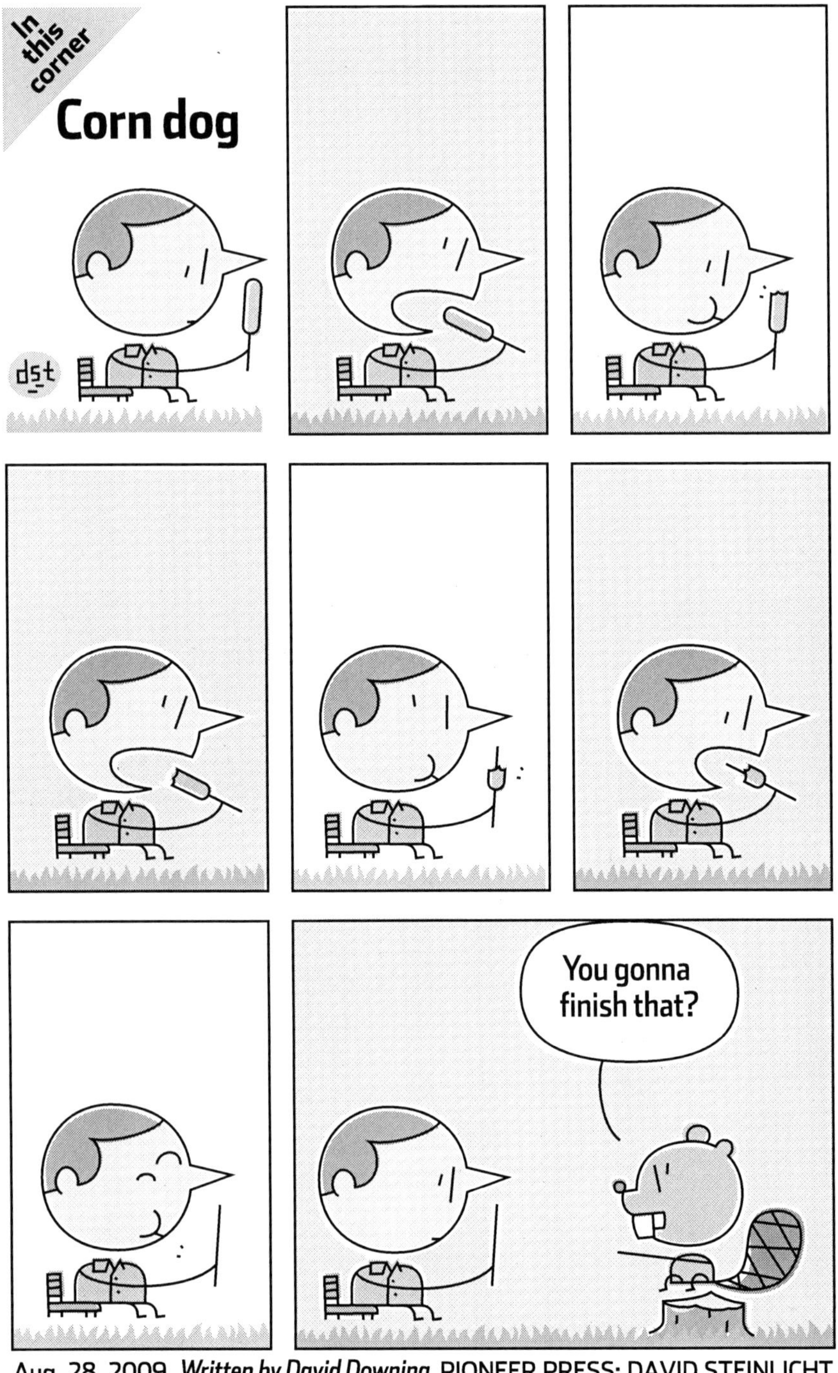
dst
You gonna finish that?

Aug. 28, 2009 *Written by David Downing* PIONEER PRESS: DAVID STEINLICHT

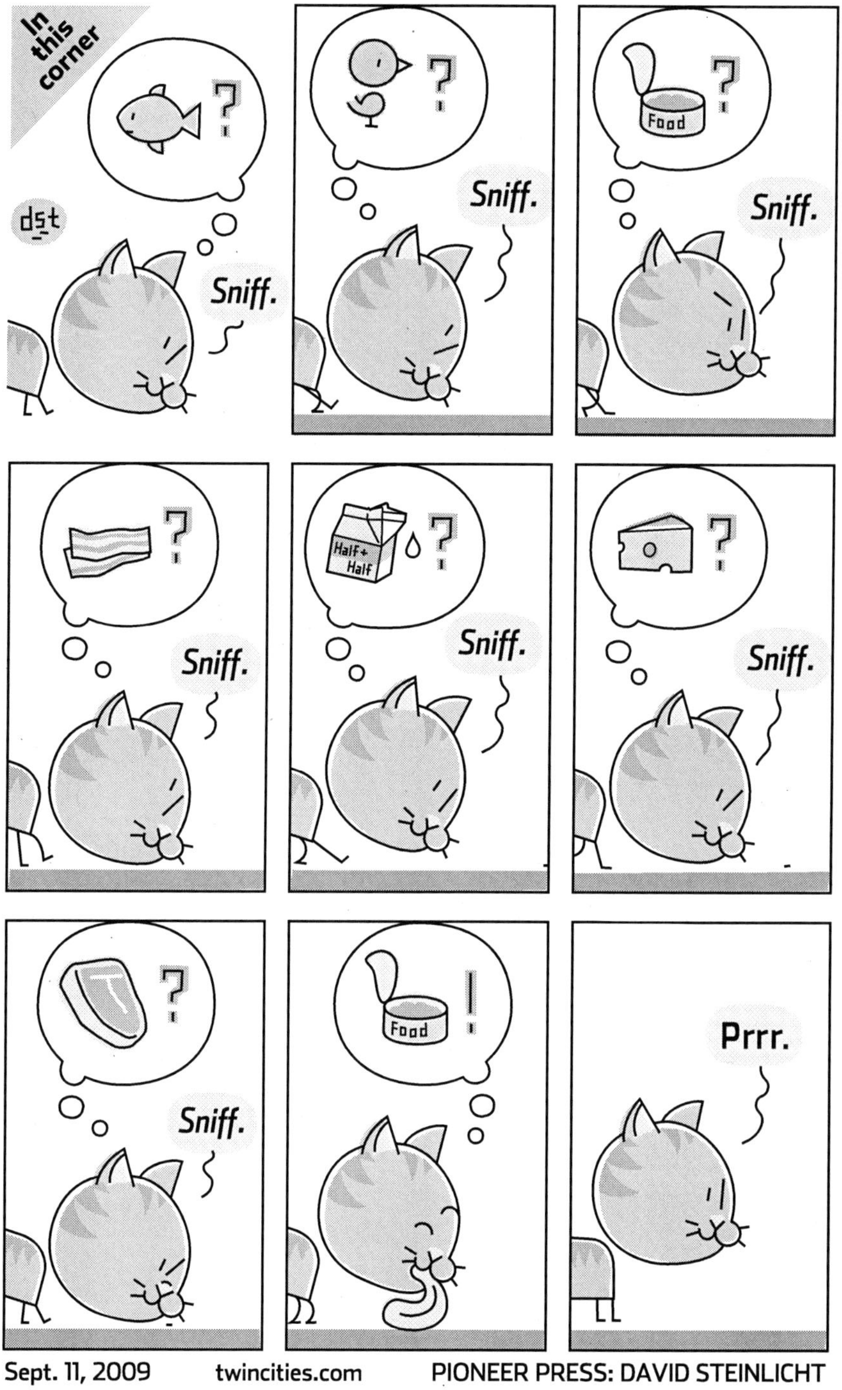
In this corner
dst
Sniff.
Sniff.
Food
Sniff.
Sniff.
Half+ Half
Sniff.
Sniff.
Sniff.
Food
Prrr.

Sept. 11, 2009 twincities.com PIONEER PRESS: DAVID STEINLICHT

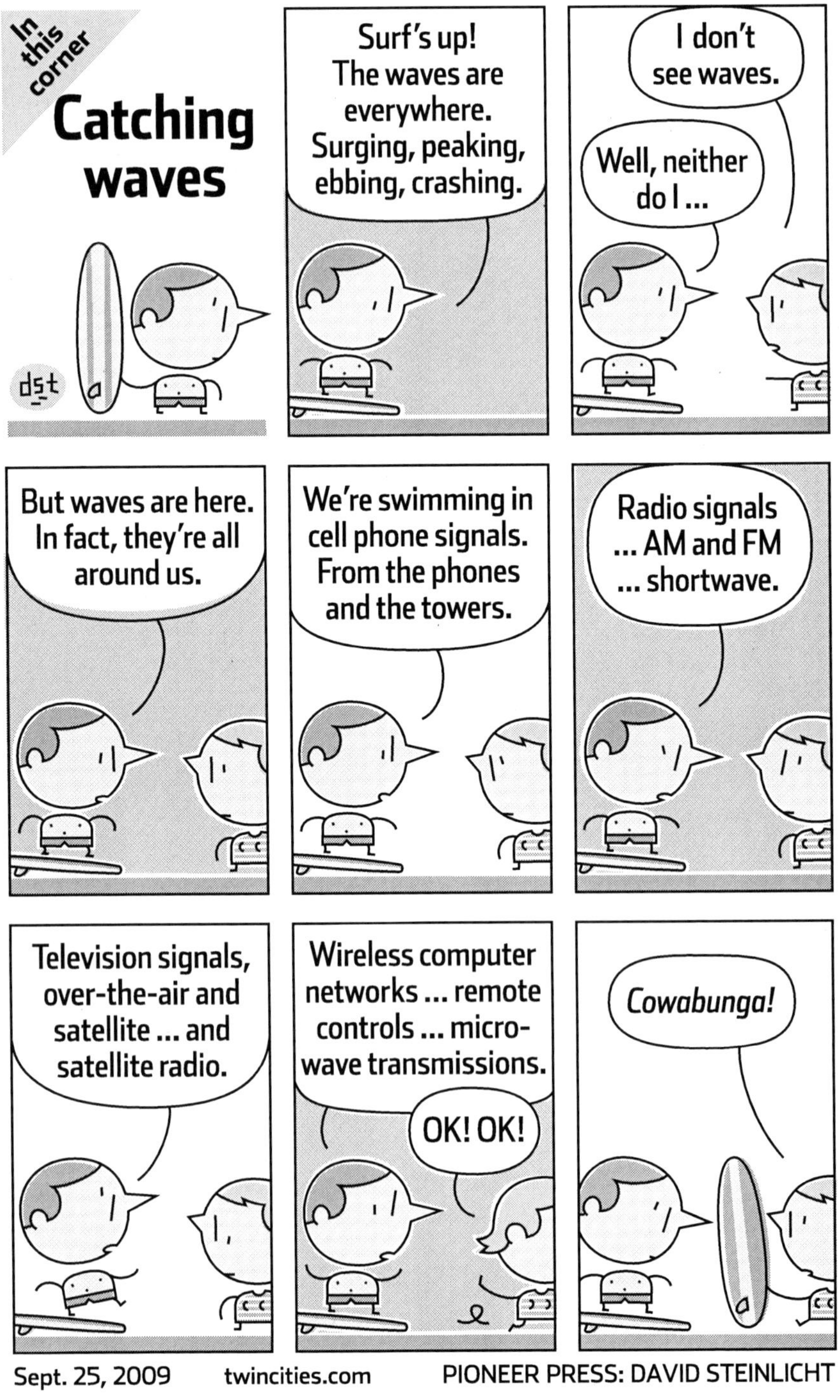
In this corner
Catching waves
dst
Surf's up! The waves are everywhere. Surging, peaking, ebbing, crashing.
I don't see waves.
Well, neither do I ...
But waves are here. In fact, they're all around us.
We're swimming in cell phone signals. From the phones and the towers.
Radio signals ... AM and FM ... shortwave.
Television signals, over-the-air and satellite ... and satellite radio.
Wireless computer networks ... remote controls ... micro-wave transmissions.
OK! OK!
Cowabunga!

Sept. 25, 2009 twincities.com PIONEER PRESS: DAVID STEINLICHT

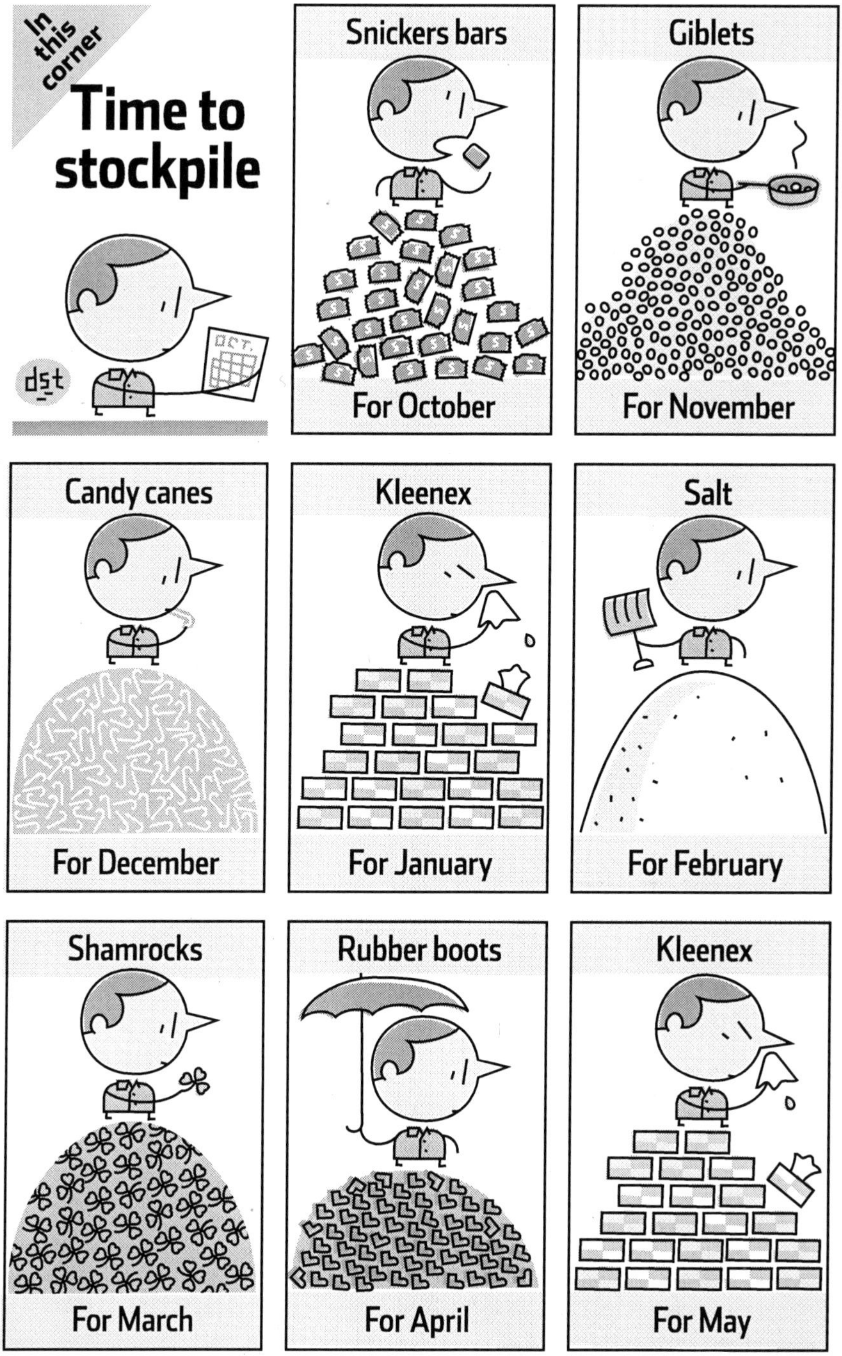
In this corner
Time to stockpile
OCT.
dst
Snickers bars
For October
Giblets
For November
Candy canes
For December
Kleenex
For January
Salt
For February
Shamrocks
For March
Rubber boots
For April
Kleenex
For May

Oct. 2, 2009 PIONEER PRESS: DAVID STEINLICHT

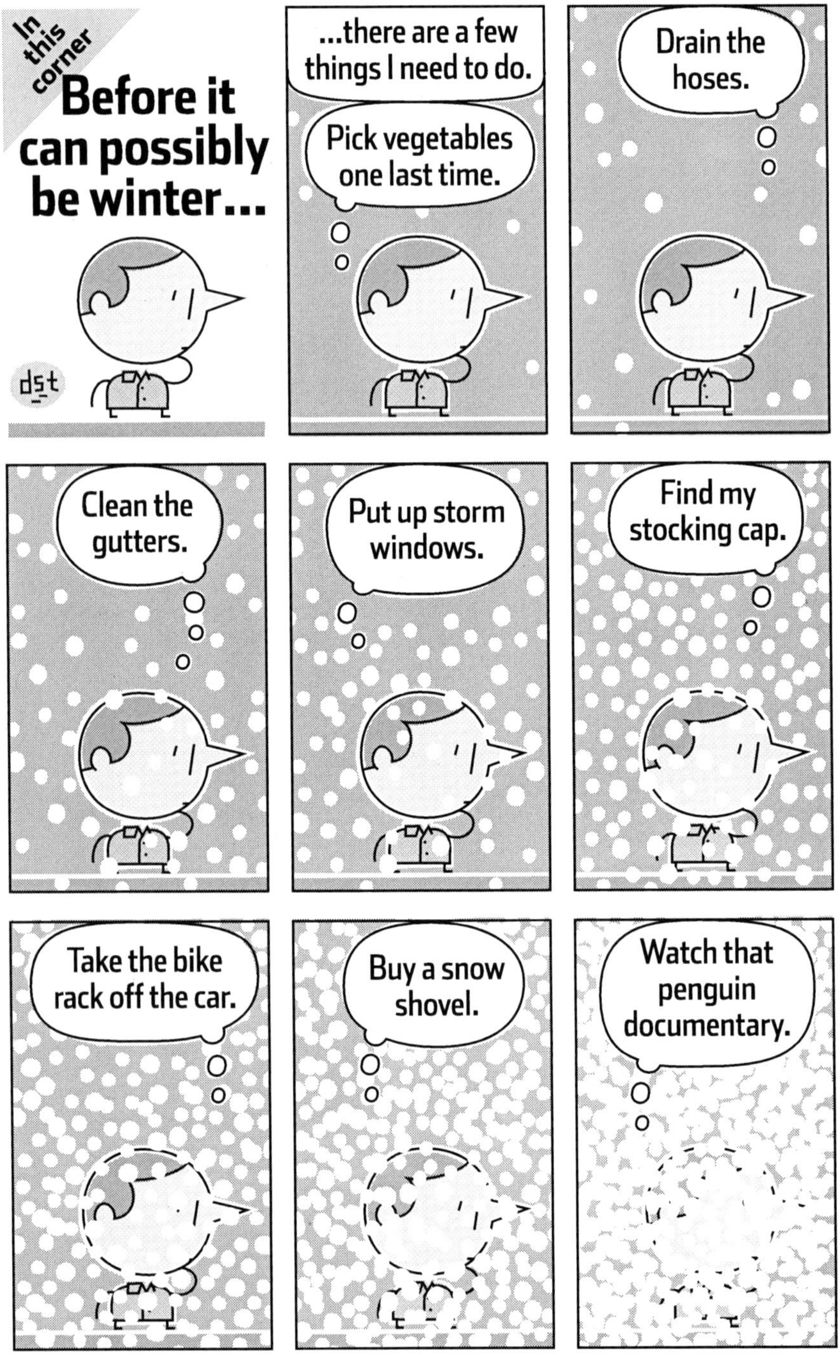
In this corner
Before it can possibly be winter...
dst
...there are a few things I need to do.
Pick vegetables one last time.
Drain the hoses.
Clean the gutters.
Put up storm windows.
Find my stocking cap.
Take the bike rack off the car.
Buy a snow shovel.
Watch that penguin documentary.

Oct. 16, 2009

PIONEER PRESS: DAVID STEINLICHT

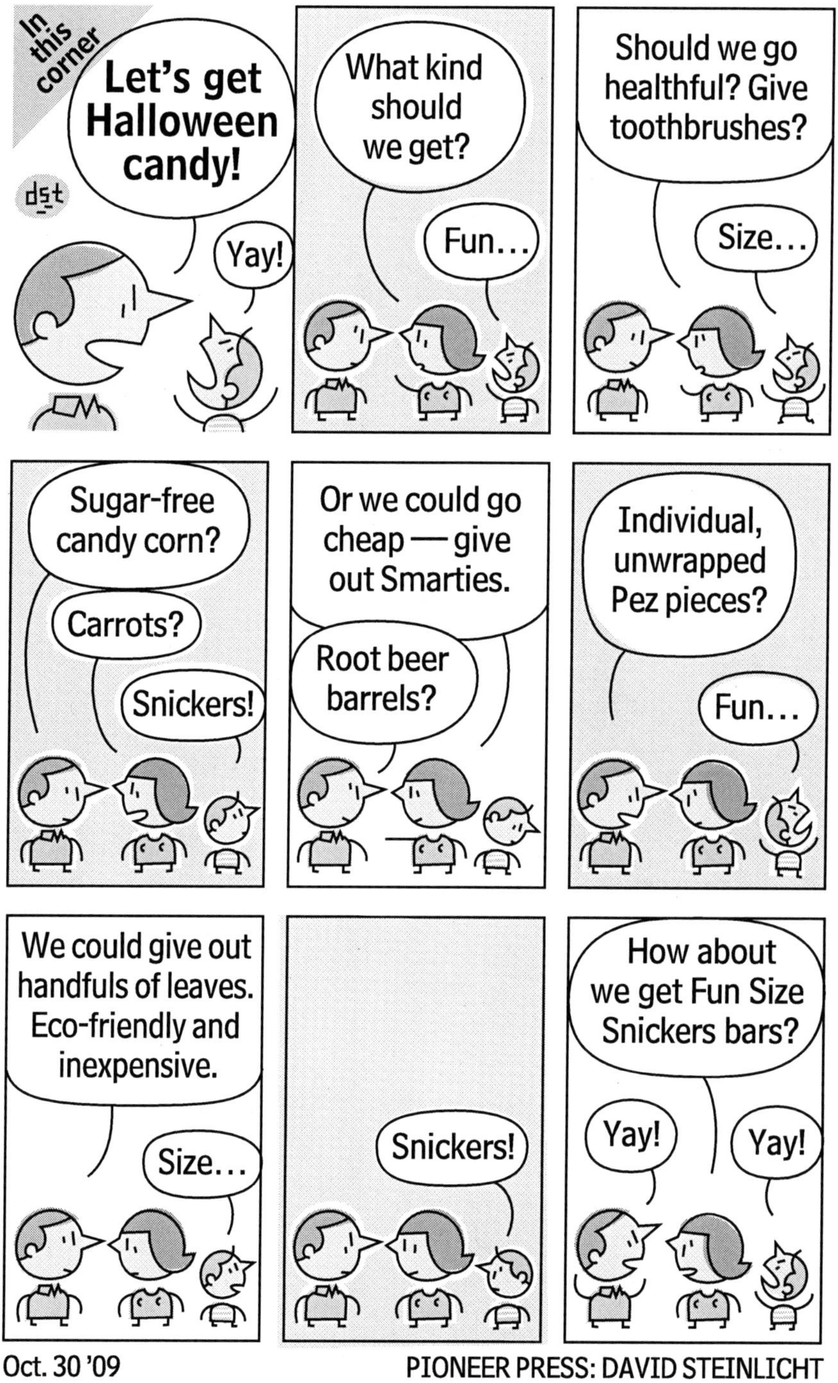
In this corner
dst
Let's get Halloween candy!
Yay!
What kind should we get?
Fun…
Should we go healthful? Give toothbrushes?
Size…
Sugar-free candy corn?
Carrots?
Snickers!
Or we could go cheap — give out Smarties.
Root beer barrels?
Individual, unwrapped Pez pieces?
Fun…
We could give out handfuls of leaves. Eco-friendly and inexpensive.
Size…
Snickers!
How about we get Fun Size Snickers bars?
Yay!
Yay!

Oct. 30 '09

PIONEER PRESS: DAVID STEINLICHT

In this corner
Bells, translated
dst
Dr-rr-rr-ring!
Goose is cooked
Zee-zee-zee!
00:00
Workout's over, thank goodness
Waa-aaa-aa-aa!
6:00 AM
Another dollar
Deedle-dee!
Where are you?
Bon-n-n-ng!
Late to church again
Ding!
This is service?
Ring-ring!
On your left or right
Clang-clang-clang!
Beans and hardtack for supper

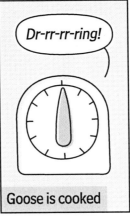

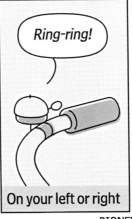

Nov. 6 '09

PIONEER PRESS: DAVID STEINLICHT

Arf!

(talking dog, page 150)

INDEX

E

F

G

272

T

(bicycle, pages 53, 60, 116, 161, 163)